THE
MOVIE QUIZ
COMPANION

THE
MOVIE QUIZ COMPANION

ALLAN FOSTER

Polygon

This book is for Chris

© Allan Foster, 2002

Polygon
An imprint of Edinburgh University Press Ltd
22 George Square, Edinburgh

Typeset in Gill Sans and Garamond
by the author, and printed and bound
in Great Britain by Bookcraft Ltd,
Midsomer Norton, Bath

A CIP Record for this book is available from
the British Library

ISBN 0 7486 6292 8 (paperback)
The right of Allan Foster
to be identified as the author of this work
has been asserted in accordance with
the Copyright, Designs and Patents Act 1988.

Picture Credits (page & column)
The illustrations in this book consist mostly of portraits and stills issued for publicity purposes by the following organisations:
Warner Bros. Inc. 11/3, 21/3, 27/3, 78/3, 81/2, 185/1, 195/3, 206/3, 209/3, 235/1, 265/1. Twentieth Century Fox Film Corp. 23/1, 87/2, 88/1, 95/2, 109/2, 147/1, 227/3, 228/2, 245/2, 274/3. 283/2. Janus Films 82/3, 271/3, 281/1. Cinecom Film Entertainment Group 241/2. Fine Line Features 243/1. Otto Preminger Films Ltd. 249/2. Universal City Studios 12/2, 13/1, 13/2, 28/3, 34/3, 39/2, 42/1, 43/1, 46/3, 49/2, 55/2, 77/1, 79/3, 91/2, 92/1, 92/2, 96/1, 96/2, 98/2, 106/1, 115/1, 116/1, 121/1, 121/2, 138/1, 142/3, 145/1, 189/3, 193/1, 196/3, 199/3, 201/3, 219/2. 229/3, 255/2, 258/1, 276/1, 277/3, 286/1, 288/2, 289/2, 292/1. Liberty Films Inc. 264/2. Orion-Nova 187/3, 215/3. New Yorker films 164/1. Pressman Williams Ltd. 164/3. Roy Export Co. 179/2, 185/3. Merchant Ivory Productions 241/1. Columbia Pictures 23/2, 22/3, 30/3, 45/1, 45/2, 53/2, 95/2, 97/2, 111/1, 188/2, 188/3, 207/1, 207/2, 283/1. Les films du Carrosse 231/3. Culver Pictures Inc. 211/3. De Laurentis Entertainment Group 217/1, United Artists Corporation 66/1, 80/1, 102/2, 138/1, 162/3, 208/2, 222/2, 257/1, 261/2, Jim Emerson Collection 291/2. Fantasay Films 157/3. Hemdale Pictures 73/3. Apollo Film 98/3. Initial Groupe 92/3. MGM Pictures Inc. 95/3, 160/1. Republic Pictures Corporation 103/1, 200/3. Touchstone Pictures 104/2. Morgan Creek Film Partners Inc. 107/3. Paradise Films Inc. 112/2. The Continental Co. Ltd. 114/1. Miramax Films 114/2, 261/1. Paramount Pictures 7/1, 15/3, 17/3, 36/3, 59/1, 63/1, 68/2, 70/1, 86/2, 98/1, 104/1, 109/3, 111/2, 112/3, 132/3, 142/1, 146/3, 170/3, 204/3, 212/3, 282/3. RKO Pictures Inc. 10/1, 190/2, 229/1, 238/2, 290/3. Rank film Distributors Ltd. 64/1, 198/3. Central Motion Picture Corporation 67/2. Richard Feiner & Co, Inc. 142/2. Metro Pictures 143/1. Carolco 72/2, 220/3, Touchstone Pictures 70/2, Romulus Films 11/2. Frank Sinatra Trust 16/3. AB Svensk Filmindustri 19/1. Teegarden/Nash Collection 21/2, 27/2, 54/1, 83/1, 123/2, 158/3, 179/3, 262/1, 270/2. Lumiere Pictures 22/2, 253/1. Initial Groupe 33/3. Cinecom Entertainment Group 37/1, 40/1. First Look Productions Inc. 45/1. Orion Pictures 50/3. Killiam Shows Inc. 56/1. Avco Embassy Pictures Corp. 50/2. TriStar Pictures Inc. 35/1, 115/1, 137/2, 178/2. Embassy Pictures Corp. 62/1, 102/1. Woodfall Films Ltd. 63/3, 250/2. Samuel Goldwyn Co. 64/2. Turner Entertainment Co. 11/3, 14/3, 19/2, 18/3, 31/1, 35/2, 36/1, 41/2, 40/3, 51/2, 74/2, 77/3, 90/3, 97/1, 100/2, 101/1, 101/3, 102/3, 103/2, 106/3, 122/1, 178/3, 181/2, 183/3, 186/1, 191/1, 199/1, 203/3, 209/2, 210/3, 214/1, 217/2, 218/2, 233/1, 244/1, 245/2, 252/2, 253/3, 273/3, 279/2, 281/3, 289/3, 292/3. Castle Hill Productions 169/2.

Although every effort has been made to trace all other present copyright owners, apologies are offered for any unintentional omissions or neglect; we will be happy to insert appropriate acknowledgements to companies or individuals in subsequent editions of the book.

CONTENTS

THEMES	8
ROLES	62
SETTINGS	94
CHARACTERS	124
CREATURES	136
CLASSIC FILMS	146
CULT MOVIES	164
PERFORMERS	172
DIRECTORS	260
ANSWERS	294

FOREWORD

Don't pick up this book late at night - certainly not if you have to get up in the morning at a normal hour. Once you get into it you simply cannot get out, such is the fascination of Allan Foster's unique and amazing collection of questions and answers.

Have you noticed how conversation after supper, chat at the hairdresser and *"when I was a lad, I paid sixpence at the Electric Palace and I saw..."* type nostalgia invariably involves the movies, old and new? *The Movie Quiz Companion* has nine sections; thousands of questions and a series of possible answers covering what you want to know about 'arguably the greatest, and certainly the most intriguing, art form of the 20th century'. Whatever turns you on - themes, cults, characters and much more. Whoever takes your fancy - Allen (Woody) to Woods (James), you will find intriguing questions as well as real and imaginary answers. There is no movie book quite like it. At a stroke, Allan has solved all your Christmas present needs. Enjoy!

Sir Sydney Samuelson CBE.

Sir Sydney Samuelson CBE is the son of film pioneer G.B. Samuelson and has relished more than 60 years in the film business. In 1991 he became the first British Film Commissioner to be appointed by HM Government and was knighted for his services to the British film industry in 1995.

INTRODUCTION

"There is a tendency to class all quizzes as trivia, but every scrap of knowledge about what has been achieved on our planet must be valuable in its way, and film has long been accepted as the key art of the twentieth century."
Leslie Halliwell *The Great Movie Challenge* (1989).

Who am I to disagree with the great Leslie Halliwell's noble sentiment, but are we to assume from his above statement that all quizzes should cease to be regarded as trivia and become revered as part of some global plan enriching twentieth century art? If that's the case I've just written a book to rival the likes of *The Great Gatsby* and *Huckleberry Finn* (pull the other one Les, I didn't come up the Clyde in a banana boat). Just to be on the safe side this book will have to err on the side of caution and describe itself as pure trivia, which *The Oxford English Dictionary* defines as "pieces of information of little importance or value". Nonetheless, this book has been great fun to write and is great fun to read, and not only are there thousands of questions and over one thousand pictures, there are also those infuriating film title anagrams at the top of every page, of which my favourite has to be *nightmares of absent mince*.

This book has gone through many title changes, from *The Encyclopedia of Movie Questions* to *How I Managed to Write 5,000 Movie Questions and Still Have Time to Tango,* but in the end we settled on the electrifying *Movie Quiz Companion*. I sincerely hope it drives you round the bend (as it did me), and should you get more than 4,500 questions correct, may I suggest you seek counselling.
Richard E. Grant once said, "a good proof-reader saves your arse." Mine was saved by my wife Chris who proofed the entire book and whose eagle eye spotted rogue questions such as the one on *Midnight Express* which read: "In which film was Billy Hayes imprisoned in a Turkey?" Any remaining errors, however, are entirely my responsibility.

Allan Foster

Thanks to: My wife Chris, Jack Foster, Chloe Foster, Kit Foster, Lucy Foster, Maureen Still, Ian Rintoul, Bob Henderson, David Skelsey, Sir Sydney Samuelson CBE, Derek Doig, Scott Keir, Tony Hillman, Ian Kerr, Fred O'Brien, Kath McDonald, Dorothy Marlborough, computer wizard Thomas Hartmann, Jackie Jones, Ian Davidson and Sarah Edwards, who all helped me write this book by commenting on parts, or all of it, at various stages throughout its long history. Finally thanks to my mum, Cissie, for instilling in me a life-long love of the movies and who would have given anything to have stood with Robert Taylor on *Waterloo Bridge*.

Tips: The questions work with or without the pictures. So if you're asking questions to a group you can ignore the picture clues if you wish. A simple points system is 5 points for answering a question correctly without using the multiple-choice answers, 3 points for answering a question correctly on first use of multiple-choice, 2 points for second use and 1 point for third.
N.B. The anagrams at the top of each page are all film titles.

THEMES

ABORIGINES

1) On whose novel was Fred Schepsi's 1978 drama, **The Chant of Jimmie Blacksmith** based?
a) Patrick White b) Thomas Keneally
c) Colleen McCullough d) David Malouf

2) With which 1986 film, directed by Bruce Beresford, do you associate an aboriginal family adjusting to life in a middle-class white neighbourhood?
a) Backroads b) A Far Off Place
c) Manganinnie d) The Fringe Dwellers

3) In 1977 he portrayed Australian lawyer, David Burton, who defends a group of aborigines accused of murder in **The Last Wave**. Who was he?
a) Sam Neill b) Richard Chamberlain
c) Jeff Bridges d) Elliott Gould

ABORTION

1) In 1966 he portrayed the abortionist in **Alfie**. Who was he?
a) Laurence Harvey b) Denholm Elliott
c) Peter Finch d) Joss Ackland

2) For whom did Arthur Seaton (Albert Finney) try to arrange an abortion in **Saturday Night and Sunday Morning** (1960)?
a) Rachel Roberts b) Shirley Ann Field
c) Rita Tushingham d) Simone Signoret

3) In which 1967 crime drama were the contents of a murdered industrialist's wallet going to be used to finance a girl's abortion in the southern town of Sparta, Mississippi?
a) Southern Comfort b) The Big Easy
c) In the Heat of the Night d) The Texas Chainsaw Massacre

ADDRESSES

1) On whose play was George Stevens' 1937 comedy drama, **Quality Street**, based?
a) J.M. Barrie b) George Bernard Shaw
c) J. B. Priestley d) Terence Rattigan

2) In 1987 she portrayed American writer, Helene Hanff, who corresponds with antiquarian bookseller, Frank Doel (Anthony Hopkins), for over twenty years in **84 Charing Cross Road**. Who was she?
a) Anne Bancroft b) Kathy Bates
c) Anjelica Huston d) Annette Bening

3) Who lived in **The House On 92nd Street**?
a) the FBI b) Judy Garland
c) the Boston Strangler d) Nazi spies

ADOLESCENCE

1) In which 1981 romantic comedy, directed by Bill Forsyth, does a boy pay a young girl the compliment: "She's only ten, but she has the body of a woman of thirteen."?
a) Local Hero b) That Sinking Feeling
c) Gregory's Girl d) Comfort and Joy

2) An oversexed maid caters for the adolescent fantasies of the teenage Buddy (Lukas Haas) in Martha Coolidge's 1991 romantic drama, **Rambling Rose**. Who was she?
a) Julia Roberts b) Laura Dern
c) Meryl Streep d) Nicole Kidman

a borrowing tory kneels

Themes

3) Name the 1961 film, directed by Elia Kazan, in which high-school sweethearts, Wilma (Natalie Wood) and Bud (Warren Beatty), are denied the chance of love and marriage by their domineering parents.
a) A Face in the Crowd b) Baby Doll
c) Splendor in the Grass d) America, America

ADOPTION

1) Name the actor who portrayed the adopted son of Vito Corleone in the **Godfather**.
a) James Caan b) John Cazale
c) Al Pacino d) Robert Duvall

2) Which 1981 film tells the real-life story of the adopted and abused daughter of screen legend Joan Crawford?
a) Mommie Dearest b) Miss Firecracker
c) The Official Story d) Tomorrow is Forever

3) In 1991 she portrayed Granny Wendy Darling who adopted the orphan Peter Banning in **Hook**. Who was she?
a) Ingrid Pitt b) Maggie Smith
c) Julie Andrews d) Anne Bancroft

AEROPLANES

1) In which film does aircraft engineer, Theodore Honey (James Stewart), discover that aeroplanes can suffer metal fatigue?
a) The Mortal Storm b) No Highway in the Sky
c) Strategic Air Command d) The Spirit of St. Louis

2) In 1980 he played the zany Dr. Rumack in **Airplane!**. Who was he?
a) Robert Stack b) Leslie Nielsen
c) Robert Hays d) Jerry Lewis

3) In which 1965 film does a scientist construct a single-engined plane from the wreckage of a twin-engined plane in the Sahara Desert?
a) The Flight of the Phoenix b) Flight from Ashiya
c) Wild in the Sky d) Flight for Freedom

AFTERLIFE

1) In 1946 he played "Conductor 71", a Frenchman who was beheaded in his country's Revolution, in Powell and Pressburger's **A Matter of Life and Death**. Who was he?
a) Marius Goring b) David Niven
c) Raymond Massey d) Richard Attenborough

2) In which 1987 film does Timothy Hutton die, go to heaven, and fall in love with beautiful heavenly guide, Kelly McGillis?
a) Angel on My Shoulder b) Heaven Can Wait
c) Bad Lord Byron d) Made in Heaven

3) In which 1990 horror film are the characters portrayed by Kiefer Sutherland and Julia Roberts eager to sample the afterlife?
a) At Close Range b) Flashback
c) Sleeping With the Enemy d) Flatliners

AGEING

1) Which film featured the 121 year old Jack Crabb?
a) The Old Man and the Sea b) Little Big Man
c) The Memory of Justice d) The Time Machine

2) In 1976 he played the legendary but ageing gunfighter J.B. Brooks in **The Shootist** (1976). Who was he?
a) James Stewart b) Randolph Scott
c) Robert Mitchum d) John Wayne

3) Who portrayed the elderly Mrs. Watts, who deserts her unhappy city life and goes on a journey to visit her childhood home for the last time, in **The Trip To Bountiful**?
a) Lauren Bacall b) Geraldine Page
c) Joan Plowright d) Jessica Tandy

AGE REVERSAL & EXCHANGE

1) Who played the title role in the 1945 horror film, **The Picture of Dorian Gray**, about a man whose portrait ages while he remains forever young?
a) George Saunders b) Peter Lawford
c) Louis Jourdan d) Hurd Hatfield

2) In which 1976 Disney fantasy do a quarrelling mother (Barbara Harris) and a teenage daughter (Jodie Foster) switch personalities for a day?
a) Seconds b) Freaky Friday
c) The Major and the Minor d) 18 Again

3) Who portrayed the older Josh Baskin in the 1988 body-switching comedy **Big**?
a) Arnold Schwarzenegger b) Martin Sheen
c) Tom Hanks d) Tim Robbins

AIRSHIPS & HOT AIR BALLOONS

1) What connection can you make between **The Sound of Music** and the 1975 film **The Hindenburg**?
a) Both starred Christopher Plummer b) The replica airship used in The Hindenburg was used to film the opening aerial shots in The Sound of Music c) Both starred Julie Andrews d) Both were directed by Robert Wise

2) Name the title of the 1931 film, directed by Frank Capra, and starring Fay Wray, in which an airship crashes in the Antarctic.
a) Dirigible b) The Lost Horizon
c) Disciple of Death d) A Distant Trumpet

9

The Movie Quiz Companion

3) What 1961 film involves an observation balloon being off course and landing on an uncharted island inhabited by giant animals?
a) *Mysterious Island* b) *The Island of Dr Moreau*
c) *Island of Lost Souls* d) *Island of Terror*

AIDS & HIV

1) Which 1993 drama became the first big-budget Hollywood movie to explore the AIDS epidemic?
a) *Philadelphia* b) *Sharing Richard*
c) *Our Sons* d) *Reckless*

2) French director, Cyril Collard, made a loosely autobiographical AIDS movie in 1993, and tragically died of the disease three days before it won the Cesar award for best film of the year. Name the title.
a) *Savage Nights* b) *Parting Glance*
c) *Opening Nights* d) *Longtime Companion*

3) What 1996 black comedy involves dinner parties which eliminate right-wing guests by poisoning them with arsenic, including a homophobe who states, "Homosexuality is the disease. AIDS is the cure"?
a) *It's Your Move* b) *Mother's Prayer* c) *Sex, Drugs and Democracy* d) *The Last Supper*

AMBUSHES

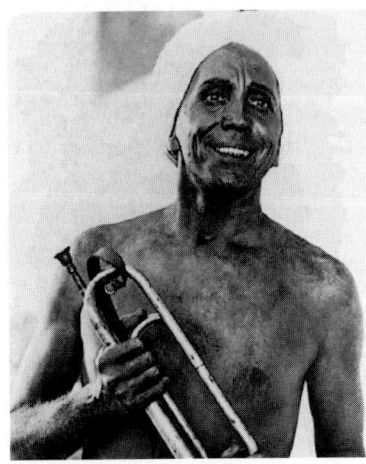

1) Water-carrier **Gunga Din** (1939) is awarded the posthumous rank of corporal in the British army for warning them with a bugle call of an approaching ambush. Who was he?
a) *Sam Jaffe* b) *Sabu*
c) *Peter Lorre* d) *Howard Keel*

2) Which 1967 film features the ambush of a young couple near Gibland, Louisiana, on May 23, 1934, when their car is raked by 187 bullets?
a) *Aces High* b) *Badlands*
c) *Bonnie and Clyde* d) *Day of the Evil Gun*

3) In which 1972 film was James Caan ambushed at a toll gate?
a) *The Rain People* b) *Slither*
c) *The Godfather* d) *Rabbit, Run*

AMERICAN CIVIL WAR

1) On whose novel was **Gone With The Wind** based?
a) *Nathaniel Hawthorne* b) *Stephen Crane*
c) *Louisa May Alcott* d) *Margaret Mitchell*

2) For what 1965 film did James Stewart portray prosperous Virginian farmer, Charlie Anderson, who tries to remain neutral towards the Civil War, but eventually changes his pacifist views in the face of ensuing events?
a) *Shenandoah* b) *The Big Country*
c) *Freedom Road* d) *Santa Fe Trail*

3) Name the 1993 civil war drama, based on Michael Shaara's Pulitzer Prize-winning novel, *The Killer Angels*.
a) *Gettysburg* b) *Glory*
c) *The Beguiled* d) *Sherman's March*

AMERICAN WAR OF INDEPENDENCE

1) In 1985 he portrayed Tom Dobb, a Glasgow-born fur trader in Hugh Hudson's **Revolution**. Who was he?
a) *Steven Berkoff* b) *Donald Sutherland*
c) *Richard Gere* d) *Al Pacino*

2) Who played the title role of the Scottish born 'Father of the American Navy' in John Farrow's 1959 biopic, **John Paul Jones**?
a) *Robert Stack* b) *Rod Taylor*
c) *Mel Ferrer* d) *Warner Baxter*

3) Who directed **The Patriot** (2000)?
a) *Rob Minkoff* b) *Alan Rudolph*
c) *Roland Emmerich* d) *John Woo*

AMNESIA

1) With which Hitchcock film do you associate Gregory Peck as an amnesiac and suspected murderer?
a) *Topaz* b) *Spellbound*
c) *Stagefright* d) *The Man Who Knew Too Much*

2) In 1945, Laird Cregar played a mad composer who murders every time he hears a loud noise, which is always accompanied by loss of memory. Name the film.
a) *Hysteria* b) *Hangover Square*
c) *Man in the Dark* d) *Somewhere in the Night*

3) For what film did Greta Garbo portray a cabaret singer who blots out her past as an Italian Countess?
a) *As You Desire Me* b) *Grand Hotel*
c) *Camille* d) *The Mysterious Lady*

ANIMAL EXPERIMENTS & VIVISECTION

1) With which film do you associate a fox terrier called Snitter and his labrador friend escaping from an animal research centre?
a) *Plague Dogs* b) *The Incredible Journey*
c) *Lassie Come Home* d) *Chicken Run*

2) Name the 1988 film, directed by George Romero, in which a monkey is injected with human brain cells.
a) *Two Evil Eyes* b) *Spanking the Monkey*
c) *Monkey On My Back* d) *Monkey Shines*

3) What 1974 film, directed by Frederick Wiseman, records electronic experiments by an American research centre on chimpanzees, orang-utangs and gorillas?
a) *Primates* b) *The Ape*
c) *The Gorilla Man* d) *Twelve Monkeys*

ANTI-SEMITISM

1) Elia Kazan's 1947 drama, starring Gregory Peck, who poses as a Jew to write magazine

fuchsia topic

Themes

articles exposing anti-semitism, is often hailed as Hollywood's first major attack on anti-semitism. Name the title.
a) Gentleman's Agreement b) The Chosen
c) Front Page d) Carbon Copy

2) Which British film was banned in the U.S.A. in 1948 for its caricature of a Jew?
a) Reach For Glory b) Oliver Twist
c) Secret Agent d) Rope

3) Name the 1971 musical, directed by Norman Jewison, which is set during the Russian pogroms in the early 1900s.
a) The Fixer b) Fiddler on the Roof
c) Funny Face d) This Is the Army

APARTHEID

1) On whose novel was Darrell James Roodt's 1995 drama, **Cry, the Beloved Country**, based?
a) Nadine Gordimer b) J.M. Coetzee
c) Alan Paton d) Doris Lessing

2) Who portrayed the naïve white schoolteacher who is awakened to the plight of blacks in South Africa, in **A Dry White Season**?
a) Adrian Dunbar b) Donald Sutherland
c) Malcolm McDowell d) Alan Bates

3) Name the title of the 1993 drama, directed by actor Morgan Freeman, about a black South African policeman whose son becomes involved in a local student strike.
a) Bopha! b) The Power of One
c) A World Apart d) Higher Learning

ARABIAN NIGHTS

1) Who provided the voice of the genie in Disney's 1992 fantasy, **Aladdin**?
a) Jonathan Freeman b) Mel Brooks
c) Robin Williams d) Mel Blanc

2) How many directors did it take to complete **The Thief of Bagdad** in 1940?
a) 4 b) 5 c) 6 d) 7

3) Who created the startling special effects for **The Seventh Voyage of Sinbad** (1958)?
a) Ray Harryhausen b) Les Bowie
c) Rick Baker d) Chris Walas

ARABS

1) Who was Charles Boyer's leading lady in the 1936 film, **The Garden of Allah**?
a) Greta Garbo b) Marlene Dietrich
c) Joan Crawford d) Claudette Colbert

2) In which 1985 film was Joan Wilder (Kathleen Turner) invited to visit the native country of a wealthy Arab?
a) Romancing The Stone b) Body Heat
c) A Breed Apart d) The Jewel of the Nile

3) With which 1954 comedy drama do you associate shipwreck survivors portrayed by Humphrey Bogart, Gina Lollobrigida, Jennifer Jones, Robert Morley and Peter Lorre, being captured by hostile Arabs?
a) Around the World in 80 Days b) Outcast of the Islands c) Beat the Devil d) Key Largo

ARMY LIFE

1) In 1960 he played Lt. Col. Jock Sinclair in **Tunes of Glory**. Who was he?
a) John Mills b) Jack Hawkins
c) Dennis Price d) Alec Guinness

2) Who directed **From Here To Eternity**?
a) Fred Zinneman b) John Frankenheimer
c) Elia Kazan d) Stanley Kramer

3) Which 1987 film was based on the book *The Short Timers*, by Gustav Hasford?
a) Full Metal Jacket b) Paths of Glory
c) Gardens of Stone d) A Walk in the Sun

ARRANGED MARRIAGES

1) With which 1993 drama, directed by Wayne Wang, do you associate a Chinese auntie "[praying] too hard" when she prays that her future husband be "not too old", and ends up with a ten year old boy?
a) The Joy Luck Club b) Smoke
c) Dim Sum: A Little Bit of Heart d) Eat a Bowl of Tea

2) Which 1937 drama features rice farmer, Wang Lung (Paul Muni), entering into an arranged marriage with kitchen slave, O-Lan (Luise Rainer)?
a) The Keys of the Kingdom b) The Bitter Tea of General Yen c) The Good Earth d) China Sky

The Movie Quiz Companion

3) In which film did Ben Kingsley portray a character who entered an arranged marriage when he was thirteen?
a) Betrayal b) Gandhi c) Silas Marner d) Harem

ART TREASURES

1) Art connoisseur and officer of the Third Reich, Col. Von Waldheim, is defeated by the French Resistance in his attempt to steal a train load of French art treasures in **The Train**. Who was he?
a) Robert Shaw b) Paul Scofield
c) Rex Harrison d) Elliott Gould

2) What famous art treasure was Professor Moriarty plotting to steal in the 1939 mystery, **The Adventures of Sherlock Holmes**?
a) the Mona Lisa b) the Crown Jewels
c) the Cape Triangular stamp d) the Hope Diamond

3) In 1539 the Knights Templar of Malta paid tribute to Charles V of Spain and sent him a small golden statuette covered in jewels. It never reached its destination as the ship carrying it was seized by pirates and its fate became a mystery. Name the film inspired by the legend.
a) Romancing the Stone b) King Solomon's Mines
c) Treasure of the Matecumbe d) The Maltese Falcon

ASSASSINATIONS

1) Who was New York cop, Dick Powell, trying to protect in Anthony Mann's 1951 noir thriller, **The Tall Target**?
a) Abraham Lincoln
b) Queen Victoria
c) Charles Dickens
d) Thomas Alva Edison

2) What book by Geoffrey Household provided the substance for Fritz Lang's 1941 thriller, **Manhunt**, in which an attempt is made to assassinate Adolf Hitler?
a) Rogue Male
b) Escape into Daylight
c) Face to the Sun
d) Rough Shoot

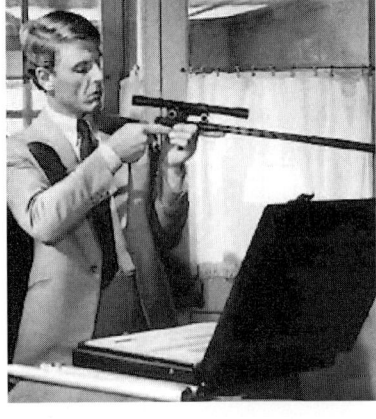

3) In which 1973 thriller is an attempt made on the life of General De Gaulle?
a) Paris is Burning b) A Killer Among Us
c) French Twist d) The Day of the Jackal

ATOMIC BOMBS

1) Name the monster who is awakened from the Arctic ice by an atomic blast in 1953.
a) The Creature from the Black Lagoon b) The Reptile c) The Beast from 20,000 Fathoms
d) Godzilla

2) On which American city is an atomic bomb dropped in **Panic in Year Zero**, directed by, and starring Ray Milland?
a) Chicago b) Los Angeles c) New York
d) Washington DC

3) Name the title of the **Planet of the Apes** sequel in which mutant humans worship an atomic bomb.
a) Beneath the Planet of the Apes b) Escape from the Planet of the Apes c) Conquest of the Planet of the Apes d) Battle for the Planet of the Apes

AUTISM

1) In which 1993 film, directed by Michael Lessac, does Ruth Mathews' (Kathleen Turner) daughter show autistic tendencies?
a) House of Cards b) Serial Mom
c) Julia and Julia d) Switching Channels

2) Which 1988 film features Raymond Babbitt, a 'high level' autistic, who has the ability to count 246 dropped toothpicks instantly?
a) Henry & June b) Weird Science
c) Rain Man d) Strange Behaviour

3) What 1986 fantasy involves an autistic orphan (Jay Underwood) being removed from the care of his drunken uncle and placed in an institution?
a) The Boy Who Had Everything b) The Boy Who Could Fly c) The Funhouse d) Half Life

AUTOBIOGRAPHICAL FILMS

1) Name the ill-fated screen legend portrayed by Carroll Baker in 1965?
a) Marilyn Monroe b) Greta Garbo
c) Jayne Mansfield d) Jean Harlow

2) Who portrayed the epigram-spouting homosexual writer, Lytton Strachey, who had a platonic love affair with Dora Carrington in **Carrington**?
a) Timothy West b) Joss Ackland
c) Jonathan Pryce d) Anthony Hopkins

3) Name the film based on the life of blind, deaf girl, Helen Keller, and her extraordinary teacher, Anne Sullivan.
a) The Miracle b) The Small Miracle
c) The Miracle Worker d) The Miracle Woman

AUTOMOBILES

1) Which Disney comedy features a diamond hidden in the petrol tank of a Volkswagen Beetle?

randy mummys threaten art

a) *The Love Bug* b) *Herbie Rides Again*
c) *Herbie Goes to Monte Carlo* d) *Herbie Goes Bananas*

2) With which film do you associate a 1904 Darracq and a 1904 Spyker?
a) *Silver Dream Racer* b) *Genevieve*
c) *Chitty Chitty Bang Bang* d) *Drive, He Said*

3) In which film do gangster's moll, Shirley MacLaine, and street photographer, Alain Delon, conduct their love-making in the back seat of a Rolls-Royce?
a) *The Yellow Rolls-Royce* b) *My Geisha* c) *Irma La Douce* d) *Sunset Limousine*

AUTO RACING

1) Name the title of John Frankenheimer's 1966 racing film which follows the lives of four professional auto racers.
a) *Pit Stop* b) *Cannonball Run*
c) *Fireball 500* d) *Grand Prix*

2) Name the start and finishing line cities in the 1965 film **The Great Race**.
a) *London to Paris* b) *New York to Paris*
c) *Paris to Peking* d) *London to Monte Carlo*

3) In which film does Elvis Presley try to raise money to purchase an engine for his racer in order that he may compete in the Grand Prix?
a) *Viva Las Vegas* b) *Blue Hawaii*
c) *Fun in Acapulco* d) *Roustabout*

BABIES

1) In 1968 he portrayed the proud father of **Rosemary's Baby**. Who was he?
a) *Dustin Hoffman* b) *John Cassavetes*
c) *Jack Nicholson* d) *Robert Redford*

2) Which 1987 comedy, directed by Leonard Nimoy, was based on the French film **Trois Hommes Et Un Couffin**?
a) *Three Men and a Cradle* b) *3 Men and a Little Lady* c) *3 Men and a Baby* d) *Three Into Two Won't Go*

3) Who provided the voice of 'Baby Mikey' in the the 1989 comedy **Look Who's Talking**?
a) *John Travolta* b) *George Segal*
c) *Bruce Willis* d) *Burt Reynolds*

BASED ON A TRUE STORY

1) Which 1988 film tells the true story of Australian woman, Lindy Chamberlain, who claimed her baby was carried away by a dingo, but was later accused of murder?
a) *Dingo* b) *A Cry in the Dark*
c) *Strange Affair* d) *I Love You to Death*

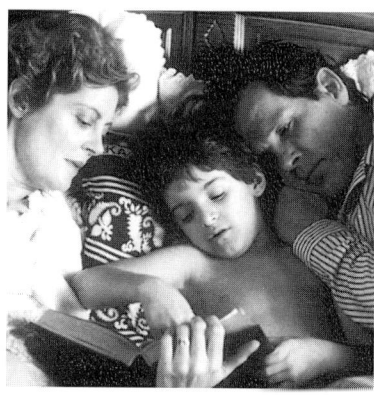

2) In which 1992 film do Michaela (Susan Sarandon) and Augusto (Nick Nolte) Odone, on discovering their son has adrenoleukodystrophy, an incurable degenerative disease, refuse to give up hope and set out to find a cure?
a) *The Awful Truth* b) *Close My Eyes*
c) *Lorenzo's Oil* d) *Child of Darkness, Child of Light*

3) Which 1978 film tells the true story of Billy Hayes who was imprisoned in Turkey for drug smuggling?
a) *Midnight Express* b) *Prisoner of the Volga*
c) *Cold Turkey* d) *Escape to the Sun*

BASKETBALL

1) In 1986 he played basketball coach, Norman Dale, in **Hoosiers**. Who was he?
a) *Dennis Hopper* b) *Gene Hackman*
c) *Clint Eastwood* d) *Jeff Bridges*

2) Name the film which was inspired by the autobiography of cult author, Jim Carroll, who descended from basketball stardom into heroin addiction.
a) *Above the Rim* b) *Iron Will*
c) *Killing Streets* d) *The Basketball Diaries*

3) In which film does Rocky Sullivan give the Dead End Kids a few tips on how to play basketball?
a) *Crime School* b) *Hit the Road*
c) *Angels With Dirty Faces* d) *Little Tough Guy*

BATTLE OF BRITAIN

1) Who portrayed Reginald Mitchell, creator of the Battle of Britain workhorse, the Spitfire, in the 1942 biopic, **The First of the Few**?
a) *David Niven* b) *Michael Redgrave*
c) *Leslie Howard* d) *John Mills*

2) Which 1956 film, directed by Lewis Gilbert, features a formation of five squadrons known as 'The Duxford Wing', whose unique tactics helped win the Battle of Britain?
a) *The Way to the Stars* b) *Fighter Squadron*
c) *Reach for the Sky* d) *Dogfight*

3) Who directed **Battle of Britain** (1969)?
a) *Guy Hamilton* b) *Hugh Hudson*
c) *John Boorman* d) *Bryan Forbes*

BEREAVEMENT

1) With which Krzysztof Kieslowski film do you associate Juliette Binoche building a new

The Movie Quiz Companion

monthly lavatories bathe wench

life for herself after her husband and daughter are killed in a car crash?
a) Three Colours: Blue b) Three Colours: Red
c) Three Colours: White d) City Life

2) John and Laura Baxter are bereaved parents whose daughter was accidentally killed in a drowning accident. While working in Venice they see a small furtive figure dressed in their daughter's clothes. Name the film.
a) Orphans b) One True Thing
c) Don't Look Now c) Sweet Hereafter

3) After the accidental death of her teenage son, Cecilia Roth leaves Madrid for another Spanish city to cope with her grief in **All About My Mother** (1999). Name the city.
a) Malaga b) Seville c) Barcelona d) Toledo

THE BIBLE

1) Who played the title role in the 1959 epic, **The Big Fisherman**?
a) Charlton Heston b) Victor Mature
c) Howard Keel d) Paul Scofield

2) On whose novel was Martin Scorsese's **The Last Temptation of Christ** based?
a) Umberto Eco b) Nikos Kazantzakis
c) Saul Bellow d) Albert Camus

3) Who directed **The Gospel According to St. Matthew** (1966)?
a) Pier Paolo Pasolini b) Jean Negulesco
c) Elia Kazan d) Werner Herzog

BICYCLES

1) With which film do you associate schoolteacher, Miss Gulch, riding a bicycle?
a) Sabrina b) The Wizard of Oz
c) The Toxic Avenger d) The Muppet Movie

2) Who portrayed Mario, the cycling postman in **Il Postino**, who died of a heart attack the day after filming was completed?
a) Massimo Troisi b) Aldo Fabrizi
c) Philippe Noiret d) Marcello Pagliero

3) In which 1982 film does Elliott's bicycle fly magically into the air?
a) One Magic Christmas b) The Muppet Movie
c) Pee Wee's Big Adventure d) E.T. The Extra-Terrestrial

BIGAMY

1) **The Remarkable Mr. Pennypacker** (1959) tells the story of a Pennsylvania businessman who leads a dual life with two families and seventeen children. Who played the title role?
a) Charles Laughton b) Robert Young
c) Claude Rains d) Clifton Webb

2) With which film do you associate Dudley Moore having two wives and making them both pregnant at the same time?
a) Micki & Maude b) Unfaithfully Yours
c) Best Defense d) Bedazzled

3) Who played the amnesia victim who discovers he has seven wives in the 1934 film **The Constant Husband**?
a) James Cagney b) Lionel Barrymore
c) Rex Harrison d) Charles Boyer

BIKER MOVIES

1) With which 1972 film do you associate a motorcycle gang called 'The Living Dead'?
a) Psychomania b) The Loveless
c) Electra Glide in Blue d) The Born Losers

2) In 1967 he played a gas pump attendant called 'Poet' who joins the 'Road Rats' gang by accident in **Hell's Angels on Wheels**. Who was he?
a) Adam Faith b) Dustin Hoffman
c) Lee Marvin d) Jack Nicholson

3) Who played the leader of the 'Stompers' in the 1967 film **The Glory Stompers**?
a) Rita Tushingham b) Jane Fonda
c) Dennis Hopper d) Willie Nelson

BISEXUALITY

1) In which film does Al Pacino portray a bisexual bank robber named Sonny?
a) Dog Day Afternoon b) Dick Tracy
c) Scarface d) The Panic in Needle Park

2) Who portrayed the handsome young slave who catches the eye of the bisexual Crassus (Laurence Olivier) in **Spartacus**?
a) John Gavin b) Woody Strode
c) John Ireland d) Tony Curtis

3) Name the 1972 film in which American singer Sally Bowles falls in love with a bisexual Englishman in 1930s Berlin.
a) Night Train to Munich b) Cabaret
c) The Face of Darkness d) Coming Home

BLACKMAIL

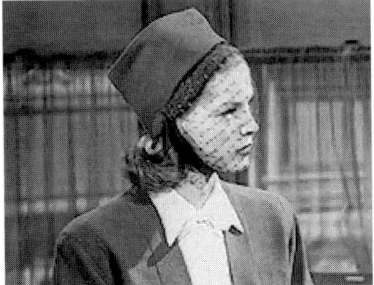

1) With which film do you associate private eye, Philip Marlowe, investigating the blackmailing of Vivian Sternwood's sister by a pornographic book dealer?
a) Murder, My Sweet b) Farewell, My Lovely
c) The Big Sleep d) The Lady in the Lake

2) In what film does Ray Milland blackmail an old university acquaintance into murdering his wife?
a) Ministry of Fear b) Dial M for Murder
c) Payment Deferred d) The Man Who Played God

3) With what 1961 thriller, starring Dirk Bogarde, do you associate a blackmail ring that preys on homosexuals?
a) Victim b) Quartet c) Desperate Moments
d) Cast a Dark Shadow

BLACK MARKETEERING

1) Who sang the song 'Black Market' in Billy Wilder's 1948 romance **Foreign Affair**?
a) Jean Arthur b) Bessie Smith
c) Judy Garland d) Marlene Dietrich

winner throttles float queen

Themes

2) With which 1949 thriller do you associate Orson Welles portraying a black marketeer?
a) Journey Into Fear
b) The Stranger
c) The Third Man d) The Lady From Shanghai

3) What film connection can you make between an enamelled cooking utensils factory, Liam Neeson and black marketeering?
a) Michael Collins b) Schindler's List c) Darkman d) The Innocent

BLAX-PLOITATION FILMS

1) In which 1970 crime comedy do 'Coffin Ed Johnson' and 'Grave Digger Jones', two Harlem detectives, investigate a shady preacher?
a) Hell Up in Harlem b) The Big Score
c) Cotton Comes To Harlem d) The Mack

2) With which 1988 comedy do you associate Jack Spade (Keenan Ivory Wayans) promising to avenge the death of his brother, who died of an O.G. (overdose of gold chains)?
a) I'm Gonna Git You Sucka b) Cool Breeze
c) The Black Gestapo d) Black Fist

3) In 1973 she played the title role in **Cleopatra Jones**. Who was she?
a) Tamara Dobson b) Whoopi Goldberg
c) Vanetta McGee d) Aretha Franklin

BLINDNESS

1) What 1962 science-fiction drama cast Howard Keel as a seaman who awakes from his hospital bed to find the world in the midst of a blindness epidemic?
a) Capricorn One b) The Day the Earth Stood Still
c) The Day of the Triffids d) The Quatermass Experiment

2) In which film does the character portrayed by Claude Rains go blind after being infected with diphtheria in a concentration camp?
a) Mr. Skeffington b) Dark Victory
c) Jezebel d) The Passionate Friends

3) Who portrayed the blind flower girl in Chaplin's 1931 comedy, **City Lights**?

a) Edna Purviance b) Merna Kennedy
c) Paulette Goddard d) Virginia Cherrill

THE BLITZ

1) In 1942, jewel thief Michael Lanyard (Warren William), battles with Nazi spies during London's Blitz in **Counter-Espionage**. By what name was he better known?
a) Boston Blackie b) The Lone Wolf
c) Torchy Blane d) The Falcon

2) Name the director who gave an autobiographical account of his WWII London childhood in **Hope and Glory**.
a) Lindsay Anderson b) Peter Greenaway
c) John Boorman d) John Schlesinger

3) Who directed **Fires Were Started** (1943), which realistically records the nightly dangers facing London's firemen during the Blitz?
a) Basil Wright b) Alberto Cavalcanti
c) Humphrey Jennings d) Edgar Anstey

THE BLUES

1) In which 1986 film does a teenager help an old blues harmonica player named Willie Brown to escape from a nursing home?
a) Mambo Kings b) Johnny Handsome
c) Rockin' the Blues d) Crossroads

2) Name the 1972 biopic about the life of the legendary Billie Holiday.
a) Honeysuckle Rose b) Night on Earth
c) What's Love Got to Do With It d) Lady Sings the Blues

3) With which film do you associate Bette Midler and the Harlettes singing the blues?
a) Divine Madness b) The Rose
c) Beaches d) Down and Out in Beverley Hills

BOER WAR

1) Bruce Beresford's **Breaker Morant** (1979) was based on the true story of three soldiers' actions during the Boer War. Who played the lead role of Lt. Harry Morant?
a) Edward Woodward b) Joss Ackland
c) Richard Attenborough d) Peter O'Toole

2) What 1943 film involves British officer Clive Candy (Roger Livesey) travelling to Germany to protest against and revoke newspaper reports describing British atrocities in South Africa?
a) The Four Feathers b) The Life and Death of Colonel Blimp c) The Silken Affair
d) A Gentleman at Heart

3) In the 1969 film **Strangers at Sunrise** an American mining engineer is accused by the British of spying for the Boers. Who was he?
a) James Garner b) Sydney Poitier
c) George Montgomery d) William Holden

BOMBING RAIDS

1) What 1955 film was adapted from Paul Brickhill's 'Enemy Coast Ahead'?

15

The Movie Quiz Companion

terrified hens bank often

a) Dawn Patrol b) Flying Leathernecks
c) The Dambusters d) The Way to the Stars

2) In 1955 he portrayed Lt. Harry Brubaker, a reserve officer who is recalled to active service, and takes part in the bombing of five strategic Korean bridges in **The Bridges at Toko-Ri**. Who was he?
a) Mickey Rooney b) John Wayne
c) Richard Widmark d) William Holden

3) What was the target **633 Squadron** were sent to demolish in Nazi occupied Norway?
a) a rocket fuel installation b) the Bismarck
c) Gestapo Headquarters d) a U-boat base

BOOTLEGGING & PROHIBITION

1) In the 1995 drama, **Legends of the Fall**, bootleggers came to kill Triston Ludlow. Who was he?
a) River Phoenix b) Brad Pitt
c) Robert Carradine d) James Spader

2) Name the slapstick comedian who starred in the 1933 prohibition comedy, **What! No Beer?**
a) Buster Keaton b) Fatty Arbuckle
c) Harold Lloyd d) Stan Laurel

3) In which film does Tom Power's (James Cagney) brother erupt at him, shouting: "You think I don't know what you two have been up to? That's not beer in that keg, but blood and beer!"?
a) Smart Money
b) The Public Enemy
c) Angels with Dirty Faces
d) The Roaring Twenties

BOXING

1) Name the film sometimes known as the boxing film to which all others are compared, in which camera man James Wong Howe wears roller skates during the fight scenes, and for which John Garfield was Oscar-nominated for his role as the Jewish prizefighter.
a) The Set-Up b) Body and Soul
c) The Harder They Fall d) Flesh and Fury

2) John G. Avildsen earned the best director and best picture Oscars for his 1976 film on a boxing theme. Name the film.
a) Heaven Can Wait b) Rocky
c) Man at the Top d) The Prizefighter

3) Which 1962 film features Mickey Rooney as a boxing trainer?
a) Requiem for a Heavyweight b) Kid Galahad
c) The Last Fight d) Leather Gloves

BRAINS

1) In the 1939 weepie, **Dark Victory**, darling socialite, Judith Traherne, dies from a brain tumour. Who was she?
a) Loretta Young b) Barbara Stanwyck
c) Grace Kelly d) Bette Davis

2) On whose novel was the 1967 spy yarn, **Billion Dollar Brain**, based?
a) Alistair MacLean b) Len Deighton
c) Ian Fleming d) Hammond Innes

3) In **The Man With Two Brains** Steve Martin falls in love with a brain in a jar. Who played the voice of the brain?
a) Sissy Spacek b) Kathleen Turner
c) Holly Hunter d) Kim Basinger

BRAINWASHING

1) In which 1965 film was an attempt made to electronically brainwash Michael Caine?
a) Gambit
b) The Ipcress File
c) Deadfall
d) Funeral in Berlin

2) With which 1962 political thriller do you associate an entire army platoon being brainwashed?
a) 36 Hours b) The Manchurian Candidate
c) Purple Noon d) Hell's Five Hours

3) In 1980, brainwashed Professor Mendelssohn (Alan Arkin), is led to believe he has come from another planet. Name the film.
a) Simon b) Ticket to Heaven c) Telefon
d) Split Image

BRITISH EMPIRE

1) Remade as **Soldiers Three** in 1951, and **Sergeants 3** in 1961, this British Empire adventure was described by the Indian press as "scandalously anti-Indian" on its release in 1939. Name the title.
a) The Drum b) The Lives of a Bengal Lancer
c) Gunga Din d) Flame Over India

2) On whose novel was the classic 1939 adventure, **The Four Feathers** based?
a) A.E.W. Mason b) Stanley Weyman
c) Rider Haggard d) Rudyard Kipling

3) Bosambo (Paul Robeson), a Congo chieftain, helped the British suppress a native uprising in a 1935 adventure. Name the title.
a) The Emperor Jones
b) King Solomon's Mines
c) Sanders of the River d) Elephant Boy

16

the inherent typists   Themes

BROTHERS

1) In which 1954 film were Rod Steiger and Marlon Brando brothers?
a) Viva Zapata b) Guys and Dolls
c) The Ugly American d) On the Waterfront

2) Karl Boehm was one of the brothers in the 1962 musical biopic, **The Wonderful World of the Brothers Grimm**. Who was the other?
a) Laurence Harvey b) Tony Curtis
c) Danny Kaye d) Fred MacMurray

3) Adam Pontabee was the first brother to marry in Stanley Donen's classic musical, **Seven Brides For Seven Brothers**. Who was he?
a) Russ Tamblyn b) Rossano Brazzi
c) Gene Kelly d) Howard Keel

BUDDHISM

1) Who portrayed the half-American, half-Chinese Buddhist monk and master of the art of self-defence in **Kung Fu** (1972)?
a) Jackie Chan b) David Carradine
c) Bruce Lee d) Jean Claude Van Damme

2) With which 1993 film, directed by Bernardo Bertolucci, do you associate a nine year old boy being the possible reincarnation of a Tibetan Buddhist lama?
a) Little Buddha b) Buddha's Lock
c) Tragedy of a Ridiculous Man d) The Spider's Stratagem

3) The Tibetan name for the Dalai Lama can be translated in English as "Ocean of Wisdom". His name in Tibetan became the title of a film. Name the film.
a) Kwaidan b) Hwaom-kyong c) Kundun
d) Siddhartha

BUDDY MOVIES

1) Who portrayed tough, streetwise cop, Nick Pulovski's (Clint Eastwood) greenhorn partner in **The Rookie**?
a) Tom Cruise b) Brad Pitt
c) Tom Berenger d) Charlie Sheen

2) Who was dubbed 'Gumby' by James Belushi in **Red Heat**?
a) Gene Hackman b) Jeff Goldblum
c) Arnold Schwarzenegger d) Eddie Murphy

3) In what 1989 film does Jack Palance play crime boss, Yves Perret, who is out to kill buddy cops Sylvester Stallone and Kurt Russell?
a) Freebie and the Bean b) Tough Guys
c) Tango & Cash d) The Hidden

BURIED ALIVE

1) A young Dutch couple are buried alive in a 1988 thriller adapted from Tim Krabbe's novel, 'The Golden Egg'. Name the title.
a) Ordeal by Innocence b) Near Dark
c) The Vanishing d) The Disappearance

2) For what Roger Corman film does Roderick (Vincent Price) bury his sister Madeline (Myrna Fahey) alive?
a) The House of Usher b) The Pit and the Pendulum c) The Undead d) The Tomb of Ligeia

3) What 1969 horror film was inspired by the Edgar Allan Poe story, The Premature Burial?
a) The Oblong Box b) Moulin Rouge
c) The Man Who Could Cheat Death d) Scream of Fear

BURIED TREASURE

1) With which 1967 musical do you associate Elvis Presley diving for buried treasure?
a) Easy Come, Easy Go b) Fun in Acapulco
c) Paradise, Hawaiian Style d) Double Trouble

2) The vast island treasure hoard in **The Count of Monte Cristo** was discovered by Robert Donat in 1934, and Jean Marais in 1954. Who discovered it in 1961?
a) Richard Chamberlain b) Louis Jourdan
c) Stewart Granger d) Gig Young

3) For what famous sleuth did **13 Lead Soldiers** contain a vital clue to buried treasure in 1948?
a) Sherlock Holmes b) Bulldog Drummond
c) Charlie Chan d) Nick Carter

BUSES

1) In which film do heiress Ellie Andrews and reporter Peter Warne sing 'The Daring Young Man on the Flying Trapeze' on a night bus from Miami to New York?
a) The Misfits b) Strange Cargo
c) It Happened One Night d) The Hucksters

2) On whose novel was the 1957 film **The Wayward Bus** based?
a) Ernest Hemmingway b) John Steinbeck
c) William Faulkner d) Ray Bradbury

3) With which film do you associate Del Griffith leading fellow bus passengers in a rendition of the 'Flintstones' theme song?
a) Mexican Bus Ride b) Where Angels go...Trouble Follows c) Planes, Trains and Automobiles
d) Brewster's Million

CAMPING

1) With which film do you associate rednecks attacking the trio - Billy, Wyatt and George - who are camping in woods?
a) Death Wish 3 b) The Color Purple
c) The Grapes of Wrath d) Easy Rider

2) In which film do three students disappear while camping in woods near Burkittsville, Maryland?
a) Picnic at Hanging Rock b) The Blair Witch Project c) The Vanishing d) The Desperate Hours

3) Whose bra catapults itself from her body in **Carry on Camping**?
a) Joan Sims b) Hattie Jacques
c) Amanda Barrie d) Barbara Windsor

17

The Movie Quiz Companion

CANNIBALISM

1) In 1957 police arrested Ed Gein after discovering dismembered bodies and corpses at his home in Plainfield, Wisconsin. Name the 1974 film supposedly based on his story.
a) The Texas Chainsaw Massacre b) Body Snatchers c) Eating Raoul d) Night of the Living Dead

2) **Silence of the Lambs** (1991) was not the first film to feature the man-eating 'Hannibal Lecter'. Name the title of the 1986 film, directed by Michael Mann, which does have this claim.
a) Raw Meat b) Spider Baby
c) Obsession d) Manhunter

3) In which film does Georgina Spica eat her lover's penis?
a) Hussy b) Caligula c) The Cook, The Thief, His Wife & Her Lover d) Savage Messiah

CAR BOMBS

1) In which film does mobster's wife, Apollonia (Simonetta Stefanelli), die in a car bomb explosion meant for her husband?
a) Married to the Mob b) Once Upon a Time in America c) The Untouchables d) The Godfather

2) When a bomb is planted in police lieutenant Dave Bannion's (Glenn Ford) car in 1953 crime thriller, **The Big Heat**, someone else is accidentally blown up. Who is it?
a) his son b) his daughter c) his wife d) his maid

3) Which 1995 film features a priest, a Hindu holy man and a rabbi stuck in a booby-trapped limousine?
a) Top Dog b) Bomb at 10:10
c) Every Man For Himself d) The Appointment

CAVALRY CHARGES

1) Major Geoffrey Vickers rides to his death in Michael Curtiz's **The Charge of the Light Brigade** (1936). Who was he?
a) Patric Knowles b) Cary Grant
c) Errol Flynn d) Van Heflin

2) Which 1965 film features the Russian cavalry charging Bolshevik marchers?
a) Rasputin - the Mad Monk b) Iron Duke
c) Song of Russia d) Doctor Zhivago

3) Name the 1987 film which re-enacts the Australian Light Horse Brigade's charge at Beersheba during WWI.
a) The Lighthorsemen b) Young Winston
c) Living Legend d) Without a Trace

CAVE DWELLERS

1) Which film featured 'The Shell People'?
a) The Tribe b) One Million B.C. c) Cavegirl
d) One Million Years B.C.

2) Who was Roger Corman's **Teenage Caveman**?
a) Robert Vaughn b) Oliver Reed
c) Jack Nicholson d) Michael Landon

3) On whose novel was the 1986 film, **The Clan of the Cave Bear** based?
a) Cynthia Freeman b) Margaret Atwood
c) Virginia Andrews d) Jean M. Auel

CELEBRATIONS

1) In which 1992 film do Lt. Col. Frank Slade and and his minder gatecrash his brother's Thanksgiving celebrations?
a) Planes, Trains & Automobiles b) Home For the Holidays c) Hannah and Her Sisters d) Scent of a Woman

2) Name the 1988 action thriller, directed by John McTiernan, in which terrorists strike during an office Christmas party at the multinational Nakatomi Corporation.
a) The Delta Force b) Executive Decision
c) True Lies d) Die Hard

3) With which film do you associate Kid Shelleen mistaking funeral candles for a birthday celebration?
a) The Dirty Dozen b) The Comancheros
c) Cat Ballou d) Raintree County

CHAIN GANGS

1) Who directed the 1932 prison drama, **I Am a Fugitive from a Chain Gang**?
a) William Wellman b) Frank Borzage
c) Henry King d) Mervyn LeRoy

2) With which 1941 film, directed by Preston Sturges, do you associate a prisoner of a chain gang laughing with his fellow prisoners at a Mickey Mouse cartoon during a film show organised by the black congregation of a local Baptist church?
a) The Power and the Glory b) Never Say Die
c) Sullivan's Travels d) The Miracle of Morgan's Creek

3) In which film does Paul Newman's character get sent to a chain gang camp for vandalising parking meters?
a) Cool Hand Luke b) The Long Hot Summer
c) The Rack d) What a Way to Go!

CHASE MOVIES

1) In what 1963 comedy do Captain C.G. Culpepper (Spencer Tracy), Ding Bell (Mickey Rooney) *et al* all have an interest in finding gangster Smiler Grogan's buried loot?
a) Coming up Roses
b) Cannonball Run
c) It's a Mad, Mad, Mad, Mad World
d) Brewster's Millions

2) In which film do 'The Great Leslie' and 'Professor Fate' compete against each other?
a) Run For Your Life b) Dirty Mary Crazy Larry
c) Tell Them Willie Boy Is Here d) The Great Race

3) Where is the finish line for the customised cars in the 1976 action comedy, **The Gumball Rally** ?
a) New York b) Long Beach
c) New Orleans d) Key West

CHESS

1) Who was Max Von Sydow's opponent in Ingmar Bergman's, **The Seventh Seal**?
a) the Devil b) Death c) himself d) a Crusader

2) In which 1968 film do the characters portrayed by Faye Dunaway and Steve McQueen make love over a chess board?
a) The Arrangement b) Towering Inferno
c) The Thomas Crown Affair d) Nevada Smith

3) In 1993 he played a chess master who is suspected of murder during a competition in **Knight Moves**. Who was he?
a) Christopher Lambert b) Dustin Hoffman
c) Robert Duvall d) Richard Gere

CHILDREN & CHILDHOOD

1) In which film do a mother and three children live in a house called 'The Three Chimneys'?
a) The Monster Squad b) Explorers
c) The Railway Children d) The Innocents

2) Who directed **Ratcatcher**?
a) Shane Meadows b) Lynne Ramsay
c) Peter Mullen d) Beeban Kidron

3) What 1985 comedy drama about childhood friendships was based on the autobiographical novella, *The Body*?
a) Stand By Me b) Cousin Bobby
c) A World Apart d) Toto le Heros

CHILD CUSTODY DISPUTES

1) Who was **The Good Father** in 1987 who lost custody of his child?
a) Anthony Hopkins b) Liam Neeson
c) Robert Redford d) Tim Roth

2) In which 1984 film does Casey Brodsky (Drew Barrymore) sue parents Lucy and Albert Brodsky (Shelley Long & Ryan O'Neal) for custody of herself?
a) Irreconcilable Differences b) This Child is Mine
c) One Potato, Two Potato d) A Place to Be Loved

3) In which 1994 thriller does Reggie Love (Susan Sarandon) lose custody of her children?
a) Bye Bye Love b) Losing Isaiah
c) House of Cards d) The Client

TALES OF CHIVALRY

1) Who portrayed the courageous Saxon leader, **Ivanhoe**, in 1952?
a) Robert Taylor b) Tony Curtis
c) Tyrone Power d) Ray Milland

2) In 1954 he played the title role in **The Black Knight**, championing the cause of King Arthur. Who was he?
a) Gene Kelly b) William Holden
c) Omar Sharif d) Alan Ladd

3) In which 1973 drama do present-day vacationers encounter The Black Knight?
a) Into the Sun b) Somewhere in Time
c) Westworld d) Navigator: A Medieval Odyssey

CHRISTMAS

1) Who goes on a shopping spree after mistakenly believing he has won a major contest in **Christmas in July**?
a) Dick Powell b) Cary Grant
c) Maurice Chevalier d) Alec Guinness

2) In which film do Bob Wallace and Phil Davis help their old army general out of a tight spot?
a) Holiday Inn b) White Christmas
c) The Holly and the Ivy d) The Miracle

3) Who portrayed Ebeneezer Scrooge in the 1938 adaptation of Dickens' classic, **A Christmas Carol**?
a) Reginald Owen b) D'Arcy Corrigan
c) Gene Lockhart d) Charles Coleman

C.I.A.

1) His code name is "Condor" in the 1975 thriller **Three Days of the Condor**. Who was he?
a) Max von Sydow b) Richard Dreyfuss
c) Robert Redford d) Alan Rickman

The Movie Quiz Companion

my fated unreliable tutu

2) What 1973 film, directed by Michael Winner, has Alain Delon pursuing Soviet defector Burt Lancaster from Washington to Europe?
a) Death Wish b) Scorpio c) Shoot to Kill
d) The Osterman Weekend

3) Who portrayed Matt Dillon's dull middle class American father who has a secret past as a CIA agent, in Arthur Penn's 1985 film, **Target**?
a) Walter Matthau b) Tommy Lee Jones
c) Gene Hackman d) Martin Sheen

CIGARS

1) Which 1988 comedy features a cartoon 'baby' lighting a cigar and telling the director to "go to hell"?
a) Fritz The Cat b) Who Framed Roger Rabbit
c) Aladdin d) An American Tail

2) Who directed **Smoke** (1995) and **Blue in the Face** (1995), two related films set in a Brooklyn cigar store?
a) Wayne Wang b) John Woo
c) Spike Lee d) Wim Wenders

3) With which film do you associate Harold Bissonette (W.C. Fields) removing a flower from his buttonhole and putting it in his mouth while dropping his cigar into the water glass?
a) The Bank Dick b) The Fatal Glass of Beer
c) It's a Gift d) Never Give a Sucker an Even Break

CINEMA AUDIENCES

1) With which 1985 comedy-fantasy do you associate a character in a movie conversing directly with a member of the audience?
a) Peggy Sue Got Married b) That Funny Feeling
c) Starstruck d) The Purple Rose of Cairo

2) In which film do secret lovers, Alec and Laura, blend into anonymity at a cinema screening of the melodrama 'Flames of Passion'?
a) Brief Encounter b) Something Wild
c) Singin' In the Rain d) Love on the Dole

3) With which Barry Levinson film do you associate a young man winning a wager with his friends that he can get a certain girl to touch his penis before the movie ends and wins his bet by placing a carton of popcorn in his lap with a strategic hole in it?
a) Silent Movie b) Diner c) Best Friends
d) Unfaithfully Yours

CLASS

1) In 1959 he played the working-class social climber Joe Lampton in **Room at the Top**. Who was he?
a) Albert Finney b) Laurence Harvey
c) Kenneth More d) Alec Guinness

2) Name Jean Renoir's 1939 film which grappled with the pre-WWII French class system.
a) The River b) La Grande Illusion
c) La Regle Du Jeu d) Diary of a Chambermaid

3) On whose novel was the 1973 film **The Hireling** based?
a) William Faulkner b) Kate Chopin
c) L.P. Hartley d) D.H. Lawrence

CLIMBING HEROES

1) San Francisco police officer, 'Scottie' Ferguson, retires from the force after a fellow officer, when trying to pull him to safety on a rooftop, loses his footing and falls to his death. Name the film.
a) The San Francisco Story b) Vertigo
c) Panic in the City d) Detective Story

2) Which building does Richard Hannay (Robert Powell) climb in 1978 to foil a plot that would have started WWI?
a) The Tower of London b) Big Ben
c) Blackpool Tower d) The Albert Hall

3) Dr. Emmett Brown scales the clock-tower in Hill Valley in order to synchronise with the electric storm whose energy will send Marty **Back to the Future**. What time is the bolt of lightning due?
a) 10.02 pm b) 10.04 pm c) 10.06 pm d) 10.08 pm

CLIMBING VILLAINS

1) After the oil tank ignites with James Cagney on top in **White Heat** (1949) cop Hank Fallon retorts - "Cody Jarrett - he finally made it to the top of the world and it blew up in his face." Who portrayed Fallon?
a) Paul Muni b) Louis Calhern
c) Edmond O'Brien d) William Bendix

2) Hoodlum Roy Earle, pursued by police, is shot by a police marksman after having climbed part of Mt. Whitney, the highest mountain in the continental United States. Name the film.
a) High Sierra b) Scarface
c) The Roaring Twenties d) Gun Crazy

3) In which film do Pendlebury and Henry Holland race down the steps of the Eiffel Tower in pursuit of a group of schoolgirls?
a) The Man in the White Suit b) The Ladykillers
c) The Way to the Stars d) The Lavender Hill Mob

CLOCKS

1) On whose novel was the 1974 French drama, **The Clockmaker** based?
a) Georges Simenon b) Jean-Paul Sartre
c) Guy de Maupassant d) Gustave Flaubert

2) Name the 1952 film which shows frequent shots of a ticking clock which coincides exactly with the film's running time?
a) 12 Angry Men b) High Noon
c) Vertigo d) Spellbound

3) With which film do you associate the mantel clock of 15th-century child-killer Gilles de Rais?
a) Interview With The Vampire b) Rage
c) Time Bandits d) Amityville 1992: It's About Time

CLOSING LINES

Name the films which had the following closing lines:

1) "Oh, good. For a moment I thought we were in trouble."
a) They Call Me Mister Tibbs! b) Butch Cassidy

and the Sundance Kid c) The Untouchables
d) The Unsinkable Molly Brown

2) "Every one of you listening to my voice, tell the world. Tell this to everybody, wherever they are. Watch the skies, everywhere, keep looking. Keep watching the skies."
a) The Thing b) Invaders From Mars
c) When Worlds Collide d) Things to Come

3) "The old man was right, only the farmers won. We lost. We'll always lose."
a) The Grapes of Wrath b) Vera Cruz
c) Days of Heaven d) The Magnificent Seven

COLD WAR

1) In 1965 he played Alec Leamus as **The Spy Who Came in From the Cold**. Who was he?
a) Edward Fox b) Michael Caine
c) Richard Burton d) Alec Guinness

2) What did Capt. Eric Finlander (Richard Widmark) monitor daily in **The Bedford Incident**?
a) Russian Submarines b) Russian agents
c) the Kremlin dustbins d) the Soviet Embassy in Washington

3) Who played the title role in Carol Reed's 1953 spy yarn, **The Man Between**?
a) James Mason b) Paul Scofield
c) Orson Welles d) Trevor Howard

COLONIALISM

1) With which 1954 film do you associate Trevor Howard as an African colonial policeman on the verge of a mental breakdown?
a) Outcast of the Islands b) The Stranger's Hand
c) The Heart of the Matter
d) Afraid of the Dark

2) Who portrayed the pacifist missionary, Otto Witt, in **Zulu**?
a) James Booth b) Jack Hawkins
c) John Mills d) Ralph Richardson

3) Name the 1988 drama, directed by Claire Denis, about a young woman's memories of her colonial childhood in French West Africa
a) Chocolat b) Back From the Dead
c) Fire Over Africa d) French Twist

COMAS

1) John Soames lives in a coma for thirty years in the 1970 sci-fi thriller, **The Mind of Mr Soames**. Who was he?
a) Christopher Walken b) Donald Pleasence
c) Terence Stamp d) Barry Foster

2) For what film did Glenn Close portray coma victim Sunny von Bulow?
a) Jagged Edge b) She Woke Up
c) Reversal of Fortune d) The Exorcist

3) On whose novel was the 1978 film **Coma** based?
a) Stephen King b) Simon Brett
c) Peter Benchley d) Robin Cook

COMMUNISM

1) Name the American playwright portrayed by Jack Nicholson in **Reds**.
a) Eugene O'Neill b) Arthur Miller
c) Edward Albee d) Tennessee Williams

2) In which 1988 film do Tereza and Tomas (Juliette Binoche & Daniel Day-Lewis) fall in love during the Soviet invasion of Czechoslovakia?
a) Pickup on South Street b) The Unbearable Lightness of Being c) The Red Danube d) Peter and Pavla

3) In the 1985 film, **Eleni**, New York Times reporter, Nick Gage, journeys to Greece in search of his past, where his mother was executed by communists. Who portrayed Gage?
a) Elliott Gould b) Dustin Hoffman
c) Harvey Keitel d) John Malkovich

COMPUTERS

1) In which film does a computer utter the line: "Everything's under control, Dave."?
a) Alien b) Logan's Run c) Explorers
d) 2001: A Space Odyssey

2) Susan Harris is impregnated by Proteus IV, a master computer system in the 1977 sci-fi drama, **Demon Seed**. Who was she?
a) Sigourney Weaver b) Jane Fonda
c) Tuesday Weld d) Julie Christie

3) In which 1969 film do the Soviet and the US defence computers link up because they become distrustful of humans?
a) The Forbin Project b) Tron c) The Tower
d) Deadly Impact

CONCERT MOVIES

1) Who directed **The Last Waltz**?
a) Bob Dylan b) Peter Bogdanovich
c) Roman Polanski d) Martin Scorsese

2) Which film celebrates a music festival in which thousands of music lovers descend on the sleepy town of White Lake in New York's Catskill Mountains?
a) Don't Look Back b) Let the Good Times Roll
c) Let's Spend the Night Together d) Woodstock

The Movie Quiz Companion

3) Name the film which documented the concert at the Altamont Speedway in California which culminated in violence and murder.
a) Fillmore b) Gimme Shelter
c) Monterey Pop d) Concert for Bangladesh

CORRUPT COPS

1) Which 1973 film, based on the book by Peter Maas, tells the true story of a NYC policeman's attempt to expose corruption within the force?
a) Getting Straight b) Labyrinth
c) Serpico d) Small Change

2) On whose book was **LA Confidential** based?
a) James Ellroy b) Elmore Leonard
c) Norman Mailer d) Raymond Chandler

3) The 1987 crime thriller, **The Big Easy**, tells the story of which city's corrupt police department?
a) Chicago b) Seattle c) Miami d) New Orleans

CORPSES

1) What film involves cop James Malone propping a corpse against a wall, and, pretending it is alive, shooting it in order to intimidate gangsters into talking?
a) Family Business b) The Molly Maguires
c) From Russia With Love d) The Untouchables

2) What 1956 spy yarn releases a corpse from a British WWII submarine with false documents in the hope of fooling the Germans into believing the allied invasion was happening in Sicily?
a) Above Us the Waves b) Run Silent, Run Deep
c) The Man Who Never Was d) In Which We Serve

3) Which film features three corpses found buried beneath snow with their faces and fingerprints removed?
a) Pet Sematary II b) Gorky Park
c) Ice Station Zebra d) Rasputin - The Mad Monk

COUNTRY & WESTERN MUSIC

1) In 1980 she portrayed country singer Loretta Lynn in the rags-to-riches biopic **Coal Miner's Daughter**. Who was she?
a) Sissy Spacek b) Faye Dunaway
c) Jodie Foster d) Barbra Streisand

2) In which 1982 film, directed by Bruce Beresford, does Robert Duvall play a drunken down-on-his-luck country singer?
a) Crazy Mama b) Payday
c) Places in the Heart d) Tender Mercies

3) Who does Jessica Lange portray in the 1985 film **Sweet Dreams**?
a) Patsy Cline b) Dolly Parton
c) Patti LaBelle d) June Carter

COURTS-MARTIAL

1) On whose novel was **The Caine Mutiny** based?
a) Jack London b) Vladimir Nabokov
c) Herman Wouk d) J.G. Farrell

2) With which film do you associate Capt. Hargreaves (Dirk Bogarde) defending Private Arthur Hamp (Tom Courtenay) on a charge of desertion in 1964?
a) Paths of Glory b) King and Country
c) Conduct Unbecoming d) The Man in the Middle

3) Who was expelled from naval college when he was accused of stealing a five-shilling postal order from another cadet?
a) Private Potter b) Sergeant Rutledge
c) The Winslow Boy d) Roxie Hart

COURTROOM DRAMAS

1) Who directed the classic courtroom drama **12 Angry Men**?
a) Elia Kazan b) John Ford
c) Arthur Hiller d) Sidney Lumet

2) With which Fritz Lang film do you associate Dana Andrews and Joan Fontaine attempting to expose the unsoundness of circumstantial evidence?
a) Beyond Reasonable Doubt b) Confirm or Deny
c) You Only Live Once d) Fury

3) Name Otto Preminger's courtroom drama which shocked 1950's audiences with its direct approach to sex, rape, and contraceptives.
a) Margin for Error b) Whirlpool
c) Advise and Consent d) Anatomy of a Murder

COWARDICE

1) In which 1965 adventure is the character portrayed by Peter O'Toole accused of cowardice for deserting a sinking ship which goes down with 400 passengers?
a) Murphy's War b) The Savage Innocents
c) Lord Jim d) Brotherly Love

2) In which 1957 film is an entire regiment accused of cowardice?
a) Kings Go Forth b) Hell is For Heroes
c) Operation Daybreak d) Paths of Glory

vicars favourite egos   **Themes**

3) With which film do you associate college kids, Jim and Buzz, proving they aren't "chicken" by driving at speed towards a cliff edge?
a) Rebel Without a Cause b) Grease 2
c) Teen Wolf d) The Incredibly Strange Creatures Who Stopped Living and Became Mixed Up Zombies

CRASHES, CAR

1) Name the 1983 Mike Nichols film in which the character portrayed by Meryl Streep dies in a suspicious car crash involving no other vehicles.
a) Postcards From the Edge b) The Longshot
c) Silkwood d) The Fortune

2) With which 1981 comedy horror movie do you associate a multiple car crash in London's Piccadilly Circus?
a) An American Werewolf in London b) The Rocky Horror Picture Show c) Rabid
d) Crash Dive

3) In which 1989 comedy drama does Miss Werthan continually crash her car?
a) Fried Green Tomatoes b) Cocoon
c) Driving Miss Daisy d) Batteries Not Included

CRASHES, PLANE

1) The 1987 biopic **La Bamba** tells the story of a seventeen year old rock'n'roll star who died in a plane crash on February 3, 1959, along with Buddy Holly and the Big Bopper. Who was he?
a) Eddie Cochrane b) Ricky Nelson
c) Frankie Avalon d) Ritchie Valens

2) Born Jane Peters, this actress died in a plane crash during a tour selling defense bonds in 1942. By what name was she better known?
a) Jean Arthur b) Jayne Mansfield
c) Agnes Moorehead d) Carole Lombard

3) In the 1941 fantasy, **Here Comes Mr. Jordan**, prizefighter Joe Pendleton crashes his private plane and is accidentally sent to heaven by a novice angel (Edward Everett Horton). Who portrayed Joe?
a) Robert Montgomery b) Bob Hope
c) Glenn Ford d) David Niven

CRASHES, TRAIN

1) With which 1935 horror film do you associate a famous pianist losing both hands in a train crash?
a) Freaks b) Mad Love
c) The Face of Darkness d) The Hand

2) In which film did a train seconded by German colonel, von Waldheim, encounter frequent crashes engineered by the resistance, in his efforts to transport Impressionist paintings to Berlin?
a) The Train b) Von Ryan's Express
c) Berlin Express d) Night Train to Munich

3) During the looting of a crashed train in **Lawrence of Arabia**, Auda Abu Tayi retrieves a clock. Who was he?
a) Omar Sharif b) Jose Ferrer
c) Anthony Quinn d) Anthony Quayle

CULTS

1) In which 1939 film do Sgts. Cutter, MacChesney and Ballantine battle with the Thuggee cult in 19th century India?
a) The Lives of a Bengal Lancer b) The Drum
c) The Charge of the Light Brigade d) Gunga Din

2) What film connection can you make with Sherlock Holmes and an Ancient Egyptian cult?
a) Sherlock Holmes and the Voice of Terror
b) The Pearl of Death c) Young Sherlock Holmes
d) Sherlock Holmes Faces Death

3) Name the 1981 film, directed by Joe Dante, in which Dr. George Waggner's (Patrick Macnee) cult members are all werewolves.
a) The Howling b) Fright Night c) Wolf d) Wolfen

CURSES

1) In which 1988 horror film is a curse passed on by a kiss?
a) The Kiss b) Kiss Me...Kill Me c) Kiss of Death
d) Kiss of the Spider Woman

2) What film was inspired by the novel, The Curse of Capistrano, by Johnston McCulley?
a) Captain Blood b) Phantom of the Opera
c) The Shining d) The Mark of Zorro

3) With which 1983 horror film do you associate a town haunted by a 300 year old curse?
a) The Amityville Horror b) The Legacy
c) The Devonsville Terror d) I Don't Want to be Born

DANCE

1) Name the 1983 sequel to **Saturday Night Fever**?
a) Staying Alive b) Grease
c) The Music Machine d) Flashdance

2) Who danced the **Bolero** with Carole Lombard in 1934?
a) Fred Astaire b) Nelson Eddy
c) Dick Powell d) George Raft

The Movie Quiz Companion

irritating handsome hero flattened

3) What style of dancing do the rebellious Scott and Fran (Paul Mercurio & Tara Morice) practise in 1990s Australia?
a) Rumba b) Tapdancin' c) Strictly Ballroom d) Wild Style

DAUGHTERS

1) With which film do you associate Mrs Bennet's (Mary Boland) continual search for husbands for her five marriageable daughters?
a) The Little Foxes b) Little Women
c) Pride and Prejudice d) The Philadelphia Story

2) Which film features the impoverished widow Dashwood and her three daughters?
a) Little Dorrit b) David Copperfield
c) Sense and Sensibility d) A Tale of Two Cities

3) Name the film which ends with a father discovering his daughter's diary, saying: "She puts me to shame"?
a) The Diary of Ann Frank b) Diary of a Country Priest c) Guadalcanal Diary d) Diary of a Madman

D-DAY INVASION

1) After the film was released, the Normandy cemetery, where 9,386 soldiers who died in the invasion are buried, reported a marked increase in visitors, with many searching for the grave of the fictitious Captain John Miller. Name the film.
a) The Big Red One b) D-Day the Sixth of June
c) Saving Private Ryan d) Up From the Beach

2) On whose novel was the 1962 epic, **The Longest Day**, based?
a) Paul Brickhill b) Cornelius Ryan
c) Irwin Shaw d) Alistair MacLean

3) In **Battle of the Commandos** (1969), Jack Palance leads a unit of commandos behind German lines on a mission to destroy something that has to be put out of action before the D-Day invasion. What is it?
a) a code machine b) a Stuka squadron
c) a cannon d) a V2 launch site

DEAFNESS

1) Name the deaf actress who won a Best Actress Oscar for the 1986 film, **Children of a Lesser God**?
a) Angela Molina b) Marlee Matlin
c) Jennifer O'Neil d) Patti Love

2) In 1944 she portrayed a deaf socialite in love with poor physician Alan Ladd in **And Now Tomorrow**. Who was she?
a) Loretta Young b) Helen Hayes
c) Dorothy McGuire
d) Maureen O'Hara

3) For what film did Jane Wyman induce deafness by stuffing her ears with wax to try to accurately portray a deaf mute?
a) Gigot b) The Man Who Played God
c) Johnny Belinda
d) The Chosen

DEAD - BUT NOT REALLY DEAD

1) For what film does Robert Patrick portray a T-1000 android, which, no matter how many times it appears to have been destroyed, always manages to reconstruct itself?
a) Robocop 2 b) Terminator 2: Judgment Day
c) Westworld d) Godzilla Vs the Cosmic Monster

2) Jason (Todd Armstrong) kills the seven-headed hydra thinking his path is clear to take the golden fleece, but he doesn't count on the seven sword-wielding skeletons which grow out of part of its anatomy in **Jason and the Argonauts** (1963). From what part of the hydra's body do they grow?
a) its eyes b) its blood c) its tail d) its teeth

3) What thriller involves Alex Forrest seemingly rising from the dead after having been drowned in a bath tub?
a) Jagged Edge b) Something About Amelia
c) Fatal Attraction d) Mary Reilly

DEATH INCARNATE

1) In 1934 he portrayed Death in the romantic fantasy **Death Takes A Holiday**. Who was he?
a) Fredric March b) W.C. Fields
c) Danny Kaye d) Charles Boyer

2) Who directed **Orpheus**, a film in which Jean Marais encounters The Princess of Death?
a) Jean-Luc Godard b) Ingmar Bergman
c) Rainer Fassbinder d) Jean Cocteau

3) On whose story was Roger Corman's **The Masque of the Red Death** based?
a) Stephen King b) Henry James
c) Edgar Allan Poe d) Bram Stoker

DECAPITATION

1) In which film is the severed head of the wife of homicide detective, Mills, delivered to him in a box?
a) The Naked Prey b) Payday c) Persona d) Seven

2) Who directed **Bring Me the Head of Alfredo Garcia**?
a) Sam Peckinpah b) Robert Altman
c) Peter Bogdanovich d) Cy Enfield

3) With which film do you associate Peachy Carnehan carrying the head of his friend, Daniel Dravot?
a) The Man Who Would Be King b) Northwest Passage c) King Rat d) Empire of the Sun

DELINQUENTS

1) Who played the title role in the 1957 comedy, **The Delicate Delinquent**?
a) Rock Hudson b) Adam Faith
c) Jerry Lewis d) Natalie Wood

2) With which 1955 drama do you associate idealistic teacher, Glenn Ford, teaching a class of delinquent boys?
a) Blackboard Jungle b) West Side Story
c) Boys Town d) The Happiest Days of Your Life

3) Who played the title role in **Cry-Baby**?
a) Johnny Depp b) Brad Pitt
c) Russell Crowe d) Keanu Reeves

DEMONIC POSSESSION

1) Name the title of the 1961 horror film about two Victorian children, based on Henry James' thriller, *The Turn of the Screw*.
a) Demons b) The Innocents
c) House of Mortal Sin d) Tomorrow Never Comes

2) In which 1968 film does Mrs Woodhouse dream about being raped by a savage demonic beast?
a) The Sexorcist b) The Possession of Joel Delaney
c) Rosemary's Baby d) Cathy's Curse

3) What 1973 film was based on William Peter Blatty's bestselling tale of horror and religious perversion?
a) White Zombie b) The Village of the Damned
c) Demon Seed d) The Exorcist

DEPARTMENT STORES

1) In what famous New York department store is the 1947 version of **Miracle on 34th Street** set?
a) Bloomingdale's b) Macy's
c) Sak's d) Marshal Fields

2) Name the comedy team that causes havoc in MGM's 1941 comedy, **The Big Store**.
a) Abbott and Costello b) The Marx Brothers
c) The Three Stooges d) The Dead End Kids

3) Who falls in love with elevator operator, Jill St. John, in the 1963 comedy, **Who's Minding the Store**?
a) Bob Hope b) Jerry Lewis
c) James Cagney d) Fred Astaire

DEPRESSION ERA

1) In 1969 he played Byron Barr, the sleazy master of ceremonies of a 1920s dance marathon in **They Shoot Horses, Don't They?** Who was he?
a) Roy Scheider b) Gig Young
c) George Coe d) Tom Skerritt

2) Name the 1940 John Ford film which recounts the migration of the Joad family from the dustbowl to California during the depression era.
a) Each Dawn I Die b) Places in the Heart
c) The Long Voyage Home d) The Grapes of Wrath

3) What famous entertainer starred in Lewis Milestone's musical, **Hallelujah, I'm a Bum**?
a) Al Jolson b) George M. Cohan
c) Enrico Caruso d) Paul Robeson

DESERTERS

1) Army deserter, Learoyd, becomes the leader of a Borneo tribe in the 1989 war film, **Farewell to the King**. Who portrayed him?
a) Nigel Havers b) James Fox
c) Nick Nolte d) Powers Boothe

2) In which film does Vivien Leigh shoot an army deserter attempting to steal her mother's jewellery?
a) Dark Journey b) Ship of Fools
c) Gone With the Wind d) Storm in a Teacup

3) In 1951, Audie Murphy portrayed an American Civil War deserter who has a change of heart, and returns to the battlefront without anyone realising it. Name the film.
a) The Red Badge of Courage b) Beyond Glory
c) Drums Across the River d) Another Part of the Forest

DEVIL WORSHIP

1) Name the 1943 horror film, produced by Val Lewton, in which Mary Gibson (Kim Hunter) discovers that her missing sister is under the influence of a group of satanists in New York.
a) I Walked With a Zombie b) The Seventh Victim
c) Please Believe Me d) Isle of the Dead

2) With which 1987 comedy do you associate Sgt. Joe Friday (Dan Aykroyd) and Detective

The Movie Quiz Companion

Pep Streebek (Tom Hanks) investigating satanic rites in LA?
a) *The Devil and Max Devlin* b) *Turner & Hooch*
c) *Dragnet* d) *Ghostbusters*

3) Private eye, Harry Angel, visits a devil worship cult in Harlem in Alan Parker's 1987 thriller, **Angel Heart**. Who is he?
a) *Robert De Niro* b) *Mickey Rourke*
c) *Johnny Depp* d) *Russell Crowe*

DISABILITY

1) In 1946 he played Professor Warren, the maniac who murders three physically handicapped girls in Robert Siodmak's thriller **Spiral Staircase**. Who was he?
a) *George Brent* b) *Leslie Howard*
c) *Zachary Scott* d) *Herbert Lom*

2) In which film does Stan Laurel fool Ollie into believing he had lost both legs during WW1?
a) *Blockheads* b) *Saps at Sea*
c) *A Chump at Oxford* d) *Sons of the Desert*

3) Who portrayed Ronny Cammareri, the N.Y. baker with an artificial hand, in the 1987 romantic comedy, **Moonstruck**?
a) *Joe Pesci* b) *Sylvester Stallone*
c) *Randy Quaid* d) *Nicolas Cage*

DISASTER MOVIES

1) On whose novel was the 1972 film **The Poseidon Adventure** based?
a) *Paul Gallico* b) *Wilbur Smith*
c) *Alistair Maclean* d) *Hammond Innes*

2) Who was Clark Gable's leading lady in the 1936 romantic drama **San Francisco**?

a) *Lana Turner* b) *Bette Davis*
c) *Rita Hayworth* d) *Jeanette MacDonald*

3) Which disaster did director Roy Ward Baker's drama, **A Night to Remember** reconstruct in 1958?
a) *the Hindenburg inferno* b) *the sinking of the Titanic* c) *the Tay Bridge disaster* d) *Krakatoa*

DISFIGUREMENT & DEFORMITY

1) Who portrayed the facially disfigured and withdrawn war veteran, who, while staying at **The Enchanted Cottage** (1945), appears healed to Laura Pennington (Dorothy McGuire)?
a) *Walter Pidgeon* b) *Ronald Reagan*
c) *Robert Young* d) *Ray Milland*

2) Who played the title role in the 1971 horror film, **The Abominable Dr. Phibes**, in which a man, disfigured in a car crash, is out for revenge on the nine medical staff present when his wife died during surgery?
a) *Christopher Walken* b) *Lee Van Cleef*
c) *Vincent Price* d) *James Woods*

3) In which 1953 crime thriller does Vince Stone (Lee Marvin) throw scalding coffee into the face of his mistress, Debby Marsh (Gloria Grahame), horribly disfiguring one side of her face?
a) *Shout at the Devil* b) *The Killers*
c) *The Big Heat* d) *The Klansman*

DISGUISES

1) A variety of disguises are employed by Rod Steiger portraying a psychotic murderer who strangles middle-aged women in a 1968 thriller directed by Jack Smight. Name the title.
a) *The Amityville Horror* b) *Eyes of a Stranger*
c) *No Way to Treat a Lady* d) *The Midnight Man*

2) Julie's father, Les, has a crush on Dorothy, who is really Michael in drag. Name the title of this 1982 romantic comedy.
a) *Charley's Aunt* b) *Yentl*
c) *The Ballad of Little Jo* d) *Tootsie*

3) Robert Mitchum, Frank Sinatra, Burt Lancaster, Kirk Douglas, and Tony Curtis are all heavily disguised in John Huston's 1963 mystery. Name the title.
a) *Witness for the Prosecution* b) *Deadly Strangers* c) *The Major and the Minor* d) *The List of Adrian Messenger*

DIVORCE

1) Name Alan Parker's 1982 film which tells the story of the break-up of the marriage of George and Faith Dunlap (Albert Finney and Diane Keaton).
a) *Always* b) *Shoot the Moon*
c) *One More River* d) *No Hard Feelings*

2) In order for Mimi Glossop (Ginger Rogers) to get a divorce in the 1934 musical comedy, **The Gay Divorcee**, her lawyer arranges for a witnessed assignation to take place with professional correspondent, Rodolfo Tonetti. Who played Tonetti?
a) *Erik Rhodes* b) *Edward Everett Horton*
c) *Charles Coleman*
d) *Eric Blore*

3) In which 1951 thriller does Miriam refuse to give tennis star Guy Haines a divorce so he can marry Anne and live happily ever after?
a) *Dark Victory* b) *Act of Vengeance*
c) *Strangers on a Train*
d) *All About Eve*

DOUBLES

1) On whose novel was the 1937 role-switching adventure, **The Prince and the Pauper** based?
a) Anthony Hope b) Mark Twain
c) Alexandre Dumas d) Rudyard Kipling

2) In which 1956 sci-fi thriller are doubles hatched from 'pods'?
a) Demon Seed b) Children of the Damned
c) Not of This Earth d) Invasion of the Body Snatchers

3) In which film does John Ferguson dress Judy Barton in the image of his dead lover?
a) Stolen Face b) Vertigo c) Night Passage d) The Man Who Knew Too Much

DREAMS

1) Who played the title role in **The Secret Life of Walter Mitty**?
a) Danny Kaye b) Bob Hope
c) Dick Powell d) Peter Sellers

2) Name the avant-garde artist who created the surrealist dream sequence in Hitchcock's **Spellbound**.
a) Pablo Picasso b) Jackson Pollock
c) Salvador Dali d) Rene Magritte

3) In which Ingmar Bergman film does Professor Isak Borg (Victor Seastrom) dream about his own funeral?
a) Smiles of a Summer Night b) The Virgin Spring
c) Through a Glass Darkly d) Wild Strawberries

DROWNING

1) Manuel, the Portuguese fisherman, is pulled under the ocean by his ship's mast in **Captains Courageous**. Who was he?
a) Lionel Barrymore b) Melvyn Douglas
c) Mickey Rooney d) Spencer Tracy

2) In which Ken Russell film is an estate's lake drained and the bodies of two newlyweds discovered entwined in the mud?
a) The Music Lovers b) Women in Love
c) The Devils d) Mahler

3) Which 1978 biopic was based on the life of the poet who wrote the lines:
"I was much too far out all my life
And not waving, but drowning"?
a) The Lost Moment b) Stevie c) Tom & Viv
d) An Angel at My Table

DRUGS & DRUG ADDICTION

1) What 1955 drama, directed by Otto Preminger, portrayed Frank Sinatra as a heroin addict?
a) Pal Joey b) The Manchurian Candidate
c) Cast a Giant Shadow d) The Man With the Golden Arm

2) Who directed the 1967 cult favourite **The Trip**?
a) Roger Corman b) Roman Polanski
c) Peter Fonda d) Jack Nicholson

3) He portrayed real-life comedian Lenny Bruce who became hooked on drugs in the 1974 film **Lenny**. Who was he?
a) Jack Lemon b) Steve Martin
c) Warren Beatty d) Dustin Hoffman

DRUNK SCENES

1) What makes Tom Doniphon (John Wayne) get drunk and burn his house down in John Ford's western classic, **The Man Who Shot Liberty Valance**?
a) Ransom Stoddard (James Stewart) stole his girl
b) Liberty Valance killed his negro hired hand
c) the railroad was coming to town
d) Dutton Peabody, a local newspaper man, had been murdered

2) In which film does Frank Bryant utter the line - "Life is such a rich and frantic form that I need the drink to help me step delicately through it"?
a) Sleuth b) Alfie c) Educating Rita d) Mona Lisa

3) With which film do you associate villain Phillip Vandamm and associates forcing Roger Thornhill to consume copious quantities of bourbon and then putting him in the driver's seat of a car on a dangerous mountain road?
a) The Desperate Hours b) Detour
c) North by Northwest d) Miller's Crossing

DUELS

1) With which 1975 film do you associate Ryan O'Neal fighting a duel?
a) Wild Rovers b) What's Up Doc?
c) Barry Lyndon d) The Thief Who Came to Dinner

2) Captain Esteban Pasquale fought Don Diego Vega (Tyrone Power) in a memorable duel in the finale of **The Mark of Zorro** (1940). Who was he?
a) Charles Boyer b) Basil Rathbone
c) Paul Henreid d) Claude Rains

3) The characters portrayed by Ronald Colman and Douglas Fairbanks Jnr. fought a duel in 1937 in a film based on a novel by Anthony Hope. Name the title.
a) The Prisoner of Zenda b) The Corsican Brothers c) Catherine the Great d) Gunga Din

EARTHQUAKES

1) With which 1965 film do you associate scientist Stephen Sorensen (Dana Andrews)

The Movie Quiz Companion

causing an earthquake with missile tests while trying to harness energy from the Earth's core?
a) The Day the Earth Moved b) Crack in the World c) The Night the World Exploded d) Life on the Edge

2) In which 1962 Disney film do Hayley Mills and Maurice Chevalier encounter an earthquake?
a) Journey to the Centre of the Earth b) Summer Magic c) In Search of the Castaways d) Mr Forbush and the Penguins

3) With which 1985 film do you associate the swordsman, Kalidor (Arnold Schwarzenegger) entering the temple of Queen Gedren, who has stolen an emerald that will destroy the world in thirteen days, by flood and earthquake?
a) Conan the Barbarian b) Hercules in New York c) Red Sonja d) Conan the Destroyer

ELECTRIC CHAIR & GAS CHAMBER

1) Who portrayed the real life criminal, Barbara Graham, who was sentenced to the gas chamber, in Robert Wise's 1958 crime drama **I Want to Live!**?
a) Susan Hayward b) Ava Gardner c) Joan Fontaine d) Barbara Stanwyck

2) Tom Connors (Spencer Tracy) goes willingly to the chair for a murder committed by his girlfriend in **20,000 Years in Sing Sing**. Who portrayed his girlfriend?
a) Lana Turner b) Lauren Bacall c) Jean Harlow d) Bette Davis

3) Name the 1944 thriller which had its gas chamber scene cut by the official censor after its premiere.
a) Night of the Hunter b) Double Indemnity c) High Sierra d) Anatomy of a Murder

END OF THE WORLD & POST-APOCALYPSE

1) On the novel of which writer was Stanley Kramer's 1959 end-of-world drama **On the Beach** based?

a) J.G. Ballard b) John Wyndham c) H.G. Wells d) Nevil Shute

2) Who directed **The War Game**?
a) Peter Watkins b) Fritz Lang c) John Frankenheimer d) Peter Weir

3) Who provided the voice of Jim Bloggs in the 1988 animated film **When the Wind Blows**?
a) John Gielgud b) Joss Ackland c) James Mason d) John Mills

EPIDEMICS

1) With which 1938 film do you associate Bette Davis in the middle of a yellow jack (yellow fever) epidemic?
a) The Letter b) Dark Victory c) Jezebel d) Juarez

2) Crusader knight, Antonius Block, returns from the Crusades to find his country in the grip of a plague and witchhunts in Ingmar Bergman's **The Seventh Seal**. Who was he?
a) Yves Montand b) Gunnar Björnstrand c) Max von Sydow d) Curt Jurgens

3) Name the 1940 drama, based on a novel by A.J. Cronin, which features an epidemic of cerebrospinal fever.
a) Eighty Thousand Suspects b) Vigil in the Night c) Isle of the Dead d) The Rains Came

ETERNAL YOUTH & REJUVENATION

1) On whose novel was Frank Capra's 1937 tale of Shangri-La, **The Lost Horizon** based?
a) Sir Arthur Conan Doyle b) John Buchan c) James Hilton d) Daniel Defoe

2) In which film does Ayesha (Ursula Andress) try to entice a traveller to bathe in the mysterious Flame of Life?
a) The Wasp Woman b) The Thirsty Dead c) She d) Evil Spawn

3) With which 1993 film do you associate Tilda Swinton's character changing sex and living for 400 years?
a) Death Becomes Her b) Orlando c) Metamorphosis d) The Immortal

EXPEDITIONS

1) Where did Lord Roxton (Michael Rennie) and Professor Challenger (Claude Rains) lead an expedition to in a 1960 adventure?
a) Island of the Lost b) The Treasure of the Amazon c) The Lost World d) The Mummy's Tomb

2) In which film does an Amazon expedition encounter the half fish, half human, Gill Man?
a) It's Alive b) Isle of the Dead c) The Beast From 20,000 Fathoms d) Creature From the Black Lagoon

3) With which 1972 historical drama do you associate Pizarro's expedition in search of the seven cities of gold in 1560?
a) Aguirre: The Wrath of God b) The Royal Hunt of the Sun c) The Exterminating Angel d) The Navigator

EXPLOSIONS

1) In which film does Cody Jarrett meet his end on the top of an exploding oil tank in 1949?
a) The Asphalt Jungle b) Ministry of Fear c) White Heat d) The Beast From 20,000 Fathoms

2) Dr. Andrew Manson dynamites the sewers which are the cause of so much disease in a Welsh mining town in the 1938 drama, **The Citadel**. Who was he?
a) Walter Pidgeon b) Jack Hawkins c) John Mills d) Robert Donat

3) In 1969 railroad employee, Woodcock, kept getting his baggage car (which held the safe), blown to bits by outlaws. Who were they?
a) The Wild Bunch b) The Long Riders
c) Butch Cassidy and the Sundance Kid d) Buck and the Preacher

FAMILY LIFE

1) On whose play was David Lean's 1944 drama **This Happy Breed** based?
a) Terence Rattigan b) John Osborne
c) Shelagh Delaney d) Noel Coward

2) Name the 1970 film, starring Jack Nicholson and Karen Black, which scrutinised the upper middle class American way of life.
a) Five Easy Pieces b) House of Strangers
c) Nothing in Common d) Long Day's Journey into Night

3) In what city is Terence Davies' autobiographical **Distant Voices, Still Lives** set?
a) Birmingham b) Glasgow
c) Liverpool d) Newcastle-upon-Tyne

FASCISM

1) Klaus Brandauer (Hendrik Hofgen) sells his soul to the Nazis in Istvan Szabo's 1981 film based on a novel by Klaus Mann (son of Thomas). Name the title.
a) Mephisto b) My Life as a Dog
c) Lacombe Lucien d) The Unbearable Lightness of Being

2) In 1964 she portrayed Parisian chambermaid Celestine in Luis Bunuel's **Diary of a Chambermaid**, whose diary records the conditions which made the rise of European fascism inevitable. Who was she?
a) Susan Hayward b) Jeanne Moreau
c) Charlotte Rampling d) Jean Simmons

3) Former Beatle George Harrison's first venture into film-making was a story based on David Halliwell's play of a young man who forms a neofascist group. Name the title.
a) The Cannibals b) Little Malcolm and His Struggle Against the Eunuchs c) The Conformist d) The Last of England

FASHION WORLD

1) Who directed **Pret-a-Porter**?
a) Robert Altman b) John Boorman
c) David Lynch d) Steven Soderbergh

2) In which 1995 film is fashion designer, Isaac Mizrahi, inspired to design: "A wild fake fur coat that covers you from your neck to your ankles, so you can go out of the house wearing absolutely nothing underneath, and go down to the corner, and look fabulous…"?
a) Unzipped b) Belle De Jour
c) Hollow Image d) Fellini's Roma

3) With which 1934 musical do you associate designer Bette Davis and con-man William Powell immersing themselves in the world of Paris fashions?
a) Front Page Woman b) Housewife
c) Fashions d) The Rich Are Always With Us

FATHERS

1) Who was **Father of the Bride** in 1991?
a) Danny Aiello b) John Candy
c) Chevy Chase d) Steve Martin

2) In which film does the father of Chelsea Thayer (Jane Fonda) say to his wife Ethel: "Do you wanna dance, or would you rather just suck face?"?
a) On Golden Pond b) Cat Ballou
c) Barefoot in the Park d) California Suite

3) Who portrayed James Dean's father, Adam Trask, in Elia Kazan's 1955 drama, **East of Eden**?
a) Lionel Barrymore b) Raymond Massey
c) Louis Calhern d) Glenn Ford

FBI

1) To ensure Hollywood told the story the way he wanted it, J. Edgar Hoover loaned real agents to appear in James Cagney's 1935 crime drama. Name the title.
a) The FBI Story b) "G" Men
c) I Was a Communist for the FBI d) The Private Files of J. Edgar Hoover

2) Name the actress who portrayed the FBI Agent who fell in love with Gary Simmons (Tom Berenger) in the 1988 thriller **Betrayed**.
a) Cher b) Debra Winger
c) Nicole Kidman d) Demi Moore

3) For which film was Jodie Foster awarded an AA for Best Actress for her portrayal of FBI agent Clarice Starling?
a) Manhunter b) Eyes of a Stranger
c) Prizzi's Honor d) Silence of the Lambs

FEMINISM

1) Who portrayed Beryl Thibodeaux, the feminist who teaches women's self-defence classes in the 1984 thriller, **Tightrope**?
a) Catherine Deneuve b) Mia Farrow
c) Annette Bening d) Michelle Pfeiffer

2) Jenny Fields had sex with a dying man because she wanted a child, but not a relationship, in **The World According to Garp**. Who was she?
a) Jane Fonda b) Glenn Close
c) Diahnne Abbott d) Talia Shire

3) On whose novel was the 1980 film **The Women's Room** based?
a) Marilyn French
b) Virginia Woolf
c) Lynne Reid Banks
d) Margaret Atwood

The Movie Quiz Companion

fetish of retired pet

FEUDS

1) With which Disney animated feature do you associate a long-standing feud between a caterpillar and a woodpecker?
a) The Fox and the Hound b) The Sword and the Stone c) Pocahontas d) The Beauty and the Beast

2) In which 1977 film do French officers D'Hubert (Keith Carradine) and Feraud (Harvey Keitel) conduct a long-running feud?
a) Desert Legion b) Belizaire the Cajun
c) The Duellists d) Beau Geste

3) With which well known comedian does Fred Allen conduct a fued in the 1940 comedy, **Love Thy Neighbor**?
a) Jack Benny b) Arthur Askey
c) Bob Hope d) George Burns

FIGHTS

1) Who portrayed the corrupt union boss, Johnny Friendly, who fights Terry Malloy (Marlon Brando) on New York's dockside in **On the Waterfront**?
a) Rod Steiger b) Robert Shaw
c) Lee J. Cobb d) Sterling Hayden

2) The saloon brawl in Michael Curtiz's classic 1939 western, starring Errol Flynn, is used as stock footage in countless other films. Name the title.
a) They Died With Their Boots On b) Dodge City
c) The Man From Laramie d) The Kentuckian

3) **Shane** (Alan Ladd) fights Joe Starrett to prevent him going into town where he faced certain death in a gunfight? Who portrayed Joe?
a) Van Heflin b) Glenn Ford
c) Victor Mature d) Tyrone Power

FIRES

1) What 1938 film, directed by Henry King, tells the story of the great Chicago fire of 1871?
a) In Old Chicago b) City on Fire
c) The Shining Hour d) The Glorious Adventure

2) In 1958 he played suspected "barn burner" Ben Quick, whose father likes to resolve an argument by burning people's barns to the ground in **The Long, Hot Summer**. Who was he?
a) Paul Newman b) Rock Hudson
c) Robert Mitchum d) Frank Sinatra

3) It took director Mervyn LeRoy 24 days to shoot the burning of ancient Rome in his 1951 historical spectacular. Name the title.
a) Demetrius and the Gladiators b) Julius Caesar
c) Quo Vadis d) Spartacus

FIRING SQUADS

1) In 1958 she portrayed wartime agent, Violet Szabo, who won a posthumous George Cross and was executed by the Nazis in **Carve Her Name With Pride**. Who was she?
a) Virginia McKenna b) Claudette Colbert
c) Mary Astor d) Jean Simmons

2) Why was the eponymous heroine of **Nurse Edith Cavell** (1939) executed by the Germans during WW1?
a) for spying b) for working with the Belgian underground c) for stealing drugs d) for making derogatory remarks about the Kaiser

3) In which film does a character portrayed by Nicolas Cage survive a firing squad?
a) Trapped in Paradise b) Zandalee
c) Firebirds d) Captain Corelli's Mandolin

FISHING

1) In **The Godfather Part II** Fredo is murdered by a hit man while fishing on Lake Tahoe. Who portrayed Fredo?
a) Tim Carey b) Richard Conti
c) Guy Stockwell d) John Cazale

2) Who played the title role in the 1958 version of **The Old Man and the Sea**?
a) William Bendix
b) Spencer Tracy
c) Burt Lancaster
d) Dick Powell

3) Reverend MacLean teaches his sons the art of fly-fishing in **A River Runs Through It** (1992). Who was he?
a) Robert Redford b) Tom Skerritt
c) Tom Berenger d) Willem Dafoe

FLYING

1) In 1970, Bud Cort played the title role in a Robert Altman film about a young boy who is desperate to fly. Name the film.
a) Brewster McCloud b) Oscar
c) The Jester d) Mr. Klein

2) Which film features a street urchin holding on to a genie's pigtail and flying through the skies towards the All-Seeing Eye?
a) Son of Sinbad b) 1001 Arabian Nights
c) Flying Wild d) The Thief of Bagdad

3) On whose original story was the 1968 musical fantasy **Chitty Chitty Bang Bang** based?
a) Ian Fleming b) Paul Theroux
c) C.S. Lewis d) Edith Nesbit

FOG

1) With which film do you associate Ronald Colman escaping in the fog from Medbury Asylum during WW1 armistice celebrations?
a) The Light That Failed b) Condemned
c) The Masquerader d) Random Harvest

2) As Rick and Renault walk across a runway enveloped by fog at the end of **Casablanca**, Rick reminds Renault that he still owes him a 10,000 franc wager. On what conviction was the bet based?

frothier fiasco

a) the belief that Laszlo would escape
b) that Rick would kill Major Strasser if he had to
c) that Renault had a heart after all
d) that they would both end up fighting for the same side

3) Who directed the 1980 supernatural thriller **The Fog**?
a) Sidney Lumet b) Stanley Kubrick
c) David Lynch d) John Carpenter

FOREIGN LEGION

1) With which Foreign Legion adventure do you associate the fabulous gemstone called "the Blue Water"?
a) Beau Ideal b) Beau Geste c) Desert Legion
d) Abbott and Costello in the Foreign Legion

2) With which film do you associate Laurel and Hardy joining the Foreign Legion?
a) The Midnight Patrol b) Nothing But Trouble
c) Sons of the Desert d) The Flying Deuces

3) What book by Ouida, pen name of British romantic novelist Marie Louise de la Ramee, provided the substance for 20th Century Fox's 1936 classic tale of the Legion, starring Ronald Colman and Claudette Colbert?
a) Legion of the Doomed b) The Lost Patrol
c) Under Two Flags d) Beau Ideal

FRENCH RESISTANCE

1) What 1944 film connection can you make between Humphrey Bogart and the French Resistance?
a) To Have and Have Not b) Sahara
c) Casablanca d) Dark Passage

2) Who portrayed English agent, Susan Traherne, who works with the French Resistance in the 1985 drama, **Plenty**?
a) Tracey Ullman b) Meryl Streep
c) Natasha Richardson d) Julie Christie

3) With which Louis Malle film do you associate a young farm boy being rejected by the French Resistance for being too young and who joins the Gestapo instead?
a) Pretty Baby b) The Fire Within c) The Thief of Paris d) Lacombe, Lucien

THE FUTURE

1) Who portrayed the confused hero, Winston Smith, in the 1984 version of **1984**?
a) Richard Burton b) Edmond O'Brien
c) John Hurt d) Denholm Elliott

2) In which 1995 film does James Cole travel from the future back to the year 1990 to trace the source of a plague virus which would wipe out five billion people?
a) Terminator b) Twelve Monkeys
c) Soylent Green d) Quatermass II

3) Who directed the classic silent-film fantasy, **Metropolis**?
a) Sergei Eisenstein b) Edmund Goulding
c) Ernst Lubitsch d) Fritz Lang

GAME SHOWS

1) Who becomes a national celebrity on a TV quiz show in the 1950 comedy, **Champagne for Caesar**?
a) Charles Coburn b) Ann Sheridan
c) Googie Withers d) Ronald Colman

2) In which film do burglars participate in a radio quiz show while robbing a house, and in the process win new furniture for the householder?
a) Stay Tuned b) National Lampoon's European Vacation c) Radio Days d) Take It or Leave It

3) Lynda Dummar wins $10,000 tap dancing to a Rolling Stones song on a TV game show in the 1980 comedy, **Melvin and Howard**. Who was she?

a) Mary Steenburgen b) Tilda Swinton
c) Sally Field d) Nancy Spungen

GERM WARFARE

1) In 1953 he portrayed Jungle Jim who does battle against white hunters who are testing germ warfare weapons on animals in **Killer Ape**. Who was he?
a) Johnny Weissmuller b) Steve Reeves
c) Jock Mahoney d) Buster Crabbe

2) Which 1971 film tells the story of the sole survivor of a bacteriological war who is besieged by the zombie-like survivors?
a) The Andromeda Strain b) The Omega Man
c) X The Unknown d) Alphaville

3) Who portrayed the character who is involved in an accident at a germ warfare research lab and its tragic consequences in the 1985 thriller, **Warning Sign**?
a) Joe Sheridan b) Denis Carey
c) Sam Waterston d) Bruce Glover

GETAWAY CARS

1) With which 1947 crime thriller, directed by Carol Reed, do you associate wounded IRA fugitive, Johnny McQueen, falling from a getaway car after a daring robbery?
a) The Fallen Idol b) The Running Man
c) The Man Between d) Odd Man Out

The Movie Quiz Companion

semen eradicates trader

2) Who played the title role in **The Driver** (1978)?
*a) Bruce Dern b) Kevin Kline
c) Ryan O'Neal d) Oliver Reed*

3) Who was Steve McQueen's leading lady in **The Getaway**?
*a) Ali MacGraw b) Barbra Streisand
c) Charlotte Rampling d) Faye Dunaway*

GIANTS

1) On which H.G. Wells story was the 1965 film, **Village of the Giants** based?
a) The Island of Dr Moreau b) The Food of the Gods c) When the Sleeper Awakes d) The First Men in the Moon

2) Who or what was **The Giant Behemoth** (1959)?
a) a radioactive dinosaur b) a plague-carrying gorilla c) a poison-spitting spider d) a bloodsucking leech

3) Which 1963 fantasy features the giant bronze god, Talos?
a) Jason and the Argonauts b) The Giants of Thessaly c) The 300 Spartans d) Goliath Against the Giants

GOLD

1) Name the 'Road' film which takes Hope and Crosby in search of gold in 1945.
*a) Road to Utopia b) Road to Rio
c) Road to Hong Kong d) Road to Bali*

2) In which film does a villain threaten to contaminate the U.S. gold supplies at Fort Knox with lethal radiation?
*a) Goldfinger
b) The Parallax View
c) State of Siege
d) The World of Henry Orient*

3) With which film do you associate a prison inmate named Mr. Bridger masterminding a $4,000,000 gold bullion robbery?
*a) El Condor
b) The Heist
c) The Italian Job
d) The Thomas Crown Affair*

GOLF

1) On the life of which famous golfer was the film, **Follow the Sun** based?
*a) Ben Hogan b) Willie Park
c) Arnold Palmer d) Nick Faldo*

2) For what film did Katherine Hepburn portray a golf pro with Spencer Tracy playing her shady promoter?
*a) Woman of the Year b) Adam's Rib
c) Suddenly Last Summer d) Pat and Mike*

3) Name the comedy duo who starred in the 1953 golfing caper, **The Caddy**.
a) Bing Crosby and Bob Hope b) Dean Martin and Jerry Lewis c) Arthur Askey and Richard Murdoch d) Abbott and Costello

GRANDFATHERS

1) Which film features Sean Connery as the grandfather of Matthew Broderick?
*a) Medicine Man b) A Good Man in Africa
c) Rising Sun d) Family Business*

2) Paul McCartney's grandfather in **A Hard Day's Night** was described as a "clean old man". Who portrayed him?
*a) Wilfred Hyde White b) Peter Sellers
c) Wilfrid Brambell d) Norman Rossington*

3) In which 1937 comedy drama, set on a British Army outpost in India, does Priscilla (Shirley Temple) charm her grandfather, quintessential old soldier, Colonel Williams (C. Aubrey Smith)?
*a) The Little Princess b) The Little Colonel
c) Captain January d) Wee Willie Winkie*

GRANDMOTHERS

1) With which animated Disney adventure do you associate 'Old Grandmother Willow'?
*a) Cinderella b) Bambi c) Pocahontas
d) The Aristocats*

2) Who portrayed Finn's (Winona Ryder) grandmother in the 1995 romantic drama, **How to Make an American Quilt**?
*a) Ellen Burstyn b) Jessica Tandy
c) Anne Bancroft d) Lauren Bacall*

3) In the 1958 musical, **Gigi**, she portrayed Leslie Caron's grandmother, Mme Alvarez. Who was she?
*a) Eva Gabor b) Mitzi Gaynor
c) Dame Flora Robson d) Hermione Gingold*

THE GUILLOTINE

1) In 1935 he portrayed Sir Percy Blakeney, an English aristocrat who rescued countless French nobles from the guillotine in Alexander Kordas's classic adventure, **The Scarlet Pimpernel**. Who was he?
*a) David Niven b) Fredric March
c) Leslie Howard d) John Barrymore*

2) Dirk Bogarde portrayed the doomed hero Sydney Carton in the 1958 version of **A Tale of Two Cities**. Who portrayed him in the 1936 version?
*a) Ronald Colman b) Robert Donat
c) Walter Pidgeon d) William Powell*

3) Name the actor who is led to the guillotine in the opening scenes of Raoul Walsh's **Uncertain Glory**.
*a) John Wayne b) Errol Flynn c) Boris Karloff
d) Gary Cooper*

GUNFIGHTS

1) Lin McAdam has a shootout with his brother, Dutch Henry Brown, in the final

Themes

scenes of **Winchester '73** (1950). Who portrayed Dutch?
a) Millard Mitchell b) Dan Duryea
c) Stephen McNally d) Rock Hudson

2) In which film does Marshal Kane fight it out with Frank Miller and his gang?
a) The Unforgiven b) My Darling Clementine
c) The Man From Laramie d) High Noon

3) In which 1969 drama do the 'banditos Yanqui' die in a gunfight?
a) Butch Cassidy and the Sundance Kid
b) Ulzana's Raid c) Shalako d) El Dorado

GUNS

1) Marsh Williams invented the 'floating chamber' for his famous rifle while serving a prison sentence in Richard Thorpe's 1952 biopic, **Carbine Williams**. Who portrayed him?
a) Joel McCrea b) James Stewart
c) Alan Ladd d) Tyrone Power

2) What 1957 film, directed by Stanley Kramer, was based on C.S. Forester's novel, *The Gun*?
a) The Pride and the Passion b) Home of the Brave c) Invitation to a Gunfighter
d) The Defiant Ones

3) Who played the title role in the 1958 western, **The Last of the Fast Guns**?
a) Jeff Chandler b) Audie Murphy
c) Randolph Scott d) Jock Mahoney

GYPSIES

1) In which film do Laurel and Hardy play a couple of implausible gypsies?
a) The Bohemian Girl b) Busy Bodies
c) The Music Box d) Our Relations

2) Who made a cameo appearance as a gypsy stableman in John Huston's **The List of Adrian Messenger**?
a) Robert Mitchum b) Burt Lancaster
c) Tony Curtis
d) Frank Sinatra

3) In 1957 she played the beautiful gypsy Esmeralda in **The Hunchback of Notre Dame**. Who was she?
a) Gina Lollobrigida b) Ava Gardner
c) Shirley Jones d) Heather Sears

HALLUCINATIONS

1) Who directed the 1965 horror film, **Repulsion**, depicting the mental decline of the sexually repressed Carol Ledoux (Catherine Deneuve) who hallucinates in her sister's apartment?
a) Roger Corman b) Roman Polanski
c) Andy Warhol d) Nicholas Roeg

2) In Martin Scorsese's religious epic, **The Last Temptation of Christ**, Jesus hallucinates during his crucifixion about what his life would have been like if he had been an ordinary man and married Mary Magdalene. Who portrayed Mary Magdalene?
a) Amy Robinson b) Holly Hunter
c) Jessica Lange d) Barbara Hershey

3) Name the Sherlock Holmes adventure in which all the victims die while hallucinating.
a) Sherlock Holmes in Washington b) Sherlock Holmes and the Spider Woman c) Young Sherlock Holmes d) The Private Life of Sherlock Holmes

HEIST & CAPER FILMS

1) With which city do you associate the theft of a priceless dagger from a museum in the 1964 comedy, **Topkapi**?
a) Athens b) Istanbul c) Cairo d) Baghdad

2) For which film did Jack Hawkins portray ex-army colonel Hyde, who masterminds a million-pound bank heist in 1961?
a) The League of Gentlemen b) The Ladykillers
c) It Takes a Thief d) Rififi

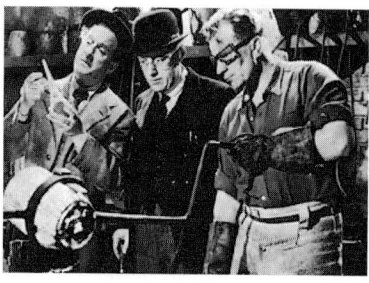

3) With which film do you associate gold bullion being melted down and smuggled out of the country as Eiffel Tower souvenirs?
a) Gambit b) Ocean's Eleven
c) Made in Heaven
d) The Lavender Hill Mob

HELICOPTERS

1) What James Bond film opens with 007 trapped inside a remote controlled helicopter?
a) Live and Let Die b) Never Say Never Again
c) Diamonds Are Forever d) For Your Eyes Only

2) Name the 1983 action film, directed by John Badham, which was based on LA's police helicopter surveillance team.
a) Fire Birds b) Sky Heist
c) Blue Thunder d) Birds of Prey

3) What 1960 film opens with a large statue of Jesus suspended from a helicopter above the streets of Rome?
a) Roman Holiday
b) La Dolce Vita
c) Umberto D
d) Bicycle Thieves

The Movie Quiz Companion

HIJACKING

1) Name the title of the film which was the official Israeli version of the 1976 Entebbe highjacking.
a) Raid on Entebbe b) Operation Thunderbolt
c) Victory at Entebbe d) Operation Snatch

2) What 1986 film was inspired by the real-life hijacking of a TWA airliner to Beirut?
a) Passenger 57 b) The Delta Force
c) The Outside Woman d) The Terrorists

3) Who portrayed the U.S. judge in **Judgement in Berlin**, who has to ascertain whether or not it is justifiable for a young couple to hijack an airliner from East to West Berlin?
a) Willem Dafoe b) Martin Sheen
c) Nick Nolte d) Sam Shepard

HINDUISM

1) Lady Edwina Esketh attempts to seduce Hindu doctor, Major Rama Safti (Tyrone Power) in the 1939 drama, **The Rains Came**. Who was she?
a) Myrna Loy b) Bette Davis
c) Mae West d) Donna Reed

2) Which film featured 'Hindu - The Living Torso'?
a) Night People b) The Greatest Show on Earth
c) The Island of Dr. Moreau d) Freaks

3) In which Pink Panther movie does 'Hindu Harry' (Bill Cummins) appear?
a) The Pink Panther b) The Pink Panther Strikes Again c) The Return of the Pink Panther d) The Revenge of the Pink Panther

HITCH-HIKING

1) With which film do you associate audacious heiress, Ellie Andrews, giving itinerant reporter, Peter Warne, a hitch-hiking lesson?
a) How to Marry a Millionaire b) The Miracle of Morgan's Creek c) It Happened One Night d) Lost in America

2) Which Roman Polanski film involves a couple picking up a hitch-hiker and asking him to join them on a boating holiday?
a) Knife in the Water b) Repulsion
c) The Fearless Vampire Killers d) Cul de Sac

3) Who portrayed Alan Squier, the penniless traveller who hitch-hikes through **The Petrified Forest** in 1936.
a) John Garfield b) Peter Lorre
c) Humphrey Bogart d) Leslie Howard

HOLIDAYS

1) Who directed **Roman Holiday** (1953)?
a) William Wyler b) Elia Kazan
c) Otto Preminger d) George Stevens

2) What 1987 film involves two out of work actors going on holiday "by mistake" to a remote cottage in the Lake District?
a) Where the Boys Are b) Strange Holiday
c) Two of a Kind d) Withnail & I

3) In which 1988 film does the character portrayed by John Candy have his summer holiday ruined by his in-laws?
a) The Great Outdoors b) National Lampoon's Vacation c) Summer Rental d) Nothing But Trouble

HOLLYWOOD & THE MOVIE BUSINESS

1) With which film do you associate Esther Blodgett and Vicki Lester?
a) Nickelodeon b) Two Weeks in Another Town
c) Valley of the Dolls d) A Star is Born

2) Who directed playwright Clifford Odet's gloomy view of Hollywood in the 1955 drama, **The Big Knife**?
a) Robert Aldrich b) George Cukor
c) Elia Kazan d) King Vidor

3) Name the film which was based on a story called *A Can of Beans*, by Charles Brackett and Billy Wilder.
a) The James Dean Story b) Goodbye, Norma Jean
c) The Bad and the Beautiful
d) Sunset Blvd.

THE HOLOCAUST

1) On whose novel was 1982 drama, **Sophie's Choice** based?
a) Irwin Shaw b) Isaac Singer
c) Saul Bellow d) William Styron

2) Who directed **The Pawnbroker**?
a) Sidney Lumet b) Luis Buñuel
c) Jean Negulesco d) Ernst Lubitsch

3) Claude Lanzmann's 1985 documentary, **Shoah**, chronicles the memories of Holocaust survivors. What does 'Shoah' mean in Hebrew?
a) annihilation b) life c) solution d) survive

HOMECOMINGS

1) With which 1941 film do you associate the homecoming of Alvin (Gary Cooper), when the entire population of Three Forks of the Valley of the Wolf, Tennessee, turn out to greet him?
a) Meet John Doe b) Sergeant York
c) Mr. Deeds Goes to Town d) The Real Glory

2) Ma Powers was busy making preparations for her son Tom's homecoming. When she answers the doorbell Tom falls into the hallway wrapped in bandages and a blanket with a gunshot wound through his head. Name the film.
a) The Public Enemy b) The Roaring Twenties
c) Little Caesar d) G Men

3) With which film do you associate boxer Sean Thornton returning to his birthplace, White O' Morn Cottage?
a) Gentleman Jim b) Here Comes Mr. Jordan
c) The Quiet Man d) Kid Galahad

snoring rat ran teas

Themes

HOMELESSNESS

1) What 1992 film involves Joan Bethel (Pauline Collins) running a clinic for the sick and homeless in Calcutta?
a) Where Angels Fear to Tread b) Heat and Dust c) Bandit Queen d) City of Joy

2) Who portrayed the homeless widow who implores bounty hunter Thomas Price (Robert Culp) to teach her to shoot, thus enabling her to exact revenge in **Hannie Caulder** (1972)?
a) Jessica Tandy b) Raquel Welsh c) Jane Fonda d) Kathleen Turner

3) Name the 1991 fantasy comedy in which a homeless man is convinced the Holy Grail is in the possession of a New York billionaire.
a) Manhattan Melodrama b) Rich and Strange c) Memoirs of a Survivor d) The Fisher King

HOMOSEXUALITY

1) In which film is composer, Gustav Von Aschenbach, completely entranced by a beautiful boy named Tadzio (Bjorn Andresen)?
a) The Music Lovers b) Law of Desire c) Reflections in a Golden Eye d) Death in Venice

2) In which 1994 film is a director, who is dressed in women's clothes, asked the question: "Are you a homosexual?", to which he replies: "No! I'm a cross-dresser!"
a) Some of My Best Friends Are b) A Different Story c) Ed Wood d) The Queens

3) For what 1941 film did Warner Brothers downplay the homosexual element in a character portrayed by Peter Lorre to please the censors?
a) Casablanca b) The Mask of Dimitrios c) Passage to Marseilles d) The Maltese Falcon

HORSE RACING

1) On whose novel was the 1944 drama **National Velvet** based?
a) Enid Bagnold b) Josephine Saxton c) Jane Rogers d) Dodie Smith

2) Name the 1983 film which tells the true story of a legendary Australian racehorse which met a mysterious death in California in 1932.
a) Bite the Bullet b) Sylvester c) Phar Lap d) The Longshot

3) With which film do you associate movie director Jack Woltz waking up beside his prized racehorse?
a) Killer's Kiss b) The Godfather c) Fear and Desire d) Blue Blood

HOSTAGES

1) Name the **Star Trek** film which opens with the taking of three hostages on a desert planet.
a) Star Trek - The Motion Picture b) Star Trek: Generations c) Star Trek III: The Search for Spock d) Star Trek V: The Final Frontier

2) In 1996 Harvey Keitel plays a Baptist minister who is held hostage. Name the film.
a) Mortal Thoughts b) From Dusk Till Dawn c) Wise Guys d) Eagle's Wing

3) Marion Ravenwood, the tough-talking partner of Indiana Jones, is taken hostage in Egypt and taken into the desert by Nazi agent, Belloq (Paul Freeman), in **Raiders of the Lost Ark** (1981). Who portrayed Marion?
a) Karen Allen b) Alison Doody c) Kate Capshaw d) Nina Almond

HYMNS

1) Which 1942 film features Charles Rainier (Ronald Colman) and Kitty (Susan Peters) choosing the hymn 'O Perfect Love' for their wedding day?
a) The Light that Failed b) A Tale of Two Cities c) Random Harvest d) Arrowsmith

The Movie Quiz Companion

2) Name the hymn which is sung by the congregation amid the ruined shell of Belham church in the closing scenes of **Mrs. Miniver**?
a) Fight the good fight
b) Who would true valour see
c) Onward Christian soldiers d) Jerusalem

3) What hymn was the ship's orchestra playing as the Titanic sank in the 1958 disaster film, **A Night to Remember**?
a) Nearer My God to Thee
b) The Old Rugged Cross c) Abide With Me
d) The Lord is My Shepherd

ICE DRAMAS

1) What ice drama film connection can you make between Clark Gable and Charlton Heston?
a) On Thin Ice b) White Fang
c) Call of the Wild d) The White Dawn

2) On whose novel was John Sturges' 1968 adventure, **Ice Station Zebra** based?
a) Hammond Innes
b) John Le Carre
c) Nevil Shute
d) Alistair MacLean

3) With which film do you associate characters portrayed by Ronald Colman, Edward Everett Horton, John Howard, Isabel Jewell and Thomas Mitchell crash- landing their plane in the Valley of the Blue Moon?
a) The Ice Palace
b) The White Dawn
c) The Lost Horizon
d) The Abominable Snowman

ILLEGITIMACY

1) Who portrayed Sonny Corleone's illegitimate son, Vincent Mancini, in **The Godfather Part III**?
a) Richard Dreyfuss b) Joe Mantegna
c) George Hamilton d) Andy Garcia

2) Name the young actress who won a Best Supporting Actress Oscar in 1993 for her portrayal of the illegitimate daughter of Ada McGrath (Holly Hunter) in **The Piano**.
a) Anna Paquin b) Liesel Matthews
c) Jayne Atkinson d) Samantha Mathis

3) Name the 1963 musical in which Judy Garland travels to England to find her illegitimate son.
a) I Could Go on Singing b) Pepe
c) Gay Purr-ee d) A Child is Waiting

ILLITERACY

1) Which film features a bakery worker teaching a co-worker how to read?
a) Agnes of God b) Tall Story
c) Stanley & Iris d) Hurry Sundown

2) Who portrayed the illiterate and unenterprising bootmaker, Willie Mossop, in the 1954 comedy, **Hobson's Choice**?
a) Robert Donat b) Alec Guinness
c) Kenneth More d) John Mills

3) For what 1938 film did Wendy Hiller portray an illiterate cockney?
a) Champagne Charlie b) Pygmalion
c) The Good Companions d) Gaslight

IMMORTALITY

1) The 200 year old vampire, Louis de Pointe du Lac is doomed to immortality in the 1994 film, **Interview With The Vampire**. Who was he?
a) Tom Cruise b) Brad Pitt
c) Christian Slater d) John Cusak

2) Who directed the 1986 fantasy, **Highlander**, about immortals pursuing and battling with each other across the centuries?
a) Michael Caton-Jones b) Russell Mulcahy
c) Michael Ritchie d) Terry Gilliam

3) Which 1990 film tells the story of a professor who uses an experimental immortality drug on himself with tragic consequences?
a) Metamorphosis b) Changes
c) Turn Back the Clock d) Never Say Goodbye

IMPERSONATION

1) With which 1973 film do you associate soldier Brian Deacon trying to avoid returning to the front by dressing as a woman to conceal his identity?
a) Just Before Nightfall b) Improperly Dressed
c) Forbidden Relations d) Triple Echo

2) A family attorney convinces Gordon Craven to impersonate Uncle Fester, the long-lost brother of **The Addams Family** (1991). Who portrayed him?
a) Christopher Lloyd b) Chevy Chase
c) Danny De Vito d) Zero Mostel

theory of retirement

3) In the 1975 film, **Royal Flash**, Harry Flashman is forced to impersonate a Prussian nobleman. Who portrayed him?
a) Malcolm McDowell b) Alan Bates
c) Oliver Reed d) Bob Hoskins

IMPALEMENT

1) With which 1981 Walter Hill film, set in the Cajun country of Louisiana, do you associate the impalement of a National Guardsman in the bayous?
a) Belizaire the Cajun b) A Soldier's Story
c) The Big Easy d) Southern Comfort

2) In which 1981 film is the guide of the character portrayed by Harrison Ford impaled ?
a) Raiders of the Lost Ark b) Force 10 From Navarone c) The Mosquito Coast d) The Empire Strikes Back

3) Kurtz made sure that the heads of dissident Montagnard tribesmen were impaled on poles and put on display for all to see. Name the 1979 film.
a) Farewell to the King b) The Emerald Forest
c) The Mosquito Coast d) Apocalypse Now

IMPOTENCE & INFERTILITY

1) What does Ayre McGillvary (Bo Derek) believe was the cure for her man's impotence in the 1984 drama, **Bolero**?
a) to drink tequila at breakfast b) to dress like a man c) to wear fur knickers d) to become a bullfighter

2) Name the 1990 drama, based on the novel by Margaret Atwood, which depicts a futuristic Earth where most of the women are infertile.

a) The Painted Veil b) The Handmaid's Tale
c) Women of Valour d) Ladyhawke

3) In which 1970 comedy does army dentist, Painless Pole (John Schuck) decide to commit suicide after experiencing a period of impotence?
a) M*A*S*H b) How I Won the War
c) Good Morning Vietnam d) Sergeants 3

IMPREGNABLE BUILDINGS

1) Who directed the 1957 film **Colditz**, based on P.R. Reid's experiences as a prisoner-of-war in the 'impregnable' Saxony fortress of Colditz Castle?
a) Robert Hamer b) Alexander Mackendrick
c) Guy Hamilton d) Carol Reed

2) In 1964 Auric **Goldfinger** infiltrated the seemingly impregnable Fort Knox. Which 1979 Bond film also used Fort Knox as a location?
a) The Spy Who Loved Me b) Moonraker
c) For Your Eyes Only d) Live and Let Die

3) In the 1989 film, **Glory**, Col. Robert Gould Shaw leads a suicidal assault on the impregnable harbour fortification of Fort Wagner with the 54th. regiment of Massachusetts Volunteer Infantry, the first black unit in the Union army. Who portrayed Col. Shaw?
a) Matthew Broderick b) Martin Sheen
c) Tim Robbins d) Tom Hanks

INCEST

1) On whose best-selling novel of incest and sadomasochism was the 1987 thriller, **Flowers in the Attic** based?
a) Roald Dahl b) Virginia Andrews
c) Stephen King d) William Blatty

2) In which film in the **Amityville** series does a brother seduce his sister?
a) Amityville: A New Generation b) Amityville II: The Possession c) Amityville 4: The Evil Escapes
d) The Amityville Curse

3) In the 1981 film **Excalibur** she portrayed Morgana, the incestuous half-sister of King Arthur who bears him a son named Mordred. Who was she?
a) Helen Mirren b) Cherie Lunghi
c) Lily Tomlin d) Nastassja Kinski

INDIANS

1) Name the Indian tribe befriended by Lt. John Dunbar (Kevin Costner) in the 1990 western, **Dances With Wolves**?
a) Apache b) Sioux c) Arapaho d) Cheyenne

2) With which 1956 western do you associate Chief Scar?
a) Hondo b) Apache
c) The Searchers d) Broken Arrow

3) Name the actor who portrayed Indians regularly, and who has played Cochise on three occasions.
a) Jeff Chandler b) George O'Brien
c) Henry Brandon d) Richard Basehart

INFIDELITY

1) With which 1987 thriller do you associate New York attorney, Dan Gallagher, having an extramarital affair with Alex Forrest?
a) The Honeymoon Killers b) Fatal Attraction
c) Sorry, Wrong Number d) Night Moves

2) In which film does brilliant violinist, Holger Brandt (Leslie Howard), fall in love with Anita, his children's piano teacher?
a) Intermezzo b) The Lady is Willing
c) Of Human Bondage d) Sparrows Can't Sing

The Movie Quiz Companion

3) Greta Garbo succumbed to the charms of diplomat George Brent in **The Painted Veil**. In which country was the film set?
a) India b) Kenya c) China d) Malaya

INHERITANCE

1) Who inherits his uncle's colossal fortune in Frank Capra's **Mr. Deeds Goes to Town**?
a) Cary Grant b) Gary Cooper
c) Joel McCrea d) James Stewart

2) In 1945 Dennis O'Keefe inherits an estate worth $8,000,000. The catch is that he has to spend $1,000,000 in two months, or he will receive none of it. Name the film.
a) Brewster's Millions b) Mr. Billion
c) If I Had a Million
d) Better Late Than Never

3) Louis Mazzini sets about knocking off all his relatives to gain his rightful title and inheritance in **Kind Hearts and Coronets**. Who was he?
a) George Cole b) Bernard Miles
c) Leslie Banks d) Dennis Price

INSANITY

1) The naïve Parris Mitchell (Robert Cummings) falls in love with the mysterious Cassie Tower who would one day succumb to hereditary insanity in Sam Wood's 1942 drama, **Kings Row**. Who portrayed Cassie?
a) Constance Cummings b) Betty Field
c) Ann Sheridan d) Carol Marsh

2) In which film is someone assumed to be insane when their mental state is caused by porphyria, a metabolic imbalance?
a) The Madness of King George
b) Nuts c) Me and My Brother
d) Madhouse

3) Olivia de Havilland starred in one of the first films to treat mental illness seriously in 1948. Name the title.
a) Suddenly Last Summer b) Twisted Nerve
c) The Snake Pit d) Night Must Fall

INVASIONS & COUPS D'ETAT

1) What 1969 French political thriller is based on the real-life killing of the Greek liberal and peace campaigner, Gregorious Lambrakis in 1963?
a) Missing b) State of Siege
c) Z d) The Sleeping Car Murder

2) In 1964 he played U.S. President, Jordan Lyman, in John Frankenheimer's political thriller, **Seven Days in May**. Who was he?
a) Edmond O'Brien b) Fredric March
c) Kirk Douglas d) Martin Balsam

3) Name the invasion film directed by Ken Annakin, Bernhard Wicki, Andrew Marton, and Gerd Oswald in 1962.
a) Invasion U.S.A. b) Invaders From Mars
c) D-Day the Sixth of June d) The Longest Day

INVISIBILITY

1) Flora Cranley was the demented Jack Griffin's confused girlfriend in **The Invisible Man** (1933). Who portrayed her?
a) Gloria Stuart b) Jane Darwell
c) Paulette Goddard d) Binnie Barnes

2) Who directed the classic 1933 version of **The Invisible Man**?
a) James Whale b) Fritz Lang
c) Jacques Tourneur d) Robert Wise

3) Who played the title role in Universal's 1940 attempt to repeat the success of the original in **The Invisible Man Returns**?
a) Douglas Fairbanks Jnr. b) Lionel Barrymore
c) Vincent Price d) Basil Rathbone

ISLAM

1) Who directed the 1992 biopic, **Malcolm X**, based on the life of Malcolm Little (Denzel Washington) who fell under the influence of the Black Muslim movement of Elijah Muhammad?
a) Carl Lerner b) Carl Franklin
c) Spike Lee d) Bill Duke

2) Who portrayed the Islamic terrorist Nagi Hassan, who plans to poison "the entire Eastern Seaboard of the United States" in the 1995 disaster thriller, **Executive Decision**?
a) David Suchet b) Tommy Lee Jones
c) John Malkovich d) David Caruso

3) Which 1991 film, based on the true story of Betty Mahmoody, tells the story of an American woman (Sally Field) who marries an Iranian and returns to his homeland with their daughter for a holiday, but who then, at the insistence of her husband, realises the family must stay there permanently?
a) Not Without My Daughter b) Kidnap Syndicate
c) Maybe I'll Come Home In the Spring d) Kiss Me Goodbye

ITALIAN AMERICANS

1) In which 1992 film do Niccolo Vittelli (John Turturro) and his Italian American brothers start their own construction company?
a) Men of Respect b) Mac c) Five Corners
d) Do the Right Thing

2) With which film do you associate mashed potatoes dyed to match the colour of the bridesmaids' dresses at an Italian-American wedding?

a) True Love b) Wise Guys c) Spike of Bensonhurst d) Married to the Mob

3) What 1987 romantic comedy about Italian Americans features Dean Martin singing "When the moon hits your eye, like a big-a pizza pie—that's amore!"?
a) Mermaids b) Radio Days c) Cookie d) Moonstruck

JAIL BREAKS

1) With which film do you associate convict Andy Dufresne escaping from prison with the help of a Rita Hayworth poster?
a) San Quentin b) Unchained c) The Shawshank Redemption d) 20,000 Years in Sing Sing

2) Who directed **Escape From Alcatraz**?
a) Don Siegel b) John Carpenter c) Ridley Scott d) Otto Preminger

3) In which film does silver-tongued petty criminal, Everett Ulysses McGill, escape from his term of hard labour in Mississippi with sidekicks, Delmar and Pete?
a) Caged Heat b) Jailhouse Rock c) O Brother, Where Art Thou? d) Riot in Cell Block 11

JAZZ

1) Who played the title role of Charlie "Yardbird" Parker in director Clint Eastwood's 1988 biopic, **Bird**?
a) Sidney Poitier b) Forest Whitaker c) Eddie Murphy d) Richard Roundtree

2) In which film does Dexter Gordon portray black bebop tenor saxophone player Dale Turner?
a) Jazz in Exile b) Round Midnight c) The Last of the Blue Devils d) The Cool World

3) Who starred in the third screen version of **The Jazz Singer** in 1980?
a) John Travolta b) Paul Nicholas c) Neil Diamond d) Glen Campbell

JOURNEYS & MARCHES

1) In which film does a servant girl pay for her ticket on the Trans-Siberian Express by weekly instalments to the travel agent, Thomas Cook?
a) The Inn of the Sixth Happiness b) The Keys of the Kingdom c) The Long Journey Home d) Gallant Journey

2) In 1956 Japanese POW Jean Paget and other women prisoners are forced to march from one camp to another in wartime Malaya with many dying along the way, in **A Town Like Alice**. Who portrayed Jean Paget?
a) Renee Houston b) Celia Johnson c) Deborah Kerr d) Virginia McKenna

3) What 1963 film about a hazardous trek through the wilderness was inspired by a book by Sheila Burnford?
a) The Journey of Natty Gann b) Journey to Freedom c) The Incredible Journey d) Miraculous Journey

KIDNAPPING

1) Which 1992 drama features a British squaddie who is kidnapped by the IRA?
a) Deathtrap b) Fools of Fortune c) The Outsider d) The Crying Game

2) In 1971 he portrayed Alan Breck in a U.K. film version of Robert Louis Stevenson's adventure classic, **Kidnapped**. Who was he?
a) Sean Connery b) Michael Caine c) Ryan O'Neal d) Richard Gere

3) With which 1956 Hitchcock mystery do you associate a young girl being kidnapped to prevent her parents from revealing their knowledge about an assassination plot?
a) The Man Who Knew Too Much b) Foreign Correspondent c) Blackmail d) Torn Curtain

KNIVES

1) Riff, the leader of the Jets, dies in a knife fight in **West Side Story**. Who was he?
a) Richard Beymer b) Eliot Feld c) George Chakiris d) Russ Tamblyn

2) Who uses a knife to split the nostril of private investigator, J.J. Gittes, in **Chinatown**?
a) John Huston b) Danny DeVito c) Roman Polanski d) Tommy Lee Jones

3) In which film does Sgt. 'Fatso' Judson (Ernest Borgnine) pull a switchblade on Angelo Maggio (Frank Sinatra)?
a) The Man with the Golden Arm b) Pal Joey c) From Here to Eternity d) Ocean's Eleven

KOREAN WAR

1) Who portrayed the army sergeant suspected of being a traitor during the Korean War in the 1968 drama, **Sergeant Ryker**?
a) Sidney Poitier b) Michael Sarrazin c) Lee Marvin d) Lee J. Cobb

2) On whose novel was **The Bridges at Toko-Ri** based?
a) Ring Lardner b) Jack Higgins c) Douglas Reeman d) James A. Michener

3) James Dean made his film debut in a 1951 Korean war drama directed by Sam Fuller. Name the title.
a) The Big Red One b) Fixed Bayonets c) The Steel Helmet d) The Command

KU KLUX KLAN

1) Name the film criticised for its glorification of the KKK which was based on Thomas Dixon Jr.'s book *The Clansmen*.

The Movie Quiz Companion

a) *Cross of Fire* b) *Brotherhood of Death*
c) *In the Homeland* d) *Birth of a Nation*

2) Frank Taylor (Humphrey Bogart) was recruited into the KKK, though never actually named as such, in a 1936 drama. Name the title.
a) *King of the Underworld* b) *Black Legion*
c) *Bullets or Ballots* d) *Dead End*

3) Marsha Mitchell (Ginger Rogers) discovers that her sister has married a Klansman in the 1951 film, **Storm Warning**. Who was the sister?
a) Doris Day b) Joan Fontaine
c) Vivien Leigh d) Joan Blondell

LABOUR RELATIONS & STRIKES

1) Bo Widerberg's 1971 biopic, **Joe Hill**, shows the famed labour leader getting involved with the "Industrial Workers of the World". By what name were they better known?
a) *Union Maids* b) *Babies with Banners*
c) *Sleeping Dogs* d) *The Wobblies*

2) Name the title of John Sayle's 1987 film, based on the true story of a West Virginian coal mining town's violent struggle to establish a union in the 1920s.
a) *Harlan County USA* b) *So That You Can Live*
c) *Comrades* d) *Matewan*

3) In 1992 he portrayed the controversial Teamster boss, Jimmy Hoffa, in **Hoffa**. Who was he?
a) James Woods b) Sean Penn
c) Jack Nicholson d) Elliott Gould

LANDSLIDES & AVALANCHES

1) In which 1938 spy mystery does an avalanche block a railway line and delay a train, compelling folklore student, Gilbert Redman, to rent a room in a Balkan inn?
a) *Night Train to Munich* b) *The Spy in Black*
c) *The Lady Vanishes* d) *Confidential Agent*

2) With which film do you associate girls using their red flannel petticoats as flags to warn of a concealed landslide?
a) *Dad's Army* b) *The Nutty Professor*
c) *Micki + Maude* d) *The Railway Children*

3) With which musical do you associate an avalanche blocking the pursuit of a group of country boys kidnapping some beautiful town girls?
a) *Kiss Me Kate* b) *Guys and Dolls*
c) *Seven Brides for Seven Brothers*
d) *One Hundred Men and a Girl*

LAST RITES

1) In which film does Dan Tobin (Francis Ford) jump from his deathbed just as he is being given the last rites, postponing his death until he has seen the fight of the century between Sean Thornton and Red Will Danaher?
a) *Gentleman Jim*
b) *The Fighting Kentuckian*
c) *The Quiet Man* d) *The Fighting O'Flynn*

2) Name the 1995 comedy drama in which a stone angel in a churchyard uses its wing to strike a priest who refuses a man the last rites because he has sheltered Jews from the Nazis.
a) *Antonia's Line* b) *To Die For*
c) *Trees Lounge* d) *Slacker*

3) Who portrayed gangster **Pepe Le Moko** who hides from the police in the Casbah of Algiers, and is fond of saying that if the police were ever to kill him, hundreds of widows would come to hear his last rites?
a) Yves Montand b) Jean Gabin
c) Alain Delon d) Jean Marais

LESBIANISM

1) With whom does soap opera actress June (Beryl Reid) have a lesbian relationship, in **The Killing of Sister George**?
a) Susannah York b) Lynn Redgrave
c) Rita Tushingham d) Dora Bryan

2) In which film does Jo Courtney (Barbara Stanwyck), the lesbian madam of a New Orleans brothel, have a relationship with one of her prostitutes?
a) *Beyond the Valley of the Dolls* b) *The Silence*
c) *Tony Rome* d) *A Walk on the Wild Side*

3) In which film are schoolmistresses Audrey Hepburn and Shirley Maclaine accused of lesbianism?
a) *The Class of Miss Michael* b) *The Children's Hour* c) *Almost Summer* d) *Irma La Douce*

LETTERS

1) On whose novel was based the oft-filmed **The Scarlet Letter** (1926, 1934, 1973, 1995), which tells the story of the 17th century Hester Prynne who does public penance for her adultery in puritan Salem?
a) Henry James b) James Fenimore Cooper
c) Paul Bowles d) Nathaniel Hawthorne

2) Who directed Fox's 1948 drama, **A Letter to Three Wives** (1949)?
a) Joseph L. Mankiewicz b) Henry Hathaway
c) Elia Kazan d) Billy Wilder

3) On whose story was the 1940 drama, **The Letter** based, which involves characters portrayed by Bette Davis and Herbert Marshall in murder on a Malayan rubber plantation?
a) Lillian Hellman b) Anais Nin
c) Dorothy Parker d) Somerset Maugham

destitute hare aroma refresher

Themes

LONG SUPPOSED DEAD

1) In 1982 he played a 16th century peasant whose true identity is questioned when he returns to his family after nine years at war, in **The Return of Martin Guerre**. Who was he?
a) Richard Chamberlain b) Harvey Keitel c) John Hurt d) Gerard Depardieu

2) Name the title of the 1993 remake of **The Return of Martin Guerre**.
a) Sommersby b) The Return c) The Whole Town's Talking d) A Man Named John

3) With what 1973 film do you associate Elliott Gould deliberately shooting a friend he had presumed was dead?
a) The Silent Partner b) California Split c) The Night They Raided Minsky's d) The Long Goodbye

LOTTERIES

1) In which 1954 comedy does the character portrayed by David Niven agree to be a lottery prize?
a) The Moon is Blue b) The Lottery Bride c) Happy Go Lovely d) The Love Lottery

2) In which 1944 film does a young Mexican boy sell a lottery ticket to Fred C. Dobbs?
a) China Clipper b) San Quentin c) It All Came True d) The Treasure of the Sierra Madre

3) What 1991 comedy tells the story of Frank Pesce, the real-life winner of the 1976 New York State Lottery?
a) 29th Street b) Lots of Luck c) The Music of Chance d) Uptown Saturday Night

LYNCHING

1) In which Fritz Lang film does Spencer Tracy portray the innocent victim of a lynch mob, who becomes intent on bringing his tormentors to justice?
a) The Murder Man b) 20,000 Years in Sing Sing c) Fury d) State of the Union

2) Who portrayed the survivor of his own hanging in **Hang 'em High** (1968), a character who swears vengeance on those who lynched him?
a) Gene Hackman b) Jeff Bridges c) Jeff Goldblum d) Clint Eastwood

3) On whose novel was Clarence Brown's 1949 drama, **Intruder in the Dust** based?
a) F. Scott Fitzgerald b) William Faulkner c) James Fenimore Cooper d) Pearl S. Buck

McCARTHYISM

1) Fictional director, David Merrill, is blacklisted by the House Un-American Activities Committee (HUAC) in Irvin Winkler's 1991 Hollywood witch hunt drama, **Guilty By Suspicion**. Who portrayed Merrill?
a) James Woods b) Robert De Niro c) Bob Hoskins d) Dennis Hopper

2) The screenwriter of **Laura** and **M.A.S.H.** was blacklisted by the HUAC and served a term in prison. Who was he?
a) Ring Lardner Jr. b) Lester Cole c) Ben Hecht d) Dalton Trumbo

3) What 1956 science fiction film was said to be a discerning attack on McCarthyism and the political witchhunts of the fifties?
a) Night of the Demon b) Invasion of the Body Snatchers c) The Thing From Another World d) War of the Worlds

THE MAFIA

1) In which 1995 film is Miami dry cleaner, Leo Devoe (David Paymer), pursued by Chili Palmer for a debt he owes to Mafia boss, 'Bones' Barboni (Dennis Farina)?
a) Hoffa b) Last Rites c) Married to the Mob d) Get Shorty

2) On whose novel was **The Sicilian** based?
a) Judith Krantz b) Harold Robbins c) Taylor Caldwell d) Mario Puzo

3) Who "sleeps with the fishes" in **The Godfather**?
a) Clemenza b) Luca Brasi c) Barzini d) Sollozo

MARRIAGE BROKERS

1) Name the musical remake of the 1958 comedy, **The Matchmaker**?
a) Fiddler on the Roof b) Hello, Dolly! c) Show Boat d) Pal Joey

2) With which film do you associate bookstore assistant, "Izzy" Grossman's Jewish grandmother hiring the services of a matchmaker?
a) Crossing Delancey b) Singles c) Sleepless in Seattle d) Hunting

3) In which 1972 comedy does Bud Cort's character's mother sign him up with a computer dating agency?
a) Brewster McCloud b) Sweet Charity c) Electric Dreams d) Harold and Maude

MARTIAL ARTS

1) The 1980 action comedy **The Big Brawl** starred one of Asia's biggest stars. Who was he?
a) Nora Miao b) Bruce Lee c) Jackie Chan d) Mako Iwamatsu

2) Who portrayed the fugitive Buddhist monk, Kwai Chang Caine, who roamed the American West in **Kung Fu: The Movie**?
a) David Carradine b) Chuck Conners c) Rick Moranis d) Bruce Lee

41

The Movie Quiz Companion

3) Who played the title role in **Dragon: The Bruce Lee Story**?
a) Kay Tong Lim b) Jason Scott Lee
c) Ned Beatty d) Mickey Rourke

MASSACRES

1) In which film do Pike Bishop, Dutch Engstrom, Tector and Lyle Gorch knowingly walk into their own massacre?
a) The Untouchables b) The Wild Bunch
c) The Roaring Twenties d) Bonnie & Clyde

2) Name the John Ford western based on the story *Massacre* by James Warner Bellah.
a) Fort Apache b) She Wore a Yellow Ribbon
c) The Man Who Shot Liberty Valance d) My Darling Clementine

3) What D.W. Griffith film do you associate with the St. Bartholomew's Day Massacre of the Huguenots in 1572?
a) The Birth of a Nation b) Orphans of the Storm
c) Broken Blossoms d) Intolerance

MEETINGS

1) Who met pulp novelist, Holly Martins, in a deserted amusement park in 1949?
a) Phillip Marlowe b) Dracula
c) Harry Lime d) Richard Hannay

2) In **Blue Velvet** (1986), college kid Jeffrey Beaumont takes photos of deviant Frank Booth's (Dennis Hopper) secret meetings. Who portrayed Jeffrey Beaumont?
a) Dean Stockwell b) John Belushi
c) Warren Oates d) Kyle MacLachlan

3) Who held gang council meetings above the parlour in their family home?

a) Machine Gun Kelly b) Little Caesar
c) The Krays d) Dillinger

MEXICANS

1) In 1958 he portrayed Mexican lawyer, Ramon Miguel 'Mike' Vargas, in **Touch of Evil**. Who was he?
a) Dennis Weaver b) Orson Welles
c) Joseph Cotten d) Charlton Heston

2) With which film do you associate the tea which "a million Mexicans drink"?
a) Juarez b) The Night of the Iguana
c) The Lady Vanishes d) The Grapes of Wrath

3) By what name was the Mexican actress, Lupe Velez, better known?
a) Tijuana Rita b) The Mexican Maiden
c) The Mexican Spitfire d) Mexico Minnie

MICROFILM

1) Who portrayed the pickpocket who unwittingly steals microfilm from a woman's purse and finds himself dealing with communist agents in **Pickup on South Street** (1953)?
a) Richard Widmark b) Peter Lorre
c) James Mason d) Jack Palance

2) Which 1943 mystery features Sherlock Holmes tracking down missing microfilm?
a) Sherlock Holmes Faces Death b) Sherlock Holmes in New York c) Sherlock Holmes and the Secret Weapon d) Sherlock Holmes in Washington

3) With which film do you associate James Bond photographing the contents of billionaire Hugo Drax's safe, using a mini camera which has the lens positioned in the middle of the '0' on the '007' etched onto the casing?
a) Moonraker b) For Your Eyes Only
c) Octopussy d) A View to a Kill

MIDDLE AGES

1) With which 1985 fantasy do you associate a romance between Princess Isabeau (Michelle Pfeiffer) and the noble Navarre (Rutger Hauer)?
a) Dragonslayer b) The Dark Crystal
c) Ladyhawke d) Krull

2) Name the title of Bertrand Tavernier's 1988 historical saga set during the Hundred Years War in which a bullying father returns home from the conflict to his family.
a) Beatrice b) The Undeclared War
c) Spoiled Children d) The Daughter of D'Artagnan

3) In 1950 he played Dardo, a rebel leader in medieval Italy in **The Flame and the Arrow**. Who was he?
a) Errol Flynn b) Burt Lancaster
c) Kirk Douglas d) Richard Todd

MILLIONAIRES

1) In which film does Richard Widmark portray obnoxious American millionaire, Ratchett, who is stabbed to death on a train?
a) Night Passage b) Last Train From Gun Hill
c) Murder on the Orient Express d) Berlin Express

2) Who played the title role in the 1949 adaptation of F. Scott Fitzgerald's **The Great Gatsby**?
a) Alan Ladd b) Tyrone Power
c) Dick Powell d) Glenn Ford

3) In 1967 he portrayed eccentric millionaire, Anthony J. Drexel Biddle, in the Disney musical, **The Happiest Millionaire**. Who was he?
a) Tommy Steele b) Fred MacMurray
c) Terry Thomas d) Jerry Lewis

MINIATURIZATION

1) With which film do you associate Dr. Septimus Pretorius (Ernest Thesiger) creating miniature people and displaying them in belljars?
a) The Curse of Frankenstein b) Bride of Frankenstein c) House of Frankenstein d) Frankenstein Must Be Destroyed

2) What does Scott Carey (Grant Williams) encounter that turns him into **The Incredible Shrinking Man**?
a) a gas cloud b) a curse
c) radiation d) poisonous chemicals

3) In 1936 he played Paul Lomond, an escaped convict who shrank humans to the size of dolls in **The Devil Doll**. Who was he?
a) Jackie Coogan b) Louis Calhern
c) Fredric March d) Lionel Barrymore

MIRACLES

1) In which 1947 film does history Professor Wutheridge's (Monty Woolley) bottle of sherry miraculously never empty?
a) The Man Who Came to Dinner b) Miracle Mile
c) Miss Tatlock's Millions d) The Bishop's Wife

2) Name the postulant nun who falls in love with soldier, Captain Michael Stuart (Roger Moore) during the Napoleonic wars in **The Miracle** (1959).
a) Hope Lange b) Sophia Loren
c) Carroll Baker d) Maureen O'Hara

3) Who or what does Margo the carnival dancer find on Christmas Eve in the 1939 film, **Miracle on Main Street**?
a) an abandoned baby b) Father Christmas
c) her future self d) Francis of Assisi

MIRRORS

1) In which film do Groucho and Harpo Marx imitate each other's movements in an imaginary mirror?
a) A Night at the Opera b) Horse Feathers
c) Monkey Business d) Duck Soup

2) Name the Orson Welles film which has a shoot-out in a carnival hall of mirrors for its finale.
a) The Stranger b) The Lady From Shanghai
c) Touch of Evil d) The Trial

3) Joan Courtland is given an antique mirror by her fiancé which reflects a Victorian room where a murder is being committed in **Dead of Night** (1945). Who was she?
a) Googie Withers b) Wendy Hiller
c) Sybil Thorndike d) Deborah Kerr

MISTAKEN IDENTITY

1) In which film is the character portrayed by Joel McCrea convicted of his own murder after a tramp carrying his stolen ID is killed by a train?
a) The Most Dangerous Game b) Foreign Correspondent c) Sullivan's Travels d) Dead End

2) Who was mistakenly assumed by the Germans to be a Nazi spy posing as the waiter of a Saharan hotel in **Five Graves to Cairo** (1943)?
a) Paul Henreid b) Franchot Tone
c) Clark Gable d) Gig Young

3) In which film is New York advertising executive, Roger Thornhill, kidnapped because he is mistaken for a man named George Kaplan?
a) Three Brothers b) The Wrong Man
c) Nothing But a Man d) North by Northwest

MORMONS

1) Who played the title role in the 1940 biopic, **Brigham Young - Frontiersman**?
a) Tyrone Power b) Vincent Price
c) Fredric March d) Dean Jagger

2) In 1980 he portrayed Howard Hughes, who left $156 million in the so-called 'Mormon Will' to a stranger who once gave him a lift in his pickup truck, in **Melvin and Howard**. Who was he?
a) Gene Hackman b) Jason Robards
c) Burt Lancaster d) Alan Arkin

3) With which 1988 film, starring Charles Bronson, do you associate a murder mystery concerning two rival Mormon sects?
a) Messenger of Death b) The Stone Killer
c) Ten to Midnight d) Borderline

MOTHERS

1) In which 1949 film does James Cagney's character hear the news of his mother's death in a prison mess hall?
a) Each Dawn I Die b) White Heat
c) The Roaring Twenties d) The Public Enemy

2) With which 1983 horror film do you associate Norman Bates' (Anthony Perkins) long dead mother telephoning him?
a) Psycho b) Psycho II c) Psycho III d) Psycho IV

3) Who portrayed the unmarried mother who gives up her baby in the 1946 tearjerker, **To Each His Own**?
a) Claudette Colbert b) Jean Arthur
c) Maureen O'Hara d) Olivia De Havilland

MOTORCYCLES

1) German naval officer, Capt. Hardt, is put ashore on the Orkney Islands from his submarine complete with motor-cycle in Powell and Pressburger's **The Spy in Black**.

The Movie Quiz Companion

anointed hems

Who was he?
a) Conrad Veidt b) Erich Von Stroheim
c) Max Von Sydow d) George Voskovec

2) Name the 1962 film in which the hero is killed in a motor-cycle accident in the opening scene.
a) Dr. No b) In Like Flint
c) Lawrence of Arabia d) Mogambo

3) The motor-cycle crash which caused the death of Dr. Reeves in Michael Powell's **A Matter of Life and Death** enabled him to plead in heaven for the life of RAF pilot, Peter Carter (David Niven). Who was he?
a) Raymond Massey b) James Robertson Justice
c) Peter Ustinov d) Roger Livesey

MOVIES ABOUT MOVIES

1) Who portrayed the young NY playwright who journeys to Hollywood to write for the movies in the Coen Brothers 1991 comedy drama, **Barton Fink**?
a) John Turturro b) Michael Keaton
c) Tom Hanks d) Dustin Hoffman

2) What film did Billy Wilder direct about Hollywood and its film community in 1950?
a) The Lost Weekend b) Sunset Blvd.
c) Sabrina d) Hold Back the Dawn

3) In 1952 he played ruthless Hollywood producer, Jonathan Shields, in **The Bad and the Beautiful**. Who was he?

a) Dick Powell b) Burt Lancaster
c) Karl Malden d) Kirk Douglas

MULTIPLE PERSONALITIES

1) In 1957 she portrayed a woman with three personalities in **The Three Faces of Eve**. Who was she?
a) Joanne Woodward b) Dorothy McGuire
c) Linda Darnell d) Martha Scott

2) Who portrayed the actor who becomes dominated by his role of Othello in George Cukor's **A Double Life**?
a) Edward G. Robinson b) Robert Young
c) Ronald Colman d) George Sanders

3) Who played a character with a personality disorder which makes him speak in the voices of Captain Kirk, Pee-wee Herman, and Tweetie Pie, in the 1990 comedy, **Loose Cannons**?
a) Nicolas Cage b) Walter Matthau
c) Gene Wilder d) Dan Aykroyd

MULTIPLE ROLES

1) In which film does Peter Sellers portray Tully Bascombe, Count Mountjoy, and the Grand Duchess Gloriana XII ?
a) The World of Henry Orient b) What's New Pussycat? c) I'm Alright Jack d) The Mouse That Roared

2) On whose story was **The Secret Life of Walter Mitty** based?

a) Leon Garfield b) James Thurber
c) S.J. Perelman d) G.K. Chesterton

3) Who played the title role in the 1964 fantasy, **7 Faces of Dr. Lao**?
a) Tony Randall b) Robert Duvall
c) Leo G. Carroll d) Ron Moody

MURDERERS, REAL LIFE

1) What Hitchcock film was inspired by the Leopold-Loeb murder case in 1920s Chicago?
a) Frenzy b) Rope
c) Shadow of a Doubt
d) The Paradine Case

2) On the life of which notorious criminal was Tom Griess's 1996 film, **Helter Skelter** based?
a) Charles Manson b) Jack the Ripper
c) Dr Crippen d) The Boston Strangler

3) With which film do you associate Caryl Chessman, the "red light bandit", who was finally executed in 1960 after spending 12 years on San Quentin's death row?
a) I Want to Live
b) Kill Me If You Can
c) Yield to the Night d) Rotten to the Core

MUTATION & METAMORPHOSIS

1) What is responsible for the overnight growth of Allison Hayes in **The Attack of the 50 Foot Woman**?
a) a growth serum b) an ancient curse
c) a bolt of lightning d) ray burns from an alien

2) In the 1973 horror film, **The Mutations**, what does scientist Donald Pleasence crossbreed with humans?
a) insects b) plants c) fish d) wolves

3) Into what did characters portrayed by Al Hedison, Jeff Goldblum and Eric Stoltz mutate in 1958, 1986 and 1989 respectively?
a) The Amazing Colossal Man
b) The Incredible Shrinking Man
c) The Reptile
d) The Fly

44

MUTINY

1) In 1935 he portrayed 1st Mate Fletcher Christian in MGM's **Mutiny on the Bounty**. Who was he?
a) Errol Flynn b) Clark Gable
c) Gary Cooper d) John Garfield

2) Which film opens with the clerks of an insurance company staging a mutiny and turning their office building into a ship?
a) Brazil b) Monty Python's The Meaning of Life
c) The Adventures of Baron Munchausen
d) Jabberwocky

3) Lt. Steve Maryk mutinies against the paranoid Captain Queeg (Humphrey Bogart) and is subsequently court martialled in **The Caine Mutiny** (1954). Who portrayed Maryk?
a) Van Johnson b) Fred MacMurray
c) Lee Marvin d) José Ferrer

MYTHS & LEGENDS

1) Which 1994 drama tells the legend of a man who marries a creature known as a Selky, who is both woman and seal?
a) Secrets of a Married Man b) The Secret Life of Kathy McCormick c) Secret People d) The Secret of Roan Inish

2) On whose classic story was Tim Burton's **Sleepy Hollow** based?
a) Edgar Allan Poe b) Nathaniel Hawthorne
c) Mark Twain d) Washington Irving

3) In **Pandora and the Flying Dutchman** (1951), a sea captain is condemned to sail the seven seas for eternity until he finds the thing that can save his soul. What is he searching for?
a) a woman willing to die for love b) the Fountain of Youth c) Neptune's trident d) his brother's murderer

NEWSPAPERS

1) With which film do you associate a mother placing an ad in the Chicago Times offering a $5,000 reward for information which could quash the nine years sentence her son is serving for a murder he didn't commit?
a) Anatomy of a Murder b) Thunder Bay
c) That Rare Breed d) Call Northside 777

2) What film did critic Pauline Kael describe as "... the greatest newspaper comedy of all time"?
a) Front Page Story b) His Girl Friday
c) Pat & Mike d) The Front Page

3) In which 1994 film did telegraph operator, Renato Scarpa, collect newspaper cuttings about the famous Chilean poet, Pablo Neruda?
a) Fellini's Roma b) Last Tango in Paris
c) The Decameron d) Il Postino

NUCLEAR ENERGY

1) For what 1979 drama does Jack Lemmon portray an engineer at a nuclear plant who discovers a leak caused by faulty welding due to the plant's cost-cutting policy?
a) The China Syndrome b) Missing
c) Silkwood d) The Incident

2) What 1958 film, directed by Irving Lerner, tells the story of an escaped convict who has in his possession a canister which he believes contains $1m worth of heroin, but actually contains radioactive cobalt?
a) City on Fire b) City of Fear
c) City Heat d) City of the Living Dead

3) With which 1986 film do you associate a high school being contaminated by a leak from a nearby nuclear power plant?
a) Class of Nuke 'Em High b) Dark Circle
c) Meet the Applegates d) The River's Edge

NUCLEAR WEAPONS

1) Name the 1994 drama, directed by Tony Richardson, in which army officer, Major Hank Marshall (Tommy Lee Jones), is involved in a cover-up of radiation levels following nuclear weapon testing.
a) Shadow on the Sun b) Blue Sky
c) A Delicate Balance d) Penalty Phase

2) In which 1950 thriller film does a scientist threaten to blow up London with a nuclear bomb unless the government abandons its nuclear weapon programme?
a) The Day the World Ended b) Defence of the Realm c) Seven Days to Noon d) The Last Battle

3) Who portrayed the President of the U.S.A. in the 1964 nuclear drama, **Fail Safe**?
a) Walter Matthau b) Henry Fonda
c) Burt Lancaster d) Karl Malden

NUDITY

1) What film has for its finale, Jack and Parry lying naked in Central Park, singing "I like New York in June, How About You?"
a) Arthur b) The Fisher King c) Broadway Danny Rose d) The Goodbye Girl

2) Who portrays Jacy Farrow, who attends a nude bathing party for the purpose of meeting rich boy, Bobby Sheen (Gary

The Movie Quiz Companion

Brockette) in **The Last Picture Show**?
a) Ellen Burstyn b) Dyan Cannon
c) Anne Archer d) Cybil Shepherd

3) Which film was critic Roger Ebert discussing when he commented: "And the Polynesians, for once, are all allowed to go topless all the time (the movie nevertheless gets the PG rating, qualifying under the National Geographic loophole in which nudity doesn't count south of the equator)"?
a) The Bounty b) Rapa Nui c) Castaway d) Bird of Paradise

NYMPHOMANIACS

1) Who portrayed the nymphomaniac sister of millionaire playboy, Kyle Hadley (Robert Stack), in the 1965 drama, **Written on the Wind**?
a) Janet Leigh b) Dorothy Malone
c) Julie Harris d) Judi West

2) In which 1989 comedy does Dexter King (Jeff Goldblum) rent a room in a nymphomaniac's apartment?
a) The Tall Guy b) Beyond Therapy
c) Earth Girls Are Easy d) Vibes

3) With which 1956 crime drama do you associate Jane Mansfield portraying a nymphomaniac?
a) Female Jungle
b) The Girl Can't Help It
c) Kiss Them For Me
d) Too Hot to Handle

OLD AGE

1) Katie Johnson became a star at the age of 78 with her portrayal of scatty landlady, Mrs. Wilberforce, in a 1956 Ealing comedy. Name the title.
a) The Lavender Hill Mob b) Passport to Pimlico
c) The Ladykillers d) Whisky Galore

2) In 1991 she played octogenarian storyteller, Ninny Threadgoode, in **Fried Green Tomatoes**. Who was she?
a) Vivien Leigh b) Josephine Hull
c) Joan Plowright d) Jessica Tandy

3) In which Will Hay comedy does the aged Harbottle (Moore Marriott) portray his own father?
a) Oh Mr Porter b) Convict 99
c) Where's That Fire? d) Ask a Policeman

OPERA

1) Name the Verdi opera which the cast attempts to perform in the finale of the Marx Brothers' **A Night at the Opera** (1935).
a) Il Trovatore b) Rigoletto
c) La Traviata d) Nabucco

2) Who portrayed "Porgy" in the 1958 folk opera, **Porgy and Bess**?
a) Harry Belafonte b) Paul Robeson
c) Sammy Davis Jr. d) Sidney Poitier

3) Name the opera Ronny (Nicolas Cage) takes Loretta (Cher) to see at the New York Met in the 1987 romantic comedy, **Moonstruck**?
a) Carmen b) La Boheme
c) The Magic Flute d) Aida

ORPHANS

1) Who played the title role of the orphan who becomes a governess in the 1944 version of **Jane Eyre**?
a) Elizabeth Taylor b) Joan Fontaine
c) Deborah Kerr d) Ava Gardner

2) With which 1977 Disney comedy do you associate orphan Casey (Jodie Foster) trying to persuade Lady St. Edmund (Helen Hayes)

a macho waterfront fish

she is her lawful heir?
a) Candleshoe b) No Deposit, No Return
c) The Cat From Outer Space d) Gus

3) Name the orphaned dinosaur who journeys to the Great Valley in **The Land Before Time**?
a) Petrie b) Cera c) Littlefoot d) Sharptooth

PACIFISM

1) On whose novel was Lewis Milestone's 1930 anti-war classic, **All Quiet on the Western Front** based?
a) Siegfried Sassoon b) Erich Maria Remarque
c) Ernest Hemingway d) Vera Brittain

2) Name the Jean Renoir film which was banned in Germany by Nazi Propaganda Minister Josef Goebbels, who called it "Cinema-tographic Enemy No. 1"?
a) La Regle du Jeu b) Madame Bovary
c) La Grande Illusion
d) Diary of a Chambermaid

3) What 1941 film tells the true story of a deeply religious pacifist who tries to avoid service in WW1, and ends up single-handedly capturing 132 enemy soldiers and being awarded the Congressional Medal of Honor?
a) The Way Ahead b) Sergeant York
c) None But the Brave d) Kings Go Forth

PAINTINGS

1) With which film do you associate a museum portrait of Carlotta Valdes?
a) The Life and Death of Colonel Blimp b) Hello, Dolly! c) The Crow d) Vertigo

2) In which 1939 mystery does a portrait of Sir Hugo assist Sherlock Holmes in solving a murder?

astounding handyman industry rag

Themes

a) *Sherlock Holmes Faces Death* b) *The Hound of the Baskervilles* c) *The Return of Sherlock Holmes* d) *The Adventures of Sherlock Holmes*

3) With which Marx Brothers comedy do you associate Captain Spaulding the explorer, art expert Abey the Fishmonger, and a stolen painting?
a) *Cocoanuts* b) *Animal Crackers*
c) *Monkey Business* d) *Horse Feathers*

PERSONAL ADS

1) In 1985 bored housewife, Roberta, answers a classified ad which was **Desperately Seeking Susan**. Who was she?
a) *Rosanna Arquette* b) *Lois Hall*
c) *Cathy Tyson* d) *Zena Walker*

2) Who advertises for a room-mate but gets a female slasher instead in **Single White Female**?
a) *Jennifer Jason Leigh* b) *Kate Nelligan*
c) *Gena Rowlands* d) *Bridget Fonda*

3) With which 1991 romantic drama do you associate Hillary O'Neil (Julia Roberts) answering a classified ad calling for a "young and attractive woman, with some nursing experience"?
a) *Sleeping With the Enemy* b) *I Love Trouble*
c) *Dying Young* d) *Blood Red*

PINBALL & VIDEO GAMES

1) Who portrayed "the pinball wizard" in Ken Russell's **Tommy** (1975)?

a) Eric Clapton b) Elton John
c) Jack Nicholson d) Roger Daltrey

2) King Koopa rules Dinohattan, the subterranean world of lizard humans in **Super Mario Bros.** Who was he?
a) *Dennis Hopper* b) *Bob Hoskins*
c) *Willem Dafoe* d) *David Bowie*

3) In which 1982 Disney feature is computer games designer, Flynn (Jeff Bridges), trapped inside a computer world where he is compelled to play a real video game to stay alive?
a) *Weird Science*
b) *Electric Dreams*
c) *Tron* d) *Jumpin' Jack Flash*

PLAGUES & DISEASES

1) Name the 1950 Elia Kazan drama in which two killers, Blackie and Fitch (Jack Palance and Zero Mostel), are suspected carriers of pneumonic plague.
a) *Plague* b) *The Search*
c) *Panic in the Streets* d) *Manhunt*

2) On whose story was Roger Corman's **The Masque of the Red Death** based, in which the evil Prince Prospero (Vincent Price) leads a life of debauchery in his castle, while the surrounding countryside is ravaged by plague?
a) *Stephen King* b) *Edgar Allan Poe*
c) *M.R. James* d) *Sir Arthur Conan Doyle*

3) Which 1990 film features Dr. Malcolm Sayer (based on British-born New York neurologist, Oliver Sacks) who discovered L-dopa in 1969, a new drug for the treatment of Parkinson's disease?
a) *Dying Young* b) *Lorenzo's Oil*
c) *Awakenings* d) *Damaged Lives*

PLANTS & TREES

1) In which film does Francie Nolan (Peggy Ann Garner) liken her life to a tree which grows outside her tenement window?
a) *Tree of Hands* b) *A Tree Grows in Brooklyn*
c) *The Far Country* d) *Raintree County*

2) By growing what variety of flower does Ugolin Soubeyran (Daniel Auteuil) hope he will make his fortune in **Jean De Florette**?
a) *rose* b) *sunflower* c) *tulip* d) *carnation*

3) What was the plant, Triffidus Celestus, attracted to, which eventually enabled Bill Masen (Howard Keel) to lead it to its doom, in **The Day of the Triffids**?
a) *light* b) *water* c) *sound* d) *heat*

PLASTIC SURGERY

1) In which 1947 crime drama does Vincent Parry (Humphrey Bogart) receive plastic surgery?
a) *Dark Passage* b) *Dead Reckoning*
c) *All Through the Night* d) *Thank Your Lucky Stars*

2) Dr. Gustav Segert operated on Anna Holm's (Joan Crawford) facial disfigurement transforming her not only physically, but spiritually as well, in **A Woman's Face** (1941). Who portrayed Dr. Segert?
a) *Cedric Hardwicke* b) *Leslie Howard*
c) *Conrad Veidt* d) *Melvyn Douglas*

3) In which 1985 film is Ida Lowry (Katherine Helmond) obsessed with plastic surgery?
a) *Rabid* b) *Brazil*
c) *Perfect* d) *Johnny Handsome*

PORNOGRAPHY

1) Name the 1980 porno film produced by *Penthouse* magazine and set in ancient Rome.
a) *Caligula* b) *The Arena* c) *Gospa*
d) *Roman Scandals*

2) Who played the title role in the soft-core skin flick, **Emmanuelle**?
a) *Ingrid Thulin* b) *Stacy Keach*
c) *Britt Ekland* d) *Sylvia Kristel*

3) Which film features George C. Scott as a Calvinist father from Grand Rapids who descends into the Californian porno-prostitution world in search of his runaway daughter?

47

The Movie Quiz Companion

any posh ceramic

a) Hardcore b) My Father is Coming
c) Shattered Innocence d) Devil in the Flesh

POVERTY

1) In which 1937 drama does a mother feed her starving family cooked earth?
a) The Good Earth b) Lies My Father Told Me
c) Dark Enemy d) This Above All

2) Name the North of England town which provided the setting for the 1941 drama, **Love on the Dole**.
a) Bradford b) Salford c) Rochdale d) Oldham

3) What 1941 film, directed by John Ford, portrayed the misery of the poverty stricken Lester family of Georgia?
a) Our Daily Bread b) The Grapes of Wrath
c) The Sun Shines Bright d) Tobacco Road

PREGNANCY & CHILDBIRTH

1) Kristy Briggs gives birth nine months after copulation with her husband to the strains of the song 'Workin' on the Chain Gang' in **She's Having a Baby** (1988). Who was she?
a) Judy Davis b) Tracey Walter
c) Tess Harper d) Elizabeth McGovern

2) In which film does Jo (Rita Tushingham) become pregnant to a black sailor she meets in Blackpool docks?
a) Girl with the Green Eyes b) A Taste of Honey
c) The Knack d) The Bed-Sitting Room

3) Who couldn't remember who was the father of her child because she was drunk at the time of conception, in **The Miracle of Morgan's Creek**?
a) Betty Hutton b) Maureen O'Hara
c) Margaret Sullavan d) Jean Arthur

PROSTITUTION

1) In which country is **The World of Suzie Wong** set?
a) Hong Kong b) China c) Macao d) U.S.A.

2) In Luis Buñuel's 1967 drama, **Belle de Jour**, bored housewife turned prostitute, Severine Serizy (Catherine Deneuve), is presented with an ornate box from a client, the contents of which he wants to employ during his session with her. What is in the box?
a) a whip b) a mask
c) a vibrator d) we are never told

3) Name the 1987 film, directed by Terry Jones, which documents the life of real-life madam, Cynthia Payne.
a) Personal Services b) Lady Be Good
c) Hussy d) The Happy Hooker

PROTECTION RACKETS

1) What 1973 film involves Charlie (Harvey Keitel) as a collector for his uncle's protection racket?
a) Mean Streets b) Taxi Driver c) Alice Doesn't Live Here Anymore d) Who's That Knocking at my Door?

2) Who portrayed the dedicated police lieutenant, Joseph Petrosino, who fights against the protection rackets of The Black Hand, eventually paying for them with his life, in the 1960 drama, **Pay or Die**?
a) Ernest Borgnine b) Karl Malden
c) Robert Mitchum d) Robert Ryan

3) In which film is Robert De Niro's character reluctantly ousted from his job by his employer who is forced to substitute the nephew of local protection racketeer, Don Francesco?

a) Once Upon a Time in America b) Bloody Mama c) The Godfather Part II d) A Bronx Tale

PSYCHIATRY & PSYCHOLOGY

1) In 1946 psychiatrist Lew Ayres analyses two identical twins, one of whom is a killer, in **The Dark Mirror**. Who portrayed both twins?
a) Olivia de Havilland b) Bette Davis
c) Barbara Stanwyck d) Rosalind Russell

2) In which film does Alan Strang (Peter Firth) have a compulsion for blinding horses?
a) The Electric Horseman b) Stallion Road
c) Equus d) Eagle's Wing

3) The 1987 film, **The Man Who Mistook His Wife for a Hat**, is the case-history of a man who suffers from the inability to recognise everyday objects. What is the medical term for this condition?
a) logophobia b) agnosia
c) scopophilia d) russophobia

PUNKS & PUNK FILMS

1) What nationality was the punk band **Dogs in Space** in the 1986 film of the same name?
a) Dutch b) American c) Russian d) Australian

2) What film, featuring themselves, did The Clash disown in 1980?
a) Rude Boy b) The Great Rock 'n' Roll Swindle
c) The Return of the Living Dead d) Union City

3) Considered by many to be the best punk movie ever made, name the title of this 1977 punk documentary by Don Lett which featured Wayne County, Siouxsie, Johnny Rotten and others.
a) Punk in London b) The Punk Rock Movie
c) The Wild Side d) Smithereens

PUPPETS

1) In 1974 he played a puppeteer who could re-animate dead bodies in **Shanks**. Who was he?

48

a) Michael Crawford b) Marcel Marceau
c) Mel Brooks d) Joe Pesci

2) Who danced with life-sized puppets in the 1953 film, **Lilli**?
a) Moira Shearer b) Cyd Charisse
c) Debbie Reynolds d) Leslie Caron

3) Who played the title role in the 1989 horror film, **Puppetmaster**?
a) Paul Le Mat b) Matt Roe
c) Denis Leary d) William Hickey

QUAKERS

1) Name the 1971 children's fantasy which was financed by the Quaker Oats Company.
a) The Railway Children
b) Willie Wonka and the Chocolate Factory
c) Tarka the Otter
d) Charlotte's Web

2) Who portrayed the WWII naval officer who loses the respect of his crew because of his Quaker beliefs in the 1958 war film, **The Deep Six**?
a) William Bendix b) Glenn Ford
c) Richard Todd d) Alan Ladd

3) What 1956 drama, directed by William Wyler, tells the story of a Quaker family trying to preserve its religious beliefs during the Civil War?
a) Devil's Doorway b) Friendly Persuasion
c) Unconquered d) In Harm's Way

RACE

1) With which film do you associate Ava Gardner portraying an Anglo-Indian falling for army officer, Col. Rodney Savage (Stewart Granger), during the last days of British rule in India?
a) Bhowani Junction b) The Drum
c) The Brigand of Kandahar d) The Rains of Ranchipur

2) Who is Mr. and Mrs. Drayton's guest in Stanley Kramer's 1967 drama, **Guess Who's Coming to Dinner**?
a) Sidney Poitier b) Sammy Davis Jr.
c) Richard Roundtree d) Richard Pryor

3) In which 1984 drama does Dr. Aziz befriend Adela Quested?
a) Chato's Land b) Heat and Dust
c) The Sandpiper d) A Passage to India

RACISM

1) Which 1987 film highlighted the struggle of the young leader of the Black Consciousness Movement?
a) Cry Freedom b) A World Apart
c) Mandela d) The Power of One

2) Name the 1967 film whose racial issues were deemed too controversial to film in the story's original Mississippi setting, and had to be shot in Tennessee.
a) To Kill a Mockingbird b) Watermelon Man
c) In the Heat of the Night d) Edge of the City

3) Name the title of Spike Lee's powerful 1989 testimony on U.S race relations, starring Danny Aiello and Ossie Davis.
a) School Daze b) Do the Right Thing
c) She's Gotta Have It d) Mo' Better Blues

RADIO

1) Bing Crosby first sang the song which became his theme song in the 1932 musical comedy, **The Big Broadcast**. Name the song.
a) White Christmas b) When the Blue of the Night Meets the Gold of the Day c) True Love d) Don't Fence Me In

2) In which film does "The Crimson Avenger" make a brief appearance?
a) Talk Radio b) Play Misty for Me
c) Radio Days d) The Great American Broadcast

3) Name the title of the 1950 drama in which 'God' speaks over the radio.
a) The Unsuspected b) I'll Tell the World
c) Wake Up and Live d) The Next Voice You Hear

RAIN

1) In which Hitchcock film is a Dutch diplomat assassinated on the steps of an Amsterdam building in torrential rain?
a) Saboteur b) Torn Curtain
c) Foreign Correspondent
d) Secret Agent

2) With which 1950 drama, set in 11th century Japan and directed by Akira Kurosawa. do you associate a woodcutter, a priest and a commoner taking refuge from a rainstorm?
a) Sanjuro b) The Seven Samurai
c) Rashomon d) Throne of Blood

3) Who was the character portrayed by Irene Dunne stranded with overnight in an isolated church during a rainstorm in **When Tomorrow Comes** (1939)?
a) Joseph Cotten b) Charles Boyer
c) Clark Gable d) James Mason

THE RAJ

1) In 1967 he portrayed the Bhanta tribal leader who leads a revolt against the British Raj in **The Long Duel**. Who was he?
a) Jack Palance b) Yul Brynner
c) Omar Sharif d) Anthony Quinn

The Movie Quiz Companion

2) Who played the title role in the 1935 biopic, **Clive of India**?
a) Robert Donat b) Ronald Colman
c) Leslie Howard d) Basil Rathbone

3) Name the classic 1935 adventure film about life in the British Raj, directed by Henry Hathaway, which was nominated for seven Oscars.
a) Kim b) The Drum
c) Gunga Din d) Lives of a Bengal Lancer

RAPE

1) District Attorney, Kathryn Murphy, takes up the case of Sarah Tobias (Jodie Foster) who was gang-raped in a neighbourhood bar in **The Accused** (1988). Who was she?
a) Kelly McGillis b) Ann Hearn
c) Dyan Cannon d) Cynthia Harris

2) In which 1972 adventure film is Bobby (Ned Beatty) raped by hillbillies in the Appalachians?
a) Deliverance b) Extremities
c) Act of Vengeance d) Incubus

3) For what western did Kirk Douglas portray Marshal Matt Morgan whose young Indian wife is raped by the son of his friend?
a) The Half-Breed b) Last Train From Gun Hill
c) Dakota Incident d) The Man Without a Star

REINCARNATION

1) Dr. Marc Chabot (Yves Montand) discovers that Daisy Gamble has lived in 19th century England in a previous life in the 1970 musical **On a Clear Day You Can See For Ever**. Who was she?
a) Ellen Burstyn b) Barbra Streisand
c) Natalie Wood d) Shirley MacLaine

2) In which 1964 comedy does a gangster come back to earth as a character played by Debbie Reynolds?
a) Goodbye Charlie b) When a Stranger Calls
c) You'll Like My Mother d) Somewhere in Time

3) The soul of a murdered man exists inside the body of Peter Proud in the 1975 thriller, **The Reincarnation of Peter Proud**. Who portrayed Peter?
a) Michael O'Keefe b) Charles Grodin
c) Michael Jayston d) Michael Sarrazin

RELIGION

1) In 1943 she portrayed the young French girl, Bernadette Soubirous, who had a vision of the Virgin Mary in Lourdes in **The Song of Bernadette**. Who was she?
a) Ava Gardner b) Jennifer Jones
c) Elizabeth Taylor d) Audrey Hepburn

2) With which 1962 film do you associate a couple allowing their eight year old daughter to die by refusing to give permission for a blood transfusion because of their religious beliefs?
a) Improper Conduct b) Heaven Help Us
c) The Refusal d) Life For Ruth

3) Of what religious group was Lindy Chamberlain, who was accused of murdering her baby in the 1988 docudrama, **A Cry in the Dark**?
a) Seventh Day Adventist b) Baptist
c) Jehovah's Witness d) Mormon

RETIREMENT

1) In which film do retirement home residents, portrayed by Wilford Brimley, Don Ameche and Hume Cronyn, discover "a fountain of youth" in a local swimming pool?
a) Destiny b) Daddy Nostalgia
c) Easy Living d) Cocoon

2) In 1951 and 1994 respectively, Michael Redgrave and Albert Finney portrayed schoolmaster, Andrew Crocker-Harris, who was forced into retirement at an English public school. Name the film.
a) Goodbye Mr. Chips b) The Browning Version
c) The Lady Vanishes d) A Man of no Importance

3) What 1949 western involved Capt. Nathan Brittles (John Wayne) and Sgt. Quincannon (Victor McLaglen) pondering their imminent retirement from the US Cavalry?
a) Rio Grande b) She Wore a Yellow Ribbon
c) The Horse Soldiers d) Hondo

REVENGE

1) In which 1987 drama does policeman, Alex J. Murphy, seek revenge on a gang of killers?
a) Kickboxer b) Ricochet
c) Robocop d) Massacre at Central High

2) Henry James' classic tale of revenge, *Washington Square*, was filmed by William Wyler in 1949. Name the title of the film.
a) The Gay Deception b) The Little Foxes
c) The Heiress d) Friendly Persuasion

3) The eponymous heroine of **Hannie Caulder** (1972) resolves to wreak vengeance on the Clemens brother who raped her and murdered her husband. Who was she?
a) Raquel Welch b) Jane Fonda
c) Diane Keaton d) Sissy Spacek

REVOLUTIONS

1) What is the connection between the characters played by Gene Wilder and Donald Sutherland in the 1970 comedy, **Start the Revolution Without Me**.
a) stepbrothers b) father and son
c) twins d) master and slave

2) In which 1974 film is the Mafia forced to flee Cuba during the 1959 revolution which overthrew the Batista regime?
a) The Don is Dead b) The Brotherhood
c) The Sicilian d) The Godfather Part II

3) Douglas Fairbanks Jr. portrayed an officer in the Tsar's army who is forced to abscond after the Russian Revolution with his former female servant in William Dieterle's 1932 romantic adventure, **Scarlet Dawn**. Who portrayed the servant?
a) Miriam Hopkins b) Nancy Carroll
c) Elizabeth Allen d) Dolores Del Rio

REWARDS

1) In a 1973 crime drama, murderer Kit Carruthers says : "I killed them because they was bounty hunters who wanted the reward money. If they was policemen, just being paid for doing their job, that would have been different." Name the film.
a) Out of the Darkness b) Badlands
c) Sweet Hostage d) The Story of Pretty Boy Floyd

2) Gypo Nolan (Victor McLaglen) betrays his friend for a police reward during the Sinn Fein rebellion of 1922 in John Ford's 1935 drama, **The Informer**. On whose novel was the film based?
a) Flann O'Brien b) Sean O'Faolain
c) Frank O'Connor d) Liam O'Flaherty

3) With which Laurel and Hardy film do you associate the duo getting a reward for catching a bank robber who slipped on a banana skin they'd dropped?
a) A Chump at Oxford b) The Music Box
c) Busy Bodies d) Bonnie Scotland

ROAD MOVIES

1) Three brothers drive a classic 1954 Cadillac down to Florida in the 1990 film, **Coupe de Ville**. From which city do they begin their odyssey?
a) Chicago b) Detroit
c) Kansas City d) Indianapolis

2) What 1973 road movie was based on Joe David Brown's novel, *Addie Pray*?
a) Sugarland Express b) The Last of the Cowboys
c) Paper Moon d) Hearts of Fire

3) In Paul Mazursky's 1974 drama, **Harry and Tonto**, who or what was Tonto?
a) a cat b) a dog
c) a rabbit's foot d) a stuffed parrot

ROBBERIES

1) In 1950 he portrayed master criminal "Doc" Erwin Riedenschneider who plans a jewel robbery while serving a prison sentence in **The Asphalt Jungle**. Who was he?
a) Louis Calhern b) Robert Ryan
c) Sam Jaffe d) Don Ameche

2) Name Lewis Milestone's 1960 drama about eleven ex-army buddies who attempt to rob five Las Vegas Hotels.
a) Ocean's Eleven b) They Came to Rob Las Vegas
c) Grand Slam d) The Biggest Bundle of Them All

3) As what were the characters portrayed by Alec Guinness, Stanley Holloway, Sidney James and Alfie Bass collectively known in 1951?
a) The Ladykillers b) The League of Gentlemen
c) Persons Unknown d) The Lavender Hill Mob

ROCK 'N' POP

1) Name the title of D.A. Pennebaker's film which chronicled Bob Dylan's 1965 concert tour of Great Britain.
a) Purple Rain b) Can't Stop the Music
c) Take It or Leave It d) Don't Look Back

2) Who portrayed the successful rock musician who worries about ageing and loneliness in **Who is Harry Kellerman and Why is He Saying Those Terrible Things About Me?**
a) Dustin Hoffman b) Gerry Marsden
c) Rock Hudson d) Jerry Lewis

3) With which film do you associate Mick Jagger portraying a rock star named Turner?
a) Blame It on the Night b) Popcorn
c) Burden of Dreams d) Performance

ROCK 'N' ROLL

1) In 1974 he portrayed Jim Maclaine in **That'll Be the Day**. Who was he?
a) Ringo Starr b) Billy Fury
c) David Essex d) James Booth

2) What film connection can you make between 1950's Rydell High and the characters, Danny and Sandy?
a) American Graffiti b) Grease
c) Eddie and the Cruisers d) Bye Bye Birdie

3) Who sang the title song in Frank Tashlin's 1956 film, **The Girl Can't Help It**?
a) Fats Domino b) Gene Vincent
c) Little Richard d) The Platters

The Movie Quiz Companion

sarcastic man waxes sheathe

ROLLER SKATING & SKATEBOARDS

1) In which musical does Barbra Streisand's screen character attempt a roller skating routine, with disastrous results?
a) *Funny Girl* b) *A Star is Born*
c) *Hello, Dolly!* d) *Yentl*

2) The title of the 1989 action film, **Gleaming the Cube** is skateboard jargon. What does it mean?
a) *to accomplish the utmost* b) *to clean your board* c) *to somersault backwards* d) *to have a fatal accident*

3) With which drama, directed by Frederico Fellini, do you associate roller skating priests and nuns?
a) *La Dolce Vita* b) *Armacord*
c) *La Strada* d) *Fellini's Roma*

SABOTAGE

1) Who is falsely accused of sabotage in Alfred Hitchcock's 1942 spy yarn, **Saboteur**?
a) *Robert Cummings* b) *Robert Donat*
c) *Joan Fontaine* d) *Mary Astor*

2) What do the miners sabotage in the 1970 film, **The Molly Maguires**?
a) *coal trains* b) *the pit boss's car*
c) *a police station* d) *a dam*

3) Mrs Verloc's younger brother unwittingly carries a bomb inside a film can which her husband has given him to deliver in Alfred Hitchcock's 1936 thriller **Sabotage**. Who portrayed Mrs Verloc?
a) *Nova Pilbeam* b) *Joan Barry*
c) *Irene Dunn* d) *Sylvia Sidney*

SADISM & SADOMASOCHISM

1) Dorothy Vallens (Isabella Rossellini) has a terrifying sadomasochistic relationship with Frank Booth in **Blue Velvet** (1986). Who was he?
a) *Dean Stockwell* b) *Brad Dourif*
c) *Kyle MacLachlan* d) *Dennis Hopper*

2) With which 1974 film do you associate a sadomasochistic relationship between a former Nazi and a woman he sexually abuses in a concentration camp?
a) *The Skin Game* b) *Revenge is my Destiny*
c) *The Night Porter* d) *Unholy Partners*

3) John Maybury's film, **Love is the Devil - Study for a Portrait of Francis Bacon** (1998), chronicles the ruthless and sadistic relationship between painter Bacon and his model George Dyer. Who portrayed Bacon?
a) *Nigel Hawthorne* b) *Derek Jacobi*
c) *Ian Holm* d) *Colin Firth*

SALVATION ARMY

1) Who portrayed Bat Masterson's Salvation Army "doll" in Joseph L. Mankiewicz's 1955 musical, **Guys and Dolls**?
a) *Natalie Wood* b) *Audrey Hepburn*
c) *Jean Simmons* d) *Shirley MacLaine*

2) Which Alfred Hitchcock film features a fugitive concealing himself in a crowd marching behind a Salvation Army band?
a) *Sabotage* b) *The 39 Steps*
c) *Blackmail* d) *The Wrong Man*

3) Who played the title role in the 1941 comedy, **Major Barbara**?
a) *Joan Fontaine* b) *Mary Astor*
c) *Wendy Hiller* d) *Deanna Durbin*

SCISSORS

1) In which 1987 comedy does mother-hating Owen Lift fantasise about driving a pair of scissors into his mum's (Anne Ramsey) ear?
a) *Wait Till Your Mother Gets Home* b) *Mother's Day* c) *My Mother's Secret Life* d) *Throw Momma From the Train*

2) Name the Hitchcock thriller in which intended murder victim, Margot Wendice, turns the tables on her attacker and stabs him in the back with a pair of scissors.
a) *Topaz* b) *Torn Curtain*
c) *Dial M For Murder* d) *To Catch a Thief*

3) Which 1987 Peter Greenaway drama features someone being circumcised with scissors?
a) *The Cook, The Thief, His Wife & Her Lover*
b) *Prospero's Books* c) *The Draughtsman's Contract* d) *Drowning By Numbers*

SECRET IDENTITIES

1) Which 1995 crime thriller features a club-footed criminal called 'Verbal' whose real identity is the terrifying Hungarian mobster, Keyser Söoze?
a) *Seven* b) *The Usual Suspects*
c) *Black Rainbow* d) *Death and the Maiden*

2) What was the secret identity of Don Diego de la Vega?
a) *Pancho Villa* b) *The Lone Wolf*
c) *Zorro* d) *The Cisco Kid*

3) Who played the title role in the 1981 western, **The Legend of the Lone Ranger**?
a) *John Hart* b) *Michael Horse*
c) *Klinton Spilsbury* d) *Matt Clark*

SECRET SOCIETIES

1) Name the 1935 Sherlock Holmes mystery about a secret society of coal miners which was based on Conan Doyle's *The Valley of Fear*?
a) *Terror By Night* b) *The Triumph of Sherlock Holmes* c) *The Pearl of Death* d) *The Scarlet Claw*

2) Which film features a secret society named The Foot?
a) *Teenage Mutant Ninja Turtles* b) *The Witches*
c) *The Secret of NIMH* d) *Meet the Applegates*

3) What 1967 film, starring James Coburn, involves a secret society of women plotting to take over the world?
a) The President's Analyst b) The Carey Treatment
c) Our Man Flint d) In Like Flint

SERMONS

1) In which film is part of the Sermon on the Mount interpreted by one of the faithful as: "The Greek shall inherit the Earth. Blessed are the cheesemakers."?
a) National Lampoon's Christmas Vacation
b) Blazing Saddles c) Monty Python's Life of Brian
d) The Muppet Movie

2) Name the evangelist (which is also the title of the film) whose sermons frequently include the line, "Love is like the morning and the evening star..."
a) Luther b) The Apostle
c) Cousin Bobby d) Elmer Gantry

3) Who portrayed the confused Bishop, whose Christmas sermon is rewritten by an angel called Dudley (Cary Grant) in the 1947 fantasy, **The Bishop's Wife**?
a) Nigel Bruce b) Louis Calhern
c) Thomas Mitchell d) David Niven

SEX

1) In which 1961 film, directed by Elia Kazan, does Hollywood's first French kiss appear?
a) A Streetcar Named Desire b) East of Eden
c) Splendor in the Grass d) Baby Doll

2) Phoolan Devi was married at the age of 11 and forced into sex by her 33-year-old husband. By what name is she better known?
a) The Diamond Queen b) Madame Sousatzka
c) Bandit Queen d) The Bandit of Zhobe

3) Lonely housewife, Ruth Popper (Cloris Leachman), has regular sex with teenager Sonny Crawford in Peter Bogdanovich's 1971 drama, **The Last Picture Show**. Who was he?
a) Timothy Bottoms b) Jeff Bridges
c) Randy Quaid d) Richard Dreyfuss

SEX CHANGE

1) With which 1975 film do you associate a bisexual man attempting to rob a bank to finance his transvestite lover's sexchange operation?
a) The Fruits of Passion b) Dog Day Afternoon
c) That Obscure Object of Desire d) Skin Deep

2) On whose novel was the 1970 transsexual satire, **Myra Breckinridge** based?
a) Mary McCarthy b) Flannery O'Connor
c) Gore Vidal d) Philip Roth

3) Name the title of Irving Rapper's 1970 film which tells the true story of the first man to undergo a sex-change operation in 1952.
a) The Christine Jorgensen Story b) Homicidal
c) In a Year with 13 Moons d) I Want What I Want

SIAMESE TWINS

1) Which 1932 horror film, adapted from the circus story 'Spurs', by Tod Robbins, features the Siamese twins Daisy and Violet Hilton?
a) Island of Lost Souls b) Freaks
c) The Ghoul d) The Cabinet of Dr. Caligari

2) Who directed **Sisters** (1973), a thriller about separated Siamese twins, one of whom is a murderer?
a) Brian DePalma b) Roger Corman
c) Tim Burton d) Sally Potter

3) In which film do Siamese twins decide to track down their mother who abandoned them as babies?
a) Twins of Evil b) The Savage Innocents
c) Twin Falls Idaho d) The Search

SISTERS

1) By what name were the 'March sisters' better known?
a) The Joy Luck Club b) Two English Girls
c) Little Women d) Seven Beauties

2) The Brewster sisters, Abby (Josephine Hull) and Martha (Jean Adair), have been poisoning elderly gentlemen for years before their nephew, Mortimer (Cary Grant), discovers what they are up to in **Arsenic and Old Lace** (1944). Who portrayed Abby?
a) Beulah Bondi b) Josephine Hull
c) Jean Adair d) Priscilla Lane

3) In 1986 she played Lee, sister of Hannah and Holly in **Hannah and Her Sisters**. Who was she?
a) Carrie Fisher b) Dianne West
c) Theresa Russell d) Barbara Hershey

SKIING

1) Who played the title role in **Downhill Racer**?
a) Bruce Dern b) Robert Redford
c) Steve McQueen d) Michael Sarrazin

2) In which 1978 film does the stubborn character portrayed by Rock Hudson build a ski lodge in a hazardous spot, ignoring all warnings?
a) Avalanche b) The Silent Wilderness
c) A Dangerous Summer d) Obsession

3) In which 1945 film does an amnesiac subconsciously depict ski tracks by gouging a table with a fork?
a) Fear is the Key b) Secret Beyond the Door
c) Spellbound d) Prizzi's Honor

SLASHER MOVIES

1) Which film features a killer known as 'The Shape'?
a) A Nightmare on Elm Street b) Halloween
c) There's Nothing Out There d) Splatter University

2) With which 1980 film do you associate a New Jersey summer camp being re-opened after being closed for twenty years because of a history of 'accidental' deaths?
a) April Fool's Day b) Cheerleader Camp
c) Deadly Lessons d) Friday the 13th

3) With which film do you associate a masked killer stalking a group of teenagers who are responsible for the death of a ten-year-old girl?
a) Prom Night b) Slaughter High
c) Bad Dreams d) Death Valley

SLAVERY

1) On whose novel was the 1975 film **Mandingo** based?

a) Kyle Onstott b) Toni Morrison
c) Frank Norris d) Danielle Steel

2) Who played the title role of the Brazilian slave trader in Werner Herzog's **Cobra Verde**?
a) Klaus Kinski b) Wolfgang Reichmann
c) Ken Takakura d) Gerard Depardieu

3) With which film do you associate the ruthless slave trader, Mendoza, who enslaved the Guarani Indians in 1750s South America?
a) Captain Blood b) The Mission
c) Saratoga Trunk d) A High Wind in Jamaica

SMALL TOWN LIFE

1) Name the Groundhog Capital of Pennsylvania where weatherman Phil (Bill Murray) is trapped in a 24-hour replay in the 1993 comedy, **Groundhog Day**?
a) Paducah b) Waynesboro
c) Punxsutawney d) Chickasha

2) One of the attractions of Brainerd, Minnesota, is the gigantic statue of Paul Bunyan on the outskirts. Name the film.
a) The Last Picture Show b) Fargo
c) Bagdad Cafe d) Town Without Pity

3) What film was based on real events in Hollister, California, when 4,000 members of the 'Black Rebels' gang took over the town?
a) The Invasion of Johnson County b) Hells Angels on Wheels c) Ransom d) The Wild One

SOCCER

1) In 1982 she played Dorothy, the only female member on the school soccer team, in **Gregory's Girl**. Who was she?
a) Carol Macartney b) Clare Grogan
c) Dee Hepburn d) Caroline Guthrie

2) With what 1981 film do you associate international football legend, Pele, being imprisoned in a German POW camp during WWII?
a) Victory b) Yesterday's Hero
c) The Ball of Fortune d) Bloomfield

3) Name the Disney fantasy which features an animated soccer game in 1971.
a) The Rescuers b) The Jungle Book
c) Bedknobs and Broomsticks d) The Aristocats

SOLDIERS RETURNING

1) When Navy flyer, Johnny Morrison (Alan Ladd), returns home and discovers his wife has been unfaithful, he becomes the prime suspect following her subsequent murder. Name the title of this 1946 mystery film.
a) The Blue Dahlia b) This Gun For Hire
c) Beyond Glory d) And Now Tomorrow

2) "I don't care if it doesn't make a nickel" Samuel Goldwyn reputedly claimed, "I just want every man, woman, and child in America to see it." Name this 1946 drama about returning WWII servicemen.
a) Hail the Conquering Hero b) These Three
c) Dead End d) The Best Years of Our Lives

3) Who portrayed Paul Sutton, a young man returning from WWII who meets a young Mexican girl on a bus in the 1995 romantic drama, **A Walk in the Clouds**?
a) Matt Damon b) Keanu Reeves
c) Sean Penn d) Charlie Sheen

SOLITARY CONFINEMENT

1) Why was WWI French POW, Marechal (Jean Gabin), sentenced to solitary confinement by the Germans in **La Grande Illusion**?
a) for singing "La Marseillaise" b) for digging an escape tunnel c) for insulting the Kaiser d) for assaulting a guard

2) Name the film which dramatised the life of convicted killer, Robert Stroud, who spent forty years in solitary confinement.
a) Each Dawn I Die b) The Rise and Fall of Legs Diamond c) The Birdman of Alcatraz d) You Only Live Once

3) Who was incarcerated for years in the infamous Chateau d'If?
a) The Man in the Iron Mask b) The Count of Monte Cristo c) The Elephant Man d) Beau Geste

SONS

1) Who played the title role in the 1943 horror film, **Son of Dracula**?
*a) Boris Karloff b) Lionel Barrymore
c) John Carradine d) Lon Chaney Jr*

2) Who played the title role in Joseph Ruben's 1993 comedy, **The Good Son**?
*a) Macaulay Culkin b) Brad Pitt
c) Adam Hann-Byrd d) Robert Oliveri*

3) In 1948 he portrayed Chris Keller, who was convinced of his father's innocence when he was accused of manufacturing defective aero-engine cylinders in **All My Sons**. Who was he?
*a) Paul Newman b) Burt Lancaster
c) John Wayne d) Pat O'Brien*

SPACE EXPLORATION

1) What was Cmdr. Christopher "Kit" Draper (Paul Mantee) known as in 1964?
*a) The Man Who Fell to Earth b) Robinson Crusoe on Mars c) Doc Savage - The Man of Bronze
d) The Last Starfighter*

2) In what film does a 1960s moon landing expedition unearth a Union Jack and a note dated the previous century claiming the moon as part of the British Empire?
*a) Not of This Earth b) The First Men in the Moon
c) Destination Moon d) The Time Machine*

3) With which film do you associate astronauts landing on Jupiter's 13th moon and discovering alluring female beings?
*a) Fire Maidens of Outer Space b) Quest for Love
c) Futureworld d) Teenagers from Outer Space*

SPANISH CIVIL WAR

1) In which film does schoolgirl, Mary McGregor, journey to Spain to join her brother in the fight for the fascist cause?
a) The Fallen Sparrow b) The Prime of Miss Jean Brodie c) Burden of Dreams d) Before Hindsight

2) In 1937 Carmelita Castillo was on **The Last Train from Madrid**. Who was she?
*a) Dorothy Lamour b) Joan Fontaine
c) Mary Astor d) Claudette Colbert*

3) Who directed the 1943 drama, **For Whom the Bell Tolls**?
*a) Raoul Walsh b) John Huston
c) Howard Hawks d) Sam Wood*

SPEECHES

1) With which actor and film do you associate the following speech:
"[If] you make it a crime to teach it in the public schools, tomorrow you can make it a crime to teach it in the private schools, and tomorrow you may make it a crime to read about it, and soon you may ban books and newspapers, and then you may turn Catholic against Protestant, and Protestant against Protestant, and try to foist your own religion on the mind of man. If you can do one, you can do the other, because fanaticism and ignorance is forever busy and needs feeding. And soon... with banners flying and with drums beating we'll be marching backward. Backward! Through the glorious ages of that 16th century, when bigots burned a man who dared bring enlightenment and intelligence to the human mind."
*a) James Stewart in Mr. Smith Goes to Washington
b) Michael Redgrave in The Browning Version
c) Spencer Tracy in Inherit the Wind d) Al Pacino In Scent of a Woman*

2) Long John Willoughby makes the following radio speech in a 1941 film, directed by Frank Capra:
"To most of you, your neighbor is a stranger, a guy with a barking dog and a fence around him. Now you can't be a stranger to any guy who's on your own team. So tear down the fence that separates you. You'll tear down a lot of hate and prejudices. I know a lot of you are saying to yourself: 'He's asking for a miracle.' Well, you're wrong. It's no miracle. I see it happen once every year at Christmas time. Why can't that spirit last the whole year round? Gosh, if it ever did, we'd develop such a strength that no human force could stand against us."
Name the film.
a) Mr. Smith Goes to Washington b) Meet John Doe c) Mr. Deeds Goes to Town d) You Can't Take It With You

3) The following speech extract was made by a local vicar portrayed by Henry Wilcoxon in a 1942 war drama, and was such a successful morale-booster that it was reprinted onto thousands of leaflets and dropped over Allied-enemy positions:
"It is a war of the people, of all the people, and it must be fought not only on the battlefield but in the cities and in the villages, in the factories and on the farms, in the home and in the heart of every man, woman and child who loves freedom. Well, we have buried our dead, but we shall not forget them. Instead, they will inspire us with an unbreakable determination to free ourselves and those who come after us from the tyranny and terror that threaten to strike us down. This is the people's war. It is our war. We are the fighters. Fight it then. Fight it with all that is in us, and may God defend the right."
Name the film.
*a) In Which We Serve b) Went the Day Well?
c) Mrs. Miniver d) Twelve O'Clock High*

STABBINGS

1) With which Alfred Hitchcock film do you associate advertising executive, Roger Thornhill, being suspected of stabbing the mysterious Mr. Townsend?
*a) To Catch a Thief b) Frenzy
c) North By Northwest d) Torn Curtain*

2) In which 1937 crime drama does Baby Face Martin (Humphrey Bogart) stab Dave (Joel McCrea) and throw him into New York's East River?
*a) The Great O'Malley b) Dead End
c) Crime School d) Black Legion*

The Movie Quiz Companion

3) In a 1956 mystery, French agent Louis Bernard is stabbed in the back in the backstreets of Marrakesh and stumbles into the arms of Dr. Ben McKenna (James Stewart). Name the film.
a) The Rare Breed b) Night Passage
c) The Man Who Knew Too Much
d) Bell, Book and Candle

STORMS

1) Who or what does an electric storm bring to life in 1931?
a) The Mummy b) Frankenstein's Monster
c) Kongo d) The Ghoul

2) With which F.W. Murnau silent classic do you associate a boat rowed by a couple capsizing on a lake during a raging storm?
a) Nosferatu b) Dr Jekyll and Mr Hyde
c) Faust d) Sunrise

3) Will Hay journeys through a storm to take up a new post on an Irish bus full of superstitious locals in 1937. Name the film.
a) Convict 99 b) Ask a Policeman
c) Windbag the Sailor d) Oh! Mr Porter

STRANGULATION

1) Who played the title role in the 1968 crime thriller, **The Boston Strangler**?
a) Burt Lancaster b) Tony Curtis
c) Laurence Harvey d) Christopher Plummer

2) With which film do you associate Peter Sellers' character trying to strangle himself with his own hand?
a) Dr Strangelove b) Casino Royale
c) Being There d) The Pink Panther

3) In which 1951 thriller is the strangling of Miriam (Laura Elliot) seen through the lens of spectacles?
a) Criss Cross
b) Strangers on a Train
c) Stage Fright d) Whirlpool

STRIKES

1) With which film do you associate Doris Day as a "grievance committee chairman"?
a) Pillow Talk b) Young at Heart c) Please Don't Eat the Daisies d) The Pajama Game

2) In 1959 he portrayed crooked capitalist, Sidney de Vere Cox, who tries to arrange a strike at Price's factory in the 1959 comedy, **I'm All Right Jack**. Who was he?
a) Peter Sellers b) Ian Carmichael
c) Richard Attenborough d) Terry Thomas

3) **The Second Greatest Sex** (1955), was based on the ancient Greek comedy, *Lysistrata*, in which the women of Athens, tired of war, take strike action and refuse to make love to their husbands to force a restoration of peace. Who wrote *Lysistrata*?
a) Aristophanes b) Euripides
c) Sophocles d) Aeschylus

STUDENTS

1) In what 1971 film do Jack Nicholson and Art Garfunkel portray college roommates?
a) On a Clear Day You Can See Forever
b) The Trip c) Too Soon to Love d) Carnal Knowledge

2) Which 1990 horror film features a group of medical students experimenting with life after death?
a) Flatliners b) Heathers
c) Before Sunrise d) Heart Land

3) In which 1959 film does cop killer and petty thief, Michel Poiccard, persuade an American student who sells newspapers to hide him from the police?
a) Kiss Me Deadly b) Daddy-O
c) City That Never Sleeps d) Breathless

SURFING

1) Name the fifties pop singer who portrays 'The Big Kahuna', winner of the surfing competition in the 1987 comedy, **Back to the Beach**?
a) Frankie Avalon b) Bill Haley
c) Ricky Nelson d) Ritchie Valens

2) Who sang the title music for **Ride the Wild Surf**, starring Tab Hunter?
a) Fabian b) Jan and Dean
c) Elvis Presley d) The Beachboys

3) In 1991 he played FBI agent, Johnny Utah, sent to investigate a string of bank robberies in Southern California's surfing community in **Point Break**. Who was he?
a) Patrick Swayze b) Gary Busey
c) Keanu Reeves d) Richard Gere

SUICIDE

1) On whose play was **An Inspector Calls** based, in which each member of a family bears some responsibility for a young girl's suicide?
a) Tom Stoppard
b) Peter Shaffer
c) Terence Rattigan
d) J.B. Priestley

2) With which 1968 drama do you associate deaf and mute Mr. Singer shooting himself?
a) The Heart is a Lonely Hunter
b) No Way Out
c) The Angry Silence
d) Johnny Got His Gun

field of wet urinals

3) In which film was musician Antonio Salieri (F. Murray Abraham) confined to an asylum after attempting suicide?
a) The Music Lovers b) Immortal Beloved
c) Beethoven's Great Love d) Amadeus

SURVIVAL IN THE WILDERNESS

1) With which 1972 film do you associate Robert Redford learning how to survive in the wilderness?
a) Three Days of the Condor b) Jeremiah Johnson
c) Tell them Willie Boy is Here d) Situation Hopeless but not Serious

2) Who played the title role in the 1971 drama, **Man in the Wilderness**?
a) Richard Harris b) Rod Steiger
c) Tony Curtis d) Lee J. Cobb

3) Rhonda Fleming leaves her millionaire playboy husband to die in the desert in the Roy Ward Baker's 1953 3-D drama, **Inferno**. Who was he?
a) Robert Wagner b) Sterling Hayden
c) Walter Huston d) Robert Ryan

SWIMMING

1) Who played the title role in **The Swimmer** (1968), in which a man makes his way homeward by swimming through the pools of neighbouring houses, each pool triggering a memory?
a) William Holden b) Burt Lancaster
c) Gregory Peck d) Fred MacMurray

2) With whom does Emmeline Foster (Jean Simmons) go swimming in the 1949 romantic drama, **The Blue Lagoon**?
a) John Garfield b) Donald Houston
c) Rex Harrison d) Russ Tamblyn

3) Name the Jean Vigo film in which Jean Dasté dives into water and sees an image of a smiling Dita Parlo swimming in her wedding gown?
a) Zero De Conduite
b) A Propos De Nice
c) L'Atalante
d) Taris Champion De Natation

TATTOOS

1) In which 1956 adventure film does Ishmael (Richard Basehart) share a room with a strange tattooed West Indian named Queenqueg?
a) Two Years Before the Mast b) Moby Dick
c) Captain Horatio Hornblower d) The Sea Wolf

2) What film depicts parts of a treasure map tattooed on young ladies' bottoms?
a) Get Charlie Tully
b) The Stranger and the Gunfighter
c) Double Exposure d) Octopussy

3) With which film do you associate Robert Mitchum observing an ex-con's tattoos, and commenting: "I don't know whether to look at him or read him."?
a) The Sundowners b) Pursued
c) Farewell My Lovely d) Cape Fear

Themes

TELEKINESIS

1) On whose short story was the 1936 fantasy, **The Man Who Could Work Miracles** based?
a) M.R. James b) H.G. Wells
c) Edgar Allan Poe d) Franz Kafka

2) In which 1960 science fiction film do a group of deadly children use their telekinetic energy to force a man to shoot himself with his own shotgun?
a) Cathy's Curse b) The Village of the Damned
c) The Innocents d) Return of the Living Dead

3) Who portrayed the little girl who could telekinetically start a blaze in **Firestarter**?
a) Linda Blair b) Annette Funicello
c) Drew Barrymore d) Tatum O'Neal

TELEPATHY

1) With which film do you associate scientist, Dr. Ruth (Patrick McGoohan), infiltrating a group of people who can read people's minds?
a) The Medusa Touch b) The Genius
c) Weird Science d) Scanners

2) Who or what gives people a telepathic experience in the 1983 science fiction film, **Brainstorm**?
a) a machine b) a drug
c) a prostitute d) an electric storm

3) In the 1982 film **Basket Case**, telepathic twin, Duane (Kevin Van Hentenryck), arrives in New York with a wicker basket to kill the three doctors who separated him from his Siamese twin when he was ten years old. What does he carry in the basket?
a) a rabid dog b) scorpions c) his Siamese twin
d) the heads of the doctors' wives

TELEPHONES

1) Leona Stevenson overhears a murder being planned through crossed telephone lines in the 1948 thriller, **Sorry, Wrong Number**. Who was she?
a) Gloria Grahame b) Joan Crawford
c) Barbara Stanwyck d) Ava Gardner

57

The Movie Quiz Companion

gothic rave attire

2) In which film do Jan Morrow (Doris Day) and Brad Allen (Rock Hudson) meet through a party line?
a) *That Touch of Mink* b) *Pillow Talk*
c) *Do Not Disturb* d) *Move Over Darling*

3) She portrayed answering machine operator, Ella Peterson, who falls in love with a man's voice heard over the telephone line in the musical comedy, **Bells Are Ringing** (1960). Who was she?
a) *Caroll Baker* b) *Judy Holliday*
c) *Margaret Sullavan* d) *Julie Harris*

TELEVISION

1) In **Network** (1976), veteran newsreader Howard Beale, of the United Broadcasting System, announces to his audience that he intends to commit suicide on his next broadcast. Who was he?
a) *William Holden* b) *Ned Beatty*
c) *Peter Finch* d) *Eli Wallach*

2) With which film do you associate Holly Hunter as a TV network news producer?
a) *The Front* b) *Broadcast News*
c) *Terrorvision* d) *Stay Tuned*

3) With whom does TV news reporter, Christy Colleran (Kathleen Turner), fall in love, in **Switching Channels** (1988)?
a) *Mel Gibson* b) *Al Pacino*
c) *Christopher Reeve*
d) *Tommy Lee Jones*

TENNIS

1) In the 1979 film, **Players**, the tennis pro played by Dean-Paul Martin is compelled to choose between the game and a woman. Who portrayed her?
a) *Ali MacGraw* b) *Marsha Mason*
c) *Tuesday Weld* d) *Glenda Jackson*

2) What 1979 film features real-life tennis stars Björn Borg and Bobby Riggs?
a) *Spring Fever* b) *Racquet*
c) *Little Mo* d) *Nobody's Perfect*

3) In which 1960 comedy does insurance clerk, C.C. Baxter, strain spaghetti through his tennis racquet?
a) *That Touch of Mink* b) *Diary of a Bachelor*
c) *Indiscreet* d) *The Apartment*

TERMINALLY ILL

1) Name the 1988 black comedy in which characters portrayed by Timothy Dalton and Anthony Edwards, both terminally ill with cancer, steal an ambulance and visit the flesh-pots of Amsterdam for the last time.
a) *Hawks* b) *Last Wish*
c) *Things in Their Season* d) *The Boys*

2) In the 1991 romantic drama, **Dying Young**, Hillary O'Neal (Julia Roberts) is hired by Victor Geddes (Campbell Scott) to nurse him through a life-threatening illness. Name the illness.
a) *AIDS* b) *leukaemia*
c) *pneumonic plague* d) *adrenoleukodystrophy*

3) With which film do you associate the singer C.C. Bloom losing her best friend Hillary to heart disease after a thirty-year friendship?
a) *Working Girls* b) *The Cure*
c) *High Hopes* d) *Beaches*

THANKSGIVING

1) What film, set in North Africa, had the good fortune to open at New York's Hollywood Theater on Thanksgiving Day, 1942, three weeks after the Allies actually landed in North Africa?
a) *The African Queen* b) *Casablanca*
c) *The Man Who Never Was* d) *Desert Fury*

2) What film involves a businessman and a shower-ring salesman trying to get home for Thanksgiving, and bumping into adversity at every turn?
a) *National Lampoon's Vacation* b) *Long Road Home* c) *Planes, Trains & Automobiles* d) *Home For the Holidays*

3) In which film does two people's Thanksgiving Day dinner consist of a cooked boot?
a) *The Gold Rush* b) *Orpheus*
c) *Hobson's Choice* d) *Duck Soup*

TIME TRAVEL

1) With which 1960 science fiction film do you associate time traveller, George, falling in love with the passive Eloi girl, Weena?
a) *The Time Travellers* b) *The Atomic Man*
c) *Somewhere in Time* d) *The Time Machine*

2) In which 1986 film does Kathleen Turner return to 1960?
a) *Trancers* b) *Peggy Sue Got Married*
c) *I'll Never forget You* d) *Time After Time*

3) What film tells the story of two US Navy sailors whose ship is involved in 1943 in an experiment that goes wrong, which consequently transports them through time to 1984?
a) *Quantum Leap* b) *The Blue Yonder*
c) *The Philadelphia Experiment* d) *Tomorrow*

TRANSPLANTATION

1) Name the 1971 comedy in which Hywell Bennett receives the world's first penis transplant.
a) *The Goonies* b) *It's Not Size That Counts*
c) *Percy* d) *Portnoy's Complaint*

2) Which Monty Python film features the brutal removal of a liver from a transplant "volunteer"?
a) *The Meaning of Life* b) *Life of Brian* c) *The Holy Grail* d) *And Now For Something Completely Different*

3) In which film does Joan Crawford portray an art collector who arranges an eye transplant from a donor who is still alive?
a) Night Gallery b) A Woman's Face
c) This Woman is Dangerous d) Above Suspicion

TRANSVESTITES

1) With which film do you associate the transvestite scientist, Dr. Frank N. Furter?
a) Duck Soup b) The Producers
c) The Rocky Horror Picture Show d) I Was a Male War Bride

2) In which film does Murphy (Paul Newman) try to dissuade a transvestite from committing suicide?
a) Fort Apache, The Bronx b) When Time Ran Out
c) The Drowning Pool d) Harry and Son

3) In which 1994 drama, directed by John Dahl, is regular guy Mike Swale briefly married to a transvestite?
a) The Last Seduction b) Kill Me Again
c) Red Rock West d) The Death Mutants

TRAPPED

1) Who directed the 1951 drama, **Ace in the Hole** (aka The Big Carnival), about an ambitious newspaper reporter who delays the rescue of a man trapped in a collapsed mine to make his scoop last longer?
a) Billy Wilder b) John Huston
c) Howard Hawks d) King Vidor

2) With which 1941 drama do you associate Mr. Morgan (Donald Crisp) being trapped in a mine shaft?
a) Lassie Come Home b) Greyfriars Bobby c) How Green Was My Valley d) Valley of the Giants

3) Which Woody Allen film features the rescue of a little girl who is trapped at the bottom of a well, and is eventually discovered to be dead?
a) Radio Days b) Love and Death
c) Stardust Memories d) Manhattan Murder Mystery

TRIAD GANGS

1) Who directed the 1995 drama, **Shanghai Triad**?
a) Wim Wenders b) Zhang Yimou
c) Sam Mendes d) Oliver Stone

2) Name the 1991 John Woo film in which Triad gun-runners use a hospital morgue to store their arms.
a) Bullet in the Head b) Broken Arrow
c) A Better Tomorrow d) Hard-Boiled

3) Which film in the **Lethal Weapon** series involves Gibson and Glover investigating a Triad gang selling Chinese immigrants into slavery?
a) Lethal Weapon b) Lethal Weapon 2
c) Lethal Weapon 3 d) Lethal Weapon 4

TRUCK-DRIVING MOVIES

1) What type of explosives do the two trucks carry in Henri-Georges Clouzot's, **The Wages of Fear**?
a) nitroglycerine b) dynamite
c) land mines d) gelignite

2) In which 1940 drama, directed by Raoul Walsh, do George Raft and Humphrey Bogart portray truck-driving brothers?
a) Thieves' Highway b) Every Night at Eight
c) St. Louis Blues d) They Drive by Night

3) Name the trucker who gets into **Big Trouble in Little China** in 1986?
a) Chris Makepeace b) Bill Paxton
c) Kurt Russell d) Treat Williams

TWINS

1) Who portrayed both twins in the 1941 film of Alexandre Dumas's novel, **The Corsican Brothers**?
a) Douglas Fairbanks Jr. b) Errol Flynn
c) Louis Calhern d) Gary Cooper

2) In which film are siblings Julius and Vincent Benedict separated at birth and reunited thirty five years later?
a) Double Impact b) Twins
c) Take Two d) Twins of Evil

3) In 1964 she portrayed both twins, Margaret and Edith, in **Dead Ringer**. Who was she?
a) Bette Davis b) Doris Day
c) Natalie Wood d) Elizabeth Taylor

VIETNAM WAR

1) Name the film which contains the following dialogue:
Joker: "How can you shoot women and children?"
Cobra gunner: "Easy, you just don't lead 'em so much."
a) Gardens of Stone b) Missing in Action
c) Rolling Thunder d) Full Metal Jacket

2) In 1978 he portrayed Major Asa Barker in **Go Tell the Spartans**. Who was he?
a) Martin Sheen b) Burt Lancaster
c) James Caan d) Richard Dreyfuss

3) Name the Vietnam war movie which is famous for its final scene depicting the sun setting in the east.
a) The Green Berets b) Fatal Mission
c) The Iron Triangle d) Jacob's Ladder

VIGILANTES

1) How many sequels to **Death Wish** have there been to date?
a) 2 b) 3 c) 4 d) 5

2) With which 1983 thriller do you associate criminal judges turning into vigilantes?
a) The Star Chamber b) The Death Squad
c) Brotherhood of Justice d) Fighting Back

3) In which 'Dirty Harry' film does Clint Eastwood investigate a group of vigilante cops?

The Movie Quiz Companion

a) Magnum Force b) The Enforcer
c) Sudden Impact d) The Dead Pool

VIKINGS

1) Who played the title role in the 1989 fantasy, **Eric the Viking**?
a) John Cleese b) Tim Robbins
c) Bill Murray d) Jim Carrey

2) With which film do you associate a Viking quest to find the legendary Golden Bell?
a) The Long Ships b) The Golden Lady
c) Death in the Sun d) When Time Ran Out

3) In 1958 he portrayed the Viking chieftain, Ragnar, who is thrown into a pit of wolves by the English, in **The Vikings**. Who was he?
a) Tony Curtis b) Curt Jurgens
c) Lon Chaney Jr. d) Ernest Borgnine

VOODOO

1) What 1940 voodoo connection can you make between Bob Hope and Paulette Goddard?
a) The Cat and the Canary b) The Ghost Breakers
c) Where There's Life d) Let's Face It

2) In 1932 he portrayed "the Voodoo Master" in **White Zombie**. Who was he?
a) Bela Lugosi b) Lionel Barrymore
c) Peter Lorre d) Boris Karloff

3) With which 1987 film do you associate the Caribbean voodoo cult, Santeria, which practises the sacrifice of young boys?
a) Island of Mutation b) The Serpent and the Rainbow c) Lifeforce d) The Believers

WAR CRIMINALS

1) Name the Nazi war criminal who murdered thousands of Jews during genetics experiments and was portrayed by Gregory Peck in the 1978 thriller, **The Boys From Brazil**.
a) Reinhard Heydrich
b) Klaus Barbie
c) Adolf Eichman
d) Joseph Mengle

2) With which film do you associate Dirk Bogarde as an ex-SS officer trying to keep a low profile in 1950s Vienna?
a) They Who Dare b) The Spanish Gardener
c) The Night Porter d) Song Without End

3) Journalist Peter Miller tracks down former Nazi war criminals in the 1974 thriller, **The Odessa File**. Who was he?
a) John Voight b) Randy Quaid
c) Mark Lester d) Harry Dean Stanton

WAR HEROES

1) Name the film which was based on the autobiography of Audie Murphy, America's most decorated soldier.
a) Objective Burma! b) Kings Go Forth
c) To Hell and Back d) They Were Expendable

2) In which 1946 drama does James Stewart portray a character whose pilot brother is decorated at the White House for saving the lives of everyone on a naval transport?
a) Navy Blue and Gold b) The Mortal Storm
c) It's a Wonderful Life d) Strategic Air Command

3) The 1961 biopic, **The Outsider**, starred Tony Curtis as the Pima Indian who was one of the US marines who raised the famous flag at Iwo Jima. Name the Indian he portrayed?
a) Guy Gabaldon b) Ernie Pyle
c) John Hoskins d) Ira Hayes

WHEELCHAIRS

1) In 1994 he portrayed Lieutenant Dan Taylor, the wheelchair-bound friend of **Forrest Gump**. Who was he?
a) Gary Sinise b) Ben Lang
c) Wendell Wellman d) Jerry Orbach

2) With which 1993 drama do you associate the stern housekeeper, Mrs. Medlock (Maggie Smith) caring for a wheelchair-bound invalid?
a) The Pumpkin Eater b) A Private Function
c) The Lonely Passion of Judith Hearne d) The Secret Garden

3) What romantic drama about a failed American writer who is confined to a wheelchair did Roman Polanski direct in 1992?
a) Bitter Moon b) Boxing Helena
c) Cul de Sac d) The Slender Thread

WITCHCRAFT

1) On whose novel was Ken Russell's **The Devils** based?
a) Aldous Huxley b) Dennis Wheatley
c) Edgar Allan Poe d) Albert Camus

2) What animal does a 15th century French lawyer defend when it is accused of witchcraft in the 1994 historical drama, **The Advocate**?
a) a dog b) a goat c) a pig d) a raven

3) Barbara Clarke is accused of witchcraft by Ann Goode (Bonita Granville) in Frank Lloyd's 1937 historical drama, **Maid of Salem**. Who portrayed Barbara?
a) Jean Arthur b) Mary Astor
c) Donna Reed d) Claudette Colbert

WITNESS-TO-CRIME STORIES

1) In which Hitchcock thriller does L.B. "Jeff" Jeffries witness events that convince him Lars Thorwald (Raymond Burr) has murdered his wife?
a) Dial M For Murder b) Blackmail
c) The Paradine Case d) Rear Window

2) With which film do you associate 12-year-old tomboy, Gillie, peering through a letter-box and witnessing a Polish sailor murdering his girlfriend?
a) Deadly Strangers b) Tiger Bay
c) Whistle Down the Wind d) The Moonspinners

3) Name the title of the 1962 thriller based on Agatha Christie's 4:50 From Paddington, in which Miss Marple witnesses a murder.
a) Murder She Said b) Evil Under the Sun
c) Spider's Web d) Witness for the Prosecution

WORLD WAR I

1) With which film do you associate an all-out assault on an impregnable German

position nicknamed The Ant Hill?
a) Paths of Glory b) Sergeant York
c) All Quiet on the Western Front d) Gallipoli

2) With which WWI anti-war film do you associate a cricket scoreboard keeping a tally of casualties?
a) Isn't Life Wonderful? b) We're in the Army Now
c) The Blue Max d) Oh What a Lovely War

3) On whose novel was Gilles MacKinnon's **Regeneration** based, about a real-life encounter between writer, Siegfried Sassoon, and army psychologist, W.H.R. Rivers?
a) Anita Brookner b) Pat Barker
c) J.G. Farrell d) Robert Graves

WORLD WAR II

1) Based on a Graham Greene story called *The Lieutenant Died Last,* this 1942 film tells the story of the invasion of an isolated English village by German paratroopers disguised as Royal Engineers. Name the title.
a) Went the Day Well? b) The Imitation Game
c) The Way Ahead d) This Above All

2) What does the Seabee stand for in the 1944 war film, **The Fighting Seabees**, starring John Wayne and Dennis O'Keefe?
a) Construction Battalion b) Commando Battalion c) Catering Battalion d) Canadian Battalion

3) During WWII, the Niland family received reports that three of their four sons had been killed in action. Name the film based on this true story.
a) Simple Men b) The Seven Little Foys
c) Saving Private Ryan d) Brothers in Arms

WRESTLING

1) With which wrestling star do you associate the film **No Holds Barred**?
a) Mad Dog Joe De Curso b) Kendo Nagasaki
c) Hulk Hogan d) Andy Robbins

2) In which film do Rupert Birkin and Gerald Crich wrestle in the nude?
a) The Fighting Kentuckian
b) Women in Love
c) Sid and Nancy d) The Sons of Katie Elder

3) In what 1987 film does Sylvester Stallone portray a character who competes in an arm-wrestling championship in Las Vegas?
a) Over the Top b) Paradise Alley
c) Death Race 2000 d) The Prisoner of Second Avenue

YEAR IN TITLE

1) With which film do you associate android schoolteachers armed, by the DED (Dept. of Educational Defense), with rocket launchers?
a) Class of 1999 b) Class of 1984
c) The Spirit of '76 d) 1990: The Bronx Warriors

2) In which film do Ray Milland and family escape a nuclear attack by sheltering in an isolated cave?
a) Terror From the Year 5000 b) Panic in Year Zero c) 2000 Years Later d) Daleks-Invasion Earth 2150 A.D.

3) Who portrayed Berlinghieri's (Robert De Niro) grandfather in Bertolucci's **1900**?
a) Donald Sutherland b) Yves Montand
c) Orson Welles d) Burt Lancaster

ROLES

ACCOUNTANTS

1) With which film do you associate Broadway producer, Max Bialystock, persuading neurotic accountant, Leo Bloom, to help him find the worst play ever written?
a) Broadway Melody of 1938 b) Meet Me After the Show c) The Producers d) Broadway Danny Rose

2) Who portrayed the conscientious Jewish accountant, Itzhak Stern, in **Schindler's List**?
a) Richard Dreyfuss b) William Sadler
c) David Caruso d) Ben Kingsley

3) Which 1959 drama features Laurence Harvey as a lowly government accountant in the Yorkshire mill town of Warnley?
a) Saturday Night and Sunday Morning
b) Room at the Top c) Darling
d) Of Human Bondage

ADMIRALS

1) James Cagney portrayed WWII Admiral 'Bull' Halsey in the 1960 war film, **The Gallant Hours**. Name the battle in the film which is the turning point for American victory in WWII.
a) Bataan b) Iwo Jima
c) Guadacanal d) Toko-Ri

2) In which film did Reginald Owen portray a retired admiral whose house resembles a ship, and who fires his ship's cannon at six on the dot every evening?
a) Mary Poppins b) Chitty Chitty Bang Bang
c) Doctor Doolittle d) The Great Race

3) In 1992 and 1994 respectively he portrayed Admiral James Greer in **Patriot Games** and **Clear and Present Danger**. Who was he?
a) James Earl Jones b) Donald Moffat
c) Willem Dafoe d) Henry Czerny

ADVERTISING EXECUTIVES

1) With which 1959 film do you associate Cary Grant portraying an advertising executive?
a) His Girl Friday b) North By Northwest
c) That Touch of Mink d) An Affair to Remember

2) Which 1975 comedy involves advertising executive Jack Lemmon having a nervous breakdown?
a) Save the Tiger b) The China Syndrome
c) The Prisoner of Second Avenue d) Days of Wine and Roses

3) In 1989 he played a top advertising executive in the 1989 film, **How To Get Ahead in Advertising**. Who was he?
a) Nicholas Cage b) Anthony Hopkins
c) Sean Penn d) Richard E. Grant

ALCOHOLICS

1) In 1948 she portrayed Gaye Dawn, Johnny Rocco's (Edward G. Robinson) alcoholic

girlfriend in **Key Largo**. Who was she?
a) Claire Trevor b) Ida Lupino
c) Mary Astor d) Peggy Ann Garner

2) With which film do you associate Fredric March portraying an alcoholic, who, believing he is an enormous burden on his wife, commits suicide by drowning?
a) Man on a Tightrope b) A Star is Born
c) It's a Big Country d) We Live Again

3) On which actress's biographical novel was the 1990 comedy, **Postcards From the Edge** based, which chronicles her struggle with alcohol addiction?
a) Drew Barrymore b) Carrie Fisher
c) Helen Morgan d) Jean Harlow

ARISTOCRATS

1) English aristocrat, Lord John Morgan, was captured by Sioux Indians in a 1970 western. Name the film.
a) Chato's Land b) Breakheart Pass
c) Hannie Caulder d) A Man Called Horse

2) Who portrayed the haughty Russian aristocrat, Dragomiroff, in the 1974 mystery, **Murder on the Orient Express**?
a) Rachel Roberts
b) Vanessa Redgrave
c) Wendy Hiller
d) Ingrid Bergman

3) In which film does the character portrayed by Greta Garbo fall in love with Count Leon Dolga (Melvyn Douglas)?
a) Ninotchka
b) Camille
c) Queen Christina
d) Anna Karenina

ARTISTS

1) In 1948 struggling artist, Eben Adams, is inspired to paint the haunting **Portrait of Jennie**. Who was he?
a) Gregory Peck b) John Garfield
c) Joseph Cotten d) Victor Mature

2) On the life of what famous artist is the 1942 film, **The Moon and Sixpence** based?
a) Paul Gaugin b) Francisco Goya
c) Picasso d) Modigliani

3) Who played the title role in Alexander Korda's 1936 production, **Rembrandt**?
a) Robert Donat b) Charles Laughton
c) Sydney Greenstreet d) Mel Ferrer

ARCHAEOLOGISTS

1) In which 1980 horror film does British archaeologist, Matthew Corbeck (Charlton Heston) discover the undisturbed tomb of the Egyptian Queen Kara?
a) King Solomon's Mines b) The Awakening
c) Nairobi Affair d) The Mummy

2) With which film do you associate archaeologist, Angus Flint (Peter Capaldi), discovering a bizarre fossil in the Scottish Highlands?
a) The Black Hole b) The Quatermass Conclusion
c) Digger d) The Lair of the White Worm

3) Name the actor who portrayed the archaeologist responsible for desecrating the tomb of the Egyptian Princess Ananka in Hammer's 1959 horror film, **The Mummy**.
a) Christopher Lee b) Peter Cushing
c) Laurence Payne d) Anthony Quayle

ASSASSINS

1) Who played the title role in **Ruby** (1992), about the life of assassin Jack Ruby?
a) Harvey Keitel b) Rod Steiger
c) Danny Aiello d) Kevin Kline

2) Who portrayed the assassin 'Scaramanga' in **The Man With the Golden Gun**?
a) Donald Pleasence b) Michael Lonsdale
c) Christopher Lee d) Louis Jourdan

3) With which 1957 comedy do you associate Alastair Sim as a part-time assassin?
a) The Green Man b) Rogue Male
c) Laughter in Paradise d) Cottage to Let

ASTRONAUTS

1) In what film do NASA astronauts try to fool the world through TV networks that they have successfully landed a manned mission on Mars?
a) Conquest of Space b) Logan's Run
c) Capricorn One d) Not of This Earth

2) With which film do you associate a traveller emerging from his craft wearing a black spacesuit and a glass helmet, announcing that he is a representative of "Wings Over the World"?
a) Things to Come b) Star Wars c) Metropolis
d) Dark Star

3) What is the astronaut's mission assignment in the 1974 film, **Dark Star**?
a) to blow up planets with unsuitable life forms
b) to collect alien life forms
c) to destroy Earth d) to colonize Mars

ATHLETES

1) In 1962 he portrayed distance runner, Colin Smith, who is sent to reform school for robbing a bakery in **The Loneliness of the Long Distance Runner**. Who was he?
a) Alan Bates b) Tom Courtenay
c) Richard Harris d) Albert Finney

2) What 1981 film tells the story of athletes Eric Liddell and Harold Abraham's victory at the 1924 Olympics in Paris?

The Movie Quiz Companion

a) Some Came Running b) Triumph of the Will
c) Chariots of Fire d) Each Dawn I Die

3) Sioux Indian, Billy Mills, left his reservation to become an Olympic athlete and win the gold medal for the 10,000 metres in Tokyo in 1964. Name the title of the film which chronicles his life.
a) Running Brave b) Running Scared
c) The Running Man d) Run of the Arrow

BABYSITTERS

1) Who portrayed the irascible intellectual bachelor, who becomes a full-time babysitter in the 1948 comedy, **Sitting Pretty**?
a) Charles Coburn b) Cary Grant
c) Robert Cummings d) Clifton Webb

2) In which 1978 horror film do babysitters watch **The Thing (From Another World)** on television?
a) Halloween b) A Nightmare on Elm Street
c) The Amityville Horror d) Poltergeist

3) From what does the old lady die in **Don't Tell Mom the Babysitter's Dead**?
a) a heart attack b) poison c) a drug overdose
d) she is run over by a supermarket trolley

BALLERINAS

1) Who portrayed the young ballerina, Victoria Page, in Powell and Pressburger's **The Red Shoes**?
a) Deborah Kerr
b) June Duprez
c) Wendy Hiller
d) Moira Shearer

2) Which 1932 drama features Greta Garbo as a lonely ballerina?
a) Grand Hotel b) Camille
c) The Painted Veil d) Two-Faced Woman

3) In which 1953 musical does Tony Hunter (Fred Astaire) fall in love with ballerina Gaby Gerard (Cyd Charisse)?
a) Silk Stockings b) The Band Wagon
c) Invitation to the Dance d) Singin' in the Rain

BANKERS

1) In 1946, infantry sergeant, Al Stephenson, returns from WWII to take up his old job as banker in his mid-west home town, in William Wyler's, **The Best Years of Our Lives**. Who was he?
a) Dana Andrews b) William Bendix
c) Fredric March d) Dick Powell

2) Which film weaves the true events of a Vatican bank scandal and the hanging of a Vatican banker from London bridge into its plot?
a) The Sicilian b) Vendetta: Secrets of a Mafia Bride c) The Godfather Part III
d) The Pope Must Die

3) Who portrayed the greedy, grasping, miserly banker, 'old man' Potter, in **It's a Wonderful Life**?
a) Raymond Massey
b) Sydney Greenstreet
c) Cedric Hardwicke
d) Lionel Barrymore

BARBERS & HAIRDRESSERS

1) In which 1952 western is the Hadleyville barber "pretty sure" he saw outlaws Jack Colby, Pierce and Ben Miller ride past his shop?
a) Gunfight at the OK Corral b) Rancho Notorious
c) High Noon d) The Naked Spur

2) With which film do you associate a hairdresser turned Open University student giving a much needed haircut to her tutor, Dr. Frank Bryant.
a) Claire's Knee b) Lucky Jim
c) A World Apart d) Educating Rita

3) Who portrayed the amorous Beverley Hills hairdresser in **Shampoo**?
a) Warren Beatty b) Eddie Murphy
c) Woody Harrelson d) Woody Allen

BARTENDERS & PUBLICANS

1) In 1988 he portrayed the bottle juggling bartender, Brian Flanagan, in **Cocktail**. Who was he?
a) Jeff Goldblum b) Nicholas Cage
c) Michael J. Fox d) Tom Cruise

2) Which film features publican Pat Cohan?
a) Odd Man Out b) The Quiet Man
c) Ryan's Daughter d) Michael Collins

3) Name the silent-screen slapstick comedian who played the role of a publican in Alfred Hitchcock's 1944 thriller, **The Lodger**?
a) Harold Lloyd b) Oliver Hardy
c) Billy Bevan d) James Finlayson

BASEBALL PLAYERS

1) Who played the title role of the great American baseball hero, George Herman 'Babe' Ruth, in the 1992 film, **The Babe**?
a) John Belushi b) John Goodman c) Tom Hanks
d) Tim Robbins

2) Who portrayed baseball giant Lou Gehrig, the 'Iron Man', first baseman for the NY Yankees, in **The Pride of the Yankees**?
a) Sterling Hayden b) Burt Lancaster
c) Gary Cooper d) Robert Mitchum

3) Which baseball movie features catcher, Crash Davis, and pitcher, 'Nuke' LaLoosh?
a) Bull Durham b) The Natural
c) Field of Dreams d) A League of Their Own

BEATNIKS & HIPPIES

1) In 1965 she played the beatnik artist, Laura Reynolds, in **The Sandpiper**. Who was she?
a) Audrey Hepburn b) Eva Marie Saint
c) Elizabeth Taylor d) Debbie Reynolds

2) What 1965 film involves New York hippies and the song, 'Let the Sun Shine In'?
a) I Love You Alice B. Toklas b) Woodstock
c) Hallucination Generation d) Hair

3) Name the title of Joyce Johnson's 1985 documentary about a famous anti-establishment beatnik.
a) Ginsberg b) Ferlinghetti
c) Kerouac d) Burroughs

BODYGUARDS

1) Who portrayed the police bodyguard assigned to protect a witness to a murder in Ridley Scott's **Someone to Watch Over Me**?
a) Tom Berenger b) James Woods
c) Al Pacino d) Bruce Willis

2) Which film features professional bodyguard, Frank Farmer, falling in love with his superstar charge, Rachel Marron?
a) Dick Tracy b) Fatal Beauty
c) Guarding Tess d) The Bodyguard

3) Name the Woody Allen film in which gangster's bodyguard, Cheech (Chazz Palminteri) becomes an effective drama critic.
a) Scenes From a Mall b) Bullets Over Broadway
c) New York Stories d) Broadway Danny Rose

BOMB DISPOSAL EXPERTS

1) Who portrayed the melancholy and crippled WWII bomb disposal expert, Sammy Rice, in Powell and Pressburger's, **The Small Back Room**?
a) Peter Finch b) David Farrar
c) Eric Portman d) Conrad Veidt

2) Joe Morton played a bomb disposal expert with a cracked vertebrae and a nerve gas bomb to diffuse aboard an airliner. Name the 1995 thriller.
a) Executive Decision b) Airplane II: The Sequel
c) The Mad Bomber d) Air America

3) Which film features a Sikh British army disposal expert named Kip?
a) The Longest Day b) Bhowani Junction
c) A Bridge Too Far d) The English Patient

BOMBER PILOTS

1) **Pearl Harbour** (2001) recreates factual events in which, two weeks after the attack, President Roosevelt gathered his military leaders at the White House to discuss how to strike back at the Japanese, which resulted in a daring bombing raid on Tokyo. By what name did the hand-picked pilots on the mission become known?
a) The Tokyo Wing b) The Eagle Squadron
c) The Sky Commandos d) The Doolittle Raiders

2) Name the film in which Squadron Leader Peter Carter's last words into the radio of his crashing bomber before baling out without a parachute are. "I love you, June. You're life, and I'm leaving it"?
a) Memphis Belle b) High Wall c) A Matter of Life and Death/Stairway to Heaven d) They Were Expendable

3) In 1943 John Ridgely and Gig Young were cast as the pilots of a Flying Fortress nicknamed Mary Ann in a film directed by Howard Hawks. Name the title.
a) Air Force b) The Big Sky
c) Ball of Fire d) Only Angels Have Wings

BOUNTY HUNTERS

1) Bounty hunter, Howard Kemp, relentlessly pursues outlaw Ben Vandergroat (Robert Ryan) in the 1953 western **The Naked Spur**. Who was he?
a) Van Heflin b) Jack Palance
c) Ernest Borgnine d) James Stewart

2) Which film featured Robert De Niro as bounty hunter Jack Walsh?
a) Bloody Mama b) True Confessions
c) Midnight Run d) This Boy's Life

3) In the 1957 western, **The Tin Star**, greenhorn Sheriff Ben Owens (Anthony Perkins) asks bounty hunter, Morg Hickman,

to help him tame the town. Who portrayed Hickman?
a) Gary Cooper b) John Gavin c) Robert Taylor d) Henry Fonda

BOXERS

1) Which famous boxer was portrayed by Paul Newman in the 1956 film, **Somebody Up There Likes Me**?
a) Rocky Graziano b) Sugar Ray Robinson c) Jack Dempsey d) Joe Louis

2) Which 1980 film tells the story of Jake LaMotta?
a) The Main Event b) Raging Bull c) The Greatest d) The Last Fight

3) Who portrayed John L. Sullivan in the 1942 film, **Gentleman Jim**?
a) Robert Ryan b) Errol Flynn c) Ward Bond d) Victor McLaglen

BULLIES

1) In which film is a character portrayed by Crispin Glover continually bullied by Tannen (Thomas F. Wilson)?
a) This is Spinal Tap b) The Rocky Horror Picture Show c) Grease d) Back to the Future

2) In 1921 he portrayed the neibourhood bully in Chaplin's **The Kid**. Who was he?
a) Eric Campbell
b) Tom Murray
c) Charles Riesner
d) Stanley 'Tiny' Sandford

3) In which Marx Brothers film does Groucho utter the inane lines: "You big bully, why are you hitting that little bully? "
a) A Night at the Opera b) Duck Soup c) Monkey Business d) Horse Feathers

BURGLARS

1) As well as starring in this 1991 action comedy about a cat burglar, Bruce Willis also co-wrote the script and the title song. Name the title.
a) Striking Distance b) Death Becomes Her c) Hudson Hawk d) The Last Boy Scout

2) Who portrayed the cat burglar in Hitchcock's **To Catch a Thief**?
a) Paul Newman b) Cary Grant c) Rod Taylor d) James Stewart

3) Who played the title role in the 1987 romantic comedy, **Burglar**?
a) Whoopi Goldberg b) Goldie Hawn c) Michelle Pfeiffer d) Meg Ryan

BUTCHERS

1) Who portrayed Helene, the spinster schoolteacher who unknowingly befriends Popaul (Jean Yanne) the butcher and serial killer in Claude Chabrol's 1969 psychological thriller, **Le Boucher / The Butcher?**
a) Stephane Audran
b) Bernadette Lafont
c) Nathalie Baye
d) Sabine Axema

2) Which 1955 drama won an Oscar for Ernest Borgnine for his portrayal of a Bronx butcher?
a) Man on a String b) Violent Saturday c) Marty d) Run For Cover

3) In 1991 she portrayed Marina, the wife of a Greenwich Village butcher in the romantic fantasy, **The Butcher's Wife**. Who was she?
a) Andie MacDowell b) Mary Steenburgen c) Julia Roberts d) Demi Moore

BUTLERS

1) On whose play was the 1957 comedy, **The Admirable Crichton** based, in which a butler who is marooned on a desert island with his aristocratic employers succeeds in reversing his servant role to that of master?
a) Terence Rattigan b) J.M. Barrie c) Arnold Wesker d) P.G. Wodehouse

2) Who portrayed the embassy butler who is idolized by the ambassador's young son in the 1948 thriller, **The Fallen Idol**?
a) Michael Horden b) Ralph Richardson c) Emlyn Williams d) Cedric Hardwicke

3) Which 1993 drama features a butler named Stevens?
a) King Ralph b) The Remains of the Day c) Other People's Money d) Miller's Crossing

CARETAKERS & NIGHTWATCHMEN

1) What Mike Leigh film involves a nightwatchman taking Johnny (David Thewlis) on an after dark tour of an office block?
a) Naked b) High Hopes c) Life is Sweet d) Meantime

2) In 1980, Jack Torrance becomes the off-season caretaker of the Overlook Hotel in Colorado. Name the film.
a) Nowhere to Run b) The Amityville Horror c) The Shining d) Hotel Terminus: The Life and Times of Klaus Barbie

3) With which Charlie Chaplin comedy do you associate him finding employment as a

enormous fancy bar be frock

Roles

nightwatchman in a department store and using roller skates to speed up his rounds?
a) *Modern Times* b) *The Rink*
c) *Easy Street* d) *A Woman of Paris*

CHAUFFEURS

1) With which film, based on an adaptation of Alfred Uhry's stage play, do you associate the chauffeur, Hoke Colburn?
a) *The Magnificent Ambersons* b) *Driving Miss Daisy* c) *Sabrina* d) *Stormy Weather*

2) Which 1986 crime drama features a chauffeur named George, who is given the job of driving Simone, a high class prostitute?
a) *Vice Versa* b) *The Hireling*
c) *Mona Lisa* d) *Mrs. Winterbourne*

3) Of what crime is the chauffeur (Jean-Paul Belmondo) wrongly accused, resulting in his imprisonment, in Claude Lelouch's 1995 version of **Les Miserables**?
a) stealing a loaf of bread b) the death of his employer c) treason d) kidnapping

CHEERLEADERS

1) Who played the title role in **The Positively True Adventures of the Alleged Texas Cheerleader-Murdering Mom**?
a) *Holly Hunter* b) *Jessica Lange*
c) *Susan Sarandon* d) *Uma Thurman*

2) With which 1991 drama do you associate wealthy voyeur, Bubba (Maury Chaykin), hiring an entire football team for his exhibitionist wife (Gabrielle Rose) to perform her cheerleader fantasies in front of?
a) *Middle Age Crazy* b) *The Adjuster*
c) *Party Girl* d) *Dallas Cowboys Cheerleaders II*

3) What 1992 horror film is set in a school for cheerleaders?
a) *Pandemonium* b) *Satan's Cheerleaders*
c) *Life Begins at College* d) *Say Anything...*

CHEFS & COOKS

1) Which film features a French chef who attempts to cook a crab named Sebastian?
a) *Pal Joey* b) *The Muppet Christmas Carol*
c) *Fun in Acapulco* d) *The Little Mermaid*

2) Name the comedy drama, directed by Ang Lee, in which Mr Chu (Sihung Lung), a Taiwanese master chef, prepares meals each evening for his three unmarried daughters.
a) *Eat Drink Man Woman* b) *The Wedding Banquet* c) *East to West* d) *Fine Line*

3) Who directed **The Cook, The Thief, His Wife & Her Lover**?
a) Ken Russell b) Derek Jarman
c) Peter Greenaway d) Peter Weir

CHORUS GIRLS

1) In which 1968 film does Barbra Streisand lose her job in a chorus line?
a) *On a Clear Day You Can See Forever* b) *Funny Girl* c) *Hello, Dolly* d) *A Star is Born*

2) Which 1933 musical features Ginger Rogers leading a chorus dressed in gold coin outfits singing 'We're In the Money'?
a) *42nd Street* b) *Gold Diggers of 1933*
c) *Gold Diggers of 1935* d) *Gold Diggers of 1937*

3) Who played the title role of the brassy chorus girl in MGM's **Maisie** series between 1939 and 1947?
a) Ann Sothern b) Judy Holliday
c) Nancy Kelly d) Binnie Barnes

CLAIRVOYANTS & FORTUNE-TELLERS

1) In 1939 he played Professor Marvel who is "acclaimed by the Crowned Heads of Europe" in **The Wizard of Oz**. Who was he?
a) Clifton Webb b) Frank Morgan
c) Claude Rains d) Bert Lahr

2) Name the actor who foretells the future in David Cronenberg's **The Dead Zone**?
a) Patrick McGoohan b) Michael J. Fox
c) Kevin Costner d) Christopher Walken

67

The Movie Quiz Companion

men repelled ants shit

3) Who played the title role in the 1978 film, **Eyes of Laura Mars**?
a) Faye Dunaway b) Lauren Bacall
c) Bette Midler d) Jessica Tandy

CLOWNS

1) With which film do you associate Michael Caine dressing up as a clown to steal jewels?
a) Sleuth b) The Wrong Box
c) Dirty Rotten Scoundrels d) The Jigsaw Man

2) In 1952 he portrayed 'Buttons' the clown in Cecil B. De Mille's **The Greatest Show on Earth**. Who was he?
a) Bob Hope b) James Stewart
c) Cornel Wilde d) Peter Lorre

3) **The Man Who Laughs** (1928), tells the story of a child of the 17th-century who is kidnapped and has his face mutilated and carved into a permanent grin and so is tragically destined to become a clown. On whose story was the film based?
a) Edgar Allan Poe b) H.G. Wells
c) Victor Hugo d) Rumer Godden

COLONELS

1) Which film features foul-mouthed ex-army colonel, Frank Slade?
a) Scent of a Woman b) True Lies
c) Rio Lobo d) Seven Days in May

2) Who directed **The Life and Death of Colonel Blimp**?
a) Carol Reed b) Michael Powell
c) Edmund Goulding d) Charles Crichton

3) Who played the title role in the 1935 drama, **The Little Colonel**?
a) Freddie Bartholomew b) Jackie Coogan
c) Deanna Durbin d) Shirley Temple

COMMERCIAL PILOTS

1) Who portrayed Albain, the crazy crop-dusting pilot who teams up with Elliott Gould in the 1978 thriller, **Capricorn One**?
a) O.J. Simpson b) Lee Marvin
c) Richard Harris d) Telly Savalas

2) Name the 1980 comedy which involves the following corny dialogue -
Captain: "Surely you can't be serious!"
Doctor: "Of course I am! And stop calling me Shirley!"
a) How to Steal an Airplane b) L.A. Story
c) Airplane! d) Airplane II: The Sequel

3) In 1989 he played daredevil aerial fire-fighter, Pete Sandich, who loses his life in Stephen Spielberg's romantic fantasy, **Always**. Who was he?
a) Michael Keaton b) Richard Dreyfuss
c) Tim Robbins d) Dennis Quaid

COMPOSERS, CLASSICAL

1) Who directed the 1984 biopic, **Amadeus**?
a) Robert Wise b) Robert Rossen
c) Milos Forman d) George Cukor

2) On whose life was Ken Russell's **The Music Lovers** based?
a) Mahler b) Tchaikovsky
c) Beethoven d) Mozart

3) Name the title of the 1956 musical biography of Richard Wagner.
a) Magic Fire b) Song of Love
c) The Magnificent Rebel d) The Magic Bow

COMPOSERS, POPULAR

1) In a 1951 musical biopic Doris Day portayed Grace Khan, wife of the composer, Gus Khan, who wrote such evergreens as 'Ain't We Got Fun' and 'It Had to Be You'. Name the film.
a) I'll See You in My Dreams b) Young Man With a Horn c) Lullaby of Broadway d) On Moonlight Bay

2) Who portrayed composer George Gershwin in the 1945 Hollywood biopic, **Rhapsody in Blue**?
a) Gordon MacRae b) Robert Young
c) Fredric March d) Robert Alda

3) Name the composer/songwriter who appears as saloon owner, Butch Engle, in **The Best Years of Our Lives**?
a) Oscar Levant b) Hoagy Carmichael
c) Arthur Freed d) Jule Styne

COMPUTER NERDS & HACKERS

1) Which film features the evil hacker code-named 'Plague'?
a) Hackers b) The Matrix c) Angus d) Assassins

2) What do two computer nerds programme their computer to create in **Weird Science**?
a) the perfect woman b) the fountain of youth
c) a stairway to heaven d) the real identity of Jack the Ripper

3) What film involves a computer nerd named Michael (Edward Furlong) being trapped inside a deadly computer game?
a) Innerspace b) Drop Zone
c) Brainscan d) Virtuosity

CONFIDENCE TRICKSTERS

1) In 1992 he played Florida con man, Thomas Jefferson Thompson, in **The Distinguished Gentleman**. Who was he?
a) Bob Hoskins b) Joe Don Baker
c) Steve Buscemi d) Eddie Murphy

2) Name the young actress who made her film debut as trainee con-artist, Addie Loggins, in Peter Bogdanovich's 1973 comedy drama, **Paper Moon**?
a) Jodie Foster b) Tatum O'Neal
c) Jamie Lee Curtis d) Drew Barrymore

3) Which film features con men Daniel Dravot and Peachy Carnehan?
a) Dirty Rotten Scoundrels b) The Man Who Would Be King c) The Sting d) Midnight Cowboy

COURAGEOUS SOLDIERS

1) Which film re-enacts the battle which resulted in the awarding of 11 Victoria Crosses, the highest number for any single engagement in British history?
a) The Charge of the Light Brigade b) The Longest Day c) Battle of El Alamein d) Zulu

2) As what were Dr. Rolf Pedersen (Kirk Douglas) and Knut Straud (Richard Harris) known in a 1965 war drama directed by Anthony Mann?
a) The Hunters
b) The Heroes of Telemark
c) The Lost Patrol d) Merrill's Marauders

3) Sgt. Bill Dane led the brave patrol which guarded a road against the Japanese advance in **Bataan**. Who was he?
a) John Garfield b) Lloyd Nolan
c) John Wayne d) Robert Taylor

COWARDLY SOLDIERS

1) Harry Faversham (John Clements) resigns his commission prior to the 1898 Sudan campaign and is accused of cowardice by his friends and fellow officers, Capt. Durrance (Ralph Richardson), Peter Gurroughs (Donald Gray), and Lt. Willoughby (Jack Allen). Name the film.
a) The Light That Failed b) East of Sudan
c) The Four Feathers d) Khartoum

2) Who portrays the cowardly soldier who regains his courage and returns to the front in John Huston's 1951 Civil War classic, **The Red Badge of Courage**?
a) Douglas Dick b) Robert Easton
c) Audie Murphy d) Jim Hayward

3) Which 1959 drama features Major Thomas Thorn (Gary Cooper) being accused of cowardice?
a) They Came to Cordura b) For Whom the Bell Tolls c) The Naked Edge d) Man of the West

CRIMINALS, MASTER

1) Name the crime thriller in which master criminal, Neil McCauley (Robert De Niro), informs a world-weary cop: "You see me doing thrill-seeking holdups with a 'Born to Lose' tattoo on my chest?"
a) Midnight Run b) Goodfellas
c) Angel Heart d) Heat

2) Professor James Moriarty was the Napoleon of crime. Name the sleuth who was his intellectual equal.
a) Sexton Blake b) Miss Marples
c) Sherlock Holmes d) Charlie Chan

3) Dr. Kananga is a respected Caribbean diplomat on the island of San Monique, but in the criminal fraternity he is known as international drug boss, 'Mr. Big'. In which James Bond film does he appear?
a) Live and Let Die b) You Only Live Twice
c) For Your Eyes Only d) Moonraker

CRIMINALS, REAL LIFE

1) Name the murderer featured in the 1971 crime thriller, **10 Rillington Place**.
a) John Christie b) Buck Ruxton
c) Dr. Crippen d) Timothy Evans

2) On whose non-fiction novel was the film **In Cold Blood** based, which documented the mass murder of the Clutter family in Holcomb, Kansas, by two psychopathic killers in 1959?
a) Damon Runyon b) Bernard Malamud
c) Ring Lardner d) Truman Capote

3) What 1965 film, starring John Neville and Donald Houston, pits Sherlock Holmes against Jack the Ripper?
a) Fear in the Night b) A Study in Terror
c) The Scarlet Claw d) Sudden Fear

DANCERS

1) Who wrote the score which accompanied Basil (Alan Bates) and Alexis Zorba's (Anthony Quinn) memorable dance on a Cretan beach in **Zorba the Greek** (1964)?
a) Nikos Kazantzakis b) Michael Cacoyannis
c) Yorgo Voyagis d) Mikis Theodorakis

2) Tula Ellice Finklea became one of Hollywood's greatest dancers. By what name was she better known?

The Movie Quiz Companion

a) Ginger Rogers b) Ruby Keeler
c) Mitzi Gaynor d) Cyd Charisse

3) In which 1992 film do Scott and Fran (Paul Mercurio & Tara Morice) enter the Pan-Pacific Grand Prix Amateur Dancing Championships?
a) Strictly Ballroom b) Give My Regards to Broad Street c) Muriel's Wedding d) Cousins

DENTISTS

1) In 1941 he portrayed a turn-of-the-century dentist bewitched by Rita Hayworth in **The Strawberry Blonde**. Who was he?
a) Charles Boyer b) Louis Calhern
c) James Cagney d) Dick Powell

2) In which film does Steve Martin portray a motorcycle-riding dentist named Orin Scrivello?
a) Three Amigos! b) The Man With Two Brains
c) The Jerk d) Little Shop of Horrors

3) Which film features Babe Levy being tortured by a Nazi dentist named Szell?
a) Indiana Jones and the Last Crusade b) Rogue Male c) Marathon Man d) Death and the Maiden

DETECTIVES

1) Who directed the 1951 film, **Detective Story**, about life at a New York City precinct, starring rancorous detective, Jim McLeod (Kirk Douglas) and his neglected wife Mary (Eleanor Parker)?
a) William Wyler b) Fred Zinneman
c) Sam Wood d) Anthony Mann

2) Name the great crime detective created by the comic-strip of Chester Gould.
a) Charlie Chan b) Dick Tracy
c) Nick Carter d) Dick Barton

3) Charles Laughton and Richard Harris both played the same detective in 1949 and 1988 respectively. Who was he?
a) Hercule Poirot b) Paul Temple
c) Maigret d) Father Brown

DIVERS

1) With which film do you associate Oldsen (Peter Capaldi) becoming besotted with a female diver named Marina (Jenny Seagrove)?
a) The Big Blue b) Tender is the Night
c) Jaws d) Local Hero

2) In which film does Ben Braddock escape his interfering and fussing parents by scuba-diving in the family pool?
a) Ordinary People b) Teen Wolf
c) The Graduate d) Beethoven's 2nd

3) What 1953 adventure involves Robert Ryan and Anthony Quinn as treasure-hunting deep-sea divers in the Caribbean?
a) City Beneath the Sea b) Fathom
c) The Silent World d) Volcano

DISC JOCKEYS

1) Robin Williams portrayed an Armed Forces Radio DJ in **Good Morning Vietnam**. What was his name in the film, (which was also the name of the real-life DJ on whom his character was based)?
a) Alan Freed b) Walt Bennett
c) Adrian Cronauer d) Joe Reaves

2) Who portrays DJ 'Hard Harry', the high school student who runs a pirate radio station in **Pump Up the Volume**?
a) Christian Slater b) John Turturro
c) Ben Affleck d) Johnny Depp

3) Which film features DJ 'Wolfman Jack', playing classics such as 'The Book of Love' and 'Gonna Find Her'?
a) Can't Stop the Music b) Radio On
c) Stormy Monday d) American Graffiti

DISTRICT ATTORNEYS

1) In which film does D.A. Jim Garrison investigate the death of a Kennedy?
a) JFK b) Young Joe, The Forgotten Kennedy
c) The Unfinished Journey of Robert Kennedy
d) Hoover vs the Kennedys: The Second Civil War

2) Who portrays the D.A's special prosecutor, Anne Osborne, who becomes romatically involved with homicide detective, Remy McSwain (Dennis Quaid), in the 1987 crime thriller, **The Big Easy**?
a) Michelle Pfeiffer
b) Meg Ryan
c) Kim Basinger
d) Ellen Barkin

3) Assistant district attorney, Cleve Marshal falls in love with Thelma Jordan (Barbara Stanwyck) who is on trial for murder, and deliberately loses the case in the 1949 thriller, **The File on Thelma Jordan**. Who portrayed Cleve Marshall?

a) Louis Calhern b) Wendell Corey
c) John Payne d) Cornel Wilde

DOCTORS

1) In 1938 he portrayed Dr. Andrew Manson who begins his career as a young idealist treating Welsh miners, but, disillusioned, he is seduced by the big money of Harley Street in **The Citadel**. Who was he?
a) Leslie Howard b) Ronald Colman
c) Robert Donat d) Peter Finch

2) With which Michael Crichton thriller do you associate Dr. Susan Wheeler (Geneviève Bujold) havings suspicions that something is amiss at the Boston Memorial Hospital?
a) The Carey Treatment b) The Terminal Man
c) Physical Evidence d) Coma

3) Which Marx Brothers comedy features Groucho posing as neurologist, Dr. Hugo Z. Hackenbush?
a) The Big Store b) Animal Crackers
c) A Day at the Races d) Room Service

DRILL SERGEANTS

1) In 1987 Lee Ermey portrayed Gunnery Sgt. Hartman who put marines through their basic training on Parris Island. An ex-Marine sergeant, he got the part because during his audition he managed to spout obscenities for fifteen minutes without repeating himself while having tennis balls and oranges thrown at him. Name the film.
a) The Boys in Company C b) From Here to Eternity c) Fletch Lives d) Full Metal Jacket

2) Drill Sgt. Foley (Lou Gossett, Jr.) knocks Naval Officer Zack Mayo into shape in **An Officer and a Gentleman**. Who portrayed Mayo?
a) Kevin Costner b) Richard Gere
c) Clint Eastwood d) Mickey Rourke

3) With which 1988 comedy drama do you associate Christopher Walken as an army drill sergeant?
a) Biloxi Blues b) Hot Shots!
c) In the Army Now d) Stripes

DRUG DEALERS

1) Who portrays the Hispanic drug dealer, Bobby Texador, in Sidney Lumet's **Q&A** (1990)?
a) Antonio Banderas b) Armand Assante
c) Francisco Rabal d) Antonio Moreno

2) Former drug dealer, Dale McKussic, is terrified he will lose custody of his young son to his ex-wife in **Tequila Sunrise** (1988). Who was he?
a) Mel Gibson b) Samuel L. Jackson
c) Kurt Russel d) Patrick Swayze

3) In 1993 he portrayed the dreadlocked drug dealer, Drexl Spivey, in **True Romance**. Who was he?
a) Wesley Snipes b) Val Kilmer
c) Gary Oldman d) Peter Weller

DRUNKS

1) In which film does Dean Martin portray a town drunk named 'Dude'?
a) Four For Texas b) Ocean's Eleven
c) Rio Bravo d) Pardners

2) In the drunk scene with Sgt. Warden (Burt Lancaster) and Robert E. Lee Prewitt in **From Here to Eternity**, Prewitt was intoxicated for real. Who was he?
a) Frank Sinatra b) Montgomery Clift
c) Ernest Borgnine d) William Bendix

3) With which film do you associate the gin-guzzling mariner, Charlie Allnut, ridiculing his passenger by calling her a "crazy psalm-singing skinny old maid!"
a) South Pacific b) Lifeboat
c) Show Boat d) The African Queen

EDITORS

1) Who portrays the crusading newspaper editor, Dutton Peabody, in John Ford's **The Man Who Shot Liberty Valance** (1962)?
a) Thomas Mitchell b) Brian Aherne
c) Walter Connolly d) Edmond O'Brien

2) Which 1940 comedy features Cary Grant as overbearing newspaper editor, Walter Burns?
a) Once Upon a Time b) His Girl Friday
c) The Awful Truth d) My Favorite Wife

3) Donald Woods was the outspoken editor of the East London (South Africa) Daily Dispatch and fervent anti-apartheid campaigner. Which film chronicles his family's escape from the South African authorities?
a) Cry, The Beloved Country b) Mandela
c) A World Apart d) Cry Freedom

EMPERORS

1) Who played the title role in the 1933 drama, **The Emperor Jones**, about railroad porter, Brutus Jones, who becomes leader of a Caribbean island?

The Movie Quiz Companion

loathsome fetish chant

a) Paul Robeson b) Richard Barthelmess
c) Edward G. Robinson d) Walter Connolly

2) What is the Emperor Caligula (Jay Robinson) searching for in Delmer Daves' 1954 drama, **Demetrius and the Gladiators**?
a) the cup of Christ b) the crown of Christ
c) the robe of Christ d) the cross of Christ

3) Napoleon Bonaparte, Emperor of France, has his life chronicled in the breathtaking 1927 silent epic, **Napoleon**. Who directed it?
a) Jean Renoir b) Andre Delvaux
c) Abel Gance d) Jean Vigo

ENGINE DRIVERS

1) Who portrays the doomed engine driver of the Euston-Liverpool express in Ealing's 1949 drama, **Train of Events**, which tells the story of three unconnected people who end up in the same train crash?
a) Stanley Holloway b) Jack Warner
c) Frankie Howard d) John Gregson

2) In 1965 he portrayed engine driver and French Resistance fighter, 'Labiche', who runs rings around Nazis trying to steal French art treasures in John Frankenheimer's **The Train**. Who was he?
a) Frank Sinatra b) Charles Bronson
c) Gregory Peck d) Burt Lancaster

3) With which 1953 comedy do you associate a train being driven by a Reverend and a Bishop?
a) Oh, Mr Porter! b) Runaway Train
c) Lady on a Train d) The Titfield Thunderbolt

EVANGELISTS

1) On whose novel was **Elmer Gantry** (1960) based?
a) William Faulkner b) Taylor Caldwell
c) Carson McCullers d) Sinclair Lewis

2) In 1931 she portrayed evangelist, Florence 'Faith' Fallon (based on the life of Aimee Semple McPherson) in Frank Capra's **The Miracle Woman**. Who was she?

a) Jane Wyatt b) Beulah Bondi
c) Jean Arthur d) Barbara Stanwyck

3) Who portrays Jerry Lee Lewis's (Dennis Quaid) evangelist cousin, Jimmy Swaggart, in the 1989 biopic, **Great Balls of Fire**?
a) Dean Stockwell b) Alec Baldwin
c) Matthew Modine d) Bill Paxton

EXPLORERS

1) Who portrays the Belgian explorer, Captain D'Arnot, who discovers Tarzan and returns him to his ancestral home in **Greystoke: The Legend of Tarzan, Lord of the Apes**?
a) Joss Ackland b) Ian Holm
c) Charles Dance d) Ian Charleson

2) Name the 1990 film which describes the events surrounding Sir Richard Burton's search for the source of the Nile in 1856.

a) Old Explorers b) The Searching Wind
c) Storm Over the Nile d) Mountains of the Moon

3) Who plays the title role in the 1938 adventure yarn, **The Adventures of Marco Polo**?
a) Gary Cooper b) Rory Calhoun
c) Ronald Colman d) George Sanders

FARMERS

1) In which film does farmer Hugh Romney announce - "Folks, we're planning breakfast in bed for 400,000 people"?
a) Gimme Shelter b) Monterey Pop
c) Woodstock d) Celebration at Big Sur

2) On whose novel was **Jean de Florette** based, in which farmers Cesar and Ugolin Soubeyran deceive a greenhorn farmer, who eventually loses his life and land?
a) Françoise Sagan b) Alain Fournier
c) George Perec d) Marcel Pagnol

3) With which film do you associate Ernest Borgnine portraying an Amish farmer?
a) Witness b) Jubal c) McHale's Navy
d) Violent Saturday

FASHION MODELS

1) Who portrays the bookstore assistant who is transformed into a Paris model in Stanley Donen's 1957 musical, **Funny Face**?
a) Natalie Wood b) Audrey Hepburn
c) Debbie Reynolds d) Doris Day

2) In which Krzysztof Kieslowski film does fashion model, Valentine (Irène Jacob) develop a relationship with retired judge, Joseph Kern (Jean-Louis Trintigant)?
a) The Double Life of Veronique b) Blue
c) Red d) A Short Film About Love

3) Which 1992 film features Jamaican-born model, singer and actress, Grace Jones, as the supermodel 'Strange', who shows up at a product launch in a chariot pulled by four half-naked men?
a) Boomerang b) Sirens
c) Vamp d) Bad Girls

eager oaf butchered dog

Roles

FIGHTER PILOTS

1) What is Lt. Pete Mitchell's (Tom Cruise) code name in **Top Gun**?
a) Mad Mitch b) Maverick c) Angel d) Mark'em

2) **Reach For the Sky**, about legless airman Douglas Bader, who overcame all odds to become a WWII fighter pilot, was based on whose book?
a) P.R. Reid b) Eric Ambler
c) Paul Brickhill d) Eric Williams

3) In which film does the Countess Kasti become romantically involved with WWI pilot, Bruno Stachel?
a) Wings b) Aces High
c) Von Richthofen and Brown d) The Blue Max

FIRE-FIGHTERS

1) Audrey Hepburn's final film appearance was in a 1989 romantic fantasy about fire-fighters, in which she portrayed an angel. Name the title.
a) Firefox b) Love Among Thieves
c) Fire on the Mountain d) Always

2) With which film do you associate fire chief, C.D. Bales, whose firemen are so incompetent he hires a firefighting expert to train them?
a) The Shining Hour b) Roxanne
c) Fireman Save My Child d) Fire Maidens From Outerspace

3) Which 1969 film featured John Wayne as a firefighter whose character is based on real-life firefighter Red Adair?
a) Hellfighters b) Fires Were Started
c) The Firechasers d) Maracaibo

FORGERS & COUNTERFEITERS

1) Who portrays 'The Forger' in **The Great Escape**?
a) James Garner b) Richard Attenborough
c) James Coburn d) Donald Pleasence

2) In which film does Dustin Hoffman portray French counterfeiter, Louis Dega?
a) Straight Time b) Papillon
c) Alfredo, Alfredo d) Madigan's Million

3) In 1942 George Sanders portrayed the master forger, Fleg, who steals a rare volume of Shakespeare and replaces it with a forgery. Name the film.
a) Quiet Please, Murder b) The Light Touch
c) Bitter Sweet d) Tales of Manhattan

GAMBLERS

1) Who plays the title role in the 1934 drama, **Gambling Lady**?
a) Claudette Colbert b) Mary Astor
c) Barbara Stanwyck d) Margaret O'Brien

2) Which 1968 film features Omar Sharif as the shifty gambler, Nick Arnstein?
a) Funny Girl b) Mackenna's Gold
c) Juggernaut d) The Last Valley

3) Who portrays the beautiful female gambler, Laura Denbow, in the 1957 western, **Gunfight at the O.K. Corral**?
a) Ida Lupino b) Rhonda Fleming
c) Maureen O'Hara d) Ann Blyth

GARDENERS

1) On whose novel was the 1956 drama, **The Spanish Gardener** based?
a) Nevil Shute b) Somerset Maugham
c) Doris Lessing d) A.J. Cronin

2) What film involves Peter Sellers playing a mentally retarded gardener named 'Chance'?
a) Being There b) The Magic Christian
c) Lolita d) The Battle of the Sexes

3) In which film does gardener Aisin-Gioro 'Henry' Pu Yi appear?
a) Tampopo b) Raise the Red Lantern
c) The Last Emperor d) Akira

GANGSTERS

1) Who plays the title role in the 1957 crime drama, **Baby Face Nelson**?
a) James Cagney b) John Payne
c) Farley Granger d) Mickey Rooney

2) Lawrence Tierney and Warren Oates both portrayed the same gangster in 1945 and 1973 respectively. Who was he?
a) Al Capone b) Dillinger
c) Lucky Luciano d) Machine-Gun Kelly

3) Who directed the 1931 gangster classic, **The Public Enemy**?
a) Joseph Lewis b) William Wellman
c) Lewis Milestone d) Fritz Lang

GENERALS

1) In which 1970 film does a general slap a soldier, call him a coward, and is subsequently ordered to apologise to his entire division?
a) The Devil's General b) Battle of the Bulge
c) Patton d) Glory

2) Errol Flynn, Robert Shaw and Richard Mulligan have all portrayed the same general in different films. Who was he?

73

The Movie Quiz Companion

a) General Eisenhower b) General Custer
c) General Sherman d) General Ulysses Grant

3) Who was the target for assassination in Anatole Litvak's, **Night of the Generals**?
a) Benito Mussolini b) Erwin Rommel
c) Adolf Hitler d) Winston Churchill

GIGOLOS

1) In 1962 he portrayed the gigolo, Chance Wayne, in Richard Brooks' version of Tennessee Williams' **Sweet Bird of Youth**. Who was he?
a) Paul Newman b) Marlon Brando
c) Montgomery Clift d) Rock Hudson

2) Who directed **American Gigolo**?
a) Eric Rohmer b) John Landis
c) Paul Schrader d) David Cronenberg

3) In which film is Joe Gillis the reluctant gigolo of Norma Desmond?
a) Gold Diggers of 1933 b) Hold Back the Dawn
c) Midnight Cowboy d) Sunset Boulevard

GLADIATORS

1) Who directed **Gladiator** (2000)?
a) Cy Enfield b) Michael Mann
c) Ridley Scott d) John Boorman

2) In which film does the black gladiator, Draba (Woody Strode), spare the life of his friend and opponent, only to have his throat cut by senator Marcus Licinius Crassus?

a) Sign of the Gladiator b) Barabbas
c) Spartacus d) Revenge of the Gladiators

3) Who portrayed Marcus the gladiator in **The Last Days of Pompeii** (1935)?
a) Preston Foster b) Louis Calhern
c) Leslie Banks d) Ralph Ince

GOLD PROSPECTORS

1) Howard, Curtin and Fred C. Dobbs set off from Tampico, Mexico, on the gold prospecting trail in 1948. Name the film.
a) The Treasure of Pancho Villa b) Gold Raiders
c) The Treasure of the Sierra Madre d) Gold For the Caesars

2) In which 1969 western do two gold prospectors, Pardner and Ben Rumson, share a wife they bought at an auction?
a) Paint Your Wagon b) The Cheyenne Social Club c) The Ballad of Cable Hogue d) Buck and the Preacher

3) Which 1960 western features John Wayne and Stewart Granger as gold prospectors?
a) Dakota b) The Big Trail
c) California Straight Ahead d) North to Alaska

GOVERNESSES

1) The story of the widowed schoolteacher who travels to Siam to become governess to the King's children in **The King and I** was based on whose book?
a) Iris Gower b) Gladys Huntington
c) Edith Pargeter d) Margaret Landon

2) In 1961 she portrayed Miss Giddens, governess of the eerie and mysterious Flora and Miles in **The Innocents**. Who was she?

a) Megs Jenkins b) Joan Fontaine
c) Deborah Kerr d) Kim Hunter

3) With which 1952 comedy do you associate the governess Miss Prism (Margaret Rutherford), who lost Algernon's brother many years ago at a railway station?
a) The Importance of Being Earnest b) The Yellow Canary c) Murder Most Foul d) Blithe Spirit

GRAVE ROBBERS

1) What 1959 science fiction drama involves aliens trying to take over the Earth by resurrecting buried corpses?
a) Attack of the Puppet People b) I Married a Monster From Outer Space c) Plan 9 From Outer Space d) Night of the Blood Beast

2) On whose story was the 1945 horror film **The Body Snatcher** based?
a) Leo Tolstoy b) M.R. James
c) Robert Louis Stevenson d) James Hogg

3) In which 1974 horror film does Sally (Marilyn Burns), disturbed by news reports of the desecration of the cemetery where her grandfather is buried, decide to investigate?
a) The Texas Chainsaw Massacre b) Body Parts
c) Dracula Has Risen From the Grave d) Pet Sematary

GUNFIGHTERS

1) In which western does cattleman Ryker (Emile Meyer) hire professional gunfighter, Wilson (Jack Palance), to drive homesteaders off the range?
a) Red River b) El Dorado
c) Wyoming d) Shane

2) Which film features gunfighter, William Munny, killer of women and children, now turned single parent and hog farmer?
a) Unforgiven b) Django
c) My Name is Nobody d) Chuka

3) Who plays the title role in Henry King's 1950 western, **The Gunfighter**?
a) Burt Lancaster b) Gregory Peck
c) Lee Van Cleef d) Kirk Douglas

arrogance by creed

Roles

GUN-RUNNERS

1) Don Siegel's 1958 adventure, **The Gun-Runners**, was a remake of a classic Humphrey Bogart movie. Name the title.
a) Key Largo b) Dark Passage
c) Dead Reckoning d) To Have and Have Not

2) Who portrayed the undercover agent, John Deakin, who tracked down gun-runners in the 1976 western, **Breakheart Pass**?
a) Charles Bronson b) Robert Redford
c) Burt Reynolds d) Elliott Gould

3) In which 1937 comedy do the railway employees of Buggleskelly Station lay on an excursion train for Irish gun-runners?
a) The Flying Irishman b) Runaway Train
c) Oh, Mr Porter! d) Mystery Train

HEADMASTERS

1) Name the Scottish comedian who portrayed the headmaster in the 1981 romantic comedy, **Gregory's Girl**?
a) Rikki Fulton b) Jimmy Logan
c) Chic Murray d) Stanley Baxter

2) Robert Newton portrayed the stern, but humane headmaster, Dr. Arnold, in the 1951 version of **Tom Brown's Schooldays**. Who portrayed him in the 1940 version?
a) Lionel Barrymore b) Emlyn Williams
c) Finlay Currie d) Cedric Hardwicke

3) Who was the inept headmaster in the 1935 comedy, **Boys Will Be Boys**?
a) George Formby b) Will Hay
c) Arthur Askey d) Stanley Holloway

HIGHWAYMEN & WOMEN

1) In 1953 he played dashing highwayman Captain MacHeath in the 1953 film, **The Beggar's Opera**. Who was he?
a) Ralph Richardson b) Stewart Granger
c) Basil Rathbone d) Laurence Olivier

2) Who played the title role in Leslie Arliss's 1945 historical adventure, **The Wicked Lady**?
a) Valerie Hobson b) Margaret Lockwood
c) Anna Neagle d) Kay Kendall

3) Name the Hollywood western hero who played the legendary highwayman, **Dick Turpin**, in 1925.
a) Hoot Gibson b) William S. Hart
c) Tom Mix d) William Boyd

HIT MEN & WOMEN

1) In 1985 Kathleen Turner portrayed beautiful blonde mob hit-woman, Irene Walker. Name the film.
a) Body Heat b) A Breed Apart
c) Married to the Mob d) Prizzi's Honor

2) With which film do you associate a hit man attending his high school reunion while on an assignment?
a) Assassins b) Grosse Pointe Blank
c) The Hit List d) The Exterminator

3) Who plays the title role in **The Specialist** (1994), and remarks in the apartment of mobster Tomas Leon (Eric Roberts): "The next time you order a hit, you might consider taking out your decorator."?
a) Sharon Stone b) Susan Sarandon
c) Jennifer Lopez d) Kathy Bates

HOUSEKEEPERS

1) In which 1940s thriller does a jealous housekeeper despise the lady of the house saying, "Why don't you go?..... He doesn't need you, he's got his memories. He doesn't love you. He wants to be alone again with her. You've nothing to stay for. You've nothing to live for really, have you?"
a) Love From a Stranger b) Gaslight
c) Rebecca d) The Woman in the Window

2) Mrs. Pearce (Jean Caldwell) the housekeeper, forces a grimy and protesting street trader to take a bath in Anthony Asquith's 1938 comedy. Name the film.
a) It Happened One Night b) The Ghost Goes West
c) The Cat and the Canary d) Pygmalion

3) Mrs. Hudson, whom Doctor Watson observed had a "stately tread", was housekeeper to Sherlock Holmes (Basil Rathbone) on screen and radio at 221b Baker Street. Who was she?
a) Constance Collier b) Hermione Gingold
c) Mary Gordon d) Dame May Whitty

HUNTERS

1) In which 1995 adventure fantasy is big-game hunter, Van Pelt (Jonathan Hyde), a prisoner of a game?
a) The Beastmaster b) Games of Desire
c) Jumanji d) A Game of Death

2) In which 1985 romantic drama, directed by Sydney Pollack, are the baroness and the big-game hunter, Denys Finch Hatton, attacked by a pride of lions?
a) Congo b) Backroads
c) Nairobi Affair d) Out of Africa

75

3) Cedric Hardwicke and Stewart Granger both portrayed the great white hunter, Allan Quartermain in 1937 and 1950 respectively. Name the film.
a) Flame Over India b) White Hunter, Black Heart c) King Solomon's Mines d) African Treasure

HYPNOTISTS

1) Who plays the title role of **Svengali** (1931) who puts a young singer into a mesmerizing trance and transforms her into a great artist?
a) John Barrymore b) Richard Cromwell c) Guy Standing d) Paul Lukas

2) In which film does the ventriloquist, 'The Great Vorelli' (Bryant Halliday), try to convey the soul of Marianne (Yvonne Romain) into a dummy through hypnotism?
a) Devil Doll b) Dollman c) Doll Face d) China Doll

3) Name the Merchant/Ivory film in which James Wilby seeks the help of a hypnotist to overcome the trauma he is suffering after his male lover decides to get married.
a) Heat and Dust b) The Bostonians c) In Custody d) Maurice

ICE SKATERS

1) Who does Cary Grant teach to skate in **The Bishop's Wife**?
a) Loretta Young b) Jean Arthur c) Lana Turner d) Grace Kelly

2) She was a world figure skating champion at fifteen, and after three Olympic wins, began her film career, aged twenty six, with Twentieth Century-Fox in **One in a Million** (1936). Who was she?
a) Vera Hruba Ralston b) Tai Babilonia c) Sonja Henie d) Belita

3) Name the James Bond movie in which ice skating champion, Lynn-Holly Johnson, makes a brief appearance.
a) From Russia With Love
b) Live and Let Die
c) For Your Eyes Only
d) The Living Daylights

INFORMERS

1) In 1949 he portrayed police informant, Hank Fallon, who is planted in the prison cell of Cody Jarrett (James Cagney) in **White Heat**. Who was he?
a) Tyrone Power b) John Dall c) Edmond O'Brien d) Dan Duryea

2) With which film do you associate informer, Johnny Hooker Kelly (Robert Redford)?
a) Brubaker b) Up Close and Personal c) The Sting d) The Candidate

3) Who portrays the informer, Raisinoff, who alerts the sadistic Sgt Markov (Brian Donlevy) to the existence of the 'Blue Water diamond' in the 1939 version of **Beau Geste**?
a) J. Carrol Naish b) Lewis Stone c) Warner Oland d) Sidney Toler

IMPRESARIOS

1) Which film features Anton Walbrook as the imperious ballet impresario, Boris Lermontov?
a) An American in Paris b) Nijinsky c) The Red Shoes d) Flashdance

2) With which Walt Disney film do you associate the stage impresario, 'Stromboli'?
a) Darby O'Gill and the Little People b) Lady and the Tramp c) Son of Flubber d) Pinocchio

3) Who played the title role in the 1936 musical biopic **The Great Ziegfeld**, based on the life of the extravagant impresario, Florenz Ziegfeld?
a) William Powell b) Charles Coburn c) Lionel Barrymore d) Edward G. Robinson

INNKEEPERS

1) In which film does an innkeeper warn Renfield of the dangers of travelling through the Borgo Pass?

a) *A Study in Terror* b) *The Curse of the Werewolf*
c) *Dracula* d) *The Two Faces of Dr. Jekyll*

2) Which 1949 drama tells the story of a shy draper's clerk (John Mills) who chucks it all in to settle down to a life of innkeeping with a 'plump woman' (Megs Jenkins)?
a) *Hobson's Choice* b) *Mr. Denning Drives North*
c) *The History of Mr. Polly* d) *Cottage to Let*

3) Who portrays Urquhart, the roguish Ferness innkeeper in the 1983 comedy, **Local Hero**?
a) Bill Paterson b) Denis Lawson
c) Rikki Fulton d) Gordon John Sinclair

INSURANCE INVESTIGATORS & SALESMEN

1) In 1968 she portrayed insurance investigator, Vicky Anderson, in the crime caper, **The Thomas Crown Affair**. Who was she?
a) Audrey Hepburn b) Jane Fonda
c) Dyan Cannon d) Faye Dunaway

2) What 1963 thriller, directed by Carol Reed, cast Alan Bates as an insurance agent falling for fraudster's wife Lee Remick?
a) *The Running Man* b) *The Man Between*
c) *The Public Eye* d) *It's Never Too Late*

3) Name the 1944 film, in which insurance salesman, Walter Neff, dupes the wealthy Mr Dietrichson into signing a new policy.
a) *The Big Steal* b) *Dead End*
c) *Double Indemnity* d) *The Reckless Moment*

INVENTORS

1) Who plays the title role in the 1940 biopic, **Edison, the Man**?
a) Walter Pidgeon b) James Stewart
c) Spencer Tracy d) Robert Cummings

2) Inventor William Friese-Greene's contribution to motion pictures' history was nothing if not prolific. Almost forgotten today, he died virtually penniless when he collapsed at a meeting. On his body they found the sum of one and tenpence, exactly the price of a cinema seat. Name the 1951 film which chronicles his life.
a) *The Magic Box* b) *The Movie Maker*
c) *The Light Ahead* d) *Moving the Mountain*

3) In which film did Anthony Hopkins portray the inventor of corn flakes, John W. Kellogg?
a) *One Man's War* b) *The Dawning*
c) *A Change of Seasons* d) *The Road to Wellville*

JAILERS

1) Who portays the Foreign Legion jailer who locks up Laurel and Hardy in the 1939 comedy, **The Flying Deuces**?
a) Walter Long b) Dick Cramer
c) James Finlayson d) Charles Middleton

2) Name the 1982 Wes Craven film in which a jailer quotes the title of a Werner Herzog movie: "It's every man for himself, and God against all!"
a) *Swamp Thing* b) *Last House on the Left*
c) *Deadly Blessing* d) *Invitation to Hell*

3) Which film features a brutal jailer named Hamidou (Paul Smith)?
a) *Lawrence of Arabia* b) *Midnight Express*
c) *Journey Into Fear* d) *Topkapi*

JESUIT PRIESTS

1) Which 1991 historical drama tells the story of the Huron Indians' first contact with French Jesuit priests in 17th-century Quebec?
a) *The Last of the Mohicans* b) *Indian Summer*
c) *Black Robe* d) *The Deerslayer*

2) In 1951 he portrayed Jesuit priest, Father Marc Arnoux, who has doubts about a purported miracle in **The First Legion**. Who was he?
a) Charles Boyer b) Trevor Howard
c) Pat O'Brien d) Spencer Tracy

3) Who wrote the screenplay for the 1986 film, **The Mission**, about Jesuit exploits and politics in 18th-century Brazil?
a) Werner Herzog b) Robert Bolt
c) Michael Mann d) Michael Blake

JEWEL THIEVES

1) In the 1932 film, **Grand Hotel**, he played Baron Felix von Gaigern, the jewel-thief lover of Greta Garbo. Who was he?
a) Melvyn Douglas b) Lewis Stone
c) Wallace Beery d) John Barrymore

2) Which 1964 comedy features notorious jewel thief 'The Phantom'?
a) *The Pink Panther* b) *The Jokers*
c) *It's a Mad Mad Mad Mad World* d) *The Great Race*

3) Who directed the classic 1950 jewel heist movie, **The Asphalt Jungle**?
a) Elia Kazan b) John Huston
c) Sam Fuller d) Robert Wise

JOURNALISTS & REPORTERS

1) In which film does a newspaper reporter state: "This is the West. When the legend becomes the fact, print the legend"?

The Movie Quiz Companion

inhuman chant eradicated

a) My Darling Clementine b) Rio Bravo
c) High Noon d) The Man Who Shot Liberty Valance

2) Who directed the 1952 period newspaper story, **Park Row**, starring Gene Evans as reporter Phineas Mitchell?
a) George Cuckor b) Henry Hathaway
c) Howard Hawks d) Sam Fuller

3) Which 1936 Frank Capra comedy features reporter Babe Bennett (Jean Arthur) writing articles about the 'Cinderella Man'?
a) Mr. Smith Goes to Washington b) Mr. Deeds Goes to Town c) Meet John Doe d) You Can't Take it With You

JUDGES

1) In 1961 he portrayed venerable and humane Judge Dan Haywood in Stanley Kramer's **Judgement at Nuremberg**. Who was he?
a) Raymond Massey b) Spencer Tracy
c) Fredric March d) Burt Lancaster

2) Who directed the 1972 comedy western, starring Paul Newman as the self-appointed autocratic judge, in **The Life and Times of Judge Roy Bean**?
a) Michael Cimino b) Billy Wilder
c) John Huston d) John Schlesinger

3) Who plays the title role in **Judge Dredd** (1995)?
a) Sylvester Stallone b) Jean Claude Van Damme
c) Arnold Schwarzenegger d) Richard Harris

KINGS

1) What king did John Goodman portray in 1991?
a) King Ralph b) King of Hearts
c) King of the Zombies d) King David

2) With which film do you associate Charlie Chaplin as the deposed Ruritanian monarch, King Shadhov?
a) A Countess From Hong Kong b) A King in New York c) A Woman of Paris d) Shoulder Arms

3) Kaspa the Lion Man was **King of the Jungle** in 1933. Who was he?
a) Buster Crabbe b) Bruce Bennett
c) Lex Barker d) Johnny Weismuller

LAWYERS

1) Name the 1935 drama which features happy-go-lucky lawyer Sydney Carton.
a) The Murder Man b) Bell, Book and Candle
c) Dear Brigitte d) A Tale of Two Cities

2) Who portrayed the eccentric Old Bailey defence counsel, Sir Wilfred Robarts, in William Wilder's 1957 mystery, **Witness for the Prosecution**?
a) C. Aubrey Smith b) Charles Laughton
c) Claude Rains d) Spencer Tracy

3) Gregory Peck won an Oscar for his portrayal of Southern lawyer, Atticus Finch, who defends a black man accused of rape. Name the film.
a) Only the Valiant b) The Paradine Case
c) Beloved Infidel d) To Kill a Mockingbird

LIBRARIANS

1) With which 1946 drama do you associate Donna Reed portraying an old maid librarian in Pottersville?
a) Thousands Cheer b) It's a Wonderful Life
c) They Were Expendable d) From Here to Eternity

2) In 1962 she played the stiff librarian Marian Paroo who questions the credibility of con man travelling salesman, Prof. Harold Hill, in **The Music Man**. Who was she?
a) Shirley Jones b) Dorothy Lamour
c) Jean Peters d) Kim Hunter

3) Name the 1963 horror film, starring Laurence Payne, and based on an Edgar Allan Poe story about a librarian who develops an obsession for his female neighbour who becomes more interested in his best friend.
a) The Tell-Tale Heart b) Deathwatch
c) The Murders in the Rue Morgue d) Quiet Little Neighborhood

MAD SCIENTISTS

1) Name the actor who made his screen debut as mad scientist, Jack Griffin, in the title role of James Whale's **The Invisible Man**?
a) Boris Karloff b) Lionel Barrymore
c) Fredric March d) Claude Rains

2) This 1956 film, in which Prospero the magician becomes the mad scientist, Dr. Morbius, was based on Shakespeare's 'The

Tempest'. Name the film.
a) It Came From Beneath the Sea b) The Thing (From Another World) c) Forbidden Planet d) When Worlds Collide

3) Who portrayed the mad transvestite scientist, Dr. Frank N. Furters, in **The Rocky Horror Picture Show**?
a) Barry Bostwick b) Charles Gray
c) Tim Curry d) Richard O'Brien

MAGICIANS

1) In which film do Michael Redgrave and Margaret Lockwood's characters tussle with 'The Great Doppo' and temporarily vanish in his 'disappearing cabinet' on board a train?
a) The Lady Vanishes b) Night Train to Munich
c) Mystery Train d) Terror on a Train

2) Which fantasy features Conrad Veidt as the evil magician, Grand Vizier Jaffar?
a) The Golden Voyage of Sinbad b) 1001 Arabian Nights c) The Thief of Bagdad d) Sinbad the Sailor

3) Who directed **The Magician**, which tells the story of 19th-century magician, Albert Emanuel Vogler (Max von Sydow)?
a) Ingmar Bergman b) Bo Widerberg
c) Gabriel Axel d) Lasse Hallstrom

MAIDS

1) Who won a Best Supporting Actress Oscar for her portrayal of Scarlett O'Hara's maid 'Mammy' in **Gone With the Wind**?
a) Pearl Bailey b) Hattie McDaniel
c) Dorothy Dandridge d) Diahann Carroll

2) With which film do you associate Loretta Young playing a Swedish housemaid who becomes a congresswoman?
a) The Farmer's Daughter b) Washington Story
c) I Like Your Nerve d) Employees Entrance

3) Who portrays 'Birdie', the streetwise maid of Margo Channing (Bette Davis), in Joseph L. Mankiewicz's **All About Eve** (1950)?
a) Ethel Barrymore b) Helen Hayes
c) Thelma Ritter d) Coleen Gray

MATADORS

1) Who played the title role in Budd Boetticher's 1955 drama, **The Magnificent Matador**?
a) John Garfield b) Anthony Quinn
c) Steve Reeves d) Jock Mahoney

2) With which Rouben Mamoulian film do you associate seductress Dona Soldes des Muire (Rita Hayworth) tempting matador Juan (Tyrone Power) away from angelic wife Carmen (Linda Darnell)?
a) Love Me Tonight b) The Wild Heart
c) Blood and Sand d) The Gay Desperado

3) What famous comedy duo made **The Bullfighters** in 1945?
a) Laurel & Hardy b) Abbott & Costello
c) Basil Radford & Naunton Wayne d) Tom & Jerry

MAYORS

1) In which film is ex-convict, Jean Valjean, elected town mayor?
a) The Count of Monte Cristo b) Madame Bovary
c) Les Miserables d) The Life of Emile Zola

2) Name the 1955 crime comedy which features a criminal nicknamed 'The Mayor'?
a) The Lavender Hill Mob b) Indiscreet
c) The Green Man d) The Ladykillers

3) Sidney Blackmer's role of 'The Big Boy' in a 1930s crime drama was based on the real-life corrupt mayor of Chicago and Al Capone puppet, Big Bill Thompson. Name the film.
a) Little Caesar b) The Public Enemy
c) The Mayor of Hell d) Smart Money

MECHANICS

1) With which 1962 musical do you associate Elvis Presley portraying mechanic, Walter Gulick?
a) Roustabout b) Kid Galahad
c) Jailhouse Rock d) Follow that Dream

2) In 1964 Genevieve Emery falls hopelessly in love with a garage mechanic named Guy (Nino Castelnuovo) in Jacques Demy's **The Umbrellas of Cherbourg**. Who was she?
a) Anouk Aimee b) Brigitte Bardot
c) Catherine Deneuve d) Simone Signoret

3) Which 1971 drama features Dennis Wilson as 'The Mechanic' and James Taylor as 'The Driver' of a 1955 Chevy racing across the American Southwest?
a) Silver Dream Racer b) The Cool Ones
c) Two-Lane Blacktop d) Fast Forward

The Movie Quiz Companion

MEDIUMS

1) Carnival hustler, Stanton Carlisle, tricks his way to becoming a successful medium in the 1947 crime drama, **Nightmare Alley**. Who was he?
a) Tyrone Power b) Paul Muni
c) Glenn Ford d) John Payne

2) Who portrays deceased investment counsellor, Sam Wheat, who takes over the body of fake medium, Oda Mae Brown (Whoopi Goldberg) in **Ghost**?
a) Sean Penn b) Richard Dreyfuss
c) Patrick Swayze d) Sean Bean

3) With which film do you associate the medium, Madame Arcati?
a) Miracles For Sale b) Poltergeist
c) Houdini d) Blithe Spirit

MERCENARIES

1) Who portrays the leader of the mercenaries who rescue a kidnapped African statesman in the 1978 adventure, **The Wild Geese**?
a) Richard Burton b) Hardy Kruger
c) Richard Harris d) Roger Moore

2) Who directed the 1968 drama, **The Mercenaries**?
a) John Sturges b) Jack Cardiff
c) Samuel Fuller d) Arthur Penn

3) In which film does Christopher Walken portray a mercenary named Shannon?
a) The Dogs of War
b) High Risk
c) Shoot the Sun Down
d) The Enforcer

MINERS

1) On whose novel was John Ford's 1941 Oscar-winning masterpiece, **How Green Was My Valley** based?
a) A.J. Cronin b) George Orwell
c) Richard Llewellyn d) Neil Gunn

2) In 1939 he portrayed the exasperated idealist, David Fenwick, who is born and bred in a Welsh mining town and who dreams of one day improving mining conditions in Carol Reed's **The Stars Look Down**. Who was he?
a) Robert Donat b) James Mason
c) Michael Redgrave d) Peter Finch

3) Based on the novel by Emile Zola, **Germinal** (1993) tells the story of the appalling conditions French miners worked under in the late 1800s. Who directed?
a) Claude Berri b) Marcel Pagnol
c) Claude Chabrol d) Luc Besson

MISSIONARIES

1) Who directed the 1966 drama, **7 Women**, about a group of missionaries in 1935 China?
a) Elia Kazan b) Lindsay Anderson c) John Ford
d) Richard Lester

2) Gladys Aylward accused the makers of **The Inn of the Sixth Happiness** (1958) of shamefully glamourizing her life, and referred to Ingrid Bergman as "that wicked woman", - a reference to Bergman's affair with Roberto Rossellini with whom she had a child out of wedlock. She also objected to the invented romance with the Eurasian Colonel, commenting: "I never had a love affair in my life". Who played the Colonel?
a) Curt Jurgens b) Nils Asther
c) Sessue Hayakawa d) Charles Boyer

3) In 1939 he portrayed missionary explorer David Livingstone in **Stanley and Livingstone**. Who was he?
a) Spencer Tracy b) Raymond Massey
c) Thomas Mitchell d) Cedric Hardwicke

MONKS

1) Who portrays the gangster turned monk in the 1940 crime drama, **Brother Orchid**?
a) George Raft b) Edward G. Robinson
c) James Cagney d) Dick Powell

2) Which film features sleuth monk, William of Baskerville?
a) The Hound of the Baskervilles b) Father Brown
c) Mystery of the Wax Museum d) The Name of the Rose

3) In 1966 he played **Rasputin-the Mad Monk**. Who was he?
a) Gert Fröbe b) Andre Morell
c) Christopher Lee d) Michael Gough

MOUNTAINEERS

1) Which 1937 fantasy features mountaineer and adventurer, Robert Conway, whose character was based on George Leigh-Mallory who vanished on Everest in 1924?
a) Lost Horizon b) Climb an Angry Mountain
c) White Wilderness d) The Far Horizons

2) Name the 1993 action adventure in which Sylvester Stallone plays mountain climber and rescue specialist, Gabe Walker.
a) Staying Alive b) Over the Top
c) Cliffhanger d) The Specialist

3) Who leads the group of mountaineers who attempt to climb the Alps in the 1950 adventure yarn, **The White Tower**?
a) Glenn Ford b) Fred MacMurray
c) Mickey Rooney d) Gregory Peck

MOUNTIES

1) In which film does Sgt Bruce (Nelson Eddy) of the Mounties sing the 'Indian Love Call'?
a) Naughty Marietta b) Rosalie
c) Maytime d) Rose Marie

2) Who directed the 1940 adventure **North West Mounted Police**?
a) Cecil B. De Mille b) John Ford
c) Anthony Mann d) Fred Zinneman

3) Name the 1987 crime thriller, directed by Brian De Palma, in which Mounties assisted federal agents in ambushing bootleggers on a bridge.
a) Scarface b) Wise Guys
c) The Untouchables d) Carlito's Way

MOVIE DIRECTORS

1) On whose life was the 1998 biopic, **Gods and Monsters** based?
a) D.W. Griffith b) James Whale
c) Cecil B. De Mille d) Alfred Hitchcock

2) In 1962 he portrayed Maurice Kruger, a once famous director experiencing hard times, in Vincente Minnelli's **Two Weeks in Another Town**. Who was he?
a) Kirk Douglas b) George Hamilton
c) Edward G. Robinson d) George Macready

3) Who portrayed silent screen slapstick director, Mack Sennett, in Richard Attenborough's 1992 biopic, **Chaplin**?
a) Kevin Kline b) Dan Aykroyd
c) James Woods d) Anthony Hopkins

MPs

1) In which film does Ronald Colman portray the MP Sir Charles Rainier?
a) The Light That Failed b) Clive of India
c) Random Harvest d) Raffles

2) Which film is critic Roger Ebert reviewing in the following extract?
"I'm writing this review in London, where the papers for the last few days have been filled with the scandal of the Conservative member of Parliament who had to resign his constituency after being convicted of spanking two male prostitutes who were younger than twenty-one, which is the age of consent for homosexual spankings in Britain. (Female prostitutes can legally be spanked once they are sixteen. There'll always be an England)."
a) Scandal b) A Man of No Importance
c) Personal Services d) Wish You Were Here

3) Which film features screenwriter and playwright Alan Bennett in a cameo part as a member of parliament?
a) A Private Function b) Little Dorrit
c) Prick up Your Ears d) The Madness of King George

MUSICIANS

1) What were the Castillo brothers (Armand Assante and Antonio Banderas) better known as?
a) Swing Kids b) Los Olvidados
c) The Mambo Kings d) Playmates

2) Name the 'Road movie' in which Bob Hope and Bing Crosby play a pair of broke musicians rescuing Dorothy Lamour from a wicked aunt (Gale Sondergaard) and an arranged marriage.
a) Road to Rio b) Road to Singapore
c) Road to Utopia d) Road to Zanzibar

3) Which Sergio Leone film features Union troops forming an orchestra of musicians from Confederate prisoners of war, to mask the cries of torture victims?
a) The Good, the Bad, and the Ugly b) Once Upon a Time in the West c) A Fistful of Dollars d) For a Few Dollars More

NANNIES

1) Who portrays Peyton Flanders, the nanny out for revenge in **The Hand That Rocks the Cradle**?
a) Catherine Zeta-Jones b) Rebecca De Mornay
c) Glenne Headly d) Rachel Weisz

2) Name the nanny who came to look after the Banks family.
a) Jane Eyre b) Mrs. Doubtfire
c) Mary Poppins d) Lyn Belvedere

3) Who plays the title role in the 1965 horror film, **The Nanny**?
a) Ingrid Pitt b) Adrienne Corri
c) Bette Davis d) Lee Remick

NUNS

1) In 1946 she portrayed the randy nun, Sister Ruth, who makes a pass at British agent, Mr. Dean (David Farrar), in **Black Narcissus**. Who was she?
a) Deborah Kerr b) Valerie Hobson
c) Greer Garson d) Kathleen Byron

2) Who directed the 1959 drama, **The Nun's Story**?
a) Robert Wise b) Fred Zinnemann
c) Jean Negulesco d) William Dieterle

3) Which 1971 film features Vanessa Redgrave as Sister Jeanne?
a) The Rosary Murders b) Therese
c) Choices of the Heart d) The Devils

The Movie Quiz Companion

ignite a dry red ass

NURSES

1) Helen Hayes and Jennifer Jones both portrayed WWI Nurse Catherine Barkley in 1932 and 1957 respectively. Name the film.
a) Dawn Patrol b) Beau Geste c) A Farewell to Arms d) All Quiet on the Western Front

2) In which 1981 horror film does Nurse Alex Price fall in love with a werewolf?
a) Wolf b) The Howling c) Innocent Blood d) An American Werewolf in London

3) Who portrayed the priggish head nurse, Major Hot Lips Houlihan, in Robert Altman's 1970 comedy **M*A*S*H**?
a) Ellen Burstyn b) Sylvia Miles
c) Sally Kellerman d) Stacy Keach

OUTLAWS, FICTIONAL

1) Who plays the title role in the 1970 comedy western, **Dirty Dingus Magee**?
a) Frank Sinatra b) James Garner
c) Paul Newman d) Dennis Hopper

2) Which John Ford western features 'The Ringo Kid'?
a) My Darling Clementine b) The Iron Horse
c) Rio Grande d) Stagecoach

3) Farmer Dan Evans (Van Heflin) holds outlaw Ben Wade until the **3:10 to Yuma** arrives. Who portrayed Wade?
a) Glenn Ford b) Jack Palance
c) Ernest Borgnine d) Anthony Quinn

OUTLAWS, REAL-LIFE

1) Who does Jesse James meet in William Beaudine's 1966 western horror, **Jesse James Meets...**?
a) Dracula b) Frankenstein's Daughter
c) The Wolf Man d) Jack the Ripper

2) In 1952 he portrayed medieval outlaw Robin Hood in Disney's **The Story of Robin Hood and His Merrie Men**. Who was he?
a) Errol Flynn b) Cornel Wilde
c) Richard Greene d) Richard Todd

3) Who directed **Butch Cassidy and the Sundance Kid**?
a) John Frankenheimer b) John Huston
c) Arthur Penn d) George Roy Hill

PHOTOGRAPHERS

1) In which 1988 biopic does passionate animal lover, Dian Fossey, become romantically involved with National Geographic photographer, Bob Campbell (Bryan Brown)?
a) Elephant Walk b) Save the Tiger
c) Out of Africa d) Gorillas in the Mist

2) Who portrayed photographer Irving Radovich, sidekick of reporter Joe Bradley (Gregory Peck) in the 1953 romantic comedy, **Roman Holiday**?
a) Eddie Albert b) Arthur Kennedy
c) Charles Bickford d) Ray Walston

3) Which 1979 war film features Dennis Hopper as a disturbed and irrational photojournalist?
a) Catch-22 b) Apocalypse Now
c) Slaughterhouse-Five d) Kelly's Heroes

PIANISTS

1) Who portrays the concert pianist who turns his back on fame to play in a scruffy Parisian cafe, in François Truffaut's 1960 crime drama, **Shoot the Piano Player** (Tirez Sur Le Pianiste)?
a) Jean-Pierre Léaud b) Charles Aznavour
c) Oskar Werner d) Jean Paul Belmondo

2) With which 1970 film do you associate Jack Nicholson training as a child to become a concert pianist?
a) Five Easy Pieces b) Ironweed
c) Carnal Knowledge d) Easy Rider

3) Which 1941 WWII drama features a concert pianist (Anton Walbrook) who becomes a fighter pilot?
a) Dangerous Moonlight b) Wing and a Prayer
c) Somewhere I'll Find You d) This Above All

PICKPOCKETS

1) In which 1946 romantic comedy does Ginger Rogers portray a pickpocket?
a) I'll Be Seeing You b) Tales of Manhattan
c) The Mayor and the Minor d) Heartbeat

2) Name the Jack Lemmon comedy in which a relatively unknown Sylvester Stallone is cast as an alleged pickpocket.

a) The Prisoner of Second Avenue b) Irma La Douce c) The Odd Couple d) How to Murder Your Wife

3) Who portrays the beautiful gypsy pickpocket 'Venus', in Philippe de Broca's 1964 comedy, **Cartouche**?
a) Claudia Cardinale b) Virna Lisi
c) Gina Lollobrigida d) Sophia Loren

PIMPS

1) Who portrays Lenny, the pimp son of Max (Paul Rogers), in Peter Hall's 1973 adaptation of Harold Pinter's **The Homecoming**?
a) Terence Rigby b) Michael Jayston
c) Ian Holm d) James Fox

2) Who portrays the American exile pimp, Jack Flowers, in Peter Bogdanovich's 1979 drama, **Saint Jack**?
a) Val Kilmer b) Dennis Hopper
c) Christopher Walken d) Ben Gazzara

3) Name the 1987 crime drama in which journalist Christopher Reeves fabricates a story about a Times Square pimp.
a) Street Smart b) Trick Baby
c) Streetwalkin' d) Risky Business

PIRATES, FICTIONAL

1) Which 1935 swashbuckler, directed by Michael Curtiz, was based on a novel by Rafael Sabatini?
a) The Spanish Main
b) The Black Pirate
c) Frenchman's Creek
d) Captain Blood

2) Wallace Beery and Charlton Heston both portrayed the same pirate in 1934 and 1990 respectively. Who was he?
a) Captain Hook b) Long John Silver
c) Blackbeard d) Doctor Syn

3) Who portrays the pirate intent on avenging their father's death in the 1995 adventure, **Cutthroat Island**?
a) Matthew Modine b) Jennifer Lopez
c) Geena Davis d) Frank Langella

PIRATES, REAL-LIFE

1) Who played the title role in Disney's 1968 comedy, **Blackbeard's Ghost**?
a) Rex Harrison b) Burl Ives
c) Peter Ustinov d) Martin Balsam

2) Which 1938 film, directed by Cecil B. De Mille, tells the story of pirate-hero Jean Lafitte's (Fredric March) role in the Battle of New Orleans?
a) The Buccaneer b) The Rover
c) Pirates d) The Mutineers

3) Who portrays **Morgan the Pirate** in André De Toth's 1961 swashbuckler?
a) Anthony Quinn
b) Victor Mature
c) Steve Reeves d) Cornel Wilde

PLASTIC SURGEONS

1) Deranged plastic surgeon, Prof. Genessier (Pierre Brasseur) tries to reconstruct his daughter's disfigured face by kidnapping young women, removing their faces and grafting them onto his daughter's. Name the film.
a) Eyes Without a Face b) The Face Behind the Mask c) Doll Face d) The Naked Face

2) With which film do you associate plastic surgeon, Paul Henreid, attempting to turn a female convict into a carbon copy of the woman he loves?
a) Sweet Dreams b) A Stolen Face
c) The Promise d) A Stolen Life

3) In which 1981 drama does Albert Finney portray a Beverly Hills plastic surgeon investigating a series of murders?
a) Looker b) The Image
c) The Dresser d) Wolfen

POACHERS

1) In which Disney film were an eagle and a little boy kidnapped by the evil poacher, McLeach?
a) Old Yeller b) The Rescuers Down Under
c) Savage Sam d) A Far Off Place

2) The first of six MGM Johnny Weissmuller and Maureen O'Sullivan 'Tarzan' adventures dealt with ivory poachers trying to get Tarzan to lead them to the elephant graveyard. Name the title.
a) Tarzan Escapes b) Tarzan and His Mate
c) Tarzan's Peril d) Tarzan, the Ape Man

3) Which Jean Renoir film features Marceau (Julien Carette) the poacher?
a) Rules of the Game b) Diary of a Chambermaid
c) Grand Illusion d) The Elusive Corporal

POETS

1) Famous poet, Pablo Neruda's (Philippe Noiret) exile in Italy is chronicled in the 1994 drama, **Il Postino**. Name Neruda's native country.
a) Argentina b) Bolivia c) Peru d) Chile

2) Name the poet whose relationship with socialite Vivienne Haigh-Wood (Miranda Richardson) is recounted in **Tom & Viv**?
a) T.S. Eliot b) Thomas Hardy
c) Thomas Gray d) Sir Thomas Wyatt

The Movie Quiz Companion

3) Who portrays the bedridden poet, Elizabeth Barrett, in the 1934 version of **The Barretts of Wimpole Street**?
a) Jennifer Jones b) Maureen O'Sullivan
c) Olivia De Havilland d) Norma Shearer

POLICE CHIEFS & COMMISSIONERS

1) Which film features pregnant police chief, Marge Gunderson?
a) Forrest Gump b) Jaws 2 c) Fargo
d) Tough Guys Don't Dance

2) In 1981 he portrayed NYC Police Commissioner Waldo in Milos Forman's adaptation of E.L. Doctorow's best-selling novel, **Ragtime**. Brought out of retirement to play the role - who was he?
a) James Cagney b) Edward G. Robinson
c) Fred Astaire d) Ray Milland

3) Which 1968 crime thriller, directed by Don Siegel, features Henry Fonda as Police Commissioner Anthony X. Russell?
a) Madigan b) The Killers
c) Coogan's Bluff d) Dirty Harry

POLICEMEN

1) Who portrays the policeman who courted the widow Katie Nolan in Elia Kazan's 1945 drama, **A Tree Grows in Brooklyn**?
a) Jack Oakie b) Wallace Beery
c) Lloyd Nolan d) James Dunn

2) Where was constable George Dixon (Jack Warner) gunned down by young thug Tom Riley (Dirk Bogarde) in **The Blue Lamp**?
a) a jeweller's shop b) a cinema foyer
c) a garage d) a bank

3) To what branch of the police department does cop John Wintergreen (Robert Blake) belong in **Electra Glide in Blue**?
a) the mounted police b) motorcycles
c) highway patrol d) traffic

POLITICIANS

1) In 1983 he portrayed local politician, Greg Stillson, who would eventually become President (unless stopped) and trigger a nuclear war in David Cronenberg's adaptation of Stephen King's novel, **The Dead Zone**. Who was he?
a) Peter Weller b) Herbert Lom
c) Jeremy Irons d) Martin Sheen

2) What 1949 political drama describes the rise and fall of Willie Stark (Broderick Crawford), whose character was supposedly modelled on corrupt Louisiana politician, Huey Long?
a) The Glass Key b) State of the Union
c) All the King's Men d) Dirty Hands

3) In which 1987 Roger Vadim drama did prison escapee, Rebecca De Mornay, hitch a ride in the limousine of politician Frank Langella?
a) And God Created Woman b) La Ronde
c) Night Games d) Circle of Love

POPES & CARDINALS

1) Who portrays Pope Julius II, who squabbled with sculptor Michelangelo (Charlton Heston) in **The Agony and the Ecstasy**?
a) Paul Scofield b) Rex Harrison
c) Harry Andrews d) Derek Jacobi

2) In which film does craggy-featured Scots character actor, Finlay Currie, play Pope Innocent III?
a) The Angel Wore Red
b) Saint Joan
c) Francis of Assisi
d) The Rome Express

3) Many actors have portrayed the scheming Cardinal Richelieu in various versions of **The Three Musketeers** legend. Who portrayed him in 1993?
a) Miles Mander b) Massimo Serato
c) Tim Curry d) Charlton Heston

POOL HUSTLERS

1) Who portrays legendary pool player, 'Minnesota Fats', who took drifter-come-hustler, 'Fast' Eddie Felson (Paul Newman) under his wing in **The Hustler** (1961)?
a) Sidney Blackmer b) Frank Cady
c) Jim Backus d) Jackie Gleason

2) In 1986 he portrayed 'Vincent', 'Fast' Eddie's greenhorn protégé in Martin Scorsese's **The Color of Money**. Who was he?
a) Brad Pitt b) Tim Robbins
c) Tom Hanks d) Tom Cruise

3) With which film do you associate James Coburn as pool hustler, Nick Casey?
a) The Baltimore Bullet b) Shoot
c) The Last American Hero d) Kiss Shot

POSTMEN

1) Name the 1949 comedy in which François (Jacques Tati), the village postman, becomes obsessed with the ultra-modern methods of the American postal system.
a) Le Diable au Corps b) L'ecole de Facteurs
c) Jour de Fete d) Mon Oncle

2) On whose novel was Tay Garnett's 1946 thriller, **The Postman Always Rings Twice**, based?
a) James M. Cain b) Dashiell Hammett
c) Patricia Highsmith d) Chester Himes

3) Which Scottish comedian portrays the postman in Frank Launder's 1956 comedy, **Wee Geordie**?
a) Jimmy Logan b) Stanley Baxter
c) Rikki Fulton d) Will Fyffe

PREACHERS

1) In which comedy does a preacher proclaim: "Our women have been stampeded and our cattle raped"?
a) Naked Gun b) Hairspray
c) Blazing Saddles d) Horse Feathers

2) With which film do you associate black actor, Christopher Asante, portraying the Rev. Macpherson?
a) Cry Freedom b) Road to Zanzibar
c) Local Hero d) Coming to America

3) In the 1972 western, **Buck and the Preacher**, Sidney Poitier plays Buck. Who portrays 'Preacher'?
a) Harry Belafonte b) Cleavon Little
c) James Whitmore d) Richard Roundtree

PRESIDENTS

1) Which 1942 musical features President Franklin D. Roosevelt (Wallis Clark) summoning the great vaudevillian and showman, George M. Cohan (James Cagney) to the White House?
a) The Seven Little Foys
b) Little Nellie Kelly
c) Stage Struck
d) Yankee Doodle Dandy

2) Which U.S. President has been portrayed by both Walter Huston and Raymond Massey?
a) George Washington
b) Abraham Lincoln
c) Thomas Jefferson
d) John Quincy Adams

3) Name the D.W. Griffith film President Woodrow Wilson was describing, which he observed (and was later to regret) was "Like history written in lightning."
a) The Birth of a Nation b) Intolerance
c) Broken Blossoms d) The Greatest Question

PRIESTS

1) In which film is Father Logan (Montgomery Clift) faced with the dilemma of revealing a murderer's confession or facing a murder charge?
a) Confession b) The Confessional
c) I Confess d) Double Confession

2) Which Italian film features film censor, Father Adelfio (Leopoldo Trieste)?
a) La Dolce Vita b) Cinema Paradiso
c) Baccaccio d) Sotto, Sotto

3) Name the 1989 road movie in which the doyen of Beat novelists, William Burroughs, portrays a defrocked priest addicted to heroin?
a) Badlands
b) Drugstore Cowboy
c) Honkytonk Man
d) Coupe de Ville

PRIME MINISTERS

1) Which British Prime Minister did Alec Guinness portray in **The Mudlark**, a 1950 drama about a street urchin who sneaks into Windsor Castle.
a) Gladstone b) Disraeli c) Peel d) Pitt

2) Who directed the 1972 political biopic, **Young Winston**?
a) Richard Attenborough b) Hugh Hudson
c) Bryan Forbes d) John Boulting

3) Who played the title role in the 1942 biopic, **The Young Mr. Pitt**?
a) Leslie Howard b) George Arliss
c) Robert Donat d) Robert Morley

PRINCES

1) In 1938 he portrayed the Regent of England, Prince John, in **The Adventures of Robin Hood**. Who was he?
a) Basil Rathbone b) Louis Calhern
c) Vincent Price d) Claude Rains

2) On whose story, in which an urchin exchanges places with a prince, was the adventure film, **The Prince and the Pauper** based?
a) Hans Andersen b) Mark Twain
c) Jonathan Swift d) Edmond Rostand

3) Which 1957 comedy features Laurence Olivier as Prince Regent of Carpathia?
a) The Beggar's Opera b) That Hamilton Woman
c) The Prince and the Showgirl d) The Devil's Disciple

PRINCESSES

1) What danger awaits Buttercup, **The Princess Bride**, when she tries to escape from her captors by jumping out of a boat?
a) screaming eels b) a giant piranha fish
c) radioactive jellyfish d) flesh-eating leeches

2) Name the film which was inspired by a newspaper article about the Canadian government bestowing Dutch sovereignty on the room where the exiled Princess Juliana of the Netherlands was about to give birth.

Although her daughter was born in Canada, the room was technically and legally on Dutch soil, making her daughter legal heir to the throne.
a) The King Steps Out b) Passport to Pimlico c) Duck Soup d) A King in New York

3) In which horror 1932 film is Helen Grosvenor (Zita Johann) the incarnation of the Egyptian Princess Anck-es-en-Amon?
a) The Mummy b) The Devil-Doll c) Pharaoh's Curse d) The Mummy's Hand

PRISONERS

1) On whose novel was **The Prisoner of Zenda** based?
a) Alexandre Dumas b) H. Rider Haggard c) Anthony Hope d) A.E.W. Mason

2) In which 1994 prison adventure is a prisoner named Robbins (Ray Liotta) sent to Absolom Island which is inhabited by two warring factions of convicts?
a) No Escape b) Menace II Society c) Alienator d) Gulag

3) Innocent Dr. Samuel Mudd (Warner Baxter) was sentenced to life imprisonment for conspiracy to murder President Lincoln. By what name was he better known?
a) The Prisoner of Shark Island b) The Last American Hero c) Convict Cowboy d) Prisoner of Honor

PRISONERS OF WAR

1) Which P.O.W. drama was based on Eric William's novel, *The Tunnel Escape* ?
a) Grand Illusion b) The Great Escape c) The Wooden Horse d) Colditz

2) In 1953 he played arrogant loner POW, 'Sefton', who is suspected of being a Nazi spy in Billy Wilder's **Stalag 17**. Who was he?
a) Burt Lancaster b) William Holden c) Jack Lemmon d) Sterling Hayden

3) Name the film, starring Claudette Colbert, which is based on Agnes Newton Keith's autobiographical tale of her imprisonment on Japanese occupied Borneo.

a) Three Came Home b) Another Time, Another Place c) Godchild d) A Town Like Alice

PRIVATE INVESTIGATORS

1) Who plays the vaudevillian turned private eye in **Gumshoe**?
a) Richard Harris b) Albert Finney c) Alan Bates d) Peter O'Toole

2) With which film do you associate a gangster smashing his moll in the face with a bottle and then growling at private eye, Philip Marlowe: "Now that's someone I love. Think what could happen to you."?
a) Farewell My Lovely b) The Big Sleep c) Lady in the Lake d) The Long Goodbye

3) Who plays the title role in **Tony Rome** (1967)?
a) Richard Conte b) Dean Martin c) Jack Lemmon d) Frank Sinatra

PROFESSORS

1) In which comedy does clumsy, wimpy, chemistry Professor, Julius Ferris Kelp, drink a formula which transforms him into cool, hip singer, 'Buddy Love'?
a) The Absent Minded Professor b) The Nutty Professor c) Professor Beware d) College Confidential

2) Which film features Harpo Marx as 'The Professor'?
a) Animal Crackers b) A Night at the Opera c) Duck Soup d) Monkey Business

3) Name the film in which retired don, Professor Waxflatter (Nigel Stock), attempts to invent the first flying machine?
a) The Great Race b) Young Sherlock Holmes c) In Search of the Castaways d) Young Einstein

PROJECTIONISTS

1) In which 1971 comedy drama does a daydreaming projectionist imagine he is a superhero called 'Captain Flash'?
a) The Smallest Show on Earth b) Dancing in the Dark c) The Projectionist d) Dream a Little Dream

2) After a disastrous sexual encounter with a young bus conductor, Lynda (Emily Lloyd) has an affair with a middle-aged cinema projectionist who "smells of booze and fags", in **Wish You Were Here**. Who was he?
a) Colin Blakely b) Tom Bell c) Steven Berkoff d) Victor Spinetti

3) Name the 1991 drama in which a projectionist is chosen to be Stalin's official projectionist inside the Kremlin.
a) The Inner Circle b) The Fear Inside c) The Kremlin Letter d) Beyond the Walls

PROSTITUTES

1) Name the film for which Lila Kedrova won an Oscar for her role as the dying prostitute, Mme. Hortense.
a) Never on a Sunday b) La Strada c) Zorba the Greek d) Last Tango in Paris

2) In which Mike Figgis film does Ben Sanderson (Nicolas Cage) meet street-walking prostitute Sera (Elizabeth Shue)?
a) Honeymoon in Vegas b) Raising Arizona
c) Guarding Tess d) Leaving Las Vegas

3) Miriam Hopkins and Ingrid Bergman portrayed Ivy the prostitute in 1932 and 1941 respectively. Name the film.
a) Dead End b) Paisan c) The Life of Emile Zola
d) Dr. Jekyll and Mr. Hyde

PSYCHIATRISTS

1) In which 1942 drama does Dr. Jaquith explain his vocation to the cantankerous Mrs. Henry Windle Vale as follows - "There's nothing shameful about my work, or frightening, or anything else. It's very simple really what I try to do. People walk along the road. They come to a fork in the road. They're confused. They don't know which way to take. I just put up a signpost. Not that way - this way."
a) Kings Row b) Juarez
c) Now, Voyager d) Forever and a Day

2) Which film features a patient confiding to Dr. Chumley (Cecil Kellaway): "Well, I wrestled with reality for 35 years, doctor, and I'm happy to state I finally won out over it"?
a) Seventh Heaven b) You Gotta Stay Happy
c) Harvey d) Rage in Heaven

3) Name the film in which a psychiatrist is mauled to death by a panther after attempting to seduce an emotionally disturbed woman.
a) Cat People b) Cat Girl
c) Curse of the Cat People d) Cat's Eye

QUEENS

1) In 1937 she played Queen Victoria in Herbert Wilcox's biopic, **Victoria the Great**. Who was she?
a) Deborah Kerr b) Flora Robson
c) Anna Neagle d) Peggy Ashcroft

2) Who portrays Queen Morgan Le Fay in the 1931 version of **A Connecticut Yankee**?

a) Myrna Loy b) Helen Hayes
c) Beulah Bondi d) Maureen O'Sullivan

3) Katherine Hepburn and Vanessa Redgrave both portrayed the same queen in 1936 and 1971 respectively. Who was she?
a) Queen Elizabeth I b) Mary, Queen of Scots
c) Queen of Sheba d) Guinevere

RACING DRIVERS

1) Who portrays brash racing driver, Joe Greer, in Howard Hawks' **The Crowd Roars**?
a) Clark Gable b) James Cagney
c) Gene Kelly d) Joel McCrea

2) In which film do racing fanatics, Peter Fonda and Adam Roarke, steal $150,000 from a supermarket to fund the purchase of a racing car?
a) Dirty Mary Crazy Larry b) Race with the Devil
c) The Wild Angels d) The Trip

3) Name the title of the 1977 biopic about the life of Wendell Scott, the first black American racing driver.
a) Greased Lightning b) Live Fast, Die Young
c) Speed to Spare d) Thunder in Carolina

RUSTLERS

1) With which William 'Wild Bill' Wellman film do you associate three innocent men (Dana Andrews, Anthony Quinn and Francis Ford) being hanged for suspected rustling?
a) Yellow Sky
b) Across the Wide Missouri
c) The Ox-Bow Incident
d) Buffalo Bill

2) Which 1975 comedy western features cattle rustlers, Jeff Bridges and Sam Waterston, who do it "to keep from falling asleep."?
a) Hearts of the West b) In Search of America
c) Bad Company d) Rancho Deluxe

3) In Gary Cooper's first talkie he portrayed a lawman who hangs his best friend for cattle-rustling. Name the title.
a) The Big Trail b) Cimarron
c) The Virginian d) The Golden West

SAILORS

1) With which film do you associate sailors Gabey, Chip and Ozzie searching New York City on a 24-hour pass for 'Miss Turnstiles'?
a) Anchors Aweigh b) Sailor Beware
c) Three Sailors and a Girl d) On the Town

2) Able seaman Billy Mitchell proposes marriage to Queenie (Kay Walsh) in David Lean's WWII drama, **This Happy Breed** (1944). Who was he?
a) Stanley Holloway b) John Mills
c) Michael Wilding d) Bernard Miles

3) John Dyckman Brown III and Patsy and Jean Deyo (June Allyson & Gloria DeHaven) were **Two Girls and a Sailor** in the 1944 musical. Who portrayed the sailor?
a) William Bendix b) Gene Kelly
c) Van Johnson d) Howard Keel

SALESMEN

1) What product do the salesmen sell in David Mamet's **Glengarry Glen Ross**?
a) automobiles b) real-estate
c) insurance d) swimming pools

The Movie Quiz Companion

2) Salesmen, Bill 'BB' Babowsky and Ernest Tilley become mortal enemies after crashing into each other in a car accident. Name the film.
a) Ruthless People b) Wise Guys
c) Crash! d) Tin Men

3) Who played the title role in Laslo Benedek's 1951 drama, **Death of a Salesman**?
a) Paul Muni b) Ray Milland
c) Fredric March d) John Garfield

SALOON GALS

1) In 1942 she played Yukon saloon gal 'Cherry Malotte' in **The Spoilers**. Who was she?
a) Lana Turner b) Barbara Stanwyck
c) Marlene Dietrich d) Tallulah Bankhead

2) Which western features Linda Darnell as 'Chihuahua', saloon gal singer and girlfriend of Doc Holliday?
a) Gunfight at the OK Corral b) The Outlaw
c) Frontier Marshal d) My Darling Clementine

3) In which western does 'Frenchy' (Marlene Dietrich) the saloon gal sing 'See What the Boys in the Back Room Will Have'?
a) Pony Express b) Alias Jesse James
c) Destry Rides Again d) Rancho Notorius

SAMURAI WARRIORS

1) Name the western inspired by **Yojimbo** (1961), Akira Kurosawa's tale of wandering samurai, Sanjuro Kuwabatake (Toshiro Mifune).
a) The Wild Bunch b) The Magnificent Seven
c) A Fistful of Dollars d) Once Upon a Time in the West

2) In which film does a disgraced samurai warrior journey across Japan with his young son in a push-cart?
a) Lightning Swords of Death b) Ikuru
c) Kwaidan d) Chushigura

3) The title of a 1980 Akira Kurosawa samurai drama means 'shadow warrior'. Name the film.
a) Kagemusha b) Rashomon c) Ran d) Sanjuro

SANTA CLAUS

1) 20th Century-Fox producer and executive, Darryl Zanuck, was so unimpressed with this 1947 fantasy, he released it during the summer rather than wait for Christmas. **Miracle on 34th Street** went on, however, to win an Oscar for its star's portrayal of Santa Claus. Who was he?
a) Charles Coburn b) Edmund Gwenn
c) Henry Travers d) Walter Connolly

2) What 1993 musical fantasy involves Santa getting kidnapped by Jack Skellington?
a) Ernest Saves Christmas b) It Nearly Wasn't Christmas c) Tim Burton's Nightmare Before Christmas d) One Magic Christmas

3) Name the 1984 horror film in which a psychopath dressed as Santa Claus commits savage axe murders.
a) Silent Night, Deadly Night b) Black Christmas
c) The Snow Creature d) All I Want For Christmas

SCHOOL TEACHERS

1) Which rock singer has a cameo role as a high-school teacher in **Back to the Future**?
a) Bruce Springsteen b) Sting
c) Huey Lewis d) Alice Cooper

2) With which film do you associate the lines: "Give me a girl at an impressionable age, and she is mine for life."
a) Picnic at Hanging Rock b) The Belles of St. Trinians c) The Prime of Miss Jean Brodie
d) School For Scoundrels

3) Name the film which was inspired by the life of Cambridge schoolmaster, William Balgarnie?
a) The Browning Version b) Goodbye Mr. Chips
c) Dead Poets Society d) Tom Brown's Schooldays

SCIENTISTS

1) Who portrays scientist Dr. Barnhardt (Sam Jaffe) who summons scientists from all over the world at Klaatu's request in **The Day the Earth Stood Still**?
a) Reginald Owen b) Lester Allen
c) Sam Jaffe d) James Whitmore

2) Name the disease German scientist, Paul Ehrlich (Edward G. Robinson), developed a cure for in **Doctor Ehrlich's Magic Bullet**.
a) polio b) syphilis c) yellow fever d) leprosy

3) Critic Pauline Kael described the actress who portrayed scientist **Madame Curie** as "an actress who turns restraint into a cover for obscene self-assurance; when she discusses laboratory formulas she manages to invest every syllable with sanctity." Who was she?
a) *Anna Neagle* b) *Greer Garson*
c) *Claudette Colbert* d) *Loretta Young*

SCULPTORS

1) Pendlebury (Stanley Holloway) fancies himself as a bit of a sculptor, although his real job is manufacturing cheap souvenirs and paperweights, and his new Eiffel Tower paperweights are priceless! Name the film.
a) *Innocents in Paris* b) *Man With a Million*
c) *The Lavender Hill Mob* d) *A Run For Your Money*

2) In which film does Cher portray a sculptor?
a) *Silkwood* b) *Mermaids*
c) *Mask* d) *The Witches of Eastwick*

3) In 1953 he portrayed deranged sculptor, Prof. Henry Jarrod, who fills his wax museum with real human victims in **House of Wax**. Who was he?
a) *Bela Lugosi* b) *Peter Lorre*
c) *Vincent Price* d) *Christopher Lee*

SEA CAPTAINS

1) Who portrays the terrifying and inhuman skipper, Wolf Larsen, in Michael Curtiz's 1941 adaptation of Jack London's novel, **The Sea Wolf**?
a) *James Mason* b) *Burt Lancaster*
c) *Edward G. Robinson* d) *J. Carrol Naish*

2) Danish merchant sea captain, Conrad Veidt, and his mysterious passenger, Valerie Hobson, become embroiled in espionage in Powell and Pressburger's 1940 spy drama. Name the title.
a) *Battle of the River Plate* b) *The Spy in Black*
c) *49th Parallel* d) *Contraband*

3) What 1953 comedy involves Captain Henry St. James (Alec Guinness) having two very contrasting wives in different ports?
a) *A Run For Your Money* b) *The Captain Hates the Sea* c) *All at Sea* d) *The Captain's Paradise*

SECRETARIES

1) Name the secretary who falls in love with handsome boss George Brent in the 1936 comedy, **More Than a Secretary**.
a) *Jean Arthur* b) *Myrna Loy*
c) *Peggy Ann Garner* d) *Ida Lupino*

2) When James Bond's formidable adversary, Auric **Goldfinger**, discovers he has seduced his secretary he has her body covered in gold paint which seals her pores and suffocates her. Who was she?
a) *Molly Peters* b) *Diana Rigg*
c) *Shirley Eaton* d) *Lois Maxwell*

3) Who portrays ambitious secretary, Tess McGill, in Mike Nichols' 1988 romantic drama, **Working Girl**?
a) *Melanie Griffith* b) *Holly Hunter*
c) *Meg Ryan* d) *Andie MacDowell*

SENATORS

1) Which film features Senator Geary (G.D. Spradlin), a greasy Nevada politician who is set up by the Mafia when he wakes up next to a dead prostitute after a drunken binge?
a) *The Big Easy* b) *Harlem Nights*
c) *Prizzi's Honor* d) *The Godfather Part II*

2) Novelist and screenwriter, Gore Vidal, has been unsuccessful in the political arena in real life, but in 1992 he was cast as an old liberal senator named Brickley Paiste in a 1992 political comedy. Name the film.
a) *The Seduction of Joe Tynan* b) *Bob Roberts*
c) *Brubaker* d) *Citizen Cohn*

3) A 1939 film about a young idealist senator was condemned by most of Washington's politicians and press on its release because of its portrayal of corruption in the Senate. Name the film.
a) *Mr. Smith Goes to Washington* b) *All the King's Men* c) *State of the Union* d) *The Senator was Indiscreet*

SHERIFFS

1) Who portrays greenhorn sheriff, Ben Owens, who seeks the help of a bounty hunter to confront outlaws harassing his town in Anthony Mann's 1957 western, **The Tin Star**?
a) *Anthony Perkins* b) *James Stewart*
c) *Tony Curtis* d) *Montgomery Clift*

2) Joel McCrea, Kenneth Tobey, Randolph Scott and Albert Dekker all played the same real-life lawman in **The Gunfight at Dodge City**, **Gunfight at the O.K. Corral**, **Trail Street**, and **The Woman of the Town**, respectively. Who was he?
a) *Pat Garrett* b) *Wyatt Earp*
c) *Wild Bill Hickok* d) *Bat Masterson*

3) Who was **The Sheriff of Fractured Jaw**?
a) *Bob Hope* b) *Jack Lemmon*
c) *Kenneth More* d) *Rock Hudson*

SHOPKEEPERS

1) Which film features henpecked shopkeeper, Harold Bissonette (W.C. Fields), a grocer who purchases a seemingly worthless orange grove?
a) *It's A Gift* b) *Running Wild* c) *Never Give a Sucker an Even Break* d) *Tillie and Gus*

2) Michael Redgrave portrays an orphan who works in a draper's shop in a 1941 comedy adapted from an H.G. Wells novel. Name the film.

The Movie Quiz Companion

a) *The History of Mr. Polly* b) *The Man Who Could Work Miracles* c) *Kipps* d) *First Men in the Moon*

3) In which comedy does shop assistant, Louis Mazzni encounter his first murder victim, the arrogant Ascoyne d'Ascoyne?
a) *A Run For Your Money* b) *Our Man in Havana* c) *Hotel Paradiso* d) *Kind Hearts and Coronets*

SMUGGLERS

1) Who thwarted the villainous German smugglers in the 1948 crime comedy, **Smuggler's Cove**?
a) Abbott & Costello b) The Bowery Boys c) The Three Stooges d) Old Mother Riley

2) What 1939 film connection can you make between Alfred Hitchcock and smuggling during the reign of King George IV?
a) *Secret Agent* b) *Foreign Correspondent* c) *Jamaica Inn* d) *Saboteur*

3) Tourist Nicky Ferris (Hayley Mills) becomes involved with smugglers in Disney's 1964 children's mystery, **The Moon-Spinners**. What were they smuggling?
a) jewellery b) guns c) antiques d) rare birds

SODA JERKS

1) Who portrays the soda jerk who is inspired to make friends with his crotchety neighbour, Sourpuss Smithers, after listening to Long John Willoughby's (Gary Cooper) radio speech in **Mr. Deeds Goes to Town**?

a) Lionel Stander b) Arthur Hoyt c) Regis Toomey d) H.B. Warner

2) Air Force captain, Fred Derry, who was employed as a soda jerk before he enlisted, finds his marriage in ruins on his return from WWII in **The Best Years of Our Lives**. Who was he?
a) Fredric March b) William Bendix c) Dana Andrews d) Alan Ladd

3) Who portrays the soda jerk who becomes involved with gangsters in the 1938 comedy, **Wide Open Faces**?
a) Joe E. Brown b) Fred Astaire c) Andy Devine d) Bob Hope

SPIES & SECRET AGENTS

1) Who plays the title role in Powell and Pressburger's 1939 thriller, **The Spy in Black**?
a) Eric Portman b) Niall MacGinnis c) Roger Livesey d) Conrad Veidt

2) In which film does secret agent, Alec Leamas, fall for East German librarian, Nan Perry?
a) *Three into Two Won't Go* b) *Brainwashed* c) *The Spy Who Came in From the Cold* d) *The Spy With My Face*

3) On whose novel was **Eye of the Needle** based, in which a German agent (Donald Sutherland), stranded on a Scottish island, is thwarted by the wife of a legless airman?
a) Frederick Forsyth b) Ken Follett c) Geoffrey Household d) Alistair MacLean

SPORTSMEN & WOMEN

1) Who plays the title role of the great American Indian athlete in **Jim Thorpe-All American**?
a) Audie Murphy b) Glenn Ford c) Burt Lancaster d) Rip Torn

2) Which 1982 film tells the story of the lesbian relationship between athletes Chris Cahill (Mariel Hemingway) and Tory Skinner (Patrice Donnelly) during training for the 1980 Olympics?
a) *Walk, Don't Run* b) *Personal Best* c) *A Million to One* d) *American Anthem*

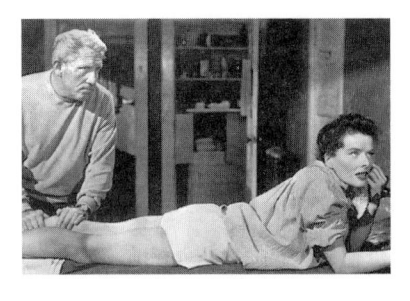

3) World class athletes, Gussie Moran and Babe Didrikson Zaharias, appeared in a 1952 George Cuckor comedy about an all-round female athlete played by Katherine Hepburn. Name the title.
a) *Pat and Mike* b) *It Should Happen to You* c) *Woman of the Year* d) *Winged Victory*

STOWAWAYS

1) Name the 1931 comedy in which the Marx brothers stow away on an ocean liner and encounter bootleggers.
a) *Monkey Business* b) *A Night at the Opera* c) *Animal Crackers* d) *Horse Feathers*

2) Puncher Roberts hides a stowaway baby on board ship in **The Baby and the Battleship**. Who was he?
a) Donald Sinden b) John Mills c) Stanley Holloway d) Bob Hope

3) Helen Hayes won a Best Supporting Actress Oscar in 1970 for her portrayal of an ageing stowaway. Name the film.
a) *Airport* b) *The Poseidon Adventure* c) *A Countess From Hong Kong* d) *Flight From Ashiya*

agitate the orphan — Roles

STRIPPERS

1) Who portrayed the ex-stripper who becomes the head teacher of a college science department in the 1960 comedy, **Sex Kittens Go to College**?
a) Mamie Van Doren b) Jayne Mansfield
c) Candice Bergen d) Marisa Pavan

2) Name the film based on the play *A Loss of Roses*, by William Inge, about an ageing stripper (Joanne Woodward) falling in love with an adolescent boy.
a) The Naked Cage b) Portrait of a Stripper
c) Through Naked Eyes d) The Stripper

3) In which film does Rita Hayworth perform a fully dressed striptease while singing 'Put the Blame on Mame'?
a) Miss Sadie Thompson b) Salome
c) Gilda d) My Gal Sal

SURGEONS

1) In 1970 he portrayed incompetent army surgeon, Major Frank Burns, in **M*A*S*H**. Who was he?
a) Tom Skerritt b) Richard Dreyfuss
c) Roger Bowen d) Robert Duvall

2) Which film features Alistair Sim as a surgeon who doesn't question the source of the bodies he uses for experiments?
a) The Anatomist b) The Body Snatchers
c) The Missing Corpse d) Foreign Body

3) In 1935 and 1954 respectively, Robert Taylor and Rock Hudson both portrayed drunken wastrel Bob Merrick, who, after blinding a woman in a car accident, studies to become a surgeon, and eventually restores her eyesight. Name the film.
a) Magnificent Obsession b) Close My Eyes
c) Some Kind of Miracle d) Journey Into Light

TAXI DRIVERS

1) Who drove **The Purple Taxi** (1977)?
a) Margaret Rutherford b) Jack Lemmon
c) Fred Astaire d) James Garner

2) In which film does Sylvester's taxi take Julia and Dudley the angel to a frozen lake?
a) And Now Tomorrow b) The Bishop's Wife
c) The Devil to pay d) Christmas Comes to Willow Creek

3) Name the 1981 film in which hard-boiled 'Cabbie' (Ernest Borgnine), drives Snake Plissken (Kurt Russell) through a ruined city.
a) Escape From New York b) Slaughter in San Francisco c) Nightmare in Chicago d) Big One: The Great Los Angeles Earthquake

TERRORISTS

1) The plan was to fly an airship over a Super Bowl audience and drop an explosive device filled with 212,000 steel darts into its midst. Name the film.
a) Black Sunday b) Silent Assassins
c) The Delta Force d) Beyond the Limit

2) In a 1988 film Natasha Richardson's character is kidnapped by the Symbionese Liberation Army. Name the title.
a) The Comfort of Strangers b) Under Siege
c) Patty Hearst d) The Amateur

3) In which film does terrorist, Hans Gruber, strike at the multinational Nakatomi Corp.?
a) Navy SEALS b) Executive Decision
c) Die Hard d) Patriot Games

TEXAS RANGERS

1) Which western features Ward Bond as Captain Samuel Clayton of the Texas Rangers?
a) The Searchers b) Santa Fe Trail
c) Kit Carson d) The Big Trail

2) Who directed the 1936 western, **The Texas Rangers**?
a) John Ford b) King Vidor c) Lewis Milestone
d) Clarence Brown

3) For what 1987 drama did Nick Nolte portray a Texas Ranger named Frank Benteen?
a) Return to Macon County b) Three Fugitives
c) North Dallas Forty d) Extreme Prejudice

TRAMPS & HOBOS

1) Who portrays the legendary hobo, 'A No.1', in Robert Aldrich's 1973 action movie, **Emperor of the North**?
a) Charles Bronson
b) Lee Marvin
c) Keith Carradine
d) Burt Reynolds

2) Name the 1987 film about two alcoholic hobos which was adapted from William Kennedy's Pulitzer Prize-winning novel.
a) The Journey of Natty Gann
b) Ironweed
c) Down and Out in Beverley Hills
d) The Littlest Hobo

The Movie Quiz Companion

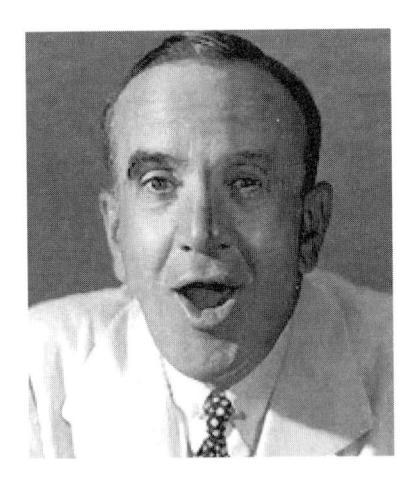

ah splotchy beer mat

3) In 1933 he portrayed 'Bumper', the 'mayor' of a collection of Central Park hobos who falls in love with an amnesiac girl (Madge Evans) in Lewis Milestone's musical comedy, **Hallelujah, I'm a Bum**. Who was he?
a) Jack Buchanan b) Al Jolson
c) Melvyn Douglas d) Ernest Thesiger

TRUCK DRIVERS

1) Who portrays the tough ex-con truck driver attempting to expose his employer's dangerous practice of forcing drivers in clapped-out trucks to drive at speed in order to meet their quotas in **Hell Drivers** (1957)?
a) Sean Connery b) Dirk Bogarde
c) Peter Finch d) Stanley Baker

2) What 1971 thriller involves businessman, Dennis Weaver, being pursued by a truck in which neither the driver, nor his motive, is ever identified?
a) Death Game b) The Driver
c) Duel d) The Truck

3) In which film does truck driver, Paul Fabrini (Humphrey Bogart), fall asleep at the wheel and lose his arm in the ensuing crash?
a) Drive a Crooked Road b) Dead End
c) They Drive By Night d) The Desperate Hours

TRUMPET PLAYERS

1) Name the 1950 musical drama, directed by Michael Curtiz, which was inspired by the life of Bix Beiderbecke.
a) Young Man With a Horn b) Dancers in the Dark c) Strike Up the Band d) A Distant Trumpet

2) In 1963 he portrayed trumpet player, Rocky Papasano, in love with Angie Rossini (Natalie Wood) in **Love With the Proper Stranger**. Who was he?
a) Russ Tamblyn b) Steve McQueen
c) Paul Newman d) Richard Conte

3) With which Spike Lee film do you associate Denzel Washington portraying a trumpet player named Bleek Gilliam?
a) Mo' Better Blues b) Jungle Fever
c) Malcolm X d) She's Gotta Have It

UNDERTAKERS

1) On being offered a free funeral, tombstone, coffin and flowers from an undertaker, John Wayne replies: "You son of a bitch, you aim to do to me what they did with John Wesley Hardin. Lay me out and parade every damn fool in the state past me at a dollar a head, half price for children, and then stuff me in a gunny sack and shovel me under." Name the film.
a) Rio Bravo b) They Were Expendable
c) The Fighting Kentuckian d) The Shootist

2) Who becames an undertaker's apprentice for Mr. & Mrs. Sowerberry?
a) Tom Jones b) Oliver Twist c) Peter Ibbetson
d) David Copperfield

3) In which film does Bonasera (Salvatore Corsitto) the undertaker seek 'justice' for his raped daughter?
a) Buona Sera, Mrs Campbell b) The Italian Connection c) The Godfather d) Goodfellas

VENTRILOQUISTS

1) Schizophrenic ventriloquist, Michael Frere (Michael Redgrave), believed his dummy was manipulating him, slowly taking over his personality and driving him insane. Name the title of this 1945 ghost story.
a) Night World b) A Double Life
c) Dead of Night d) Dummy

2) Which film features Anthony Hopkins as 'Corky' the ventriloquist?
a) Magic b) Knock on Wood
c) Devil Doll d) The Good Father

3) Lon Chaney portrayed ventriloquist, 'Prof. Echo', in 1930 - his only talkie performance. Name the title.
a) The Unholy Three b) The Big City
c) West of Zanzibar d) The Unknown

VETS

1) In 1974 he portrayed Siegfried in **All Creatures Great and Small**. Who was he?
a) Joss Ackland b) Anthony Hopkins
c) Ralph Richardson d) Christopher Plummer

2) Which film features James Stewart as a German vet in love with Margaret Sullavan during WWII?
a) The Mortal Storm b) No Time For Comedy
c) Made For Each Other d) Of Human Hearts

3) Who portrayed the callous vet, Andrew MacDhui, in Disney's **The Three Lives of Thomasina** (1964) ?
a) Richard Attenborough b) Dennis Price
c) Patrick McGoohan d) Wendell Corey

VIETNAM VETERANS

1) Vietnam vet 'Megs' Megessey, attempts to get his army buddy, Dave (Ed Harris), to confront his buried memories of the war in **Jacknife**. Who was he?
a) Dennis Hopper b) John Cazale
c) Christopher Walken d) Robert De Niro

2) Name the 1989 biopic based on the autobiography of paralysed Vietnam vet, Ron Kovic?
a) Casualties of War b) Gardens of Stone
c) Born on the Fourth of July d) Welcome Home

3) In which film does Vietnam vet, Tim Robbins, begin to suspect that he and his army buddies are part of a sinister military experiment on the battlefield after experiencing dizziness and memory loss?
a) Jacob's Ladder b) Hearts and Minds
c) Unnatural Causes d) Maya Lin: A Strong Clear Vision

VIOLINISTS

1) Joe Bonaparte has to choose between a celebrated career as a violinist or a profitable one as a prizefighter in **Golden Boy** (1939). Who was he?
a) Randolph Scott b) William Holden
c) John Clements d) Clark Gable

2) Who portrays ambitious violinist, Paul Boray's (John Garfield) wealthy patroness in **Humoresque** (1946)?
a) Bette Davis b) Lana Turner
c) Ida Lupine d) Joan Crawford

3) Name the 1946 biopic based on the life of Italian violinist Niccolo Paganini.
a) The Magic Bow b) The Italian Straw Hat
c) Intermezzo d) Duet For One

WAITERS

1) Headwaiter Carl (S.Z. Sakall aka Cuddles Sakall) attends a clandestine meeting with Victor Lazlo in 1942. Name the film.
a) The Spy in Black b) The Lady Vanishes
c) Casablanca d) Contraband

2) In 1960 he portrayed the headwaiter in **School For Scoundrels**. Who was he?
a) Alastair Sim b) Terry Thomas
c) Dennis Price d) John Le Mesurier

3) Which comedy features a waiter offering the elephantine Mr. Creosote a wafer-thin mint?
a) Meet the Applegates b) Caddyshack II
c) Monty Python's The Meaning of Life d) Airheads

WAITRESSES

1) Who portrays the housewife-turned-waitress in **Mildred Pierce**?
a) Joan Crawford b) Loretta Young
c) Greer Garson d) Ava Gardner

2) All Robert Eroica Dupea wants is toast for his breakfast, but the waitress insists toast isn't on the menu. Undeterred, Robert asks for "a chicken salad sandwich on toast, but throw the chicken away and I'll pay for the sandwich." Name the film.
a) It Happened One Night b) The Killers
c) Diner d) Five Easy Pieces

3) In which film does waitress, Carol Connelly, daily serve cantankerous romantic novelist, Melvin Lidall?
a) Frankie and Johnny b) As Good as it Gets
c) A Star is Born d) Alice's Restaurant

WITCHES

1) Joan of Arc is tried for heresy and witchcraft in the 1948 film of the same name. Who portrayed her?
a) Joan Bennett b) Rosalind Russell
c) Joan Fontaine d) Ingrid Bergman

2) Who portrayed the infamous witchhunter, Matthew Hopkins, in the 1968 horror film, **Witchfinder General** (aka The Conqueror Worm)?
a) Anthony Hopkins b) Peter Cushing
c) Vincent Price d) Oliver Reed

3) In 1939, Glinda the Good Witch of the North calmed an anxious Dorothy after her house landed on the Wicked Witch of the East freeing the Munchkins from her tyranny in **The Wizard of Oz**. Who portrayed Glinda?
a) Clara Blandick
b) Margaret Hamilton
c) Googie Withers
d) Billie Burke

SETTINGS

AIRPORTS

1) Name the airport **The V.I.P.s** (Richard Burton, Elizabeth Taylor, Margaret Rutherford, Louis Jourdan, et al.) were stranded at in Anthony Asquith's 1963 drama.
a) *London* b) *New York* c) *Paris* d) *Rome*

2) With which 1987 comedy do you associate Neal Page's (Steve Martin) flight to Chicago being diverted to Wichita airport?
a) *Leap of Faith* b) *Father of the Bride*
c) *Planes, Trains & Automobiles* d) *L.A. Story*

3) In which film did John McClane, who was waiting for his wife's flight to land at Washington's Dulles airport, become involved in a terrorist attack?
a) *Executive Decision* b) *D.O.A.*
c) *Frantic* d) *Die Hard 2*

AIRLINERS

1) Name the 1992 comedy in which a TV station offers a $1 million reward to discover the identity of 'The Angel of Flight 49', a man who rescued passengers from a crashed airliner, and then vanished into the night.
a) *Hero* b) *Hero at Large*
c) *Hero in the Family*
d) *Deadly Hero*

2) In which film was German character actor, Gert Fröbe, sucked out of an airliner's window to his death?
a) *Skyjacked* b) *Eye Witness*
c) *Goldfinger* d) *Flight From Ashiya*

3) With which 1980 film do you associate the crew and passengers of an airliner being struck with food poisoning?
a) *The Last Flight* b) *Airport*
c) *Airplane!* d) *The Disappearance of Flight 412*

AIR-RAID SHELTERS

1) The character portrayed by Greer Garson reads 'Alice in Wonderland' to her frightened children in a shelter, while overhead the Germans bombed their village. Name the film.
a) *The Way to the Stars* b) *Mrs. Miniver*
c) *Desperate Journey* d) *Home Fires*

2) Captain Roy Cronin and ballet dancer, Myra Lester, meet and fall in love in a London tube station being used nightly as an air-raid shelter. Name this great 1940 weepie.
a) *Waterloo Bridge* b) *The Clock*
c) *I'll Be Seeing You* d) *This Above All*

3) In which 1941 drama does love blossom in an air-raid shelter for wireless operator Joan Bennett, and reporter Don Ameche?
a) *Love Under Fire* b) *Confirm or Deny*
c) *Kiss the Boys Goodbye* d) *Wing and a Prayer*

ANCIENT EGYPT

1) Cecil B. De Mille made the same film set in ancient Egypt twice, in 1923 and 1956. Name the film's title.
a) *Adam's Rib* b) *The King of Kings*
c) *Cleopatra* d) *The Ten Commandments*

2) Name the Egyptian pharaoh who enslaves the Hebrews in Cecil B. DeMille's **The Ten Commandments**.
a) *Ptolemy I* b) *Amenhotep IV*
c) *Seti I* d) *Rameses I*

3) Who played the title role in Michael Curtiz's 1954 drama, **The Egyptian**?
a) *Edmund Purdom* b) *Victor Mature*
c) *Michael Wilding* d) *Ray Milland*

ANCIENT GREECE

1) Rodgers & Hart's Broadway musical, **The Boys From Syracuse**, was adapted for the movies in 1940. Set in ancient Greece, what Shakespeare play was it based on?

94

a) The Comedy of Errors b) Troilus and Cressida
c) Cymbeline d) Coriolanus

2) **The Three Hundred Spartans** (1962) hopelessly but courageously defended their country at the Battle of Thermopylae in 480 B.C. Who were they fighting?
a) the Assyrians b) the Persians
c) the Babylonians d) the Egyptians

3) Which 1963 mythological adventure, directed by Don Chaffey, features the bat-winged Harpies?
a) Hercules Unchained b) Ulysses
c) Athena d) Jason and the Argonauts

ANCIENT ROME

1) Name the 1970 film, directed by Federico Fellini, based on a poem written in ancient Rome during Nero's reign.
a) Fellini Satyricon b) Spirits of the Dead
c) Fellini's Roma d) Amarcord

2) In which ancient Rome saga does Buster Keaton portray Erronius, who is searching for his lost children?
a) Androcles and the Lion
b) A Funny Thing Happened on the Way to the Forum c) Roman Scandals
d) Julius Caesar

3) Which film features Steeve Reeves and Gordon Scott as Romulus and Remus?
a) Duel of the Titans b) The Arena
c) Fury of the Pagans d) Duel of Champions

APARTMENTS

1) Who directed **The Apartment**?
a) Robert Wise b) Sydney Pollack
c) Robert Aldrich d) Billy Wilder

2) In which film does Dr. Alec Harvey take his lover to a friend's apartment for a night of passion which never actually happens?
a) Love is a Many Splendored Thing
b) An Affair to Remember
c) Brief Encounter
d) Roman Holiday

3) Disturbed Belgian manicurist, Carol Ledoux, begins hallucinating in her sister's apartment and imagines walls cracking, lights going off and on, and a man reflected in a mirror. Name this 1965 horror film.
a) The Haunting b) Repulsion
c) Carnival of Souls d) Paranoiac

"ASYLUMS" & "MENTAL" INSTITUTIONS

1) Name the Sam Fuller film in which a journalist becomes admitted to a "mental" institution as an inmate in order to expose a murderer.
a) Shockproof b) The Naked Kiss
c) Scandal Sheet d) Shock Corridor

2) Who portrays the young bride who is committed to a "mental institution" for treatment in Anatole Litvak's 1948 drama, **The Snake Pit**?
a) Joan Crawford b) Joan Fontaine
c) Carole Lombard d) Olivia De Havilland

3) For what 1944 spy mystery does Ray Milland play a man recently released from an insane "asylum" for murdering his wife?
a) A Man Alone b) Ministry of Fear
c) The Man Who Played God d) Untamed

BAKERIES

1) In what film, directed by Martin Ritt, does Jane Fonda portray a bakery worker?
a) Coming Home b) Stanley & Iris
c) Steelyard Blues d) Hurry Sundown

2) With which comedy do you associate a group of amateur Glaswegian burglars doping the driver of a bakery truck in order to steal his vehicle for a robbery?
a) That Sinking Feeling b) Shoot to Kill
c) Comfort and Joy
d) Laughter in the Dark

3) Which film features Ted Danson portraying an ex-convict who is planning a robbery to finance his own bakery business?
a) Getting Even With Dad b) Creepshow
c) A Fine Mess d) Our Family Business

BALCONIES

1) With which film do you associate a plant pot being pushed from a balcony and falling on to the head of Iris Henderson, when it was really intended for Miss Froy?
a) Night Must Fall b) The Man in Grey
c) The Wicked Lady d) The Lady Vanishes

2) Dancer Victoria Page commits suicide by leaping from a balcony into the path of the Nice Express. Name the film.

The Movie Quiz Companion

a) *Limelight* b) *Waterloo Bridge*
c) *The Red Shoes* d) *The League of Gentlemen*

3) Unbeknown to lawyer Atticus Finch, his young children, Jem and Scout, were sitting in the courtroom balcony watching him defending a black man charged with rape. Name the film.
a) *Huckleberry Finn* b) *Anatomy of a Murder*
c) *To Kill a Mockingbird* d) *The Accused*

BALLROOMS

1) Which 1977 film, directed by James Ivory, tells the story of three people who dance at a famous New York City ballroom?
a) *Roseland* b) *One is a Lonely Number*
c) *Dance Hall* d) *Dance With a Stranger*

2) Who directed **They Shoot Horses, Don't They?**, about a 1930s dance marathon in an end of the pier ballroom?
a) Stanley Kramer b) Robert Altman c) Sydney Pollack d) Don Siegel

3) In which film does Frank Slade dance the tango with a stranger named Donna in the ballroom of the Waldorf Hotel?
a) *Dancing in the Dark* b) *Grand Hotel*
c) *A Soldier's Story* d) *Scent of a Woman*

BANKS

1) Which film re-enacted John Dillinger's gesture at Greencastle Bank, Indiana, when he allowed a farmer to keep his withdrawn cash during a robbery in 1933?
a) *Dog Day Afternoon* b) *High Sierra*
c) *The Wild Bunch* d) *Bonnie and Clyde*

2) What was W.C. Fields' character name in the 1940 comedy, **The Bank Dick**?
a) Egbert Souse "pronounced soo-zay, accent grave over the e" b) Harold Bissonette
c) A. Pismo Clam d) Elmer Prettywillie

3) On Christmas Eve Uncle Billy (Thomas Mitchell) absent-mindedly mislays $8,000 in company funds somewhere in the Bedford Falls bank. Name the film.
a) *Nothing Sacred* b) *It's a Wonderful Life*
c) *Heaven Help Us* d) *No Way Out*

BANQUETS & FEASTS

1) On whose short story was the 1987 Danish drama, **Babette's Feast** based?
a) Isak Dinesen b) Henrik Ibsen
c) Knut Hamsen d) August Strindberg

2) Who directed the 1993 comedy drama, **The Wedding Banquet**, in which a gay man tries to deceive his parents by faking his own wedding?
a) Jonathan Demme
b) Ang Lee
c) Michael Radford
d) Mike Nichols

3) When Tita prepares a wedding cake for her sister who is marrying her lover, her tears drip into the cake mix, which causes the feasting guests to weep. Name this 1992 romantic drama, directed by Mexican director, Alfonso Arau.
a) *Gas Food Lodging*
b) *Eat Drink Man Woman*
c) *Like Water for Chocolate*
d) *The Wedding Party*

BARGES

1) With which film do you associate Jean (Jean Dasté), a barge captain who lives on board with his wife Juliette (Dita Parlo), who tires of the monotonous life on the canal and longs to see the bright lights of Paris?
a) *L'Atalante* b) *A Day in the Country*
c) *Sailor's Lady* d) *Bondu Saved From Drowning*

2) Who portrayed 'Birdie', the old man who lives on a barge in the 1955 thriller, **Night of the Hunter**, who sees Willa Harper (Shelley Winters) submerged in the river in her car with her throat slashed "like another mouth"?
a) Thomas Mitchell b) Lionel Barrymore
c) Lon Chaney Jr. d) James Gleason

3) **Cleopatra** sailed up the Nile aboard her stately barge in Cecil B. De Mille's 1934 historical drama. Who portrayed the Queen of Egypt?
a) Claudette Colbert b) Mary Pickford
c) Myrna Loy d) Jean Arthur

BATHROOMS

1) In which 1941 fantasy does boxer, Joe Pendleton (Robert Montgomery), take over the body of a murdered multi-millionaire inside a steamy bathroom?
a) *Rage in Heaven* b) *Night Must Fall*
c) *Heaven Can Wait*
d) *Here Comes Mr. Jordan*

riddles of fame

Settings

2) With which film do you associate real estate secretary, Marion Crane, meeting a horrific death in a bathroom?
a) The Boston Strangler b) Murder, Inc.
c) Psycho d) Detour

3) Name the actor who kept his acting awards, which included a Best Supporting Oscar for **Topkapi**, in a glass case in his bathroom, because it was the only location in his house where he could contemplate his accomplishments without seeming egotistical.
a) Robert Morley b) Maximilian Schell
c) Peter Ustinov d) Walter Matthau

BATTLEFIELDS

1) Which film tells the true story of an American soldier during WWI's Meuse-Argonne offensive who captured 132 enemy soldiers single-handedly?
a) Over the Top b) All Quiet on the Western Front
c) Sergeant York d) Today We Live

2) Name the movie which was based on a famous battle and shot on the actual battlefield where both sides lost 43,000 men in three days.
a) Gettysburg b) Anzio
c) Battle of the Bulge d) Waterloo

3) Mel Gibson's **Braveheart** chronicles the life of that great champion of Scotland's independence, William Wallace. On which battlefield was he defeated by the English in 1298?

a) Stirling Bridge b) Falkirk
c) Culloden d) Bannockburn

BEACHES

1) On whose novel was Stanley Kramer's 1959 nuclear war drama, **On the Beach**, based?
a) Arthur C. Clarke b) Nevil Shute
c) Iras Levin d) Cornelius Ryan

2) Army base commander's gregarious wife, Karen Holmes, has a secret affair with Sgt. Warden (Burt Lancaster) and the two make memorable love on the beach in Fred Zinnemann's **From Here to Eternity** (1953). Who was she?
a) Gloria Grahame b) Grace Kelly
c) Deborah Kerr d) Donna Reed

3) Name the beach location in the 1994 comedy drama, **Bhaji on the Beach**?
a) Scarborough b) Blackpool
c) Margate d) Morecambe

BEAUTY CONTESTS

1) Carnelle Scott, a local fish-gutter whose nickname is 'Miss Hot Tamale', decides to compete in the Fourth of July beauty pageant in the 1989 romantic comedy, **Miss Firecracker**. Who was she?
a) Mary Steenburgen
b) Winona Ryder
c) Holly Hunter d) Sharon Stone

2) Name the beauty contest featured in Michael Ritchie's 1975 comedy, **Smile**?
a) Miss America b) Young American Miss c) Miss All-American d) Rose Bowl Parade Beauty Contest

3) Joan Collins made her film debut in a 1951 comedy as a contestant in a beauty contest. Name the film.
a) Lady Godiva Rides Again b) The Love Lottery
c) The Belles of St. Trinians d) A Kid For Two Farthings

BEDROOMS

1) In which film was cab driver and matchmaker, Michaeleen Flynn, confronted with a splintered bedroom door with a demolished bed inside the morning after a wedding?
a) How Green Was My Valley b) Lucky Jim
c) The Quiet Man d) As Long as They're Happy

2) Which 1972 comedy features Jack, the 14th Earl of Gurney (Peter O'Toole), taking Grace (Carolyn Seymour) into his bedroom on a tricycle?
a) Murphy's War b) The Ruling Class
c) Rosebud d) Man Friday

3) With which film do you associate a bedroom containing Bo Peep and Slinky Dog?
a) Hans Christian Andersen b) The Borrowers
c) Toy Story d) Tom Thumb

BOARDING SCHOOLS

1) In the 1944 version of **Jane Eyre** she portrayed sickly pupil, Helen Hayes, who dies due to negligence at Mr. Brocklehurst's boarding school.
Who was she?
a) Elizabeth Taylor
b) Joan Fontaine
c) Peggy Ann Garner
d) Petula Clark

2) Who directed the French thriller, **Les Diaboliques** (1954), set in a boy's boarding school where the cold-hearted headmaster's murdered body disappears?
a) Henri-Georges Clouzot
b) Claude Chabrol
c) Jacques Demy
d) Max Ophuls

The Movie Quiz Companion

3) In 1968 a director used his old boarding school (Cheltenham College) as the location for a groundbreaking film about class, homoeroticism, sexual repression and violent revolution in an English public school. Name the title.
a) School For Scoundrels b) Black Sunday
c) School Ties d) if...

BOWLING ALLEYS

1) In which film does Joe Pesci's character own a bowling alley in Jersey City?
a) Casino b) Dear Mr. Wonderful
c) A Bronx Tale d) Casino

2) Northside gangleader, Gaffney, was gunned down in a bowling alley in Howard Hawks' 1932 crime drama, **Scarface**. Who was he?
a) Paul Muni b) James Cagney
c) Humphrey Bogart d) Boris Karloff

3) Which film features Walter and 'The Dude' as regular bowling buddies?
a) The Flintstones b) The Big Lebowski
c) Hudson Hawk d) The Muppet Movie

BRIDGES

1) In which thriller does Kim Novak's character attempt suicide beneath San Francisco's Golden Gate Bridge?
a) The Man With the Golden Arm b) Bell, Book and Candle c) Vertigo d) Middle of the Night

2) Name the country the filmmakers of **The Bridge on the River Kwai** chose as their location to construct the replica bridge.
a) Laos b) Borneo c) The Phillipines d) Ceylon

3) On whose novel was the 1944 drama, **The Bridge of San Luis Rey**, based?
a) Thornton Wilder b) Scott Fitzgerald
c) Stephen Crane d) Truman Capote

BROTHELS

1) Miss Mona ran **The Best Little Whorehouse in Texas** (1982). Who was she?
a) Bette Midler b) Dolly Parton
c) Mamie Van Doren d) Joan Collins

2) The production Code office wouldn't allow a brothel scene to be filmed in a 1941 classic, so the scene took place in the *Inquirer* newsroom, complete with dancing girls instead. Name the film.
a) Exclusive Story b) The Front Page
c) His Girl Friday d) Citizen Kane

3) Name Lizzie Borden's 1986 film about a day in the life of a Manhattan brothel.
a) Working Girls b) Risky Business
c) The Men's Club d) Bad Girls

BUILDING SITES

1) In which film did LAPD's 'Hat Squad', led by Nick Nolte, investigate a girl's body discovered buried on a construction site?
a) Extreme Prejudice b) Return to Macon County
c) Mulholland Falls d) Three Fugitives

2) Name the 1991 Ken Loach film which is set around a London building site.
a) Riff Raff b) Raining Stones
c) Ladybird, Ladybird d) Poor Cow

3) Ex-IRA man, Fergus, works on a building site while searching for a dead soldier's girlfriend in **The Crying Game**. Who was he?
a) Gabriel Byrne b) Stephen Rea
c) Gary Oldman d) Colm Meaney

CAMPFIRES

1) In which film does Gordie tell his friends, who were gathered around a campfire, the story of 'Lardass' and the blueberry-pie eating contest?
a) Stand By Me b) Parent Trap
c) Bigfoot d) Running on Empty

2) With which film do you associate Ethan Edwards (John Wayne) trying to turn a small campfire into a bonfire, making sleeping Martin Pawley (Jeffrey Hunter) a conspicuous target for an approaching ambush?
a) True Grit b) Hondo
c) Red River d) The Searchers

3) What 1986 comedy involves cowboys sitting around a campfire for a sing-song, and their horses singing along too?
a) Three Amigos b) Blazing Saddles
c) Lust in the Dust d) Lightning

CARAVANS

1) Which 1954 drama features 'Zampano the strongman' pulling his caravan around the country by motorcycle?
a) The Greatest Show on Earth b) Without Pity
c) Vampire Circus d) La Strada

2) In the 1938 film **The Adventures of Robin Hood**, Robin (Errol Flynn) waylays Maid Marian's caravan in Sherwood Forest. Who portrayed Marian?
a) Joan Fontaine b) Vivien Leigh
c) Merle Oberon d) Olivia De Havilland

3) Who portrayed Rowlie, the tinker who gives Lassie a ride in his caravan during her arduous journey back to Joe Carraclough in the 1943 adventure, **Lassie Come Home**?
a) Edmund Gwenn b) Nigel Bruce
c) Arthur Shields d) Henry Travers

CAROUSELS & MERRY-GO-ROUNDS

1) With which Hitchcock thriller do you associate the operator of a merry-go-round having a heart attack and falling onto the controls which increases its speed and sends it wildly out of control?
a) Saboteur b) Strangers on a Train
c) To Catch a Thief d) Young and Innocent

2) Who portrayed the uproarious carousel barker in Henry King's 1956 musical, **Carousel**?
a) Gene Kelly b) Stubby Kaye
c) Gordon MacRae d) Donald O'Connor

3) In which Disney musical comedy do carousel horses magically gallop off across the countryside?
a) Mary Poppins b) Babes in Toyland
c) The Sword in the Stone d) Miracle of the White Stallions

CAR PARKS / PARKING LOTS

1) What 1971 crime thriller involves Cliff Brumby (Bryan Mosley) being thrown to his death from the top of a multi-storey car park?
a) Deadfall b) Gumshoe
c) The Long Good Friday d) Get Carter

2) In which Ridley Scott film was actress, Geena Davis's character, almost raped in a parking lot?
a) Someone to Watch Over Me b) Black Rain
c) Thelma & Louise d) Blade Runner

3) Unnerved by death threats received on anonymous postcards, Griffin finally narrows the culprit down to a writer he once spurned. Tracking him down, he follows him to a parking lot and kills him. Name the 1992 film.
a) Lethal Weapon 3 b) The Player
c) Red Rock West d) The Client

CASTLES

1) On whose novel was Rudolf Noelte's 1968 drama, **The Castle**, based?
a) Franz Kafka b) Bram Stoker
c) Edgar Allan Poe d) Victor Hugo

2) What fate awaits visitors to Count Drago's (Christopher Lee) **Castle of the Living Dead** (1964)?
a) mummification b) decapitation
c) starvation d) suffocation

3) In which film does Scotland's Glourie Castle end up in Sunnymede, Florida?
a) Brigadoon b) Castle of the Living Dead
c) The Maze d) The Ghost Goes West

CATTLE DRIVES

1) Name Howard Hawks' 1948 masterpiece about an epic cattle drive to Abilene, which was based on the novel *The Chisolm Trail*, by Borden Chase.
a) The Big Sky b) The Road to Glory
c) El Dorado d) Red River

2) In which western does range boss, Billy 'Green' Bush, take teenager Billy Grimes on a tough cattle drive which moulds him into a 'man'?
a) The Culpepper Cattle Company b) Blazing Saddles c) The Tall Men d) The Last Sunset

3) Which film features Joel McCrea as the boss of a cattle drive out for revenge on the cattlemen who are responsible for his imprisonment?
a) Cattle Empire b) Canyon River
c) The Cowboys d) Cattle Queen of Montana

CAVES

1) Kalibanos (Raul Julia), is a Greek goatherd who lives in a cave in a 1982 adaptation of a Shakespeare play. Name the title.
a) The Tempest b) A Midsummer Night's Dream
c) The Taming of the Shrew d) As You Like It

2) Which film features the Marabar Caves?
a) The Lord of the Rings b) The Count of Monte Cristo c) A Passage to India d) The Clan of the Cave Bear

3) What 1985 adventure involves a group of kids searching the caves of the Oregon coastline for the buried treasure of a 17th-century pirate called 'One-Eyed Willie'?
a) A Far Off Place b) The Goonies
c) The Princess Bride d) Journey of Hope

CELLARS

1) Devlin and Alicia make a clandestine visit to the wine cellar of Nazi, Alexander Sebastian in 1946, and discover a strange ore in some of the bottles. Name the thriller.
a) The Narrow Margin
b) Suspicion
c) The House on Telegraph Hill
d) Notorious

2) Which 1939 film features a farmer and his wife and their three farmhands, Zeke, Hickory and Hunk, sheltering in a storm cellar from the threat of a tornado?
a) Seven Brides For Seven Brothers
b) The Grapes of Wrath
c) The Wizard of Oz
d) Of Mice and Men

The Movie Quiz Companion

3) Who did Terence Stamp keep locked up in his cellar in the 1965 drama, **The Collector**?
a) Jane Birkin b) Samantha Eggar
c) Vanessa Redgrave d) Susan Hampshire

CHURCHES

1) Dr. Clayton Forrester calmly awaits the end of the world in a small church in the finale of **War of the Worlds** (1953). Who was he?
a) Michael Rennie b) Woody Strode
c) Dan Duryea d) Gene Barry

2) In the isolated English village of Bramley End, villagers were imprisoned in the local church by German paratroopers disguised as Royal Engineers. Name the title of this 1942 Ealing drama.
a) Went the Day Well?
b) Village of the Damned
c) Cornered d) The Imposter

3) The western townspeople of Hadleyville turn their back on their sheriff when he pleads for their help in the local church in 1952. Name the film.
a) Day of the Outlaw b) The Big Country
c) Arrowhead d) High Noon

CIRCUSES

1) Who directed the 1952 circus drama, **The Greatest Show on Earth**?
a) Michael Curtiz b) Cecil B. De Mille
c) William Wyler d) George Roy Hill

2) Which 1967 romantic drama chronicles the doomed relationship between a circus girl and a cavalry officer, with whom she eventually commits suicide?
a) Elvira Madigan b) The Duellists
c) The Life and Death of Colonel Blimp d) Polly of the Circus

3) Name Tod Browning's 1932 circus film which so repulsed audiences it remained unseen in Britain for over thirty years.
a) Circus of Horrors b) The Strong Man
c) Freaks d) Psycho Circus

CINEMAS

1) In which 1957 comedy did Matt and Jean Spenser (Bill Travers & Virginia McKenna) inherit The Bijou Cinema?
a) Starting Over b) Family Pictures
c) Dancers in the Dark d) The Smallest Show on Earth

2) **The Picture Show Man** (1977) was based on the memoirs of travelling showman, Lyle Penn, who travelled far and wide screening pictures to remote communities in the 1920s. In what country is it set?
a) Canada b) Australia
c) New Zealand d) South Africa

3) Name the 1993 comedy in which the seats of an American movie theater are wired with electrical buzzers and dry ice vapour is blown over the audience during a screening of 'Mant' - all gimmicks which were originally used by eccentric director, William Castle.
a) Matinee b) Movie Movie
c) Fright Night d) Silent Movie

CLASSROOMS

1) With which film do you associate a classroom of students standing on their desks to protest at the dismissal of their English teacher?
a) The Blackboard Jungle b) Up the Down Staircase c) Dead Poets Society d) Gregory's Girl

2) In which film does Wilkes (Michael Horden) begin his Latin class with the address: "Now, you spotty and unpleasant denizens of pond life, we will apply ourselves to Caesar's Gallic Wars."?
a) Tom Brown's Schooldays b) A Yank at Oxford
c) Boys Will Be Boys d) School For Scoundrels

3) Why was schoolteacher, Bertram T. Cates (Dick York) arrested in his Hillsboro classroom in Stanley Kramer's 1960 drama, **Inherit the Wind**?
a) teaching satanism b) teaching Darwin's theory of evolution c) promoting homosexuality
d) inciting treason

CLIFFS

1) Against impossible odds, Captain Mallory (Gregory Peck) and his hand-picked team scale the cliffs on a strategic WWII Agean Island to reach their objective. Name the 1961 film.
a) Ill Met By Moonlight
b) The Valley of Decision
c) Pork Chop Hill
d) The Guns of Navarone

2) Jim (James Dean) is challenged by a gangleader (Corey Allen) to a 'chickie run' in which both drive cars towards a cliff edge, and the first one to jump out is a coward in **Rebel Without a Cause**. The gangleader of course loses, and pays with his life. What is his nickname?
a) Moose b) Crunch
c) Buzz d) Plato

100

3) Which film features Bette Davis' and Paul Henreid's South American taxi accidentally reversing over a cliff?
a) Between Two Worlds b) Now Voyager
c) The Letter d) In This Our Life

COCKPITS

1) "Eastwood occupies the cockpit, surrounded by video screens and computer displays of flight patterns and missile trajectories, it looks as if Dirty Harry has died and gone to Atari heaven." Can you identify the Clint Eastwood movie critic Roger Ebert is discussing?
a) Pink Cadillac b) Escape From Alcatraz
c) Heartbreak Ridge d) Firefox

2) With which Harrison Ford film do you associate a snake wrapping itself around him in an aeroplane cockpit?
a) Return of the Jedi b) Blade Runner
c) The Mosquito Coast d) Raiders of the Lost Ark

3) What 1946 film involves David Niven in the cockpit of a burning bomber surrounded by his dead crew and about to bail out with no parachute?
a) The Way Ahead b) The Dawn Patrol
c) A Matter of Life and Death d) The Real Glory

COLLEGES & CAMPUSES

1) Who portrayed the title role in the 1949 comedy, **Mother is a Freshman**?
a) Shirley Maclaine b) Loretta Young
c) Katherine Hepburn d) Peggy Ashcroft

2) Which film features a campus game where students have to 'kill' each other with lumps of paint?
a) Gotcha! b) Hot Paint
c) Higher Learning d) House Party 2

3) Who was working her way through college in the 1952 musical comedy, **She's Working Her Way Through College**?
a) Virginia Mayo b) Norma Shearer
c) Myrna Loy d) Susan Hayward

CONVENTS

1) Deloris, a Reno lounge singer, accidentally witnesses a murder, and is hidden under the witness protection program in a convent. Name the film.
a) Sacred Hearts b) The Convent
c) Sister Act d) Queen Kelly

2) In which 1985 mystery does a nun become pregnant in a convent?
a) The Devil is a Woman b) Therese
c) Agnes of God d) The Dead

3) The lover of the character portrayed by Clark Gable in Victor Fleming's 1938 romance, **The White Sister**, enters a convent thinking he has died in the war. Who played his lover?
a) Helen Hayes b) Claudette Colbert
c) Mary Astor d) Myrna Loy

COURTROOMS

1) In which crime drama was Al Pacino called to testify in the courtroom of the Senate Investigative Committee?
a) The Insider b) Serpico
c) City Hall d) The Godfather Part II

2) Who directed the classic courtroom drama, **12 Angry Men**?
a) Sidney Lumet b) John Schlesinger
c) Howard Hawks d) Billy Wilder

3) With which 1949 comedy do you associate husband and wife lawyers Spencer Tracy and Katherine Hepburn on opposing sides of a courtroom battle?
a) Woman of the Year b) Guess Who's Coming to Dinner c) Adam's Rib d) Pat and Mike

CRYPTS & TOMBS

1) Who directed the 1966 horror film, **The Tomb of Ligeia**?
a) Terence Fisher b) George Romero
c) Seth Holt d) Roger Corman

2) In which film does Gary Cooper have a powerful desire to see Grant's Tomb?
a) Mr. Deeds Goes to Town b) A Farewell to Arms
c) The General Died at Dawn d) The Pride of the Yankees

3) Workmen inspecting a subway system dig through to an underground crypt decorated with beautiful frescoes in a 1972 Federico Fellini film. Name the title.
a) Spirits of the Dead b) The Clowns
c) La Dolce Vita d) Fellini's Roma

DAMS

1) In which 1939 film do Senator Joseph Paine (Claude Rains) and Governor Hubert Hopper (Guy Kibbee) make secret plans to

The Movie Quiz Companion

deviant chews owls

use a site earmarked for a boy's camp to build a purposeless dam for their own financial reward?
a) Washington Story b) Behind Locked Doors c) The Senator Was Indiscreet d) Mr. Smith Goes to Washington

2) What 1985 film involves construction engineer, Bill Markham (Powers Boothe), blowing up a South American dam to protect the rain forest and the Indians it threatens to destroy?
a) The Steel Jungle b) The Emerald Forest c) Blown Away d) Spoilers of the Forest

3) Who portrayed Wing Commander Guy Gibson who led 617 Squadron, **The Dambusters**, in the raid which successfully breached the Mohne and Eder dams using Barnes Wallis's bouncing mine in May 1943?
a) Michael Redgrave b) Robert Shaw c) Richard Todd d) Richard Attenborough

DANCE HALLS

1) Who sings to Phileas Fogg (David Niven), Passepartout (Cantinflas) and Princess Aouda (Shirley MacLaine) in the Barbary Coast dance hall in the 1956 adventure, **Around the World in 80 Days**?
a) Marlene Dietrich b) Sophie Tucker c) Shirley Bassey d) Lena Horne

2) Name the 1979 film, directed by Steven Spielberg, in which The Anderson Sisters (Andrews Sisters lookalikes) sing in a WWII dance hall.
a) The Sugarland Express b) Back to the Future c) 1941 d) Raiders of the Lost Ark

3) Shy Bronx bachelor, Ernest Borgnine, meets a girl at a local dance hall whom his buddies describe as a 'dog'. Ignoring these insulting remarks and his mother's hostility to the girl, he proposes marriage. Name the film.
a) The Best Things in Life Are Free b) Run For Cover c) Marty d) The Square Jungle

DEATH CELLS

1) Father Jerry Connelly (Pat O'Brien) persuades small-time hood Rocky Sullivan (James Cagney) to turn "yellow" in his death cell seconds before his execution, and die a coward's death in **Angels With Dirty Faces**. Why?
a) for his dying mother b) to end the hero-worship of the street kids c) to ensure his place in heaven d) to expose the horror of capital punishment

2) In his last moments Frank Chambers, who is wrongly accused of murdering his girlfriend, but is guilty of another murder, makes his peace with God and speaks to a priest in **The Postman Always Rings Twice** (1946), saying: "You know, there's something about this which is like expecting a letter you're just crazy to get, and you hang around the front door for fear you might not hear 'em ring. You never realize that he always rings twice—The truth is you always hear 'em ring the second time, even if you're way out in the back yard." Who was he?
a) Paul Muni b) John Garfield c) Fred MacMurray d) Joel McCrea

3) Charles Darnay is plucked from the death cell at the eleventh hour in 1917, 1935, 1958, and 1980. Name the film.
a) Les Miserables b) The Count of Monte Cristo c) A Tale of Two Cities d) Phantom of the Opera

DEEP SOUTH

1) In 1958 Paul Newman married Joanne Woodward; the same year they appeared in their first film together, which was based on a collection of William Faulkner stories. Name the title.
a) The Long Hot Summer b) The Southerner c) The Sound and the Fury d) The Tarnished Angels

2) On whose play was Richard Brooks' 1962 Southern drama, **Sweet Bird of Youth**, based?
a) Tay Garnett b) Maxwell Anderson c) Truman Capote d) Tennessee Williams

3) In 1938 he played Buck Cantrell, who defends the honour of Southern belle, Julie Morrison (Bette Davis) in William Wyler's **Jezebel**. Who was he?
a) Leslie Howard b) George Brent c) Joseph Cotton d) Warner Baxter

DEPARTMENT STORES

1) Name the title of Norman Wisdom's 1953 film debut which is set in a department store.
a) Who's Minding the Store b) All I Want For Christmas c) The Big Store d) Trouble in Store

2) In which 1949 film does Robert Mitchum portray a department store toy salesman who falls in love with customer Janet Leigh?

102

afternoon hit habit

a) Holiday Affair b) When Strangers Marry
c) Till the End of Time d) My Forbidden Past

3) Who poses as a humble sales assistant in his own department store to investigate the root of unrest among his employees in the 1941 comedy, **The Devil and Miss Jones**?
a) Monty Wooley b) Thomas Mitchell
c) Charles Coburn d) Frank Morgan

DESERT ISLANDS

1) Who directed **Castaway**, based on Lucy Irvine's best-seller about a year on a desert island?
a) Mark Robson b) Nicolas Roeg
c) Peter Weir d) Mike Figgis

2) Who was marooned on a desert island with pampered heiress, Carole Lombard, in the 1934 musical comedy, **We're Not Dressing**?
a) Mario Lanza b) Jack Buchanan
c) Louis Calhern d) Bing Crosby

3) With which film do you associate Ralph, Jack, Roger, Simon, and twins Sam and Eric being stranded on a desert island?
a) In Search of the Castaways b) Swiss Family Robinson c) Lord of the Flies d) The Island of Dr. Moreau

DESERTS

1) On whose novel was Bernardo Bertolucci's 1990 desert drama, **The Sheltering Sky**, based?
a) P.C. Wren b) William Styron
c) Albert Camus d) Paul Bowles

2) Who portrayed Field Marshal Rommel in both **The Desert Fox** (1951) and **The Desert Rats** (1953)?
a) Stewart Granger b) James Mason
c) Erich von Strobeim d) Robert Hossein

3) Name the desert drama, starring Victor McLaglen, directed by John Ford in 1934.
a) The Lost Patrol b) An Arabian Adventure
c) Desert Fury d) Oasis

DEVIL'S ISLAND

1) Who, in the 1937 biopic **The Life of Emile Zola**, played the title role of the character who championed the cause of the Jewish scapegoat, army captain Alfred Dreyfus, who was sentenced to life imprisonment on Devil's Island for treason?
a) Edward G. Robinson b) Walter Pidgeon
c) Robert Donat d) Paul Muni

2) Which film features Devil's Island escapee, Henri Charrìere ?
a) Passage to Marseille b) Condemned
c) Papillon d) Devil's Island

3) With which Tod Browning film do you associate Lionel Barrymore escaping from Devil's Island?
a) The Unholy Three b) The Devil-Doll
c) Inside Job d) The Black Bird

DINERS

1) In which film does movie director, Joel McCrea, meet aspiring actress, Veronica Lake, in a diner?
a) Dead End b) The Glass Key
c) Sullivan's Travels d) Hold Back the Dawn

2) Can you identify the city which was the setting for Barry Levinson's 1982 comedy drama, **Diner**?
a) Baltimore b) Boston c) Cleveland d) Pittsburgh

3) What 1946 crime thriller opens with two contract killers entering a diner and asking the proprietor if he knows the whereabouts of 'the Swede' (Burt Lancaster)?
a) The Killers b) Out of the Past
c) I Walk Alone d) Criss Cross

DOCKS & WATERFRONTS

1) Journalist Malcolm Johnson published a series of articles in the New York Sun exposing waterfront crime, which subsequently became the inspiration for a 1954 film. Name its title.
a) On the Waterfront b) Rumble on the Docks
c) Pier 13 d) I Cover the Waterfront

2) Name the Californian dock which was the setting for the 1982 drama, based on the John Steinbeck novel, **Cannery Row**.
a) Santa Cruz b) Monterey
c) Santa Barbara d) San Francisco

3) Which 1963 horror classic was set around the waterfront town of Bodega Bay?
a) Creature From the Black Lagoon b) The She Beast c) The Birds d) Reptilicus

EARTH'S CORE

1) In which 1951 science fiction film do a geologist and his colleagues burrow towards the earth's core in a mechanical digger called a 'Cyclotram'?
a) The World of Tomorrow b) Unknown World
c) Endless Descent d) Digger

2) In 1959 he portrayed expedition leader, Professor Oliver Lindenbrook, in **Journey to the Center of the Earth**. Who was he?
a) Peter Ustinov b) Peter Cushing
c) Rock Hudson d) James Mason

3) Actor and singer, Pat Boone, visited the earth's core in a film directed by Henry Levin. Name the title.

The Movie Quiz Companion

heathenish bus folk revolted

a) *No Escape* b) *Until the End of the World*
c) *The Earth Dies Screaming* d) *Journey to the Center of the Earth*

ELEVATORS

1) In the final scene of the **Maltese Falcon**, Brigid O'Shaughnessy enters an elevator with the police after Sam Spade "turns her over" for the murder of his partner. Who was she?
a) *Veronica Lake* b) *Joan Crawford*
c) *Barbara Stanwyck* d) *Mary Astor*

2) With which film do you associate C.C. Baxter (Jack Lemmon) falling in love with elevator operator Fran Kubelik (Shirley MacLaine)?
a) *Can-Can* b) *Irma La Douce*
c) *The Apartment* d) *Bell, Book, and Candle*

3) Which 1987 thriller features lawyer, Dan Gallagher, making passionate love to beguiling blonde, Alex Forest, in an elevator?
a) *Fatal Attraction* b) *Jagged Edge*
c) *Legal Eagles* d) *Golden Girl*

EMBASSIES

1) Name the 1948 thriller, directed by Carol Reed, set in the French Embassy in London.
a) *The Ambassador's Daughter* b) *The Man Between* c) *The Fallen Idol* d) *Climbing High*

2) Rene Gallimard, an attaché at the French embassy in Peking, has a long-running affair with a Peking Opera star who somehow managed to disguise the fact that she was a man. Name the film.
a) *China Moon* b) *M. Butterfly*
c) *Farewell, My Concubine* d) *Peking Opera Blues*

3) Harrison Carter MacWhite is resident ambassador at the U.S. Embassy in Sarkhan in **The Ugly American**. Who was he?
a) *William Holden* b) *Burl Ives*
c) *Burt Lancaster* d) *Marlon Brando*

FACTORIES

1) What film connects Albert Finney and Nottingham's Raleigh bicycle factory?
a) *This Sporting Life* b) *Saturday Night and Sunday Morning* c) *Two for the Road* d) *The Loneliness of the Long Distance Runner*

2) Name the title of Frank Launder and Sidney Gilliat's WWII drama about the lives of aircraft factory workers coping with the stress of war.
a) *Millions Like Us* b) *So Well Remembered*
c) *The Divided Heart* d) *Chance of a Lifetime*

3) With which film do you associate Bette Midler and Lily Tomlin working in a local factory which manufactures porch swings?
a) *Big Business* b) *Nashville*
c) *All of Me* d) *Ruthless People*

FAIRGROUNDS & CARNIVALS

1) Lovers Annie Laurie Starr (Peggy Cummins) and Bart Tare (John Dall) first meet at a carnival sharpshooting sideshow, and graduate to robbing banks. Name the title of this stylish 1949 crime thriller, directed by Joseph H. Lewis.
a) *They Live By Night* b) *Side Street*
c) *Robbery Under Arms* d) *Gun Crazy*

2) In the 1983 horror film, **Something Wicked This Way Comes**, a mysterious carnival is able to fulfil the dreams of its patrons. On whose novel was it based?
a) *M.R. James* b) *Edgar Allan Poe*
c) *Ray Bradbury* d) *Sheridan Le Fanu*

3) With which film do you associate sleazy Victorian freak-show exhibitor 'Bytes' (Freddie Jones)?
a) *The Beast Must Die* b) *The Elephant Man*
c) *Secret Beyond the Door* d) *Man Beast*

FARMS

1) Who played the title role in the 1917 version of **Rebecca of Sunnybrook Farm**?
a) *Mary Pickford* b) *Louise Brooks*
c) *Mabel Normand* d) *Vilma Banky*

2) With which film do you associate Ray Kinsella hearing strange voices on his farm?
a) *A Summer Story* b) *Heartland*
c) *Field of Dreams* d) *A Far Off Place*

3) In which 1956 western do indians scatter and butcher the cattle from the farm of Lars Jorgensen (John Qualen)?
a) *Red River*
b) *The Searchers*
c) *The Badlanders*
d) *Geronimo*

104

FIRE STATIONS

1) Which 1954 comedy features Spike Jones and The City Slickers manning a fire station in 1900s San Francisco?
a) Firehouse b) Fireman Save My Child
c) City on Fire d) Fire Down Below

2) Who portrayed the incompetent fire station chief in the 1939 comedy, **Where's the Fire**?
a) Arthur Askey b) Charlie Chester
c) Will Hay d) George Formby

3) Veteran fireman, Stephen McCaffrey (Kurt Russell) is based at Engine Company 17 in Chicago's Chinatown in Ron Howard's 1991 fire-fighting thriller. Name the title.
a) Backdraft b) Fire and Rain
c) Trapped d) Firebirds

FORESTS & WOODLANDS

1) Which film features a variety of talking woodland creatures, based on a story by Felix Salten?
a) The Wind in the Willows b) The Company of Wolves c) Bambi d) Doctor Dolittle

2) With which film do you associate a horde of winged monkeys attacking a group of frightened travellers in a forest?
a) Willow b) The Dark Angel
c) The NeverEnding Story d) The Wizard of Oz

3) Who played the title role in the 1946 adventure, **The Bandit of Sherwood Forest**?
a) Cornel Wilde b) Richard Greene
c) John Derek d) Richard Todd

FORTS

1) Resentful commander, Lt. Col. Owen Thursday, feels he is denied a prestigious post in favour of the fly-blown **Fort Apache** in John Ford's 1948 western. Who was he?
a) Ronald Reagan b) J. Carrol Naish
c) John Wayne d) Henry Fonda

2) Which film opens with a column of soldiers approaching the desolate Fort Zinderneuf, where, upon investigation, they discover that all the occupants are dead?
a) The Lost Patrol b) Beau Geste
c) Sahara d) Tarzan's Desert Mystery

3) Name the film in which gunfighter Randolph Scott reforms and becomes a newspaper editor, but ends up reverting to his old ways to banish lawlessness from his town.
a) Fort Worth b) Fort Yuma
c) Fort Utah d) Fort Dobbs

FOUNTAINS

1) Three women wish for true love at Rome's Trevi Fountain in **Three Coins in the Fountain**. Jean Peters and Maggie McNamara were two of them. Who was the third?
a) Dorothy McGuire b) Gina Lollobrigida
c) Joan Blondell d) Shirley MacLaine

2) In which film do Leo and Max celebrate the birth of their "guaranteed" confidence trick in front of New York's Lincoln Center fountain?
a) Barefoot in the Park b) The Producers
c) What's New, Pussycat? d) Gambit

3) Which film features Marlon Brando being dumped in a fountain?
a) Viva Zapata!
b) Guys and Dolls
c) The Missouri Breaks
d) On the Waterfront

FOXHOLES & SHELL HOLES

1) Name the title of Edward Dmytryk's 1947 crime drama, based on the novel, *The Brick Foxhole*, by Richard Brooks.
a) Cornered b) The Hidden Room
c) Crossfire d) Walk on the Wild Side

2) Paul Baumer stabs a French soldier and spends the night watching him slowly die while trapped in a shell hole in **All Quiet on the Western Front**. Who portrayed Baumer?
a) Frank Lawton b) Bruce Cabot
c) Richard Dix d) Lew Ayres

3) With which film do you associate a London shell hole unearthing an ancient charter ceding part of the city to the Dukes of Burgundy?
a) Bombshell b) London Belongs to Me
c) Passport to Pimlico d) A Foreign Affair

FUNERALS

1) In which 1963 comedy thriller was Audrey Hepburn pursued by the mourners at her husband's funeral?
a) The Unforgiven b) Young Wives' Tale
c) Green Mansions d) Charade

2) In the 1995 comedy drama, **Antonia's Line**, Antonia returns with her daughter to her Dutch village after WWII to bury her mother, who, at the funeral, sits upright in her coffin and bursts into song.

The Movie Quiz Companion

Name the song's title.
a) My Blue Heaven b) Pennies From Heaven
c) Lili Marlene d) White Christmas

3) A celebrity up until the end, this actress, who died in 1984, was buried wearing a gold lamé evening dress with matching cape. Can you name her?
a) Tallulah Bankhead b) Mae West
c) Diana Dors d) Bette Davis

GARAGES & GAS STATIONS

1) Who drives into a gas station and encounters gullible attendant, C.W. Moss?
a) Pretty Boy Floyd b) Dillinger
c) Bonnie and Clyde d) Machine-Gun Kelly

2) Name the Hitchcock thriller in which Uncle Charlie traps young Charlie in a garage where she almost capitulates to carbon monoxide poisoning.
a) Suspicion b) Blackmail
c) Shadow of a Doubt d) The Lodger

3) Name the 1988 thriller, adapted from Tim Krabbe's novel, *The Golden Egg*, in which an innocent girl disappears at a gas station.
a) The Vanishing b) Night Games
c) The Disappearance of Aimee d) Lost and Found

GARDENS

1) On whose novel was **The Secret Garden** based?
a) Charles Kingsley b) E. Nesbit
c) Frances Hodgson Burnett d) P.L. Travers

2) Who directed the 1987 war drama, **Gardens of Stone**?
a) Francis Ford Coppola b) Robert Aldrich
c) John Schlesinger d) James Ivory

3) On whose novel was Andrew Birkin's 1992 drama, **The Cement Garden** based?
a) Ruth Rendell b) Peter Carey
c) Ian McEwan d) Keith Waterhouse

GRAVES

1) Which film features the unmarked grave of a Japanese farmer named Komoko?
a) Sanjuro b) Flowers in the Attic
c) Bad Day at Black Rock
d) Rashomon

2) Name the John Ford western in which Captain Nathan Brittles (John Wayne) regularly talks to his wife at her desert graveside.
a) Rio Grande
b) The Man Who Shot Liberty Valance
c) Fort Apache d) She Wore a Yellow Ribbon

3) What 1946 film involves George Bailey making the startling discovery of the grave of his younger brother who was drowned in a childhood accident?
a) Mortal Storm b) Bend in the River
c) It's a Wonderful Life d) Magic Town

GRAVEYARDS & CEMETERIES

1) Young Pip has a terrifying graveyard encounter with escaped convict Magwitch in David Lean's **Great Expectations**. Who portrayed Magwitch?
a) Victor McLaglen b) Boris Karloff
c) Robert Newton d) Finlay Currie

2) In which film is Mexican bandit, Tuco, dangerously perched on a tombstone with a hangman's noose around his neck and gold beneath his feet?
a) The Magnificent Seven
b) The Good, the Bad, and the Ugly
c) The Wild Bunch
d) The Ballad of Cable Hogue

3) Name the film in which Sherlock Holmes' sidekick, Watson, hallucinates in a graveyard.

stifling trophies

a) Without a Clue b) Young Sherlock Holmes
c) The Private Life of Sherlock Holmes d) Sherlock Holmes and the Spider Woman

GYMS

1) For what film does a brain damaged **Rocky** reopen his old gym and start training young hopefuls?
a) Rocky II b) Rocky III c) Rocky IV d) Rocky V

2) Arnold Schwarzenegger plays bodybuilder, Joe Santo, who works out at the local gym in an early dramatic role in 1976. Name the film.
a) Stay Hungry b) Pumping Iron
c) Hercules in New York d) The Villain

3) Holly (Mary Tyler Moore) meets Sandy (Christine Lahti) at the gym and invites her home for dinner. What Sandy doesn't realize is that Holly is married to her lover. Name the film.
a) Just Between Friends b) My Dinner With Andre
c) Mysterious Lady d) Perfect Strangers

HAUNTED HOUSES

1) Wallie Campbell solves the mystery of the haunted house in the 1939 comedy, **The Cat and the Canary**. Who was he?
a) Robert Cummings b) Nigel Bruce
c) Jackie Coogan d) Bob Hope

2) Richard Johnson, Julie Harris, Claire Bloom and Russ Tamblyn all regret the night they spend in a haunted New England mansion in 1963. Name the title.
a) The Haunted Palace b) The Haunting
c) House on Haunted Hill d) A-Haunting We Will Go

innate mild clergymen — **Settings**

3) Who directed the 1932 creepy classic where stranded travellers spend the night in **The Old Dark House**?
a) Frank Capra b) James Whale
c) Tod Browning d) Fritz Lang

HEAVEN

1) The 1978 fantasy, **Heaven Can Wait**, starring Warren Beatty, is a remake of a 1941 film in which a man is taken to heaven by mistake. Name the title.
a) All That Heaven Allows b) The Wrong Man
c) Here Comes Mr. Jordan d) Heaven Knows Mr. Allison

2) In which film did Raymond Massey portray the heavenly prosecutor with an anti-British streak, Abraham Farlan?
a) Reap the Wild Wind b) Come Fill the Cup
c) God is My Co-Pilot d) A Matter of Life and Death

3) Who descended from heaven in the body of a dog to track down his murderer in the 1980 comedy, **Oh, Heavenly Dog!**?
a) Chevy Chase b) Bob Hoskins
c) Steve Martin d) John Candy

HELL

1) **Dr. Faustus** descends into hell with Mephistopheles (Andreas Teuber) in Richard Burton's 1968 production. On whose play was it based?
a) Ben Jonson b) John Galsworthy
c) Christopher Marlowe d) George Bernard Shaw

2) In which 1991 film does Keanu Reeves visit hell?
a) Young Blood b) I Love You to Death
c) Freaked d) Bill & Ted's Bogus Journey

3) Carnival showman, Jim Carter, had a brush with hell in the 1935 drama, **Dante's Inferno**. Who was he?
a) Paul Muni
b) Spencer Tracy
c) Boris Karloff
d) Charles Coburn

HIDEOUTS

1) Back at their Mexican hideout, who discover their stolen loot is only worthless metal washers?
a) The Grissom Gang b) The Doberman Gang
c) The Wild Bunch d) The Comancheros

2) Altar Keane runs a hideout for outlaws in the 1969 western, **Rancho Notorious**. Who was she?
a) Joan Crawford b) Marlene Dietrich
c) Barbara Stanwyck d) Jane Fonda

3) Who do the police ambush in a 1967 crime drama at a seedy apartment hideout above a garage in Joplin, Missouri?
a) The Boston Strangler b) Bonnie & Clyde
c) Baby Face Nelson d) Al Capone

HOSPITALS

1) Who is the important visitor the staff of **Britannia Hospital** (1982) are expecting?
a) Fidel Castro b) Prince Okabi of Seranga
c) Queen Mother d) Prince Charles

2) Richard Hooker's novel inspired a film about a unique hospital. Name the title.
a) Emergency Ward b) Frankenstein General Hospital c) The Hospital d) M*A*S*H

3) With which film do you associate Dustin Hoffman's character working as a hospital administrator in a New York hospital?
a) Madigan's Million b) John and Mary
c) Tootsie d) Straight Time

HOTELS

1) In which city was Edmund Goulding's 1932 drama, **Grand Hotel** set?
a) New York b) Paris c) Venice d) Berlin

2) Name the 1978 Neil Simon comedy about four brawling couples set in a Beverley Hills hotel.
a) Plaza Suite b) California Suite
c) The Out of Towners d) The Goodbye Girl

3) Who played the title role in **The Bellboy**, set in Miami Beach's Fountainbleau Hotel?

a) Jack Lemmon b) Milton Berle
c) Jerry Lewis d) Red Buttons

HOUSES

1) Who or what lived in **The House on Carroll Street**?
a) Nazi war criminals b) Martians
c) the Boston Strangler d) unmarried mothers

2) With which film do you associate Melanie Griffith and Matthew Modine desperately trying to evict a strange tenant from their San Francisco house?
a) Pacific Heights b) The Lemon Sisters
c) House of Cards d) Be My Guest

3) Who lived in Manderley?
a) Emma b) Rebecca
c) Lady Caroline Lamb d) Mrs. Miniver

ISLANDS

1) An American soldier (Lee Marvin) and a Japanese soldier are stranded on a deserted Pacific Island during WWII in the 1968 film, **Hell in the Pacific**. Who portrayed the Japanese soldier?

107

a) Takashi Shimura b) Eiji Okada
c) Masayuki Mori d) Toshiro Mifune

2) On whose novel was Carol Reed's 1948 drama, **Outcast of the Islands**, based?
a) Joseph Conrad b) Graham Greene
c) Maurice Walsh d) Geoffrey Household

3) What does the Arctic expedition discover in Disney's 1974 adventure, **The Island at the Top of the World**?
a) a kingdom of dinosaurs b) Atlantis
c) a lost Viking civilization d) a time-tunnel

ISOLATED HOUSES

1) Torture victim, Paulina Escobar, waits for the arrival of her torturer at her isolated house in Roman Polanski's, **Death and the Maiden**. Who was she?
a) Kristin Scott-Thomas b) Juliette Binoche
c) Susan Sarandon d) Julie Christie

2) Which film features the remote Highland cottage 'Camusfearna'?
a) Brigadoon b) Wee Geordie
c) Ring of Bright Water d) Kidnapped

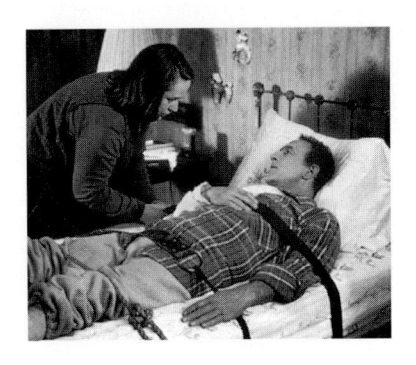

3) Injured writer, Paul Sheldon, is held prisoner at the isolated house of the deranged Annie Wilkes in Rob Reiner's 1990 horror film. Name the title.
a) Psycho II b) Misery
c) Missing Pieces d) Cat's Eye

JAILS & PRISONS

1) In which film did Alec Guinness portray a man who has been confined for twenty years in Marshalsea Jail for nonpayment of debt?
a) Doctor Zhivago b) Little Dorrit
c) The Scapegoat d) A Run for your Money

2) **The Grey Fox** (1982) tells the story of the legendary stagecoach robber, Bill Miner, who served 33 years in state prison, and on his release took to robbing trains. Name the prison he served his time in.
a) San Quentin b) Levenworth
c) Folsom d) Alcatraz

3) Dr. Benjamin Twist is the new governor of Blackdown Prison in **Convict 99**, who 'plays the market' for inmates and introduces à la carte menus. Who was he?
a) Norman Wisdom b) George Formby
c) Will Hay d) Arthur Askey

JUNGLES

1) On whose play was Leslie Norman's 1961 jungle drama, **The Long and the Short and the Tall** based?
a) Terence Rattigan b) Willis Hall
c) Robert Bolt d) Wolf Mankowitz

2) Who played the title role in the 40s and 50s film series, **Jungle Jim**?
a) Johnny Weissmuller b) Buster Crabbe
c) Jock Mahoney d) Chester Morris

3) What were Hope and Crosby looking for when travelling through the jungle in the 1941 musical comedy, **Road to Zanzibar**?
a) a script b) King Kong
c) a diamond mine d) a kidnapped princess

KITCHENS

1) What film involves a gangster named Clemenza (Richard Castellano) in the kitchen making tomato sauce for pasta?
a) Married to the Mob b) Carlito's Way
c) The Sicilian d) The Godfather

2) In which 1981 film do Cora and Frank make violent love on a kitchen table?
a) Heartburn b) The Postman Always Rings Twice
c) Sweet Dreams d) Five Easy Pieces

3) With which film do you associate a housewife regularly having a conversation with her kitchen walls?
a) East is East b) The Family Way
c) Educating Rita d) Shirley Valentine

LAKES

1) Which Frankenstein film features the monster saving a beautiful shepherdess who is so terrified of him that she falls in a lake?
a) Frankenstein b) Bride of Frankenstein
c) Frankenstein Created Woman d) The Curse of Frankenstein

2) Who portrayed Raymond Chandler's tough-talking private eye, Philip Marlowe, in the 1946 mystery, **Lady in the Lake**?
a) Robert Armstrong b) Robert Young
c) John Payne d) Robert Montgomery

3) English spinster, Miss Bentley, spends her vacation on the shores of Lake Como in the 1995 romantic drama, **A Month by the Lake**. Who was she?
a) Vanessa Redgrave b) Maggie Smith
c) Peggy Ashcroft d) Claire Bloom

LABORATORIES

1) Inventor Sidney Stratton creates an indestructable fabric in a textile mill laboratory in the 1951 comedy, **The Man in the White Suit**. Who was he?
a) Kenneth More b) Donald Sinden
c) Alec Guinness d) Peter Finch

2) In which film would you find the laboratory of the mad inventor, Rotwang (Rudolf Klein-Rogge)?
a) Things to Come b) Metropolis
c) The Man With Two Brains d) Darkman

3) Who emerges from his laboratory as the terrifying Mr. Hyde in Rouben Mamoulian's 1932 version of **Dr. Jekyll and Mr. Hyde**?
a) John Barrymore b) Spencer Tracy
c) Cedric Hardwicke d) Fredric March

LIFEBOATS

1) On whose story was Alfred Hitchcock's 1944 war drama, **Lifeboat**, based?
a) Damon Runyon b) John Steinbeck
c) Richard Hughes d) Elia Kazan

2) In which 1957 adventure did Tyrone Power portray an officer in charge of a lifeboat full of survivors from a stricken ocean liner?
a) Abandon Ship! b) The Last Survivor
c) Sea Fury d) Souls at Sea

3) Ruislip Lido in the London borough of Hillingdon, substituted for the icy North Atlantic during the filming of the lifeboat scenes in which Titanic drama?
a) A Night to Remember b) Raise the Titanic!
c) S.O.S. Titanic d) S.O.S. Iceberg

LIGHTHOUSES

1) Who was lighthouse-keeper, Fernando Rey's assistant, on a rocky South American outcrop in **The Light at the Edge of the World** (1971)?
a) Roddy McDowall b) Curt Jurgens
c) Eli Wallach d) Kirk Douglas

2) Point of Ayr Lighthouse, near Prestatyn, is where Astrid (Sheryl Lee) declares her love for Stuart Sutcliffe (Stephen Dorff). Name the film.
a) I Wanna Hold Your Hand b) Backbeat
c) Can't Buy Me Love d) Sgt. Pepper's Lonely Hearts Club Band

3) Artist Eben Adams' search for the spirit of the dead girl he has fallen in love with ends fatally beneath a storm-lashed lighthouse in **Portrait of Jennie**. Who was he?
a) Gene Kelly b) Robert Cummings
c) James Mason d) Joseph Cotton

LIMOUSINES

1) Name the legendary soul singer who draws up in his limousine alongside Jimmy Rabbitte (Robert Arkins) in the closing scenes of **The Commitments**.
a) Otis Redding b) Percy Sledge
c) Wilson Pickett d) Marvin Gaye

2) In which film does would-be television comedian, Rupert Pupkin, share a limo with pro comedy star, Jerry Langford, and try to persuade him to listen to his 'routine'?
a) The King of Comedy b) The Comedians
c) The Comedy of Terrors d) No Time For Comedy

3) Which 1994 comedy features Jim Carrey as a limousine driver?
a) Dumb & Dumber b) Pink Cadillac
c) Peggy Sue Got Married d) Earth Girls Are Easy

MEETINGS

1) Who demonstrates to Harry Burns (Billy Crystal) how to fake an orgasm in a busy restaurant in the 1989 romantic comedy, **When Harry Met Sally**?
a) Holly Hunter b) Kim Basinger
c) Melanie Griffith d) Meg Ryan

2) Who portrayed painter Jan Van Rooyen, framed for his girlfriend's murder, in Joseph Losey's 1959 mystery, **Chance Meeting**?
a) Hardy Kruger b) Richard Widmark
c) Stanley Baker d) Robert Walker

3) Reporter Joe Bradley (Gregory Peck) meets Princess Anne, a naive teenager, on a park bench in a 1953 romantic comedy. Name the title.
a) Gentleman's Agreement b) Beloved Infidel
c) Roman Holiday d) Night People

MILITARY ACADEMIES

1) General Harlan Bache was the commander of Bunker Hill Military Academy in the Harold Becker's 1981 drama, **Taps**. Who was he?
a) Richard Harris b) Walter Matthau
c) Robert Shaw d) George C. Scott

2) In which 1982 film does naval officer's candidate, Sid Worley (David Keith) hang himself?
a) An Officer and a Gentleman b) The Lords of Discipline c) Platoon d) Up the Academy

3) In the 1952 comedy **Francis Goes to West Point**, who or what is Francis?
a) an Old English sheepdog b) a girl guide
c) General Custer's horse d) a talking mule

MINES

1) With which 'Road' movie do you associate Dorothy Lamour owning a gold mine?
a) Road to Utopia b) Road to Rio
c) Road to Singapore d) Road to Zanzibar

2) In which film does Kirk Douglas portray a worker in a Libyan mine?
a) Ulysses b) The Glass Menagerie
c) Spartacus d) The Walls of Jericho

The Movie Quiz Companion

3) What film involves a young English writer named Basil, inheriting a Greek lignite mine?
a) Zorba the Greek b) The Inheritor
c) The Greek Tycoon d) Never on a Sunday

MONASTERIES

1) Larry Darrell, a young man going through a spiritual crisis, joins a monastery in the 1984 drama, **The Razor's Edge**. Who was he?
a) Mel Gibson b) Dan Aykroyd
c) William Hurt d) Bill Murray

2) Which film features Jim Carrey living in a Tibetan monastery?
a) The Dead Pool b) Once Bitten c) Earth Girls Are Easy d) Ace Ventura: When Nature Calls

3) In Powell and Pressburger's fantasy, **The Thief of Bagdad**, Abu asks the genie to take him to a mountain monastery so he can steal something. What is it?
a) the All-Seeing Eye b) a winged horse
c) a flying carpet d) magic slippers

MOUNTAINS

1) Name the 1959 Disney adventure which features young Swiss boy, Rudi Matt (James MacArthur), who is determined to climb a mountain called the Citadel?
a) Situation Hopeless - But Not Serious
b) The Hot Rock
c) Third Man on the Mountain
d) Tall Tale

2) With which film do you associate the Valley of the Blue Moon, which stands between towering mountains somewhere in Tibet?
a) The Man Who Would Be King
b) The Razor's Edge
c) Lost Horizon
d) Marco Polo

3) Name the mountains featured in the 1950 operatic drama, **The Glass Mountain**.
a) the Rocky Mountains
b) the Dolomites
c) the Pyrenees
d) the Himalayas

MUSEUMS

1) What 1966 comedy, starring Peter O'Toole and Audrey Hepburn, involves the stealing of a fake Cellini 'Venus' from a Paris art museum?
a) How to Steal a Million b) Gambit
c) Topkapi d) The Thief of Paris

2) Who directed the 3-D horror film, **House of Wax** (1953), in which a wax museum destroyed by fire is rebuilt using human victims?
a) Roger Corman b) André De Toth
c) Michael Curtiz d) Max Ophuls

3) Which Hitchcock film involves a chase on the roof of the British Museum?
a) Saboteur b) Young and Innocent
c) The Man Who Knew Too Much d) Blackmail

MUSIC HALL & VAUDEVILLE THEATERS

1) Name Mitchell Leisen's 1935 drama which is set entirely in a vaudeville theater where a convicted killer escapes en route to his execution.
a) Four Hours to Kill b) No Escape
c) Stage Fright d) Theatre of Death

2) In which film does Greer Garson do an impression of Harry Lauder in an English music hall?
a) Goodbye, Mr. Chips b) Blossoms in the Dust
c) The Youngest Profession d) Random Harvest

3) Which film features the music hall act 'Mr. Memory'?
a) Chaplin b) The 39 Steps c) Waterloo Bridge
d) Yankee Doodle Dandy

NIGHTCLUBS

1) Who directed **The Cotton Club**?
a) Francis Ford Coppola b) Robert Altman
c) Spike Lee d) Alan Parker

2) With which film do you associate Al Pacino and associates watching a knife-throwing act in a Cuban nightclub?

a) Carlito's Way b) The Godfather Part II
c) Heat d) Scarface

3) Judy Peabody was a hat-check girl in the 1945 musical comedy, **The Stork Club**, singing "Doctor, Lawyer, Indian Chief". Who was she?
a) Glenda Farrell b) Betty Grable
c) Linda Darnell d) Betty Hutton

NORTH & SOUTH POLES

1) Name the 1951 science fiction drama based on the story, Who Goes There, by Don A. Stuart, about a creature discovered buried in the Arctic ice.
a) The Thing (From Another World) b) The Beast From 20,000 Fathoms c) Godzilla d) Iceman

2) Who played the title role in the 1948 biopic, **Scott of the Antarctic**?
a) Richard Todd b) Peter Finch
c) Jack Hawkins d) John Mills

3) How do the explorers attempt to travel to the North Pole in the 1982 adventure, **The Flight of the Eagle**?
a) ballon b) hang-glider c) auto-giro d) WWII bomber

OCEAN LINERS

1) Harvey, the spoiled brat of a tycoon, falls overboard from an ocean liner heading for Europe and is picked up by a passing fishing

boat in **Captains Courageous**. Who was he?
a) Mickey Rooney b) Roddy McDowell
c) Jackie Coogan d) Freddie Bartholomew

2) In which 1957 film do Cary Grant and Deborah Kerr have a shipboard romance?
a) An Affair to Remember b) I Was a Male War Bride c) The End of an Affair d) When You're in Love

3) With which 1941 comedy do you associate department store owner, John P. Merrick, taking his entire staff on a cruise aboard an ocean liner?
a) You Can't Take it With You b) The Devil and Miss Jones c) Green Pastures d) Hope Floats

OFFICES

1) In which film do Donald Houston and Laurence Harvey work in a government accountancy office in the Yorkshire industrial town of Warnley?
a) Of Human Bondage b) Three Men in a Boat
c) Room at the Top d) The Good Die Young

2) Marion Crane steals $40,000 from the safe in her boss's real estate office and decides to buy herself a new car in a 1960 thriller. Name the title.
a) Killer's Kiss b) The Naked Edge
c) Cast a Dark Shadow d) Psycho

3) Which 1994 thriller features a virtual reality database which turns a humdrum office environment into a Greco-Roman Arcadia?
a) Disclosure b) Virtuosity
c) The Temp d) Executive Decision

OILFIELDS

1) Big John McMasters (Clark Gable) and Square John Sand (Spencer Tracy) drill for oil in a 1940 drama directed by Jack Conway. Name the title.
a) San Francisco
b) Oil For the Lamps of China
c) The Big Gusher
d) Boom Town

2) With which film do you associate Jack Nicholson playing a roughneck in a California oilfield?
a) Five Easy Pieces b) Rebel Rousers
c) Goin' South d) A Safe Place

3) Lena Doyle defends her independent oilfield from takeover by a powerful oil trust in the 1973 comedy drama, **Oklahoma Crude**. Who was she?
a) Jane Fonda b) Faye Dunaway
c) Ursula Andress d) Claudia Cardinale

OK CORRAL

1) In which western town was the O.K. Corral situated?
a) Dodge City b) Laramie
c) El Paso d) Tombstone

2) Who directed the 1957 western, **Gunfight at the O.K. Corral**?
a) John Frankenheimer b) John Sturges
c) Anthony Mann d) Henry King

3) Who said: "I knew Wyatt Earp, and he told me about the fight at the O.K. Corral. So in **My Darling Clementine** we did it exactly the way it had been."?
a) Fred Zinneman b) Howard Hawks c) John Ford d) Anthony Mann

OLD PEOPLE'S HOMES & COMMUNITIES

1) Which film features the residents of a home for the elderly watching **Top Hat** on television?
a) The Green Mile b) I Never Sang for my Father
c) Hills of Home d) Only the Lonely

2) What film connection can you make between a retirement community in St. Petersburg, Florida, and the planet Antares?
a) The Man Who Fell to Earth b) This Island Earth
c) Cocoon d) I Married a Monster From Outer Space

3) In which 1951 comedy does Clifton Webb infiltrate a home for the elderly under an assumed identity and attempt to resuscitate the dreary lives of its inhabitants?
a) Sitting Pretty b) Mr. Belvedere Rings the Bell
c) For Heaven's Sake d) The Remarkable Mr. Pennypacker

OLYMPIC GAMES

1) Name the actor/actress who was an Olympic swimming champion in 1924 and 1928.
a) Johnny Weissmuller b) Esther Williams
c) Buster Crabbe d) Steve Reeves

2) Davis Chappellet was a member of the U.S. Olympic ski team in **Downhill Racer** (1969). Who portrayed him?
a) Robert Redford
b) Steve McQueen
c) Richard Gere
d) Elliott Gould

3) How does an East German Olympic athlete, portrayed by Elke Sommer, escape to the West in the 1968 romantic comedy, **The Wicked Dreams of Paula Schultz**?
a) she toboggans into Austria
b) she polevaults over the Berlin Wall
c) she rows across the Baltic
d) she hijacks the official team train

The Movie Quiz Companion

priceless thief

OPERATING THEATRES

1) In 1946 David Niven portrayed a pilot who undergoes an operation for brain damage in a WWII operating theatre somewhere in England. Name the film.
a) The Way to the Stars b) The First of the Few c) The Way Ahead d) A Matter of Life and Death

2) With which 1947 mystery do you associate Inspector Cockrill (Alistair Sim) of Scotland Yard investigating a murder which takes place in an operating theatre?
a) Laughter in Paradise b) Doctor's Dilemma c) Green For Danger d) An Inspector Calls

3) In which 1993 thriller does top surgeon, Dr. Jed Hill (Alec Baldwin), operate on Tracy (Nicole Kidman) - the wife of an old school friend - who is suffering from abdominal pains?
a) Malice b) Consenting Adults c) Dead Connection d) Final Analysis

ORPHANAGES & CHILDREN'S HOMES

1) At St. Cloud's orphanage, Dr. Wilbur Larch's last words to the boys at the end of a day are always: "Good night, you Princes of Maine - you Kings of New England!" Name the film.
a) Boys Town b) The Dream Maker c) The Cider House Rules d) Close To My Heart

2) Who attempts to raise money for their old West Side orphanage when its future is left in the balance because of oustanding taxes?
a) The Ritz Brothers
b) The Brothers McMullen
c) The Blues Brothers
d) The Brothers Rico

3) Name the film, based on L.M. Montgomery's novel, about a headstrong young girl who is sent from a children's home by mistake to an elderly couple who requested a boy.
a) Annie
b) Anne of Green Gables
c) The Divided Heart
d) Heidi

OTHER WORLDS

1) Which Star Trek film featured the exploding planet Genesis?
a) Star Trek II: The Wrath of Khan b) Star Trek III: The Search for Spock c) Star Trek IV: The Voyage Home d) Star Trek V: The Final Frontier

2) In 1936 the planet Mongo was hurtling towards Earth in **Spaceship to the Unknown**. Who averted disaster?
a) Buck Rogers b) Captain America c) Dan Dare d) Flash Gordon

3) With which film do you associate giant mile-long sandworms guarding the spice Melange, which allows travel through Time and Space?
a) DeepStar Six b) Dune c) Leviathan d) Darkman

PARADES

1) Welsh character actor, Edmund Gwenn, won a Best Supporting Actor Oscar for his role in a 1947 fantasy which began with him unexpectedly leading a street parade. Name the film.
a) Miracle on 34th Street b) Charley's Aunt c) The Big Parade d) Street of Chance

2) Billy and Wyatt are jailed for "parading without a permit" with their bikes in a Fourth of July Parade. Name the film.
a) Hell's Angels on Wheels b) Downhill Racer c) The Wild One d) Easy Rider

3) Who went **On Dress Parade** in 1939?
a) The Dead End Kids b) Laurel and Hardy c) The Keystone Cops d) Nancy Drew

PARTIES

1) In which film does McMurphy smuggle two girlfriends into his hospital ward and throw a wild party for its inmates?
a) A Stitch in Time b) Britannia Hospital c) One Flew Over the Cuckoo's Nest d) Doctor in the House

2) With which musical do you associate Debbie Reynolds popping out of a cake at a Hollywood party?
a) The Unsinkable Molly Brown b) Carousel c) Singin' in the Rain d) Gentlemen Prefer Blondes

3) In which 1995 comedy does Cher (Alicia Silverstone) explain her party tactics as follows: "Pretend to be having a good time, pretend not to notice the guy you're interested in, and laugh and dance a lot. Also, sometimes you have to show a little skin. This reminds guys of being naked, and then they think of sex."?
a) Clueless b) Waiting to Exhale c) Bullets Over Broadway d) Earth Girls Are Easy

PENAL COLONIES

1) With which 1940 film do you associate Andre Verne (Clark Gable) escaping from a penal colony?
a) China Seas b) Saratoga c) Mogambo d) Strange Cargo

2) Innocent Adam is sent to a 19th century Australian penal colony in the 1970 drama, **Adam's Woman**. Who was he?

imprisoned jamboree fetish **Settings**

a) Tom Selleck b) Donald Sutherland
c) Beau Bridges d) James Booth

3) In 1834 six Dorset farm labourers from Tolpuddle, near Dorchester, were transported to the Australian penal colonies for forming a trade union. Following a national outcry they were released two years later. Name the 1987 film which tells their story.
a) Just Cause b) Extreme Justice
c) Fighting Back d) Comrades

PHONE BOOTHS

1) Alfred Hitchcock traditionally made brief 'walk on' appearances in many of his films. In which film does he appear outside a telephone booth?
a) Psycho b) Strangers on a Train
c) Frenzy d) Rebecca

2) Fans of a 1983 comedy like to pose for photographs in front of the phone booth in the village of Pennan in Aberdeenshire. Name the film.
a) The 39 Steps b) I Know Where I'm going
c) Wee Geordie d) Local Hero

3) The producer of the 1968 horror film, **Rosemary's Baby**, makes a short, but terrifying appearance outside a telephone booth in which Mia Farrow is frantically trying to communicate with a gynaecologist. Who was he?

a) William Castle b) Val Lewton
c) George Romero d) Roger Corman

PIERS

1) In which film do Mods sleep unknowingly beside a gang of Rockers under Brighton's West Pier?
a) Tommy b) Quadrophenia
c) Backbeat d) Don't Knock the Rock

2) With whom or what does Dennis Hopper fall in love on Santa Monica Pier in the 1963 drama, **Night Tide**?
a) a mermaid b) a living skeleton
c) the bird girl d) the turtle girl

3) A character portrayed by Robin Williams in a 1980 comedy directed by Robert Altman, has an outing to an amusement pier. Name the title.
a) Popeye b) Seize the Day c) The World According to Garp d) The Adventures of Baron Munchausen

PLANTATIONS

1) Name the British character actor who began his working life as a Ceylon tea planter.
a) Ernest Thesiger b) Sydney Greenstreet
c) Basil Radford d) Leo McKern

2) What threatens to destroy Charlton Heston and Eleanor Parker's plantation in the 1954 adventure, **The Naked Jungle**?
a) locusts b) elephants c) red ants d) baboons

3) In which film does Elizabeth Taylor join her new husband on his Ceylon tea plantation?
a) The Girl Who Had Everything b) Elephant Walk
c) A Place in the Sun d) The Sandpiper

POLICE STATIONS

1) Name John Carpenter's 1976 film about an LA police station which is a present-day reworking of Howard Hawks' **Rio Bravo**?
a) Assault on Precinct 13 b) Police Story
c) Cornered d) The Last Precinct

2) With which film do you associate an old lady popping into her local police station to tell them her friend Amelia had not seen spaceships in her garden the previous Wednesday afternoon as she had reported, but had fallen asleep listening to 'Visitors From Other Worlds' on the wireless, and the whole thing had been a dream?
a) A Kid For Two Farthings b) Hue and Cry
c) Passport to Pimlico d) The Ladykillers

3) Which 1939 comedy features Sergeant Samuel Dudfoot and the staff of Turnbottom Round police station?
a) Laughter in Paradise b) The Laughing Policeman c) Ask a Policeman d) The Lavender Hill Mob

POW CAMPS

1) What film connection can you make between POW camps and Billy Wilder?
a) Merry Christmas, Mr. Lawrence b) Stalag 17
c) Prisoners of the Sun d) Intimate Strangers

2) On whose novel was Bryan Forbes' WWII Japanese POW drama, **King Rat**, based?
a) James Clavell b) Paul Brickhill
c) Laurens Van Der Post d) Nevil Shute

3) Name the 1958 film which tells the story of Luftwaffe pilot, Franz von Werra, the only Nazi to escape from a British POW camp.
a) Journey to Freedom b) The One That Got Away
c) Some Kind of Hero d) The Last Escape

PROM NIGHTS

1) What film connection can you make between a prom night and a bucket of pig's blood?
a) Back to the Future b) Carrie
c) Class of 1984 d) Teen Wolf

2) Which film features an axe-wielding maniac out for revenge on prom night on High School kids responsible for the death of a 10-year-old girl?
a) Prom Night b) The Night Before
c) Prom Night III: The Last Kiss
d) Earth Angel

The Movie Quiz Companion

to old erotic dolt

3) With which film do you associate Vicki Carpenter (Wendy Lyon) being possessed by the spirit of a murdered prom queen?
a) Valley Girl b) Terror Train
c) Hello Mary Lou: Prom Night II d) Election

PUBS

1) George Cornell (Steven Berkoff) signs his death warrant when he calls a prominent local gangster a "fat poof", and is later shot dead while drinking at the bar of the Blind Beggar pub. Name the film.
a) Stormy Monday b) The Long Good Friday
c) Mona Lisa d) The Krays

2) Enigmatic hairdresser and part-time singer, Dil, met the man who killed her boyfriend in the Metro pub. Name the film.
a) Performance b) To the Devil - a Daughter
c) The Crying Game d) Frenzy

2) With which film do you associate Arthur Seaton getting plastered after a drinking competition, falling down stairs and throwing up over a couple of regulars in his local pub?
a) Shoot the Moon b) Saturday Night and Sunday Morning c) Charlie Bubbles d) Gumshoe

PYRAMIDS

1) Name Howard Hawks' 1955 drama about the building of the Great Pyramid.
a) Land of the Pharaohs b) Red Dust
c) A Death in Canaan d) Pharaoh's Curse

2) With which film do you associate actor Nicholas Rowe discovering a pyramid hidden in a warehouse in London's fogbound East End?
a) The Mummy's Tomb b) Street of Dreams
c) Young Sherlock Holmes d) The Saint in London

3) In which 1994 sci-fi drama was the sun god Ra clever enough to traverse galaxies at the speed of light, but had somehow not managed to get past the stage of using slaves to build his pyramids?
a) Stargate b) Space Rage
c) Star Trek: Generations d) The Big Bang

RACETRACKS

1) Rookie policeman, Andy Mitchell (Jimmy Hanley), corners his colleague's murderer, Tom Riley (Dirk Bogarde), at London's White City greyhound stadium in 1950. Name the film.
a) Eyewitness b) The Blue Lamp
c) The Sleeping Tiger d) Brighton Rock

2) Con woman Lily Dillon travels around the country to different racetracks improving the odds by placing huge last minute bets in Stephen Frears's, **The Grifters** (1990). Who was she?
a) Annette Bening
b) Jane Fonda
c) Anjelica Huston
d) Patricia Arquette

3) Name the 1956 crime thriller about a racetrack robbery based on Lionel White's novel, Clean Break ?
a) The Killing
b) The Concrete Jungle
c) Let it Ride
d) The Heist

RAFTS

1) With which film do you associate Hollywood showman, Carl Denyham (Robert Armstrong), knocking out a creature in the jungle with a gas bomb and building a special raft to transport it back to the the U.S.A.?
a) The Creature From the Black Lagoon b) Gorgo
c) King Kong d) The She Creature

2) Who rescues Marilyn Monroe from a sinking raft in the 1954 western, **River of No Return**?
a) Rory Calhoun b) Joel McCrea
c) Audie Murphy d) Robert Mitchum

3) Captain Yossarian paddles a life raft to Sweden in **Catch 22** (1970). Who was he?
a) Bob Newhart b) Jack Gilford
c) Alan Arkin d) Richard Benjamin

RAILWAY STATIONS

1) What film connection can you make between Greer Garson and Belham Station?
a) Random Harvest b) Goodbye Mr Chips
c) Mrs. Miniver d) Little Women

2) With which film do you associate Sean Thornton arriving at Castletown Station?
a) Brigadoon b) The Quiet Man
c) The Man Who Shot Liberty Valance d) Big Jim McLain

3) In which city is the station situated in Walter Salles' 1998 drama, **Central Station**?

RANCHES

1) Ex-con, Dix Handley, dreams of buying back his father's Kentucky horse ranch with his share from a jewel heist in John Huston's 1950 crime drama, **The Asphalt Jungle**. Who portrayed him?
a) Sterling Hayden b) Dana Andrews
c) Robert Mitchum d) John Garfield

2) Universal turned 20 acres of a Californian ranch into a battlefield and used over 2,000 ex-servicemen as extras to make one of the greatest WWI dramas ever made. Name the title.
a) Paths of Glory b) All Quiet on the Western Front c) A Farewell to Arms d) Sergeant York

3) Daniel Stern, Bruno Kirby and Billy Crystal sign up for a dude ranch vacation in 1991. By what name are they better known?
a) The Electric Horsemen b) The Lusty Men
c) The Last Survivors d) City Slickers

RAPIDS

1) With which film do you associate Burt Reynolds incurring a fractured leg after running rapids in the Appalachians?
a) Deliverance b) Smokey and the Bandit
c) White Lightning d) Navajo Joe

2) In which film does Lois Lane pitch herself into the rapids beneath Niagara Falls in a desperate attempt to prove Clark Kent is really Superman?
a) Superman b) Superman II c) Superman III
d) Superman IV: The Quest For Peace

3) Rosie Sayer steers a tiny steamboat through dangerous rapids in a 1951 romantic drama. Name the film.
a) River of No Return b) Steamboat 'Round the Bend c) The Sailor Takes a Wife d) The African Queen

RED INDIAN RESERVATIONS

1) Name the 1939 western in which more than 300 mounted Navajo Indians from the Arizona reservation averaged 46 miles per hour pursuing a character portrayed by John Wayne across Monument Valley.
a) Fort Apache b) Stagecoach
c) Rio Grande d) Red River

2) FBI agent, Ray Levoi, who is part-Sioux, is assigned to investigate a murder on an Oglala Sioux reservation in the 1992 thriller, **Thunderheart**. Who was he?
a) Johnny Depp b) Sam Shepard
c) Val Kilmer d) Peter Weller

3) With which film do you associate Olympic runner, Billy Mills, who left his Sioux reservation to win a gold medal at the 1964 Olympics?
a) The Indian Runner b) Running Brave
c) Prairie Gold d) Brave Warrior

REEFS & ICEBERGS

1) When the "unsinkable" **Titanic** struck an iceberg in 1912, how long did it take to sink?
a) 1 hour 40 minutes b) 2 hours 40 minutes
c) 3 hours 40 minutes d) 4 hours 40 minutes

2) Mad Count Zaroff lures ships on to the treacherous reefs that surround his remote island by shifting the channel beacons in the 1932 thriller, **The Most Dangerous Game**. Who was he?
a) Robert McWade b) Luis Alberni
c) Leslie Banks d) Warren William

3) In which 1935 film is the Pandora driven onto a reef and wrecked?
a) Mutiny on the Bounty b) Captain Blood
c) The Sea Wolf d) Captain Horatio Hornblower

RESTAURANTS

1) Which film features Daniel Day-Lewis throwing a tantrum in a restaurant, and when threatened with having his whisky removed, saying: "Touch it and I'll kick you in the only part of your anatomy that's animated"?
a) Sunday, Bloody Sunday
b) My Beautiful Laundrette
c) In the Name of the Father
d) My Left Foot

2) In a 1993 comedy, Daniel Hillard - an actor whose speciality is voice-dubbing - has to act the parts of two different people, sitting at two separate tables, in Bridges' Restaurant. Name the comedy.
a) Born Yesterday
b) Mrs. Doubtfire
c) Father of the Bride Part II
d) The Secret of My Success

The Movie Quiz Companion

3) With which film do you associate Frank Keller (Al Pacino) dating a stream of women in the same New York restaurant, and being waited upon by Sherman (John Goodman)?
a) Frankie and Johnny b) Cruising
c) Scarecrow d) Sea of Love

RIVERS

1) Name the country which was the setting for the 1982 adventure drama, **The Man From Snowy River**?
a) Canada b) Australia
c) South Africa d) New Zealand

2) On whose novel was Jean Renoir's 1951 Indian drama, **The River** based?
a) V.S. Naipaul b) John Masters
c) Rumer Godden d) Rudyard Kipling

3) Whose life was chronicled in the 1939 biopic, **Swanee River**?
a) Cole Porter b) Al Jolson
c) Mark Twain d) Stephen Foster

RIVERBOATS & PADDLE-STEAMERS

1) Who directed the 1936 version of **Show Boat**?
a) James Whale b) King Vidor
c) Raoul Walsh d) George Sidney

2) In which 1946 drama does Finlay Currie meet his end when he is sucked into the paddles of 'The Empress', a Victorian paddle-steamer?
a) Around the World in 80 Days b) The History of Mr. Polly c) Great Expectations d) The Mudlark

3) Who portrayed the comic riverboat captain, Commodore Orlando Jackson, in the 1935 musical comedy, **Mississippi**?
a) W. C. Fields b) Buster Keaton
c) Jack Benny d) Chester Conklin

RODEOS

1) Name the 1994 biopic which tells the story of Lane Frost, one of rodeo's youngest national champions.
a) 8 Seconds b) Riding Tall
c) Arena d) Born Reckless

2) Who played the title role in **Convict Cowboy** (1995), in which an ex rodeo champion manages a prison ranch?
a) Steve Martin b) Jon Voight
c) Eric Stoltz d) William Hurt

3) In 1961 he portrayed cowhand and rodeo rider, Perce Howland, in John Huston's **The Misfits**. Who was he?
a) Eli Wallach b) Clark Gable
c) Robert Ryan d) Montgomery Clift

ROOFTOPS

1) Ardent Nazi and playwright, Franz Liebkind tended his pigeons on a Yorkville rooftop in the 1968 comedy, **The Producers**. Who was he?
a) Dick Shawn b) Kenneth Mars
c) Christopher Hewett d) Michael Davis

2) Retarded teenager, Derek Bentley (Chris Eccleston), and his friend Chris, attempt to break into a building through its rooftop when they are caught by a policeman. The policeman is shot dead by Chris, but it is Derek Bentley who is hanged for the murder. Name the film.
a) Dance With a Stranger b) Deadfall
c) No Road Back d) Let Him Have It

3) In which 1948 drama does Robert Newton portray a murdering rogue who is chased across the rooftops of Victorian London?
a) A Tale of Two Cities b) David Copperfield
c) Oliver Twist d) Great Expectations

SAFARIS

1) With whom or what does Victor Mature fight in Terence Young's 1956 adventure, **Safari**?
a) the Mau Mau b) rogue elephants
c) ivory hunters d) man-eating lions

2) On whose short story was **The Macomber Affair** (1947) based, in which white hunter, Robert Wilson (Gregory Peck) leads the wealthy Macombers (Robert Preston and Joan Bennett) on an African safari?
a) Ernest Hemingway b) Joseph Conrad
c) Isak Dinesen d) Paul Bowles

3) What 1949 comedy involvs Abbott and Costello going on safari?
a) The Mask of Sheba b) Africa Screams
c) Safari Drums d) Pardon My Sarong

SEANCES

1) Name the sleuth who investigates a murder at a seance in the 1944 mystery, **Black Magic**.
a) Bulldog Drummond b) Sherlock Holmes
c) Charlie Chan d) Ellery Queen

2) In the 1991 sci-fi fantasy, **And You Thought Your Parents Were Weird**, the children of a dead inventor summon a spirit at a seance which takes possession of their father's robot. Whose is the spirit summoned?

a) Thomas Edison b) Victor Frankenstein
c) Robby the Robot d) their father's

3) Who portrayed the medium who persuades her husband to kidnap a wealthy child, collect the ransom, and then offers to find the child by using her psychic powers in Bryan Forbes' 1964 crime drama, **Seance on a Wet Afternoon**?
a) Kim Stanley b) Judith Donner
c) Nanette Newman d) Margaret Lacey

SEASIDE RESORTS

1) Tony Hancock's most memorable screen performance was as the seaside entertainer in the 1962 film, **The Punch and Judy Man**. At which seaside resort was it filmed?
a) Brighton b) Scarborough
c) Bognor Regis d) Eastbourne

2) Name the 1958 drama set in an English seaside resort which was based on a play by Terence Rattigan, and starred Deborah Kerr, Rita Hayworth, David Niven, Burt Lancaster and Gladys Cooper.
a) Separate Tables b) The V.I.P.s
c) Hotel Imperial d) French Without Tears

3) After dying a death in Las Vegas, rookie comedian, Tommy Fawkes (Oliver Platt), returns to his roots in an English seaside resort in the 1995 comedy, **Funny Bones**. Name the resort.
a) Margate b) Blackpool
c) Morecambe d) Great Yarmouth

SEWERS & DRAINS

1) What does the deranged Bruno Antony (Robert Walker) accidentally drop down a drain in Hitchcock's **Strangers on a Train**?
a) spectacles b) a lighter c) a key d) a photograph

2) Cinematographer, Robert Krasker, shot a thriller in 1949 in which the police of four countries chase a fugitive through the tunnels of a city sewer. Name the film.
a) Whirlpool b) Manhunt
c) Dark City d) The Third Man

3) Jean Valjean carries an injured young revolutionary to safety through the Paris sewers in **Les Miserables** (1935). Who was he?
a) Lew Ayres
b) Raymond Massey
c) Fredric March d) Robert Donat

SHERIFFS' OFFICES

1) In which film does Amy Kane shoot an outlaw in the back through the window of a sheriff's office?
a) Arrowhead b) High Noon
c) Colorado Territory d) The Lawless Breed

2) In Howard Hawks' classic western, **Rio Bravo**, John Wayne and his sidekicks barricade themselves inside the sheriff's office. Name Hawks' 1970 western where a similar scene is repeated.
a) Rio Lobo b) The Big Sky
c) El Dorado d) Ball of Fire

3) With which film do you associate the sheriff's office in Sparta, Mississippi?
a) Mississippi Burning b) In the Heat of the Night
c) Deliverance d) All the King's Men

SHIP'S CABINS

1) In which film does Joe attempt to woo Sugar in the cabin of a yacht moored off the Florida coast?
a) Some Like it Hot b) The Palm Beach Story
c) Monkey Business d) Key Largo

2) When con artist, Jean Pike, and her husband enter their cabin in the final scene of Preston Sturges' 1941 romantic comedy, **The Lady Eve**, Muggsy (William Demarest), her husband's bodyguard, declares: "I knew it was the same dame." Who portrayed "the dame"?
a) Claudette Colbert b) Jean Harlow
c) Joan Crawford d) Barbara Stanwyck

3) In which film does Russian emigree, Sophia Loren, stow away in the cabin of diplomat Marlon Brando?
a) Reflections in a Golden Eye b) Sayonara
c) A Countess From Hong Kong d) The Ugly American

SHIPS, CARGO

1) Name the film inspired by actual events which occurred in 1941 when the 8,000 ton cargo ship, *SS Politician*, ran aground in treacherous seas.
a) The Sea Shall Not Have Them b) Whisky Galore
c) The Wreck of the Mary Deare d) Mystery Submarine

2) What was the cargo of Charles Frend's **San Demetrio, London** (1943)?
a) wheat b) aero engines
c) oil d) munitions

3) What cargo do the canny Scots crew throw overboard from the condemned Glasgow 'puffer' boat in Ealing's 1953 comedy, **The Maggie** (aka High and Dry)?
a) antique furniture b) a limousine
c) bathroom fittings d) roof tiles

SHIPS, NAVAL

1) Name the 1953 war drama, directed by Charles Frend, which featured the plucky Corvette Class, *HMS Compass Rose*.
a) The Cruel Sea
b) The Battle of the River Plate
c) Sink the Bismarck!
d) The Bedford Incident

2) What film was based on the real events surrounding the sinking of the destroyer,

HMS Kelly, during the Battle of Crete in WWII?
a) *The Cockleshell Heroes* b) *In Which We Serve*
c) *HMS Defiant* d) *San Demetrio, London*

3) Who or what does the Royal Navy attempt to capture in Montevideo harbour in Powell and Pressburger's, **The Battle of the River Plate**?
a) *Herman Goering* b) *the Bismarck*
c) *Benito Mussolini* d) *the Graf Spee*

SHIPS, SAILING

1) In which 1996 adventure did Jeff Bridges portray the skipper of the brigantine Albatross?
a) *The Final Countdown* b) *Pascali's Island*
c) *White Squall* d) *Cutthroat Island*

2) Name director John Farrow's sea drama based on the classic book by Richard Henry Dana published to great acclaim in 1840.
a) *Two Years Before the Mast* b) *Mutiny on the Bounty* c) *A King's Cutter* d) *Mr. Midshipman Easy*

3) In which 1965 adventure film were seven children discovered in the hold of a Caribbean pirate schooner?
a) *Frenchman's Creek* b) *A High Wind in Jamaica*
c) *The Light at the Edge of the World* d) *Swiss Family Robinson*

SHIPWRECKS

1) With which film do you associate Lord and Lady Clayton being shipwrecked off the African coast?
a) *The Admirable Crichton* b) *The Blue Lagoon*
c) *Island of the Lost* d) *Greystoke: The Legend of Tarzan, Lord of the Apes*

2) Judy Cavendish was one of the **Four Frightened People** shipwrecked in Cecil B. De Mille's 1934 adventure. Who was she?
a) *Claudette Colbert* b) *Greta Garbo*
c) *Lilian Gish* d) *Ida Lupino*

3) Shipwrecked on a desert island, the **Swiss Family Robinson** encounter many hazards, but succeed in building a new life. On whose novel was the film based?
a) *Jules Verne* b) *Alexandre Dumas*
c) *Johann Wyss* d) *Johanna Spyri*

SHOWERS & BATHS

1) Someone wrote a letter to Alfred Hitchcock stating: "Sir, After seeing [this French thriller] my daughter was afraid to take a bath. Now she has seen your **Psycho** and is afraid to take a shower. What should I do with her?" Hitchcock replied: "Send her to the dry cleaner's." Name the French thriller.
a) *Eyes Without a Face* b) *Le Boucher*
c) *Les Diaboliques* d) *La Femme Infidele*

2) After discussing the ideals of the Roman Empire, Frank Pentangeli (Michael V. Gazzo) commits suicide in a bath. Name the film.
a) *The Brotherhood*
b) *Bunny Lake is Missing*
c) *The Godfather Part II*
d) *Wise Guys*

3) Name the Lindsay Anderson film which received an X rating because of its nude shower scene.
a) *if...* b) *This Sporting Life*
c) *O Lucky Man!* d) *Glory! Glory!*

SOUTH SEAS

1) In 1942 he portrayed Jonas Tuttle in **The Tuttles of Tahiti**. Who was he?
a) *Maurice Chevalier* b) *Charles Laughton*
c) *Cedric Hardwicke* d) *Victor McLaglen*

2) Viti Levu was the island used for the location of the 1953 South Sea swashbuckler, **His Majesty O'Keefe**, starring Burt Lancaster in the title role. In which group of islands is Viti Levu situated?
a) *The Fiji Islands* b) *The Gilbert Islands*
c) *The Marquesas* d) *The Marshall Islands*

3) The book, *Tales of the South Pacific*, inspired the play and finally the film, **South Pacific**. Who wrote the book?
a) *James A. Michener* b) *Anita Loos*
c) *Jack London* d) *Pearl S. Buck*

SPEAKEASYS

1) In which film did Richard Pryor portray Harlem speakeasy owner, 'Sugar Ray'?
a) *A Rage in Harlem* b) *Cotton Comes to Harlem*
c) *A Great Day in Harlem* d) *Harlem Nights*

2) With which Marx Brothers' film do you associate college president, Professor Wagstaff (Groucho), signing up Chico and Harpo to play football for the college team in a local speakeasy?
a) *Monkey Business* b) *Horse Feathers*
c) *The Cocoanuts* d) *Animal Crackers*

3) Lily 'Baby Face' Powers is a speakeasy bartender in the 1933 drama, **Baby Face**. Who was she?
a) *Ginger Rogers* b) *Norma Shearer*
c) *Barbara Stanwyck* d) *Ida Lupino*

STABLES & BARNS

1) "Finlay Currie was one of the three kings, and was in the centre of the trio as they entered the stable. The king in front of Finlay tripped up, and his turban and frankincense went flying. As he fell to the ground, he screeched, 'Jesus Christ!' Finlay quickly turned towards Joseph and Mary, saying, 'Now there's a good name to give the bairn!'" This anecdote was recounted by co-cast member Laurence Payne with reference to an incident which occured during rehearsal. Name the film in which this hilarious nativity scene never appeared.
a) *The Greatest Story Ever Told* b) *Ben-Hur*
c) *Barabbas* d) *Quo Vadis?*

2) In which film does convict on the run, Arthur Blakey (Alan Bates), hide out in a barn?

a) *Far From the Madding Crowd* b) *The Running Man* c) *It's Never Too Late* d) *Whistle Down the Wind*

3) With which film do you associate James Cagney shooting a horse dead in its stable?
a) *The Public Enemy* b) *Jimmy the Gent*
c) *The Roaring Twenties* d) *Smart Money*

STAGECOACHES

1) Which 1953 film features the Deadwood stage?
a) *Annie Get Your Gun* b) *Calamity Jane*
c) *Oklahoma!* d) *Fancy Pants*

2) In which western does James Stewart portray an Eastern lawyer who is robbed and beaten on the stage to Shinbone?
a) *The Naked Spur* b) *Destry Rides Again*
c) *Broken Arrow* d) *The Man Who Shot Liberty Valance*

3) Name the western based on Ernest Haycox's story *Stage to Lordsburg*.
a) *Dodge City* b) *Western Union*
c) *Fort Apache* d) *Stagecoach*

STAGE DOORS

1) Bill Pettigrew (James Stewart) meets contemptuous Broadway actress, Daisy Heath, at the stage door in the 1938 drama, **The Shopworn Angel**. Who was she?
a) *Marjorie Reynolds* b) *Jeanette MacDonald*
c) *Ann Harding* d) *Margaret Sullavan*

2) With which film do you associate an assassination attempt on the great tenor, Enrico Caruso (Howard Caine), outside a stage door?
a) *Tonight We Sing* b) *Pay or Die*
c) *Terror at the Opera* d) *Badge of the Assassin*

3) Who directed **Stage Door Canteen**?
a) *Frank Borzage* b) *George Cukor*
c) *Henry King* d) *Stanley Donen*

STAIRCASES

1) What was the setting for the 1967 drama, **Up the Down Staircase**?
a) a factory b) a school
c) an office block d) a department store

2) In which film does Ralph Richardson die sliding down a staircase?
a) *The Fallen Idol* b) *Doctor Zhivago*
c) *Greystoke: The Legend of Tarzan, Lord of the Apes* d) *The Heiress*

3) Who directed the 1946 thriller, **The Spiral Staircase**?
a) *Robert Siodmak* b) *Michael Curtiz*
c) *William Dieterle* d) *Fritz Lang*

SUBMARINES

1) On whose novel was the 1990 superpower thriller, **The Hunt for Red October**, based?
a) *Wilbur Smith* b) *Tom Clancy*
c) *Frederick Forsyth* d) *Alistair MacLean*

2) Which film features a submarine with a pipe organ on which the captain plays Bach?
a) *Yellow Submarine* b) *Voyage to the Bottom of the Sea* c) *The NeverEnding Story* d) *20,000 Leagues Under the Sea*

3) In which film was James Bond's assignment to recover a device known as ATAC used to programme missiles on Polaris submarines?
a) *A View to a Kill*
b) *The Living Daylights*
c) *For Your Eyes Only*
d) *Licence to Kill*

SUBWAY TRAINS

1) Who portrayed 'Blue', the former mercenary, who, together with a team of criminals, hijacks a NYC subway train in **The Taking of Pelham One Two Three**?
a) *Martin Balsam* b) *Harry Dean Stanton*
c) *George C. Scott* d) *Robert Shaw*

2) Name the director responsible for the famous scene in **The Seven Year Itch**, in which Marilyn Monroe's skirt billows up around her shoulders when a passing subway train blows air through a grating.
a) *Jean Negulesco* b) *Howard Hawks*
c) *Joseph L. Mankiewicz* d) *Billy Wilder*

3) In which film does a drug baron outsmart a narcotics detective and escape on a subway train, waving complacently as the train departs the station?
a) *Death Wish 3* b) *The French Connection*
c) *Clockers* d) *To Live and Die in L.A.*

SUMMER CAMPS

1) Separated identical twins, Sharon and Susan McKendrick, meet for the first time at summer camp in a 1961 comedy adapted from Erich Kastner's much filmed story. Name the film.
a) *Camp Nowhere* b) *Summer Magic*
c) *Parent Trap* d) *Make a Wish*

2) In 1979 he portrayed 'Tripper', the senior summer camp counsellor in **Meatballs**. Who was he?
a) *Bill Murray* b) *Chevy Chase*
c) *Mel Brooks* d) *Danny De Vito*

The Movie Quiz Companion

snarling at patios

3) In which 1980 drama do two teenage girls place bets on who will be the first to lose her virginity at summer camp?
a) The Day My Parents Ran Away b) Moving Target c) It Takes Two d) Little Darlings

SUPERMARKETS

1) With which thriller do you associate Megan Turner (Jamie Lee Curtis) shooting a man dead in a supermarket?
a) Blue Steel b) True Lies
c) The Fog d) Terror Train

2) Which film features a character portrayed by Jeff Bridges writing a cheque for 67 cents in a Los Angeles supermarket?
a) City Slickers b) Raising Arizona c) The Big Lebowski d) What's Eating Gilbert Grape?

3) In which film does Jodie Foster portray a character who visits a supermarket for the first time?
a) Bugsy Malone b) Freaky Friday
c) Nell d) Taxi Driver

SWAMPS, MARSHES & MIRES

1) Name the 1946 drama shot on Kent's St. Mary's Marshes in the Thames Estuary.
a) Jane Eyre b) Great Expectations
c) The History of Mr. Polly d) A Matter of Life and Death

2) The set which 20th Century Fox built in 1939 for Grimpen Mire - in which actor Richard Greene got lost - was then the largest in the world. Name the film.
a) The Lost World
b) The Island of Doctor Moreau
c) The Werewolf
d) The Hound of the Baskervilles

3) Name the state which was the swamp location for Walter Hill's drama, **Southern Comfort**, through which National Guardsmen are pursued by local Cajuns.
a) Georgia
b) Tennesse
c) Louisiana
d) South Carolina

SWIMMING POOLS

1) Hollywood High School at one time had a concealed underfloor swimming pool which was cleverly used for a scene in a classic 1946 film. Name the title.
a) Key Largo b) The Great Gatsby
c) Mrs. Miniver d) It's a Wonderful Life

2) Alice Moore (Jane Randolph) keeps to the centre of the unlit pool, her screams of fear echoing around the walls, almost drowning the growls of the unseen panther that stalks her. Name the title of this classic 1942 horror film.
a) Cat Girl b) Cat People
c) The Curse of the Cat People d) The Cat Creature

3) Name the 1989 sci-fi comedy in which three aliens crash land their spaceship in a swimming pool.
a) Earth Girls Are Easy b) Coneheads
c) Explorers d) My Stepmother is an Alien

TAXIS

1) Which sci-fi drama features the robotic 'Johnnycab'?
a) Blade Runner b) Total Recall
c) Brazil d) Alphaville

2) What was Bowery saloon-keeper, Lady Lou (Mae West), given in a taxi by Captain Cummings (Cary Grant) in the finale of the 1933 comedy, **She Done him Wrong**?
a) the deeds to her saloon b) a diamond ring
c) a ticket to New York d) monogrammed handcuffs

3) **The Purple Taxi** (1977) is driven by an unorthodox doctor. Who was he?
a) Peter Ustinov b) Jack Lemmon
c) Philippe Noiret d) Fred Astaire

TENTS

1) In which 1950 western do the 'Sons of the Pioneers' sing 'I'll Take You Home Again Kathleen' to Mrs. Kathleen Yorke outside her husband's tent, Lt. Col. Kirby Yorke?
a) She Wore a Yellow Ribbon b) The Horse Soldiers c) Rio Grande d) Fort Apache

2) Fred C. Dobbs, Curtin and Howard share a tent in the Mexican mountains in 1948. Name the film.
a) The Treasure of the Sierra Madre b) My Side of the Mountain c) Three Fugitives d) Journey into Fear

3) In which film were students Heather, Michael and Joshua terrorized in their tent by something out in the woods?
a) The Beast Must Die b) Bigfoot
c) The Blair Witch Project d) Arachnophobia

THEATRES

1) Name the gangster (whose name is also the film title) who was shot dead outside Chicago's Biograph Theatre, in 1934.
a) Machine-Gun Kelly b) Baby Face Nelson
c) Dillinger d) Al Capone

2) Psychopathic theatre entrepreneur and strangler of middle-aged women, Christopher Gill, is finally cornered in his own theatre by policeman, George Segal, in **No Way to Treat a Lady** (1968). Who was he?
a) James Caan b) Karl Malden
c) Christopher Plummer d) Rod Steiger

3) In **Dead Poets Society** (1989), Neil (Robert Sean Leonard) is a student who longs to go on the stage, but his despotic father (Kurtwood Smith) forbids it. Ignoring his father's "orders", he performs in a Shakespeare play at his school's theatre.. Name the title of the play.
a) Twelfth Night b) Much Ado About Nothing
c) Romeo and Juliet d) A Midsummer Night's Dream

TOILETS

1) In which film does the following dialogue appear: "Brilliant gold taps, virginal white marble, a seat carved from ebony, a cistern full of Chanel Number five, and a flunky handing me pieces of raw silk toilet roll. But

under the circumstances I'll settle for anywhere."?
a) *Spinal Tap* b) *The Rocky Horror Picture Show*
c) *Two Hundred Motels* d) *Trainspotting*

2) Danny Glover finds himself in the delicate situation of sitting on a toilet that will trigger a bomb if he stood up. Name the film.
a) *Dead Man Out* b) *Lethal Weapon 2*
c) *A Rage in Harlem* d) *Predator 2*

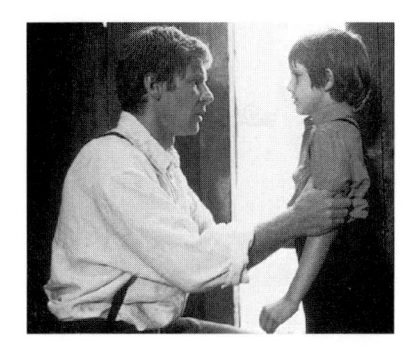

3) In which film does a small boy observe a man getting his throat cut in the toilets of Philadelphia railroad station?
a) *The Sixth Sense* b) *The Last Boy Scout*
c) *Witness* d) *Candyman*

TORTURE CHAMBERS

1) With which film do you associate Gary Cooper having wooden sticks pushed under his fingernails and set alight by his torturers?
a) *The Lives of a Bengal Lancer*
b) *Friendly Persuasion*
c) *The Plainsman*
d) *Beau Geste*

2) Roger Corman built an elaborate torture chamber for his 1961 horror film set just after the Spanish Inquisition. Name the title.
a) *The Raven* b) *The Masque of the Red Death*
c) *Tales of Terror* d) *The Pit and the Pendulum*

3) In which film is a character portrayed by Vincent Price axed to death in his own torture chamber?
a) *The Baron of Arizona*
b) *Witchfinder General*
c) *The Long Night*
d) *Tales of Terror*

TRAINS

1) Shanghai Lily (Marlene Dietrich) meets Captain Donald Harvey, one of her former lovers, on the **Shanghai Express** (1932). Who was he?
a) *Clive Brook* b) *Franchot Tone*
c) *Richard Cromwell* d) *Richard Dix*

2) Craig Belden was adamant that his old friend, Sheriff Matt Morgan (Kirk Douglas), would not board the **Last Train From Gun Hill** (1959) with his fugitive son. Who portrayed Belden?
a) *Ernest Borgnine* b) *Walter Huston*
c) *Burl Ives* d) *Anthony Quinn*

3) Name the 1987 black comedy which was inspired by Hitchcock's **Strangers on a Train**.
a) *Once Upon a Texas Train* b) *Runaway Train*
c) *Throw Momma From the Train* d) *Terror on a Train*

TRENCHES

1) In which film does Private Stan Laurel guard a WWI trench until 1938?
a) *Block-Heads* b) *Pack Up Your Troubles*
c) *Air Raid Wardens* d) *The Big Noise*

2) What was German soldier, Paul Baumer (Lew Ayres), reaching out of his trench for when he was killed by a sniper in **All Quiet on the Western Front**?
a) a photograph b) a locket
c) a flower d) a butterfly

3) With which film do you associate Kirk Douglas fighting in the trenches of WWI?
a) *The Last Sunset* b) *Paths of Glory*
c) *A Lovely Way to Die* d) *Ace in the Hole*

TUNNELS

1) Which film features the tunnels 'Tom', 'Dick' and 'Harry'?
a) *The Wooden Horse* b) *The Captive Heart*
c) *The Great Escape* d) *King Rat*

2) Bobbie, Phyllis and Peter, save the life of Jim the schoolboy when he injures his leg in a tunnel while running in a paperchase. Name the film.
a) *The Pied Piper* b) *Whistle Down the Wind*
c) *The Railway Children* d) *Thursday's Children*

3) In which film do medieval villagers tunnel through the earth and emerge in a futuristic city in the 1980s?
a) *The Navigator* b) *When Time Ran Out*
c) *Future Shock* d) *Time Bandits*

UNDERSEA WORLDS

1) Who was the **Man From Atlantis**?
a) *Chuck Connors* b) *Patrick Duffy*
c) *Eddie Byrne* d) *Michael Sarrazin*

2) With which film do you associate the god Triton ruling over an underwater kingdom?
a) *Jason and the Argonauts* b) *City Beneath the Sea* c) *The Little Mermaid* d) *The Underwater City*

3) Who played the title role in **Captain Nemo and the Underwater City**?
a) *James Mason* b) *Robert Ryan*
c) *Rex Harrison* d) *Donald Pleasence*

UNIVERSITIES

1) Name the Russian writer on whose memoirs the 1940 biopic, **My Universities**, was based.
a) *Maxim Gorky* b) *Fyodor Dostoevsky*
c) *Ivan Turgenev* d) *Leo Tolstoy*

2) In the 1993 film **Shadowlands**, American poet, Joy Gresham married C.S. Lewis, and infiltrated the male-dominated world of the Oxford don. Who was she?

a) Susan Sarandon b) Ann Bancroft
c) Debra Winger d) Annette Bening

3) Who played the title role in the 1938 comedy, **A Yank at Oxford**?
a) Walter Pidgeon b) Robert Powell
c) Henry Fonda d) Robert Taylor

VILLAGES

1) Physicist Gordon Zellaby blew up all the alien cloned children in the village school, and himself in the 1960 sci-fi thriller, **Village of the Damned**. Who was he?
a) Colin Clive b) Robert Preston
c) Walter Pidgeon d) George Sanders

2) Which 1944 film features an English village which is terrorised by the mysterious 'glue man'?
a) Windom's Way b) Ten Little Indians
c) The Last Days of Dolwyn d) A Canterbury Tale

3) In which 1978 spy yarn was the South African term, 'a one-horse dorp', used to describe a Scottish village called Strathallan?
a) Callan b) The Thirty-Nine Steps
c) The Quiller Memorandum d) The Jigsaw Man

VOLCANOES

1) On whose novel was John Huston's 1984 drama, **Under the Volcano**, based?
a) Malcolm Lowry b) Christopher Isherwood
c) William Golding d) F. Scott Fitzgerald

2) Who portrayed Father Matthew Doonan, who helps evacuate the patients of a children's hospital to safety during a volcanic eruption in the 1961 adventure, **The Devil at 4 O'Clock**?
a) Pat O'Brien b) Richard Widmark
c) Spencer Tracy d) Barry Fitzgerald

3) Name the Bond film in which SPECTRE launches rockets from a hollow volcano to capture Soviet and US space craft.
a) Live and Let Die b) Diamonds Are Forever
c) You Only Live Twice d) Moonraker

WAGON TRAINS

1) Who directed the 1950 western, **Wagon Master**, starring Ward Bond, which was the inspiration for the long-running TV series, Wagon Train?
a) Howard Hawks b) Anthony Mann
c) Fred Zinneman d) John Ford

2) In 1952 he portrayed outlaw turned wagon train guide, Glyn McLyntock, in Anthony Mann's **Bend of the River**. Who was he?
a) Arthur Kennedy b) Glenn Ford
c) John Wayne d) James Stewart

3) Robert Taylor led a wagon train full of women who were headed for California in **Westward the Women**. Who or what did the women expect would be waiting for them at their destination?
a) their chidren held hostages by the Apaches
b) mail-order husbands c) the President of the U.S.A. d) jobs as dance-hall hostesses

WATERFALLS

1) With which film do you associate Sassy the cat being swept over a waterfall?
a) Homeward Bound: The Incredible Journey
b) The Cat c) Journey Back to Oz
d) The Cat From Outer Space

2) Name the sleuth, portrayed by Christopher Lee, who is sent by King Edward to South Africa to bring back a priceless diamond in the 1991 mystery, **Incident at Victoria Falls**.
a) Sherlock Holmes b) Paul Temple
c) Hercule Poirot d) Father Brown

3) In which 1992 historical drama does a group of desperate people await the arrival of the terrifying 'Magua' (Wes Studi) under a waterfall?
a) Revolution b) Black Robe
c) Mountains of the Moon d) The Last of the Mohicans

WEDDINGS

1) In which film does Toni Collette portray a girl who enters a marriage of convenience with a gormless South African swimming champion?
a) Muriel's Wedding b) The Wedding Party
c) The Wedding Gift d) When Strangers Marry

2) Who portrayed the bride in Vincente Minnelli's 1950 comedy, **Father of the Bride**?
a) Audrey Hepburn
b) Elizabeth Taylor
c) Doris Day
d) Grace Kelly

3) Name the Frank Capra film in which the bridegroom arrives at the wedding ceremony in an autogyro to marry heiress Ellie Andrews.
a) You Can't Take it With You
b) Platinum Blonde
c) It Happened One Night
d) Broadway Bill

WESTERN SALOONS

1) With which film do you associate Alan Ladd ordering a glass of milk in a western saloon?
a) The Badlanders b) This Gun for Hire
c) Shane d) Great Guns

2) In 1937 he portrayed villainous saloon-keeper, Mickey Finn, who battles with Laurel and Hardy in **Way Out West**. Who was he?
a) James Finlayson b) Buster Keaton
c) Eric Campbell d) Ben Turpin

3) In which film does Wyatt Earp drag drunken 'Indian Charlie' out of a saloon and dump him at the feet of the town mayor, saying: "What kind of town is this, serving liquor to Indians?"?
a) My Darling Clementine b) Tombstone
c) Gunfight at the O.K. Corral d) Winchester '73

WINDMILLS

1) Which classic comedy features a windmill haunted by the ghost of a miller named 'One-eyed Joe'?
a) The Happiest Days of Your Life b) Blithe Spirit
c) Hue and Cry d) Oh, Mr Porter!

2) With which Hitchcock thriller do you associate a Dutch windmill turning against the wind?
a) Foreign Correspondent b) To Catch a Thief
c) Topaz d) Torn Curtain

3) Which film features the Oscar-winning song: 'The Windmills of Your Mind', by Michel Legrand and Alan & Marilyn Bergman?
a) The Way We Were b) The Thomas Crown Affair
c) A Time For Loving d) The Umbrellas of Cherbourg

YACHTS

1) In which 1989 thriller are Nicole Kidman and Sam Neill terrorised by a homocidal maniac on their yacht?
a) Dead Reckoning b) Storm
c) Dead Calm d) Into the Night

2) What was the name of the yacht (which was also the title of the 1974 film) in which seafarer, Robin Lee Graham, sailed on a five year voyage around the world?
a) Red Dawn b) The Dove
c) The Sea Wolf
d) The Islander

3) With which film do you associate cockney mobster, Harold Shand, living on a luxury yacht moored on the Thames?
a) Two Way Stretch b) Gumshoe
c) The Krays d) The Long Good Friday

ZOOS

1) After waking up naked in the wolf pen at London Zoo in **An American Werewolf in London**, what does David Kessler (David Naughton) steal from a child to cover his nudity?
a) balloons
b) a kite
c) a golliwog
d) candy-floss

2) Name the actress who portrayed a young girl on the run from an orphanage, who hides out at the zoo, in the 1933 romance, **Zoo in Budapest**?
a) Loretta Young
b) Greta Garbo
c) Constance Bennett
d) Katharine Hepburn

3) Name the 1976 adventure in which Bill Travers and Virginia McKenna return a lion born in London Zoo back to the wilds of Africa.
a) The Lion
b) Christian the Lion
c) The Lion at the World's End
d) The Lion Has Wings

CHARACTERS

ANDY HARDY

1) Name the town in which the the Hardy family lived.
*a) Carvel b) Cloverdale
c) Unionville d) Rockwood*

2) Who portrayed Andy Hardy's (Mickey Rooney) venerable father in the series throughout the 1930s and 40s?
*a) Lewis Stone b) John Barrymore
c) H.B. Warner d) Roscoe Karns*

3) MGM won a special Oscar for the series. What was it for?
a) launching young talent b) representing the American Way of Life c) the most popular series of all time d) upholding family values

BATMAN & ROBIN

1) Batman made his comic book debut in a spring issue of 'Detective Comics', pencilled by Bob Kane, and scripted by his Bronx neighbour, Bill Finger. Name the year.
a) 1930 b) 1936 c) 1939 d) 1943

2) Which English stately home doubled for Wayne Manor, the caped-crusader's tranquil retreat from the crime-ridden streets of Gotham, in **Batman** (1989)?
*a) Knebworth House b) Hatfield House
c) Wilton House d) Osborne House*

3) Batman's real-life identity was the astoundingly wealthy Bruce Wayne. What was Robin's?
*a) Dick Grayson b) Pete Hoffman
c) Johnny Craig d) Vic Chandler*

BATMAN VILLAINS

1) What is the occupation of the demented 'Two-Face' in **Batman Forever**?
*a) Police Commissioner b) District Attorney
c) Mayor d) Senator*

2) Fiendish tycoon, Max Shreck, plots to build a power plant which will sap all of Gotham's energy in **Batman Returns**. Who was he?
*a) Tommy Lee Jones b) Jack Palance
c) Christopher Walken d) Gary Oldman*

3) What was Uma Thurman's character name in **Batman & Robin**?
*a) Venus Batcatcher b) Poison Ivy
c) Deadly Nightshade d) Thelma Thorn*

THE BEATLES

1) Which one of The Beatles addressed the bemused audience after the live rooftop session in Lindsay Hogg's 1969 film, **Let It Be**, with the words: "I'd like to say thank you on behalf of the group and ourselves, and I hope we passed the audition!"?
a) John b) Paul c) Ringo d) George

2) What did Ringo have in his possession that a bizarre religious sect were desperate to get their hands on in Richard Lester's 1965 musical comedy, **Help!**?
*a) the key to a tomb b) a sacrificial ring
c) the lyrics of a secret chant d) a bronze idol*

3) In which film did the songs 'Only a Northern Song' and 'It's All Too Much',

appear?
a) A Hard Day's Night b) Help!
c) Yellow Submarine d) Sgt. Pepper's Lonely Hearts Club Band

BILLY THE KID

1) Who played the title role in the 1941 western, **Billy the Kid**?
a) Joel McCrea b) Victor Mature
c) Tyrone Power d) Robert Taylor

2) What was Bob Dylan's character name in Sam Peckinpah's 1973 western, **Pat Garett and Billy the Kid**?
a) Hick b) Alias c) Big Boy d) Lemuel

3) Name the title of the 1958 western, directed by Arthur Penn, in which the outlaw Billy Bonney was portrayed by Paul Newman.
a) The Left-Handed Gun b) Cast a Long Shadow
c) Bitter Creek d) The Peacemaker

BLONDIE

1) The **Blondie** series debuted in 1938, and continued with the same female lead for all of its 28 episodes over the next 12 years. Who was she?
a) Joan Davis b) Mae Clarke
c) Penny Singleton d) Joan Blondell

2) Arthur Lake portrayed Blondie's bumbling husband in the series. What was his character name?

a) Curley Harper b) Frankie Doodle
c) Slim Jim d) Dagwood Bumstead

3) Name the cartoonist who created the original comic strip character of Blondie Boopadoop in the summer of 1930.
a) Chic Young b) Bud Blake
c) Max Fleischer d) Milt Gross

BOND GIRLS

1) The epitome of the James Bond Girl, Honey Ryder (Ursula Andress) was beautiful, intelligent, bold, inventive, and she ingeniously killed a rapist in **Dr. No** (1962). How did she do it?
a) with a black widow spider b) with a vampire bat c) with a cobra d) with a weasel

2) Jill Masterson pays with her life for aiding James Bond when she is covered in gold paint and dies from skin suffocation in **Goldfinger** (1964). Who was she?
a) Tania Mallet b) Honor Blackman
c) Diana Rigg d) Shirley Eaton

3) Who portrayed 'Solitaire', the beautiful virgin whose psychic powers are indispensable to the evil Dr. Kananga in **Live and Let Die** (1973)?
a) Lana Wood b) Jane Seymour
c) Tanya Roberts d) Barbara Bach

BOND VILLAINS

1) In which film does James Bond first meet SPECTRE master criminal, Ernst Stavro Blofeld (Donald Pleasence)?
a) A View to a Kill b) You Only Live Twice
c) Moonraker d) The Man With the Golden Gun

2) Which villain tells James Bond: "You are nothing more than a stupid policeman ... whose luck has run out!"?
a) Dr. No b) Auric Goldfinger
c) Francisco Scaramanga d) Hugo Drax

3) Eccentric and dapper villain, Kamal Khan, in **Octopussy** (1983), was portrayed by a handsome romantic lead of the 1940s and 50s, whose films included **Letter From an Unknown Woman** and **Gigi**. Who was he?

a) Brian Aherne b) Michael Wilding
c) Louis Jourdan d) Robert Young

BOSTON BLACKIE

1) Boston Blackie, a former thief turned private detective, was portrayed by the same actor in 14 films from 1941 to 1949. Who was he?
a) Chester Morris b) Robert Kent
c) Ralph Meeker d) Robert Bray

2) Actor George E. Stone portrayed Blackie's comical sidekick in the majority of films in the series. What was his character name?
a) Bigsby b) Jumbo c) The Runt d) Bidder

3) **Meet Boston Blackie** (1941) was the first film in the series. The director's other films included the Marx Brothers' first film, **The Cocoanuts** (1929), **Murders in the Rue Morgue** (1932), and **The Beast With Five Fingers** (1945). He also collaborated on the original script for **Frankenstein** (1931) and in 1950 the French government made him a knight of the Légion d'Honneur for his contribution to film. Who was he?
a) Edward Dmytryk b) James Whale
c) Frank Borzage d) Robert Florey

BUGS BUNNY

1) Name the animation artist who said, "My Bugs, I think, tended to think out his problems and solve them intellectually, and I insisted upon stronger provocation. Two or three things would happen before he got mad enough—no, he wasn't mad, just the

logic would move in—and he'd say, 'Of course, you realize this means war ... "?
a) Tex Avery b) Chuck Jones
c) Frank Tashlin d) Bob Clampett

2) Bugs Bunny was created by a group of Warner Bros. artists, and the original sketch was done by Bugs Hardaway, who labelled his drawings Bugs's Bunny. Name the year this wisecracking rabbit was conceived.
a) 1932 b) 1936 c) 1942 d) 1947

3) What is the title of the first real Bugs Bunny cartoon?
a) Corny Concerto b) The Old Grey Hare
c) What's Cookin' Doc? d) A Wild Hare

BUFFALO BILL

1) Who played the title role in William Wellman's 1944 biopic, **Buffalo Bill**?
a) Joel McCrea b) Henry Fonda
c) Errol Flynn d) Howard Keel

2) Which 1950 film features Buffalo Bill (Louis Calhern) in MGM's version of a Broadway musical in which a character discovers that "you can't get a man with a gun"?
a) Showboat
b) Calamity Jane
c) Annie Get Your Gun d) Oklahoma!

3) In which film did Paul Newman portray Buffalo Bill?
a) The Left-Handed Gun b) Cariboo Trail c) Wild Bill d) Buffalo Bill and the Indians, or Sitting Bull's History Lesson

BULLDOG DRUMMOND

1) Bulldog Drummond was a tough, no-nonsense Englishman who fought clean and tackled villains with a square blow to the jaw accompanied by the phrases: "you vile hound", "blackguard", and "conceited ass". Name his creator.
a) Margery Allingham
b) James Hadley Chase
c) H.R.F. Keating
d) Herman 'Sapper' McNeile

2) **Bulldog Drummond** made his talkie debut in 1929 portrayed by Ronald Colman who comes to the rescue of American Phyllis Benton whose father is held prisoner in an insane asylum. Who was she?
a) Heather Angel b) Joan Bennett
c) Louise Campbell d) Ann Todd

3) What was the character name of Bulldog Drummond's trusty sidekick?
a) Danny b) Singer c) Jerry d) Algy

CHARLIE CHAN

1) Which actor was responsible for turning the character into a popular hit series in the 1930s?
a) Sidney Toler b) Warner Oland
c) J. Carrol Naish d) Roland Winters

2) The original novels featured Charlie Chan as an oriental sleuth on the Honolulu police force. Who wrote them?
a) Davis Grubb b) Ross MacDonald
c) Earl Derr Biggers d) Edgar Wallace

3) Name the year Charlie Chan made his screen debut.
a) 1926 b) 1930 c) 1933 d) 1936

DAVY CROCKETT

1) Which film featured John Wayne as Col. David Crockett?
a) The Big Trail b) Dakota
c) The Alamo d) The Comancheros

2) According to the lyrics of Disney's theme song for **Davy Crockett, King of the Wild Frontier** (1955), what age was Davy when he killed a bear?
a) two b) three c) four d) five

3) Fess Parker played the title role in **Davy Crockett, King of the Wild Frontier** (1955), and also in the sequel released the following year. Name the title.
a) Davy Crockett and the River Pirates b) Davy Crockett Goes to Washington c) Davy Crockett Meets Daniel Boone d) Davy Crockett's Last Command

THE DEAD END KIDS

1) The Dead End Kids series ran from 1937 to 1943. After a stint as the East Side Kids, the series was rechristened in 1946. Name the title of the new series.
a) Dead Enders
b) Street Angels
c) The Bowery Boys
d) The Kids From Hell's Kitchen

2) In which 1938 crime drama do the Dead End Kids idolize a gangster named Rocky Sullivan?
a) Mob Town
b) Little Tough Guy
c) They Made Me a Criminal
d) Angels With Dirty Faces

fetishes act woke witch

Characters

3) Who portrayed 'Dippy', the rubber-faced dim-witted buddy of gang-leader 'Spit'?
a) Huntz Hall b) Leo Gorcey
c) Billy Halop d) Bobby Jordan

DICK TRACY

1) Name the cartoonist who first created the detective thriller, Dick Tracy, on October 12, 1931.
a) Chester Gould b) Mel Graff
c) Jesse Marsh d) Joe Orlando

2) In the 1947 crime drama, **Dick Tracy Meets Gruesome**, Gruesome freezes people on the spot with an experimental gas during a bank robbery. Name the Hollywood legend who portrayed Gruesome.
a) Humphrey Bogart b) James Cagney
c) Boris Karloff d) George Romero

3) What is Madonna's character name in Warren Beatty's 1990 comedy adventure, **Dick Tracy**?
a) Tess Trueheart b) Sweet Sue
c) Kiss Kellerman d) Breathless Mahoney

DR. KILDARE

1) MGM's Dr. Kildare series ran from 1938 to 1947. Name the hospital around which it was based.
a) Hollywood Central Hospital b) Blair General Hospital c) Kruger Memorial Hospital d) St. Margaret-Rose Hospital

2) The actor who replaced Lew Ayres in the title role in **Dr. Gillespie's New Assistant** (1942), counselled Tommy (Gene Kelly) in **Brigadoon**, and fell in love with Sarah (Deborah Kerr) in **The End of the Affair**. Who was he?
a) George Montgomery b) Jose Ferrer
c) Arthur Kennedy d) Van Johnson

3) Name the veteran Hollywood actor who portrayed Dr. Gillespie in the series.
a) Fredric March b) Raymond Massey
c) Lionel Barrymore d) Charles Coburn

DRACULA

1) Who played the title role in **Nosferatu** (1922), a film which could not use the 'Dracula' name because of copyright problems with Bram Stoker's estate?
a) S.Z. Sakall b) Vladimir Sokoloff
c) Max Shreck d) Nils Kessler

2) Hammer Studios' **Dracula**, starring Christopher Lee in the title role, was shot in only twenty-five days and became a huge success. What year was it released?
a) 1958 b) 1960 c) 1962 d) 1964

3) Countess Marya Zaleska (Gloria Holden) was a descendant of Dracula in a 1936 sequel to Bela Lugosi's **Dracula** (1931). By what name was she better known?
a) Dracula's Daughter b) Dracula's Widow
c) Countess Dracula d) Lady Dracula

THE FALCON

1) George Saunders portrayed The Falcon in three films, but the character was taken over by his real-life brother in 1942. Who was he?
a) John Calvert b) Tom Conway
c) Walter Pigeon d) Buster Crabbe

2) The plot from **The Falcon Takes Over** (1942) was based on a Raymond Chandler novel. Name the title.
a) Farewell My Lovely b) The Big Sleep
c) The Long Goodbye d) Killer in the Rain

3) In which 1943 mystery is The Falcon framed for murder?
a) The Gay Falcon b) The Falcon's Alibi
c) The Falcon Strikes Back d) The Falcon Out West

FRANKENSTEIN'S MONSTER

1) In 1935 she portrayed both the author of *Frankenstein* and the **Bride of Frankenstein**. Who was she?
a) Valerie Hobson
b) Elsa Lanchester
c) Una O'Connor
d) Lillian Gish

2) Who portrayed Baron Victor Frankenstein in Hammer's 1957 horror classic, **The Curse of Frankenstein**?
a) Christopher Lee
b) Vincent Price
c) Peter Cushing d) J. Carrol Naish

3) The director of the 1974 comedy spoof, **Young Frankenstein**, once claimed: "My movies rise below vulgarity." Who was he?
a) Andy Warhol b) Ken Russell
c) Roger Corman d) Mel Brooks

FRED KRUEGER

1) Finish the rhyme: "One, two; Freddy's comin' for you / Three, four; better lock your

127

door / Five, six; grab your crucifix / Seven, eight; gonna stay up late / Nine, ten; never ...
a) go to bed again b) dream again
c) sleep again d) close your eyes again

2) Which film features Freddy penetrating the dreams of patients on a psychiatric ward?
a) A Nightmare on Elm Street, Part 2: Freddy's Revenge b) A Nightmare on Elm Street 3: Dream Warriors c) A Nightmare on Elm Street 4: The Dream Master d) A Nightmare on Elm Street 5: The Dream Child

3) In the original **A Nightmare on Elm Street** (1984), the heroine's boyfriend, Glen Lantz, is one of Freddy's victims. An unknown at the time, this actor has since become a household name. Who was he?
a) Brad Pitt b) River Phoenix
c) Michael J. Fox d) Johnny Depp

FLASH GORDON

1) Flash Gordon, Yale graduate and champion polo player, meets his future girlfriend after the airliner in which they are felllow passengers is struck by a meteor. What was her name?
a) Eve Rainsford b) Kim Lang
c) Dale Arden d) Lola Jones

2) Ming, the Merciless was a combination of the Yellow Peril and a galactic Fu Manchu and the sworn enemy of Flash Gordon. Who portrayed him?
a) George Cleveland b) Charles Middleton
c) Frank Shannon d) Richard Alexander

3) Name the race of people who live deep underground in the 1930s serial, **Flash Gordon's Trip to Mars**?
a) the Clay People b) the Fringe Dwellers
c) the Mud Monsters d) the Secret Tribe

FU MANCHU

1) Arthur Henry Ward first saw the man who inspired him to create the mysterious and inscrutable master-criminal, Fu Manchu, in 1911 in London's Chinatown, describing his face as "the living embodiment of Satan." Under what pen name did Ward begin writing about this sinister villain?
a) Emmanuel Adler b) Mark Carlson
c) Forrest Schiller d) Sax Rohmer

2) Who played the title role in the 1932 horror film, **The Mask of Fu Manchu**?
a) Bela Lugosi b) Lon Chaney
c) Boris Karloff d) J. Carrol Naish

3) Christopher Lee portrayed Fu Manchu five times. Name the title of the first film in the series.
a) The Blood of Fu Manchu b) The Vengeance of Fu Manchu c) The Brides of Fu Manchu d) The Face of Fu Manchu

GENERAL CUSTER

1) In which film did Robert Shaw portray General Custer?
a) The Legend of the Golden Gun b) Custer of the West c) Tonka d) The Great Sioux Massacre

2) Who directed Errol Flynn as the dashing Custer in the 1941 western biopic, **They Died With Their Boots On**?
a) John Ford b) Howard Hawks
c) Lewis Milestone d) Raoul Walsh

3) With which film do you associate Jack Crabb observing Custer's 'last stand' at the Battle of the Little Bighorn?
a) The Plainsman b) Santa Fe Trail
c) Warpath d) Little Big Man

HENRY ALDRICH

1) In Paramount's version of the **Andy Hardy Series**, high school teenager Henry Aldrich and family entertained audiences in the early 1940s. Who played the definitive Henry?
a) Jimmy Lydon b) Bobby Ellis
c) Jackie Cooper d) Billy Halop

2) Charles Smith portrayed Henry's devious buddy in the series. What was his character name?
a) Cookie b) Dizzy c) Shorty d) Curly

3) Who portrayed Henry's father?
a) Charles Smith b) Rod Cameron
c) John Litel d) Vaughan Glaser

HERCULE POIROT

1) In which film did Peter Ustinov first portray Agatha Christie's master sleuth?
a) Appointment With Death b) Death on the Nile
c) Evil Under the Sun d) Dead Man's Folly

2) With which film do you associate the appearance of both Hercule Poirot and Miss Marple?
a) The Alphabet Murders b) Murder on the Orient Express c) Dumb Witness d) Murder at the Vicarage

3) What nationality is Hercule Poirot?
a) French b) Dutch c) Belgian d) Austrian

HERCULES

1) Name the former "Mr. Universe" who portrayed him in Pietro Francisci's 1959 Italian production.
a) Jock Mahoney b) Buster Crabbe
c) Lex Barker d) Steve Reeves

2) What group of comedians does Hercules meet in 1962?
a) Marx Brothers b) Abbott and Costello
c) Three Stooges d) Dead End Kids

3) With which 1963 film do you associate Hercules and the quest to find the "Golden Fleece"?
a) Ulysses Against Hercules b) The Loves of Hercules c) Jason and the Argonauts d) Hercules the Invincible

HITLER, ADOLF

1) Captain Thorndike attempts to assassinate Hitler at Berchtesgaden in Fritz Lang's 1941 anti-Nazi thriller, **Man Hunt**. Who played Thorndike?
a) Robert Young b) Dick Powell
c) Walter Pidgeon d) Van Johnson

2) Chaplin's 1940 satirical comedy, **The Great Dictator**, cast Mussolini as 'Napolini', Goebbels as 'Garbitsch' and Goering as 'Herring'. What name did he use for Hitler?
a) Hynkel b) Hackle
c) Hurtkill d) Hatpin

3) In which film does a character portrayed by Orson Welles appear in a newsreel standing on a balcony with Adolf Hitler?
a) Journey Into Fear b) House of Cards
c) History of the World - Part 1 d) Citizen Kane

HOPALONG CASSIDY

1) 'Hoppy' appeared in 66 westerns and was based on the morally upstanding hero in the novels of Clarence E. Mulford. Who portrayed him?
a) Hoot Gibson b) Rory Calhoun c) William Boyd
d) Slim Pickens

2) Why was he nicknamed 'Hopalong'?
a) he was wounded by a bullet that made him limp b) he always made the baddies 'hopalong' to jail in the finale c) he always mounted his horse with a hop, skip and jump d) Hopalong was his horse - the original series was titled 'Hopalong & Cassidy'

3) What was the name of Hoppy's ranch?
a) Tumbleweed b) Bar 20
c) Arrowhead d) Ramrod

INDIANA JONES

1) What does Indiana Jones have an intense hatred of?
a) spiders b) cats
c) snakes d) horses

2) In which city are the opening scenes of **Indiana Jones and the Temple of Doom** set?
a) Venice b) San Francisco c) Shanghai d) Cairo

3) What does Indy throw across a chasm, supposedly in exchange for his whip which his treacherous guide denies him and abandons him to his doom in **Raiders of the Lost Ark** (1981)?
a) the Holy Grail b) an idol
c) the Ark of the Covenant d) a crystal

INSPECTOR CLOUSEAU

1) In which film was Inspector Clouseau on the trail of an infamous jewel thief named 'The Phantom'?
a) A Shot in the Dark b) The Pink Panther c) The Return of the Pink Panther d) The Pink Panther Strikes Again

2) Inspector Clouseau refuses to believe the beautiful Maria Gambrelli is guilty of murder in **A Shot in the Dark** (1964). Who was she?
a) Elke Sommer b) Britt Ekland
c) Ursula Andress d) Lynne Frederick

3) Which film features Inspector Clouseau faking his death and disguising himself as a sailor with a stuffed parrot stuck on his shoulder?
a) The Return of the Pink Panther b) Revenge of the Pink Panther c) Trail of the Pink Panther d) Curse of the Pink Panther

JACK THE RIPPER

1) Name the super-sleuth who investigated Jack the Ripper's gruesome murders in the 1979 mystery, **Murder By Decree**?
a) Hercule Poirot b) Sherlock Holmes
c) Ellery Queen d) Father Brown

2) In which film does Jack the Ripper depart Victorian London and escape into the future using H.G. Wells's time machine?
a) Somewhere in Time
b) A Time For Killing
c) Time After Time d) A Time to Die

The Movie Quiz Companion

ancient lore

3) Which actor played the role of the demented General Jack D. Ripper, in Stanley Kubrick's **Dr. Strangelove**?
a) George C. Scott b) James Earl Jones
c) Slim Pickens d) Sterling Hayden

JAMES BOND

1) Name the Bond film which has a famous sequence shot on the 16th, 17th, and 18th holes of Stoke Poges Golf Club in Buckinghamshire.
a) GoldenEye b) Octopussy
c) You Only Live Twice d) Goldfinger

2) Which 1977 film broke with tradition and used a Lotus Esprit (nicknamed 'Wet Nellie') as 007's personal vehicle instead of his usual Aston Martin DB5?
a) The Spy Who Loved Me b) The Man With the Golden Gun c) Moonraker d) For Your Eyes Only

3) Timothy Dalton only portrayed 007 in two films. **The Living Daylights** was one. Name the other.
a) A View to Kill b) Licence to Kill c) The Man With the Golden Gun d) For Your Eyes Only

JESSE JAMES

1) Who was mistaken for the notorious outlaw in the 1959 western comedy, **Alias Jesse James**?
a) Jack Lemmon b) Bob Hope
c) Jerry Lewis d) Rock Hudson

2) In Sam Fuller's 1949 western, **I Shot Jesse James**, Jesse is shot in the back by Bob Ford who seeks the large reward on his head. What was Bob Ford's line of work?
a) a bounty hunter
b) a gang member
c) a saloon-keeper
d) a U.S. Marshal

3) Tyrone Power played the title role in Henry King's 1939 western, **Jesse James**. Who portrayed his brother Frank James?
a) Henry Fonda
b) James Stewart
c) Joel McCrea
d) Ernest Borgnine

JESUS CHRIST

1) Who directed **Jesus Christ Superstar** (1973)?
a) Norman Jewison b) Robert Wise
c) Barry Levinson d) Jim Sharman

2) With which epic film do you associate Max von Sydow portraying Christ?
a) The Big Fisherman b) Ben Hur
c) The Greatest Story Ever Told d) Quo Vadis?

3) On whose novel was Martin Scorsese's **The Last Temptation of Christ** (1988) based?
a) Gore Vidal b) Nikos Kazantzakis
c) Malcolm Bradbury d) Anthony Burgess

KING ARTHUR

1) Which 1953 film featured Mel Ferrer as King Arthur?
a) Knights of the Round Table b) The Black Shield of Falworth c) Ivanhoe d) Sword of Lancelot

2) In which film does Morgana, Arthur's half-sister, seduce Arthur by adopting the appearance of Guinevere?
a) The Black Knight b) Arthur the King
c) Excalibur d) Camelot

3) Who is the loony horseless King Arthur in **Monty Python and the Holy Grail** (1975)?
a) Terry Jones b) Eric Idle
c) Michael Palin d) Graham Chapman

LASSIE

1) Who wrote the classic tale of the Yorkshire sheep dog which inspired the popular series of films, TV and radio shows?
a) Sheila Burnford b) Eric Knight
c) Willard Price d) Nina Bawden

2) Name the 1953 John Wayne western in which Lassie appears.
a) Hondo b) 3 Godfathers
c) Rio Grande d) The Fighting Kentuckian

3) The original Lassie, who first appeared in MGM's **Lassie Come Home** (1943), was in fact a male collie owned and trained by Rudd Weatherwax. What was his name?
a) Jim b) Shep c) Pal d) Franco

ABRAHAM LINCOLN

1) Who directed the 1939 biopic, **Young Mr. Lincoln**, with Henry Fonda in the title role?
a) Frank Borzage b) John Ford
c) Raoul Walsh d) Henry Hathaway

2) Detective John Kennedy averts an assassination attempt on Abraham Lincoln during a train journey in Anthony Mann's 1951 thriller, **The Tall Target**. Who was he?
a) Gig Young b) Adolphe Menjou
c) John Wayne d) Dick Powell

3) With which film do you associate Keanu Reeves meeting Abraham Lincoln?
a) Youngblood b) The Prince of Pennsylvania
c) My Own Private Idaho d) Bill & Ted's Excellent Adventure

THE LONE RANGER

1) The Lone Ranger began his life in comic books and on radio, and was launched as a fifteen-chapter serial by Republic in 1937. Who portrayed him?
a) Lee Powell b) William Boyd
c) Gene Autry d) Jack Carson

2) The actor who portrayed The Lone Ranger's faithful companion, Tonto (Jay Silverheels), was a full-blooded Indian. What tribe did he belong to?
a) Cheyenne b) Mohawk
c) Sioux d) Comanche

3) Clayton Moore will always be the definitive Lone Ranger, but in 1979 a restraining order (later revoked) prevented him from appearing in character. Why?
a) it was revealed he had a criminal record b) he was getting too old and a younger lead was being promoted c) he was too fat d) his politics were becoming too right-wing

MICKEY MOUSE

1) In which year did Mickey Mouse make his film debut in the animated short, **Plane Crazy**?
a) 1926 b) 1928 c) 1930 d) 1932

2) He made his feature film debut in **Fantasia** (1940) accompanied by the symphonic poem, 'L'Apprenti sorcier' (The Sorcerer's Apprentice). Who composed it?
a) Paul Dukas b) Claude Debussy c) Georges Bizet d) Jacques Offenbach

3) Walt Disney originally called Mickey by another name. What was it?
a) Mikey b) Mel c) Mortimer d) Matty

MIKE HAMMER

1) Who was Mike Hammer's creator?
a) Raymond Chandler b) Ellery Queen c) James Hadley Chase d) Mickey Spillane

2) In which 1963 film did his creator cast himself as "Mike Hammer"?
a) The Girl Hunters b) My Gun is Quick c) I, The Jury d) Murder Takes All

3) What were the contents of the Pandora's box in Robert Aldrich's, **Kiss Me Deadly**?
a) diamonds b) a human head c) radioactive material d) Mike Hammer's last will and testament

MISS MARPLE

1) On which Agatha Christie whodunnit was the 1961 Miss Marple mystery, **Murder, She Said**, based?
a) Cat Among the Pigeons b) Dumb Witness c) Murder at the Vicarage d) 4:50 From Paddington

2) Who portrayed Miss Marple in the 1980 mystery, **The Mirror Crack'd**?
a) Joan Hickson b) Angela Lansbury c) Helen Hayes d) Shelley Winters

3) Margaret Rutherford was the definitive Miss Marple. In which 1966 film did she make her last appearance as Agatha Christie's sleuth?
a) The Alphabet Murders b) Murder at the Gallop c) Murder Ahoy d) Murder Most Foul

MONSIEUR HULOT

1) In which film did French slapstick comedian, Jacques Tati, make his debut as Monsieur Hulot?
a) Playtime b) Traffic c) Mon Oncle d) Mr. Hulot's Holiday

2) With which film do you associate Monsieur Hulot lighting his pipe and tossing the lighted match into a shed full of fireworks?
a) Playtime b) Traffic c) Mon Oncle d) Mr. Hulot's Holiday

3) In the 1972 comedy, **Traffic**, Monsieur Hulot played a car designer journeying to a European city for a motor show. Name the city.
a) Paris b) Amsterdam c) Rome d) Berlin

MR. BELVEDERE

1) Pretentious bachelor, acidic wit, and self-confessed genius, no one ever got the better of Mr. Belvedere. Who portrayed him?
a) Monty Wooley b) Herbert Marshall c) Clifton Webb d) Edmund Lowe

2) Who portrayed the parents who employed Lynn Belvedere as an autocratic babysitter in the 1948 comedy, **Sitting Pretty**?
a) Robert Young & Maureen O'Hara b) Joseph Cotton & Loretta Young c) Robert Cummings & Jean Arthur d) Franchot Tone & Gloria Grahame

3) As the most zestful resident of an old folks' home in **Mr. Belvedere Rings the Bell** (1951), Lynn Belvedere convinces the residents his youthful demeanour is derived from tablets he receives regularly from Tibet. What does he steal from the local museum to make his claim seem legitimate?
a) a prayer wheel b) a Tibetan stamp c) a yak horn d) a picture of the Dalai Lama

MR. MOTO

1) Fox attempted to revive Mr. Moto in 1965 with **The Return of Mr. Moto**. Who portrayed him?
a) Henry Silva b) Cornel Wilde c) David Carradine d) Harold Sakata

2) Twentieth Century Fox made eight films about the super-sleuth and master of disguise, Mr. Moto, from 1937 to 1939. Who played the title role?

The Movie Quiz Companion

a) Charles Boyer
b) Lon Chaney Jr.
c) Boris Karloff
d) Peter Lorre

3) Name the title of the first film in the series.
a) Think Fast, Mr. Moto
b) Mysterious Mr. Moto
c) Mr. Moto Takes a Chance
d) Mr. Moto's Gamble

NANCY DREW

1) On whose juvenile mystery novels was Warner Brothers' late 30s **Nancy Drew** series based?
a) Elizabeth Smart
b) May Sarton
c) Carolyn Keene
d) Aurania Rouverol

2) Plucky, intelligent and ingenious, girl detective Nancy Drew is always capable of solving the most mysterious crime. Name the actress who portrayed her.
a) Eve Arden
b) Bonita Granville
c) Mae Busch
d) Nancy Carroll

3) In which film did Nancy Drew make her debut?

a) Nancy Drew and the Hidden Staircase
b) Nancy Drew - Troubleshooter
c) Nancy Drew - Reporter
d) Nancy Drew, Detective

OLD MOTHER RILEY

1) Irish washer woman, Old Mother Riley, was a popular variety act before becoming immortalised on screen and radio. Former music-hall comedian, Arthur Towle, portrayed her, but by the time of the success of Old Mother Riley, he had changed his surname to that of a Dublin dairy after seeing it on the side of a milkfloat. Who was he?
a) Arthur Lane
b) Arthur Wall
c) Arthur Houghton
d) Arthur Lucan

2) What was the name of Old Mother Riley's daughter?
a) Bridget
b) Kitty
c) Sally
d) Lucy

3) What was the real life relationship between the man who portrayed Old Mother Riley and her daughter?
a) husband and wife
b) father and daughter
c) brother and sister
d) grandfather and granddaughter

OUR GANG

1) Name the director who launched this popular series of comedy shorts (1922-1944) about a gang of impish kids who are always getting into trouble.
a) Frank Borzage
b) Walter Lang
c) Buster Keaton
d) Hal Roach

2) What was the name of the gang's dog, who had a black circle around his right eye?
a) Alfalfa
b) Pete
c) Loopy
d) Wheezer

all noble chefs vegetarian

3) **Our Gang** was later reissued for TV, but because MGM owned the rights to the title it had to be given another one. Can you name it?
a) The Little Rascals
b) Troublesome Imps
c) Gang of Rogues
d) The Den of Ten

PHILIP MARLOWE

1) Which Philip Marlowe movie was Howard Hawks talking about when he said: "Neither the author, the writer, nor myself knew who had killed whom." ?
a) The Long Goodbye
b) Farewell, My Lovely
c) The Lady in the Lake
d) The Big Sleep

2) Who portrayed the tough-talking private eye in **Marlowe** (1969)?
a) Elliott Gould
b) James Garner
c) Robert Mitchum
d) James Coburn

3) Which Philip Marlowe mystery features a giant thug named 'Moose Malloy'?
a) The Brasher Doubloon
b) The Big Sleep
c) The Lady in the Lake
d) Farewell My Lovely

POPEYE

1) Popeye the Sailor was originally created by newspaper cartoonist, Elzie Segar, in 1929. Name the cartoonist/animator who adapted him for the screen in 1933?
a) Max Fleischer
b) Tex Avery
c) Chuck Jones
d) Walter Lantz

2) The song 'I'm Popeye the Sailor Man' was written in less than two hours by a famous songwriter who initially didn't want it known that he was responsible for it. Who was he?
a) Sammy Cahn b) Cole Porter
c) Sammy Lerner d) Jule Styne

her thin iced yoghurt

Characters

3) Who portrayed Popeye's true love, Olive Oyl, in Robert Altman's 1980 musical comedy, **Popeye**?
a) Laura Dern
b) Shelley Duvall
c) Goldie Hawn
d) Ellen Barkin

RAMBO

1) On whose novel was the first Rambo movie, **First Blood** (1982), based?
a) David Morell
b) John Wingate
c) Dudley Pope
d) Sydney Schanberg

2) What was Rambo's mission in **Rambo: First Blood II** (1985)?
a) to assassinate Pol Pot
b) to find soldiers missing in action
c) to blow up a Cambodian weapons arsenal
d) to rescue a kidnapped U.N. delegation

3) Which 'hostile' country does Rambo visit to rescue his old Green Beret commander, Col. Trautman (Richard Crenna) in **Rambo III** (1988)?
a) Iraq
b) Afghanistan
c) Cuba
d) Burma

RICHARD HANNAY

1) Who reveals the truth about the thirty-nine steps to Richard Hannay (Robert Donat) in Hitchcock's 1935 version?

a) Miss Smith
b) Mr. Memory
c) Prof. Jordan
d) Sheriff Watson

2) Who was Kenneth More's leading lady in the 1960 remake of **The 39 Steps**?
a) Deborah Kerr
b) Celia Johnson
c) Peggy Ashcroft
d) Taina Elg

3) Who portrayed the murdered British agent who tries to convince Hannay (Robert Powell) of a Prussian plot to destabilise Europe, in Don Sharp's 1978 version of **The 39 Steps**?
a) Jack Hawkins
b) Trevor Howard
c) John Mills
d) Edward Fox

RIN TIN TIN

1) Prior to his prolific film career, this canine star was discovered by Captain Lee Duncan during WWI. Where did he find him?
a) in a German trench
b) dying on a battlefield
c) guarding an officer's mess
d) lying beside his master's grave

2) Name the title of the 1976 film which fictionalised Rin Tin Tin's career.
a) A Dog of Flanders
b) Won Ton Ton, the Dog Who Saved Hollywood
c) A Dog's Life
d) The Dog Who Had His Day

3) Rin Tin Tin died in 1932. How old was he?
a) 14 b) 16 c) 17 d) 21

ROBIN HOOD

1) Who portrayed the legendary outlaw in Richard Lester's 1976 interpretation, **Robin and Marian**?

a) Kevin Costner b) Kurt Russell
c) James Coburn d) Sean Connery

2) Hollywood character actor, Alan Hale, portrayed the same member of Robin's merry men in the 1922 silent version of **Robin Hood**, as he did in the classic **The Adventures of Robin Hood** 16 years later in 1938. Name the character.
a) Friar Tuck b) Little John
c) Alan-a-Dale d) Will Scarlet

3) Which actor led the **Rogues of Sherwood Forest** in an epic struggle to get the Magna Carta signed in 1950?
a) John Derek
b) Richard Todd
c) Cornel Wilde
d) Richard Greene

ROCKY

1) What was Rocky's surname?
a) Rossi b) Cicero c) Balboa d) Ricco

2) In which film is Rocky beaten by 'Clubber Lang' (Mr. T)?
a) Rocky II b) Rocky III
c) Rocky IV d) Rocky V

3) In **Rocky V** (1990) Rocky ends up in his hometown, shunned, broke and brain-damaged. Name his hometown.
a) Chicago
b) Baltimore
c) Philadelphia
d) Pittsburgh

The Movie Quiz Companion

THE SAINT

1) The first film in The Saint series of the late 1930s and early 40s was **The Saint in New York** (1938). Who portrayed the dapper Simon Templar?
a) Louis Hayward
b) Dudley Digges
c) Hugh Sinclair
d) Franchot Tone

2) In which country is Simon Templar's (George Sanders) working holiday in **The Saint's Vacation** (1941)?
a) Norway
b) Egypt
c) Switzerland
d) Greece

3) Who portrayed Templar in the 1997 big-budget crime thriller, **The Saint**?
a) Sean Penn
b) Ed Harris
c) Nick Nolte
d) Val Kilmer

SHERLOCK HOLMES

1) Name the year he made his first recorded screen appearance.
a) 1903 b) 1916 c) 1921 d) 1929

2) Who portrayed him in the 1959 Hammer version of **The Hound of the Baskervilles**?
a) Christopher Lee
b) Basil Rathbone
c) Peter Cushing
d) Douglas Wilmer

3) Name the villain Holmes is up against in **Study in Terror** (1965).
a) Professor Moriarty
b) Jack the Ripper
c) Spider Woman
d) Adolf Hitler

SINBAD THE SAILOR

1) For which 1974 Sinbad fantasy did special effects wizard, Ray Harryhausen, create an animated ship's figurehead?
a) The 7th Voyage of Sinbad
b) Son of Sinbad
c) The Golden Voyage of Sinbad
d) The Thief of Bagdad

2) Who played the title role in the 1947 adventure, **Sinbad the Sailor**?
a) Errol Flynn
b) Douglas Fairbanks Jr.
c) Dale Robertson
d) Victor Mature

3) With what or whom did Sinbad have a spectacular duel in **The 7th Voyage of Sinbad** (1958)?
a) the seven-headed hydra
b) a skeleton
c) the devil
d) the four horsemen of the Apocalypse

SUPERMAN

1) Name the year Superman made his movie debut in the first of a series of 17 animated cartoons produced by Max and Dave Fleischer.
a) 1938 b) 1941 c) 1945 d) 1950

2) How much did Marlon Brando allegedly earn for his miniscule cameo role as Superman's father in Richard Donner's 1978 big-budget action movie, **Superman**?
a) $2 million b) $3 million
c) $4 million d) $5 million

3) Who portrayed the Man of Steel in the 1951 adventure, **Superman and the Mole Men**, which won him the role in the popular 50s TV series?
a) Lloyd Bridges b) Tom Conway
c) George Reeves d) Kent Smith

TARZAN

1) Who was the first to portray Tarzan on the screen in the 1918 film, **Tarzan of the Apes**?
a) Lewis Stone
b) Max Linder
c) Edmund Lowe
d) Elmo Lincoln

2) Name the 1932 film in which Tarzan (Johnny Weissmuller) meets his 'mate' Jane Parker (Maureen O'Sullivan) for the first time.
a) The New Adventures of Tarzan
b) Tarzan Escapes
c) Tarzan, the Ape Man
d) Tarzan and the Lost Safari

3) Tarzan leaves his jungle paradise for the Big Apple in **Tarzan's New York Adventure** (1942) because someone had been kidnapped. Who was it?
a) Jane
b) Boy
c) Cheetah
d) Queen Melmendi

TOM SAWYER & HUCKLEBERRY FINN

1) Who played the title role in John Cromwell's 1930 classic, **Tom Sawyer**?
*a) Freddie Bartholomew b) Jackie Coogan
c) Billy Halop d) Junior Durkin*

2) *Tom Sawyer* is based on Mark Twain's own childhood in a town on the Mississippi, and appears under the same name in many of the films inspired by the novel. Name the town.
*a) Carthage b) Crystal Springs
c) Magnolia d) Hannibal*

3) For what 1939 comedy drama did Mickey Rooney portray Huck Finn?
a) The Adventures of Mark Twain b) The Adventures of Huckleberry Finn c) Ah, Wilderness d) Tom Sawyer, Detective

WILD BILL HICKOK

1) In which film did Doris Day have a stormy romance with Wild Bill Hickok?
*a) Annie Get Your Gun b) Pony Express
c) Calamity Jane d) Annie Oakley*

2) Who played the title role in Walter Hill's 1995 biopic, **Wild Bill**?
*a) Jeff Bridges b) Charles Bronson
c) William Hurt d) Keith Carradine*

3) How did Wild Bill Hickok (1837-76) die?
a) he was hanged b) he was shot in the back c) he committed suicide d) from a heart attack

WYATT EARP

1) In which 1950 western does Lin McAdam (James Stewart) encounter Wyatt Earp?
*a) The Naked Spur b) Broken Arrow
c) Bend of the River d) Winchester '73*

2) Which 1939 western biopic featured Randolph Scott as Tombstone's new marshal, Wyatt Earp?
*a) Frontier Marshal
b) Belle Starr
c) The Virginian
d) Go West, Young Man*

3) Who portrayed Wyatt Earp's (Kevin Costner) father, Nicholas, in Lawrence Kasdan's 1994 biopic, **Wyatt Earp**?
*a) Martin Sheen b) Gene Hackman
c) Peter O'Toole d) Christopher Plummer*

ZORRO

1) What does the word 'Zorro' mean in Spanish?
a) avenger b) devil c) fox d) invisible

2) Who played the title role in the 1920 silent classic, **The Mark of Zorro**?
*a) Ralph Lewis
b) Elmo Lincoln
c) Douglas Fairbanks
d) Wallace Beery*

3) In 1998 she portrayed Don Diego de la Vega's (Anthony Hopkins) estranged daughter, Elena, in **The Mask of Zorro**. Who was she?
*a) Jennifer Lopez
b) Catherine Zeta-Jones
c) Anna Paquin d) Julia Roberts*

CREATURES

ALIENS

1) Which 1985 film features aliens who are able to communicate with earthlings after having studied their language by watching vacuous television shows?
a) Strange Invaders b) Time Runner
c) Wavelength d) Explorers

2) LA cop, Matthew Sykes, has an alien as his partner who helps track down the alien killer of his former buddy in **Alien Nation** (1988). Who portrayed Sykes?
a) James Caan b) Terence Stamp
c) Jeff Bridges d) Christopher Walken

3) In 1956 Dr. Bennel (Kevin McCarthy) returns to his hometown of Santa Mira from a medical convention only to find it overrun with aliens. Name the film.
a) Invaders From Mars b) This Island Earth
c) Invasion of the Body Snatchers d) Kronos

ALLIGATORS & CROCODILES

1) Alligators delicately pranced to 'The Dance of the Hours' in Disney's **Fantasia** (1940). Who composed it?

a) Tchaikovsky b) Beethoven
c) Mussorgsky d) Ponchielli

2) With which film do you associate Pete Postlethwaite and a bag of green crocodile tongues?
a) Waterland b) Dragonheart
c) James and the Giant Peach d) A Private Function

3) Who sang 'See You Later Alligator' in the 1956 musical, **Rock Around the Clock**?
a) Freddie Bell and His Bellboys b) Tony Martinez and His Band c) The Platters d) Bill Haley and His Comets

ANDROIDS & CYBORGS

1) In 1989 Gibson Rickenbacker's mission is to escort half woman, half robot, Pearl Prophet (Dayle Haddon) safely to Atlanta in **Cyborg**. Who was he?
a) Jean-Claude Van Damme b) Sylvester Stallone
c) Val Kilmer d) Peter Weller

2) Which film features a love-affair between ex-cop, Rick Deckard, and an android named Rachel?

a) Eve of Destruction b) Universal Soldier
c) Blade Runner d) Android

3) Name the Star Trek adventure which involves android Lt. Commander Data (Brent Spinner) being able to understand old jokes after the installation of a special computer chip.
a) Star Trek IV: The Voyage Home b) Star Trek V: The Final Frontier c) Star Trek VI: The Undiscovered Country d) Star Trek: Generations

ANGELS

1) Which film features Clarence Oddbody, angel second class?

shy frigid liar — **Creatures**

a) *Heaven Can Wait* b) *Date With an Angel*
c) *It's a Wonderful Life* d) *The Miracle of the Bells*

2) In which film does Dudley the angel enter the empty life of the wealthy Mrs. Hamilton (Gladys Cooper) and dissuade her from building a huge cathedral in memory of her late husband?
a) *The Happiest Millionaire* b) *This Above All*
c) *The Bishop's Wife* d) *The Cock-eyed Miracle*

3) In 1988 an angel named Damiel becomes mortal next to the Berlin Wall, sacrificing immortality for the romantic love of a trapeze artist. Name the film.
a) *Love Under Fire* b) *Walls of Glass*
c) *Wings of Desire* d) *Almost an Angel*

APES

1) Which 1932 horror film, directed by Robert Florey and starring Bela Lugosi, features a murdering ape?
a) *Murders in the Rue Morgue* b) *Chandu the Magician* c) *Wild Company* d) *Night of Terror*

2) Cheetah the chimpanzee, comic relief and veteran of seventeen Tarzan movies, including the early O'Sullivan and Weissmuller classics, was still alive in 1998 living in Florida and enjoying the occasional cigar. How old was he?
a) 55 b) 58 c) 61 d) 65

3) Professor Peter Boyd uses a chimp for his genetic tests in the 1951 comedy, **Bedtime for Bonzo**. Who was the professor?
a) *Cary Grant* b) *Ronald Reagan*
c) *Glenn Ford* d) *Bob Hope*

BEARS

1) Zachary Bass was mauled by a grizzly bear in the 1971 adventure, **Man in the Wilderness**. Who portrayed him?
a) *Donald Sutherland* b) *Richard Harris*
c) *Charles Bronson* d) *Robert Duvall*

2) Name the title of Hanna-Barbera's first feature-length cartoon starring Yogi Bear in 1964.
a) *Yogi Bear of Yellowstone* b) *Yogi & Boo-boo*
c) *A Bear's Life* d) *Hey There Ii's Yogi Bear*

3) With which film do you associate billionaire Charles Morse (Anthony Hopkins) being pursued by a Kodiak bear after his plane crashes in the Alaskan wilderness?
a) *One Man's War* b) *The Edge*
c) *Desperate Hours* d) *The Dawning*

BIRDS

1) Name the actor who portrays a man with an obsession with birds in Alan Parker's 1984 drama, **Birdy**.
a) *Nicolas Cage* b) *Richard Dreyfuss*
c) *Jeff Bridges* d) *Matthew Modine*

2) On whose novel - said by Ray Bradbury to give him "flight" - was Hall Bartlet's 1973 drama, **Jonathan Livingston Seagull** based?
a) *Paul Auster* b) *Richard Brautigan*
c) *John Updike* d) *Richard Bach*

3) Which 1992 animated film features an irate parrot named 'Iago'?
a) *Aladdin* b) *The Lion King*
c) *Babar The Movie* d) *Beauty and the Beast*

THE BLOB

1) Name the actor who was given his first starring role in **The Blob** (1958).
a) *Paul Newman* b) *Steve McQueen*
c) *Lee Marvin* d) *Laurence Harvey*

2) Where did **The Blob** come from?
a) *a research laboratory* b) *outer space*
c) *a travelling circus* d) *a convict's spinal fluid*

3) For what does the government conspire to use **The Blob** in Chuck Russell's 1988 remake?
a) *biological warfare* b) *medical research*
c) *a deforestation agent* d) *land-fill*

BUFFALOES

1) Indian hater, Ethan Edwards (John Wayne), shoots buffalo solely to deprive the Comanches of meat. Name the film.
a) *The Horse Soldiers* b) *Hondo*
c) *Dakota* d) *The Searchers*

2) In which film did John Dunbar learn the word for buffalo in the Lakota language of the Sioux?
a) *The Sheriff of Fractured Jaw* b) *Little Big Man*
c) *Dances With Wolves* d) *She Wore a Yellow Ribbon*

3) In 1962 he portrayed moustachioed buffalo hunter, Jethro Stuart, in the epic western, **How the West Was Won** (1962). Who was he?
a) *Andy Devine* b) *Lee J. Cobb*
c) *Richard Widmark* d) *Henry Fonda*

BULLS

1) In which film does Marwood encounter a randy bull?
a) *Spanking the Monkey* b) *Uncle Buck*
c) *Withnail & I* d) *Mystic Pizza*

2) 'The Hackensack Bulls' appear in Walter Hill's 1985 comedy, **Brewster's Millions**. Who or what were they?
a) *a baseball team* b) *antique porcelain figures*
c) *a street gang* d) *John Candy's in-laws*

137

The Movie Quiz Companion

3) With which 1948 western, directed by Howard Hawks, do you associate Tom Dunson setting a bull and a cow free, saying: "Wherever they go they'll be on my land"?
a) The Big Sky b) Red River
c) The Outlaw d) Rio Bravo

CAMELS

1) Which Bob Hope film features a talking camel who complains: "This is the screwiest picture I've ever been in!" ?
a) The Cat and the Canary b) Fancy Pants
c) Beau James d) Road to Morocco

2) How does Hans Solo use a snow camel to save Luke Skywalker's life on the ice planet Hoth, in **The Empire Strikes Back**?
a) he transports Luke to safety on it b) he slashes it open and places Luke's freezing body inside c) he feeds a starving Luke raw camel meat d) the snow camel leads them both to safety through a blizzard

3) In which 1962 western does former lawman, Steve Judd (Joel McCrea), ride into the path of a race between a camel and a horse?
a) The Oklahoman b) Stranger on Horseback
c) Ride the High Country d) The Great American Cowboy

CATS

1) On whose novel was Walt Disney's **The Three Lives of Thomasina** (1964) based?
a) Paul Gallico b) Ogden Nash
c) P.L. Travers d) E.B. White

2) Name the singer, who became famous as a vocalist with the Benny Goodman band, who was the voice of Si and Am, the Siamese cats in **Lady and the Tramp**.
a) Lena Horne
b) Peggy Lee
c) Ann Sothern
d) Eartha Kitt

3) Who rescues a pussycat in the 1974 disaster movie, **The Towering Inferno**?
a) O.J. Simpson
b) Fred Astaire
c) Jennifer Jones
d) William Holden

CHILDREN RAISED BY ANIMALS

1) The legend of Romulus and Remus, who were raised by a she-wolf, was recounted in **Duel of the Titans** (1961). Gordon Scott was Remus, but who portrayed Romulus?
a) James Garner b) Steve McQueen
c) Steve Reeves d) Anthony Quinn

2) What kind of animals raised the child in the 1949 adventure, **Zamba**?
a) bears b) gorillas c) leopards d) elephants

3) Sabu portrayed Mowgli, the child raise by wolves in the 1942 adventure, **Jungle Book**. Who directed?
a) Zoltan Korda b) George Stevens
c) Carol Reed d) Edmund Goulding

CRABS & LOBSTERS

1) What part of the human anatomy do the giant crabs seek to devour in Roger Corman's 1957 thriller, **Attack of the Crab Monsters**?
a) eyes b) heart c) brains d) lungs

2) With which 1959 comedy do you associate Doris Day running a lobstery in Maine?
a) It Happened to Jane b) The Winning Team
c) The Glass Bottom Boat d) Storm Warning

3) What is the name of the crab who sings the song entitled: 'Under the Sea' in **The Little Mermaid**?
a) Carlotta b) Scuttle c) Grimsby d) Sebastian

THE DEVIL

1) Which 1943 horror film, produced by Val Lewton, about New York City devil-worshippers, begins and ends with the epigraph from the first 'Holy Sonnet' by John Donne: "I runne to death and death meets me as fast, And all my pleasures are like yesterday"?

a) Please Believe Me b) I Walked With a Zombie
c) Isle of the Dead d) The Seventh Victim

2) In which 1987 film does the devil make an appearance as Daryl Van Horne?
a) Satan's School For Girls b) She-Devil
c) The Witches of Eastwick d) Devil in the Flesh

3) Name the 1967 Hammer horror film, directed by Roy Ward Baker, which suggests that the Devil has arrived on Earth from outer space.
a) Quatermass and the Pit b) X The Unknown
c) The Damned d) Nightmare

DINOSAURS

1) In which 1938 comedy does paleontologist, David Huxley, have a crucial dinosaur bone stolen by a dog?
a) One of Our Dinosaurs is Missing b) I Love Trouble c) Bringing up Baby d) The Last Dinosaur

2) In 1993 he portrayed the evil semi-human dinosaur, King Koopa, in **Super Mario Bros.** Who was he?
a) Dennis Hopper b) Peter Mullan
c) Tommy Lee Jones d) Timothy Spall

3) Name the prehistoric beast who meets his end at Coney Island amusement park in 1953.
a) The She Creature b) Dinosaurus
c) The Beast From 20,000 Fathoms d) Godzilla

DOGS

1) A dog named 'Disraeli' has a surveillance bug planted on him when he is given as a gift to the Russian ambassador in **The Spy with a Cold Nose** (1966). What breed was he?
a) Bulldog b) Old English sheepdog
c) German shepherd d) Dalmatian

2) In which 1959 Disney comedy does an ancient spell turn a young boy into a sheepdog?
a) The Shaggy Dog b) It's a Dog's Life
c) Savage Sam d) You Never Can Tell

3) Which 1963 adventure features Bodger the Bull Terrier, Tao the Siamese Cat, and Luath the Labrador Retriever?
a) 101 Dalmatians b) The Incredible Journey
c) The Ugly Dachshund d) The Plague Dogs

DOLPHINS

1) What do George C. Scott and Trish Van Devere teach their dolphins in the 1973 drama, **The Day of the Dolphin**?
a) to detect Russian submarines b) to speak English c) to warn bathers of approaching sharks d) to retrieve sunken treasure

2) What was the real name of **Flipper** (1963), cinema's most famous dolphin?
a) Debby b) Salome c) Mitzi d) Shirley

3) In which 1964 fantasy does unassuming bookkeeper, Don Knotts, become an animated dolphin who joins the navy and helps spot Nazi subs?
a) The Incredible Mr. Limpet b) The Big Blue
c) Day of the Dolphin d) Beachhead

DONKEYS & MULES

1) Who does the little boy believe will cure his lame donkey in **The Small Miracle** (1973)?
a) St. Francis of Assisi
b) the Pope
c) The Virgin Mary
d) Saint Joan

2) With which film do you associate George C. Scott killing a donkey because it is blocking a road?
a) The Yellow Rolls-Royce
b) This Savage Land
c) The List of Adrian Messenger
d) Patton

3) Who played the empty-headed lead in most of the **Francis (The Talking Mule)** series during the fifties, and once commented: "When you've made six pictures and the mule still gets more fan mail than you do…"
a) Jay Robinson b) Frank McHugh
c) Jeffrey Lynn d) Donald O'Connor

DRAGONS

1) Which 1977 film features a dragon named Elliott, who can make himself invisible?
a) Jack the Giant Killer b) The Reluctant Dragon
c) Sleeping Beauty d) Pete's Dragon

2) Medieval locals are convinced there is a dragon in their lake in **Star Knight** (1986). They are wrong. What was it?
a) a spaceship b) a time machine
c) an amphibious alien
d) a sunken burial mound

3) Who portrayed Bowen the dragon-slayer in the 1996 adventure fantasy, **Dragonheart**?
a) Sean Connery
b) Woody Harrelson
c) Danny De Vito
d) Dennis Quaid

The Movie Quiz Companion

tolerant farm women unknown

DWARFS

1) On whose fairytale was **Snow White and the Seven Dwarfs** (1937) based?
a) Hans Andersen b) the Brothers Grimm
c) Oscar Wilde d) Margot Zemach

2) In which 1973 mystery does a deranged dwarf stab Donald Sutherland to death?
a) Castle of the Living Dead b) Oedipus the King
c) Don't Look Now d) Dr. Terror's House of Horrors

3) For what film did Ringo Starr portray 'Larry the Dwarf'?
a) The Magic Christian b) Two Hundred Motels
c) Princess Daisy d) Give My Regards to Broad Street

ELEPHANTS

1) Who helps Burt Reynolds transport a pregnant elephant to Texas in the 1980 comedy, **Smokey and the Bandit II**?
a) Sally Field b) Laura Dern
c) Tatum O'Neal d) Liza Minnelli

2) Which film features an elephant named Colonel Hathi?
a) Dumbo b) An Elephant Called Slowly
c) The Jungle Book d) Elephant Boy

3) For what film does Oliver Hardy portray a doctor who treats a sick elephant, and afterwards finds it impossible to get rid of?
a) Zenobia b) The Bashful Elephant
c) The Roots of Heaven d) Jupiter's Darling

FAIRIES & GOBLINS

1) In 1986 he portrayed Jareth, King of the Goblins, who kidnaps a baby boy in **Labyrinth**. Who was he?
a) Jonathan Pryce
b) Terry Gilliam
c) David Bowie
d) Spike Milligan

2) Who portrayed Tinkerbell in Steven Spielberg's 1991 fantasy, **Hook**?
a) Julia Roberts b) Gwyneth Paltrow
c) Glenn Close d) Maggie Smith

3) Name the 1997 film which was inspired by Elsie Wright and Frances Griffith's claim that they had photographed real-life fairies at Cottingley, West Yorkshire, in 1917.
a) One Magic Christmas b) Chasing Dreams
c) Tell No Tales d) Fairytale - A True Story

FROGS & TOADS

1) What role did Kermit the Frog play in the 1992 musical comedy, **The Muppet Christmas Carol**?
a) Charles Dickens b) Ghost of Christmas Past
c) Bob Cratchit d) Jacob Marley

2) The production designer of **Gone With the Wind** (1939), and director of **Things to Come** (1936), also directed **The Maze** (1953), about a 'frog monster' who lives in a Scottish castle. Who was he?
a) Paul Leni b) Alexander Korda
c) Sidney Franklin d) William Cameron Menzies

3) The eponymous heroine of Gary Goldman and Don Bluth's 1994 animated children's fantasy narrowly avoids marrying a toad. Name the film.
a) Thumbelina b) The Little Mermaid
c) Rock-a-Doodle d) A Troll in Central Park

GENIES

1) Street urchin Abu (Sabu) frees genie Rex Ingram from an ancient bottle where he had been imprisoned for 3,000 years in **The Thief of Bagdad** (1940). Who originally imprisoned him?
a) Allah b) King Solomon
c) Jaffar d) the Sultan of Bagdad

2) In which film does a genie bemoan:"Ten thousand years can give you such a crick in the neck", after his lengthy confinement?
a) The Brass Bottle b) The Seventh Voyage of Sinbad c) Exotica d) Aladdin

3) Name the country whose Oscar equivalent is the Genie award.
a) Italy b) Spain c) Canada d) Brazil

GHOSTS

1) Who portrayed the woman with whom the ghost (Rex Harrison) falls in love, in Joseph L. Mankiewicz's 1947 romantic fantasy, **The Ghost and Mrs. Muir**?
a) Gene Tierney b) Joan Bennett
c) Joan Fontaine d) Ida Lupino

2) Name the resident spook of Maine's Whipstaff Manor.
a) The Green Man b) The Horrible Dr. Hichcock
c) Ghost Dad d) Casper

3) Who played the title role in the 1944 comedy, **The Canterville Ghost**?
a) Robert Donat b) Charles Laughton
c) Peter Lorre d) Fredric March

HORSES

1) What does the white horse turn into in the 1985 children's fantasy, **The Legend of the White Horse**?
a) a dragon b) a witch c) a mouse d) a prince

2) In which 1974 comedy does Mongo (Alex Karras) knock out a horse with a right cross to the jaw?
a) The Shaggy D.A. b) The Bad News Bears
c) Blazing Saddles d) The Frisco Kid

3) Whose carriage is pulled by "a horse of a different color" which constantly changes its colouring as it moves along?
a) Peter Pan b) Alice in Wonderland
c) The Wizard of Oz d) The Water Babies

HUMAN ANIMALS

1) In which 1977 film do the animal-men refer to the operating room where they were medically transformed into animals as the "House of Pain"?
a) Nightbreed
b) Kiss of the Beast
c) Ladyhawke
d) The Island of Dr. Moreau

2) With which 1973 film do you associate Malcolm McDowell accidentally stumbling across a pig-boy in an experimental lab?
a) O Lucky Man!
b) Gulag
c) Figure in a Landscape
d) Voyage of the Damned

3) Benjamin Browning returns to earth in the form of a dog to solve his own murder in **Oh, Heavenly Dog!** (1980). Who was he?
a) Brad Dourif b) Harry Dean Stanton
c) Chevy Chase d) Michael McKean

INSECTS

1) In which 1991 comedy, directed by Michael Lehmann, does an insect mother tell her kids: "Clean up your sugar, and for dessert you can have some rancid trash I found in a dumpster behind the 7-11"?
a) Creepers
b) Invasion of the Bee Girls
c) Bug
d) Meet the Applegates

2) Red-haired bride by proxy, Joanna Leiningen, and her husband Christopher (Charlton Heston), fought off an army of invading red ants on their South American plantation in the 1954 adventure, **The Naked Jungle**. Who portrayed the bride?
a) Eleanor Parker b) Myrna Loy
c) Patricia Neal d) Dorothy McGuire

3) Cliff Edwards portrayed a wisecracking insect who wore a badge bearing the words: 'Official Conscience/18Kt' in a 1940 fantasy based on a story by Carlo Collodi. Name the title.

a) Hoppity Goes to Town b) Pinocchio
c) The Beginning of the End d) Once Upon a Time

LIONS & TIGERS

1) Name the Roman epic in which an old lady exclaims: "Look, there's a sweet little lion who hasn't got a Christian."
a) Julius Caesar b) Quo Vadis?
c) Cleopatra d) Demetrius and the Gladiators

2) On whose real-life exploits was Byron Haskin's 1948 adventure, **Man-eater of Kumaon** based?
a) Teddy Roosevelt b) Rudyard Kipling
c) Akos Tolnay d) Jim Corbett

3) In 1966 he won an Oscar for Best Original Music Score for the film adaptation of Joy Adamson's book about Elsa the lioness in **Born Free**. Who was he?
a) Henry Mancini b) Jerry Goldsmith
c) John Barry d) Quincy Jones

MARTIANS

1) With which film do you associate Presidential advisor Donald Kessler (Pierce Brosnan) being kidnapped by Martians?
a) Mars Attacks b) The Day Mars Invaded Earth
c) Spaced Invaders d) The Angry Red Planet

2) A TV songwriter is inadvertently responsible for millions of Martians arriving on Earth in the 1990 sci-fi comedy, **Martians Go Home**. Who portrayed him?

a) Jim Carrey b) Randy Quaid
c) John Candy d) Chevy Chase

3) Sheltering in a deserted farmhouse, Doctor Clayton (Gene Barry) chops off a piece of threatening Martian hardware with an axe in **War of the Worlds** (1953). What was it?
a) the eye of a mechanical probe b) the head of a robot c) a homing device d) a ray gun

MERMAIDS

1) In **Mr. Peabody and the Mermaid** (1948), Mr. Peabody hooks a mermaid (Ann Blyth) and deposits her in a pond close to his house. Who portrayed Mr. Peabody?
a) William Powell b) Rex Harrison
c) Kenneth More d) Walter Pidgeon

2) Who played the title role of the beautiful mermaid who hauls a doctor out of a fishing boat into the sea and will only return him to land on the condition he takes her to London in the 1948 comedy, **Miranda?**
a) Fay Holden b) Joan Greenwood
c) Kay Walsh d) Glynis Johns

3) With which romantic comedy do you associate a mermaid named 'Madison'?
a) The Little Mermaid b) Beach Blanket Bingo
c) Night Tide d) Splash

MICE

1) In which 1939 film does George (Burgess Meredith) discover Lennie (Lon Chaney Jr.) carrying around a dead mouse he has crushed to death?
a) Sullivan's Travels
b) The Awful Truth
c) The Mouse and His Child
d) Of Mice and Men

2) What kind of superintelligent animals came to the aid of the widowed mouse, Mrs Brisby, when her house and sickly baby are threatened by the farmer's tilling machinery in **The Secret of NIMH** (1982)?
a) cats b) guinea pigs
c) rats d) monkeys

3) With which film do you associate a mouse named 'Mr Jingles'?
a) An American Tail
b) The Green Mile
c) The Rescuers d) Gotcha!

MUMMIES

1) Who portrayed the avenger of the desecration of the tomb of the ancient Egyptian Princess Ananka in Hammer's **The Mummy** (1959)?
a) Andre Morell b) Ricardo Montalban
c) Christopher Lee d) Esmond Knight

2) Boris Karloff portrayed an Egyptian mummy who comes back to life three thousand years after his death to claim Helen Grosvenor (Zita Johann) because she is the incarnation of his lost love, the Princess Anck-es-en-Amon, in Universal's 1932 classic, **The Mummy**. What is Karloff's character name in the film?
a) Im-Ho-Tep b) Kharis c) Semu d) Sethi Rameses

3) Name the 1972 horror film, directed by Seth Holt, which was based on Bram Stoker's novel, *Jewel of Seven Stars* ?
a) Blood From the Mummy's Tomb
b) The Mummy's Curse
c) The Mummy's Shroud
d) The Mummy's Hand

OCTOPUSES & SQUIDS

1) In which 1954 adventure is a sea-going craft and its occupants attacked by a giant squid en route to its base on Vulcania?
a) City Beneath the Sea
b) East of Kilimanjaro
c) Sea Devils
d) 20,000 Leagues Under the Sea

2) Which film features an evil octopus named Ursula who can change into many different forms?
a) Popeye b) The Little Mermaid
c) Tentacles d) City of Lost Children

3) With which 1924 comedy do you associate Buster Keaton battling with an octopus?
a) Coney Island b) The Boat
c) Steamboat Bill, Jr. d) The Navigator

PIGS

1) In the 1984 film, **A Private Function**, chiropodist Gilbert Chilvers steals a pig which is being secretly fattened in post-WWII England when rationing is still in force. Who was he?
a) Pete Postlethwaite
b) Denholm Elliott
c) Michael Palin
d) Richard Griffiths

2) Which film features Hamm the Pig?
a) Toy Story b) Babe
c) State Fair
d) Muppet Treasure Island

3) In which film does Porky Pig confront Leon Schlesinger, the head of Warners' animation department, to demand a better deal?
a) Tiny Toon Adventures: How I Spent My Vacation b) Bugs Bunny/The Road Runner Movie c) Who Framed Roger Rabbit d) Daffy Duck's Quackbusters

PIRANHAS

1) What is hidden in the piranha infested lake in the 1979 thriller, **Killer Fish**?
a) murder victims b) stolen jewels
c) a missing airliner d) an ancient temple

2) In which film did General Mortars (William Shatner) battle with a piranha?
a) National Lampoon's Loaded Weapon I b) Bill & Ted's Bogus Journey c) Blood Sport d) Kingdom of the Spiders

3) Director James Cameron received his first directing credit in 1981 for a horror film about piranhas. Name the title.
a) A Game of Death b) Wild River
c) Piranha II: The Spawning d) Killer Instinct

RABBITS

1) With which film do you associate Elwood P. Dowd strolling home from his local bar and meeting a 6 feet, 3 inches high white rabbit leaning against a lamp post?
a) The Nasty Rabbit b) Asylum
c) Harvey d) Get to Know Your Rabbit

2) In which 1986 drama does Gérard Depardieu portray a character who attempts to breed rabbits for a living?
a) The Last Metro b) The Return of Martin Guerre
c) Danton d) Jean de Florette

3) He was only 18 inches high, constructed from aluminium alloy, rubber and sponge, and covered from head to foot in rabbit's fur, but became one of cinema's most memorable beasts. Who was he?
a) The Werewolf b) King Kong
c) The Abominable Snowman d) Chewbacca

RATS

1) Name the 1976 fantasy, adapted from a novel by H.G. Wells, which features giant rats.
a) Somewhere in Time b) The Island of Dr. Moreau c) Food of the Gods d) World Without End

2) For what 1962 thriller does Jane Hudson serve up a dead rat at mealtime for her sister Blanche?
a) Hands of a Stranger b) What Ever Happened to Baby Jane? c) The Anatomist d) Die! Die! My Darling!

3) Name the sixties pop star who emptied Hamlyn of its rats in the 1972 drama, **The Pied Piper**.
a) Ringo Starr b) Donovan
c) Cat Stevens d) Richie Havens

ROBOTS

1) Which sci-fi adventure features a robot named Gort?
a) Return of the Jedi b) Robocop 2
c) The Day the Earth Stood Still d) D.A.R.Y.L.

2) In which film does Robby the Robot battle with the monster of the Id?
a) Flash Gordon b) Eve of Destruction
c) Robot Carnival d) Forbidden Planet

3) Mad scientist, Rotwang, abducts beautiful revolutionary Maria, and creates a robot in her image to plant the seeds of revolt in a 1926 silent fantasy. Name the title.
a) The Cabinet of Dr. Caligari
b) Street Angel
c) Dr. Mabuse, King of Crime
d) Metropolis

The Movie Quiz Companion

hormones heat feet

SHARKS

1) In March 1987, Michael Caine decided against going to Hollywood to accept his Academy Award for **Hannah and Her Sisters** and remained on the set of a shark movie he was making with director Joseph Sargent. Name the title.
a) Deathtrap b) Water
c) Jaws 3-D d) Jaws the Revenge

2) Who played the title role in John Ford's 1936 prison biopic, **The Prisoner of Shark Island**?
a) Harry Carey b) Warner Baxter
c) John Carradine d) Richard Dix

3) With which Monsieur Hulot film do you associate his renting a canoe which breaks in half and by imitating the fin of a shark, terrifies bathers?
a) Playtime b) Traffic
c) Mon Oncle d) Mr. Hulot's Holiday

SNAKES

1) Who portrayed the evil High Priestess Nadja who rules over a tribe of snake worshippers in the 1944 camp classic, **Cobra Woman**?
a) Maria Montez
b) Lupe Velez
c) Dolores Del Rio
d) Carmen Miranda

2) Name the 1981 fantasy for which special effects master, Ray Harryhausen, created the snake-headed Medusa.
a) Jason and the Argonauts
b) Clash of the Titans
c) The Golden Voyage of Sinbad
d) Mysterious Island

3) Wealthy explorer, Charles Pike, claims: "snakes are my life" in Preston Sturges' 1941 comedy, **The Lady Eve**. Who was he?
a) Joel McCrea
b) Cary Grant
c) Henry Fonda
d) Eddie Bracken

SPIDERS

1) In the 1944 mystery, **Sherlock Holmes and the Spider Woman**, villainess Andrea Spedding uses poisonous spiders to drive her victims to suicide. Who portrayed her?
a) Gale Sondergaard
b) Luise Rainer
c) Myrna Loy
d) Linda Darnell

2) Name the 1931 horror film in which a real estate agent named Renfield (Dwight Frye) ends up in an asylum eating spiders and other insects.
a) The Walking Dead b) The Ghoul
c) Dracula d) The Devil-Doll

3) How did the deadly new species of South American spider manage to journey to the U.S.A. and crossbreed with domestic spiders in the 1990 comedy horror, **Arachnophobia**?
a) in a camera-case b) in a victim's coffin
c) in a woman's hairdo d) in a shrunken-head souvenir

VAMPIRES

1) As what were David (Keifer Sutherland) and his teenage gang collectively known in 1987?
a) The Bloodsuckers b) The Fearless Vampire Killers c) The Lost Boys d) Vampire Men of the Lost Planet

2) Name the director John Malkovich portrayed in **Shadow of the Vampire** (2000) about the making of **Nosferatu**, the 1922 German version of Bram Stoker's novel *Dracula*.
a) Paul Leni b) Max Reinhardt
c) Carl Dreyer d) F.W. Murnau

3) Manhattan literary agent, Peter Loew, is convinced he's been bitten by a vampire in Robert Bierman's 1989 comedy horror, **Vampire's Kiss**. Who portrayed Loew?
a) Christopher Walken b) Nicolas Cage
c) Rod Steiger d) Tim Robbins

WEREWOLVES

1) In 1957 he portrayed the problem teenager in **I Was a Teenage Werewolf**. Who was he?
a) Rock Hudson
b) Tab Hunter
c) Michael Landon
d) Tom Tully

2) For what 1961 film did Oliver Reed play a compassionate werewolf?
a) Werewolf of London b) The Curse of the Werewolf c) The Howling d) The Undying Monster

144

a lust unobserved | Creatures

3) In which 1941 film does Lon Chaney Jr. portray a character who returns to his family's castle in England after a long absence, and becomes bitten by a werewolf?
a) *The Wolf Man* b) *Cry of the Werewolf*
c) *She-Wolf of London* d) *The White Wolf*

WHALES

1) Which film features Monstro the whale?
a) *Flipper* b) *Show Boat*
c) *Free Willy* d) *Pinocchio*

2) He portrayed the obsessive Captain Ahab twice: once in a silent version called **The Sea Beast** in 1926, and in the 1930 remake, **Moby Dick**. Who was he?
a) *John Barrymore* b) *John Darrow*
c) *George O'Brien* d) *Noah Beery Sr.*

3) The terrifyingly intelligent **Orca** (1977) wreaks vengeance on a seaman who killed his pregnant mate. Who portrayed the shark-hunting seafarer?
a) *John Hurt* b) *Richard Harris*
c) *Warren Beatty* d) *Jason Robards*

WITCHES

1) Into what does The Grand High Witch of the World (Anjelica Huston) plan to turn all the children in the land, in Nicolas Roeg's 1990 fantasy, **Witches**?
a) *spiders* b) *snails* c) *mice* d) *crows*

2) Aspiring actor, Guy Woodhouse, gets involved with a witches' coven in Roman Polanski's 1968 horror film, **Rosemary's Baby**. Who was he?
a) *Alan Arkin* b) *John Cassavetes*
c) *John Kerr* d) *Tony Roberts*

3) On whose novel was George Miller's 1987 comedy horror, **The Witches of Eastwick** based?
a) *Stephen King* b) *Garrison Keillor*
c) *Joseph Heller* d) *John Updike*

WOLVES

1) In the 1984 fantasy, **The Company of Wolves**, a peasant traps a wolf in the woods and cuts off its huge paw as a trophy. What does this trophy turn into?
a) *a severed human hand* b) *another wolf*
c) *a magic talisman* d) *a pig's trotter*

2) Which 1981 fantasy features the two-headed wolf-dog, Dioskilos?
a) *The NeverEnding Story*
b) *Conan the Destroyer*
c) *Dragonslayer*
d) *Clash of the Titans*

3) Columnist and murderer, Waldo Lydecker, remarks to homicide detective, Mark McPherson: "How singularly innocent I look this morning. Have you ever seen such candid eyes?", telling him he has become "the kindest, gentlest, the most sympathetic man in the world... I should be sincerely sorry to see my neighbors' children devoured by wolves." Name the film.
a) *The Big Sleep* b) *Laura*
c) *Dial M For Murder* d) *Farewell My Lovely*

ZOMBIES

1) **The Omega Man** (1971) is besieged by a race of zombies created by the after-effects of germ warfare. Who played the title role?
a) *Donald Pleasence* b) *Anthony Hopkins*
c) *Jeff Bridges* d) *Charlton Heston*

2) Where do the four survivors in George Romero's **Dawn of the Dead** (1978) seek refuge from the roaming zombies?
a) *a deserted farmhouse* b) *a convent*
c) *a deep-freeze warehouse* d) *a shopping mall*

3) Wealthy Haiti plantation owner, Paul Holland, hires a nurse to look after his catatonic wife whom the locals believe has been turned into a zombie in Jacques Tourneur's 1943 horror classic, **I Walked with a Zombie**. Who was he?
a) *Tom Conway*
b) *George Sanders*
c) *Warner Baxter*
d) *James Ellison*

145

CLASSIC FILMS

THE ADVENTURES OF ROBIN HOOD (1938)
Michael Curtiz & William Keighley

1) This film was based on the opera Robin Hood by De Koven-Smith and a novel by Sir Walter Scott. Name the novel.
a) Guy Mannering b) The Fair Maid of Perth
c) The Fortunes of Nigel d) Ivanhoe

2) Who portrayed the villainous Sir Guy of Gisbourne?
a) Ernest Thesiger b) Claude Rains
c) Raymond Massey d) Basil Rathbone

3) What were Robin and his men disguised as when they infiltrated and wrecked Prince John's coronation in the film's finale?
a) Norman knights b) strolling players
c) monks d) servants

THE AFRICAN QUEEN (1951)
John Huston

1) James Agee and John Huston wrote the screenplay, but who wrote the original story back in 1935?
a) John Masters
b) P.C. Wren
c) Geoffrey Household
d) C.S. Forester

2) What is Rosie and Charlie's last request before they are to be hanged as spies aboard the German warship 'Louisa'?
a) one last kiss b) a swig of gin
c) to sing 'God Save the Queen' d) to be married

3) Who portrays Rev. Samuel Sayer, Rosie's (Katherine Hepburn) pompous missionary brother?
a) C. Aubrey Smith b) Sydney Greenstreet
c) Robert Morley d) Peter Bull

ALFIE (1966)
Lewis Gilbert

1) Name the actress who portrayed Lily who has an abortion in the film and was nominated for a Best Supporting Actress Oscar.
a) Shelley Winters b) Eleanor Bron
c) Vivien Merchant
d) Eva Renzi

2) The lecherous Alfie picked up Annie at a roadside cafe. Who was she?
a) Jane Asher b) Shirley Ann Field
c) Julia Foster d) Millicent Martin

3) Who wrote the music for the title song?
a) John Barry b) Richard Rodney Bennett
c) John Dankworth d) Burt Bacharach

ALIEN (1979)
Ridley Scott

1) The screenplay was written by Dan O'Bannon, but owes much of its inspiration

to a 1958 sci-fi film directed by Edward L. Cahn about a stowaway Martian monster. Name the title.
a) It! The Terror From Beyond Space b) Invisible Invaders c) The Creeping Unknown d) The Day Mars Invaded Earth

2) What is the name of the spaceship infiltrated by the alien?
a) Chronicle b) Barrier 3
c) Lone Star d) Nostromo

3) What part of Kane's (John Hurt) body does the mysterious lifeform attach itself to, rendering him unconscious?
a) his back b) his face c) his thigh d) his genitals

ALL ABOUT EVE (1950)
Joseph L. Mankiewicz

1) Who portrays sardonic critic, Addison De Witt's (George Saunders) "protégée", Miss Casswell, described by him as "a graduate of the dramatic school of Copacabana."?
a) Eva Gabor b) Jayne Mansfield
c) Marilyn Monroe d) Debbie Reynolds

2) How does Margo's friend, and playwright's wife, Karen Richards (Celeste Holm), ensure that she misses her evening performance, and so gives her understudy, Eve, the chance to prove herself?
a) their car runs out of petrol b) she locks her in her dressing-room c) she tells her the play is cancelled d) she gives her a sleeping pill

3) What does Margo Channing (Bette Davis) tell the ambitous Eve Harrington (Anne Baxter) to do with her prestigious Sarah Siddons Award?
a) put it on her grave b) to use it as a substitute for her heart c) to melt it down and use it to fill her teeth d) to use it as a door-stop

AMERICAN GRAFFITI (1973)
George Lucas

1) Name the Drive-In where everyone meets.
a) Lou's b) Al's
c) Eddie's d) Mel's

2) Curt refuses to "stay seventeen forever" and goes off to university. Who was he?
a) Charles Martin Smith b) Bo Hopkins
c) Richard Dreyfuss d) Ron Howard

3) John (Paul Le Mat) cruises down main street with "the fastest car in the valley". Name the make of car.
a) 1932 Ford Deuce Coupe b) 1958 Impala
c) 1954 Ford Thunderbird d) 1955 Chevy

APOCALYPSE NOW (1979)
Francis Ford Coppola

1) The film was inspired by a Joseph Conrad novel. Name the title.
a) Lord Jim b) Almayer's Folly
c) The Rescue d) Heart of Darkness

2) "I love the smell of napalm in the morning. It smells like... victory," eulogises Lt. Col. Kilgore prior to a raid on the Vietcong. Who was he?
a) Marlon Brando b) Robert Duvall
c) Harrison Ford d) Harvey Keitel

3) The film's production was held up for a period because Martin Sheen took ill. What happened to him?
a) he suffered from food poisoning b) he had a nervous breakdown c) he had a heart attack
d) he almost drowned

BACK TO THE FUTURE (1985)
Robert Zemeckis

1) The gull-winged DeLorean was not Robert Zemeckis' first choice for a time machine. The idea for the original machine had to be shelved because he thought it might present a danger to children who would start re-enacting the film using this common household appliance. What was it?
a) a washing machine b) a refrigerator
c) a vacuum cleaner d) a television set

2) How many 'jigawatts' did Dr. Emmett Brown (Christopher Lloyd) calculate were needed to power the flux capacitor in order for the DeLorean to break the time barrier and travel from 1955 Hill Valley back to the future?
a) 1.21 b) 2.21 c) 3.21 d) 4.21

3) The film was five weeks into production and $4 million had already been spent when the original Marty McFly (who was thought too intense) was replaced by Michael J. Fox. Who was the original actor?
a) Eric Stoltz b) Timothy Hutton
c) Joe Mastroianni d) Matthew Broderick

BAD DAY AT BLACK ROCK
(1955) John Sturges

1) The one-armed John J. MacReedy (Spencer Tracy) journeys to the western town of Black Rock to give something to the Japanese father of the dead war hero who saved his life. What is it?
a) a photo
b) a medal
c) a flag
d) a lock of hair

The Movie Quiz Companion

2) MacReedy is threatened throughout the film by local bully Coley Trimble, who almost kills him by ramming his jeep from behind, forcing him off the road. Who played Trimble?
a) Lee Marvin b) Dean Jagger
c) John Carradine d) Ernest Borgnine

3) Reno Smith (Robert Ryan), the ringleader responsible for the murder of the Japanese farmer, ambushes MacReedy and tries to kill him in the film's finale. MacReedy, however, outwits him and gives him a violent death. How does he meet his end?
a) in an avalanche b) falling down an old mine shaft c) Macreedy hurls a bottle of gasoline at him which bursts into flames d) MacReedy ties him to a jeep and pushes it over a cliff

BAMBI (1942)
David Hand

1) On whose novel was the film based?
a) Hans Andersen b) E.B. White
c) Carlo Collodi d) Felix Salten

2) What was the name of Bambi's little skunk friend?
a) Orchid b) Flower c) Petal d) Blossom

3) Who was Faline?
a) Bambi's mother b) Bambi's female deer friend
c) Bambi's father d) Thumper's sister

THE BIG SLEEP (1946)
Howard Hawks

1) What is Vivian (Lauren Bacall) complaining about when Philip Marlowe (Humphrey Bogart) retorts: "I don't like them either; I grieve over them on long winter evenings."?
a) his short legs b) his manners
c) his fees d) his close-set eyes

2) How does Eddie Mars' henchman, Canino, murder Jones (Elisha Cook, Jr.) who is involved in a blackmail scheme?
a) he garrotts him
b) he poisons him
c) he pushes him under a truck
d) he throws him from the top of a building

3) A famous American novelist, who also worked as a screenwriter, contributed to the film's script. Who was he?
a) F. Scott Fitzgerald b) John Steinbeck
c) Truman Capote d) William Faulkner

BLADE RUNNER (1982)
Ridley Scott

1) The film was based on the story *Do Androids Dream of Electric Sheep?* Who wrote it?
a) Philip K. Dick b) Ray Bradbury
c) Isaac Asimov d) J.G. Ballard

2) Who portrays the beautiful replicant 'Pris'?
a) Kelly Hine b) Daryl Hannah
c) Joanna Cassidy d) Caroly De Mirjian

3) Who or what was a 'blade runner'?
a) a machine that builds artificial humans
b) the name of the leader of the six replicants who returned from an outworld to Earth
c) a computer chip which gives replicants false memories d) a policeman who hunts down replicants

BONNIE & CLYDE (1967)
Arthur Penn

1) In reality Bonnie Parker and Clyde Barrow met each other in a restaurant where Bonnie worked as a waitress, but the film has them meet just as Clyde is about to steal something belonging to Bonnie's mother. What is it?

a) a handbag b) a car
c) her lunch d) a brass candlestick

2) Name the actor who portrays the unworldly getaway-car driver for the Barrow gang.
a) Bo Hopkins b) Denver Pyle
c) James Stiver d) Michael J. Pollard

3) After stealing Eugene Grizzard (Gene Wilder) and his fiancée's car, the gang takes them for a joy ride. After discovering Eugeune's line of work, however, Bonnie ejects them quickly from the car. What is his occupation?
a) gravedigger b) mortician
c) coffin-maker d) mortuary attendant

THE BRIDGE ON THE RIVER KWAI (1957) David Lean

1) Why did Col. Nicholson (Alec Guinness) refuse initially to co-operate with the Japanese which led to his confinement in the tiny metal sweat-box?
a) food rations were too low b) he would not allow his officers to perform manual labour
c) he was opposed to building the bridge as it was advancing the Japanese war effort d) he needed medical supplies for his men

2) Permission to use composer Kenneth J. Alford's 'Colonel Bogey March' as the main theme tune was given by his widow, but she insisted upon knowing the circumstances of the song's use in the film, well aware of soldiers' rude lyrics about bollocks etc. Only when it was established that it would be whistled was permission granted. Initially David Lean wanted to use another well known song as the film's theme tune but the rights were too expensive. Name the song.
a) Bless 'Em All b) The White Cliffs of Dover c) It's a Long Way to Tipperary d) Roll Out the Barrel

3) The real River Kwai in Burma is no more than a trickling stream whose photogenic qualities are debatable. Location scouts, however, discovered the perfect location in another country. Name the country.
a) Siam b) Malaya c) Angola d) Ceylon

Classic Films

BRIEF ENCOUNTER (1945)
David Lean

1) **Brief Encounter** was based on the one-act play *Still Life*. Who wrote it?
a) *Terence Rattigan* b) *J.B. Priestley*
c) *Noel Coward* d) *Somerset Maugham*

2) What is the name of the railway station where Alec Harvey (Trevor Howard) and Laura Jesson (Celia Johnson) first met?
a) *Burwell Junction* b) *Weybourne Junction*
c) *Allington Junction* d) *Milford Junction*

3) Whose second piano concerto is played throughout the film?
a) *Beethoven's* b) *Rachmaninov's*
c) *Schubert's* d) *Schoenberg's*

BRINGING UP BABY (1938)
Howard Hawks

1) What is David Huxley's (Cary Grant) occupation in the film?
a) *geologist* b) *archaeologist*
c) *palaeontologist* d) *Egyptologist*

2) Name the song with which Susan Vance (Katherine Hepburn) frequently serenaded her pet leopard Baby with.
a) *I Can't Give You Anything but Love* b) *It Had to be You* c) *Mary From the Dairy* d) *You Do Something to Me*

3) What is David Huxley wearing when he retorts: "I just decided to go gay all of a sudden!"?
a) *a negligee* b) *an evening gown*
c) *stiletto heels* d) *an Easter bonnet*

BUTCH CASSIDY AND THE SUNDANCE KID (1969)
George Roy Hill

1) Butch's remote hideout was located about sixty miles northwest of Casper, Wyoming, where a handful of men could defend it against an army. What was its name?
a) *Turkey Creek*
b) *Tongue River*
c) *Hole-in-the-Wall*
d) *Circle Valley*

2) Who portrays Sundance's schoolteacher lover, Etta Place?
a) *Ann-Margret* b) *Sally Field*
c) *Susan George* d) *Katherine Ross*

3) Name the screenwriter who won an Oscar for his script.
a) *Paul Mazursky* b) *John Milius*
c) *William Goldman* d) *James Clavell*

CABARET (1972)
Bob Fosse

1) Based on the stage play by Joe Masteroff and the novel *Goodbye to Berlin*, featuring cabaret artist Sally Bowles, with its well known 'I am a Camera' technique of reportage. Name the novelist.
a) *Aldous Huxley* b) *Heinrich Boll*
c) *Bertolt Brecht* d) *Christopher Isherwood*

2) Who portrays Brian Roberts, the bisexual English language teacher Sally (Liza Minnelli) begins a relationship with?
a) *Michael York* b) *David Hemmings*
c) *Robert Forster* d) *Simon Ward*

3) What is the name of the 1930s seedy Berlin nightclub where Sally Bowles performs?
a) *The Kit Kat Club* b) *Glitterland*
c) *The Danzig* d) *The Black and Scarlet*

CASABLANCA (1942)
Michael Curtiz

1) Who was supposed to have personally signed the letters of transit stolen from the two murdered German couriers?
a) *Marshal Petain* b) *General de Gaulle*
c) *Adolf Hitler* d) *Heinrich Himmler*

2) Name the title of the unpublished play, by Murray Burnett and Joan Alison, upon which **Casablanca** is based.
a) *Rick's Cafe Americain* b) *Everybody Goes to Rick's* c) *Rick and Ilsa* d) *As Time Goes By*

3) Who or what was 'The Blue Parrot'?
a) *Señor Ferrari's club* b) *Victor Laszlo's code name* c) *the password for Laszlo to enter the secret underground meeting* d) *the Parisian nightclub where Rick first met Sam*

CHINATOWN (1974)
Roman Polanski

1) Evelyn's (Faye Dunaway) incestuous and dictatorial father, Noah, commented to Jake Gittes (Jack Nicholson): "Course I'm respectable. I'm old. Politicians, ugly buildings and whores all get respectable if they last long enough."
Who was he?
a) *Sam Peckinpah*
b) *John Huston*
c) *Samuel Fuller*
d) *John Landis*

2) Name the title of the 1990 sequel to Chinatown.
a) *The Two Jakes*
b) *The Border*
c) *China Moon*
d) *Gittes*

149

The Movie Quiz Companion

wormy leg was heavenly

3) The screenplay was written by a writer who began his career writing for Roger Corman, who later evolved into one of Hollywood's top screenwriters. His work includes **The Last Detail**, **Shampoo**, **Marathon Man** and **Frantic**. Who was he?
a) Robert Towne b) Joe Eszterhas
c) Barry Levinson d) Paul Mazursky

CINEMA PARADISO (1988)
Giuseppe Tornatore

1) Who portrays Alfredo, the venerable Sicilian projectionist and mentor to the young Toto?
a) Jacques Perrin
b) Leopoldo Trieste
c) Philippe Noiret
d) Nino Terzo

2) Name the title of the sword and sandals film, directed by Mario Camerini and starring Kirk Douglas, which Salvatore (Mario Leonardi) screens outdoors and which is interrupted by torrential rain.
a) Duel of the Titans b) Ulysses
c) Atlantis, The Lost Continent d) Spartacus

3) What causes the fire in the projection room which results in Alfredo losing his sight?
a) a cigarette end b) nitrate film
c) an oil heater d) an electric storm

CITIZEN KANE (1941)
Orson Welles

1) Charles Foster Kane inherits a huge fortune from his mother. How did she acquire it?
a) a prospector unable to meet his bill left her a silver mine b) oil was discovered on her property c) she married a tycoon d) she inherited money from her long lost father

2) Actor Alan Ladd had a minor role in the film. What part did he play?
a) a head waiter b) a reporter
c) an office boy d) a policeman

3) When Kane starts out on his path as a newspaper baron he takes over the New York Enquirer and hires his old college friend Jedediah Leland as drama critic. Who portrays him?
a) Ray Collins b) Everett Sloane
c) George Coulouris d) Joseph Cotten

A CLOCKWORK ORANGE
(1971) Stanley Kubrick

1) From which British dialect does the phrase "as queer as a clockwork orange" originate?
a) Glaswegian b) Cockney
c) Geordie d) West Country

2) Name the actress who is gang-raped to the strains of the song 'Singin' in the Rain'.
a) Adrienne Cori b) Carol Marsh
c) Miriam Karlin d) Dianne Foster

3) What connection can you make between **A Clockwork Orange** and **Star Wars**?
a) George Lucas produced A Clockwork Orange b) Brunel University doubled as the Ludovico Medical Facility and was also used to shoot scenes for the Death Star c) Dave Prowse who portrayed Darth Vader played Mr. Alexander's bodyguard d) Malcolm McDowell was originally cast as Luke Skywalker

CLOSE ENCOUNTERS OF THE THIRD KIND (1977)
Steven Spielberg

1) Name the leading *la Nouvelle Vague* (the new wave) film director who portrayed Claude Lacombe, head co-ordinating scientist for the alien reception committee.
a) Claude Chabrol b) Roger Vadim
c) François Truffaut d) Jean-Luc Godard

2) Roy Neary (Richard Dreyfuss) and others become obsessed with sketching and building an oddly shaped mountain in Wyoming. The mountain's real name was used in the film and when Spielberg went to shoot there the locals were so inhospitable to his crew, they thought that aliens would have to be deranged to ever want to land there. What was the name of the mountain?
a) Devil's Tower b) Devil's Rock
c) Devil's Knee d) Devil's Finger

3) Spielberg made many changes for his 1980 'Special Edition' version of the film which included a new ending. He also included a scene where an ocean-going freighter is deposited in an absurd location. Where was it?
a) Central Park b) the Gobi Desert
c) the Grand Canyon d) the Himalayas

THE DAY THE EARTH STOOD STILL (1951)
Robert Wise

1) Screenwriter Edmund H. North based his screenplay on the story *Farewell to the Master*. Who wrote it?
a) Brian Aldiss b) Kurt Vonnegut
c) Theodore Sturgeon d) Harry Bates

150

dire hate of skeletons   **Classic Films**

2) Klaatu is sent to Earth by a federation of planets to warn its inhabitants to cease nuclear testing or suffer the consequences. Who portrays Klaatu?
a) Stewart Granger b) Michael Rennie
c) Howard Keel d) Edgar Kennedy

3) Helen Benson (Patricia Neal) prevented Klaatu's robot from obliterating Earth by uttering the words: 'Klaatu barada nikto'. What was the robot's name?
a) Garth b) Gloot c) Grode d) Gort

THE DEER HUNTER (1978)
Michael Cimino

1) After escaping from the Vietcong, Michael (Robert De Niro) and the wounded Steven join a South Vietnamese refugee column heading towards Saigon and safety. Who portrays Steven?
a) John Savage b) Christopher Walken
c) Chuck Aspergen d) John Cazale

2) What was the occupation of the three friends, Michael, Nick and Steven before they embarked for Vietnam?
a) stevedore b) coal-miner
c) construction worker d) steelworker

3) Michael returns to the States and becomes the lover of Linda, his buddy Nick's girlfriend. Who was she?
a) Janet Suzman b) Meryl Streep
c) Sissy Spacek d) Amy Wright

DOUBLE INDEMNITY (1944)
Billy Wilder

1) The film was based on a short story in the book *Three of A Kind*. Who wrote it?
a) Raymond Chandler b) Damon Runyon
c) James M. Cain d) Chester Himes

2) The US censor stipulated that scenes be cut from the film which Billy Wilder regarded as among the finest he ever directed. What did these scenes depict?
a) passionate love-making between Walter Neff and Phyllis Dietrichson b) Neff's trial and execution c) Phyllis's seduction of her future husband when she is his wife's nurse d) Phyllis seducing her stepdaughter's boyfriend

3) Who portrays the suspicious insurance company's claims adjuster, Barton Keyes?
a) William Bendix b) Warner Baxter
c) Spencer Tracy d) Edward G. Robinson

FRANKENSTEIN (1931)
James Whale

1) **Frankenstein** was actually based on a play rather than on Mary Shelley's gothic fantasy and retains only the bare bones of her novel. Who wrote the play?
a) Peggy Webling b) Thomas Otway
c) R.C. Sherrif d) Aphra Behn

2) Legendary make-up artist, Jack Pierce, created the startling make-up for the monster which took five hours to apply. Who pencilled the original sketch which inspired him?
a) Boris Karloff b) James Whale
c) Colin Clive d) Carl Laemmle Jr.

3) Who portrays Elizabeth, Henry Frankenstein's terrified fiancée?
a) Myrna Loy b) Mae Clarke
c) Loretta Young d) Fay Wray

THE FRENCH CONNECTION
(1971) William Friedkin

1) Name the cinematographer responsible for the now classic car-train chase sequence whose other credits include **The Taking of Pelham One Two Three** (1974) and **The Exorcist** (1973).
a) Gil Taylor b) Michael Ballhaus
c) Carlo Di Palma d) Owen Roizman

2) Who portrays the cunning druglord, Alain Charnier, who hid 120 pounds of heroin in a Lincoln Continental?
a) Fernando Rey b) Roy Scheider
c) Marcel Bozzuffi d) Bill Hickman

151

The Movie Quiz Companion

3) What fate do Popeye Doyle (Gene Hackman) and his buddy finally endure for their unconventional approach to the case and their offbeat behaviour?
a) they are demoted b) they are transferred to another department c) they are passed over for promotion d) they are ridiculed in the New York Times

THE GODFATHER (1972)
Francis Ford Coppola

1) Coppola cast his daughter Sofia as Michael Corleone's daughter in **The Godfather Part III** (1990). What role did she play in **The Godfather**?
a) the baby in the baptism scene b) the child who witnessed Don Corleone's death in the garden c) Michael and Kay's daughter d) one of the children attending Connie and Carlo Rizzi's wedding

2) During the war between the Corleone and Tattaglia families Don Barzini convenes a meeting with the families to discuss a truce. Who was he?
a) Al Lettieri b) Alex Rocco c) John Cazale d) Richard Conte

3) Michael is picked up by Sollozzo and McCluskey outside a famous boxer's Broadway bar and driven to Louis's Restaurant in the Bronx where he shoots them both fatally. Name the boxer who owns the Broadway bar.
a) Rocky Graziano b) Jack Dempsey c) John L. Sullivan d) Joe Louis

THE GODFATHER PART II
(1974) Francis Ford Coppola

1) Michael Corleone wants to detach himself from the old Mafia rackets and enter into the world of "legitimate" business relocating his New York crime empire in the process. In which part of the U.S.A. does he relocate?
a) Miami, Florida b) Dallas, Texas c) Chicago, Illinois d) Lake Tahoe, Nevada

2) Jewish mobster, Hyman Roth, opens an upmarket hotel-casino in Havana with Michael Corleone and is also behind the failed attempt on his life. Who was he?
a) Richard Bright b) Joe Spinell c) Lee Strasberg d) Michael V. Gazzo

3) How does the Corleone family prevent former Mafia lieutenant, Frank Pentangeli, testifying before a Senate Investigative Committee?
a) they garrotte him b) they force him to commit suicide c) they threaten to murder his brother d) they threaten to frame him for the murder of a prostitute

GOLDFINGER (1964)
Guy Hamilton

1) How does Goldfinger smuggle bullion internationally from his metallurgical base in Kent?
a) he moulds it into cheap souvenirs b) he conceals it in the casing of Oddjob's bowler hat c) he recasts parts of his Rolls-Royce in gold d) he recasts his golf clubs in gold

2) Posing as a dubious dealer in Nazi gold, 007 plays billionaire and cheat, Auric Goldfinger, for a shilling a hole at golf. Who portrayed **Goldfinger**?
a) Gustav Frölich b) Helmut Griem c) Fritz Feld d) Gert Fröbe

3) Oddjob's deadly bowler hat would eventually be his undoing, becoming instrumental in his death. How does he die?
a) he is electrocuted b) he drowns c) he is crushed to death d) his hat inadvertently sets off an explosive device

GONE WITH THE WIND (1939)
Victor Fleming, George Cuckor, Sam Wood

1) At the beginning of the film Scarlett is sitting on the verandah of her sprawling Georgian mansion flirting with suitors. What is the name of the mansion?
a) Manderley b) Tara c) Hampton d) Twelve Oaks

2) Name the character portrayed by Leslie Howard who is the object of Scarlett O'Hara's obsessive love.
a) Johnny Gallagher b) Brent Tarleton c) Rhett Butler d) Ashley Wilkes

152

3) Scarlett O'Hara and Rhett Butler have one daughter who is killed in a tragic accident. How does she die?
a) she is killed in a riding accident b) she falls downstairs c) she dies in a stable fire d) she is trampled under the hooves of Confederate cavalry

THE GOOD, THE BAD AND THE UGLY (1966)
Sergio Leone

1) What is Mexican bandit Tuco's (Eli Wallach) nickname for Joe (Clint Eastwood), the 'man-with-no-name'?
a) Loner b) Blondie c) Thinker d) Angel

2) Why do Tuco and Joe have to stay together when the dying man tells them the secret of where the gold is buried?
a) because it would need the strength of two men to lift it b) because he only tells each man half the secret c) because they only have half a map each d) because one would have to be bodyguard to the other

3) Lee Van Cleef portrayed 'the Bad'. What was his character's name?
a) Setenza b) Saratoga b) Sarata c) Sabata

GOODBYE MR CHIPS (1939)
Sam Wood

1) The story was written in only four days to meet a magazine deadline and has since been published in over twenty-two English language editions and translated into more than twenty other languages. Who wrote it?
a) A.J. Cronin b) H.E. Bates
c) James Hilton d) Terence Rattigan

2) Mr. Chipping (Robert Donat) falls in love with Katherine Ellis while on an Austrian hiking holiday. She later dies in childbirth. Who was she?
a) Valerie Hobson b) Anna Neagle
c) Jessie Matthews d) Greer Garson

3) Chips is a schoolmaster who devotes his life to his school and pupils. What is the name of the school?

a) Brookside b) Brookfield
c) Brookdean d) Brook College

GOODFELLAS (1990)
Martin Scorsese

1) The film was based on the life story of Henry Hill (portrayed by Ray Liotta in the film) which was turned into a bestselling book by journalist Nicholas Pileggi. Name the title.
a) The Whistler b) Criss Cross
c) The Clay Pigeon d) WiseGuy

2) Godfather, Paul Cicero, warns Henry Hill to steer clear of narcotics, a warning he ignores to his cost as it becomes a key factor in his downfall. Who portrays Paulie?
a) Paul Sorvino b) Frank Sivero
c) Tony Darrow d) Frank Vincent

3) Which airline's cargo depot do they rob of $6 million at New York's Idlewild Airport?
a) TWA b) Quantas c) KLM d) Lufthansa

THE GRADUATE (1967)
Mike Nichols

1) Name the actor who made his film debut as a Berkeley student in **The Graduate** who went on to become a leading actor with prominent roles in **American Graffiti**, **Jaws** and **Tin Men**?

a) Elliot Gould b) Ron Howard
c) Bo Hopkins d) Richard Dreyfuss

2) The screenplay was written by Buck Henry and Calder Willingham, based on the novel by Charles Webb. Buck Henry also appeared in the film. What role did he play?
a) Mr. DeWitt b) a hotel clerk
c) Mr. Robinson d) a minister

3) After heroically rescuing Elaine (Katherine Ross) from marrying the wrong man, Benjamin (Dustin Hoffman) and Elaine board a bus and head off towards their future in the film's finale. How did director Mike Nichols predict they would end up?
a) getting divorced b) fat and childless
c) with six kids and a mortgage d) exactly like their parents

THE GRAPES OF WRATH
(1940) John Ford

1) The Joad family decide to head out west in search of work and a new life during the depression. Where was their home state?
a) Kansas b) Illinois c) Oklahoma d) Arkansas

2) Who portrays Tom Joad, the eldest son who had just served a four-year prison term for manslaughter?
a) Henry Fonda b) John Garfield
c) Farley Granger d) Tyrone Power

3) The screenwriter who adapted John Steinbeck's novel for the screen was one of Hollywood's most prolific and admired writers whose work included **Tobacco Road**, **The Mudlark** and **The Dirty Dozen**. Who was he?
a) Ben Hecht b) Dalton Trumbo
c) Howard Koch d) Nunnally Johnson

THE GREAT ESCAPE (1963)
John Sturges

1) On whose book was the film based?
a) Hugh Trevor Roper
b) Pierre Boulle
c) Paul Brickhill
d) Len Deighton

The Movie Quiz Companion

sweet shaven he farts downwind

2) The character of Hendley (James Garner) was inspired by the exploits of Marcel Zillessen, a young pilot who was imprisoned in Stalag Luft 3 in Sagen, Germany. What is Hendley's nickname in the film?
a) The Manufacturer b) The Forger
c) The Mole d) The Scrounger

3) Who wrote the memorable score?
a) Elmer Bernstein b) Jerry Goldsmith c) Ron Grainer d) Richard Addinsell

GREAT EXPECTATIONS (1946)
David Lean

1) Estella, with whom Pip (John Mills) falls desperately in love, is the ward of the eccentric Miss Havisham. Who portrayed Estella as a young girl?
a) Margaret Lockwood
b) Moira Shearer
c) Petula Clark
d) Jean Simmons

2) Pip is apprentice to his brother-in-law Joe Gargery (Bernard Miles). What is Joe's occupation?
a) cooper b) wheelwright
c) blacksmith d) miller

3) Pip mistakenly believes his benefactor to be Miss Havisham when it is really the convict Magwitch. Who portrays him?
a) Lionel Barrymore
b) Lon Chaney Jr.
c) Finlay Currie
d) Victor McLaglen

HIGH NOON (1952)
Fred Zinnemann

1) The town location for **High Noon** was shot at the Columbia Ranch in Burbank. What was the name of the town?
a) Bradleyville b) Hadleyville
c) Shelleyville d) Radleighville

2) Harvey Pell had once been Will Kane's (Gary Cooper) faithful deputy but now wanted the retiring marshal's job for himself. Who was he?
a) Otto Kruger b) Lloyd Bridges
c) Van Heflin d) Glenn Ford

3) The screenwriter of **High Noon** was blacklisted by the HUAC when the film was released, but he went on to write many great screenplays including **The Bridge on the River Kwai** and **The Guns of Navarone**. Who was he?
a) Frank Tashlin b) Ben Hecht
c) Howard Koch d) Carl Foreman

IT HAPPENED ONE NIGHT
(1934) Frank Capra

1) In which Greyhound bus depot does hard drinking itinerant reporter, Peter Warne (Clark Gable) first meet runaway heiress, Ellie Andrews (Claudette Colbert)?
a) Chicago b) New Orleans c) Kansas d) Miami

2) Name the title of the song sung by Ellie, Peter and the entire complement of passengers on the night bus to New York before it loses control and careers off the road.
a) Anything Goes b) I Love Paris
c) It's De-Lovely d) The Daring Young Man on the Flying Trapeze

3) Something in the scene in which Peter Warne undresses in front of Ellie at an overnight motel stop set a national trend and sent women viewers into fits of ecstasy. What was it?
a) his chest hair had been shaved b) he wore no undershirt c) he wore boxer shorts d) his thigh sported an erotic tattoo

IT'S A WONDERFUL LIFE (1946)
Frank Capra

1) After George Bailey's guardian angel gives him "a great gift", a chance to see what the world would be like without him, his home town is changed into a sleazy den of iniquity called Pottersville. What was its original name?
a) Sweetwater b) Comfort Springs
c) Bedford Falls d) Chapel Hill

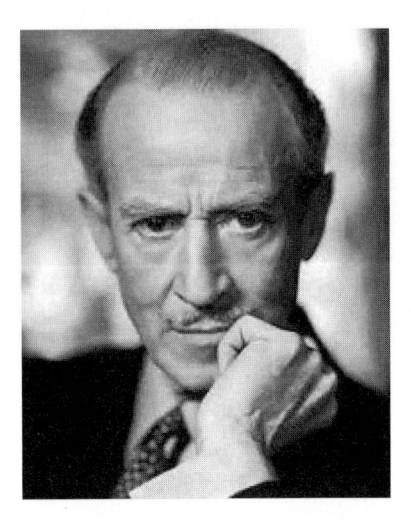

2) Mr. Gower is so distressed by the telegram informing him of the death of his son he accidentally fills a prescription with cyanide. Fortunately it is spotted in time by young George Bailey. Who portrays Mr. Gower?
a) H.B. Warner b) Thomas Mitchell
c) Samuel S. Hinds d) William Edmunds

Classic Films

the paternal dad myth

3) Clarence leaves George a copy of a book with the inscription: 'Dear George, Remember, no man is a failure who has friends.' Name the book's title.
*a) Great Expectations b) Tom Sawyer
c) Alice in Wonderland d) Robinson Crusoe*

JEAN DE FLORETTE (1986)
Claude Berri

1) Hunchback tax collector Jean de Florette Cadoret (Gérard Depardieu) and his wife Aimee struggled to produce their crops on land without water, not knowing there is a natural spring nearby. What relation is the actress who portrayed Aimee in real life to Gérard Depardieu?
*a) his daughter b) his sister
c) his wife d) his daughter-in-law*

2) The film was based on the first volume of the two-part novel, *L'Eau des Collines* (The Water of the Hills), published in 1963. Name the author - also a film-maker, who filmed **Manon Des Sources** in 1952.
*a) Claude Chabrol
b) Eric Rohmer
c) Sacha Guitry
d) Marcel Pagnol*

3) What animals did Jean de Florette Cadoret hope to breed for profit?
*a) goats
b) mules
c) rabbits
d) wild boar*

KING KONG (1933)
Merian C. Cooper, Ernest B. Shoedsack

1) Name the English thriller writer who co-wrote the screenplay with director Merian C. Cooper.
a) Geoffrey Household b) Herman 'Sapper' McNeile c) Daphne du Maurier d) Edgar Wallace

2) Hollywood showman Carl Denyham's (Robert Armstrong) enigmatic voyage leads his entourage to a strange island where the natives shelter in a walled camp and live in fear of a great beast. What is the name of the mysterious island?
*a) Shark Island b) Black Island
c) Skull Island d) Blood Island*

3) First Mate, John Driscoll, is the hero who saves Ann Darrow (Fay Wray) from the clutches of **King Kong**. Who was he?
*a) Bruce Cabot b) Robert Armstrong
c) Noble Johnson d) Frank Reicher*

L.A. CONFIDENTIAL (1997)
Curtis Hanson

1) On whose book was the film based?
*a) Erle Stanlet Gardner b) James Ellroy
c) Chester Himes d) Elmore Leonard*

2) Corrupt LA cop, Dudley Smith, steals a fortune in heroin in a drug raid and later concocts the 'Nite Owl Massacre' to confuse investigators. Who was he?
*a) Guy Pearce b) Ron Rifkin
c) Paul Guilfoyle d) James Cromwell*

3) Name the TV police series featured in the film starring Brett Chase (Matt McCoy).
*a) Dragnet b) Badge of Honor
c) Naked City d) Official Detective*

THE LADY VANISHES (1938)
Alfred Hitchcock

1) Who portrays retired governess and unlikely secret agent, Miss Froy, who vanishes on board a train bound for England?
*a) Margaret Rutherford b) Dame May Whitty
c) Gladys Cooper d) Josephine Hull*

2) What makes Gilbert (Michael Redgrave) suspicious of the nun attending to the patient swathed in bandages from head to foot?
*a) she is smoking b) she is reading a gory thriller
c) she is wearing high heels d) she is whistling a Welsh ballad*

3) Cricket fanatics, Charters and Caldicott's (Basil Radford and Naunton Wayne) prime concern throughout the entire drama is to get back to England for the test match, only to find it abandoned when they eventually do get home. For what reason is the test match abandoned?
*a) floods
b) the outbreak of war
c) a flu epidemic
d) the cricket ground was bombed*

THE LADYKILLERS (1955)
Alexander Mackendrick

1) Purporting to be classical musicians the gang members meet in a rented room to plan their robbery with a record playing in the background simulating their rehearsal. Name the piece of music they play repeatedly which is also played over the opening credits.
a) Handel's Water Music b) Boccherini's Minuet in E c) Sibelius' Finlandia d) Mozart's Eine Kleine Nachtmusik

2) Who portrays Harry the teddy boy?
a) Herbert Lom b) Cecil Parker
c) Peter Sellers d) Danny Green

3) At which London station does the robbery take place?
a) St. Pancras b) Waterloo
c) Euston d) Kings Cross

LAWRENCE OF ARABIA (1962)
David Lean

1) Journalist Jackson Bentley (based on CBS correspondent Lowell Thomas) travels with Lawrence and relays his exploits to the world's media, commenting: "It was my privilege to know him and make him known to the world. He was a poet, a scholar and a mighty warrior... he was also the most shameless exhibitionist since Barnum & Bailey." Who portrayed Bentley?
a) Jack Gwillim b) Jose Ferrer
c) Arthur Kennedy d) Frank Lovejoy

2) Who portrays General Allenby?
a) Claude Rains b) Anthony Quayle
c) Donald Wolfit d) Jack Hawkins

3) Why do Lawrence (Peter O'Toole) and Sharif Ali Ibn El Kharish (Omar Sharif) cross the burning sands of the Nefud Desert and enlist the forces of Auda Abu Tayi (Anthony Quinn)?
a) to capture Aqaba b) to circumvent a kidnapping plot against Prince Faisal
c) to capture waterholes d) to blow up a Turkish troop train

LOCAL HERO (1983)
Bill Forsyth

1) A Texas oil tycoon, with a passion for astronomy, decides to build a refinery in Scotland and tries to negotiate the purchase of an entire Highland community. The small Aberdeenshire fishing village of Pennan was the main location. What is its fictional name in the film?
a) Blackness b) Dungeness c) Ferness d) Ardness

2) Who portrays Mac, the young troubleshooting executive sent to do the negotiating, whose materialistic perspective on life is gradually eroded as he begins to appreciate the simpler pleasures, like clean air, beachcombing, and a good malt whisky?
a) Jonathan Banks b) David Patrick Kelly
c) James Remar d) Peter Riegert

3) Vital to the negotiations is the local beach which has been the legal property of the family of an old hermit named Ben for four centuries, who exclaims: "Would you give me a pound note for every grain of sand I hold in my hand? Now you can buy the beach for that." Who was he?
a) Rikki Fulton b) Ian Bannen
c) Fulton Mackay d) Brendan Gleeson

THE MALTESE FALCON (1941)
John Huston

1) "In 1539 the Knights Templar of Malta paid tribute to [a European monarch] by sending him a golden falcon encrusted from beak to claw with rarest jewels. But pirates seized the galley carrying this priceless token, and the fate of the Maltese Falcon remains a mystery to this day." Name the monarch whose tribute never arrived.
a) Charles V of Spain b) Charlemagne King of the Franks c) Peter II King of Yugoslavia d) Henry VIII

2) What is the character name of the sinister 'Fat Man' portrayed by Sydney Greenstreet?
a) Joel Cairo b) Buck Mansfield
c) Horace Vendig d) Kasper Gutman

3) The morning after a murder, Iva Archer (Gladys George) passionately embraces Sam Spade in his office. What is her connection to Sam?
a) his secretary b) his ex-wife
c) his partner's widow d) his new client

A MATTER OF LIFE AND DEATH (1946)
Michael Powell, Emeric Pressburger

1) With his instruments gone, his crew baled out and his undercarriage shot away, death seems a certainty for WWII bomber pilot Peter Carter (David Niven) as he talks over the radio to June, a ground controller back at the airfield with whom he falls in love. Who was she?
a) Kim Hunter b) Ida Lupino
c) Cathy O'Donnell d) Simone Simon

2) The prosecutor in the boundless High Court in the Other World is Abraham Farlan, the first colonial fighter killed in the

American Revolution and extremely anti-British. Who portrays him?
a) Spencer Tracy b) Walter Pigeon
c) Louis Calhern d) Raymond Massey

3) What evidence, held by Heavenly Conductor 71 (Marius Goring), is introduced to the court as proof of June and Peter's love?
a) his last radio communication from the burning bomber b) a book of Robert Browning's poems c) a tear caught on a rose petal d) a promise made in a prayer

MEET ME IN ST. LOUIS (1944)
Vincente Minnelli

1) Who portrays the Smith family's whimsical Grandpa?
a) Harry Davenport b) Henry Travers
c) Cedric Hardwicke d) Frank Morgan

2) What does little Tootie (Margaret O'Brien) bury in the back garden?
a) her grandpa's cigars
b) her dolls
c) her unwanted Christmas presents
d) her sister's love-letters

3) At the end of the film an ecstatic Smith family attends the opening of the World's Fair in St. Louis. Name the year the Fair opened.
a) 1900 b) 1904
c) 1908 d) 1912

NORTH BY NORTHWEST
(1959) Alfred Hitchcock

1) The film's title comes from a line in a Shakespeare play: "I am but mad north-northwest; when the wind is southerly I know a hawk from a handsaw." Name the play.
a) Hamlet b) Julius Caesar
c) A Midsummer Night's Dream d) Twelfth Night

2) Advertising executive, Roger Thornhill, is mistaken for a man named Kaplan during a meeting with business associates at a famous New York hotel. Name the hotel.
a) Waldorf b) Hilton c) Plaza d) Ambassador

3) Roger Thornhill is waiting to meet the mysterious Kaplan at a deserted crossroads when he is attacked by a bi-plane which forces him to seek refuge in a nearby cornfield. How does the plane flush him out into the open?
a) with machine-gun fire b) by showering him with chemicals c) by setting alight to the field d) by dropping bombs

ON THE WATERFRONT (1954)
Elia Kazan

1) Name the actor who almost landed the part of the ex-fighter, Terry Malloy, because Marlon Brando couldn't make up his mind if he wanted to play the role or not.
a) James Dean b) Frank Sinatra
c) Burt Lancaster d) Paul Newman

2) Father Barry (Karl Malden) gives the last rites to a longshoreman who was killed in a ship's hold because he dared to oppose union corruption. How did he die?
a) he was crushed by a heavy crate b) his throat was ripped with an ice hook c) he was drowned in bilge water d) he was hanged from a crane

3) Terry Malloy feels responsible for Edie Doyle's brother's death ("I thought they were only gonna lean on him a little") when Johnny Friendly's (Lee J. Cobb) henchman throws him from the roof of a building. Who portrays Edie?
a) Eva Marie Saint b) Natalie Wood
c) Audrey Hepburn d) Cathy O'Donnell

ONE FLEW OVER THE CUCKOO'S NEST (1975)
Milos Forman

1) On whose novel was the film based?
a) J.P. Donleavy b) Ken Kesey
c) Joseph Heller d) Philip Roth

2) McMurphy (Jack Nicholson) tries to strangle sadistic nurse, Mildred Ratched, after Billy Bibbit (Brad Dourif) committs suicide. Who portrays her?
a) Louise Fletcher b) Cybill Shepherd
c) Eileen Brennan d) Cloris Leachman

3) What does McMurphy want to watch on television so badly that he gets the patients to vote on changing the ward schedule?
a) the World Series b) the Harlem Globetrotters
c) the Open Golf Championships d) bowling

PLANET OF THE APES (1968)
Franklin J. Schaffner

1) Who portrays Dr. Zaius?
a) James Daly b) Maurice Evans
c) James Whitman d) Roddy McDowell

The Movie Quiz Companion

2) **Planet of the Apes** was based on the novel *Monkey Planet*. Who wrote it?
a) *Pierre Boulle* b) *Isaac Asimov*
c) *Philip K. Dick* d) *Frank Herbert*

3) What are Taylor's (Charlton Heston) first words of communication to the apes?
a) *"Touch me again you stinking baboon and I'll kill you!"* b) *"Get your stinking paws off me, you damn dirty ape"* c) *"Lay another stinking paw on me ape and you won't live to see another banana!"* d) *"Don't monkey with me you stinking ape!"*

THE PRISONER OF ZENDA
(1937) John Cromwell, George Cukor, W.S. Van Dyke II

1) On whose novel was the film based?
a) *Alexandre Dumas* b) *A.E.W. Mason*
c) *P.C. Wren* d) *Anthony Hope*

2) Commoner Rudolph Rassendyl (Ronald Colman) falls helplessly in love with the Princess Flavia. Who portrays her?
a) *Olivia de Havilland* b) *Madeleine Carroll*
c) *Joan Fontaine* d) *Ida Lupino*

3) In which mythical European kingdom is the film set?
a) *Ruritania* b) *Freedonia*
c) *Duchy of Grand Fenwick* d) *Burgonia*

PSYCHO (1960)
Alfred Hitchcock

1) Private detective, Milton Arbogast, hired to recover the $40,000 Marion stole from her employer, tracks her to the Bates Motel where he too meets his death. Who was he?
a) *Edward Binns* b) *Lew Ayres*
c) *Ed Begley* d) *Martin Balsam*

2) Alfred Hitchcock makes his traditional cameo appearance in the film outside Marion Crane's real-estate office. What is he wearing on his head?
a) *a panama hat*
b) *a ten gallon hat*
c) *a bowler hat*
d) *a clip-on sign advertising 'Ernie's Hot Dogs'*

3) Name the actor who portrayed Sam Loomis, seen having an adulterous affair with Marion Crane (Janet Leigh) in a Phoenix hotel room in the opening scenes.
a) *John Cassavetes* b) *John Gavin*
c) *Alain Delon* d) *Jason Robards*

PULP FICTION (1994)
Quentin Tarantino

1) Who portrays Lance, the drug dealer who screams at Vincent (John Travolta) following Mia's overdose - "YOU brought her here, YOU stick in the needle! When I bring an O.D. to YOUR house, I'LL stick in the needle!"?
a) *Eric Stoltz* b) *Tim Roth*
c) *Ving Rhames* d) *Frank Whaley*

2) Steve Buscemi plays a waiter in the 1950s theme restaurant, Jack Rabbit Slim's, where Mia and Vincent enter a twist contest. Who does he portray?
a) *Buddy Holly*
b) *James Dean*
c) *Ricky Nelson*
d) *Jerry Lewis*

3) On the run boxer, Butch Coolidge (Bruce Willis), makes a dangerous return trip to his apartment to retrieve a priceless family heirloom. What is it?
a) *a locket*
b) *a ring*
c) *a wristwatch*
d) *a tiepin*

REBECCA (1940)
Alfred Hitchcock

1) Producer David O. Selznick insisted Joan Fontaine play the part of Mrs. de Winter even though Hitchcock and Laurence Olivier were against it. Who did Olivier have in mind for the part?
a) *Anne Baxter* b) *Olivia De Havilland*
c) *Margaret Sullavan* d) *Vivien Leigh*

2) What did Rebecca reveal to Max de Winter which resulted in him accidentally killing her?
a) *that she was having an affair* b) *that she was pregnant with another man's child* c) *that she tried to set fire to Manderley* d) *that she had gambled away his fortune*

3) Mrs. Danvers perishes when she sets fire to Manderley. Who portrayed her?
a) *Judith Anderson* b) *Margaret Hamilton*
c) *Martita Hunt* d) *Gail Patrick*

REBEL WITHOUT A CAUSE
(1955) Nicholas Ray

1) A drunk and disorderly Jim first meets Plato (Sal Mineo) at a police station. What is Plato accused of?
a) *shoplifting* b) *attempting to murder his father* c) *killing a litter of puppies* d) *attempting to burn down his school*

2) Corey Allen portrayed the gang-leader who dies after challenging Jim to a 'chickie run' in which two speeding cars drive towards a cliff edge. What is Allen's character name in the film?
a) *Beau* b) *Chick* c) *Buzz* d) *Moose*

Classic Films

3) The actor who portrayed Jim's (James Dean) inadequate and weak-willed father was also the voice of the cartoon character Mr. Magoo. Who was he?
a) Gus Schilling b) Paul Bryan
c) Ian Wolfe d) Jim Backus

THE SEARCHERS (1956)
John Ford

1) The actor who portrayed Martin Pawley, the one eighth Cherokee and adopted son of Aaron and Martha Edwards who accompanies Ethan on his search for Debbie, died aged only 43 following a fall. Best known for his role of Jesus in Nicholas Ray's **King of Kings** (!961). Who was he?
a) Jeffrey Hunter
b) Paul Wallace
c) Millard Mitchell
d) John Dall

2) Shortly after the end of the civil war Ethan Edwards (John Wayne) arrives at his brother's ranch for the first time in years and gives his niece Debbie a present, saying: "It don't amount to much". What is it?
a) a sword b) a medal
c) a confederate gold coin d) a silver bullet

3) What is the name of the Comanche chief, portrayed by Henry Brandon, who kidnaps Debbie and Lucy, and is eventually scalped by Ethan Edwards (John Wayne)?
a) Crazy Horse b) Ten Bears
c) Scar d) Kicking Wolf

SINGIN' IN THE RAIN (1952)
Gene Kelly & Stanley Donen

1) Name the title of Don and Cosmo's (Gene Kelly & Donald O'Connor) disastrous musical talkie featuring silent star Lina Lamont's (Jean Hagen) grating voice which is eventually pulled out of distribution for being technically so awful.
a) The Dueling Cavalier b) The Dying Cavalier
c) The Dandy Cavalier d) The Dancing Cavalier

2) With which actress, who wore a "crazy veil" made from 25 feet of Chinese silk, does Don (Gene Kelly) dance in the song-and-dance routine, 'Broadway Ballet'?
a) Cyd Charisse b) Leslie Caron
c) Kathryn Grayson d) Ann Miller

3) The musical numbers in the film were lifted from previously successful MGM musicals and mostly written by Arthur Freed and Nacio Herb Brown. In which MGM musical did the title song first appear?
a) Broadway Melody b) Broadway Melody of 1936
c) Going Hollywood d) The Hollywood Revue of 1929

SNOW WHITE AND THE SEVEN DWARFS (1937)
David Hand, Perce Pearce, Larry Morey, William Cottrell, Wilfred Jackson, Ben Sharpsteen

1) Twenty-year-old Adriana Caselotti was eventually chosen to be the voice of Snow White, but the voice of a well known Canadian actress was almost used and eventually dropped because her voice sounded too mature. Who was she?
a) Deanna Durbin b) Lois Maxwell
c) Fay Wray d) Kathleen Howard

2) What do the seven dwarfs dig out daily from their mine?
a) gold b) silver c) diamonds d) emeralds

3) A well-known vaudevillian and character actor who had developed a sneezing routine and had often supported Laurel and Hardy and Charlie Chaplin, gave a memorable portrayal of Sneezy. Who was he?
a) George Chandler b) Keenan Wynn
c) William Frawley d) Billy Gilbert

SOME LIKE IT HOT (1959)
Billy Wilder

1) Itinerant musicians, Joe and Gerry (Tony Curtis and Jack Lemmon), inadvertently witness the murder of Toothpick Charlie and his gang by Spats Columbo and his mob on St. Valentine's Day, 1929. Who portrays Spats?
a) Lon Chaney Jr. b) Jackie Coogan
c) Edward G. Robinson Jr. d) George Raft

2) Singer, Sugar Kane (Marilyn Monroe), is on the look-out for a millionaire husband. Imitating a famous actor, Joe (Tony Curtis) impersonates a millionaire and convinces her his family owns Shell Oil. Name the actor he impersonates.

The Movie Quiz Companion

a) W.C. Fields b) Cary Grant
c) Marlon Brando d) Charles Boyer

3) When an excitable Jerry/Daphne (Jack Lemmon) tries to explain to millionaire Osgood E. Fielding that marriage is out of the question because they're both men he replies: "Well, nobody's perfect." Who portrays him?
a) Pat O'Brien b) Billy Gray
c) George E. Stone d) Joe E. Brown

THE SOUND OF MUSIC (1965)
Robert Wise

1) How many children were there in the Von Trapp family?
a) 5 b) 6 c) 7 d) 8

2) Capt. Von Trapp (Christopher Plummer) ends up marrying Maria (Julie Andrews), but his original intention was to marry 'The Baroness'. Who portrays her?
a) Peggy Wood b) Anna Lee
c) Norma Varden d) Eleanor Parker

3) The film's screenwriter also penned the hits **Sweet Smell of Success**, **The King and I**, **North By Northwest** and **West Side Story**. Who was he?
a) Ernest Lehman b) Stephen Sondheim
c) Richard Rogers d) Frank Loewe

STAGECOACH (1939)
John Ford

1) What is John Wayne's character name in the film?
a) The Ringo Kid b) Rusty Hart
c) The Colorado Kid d) Pawnee Bill

2) The alcoholic Dr. Boone (Thomas Mitchell) sobers up long enough to deliver a baby to Dallas, a prostitute who was run out of town by local women. Who portrayed her?
a) Maureen O'Hara b) Joanne Dru
c) Barbara Stanwyck d) Claire Trevor

3) Name the destination of the stagecoach, which is also the scene of the final gunfight.
a) Lordsburg b) Wichita Falls
c) Canyon City d) Pecos

STAR WARS (1977)
George Lucas

1) George Lucas acknowledged that the 1958 adventure film, **The Hidden Fortress**, was the primary inspiration for **Star Wars**. Who directed it?
a) Howard Hawks b) Fritz Lang
c) Jean-Luc Godard d) Akira Kurosawa

2) Name the actor who provided the unforgettable bass voice of Lord Darth Vader, second-in-command of The Imperial Galactic forces.
a) Jack Purvis b) Dave Prowse
c) James Earl Jones d) Eddie Byrne

3) In a smoke-filled Tatooine cantina, starpilot Han Solo (Harrison Ford) describes his ship to Luke Skywalker (Mark Hamill) as "...the ship that made the Kessel run in less than twelve parsecs!" What is his ship's name?
a) The Corellian b) Millennium Falcon
c) The Droid Void d) Hoth Avenger

SUNSET BLVD. (1950)
Billy Wilder

1) In Billy Wilder's attempt to recapture Hollywood's days of silent grandeur, former star, Norma Desmond (Gloria Swanson) reflects: "We didn't need dialogue. We had faces then. They don't have faces any more; maybe one..." Who was the 'one' she was referring to?
a) Ingrid Bergman b) Greta Garbo
c) Marilyn Monroe d) Jean Harlow

2) To which director (who played himself) did Norma Desmond send her 'Salome' script, hoping it would relaunch her career?
a) Cecil B. De Mille b) George Cuckor
c) D.W. Griffith d) King Vidor

3) Norma Desmond is discovered at age sixteen by film director, Max von Mayerling, whom she later marries. Who portrays him?
a) Buster Keaton b) H.B. Warner
c) Eric von Stroheim d) Jay Livingston

TAXI DRIVER (1976)
Martin Scorsese

1) Travis Bickle (Robert De Niro) developed a crush on a beautiful blonde named Betsy at the campaign offices of presidential candidate Charles Palantine (Leonard Harris), but after he takes her to a porno cinema she storms out in disgust and rejects him. Who was she?
a) Diahnne Abbott b) Marlene Jobert
c) Jill Ireland d) Cybill Shepherd

2) Name the critic turned screenwriter who collaborated with Scorsese for the first time on **Taxi Driver** and went on to pen the screenplays for **Raging Bull** (1980) and **The Last Temptation of Christ** (1988).
a) Joseph Minion b) Paul Zimmerman
c) Richard Price d) Paul Schrader

3) Harvey Keitel portrays a long-haired neighbourhood pimp who manages Iris, a 12-year-old prostitute. What is his character name in the film?
a) Sport b) Easy Andy c) Wizard d) Mafioso

THE TERMINATOR (1984)
James Cameron

1) Author Harlan Ellison successfully sued the film's producers claiming that much of the plot was derived from two scripts he wrote for a well known sci-fi television series. Name the series.
a) Lost in Space b) Weird Tales
c) The Outer Limits d) Quatermass

2) Who portrays the apparently innocent waitress, Sarah Connor, who is pursued by a cyborg sent from the future to kill her?
a) Linda Hamilton b) Barbara Powers
c) Bess Motha d) Marianne Gatto

3) When Sarah Connor realises she is being followed by Reese (Michael Biehn) she enters a nightclub to try to lose him. What is the name of the club?
a) Polanski's b) The Abyss
c) Beauty and the Beast d) Tech Noir

THE THIRD MAN (1949)
Carol Reed

1) Harry Lime's old friend Holly Martins was a writer. What type of books did he write?
a) thrillers b) westerns
c) travelogues d) short stories

2) Name the Italian actress who portrays Harry Lime's beautiful and mysterious girlfriend, Anna Schmidt.
a) Valentina Cortese b) Anna Magnani
c) Silvana Mangano d) Alida Valli

3) Harry Lime (Orson Welles) is an unscrupulous black marketeer. What had he been selling that caused the deaths of so many children?
a) contaminated blood b) faulty oxygen cylinders
c) corroded medical tubing d) diluted penicillin

THE 39 STEPS (1935)
Alfred Hitchcock

1) The enemy in the film is never identified. Why?
a) the Foreign Office had warned film-makers that hostile representation of Germany was undesirable b) the film would have been banned in Germany c) German financiers had invested heavily in the film d) producer Michael Balcon feared for the safety of his parents who were still living in Hitler's Germany

2) Wylie Watson, veteran actor of films such as **Whisky Galore**, **Brighton Rock** and **The Sundowners**, starred in the film. Who did he portray?
a) Professor Jordan b) Sheriff Watson
c) Mr. Memory d) John the farmer

3) When Richard Hannay (Robert Donat) is fleeing by train to Scotland he shares a compartment with two travelling salesmen and a minister. What does one of the salesmen pull out of his samples case?
a) a kilt and sporran b) a corset and brassiere
c) cough mixture and a spoon d) a pair of nylons

TO KILL A MOCKINGBIRD
(1962) Robert Mulligan

1) Seen only briefly in the final scenes, Arthur 'Boo' Radley is a deranged youth who is chained to his bed by his father and feared by the local children. Who portrays him?
a) Richard Dreyfuss b) Robert Duvall
c) Curt Jurgens d) Charles Bronson

2) On whose novel was the film based?
a) William Faulkner b) Harper Lee
c) Pearl Buck d) Taylor Caldwell

3) What is Scout dressed up as when she is attacked in the woods by the vengeful Bob Ewell?
a) a giant cactus b) a giant pumpkin
c) a giant corn cob d) a giant ham

TOP HAT (1935)
Mark Sandrich

1) Horace Hardwick is the confused and befuddled agent of Jerry Travers (Fred Astaire). Who portrays him?
a) Eric Blore b) Donald Meek
c) Dennis O'Keefe d) Edward Everett Horton

The Movie Quiz Companion

2) Character comedian, Erik Rhodes' caricature of a fashion designer resulted in the film being banned by one European country. To which country did it cause offence?
a) France b) Italy c) Spain d) Germany

3) Astaire and Rogers' duet, 'Cheek to Cheek', is arguably cinema's most famous. Who wrote it?
*a) Cole Porter b) Irving Berlin
c) Lorenz Hart d) Gus Kahn*

2001: A SPACE ODYSSEY (1968)
Stanley Kubrick

1) What had the primitive apeman just done before hurling his bone cudgel into orbit above the Earth?
*a) killed a tapir b) killed an enemy apeman
c) killed a leopard d) shattered a rock*

2) Scientist Dr. Heywood Floyd's (William Sylvester) space shuttle zooms through space on its journey towards a lunar station. To what well-known U.S. airline did the shuttle belong?
*a) TWA b) American Airlines
c) Pan American d) North-West Airlines*

3) The Hal 9000 computer on the Jupiter spaceship kills all the astronauts but one. After a struggle this astronaut succeeds in closing the computer down. As he slowly feels his "mind going" all Hal can remember is an old song. Name the title.
*a) Annie Laurie b) Pennies From Heaven
c) Daisy d) Moonlight Bay*

VERTIGO (1958)
Alfred Hitchcock

1) The spirit of Carlotta Valdes, who went mad and committed suicide, was presumed to be taking possession of Madeleine. Why did Carlotta kill herself?
*a) because her husband was having an affair
b) because her husband left her and took their child c) because she had a hereditary psychiatric illness d) because she was responsible for a fire which killed her child*

2) What does Judy (Kim Novak) wear when getting ready for dinner that finally convinces Scottie (James Stewart) that Judy and Madeleine were the same person?
*a) a hair clasp b) a necklace
c) a grey suit d) a bracelet*

3) Name the actress Hitchcock originally cast for the lead in **Vertigo**, who became pregnant and who lost the part to Kim Novak.
*a) Tippi Hedren b) Vera Miles
c) Janet Leigh d) Alida Valli*

WEST SIDE STORY (1961)
Robert Wise & Jerome Robbins

1) Who portrays Bernardo, the leader of the Puerto Rican gang known as The Sharks?
*a) David Winters b) Richard Beymer
c) Tony Mordente d) George Chakiris*

2) The leader of The Jets (Russ Tamblyn) is killed in a knife fight with Bernardo. What is Tamblyn's nickname in the film?
a) Riff b) Ice c) Rocco d) Action

3) Name the actress who won a Best Supporting Actress Oscar for her portrayal of Anita, the turbulent girlfriend of Bernardo?
*a) Carole D'Andrea b) Natalie Wood
c) Gina Triconis d) Rita Moreno*

WHISKY GALORE (1949)
Alexander Mackendrick

1) On whose novel was the film based?
*a) Gavin Maxwell b) George Mackay Brown
c) James Kennaway d) Compton Mackenzie*

2) The film was shot on the Hebridean island of Barra. What name was it given in the film?
a) Eriskay b) Sandray c) Todday d) Pabbay

3) Who portrays the self-important Home Guard commander Captain Waggett?
*a) Basil Radford b) James Robertson Justice
c) Anthony Quayle d) Stanley Holloway*

THE WILD BUNCH (1969)
Sam Peckinpah

1) After being ambushed during a bank raid in the small town of San Rafael the survivors of the wild bunch head for their hideout in Mexico. Which member of the gang did Ernest Borgnine portray?
*a) Angel b) Lyle Gorch
c) Tector Gorch d) Dutch Engstrom*

2) Railroad baron, Pat Harrigan (Albert Dekker), is responsible for getting ex Wild Bunch member, Deke Thornton, out of jail on the condition that he track down his old gang. Who played Deke?
*a) William Holden b) Warren Oates
c) Robert Ryan d) Edmond O'Brien*

3) Director Sam Peckinpah once commented: "I was trying to tell a simple story about bad men in changing times." In what year were the "changing times" of the film set?
a) 1895 b) 1900 c) 1913 d) 1920

THE WIZARD OF OZ (1939)
Victor Fleming, King Vidor

1) Jack Haley was only cast as the tin man after the original actor suffered from poisoning after the make-up department sprayed aluminium dust on his face and he had to be hospitalised. Who was he?
*a) Jack Carson b) Buddy Ebsen
c) Franklin Pangborn d) James Ellison*

2) When Dorothy's farmhouse lands on an evil witch the Munchkins are overjoyed and celebrate with the song 'Ding Dong the Witch is Dead'. Name the witch who was killed.
The wicked witch of the: a) north b) south c) east d) west

3) The part of the wizard was originally offered to actor Ed Wynn. After he turned it down it was offered to one of the screen's best loved comedians, who, in the end, also turned it down because the money wasn't good enough and he felt the part was beneath him. Who was he?
*a) Charlie Chaplin b) Oliver Hardy
c) Buster Keaton d) W.C. Fields*

WUTHERING HEIGHTS (1939)
William Wyler

1) Which Brontë sister wrote the tragic novel on which the film was based?
a) Maria b) Elizabeth c) Emily d) Charlotte

2) Where does Dr. Kenneth (Donald Crisp) discover Heathcliff's dead body?
a) on one of Cathy's favourite crags overlooking the moor b) on Cathy's grave c) sprawled over Cathy's deathbed d) on the Liverpool road

3) Name the cinematographer who won an Academy Award for the film's photography.
*a) Gregg Toland
b) Lucien Ballard
c) Stanley Cortez
d) James Wong Howe*

CULT MOVIES

AGUIRRE, THE WRATH OF GOD (1972)
Werner Herzog

1) The film is based on the journal of Brother Gaspar de Carvajal who was a member of a sixteenth century expedition searching for El Dorado, the lost city of gold. Name the conquistador who led the expedition.
a) Gonzalo Pizarro b) Hernando Cortez
c) Diego Velázquez d) Diego de Almagro

2) Who portrayed Spanish conquistador Don Lope de Aguirre?
a) Edward Roland b) Klaus Kinski
c) Del Negro d) Ruy Guerra

3) After all the expedition members have died from disease or been killed by Indians, Aguirre in his madness announces that he is "the wrath of God," and grabbing one of the animals which have invaded his raft, he asks, "Who is with me?" Name the animal he seizes.
a) a crocodile b) a vulture
c) a parrot d) a monkey

BADLANDS (1973)
Terrence Malick

1) The film was inspired by Charles Starkweather and Caril Ann Fugate who murdered eleven people in 1958. What nickname did the newspaper of the time give Starkweather?
a) The Bowleg Killer
b) The Mad Dog Killer
c) The Babysnatcher
d) The Stark Mad Killer

2) After his capture, what souvenirs does Kit distribute amongst the National Guardsmen who have been pursuing him?
a) photographs of himself kissing Holly
b) a road map and compass
c) Holly's schoolbooks
d) a comb, lighter and pen

3) Who portrayed Kit's (Martin Sheen) 15-year-old girlfriend, Holly, who accompanies him on a killing spree across South Dakota and later claims after realising her misdemeanour, "I made a resolution never again to take up with any hell-bent types"?
a) Sissy Spacek b) Juliette Lewis
c) Tisha Sterling d) Lee Remick

BLOW UP (1966)
Michelangelo Antonioni

1) At the start of the film, Thomas (David Hemmings), a fashionable photographer, is seen emerging dishevelled from a building where he has just spent the night on a photo

164

assignment. What was the building used for?
a) a brothel b) a doss-house
c) an insane asylum d) a porno cinema

2) What does Thomas purchase from the antique shop for £8 before his fateful visit to the park?
a) an Egyptian mummy b) a Victorian croquet set c) a brass coal scuttle d) a propellor

3) Who portrayed the mysterious Jane who objects to him taking photographs of her with her lover in the park?
a) Sarah Miles b) Susan Hampshire
c) Vanessa Redgrave d) Rita Tushingham

BRAZIL (1985)
Terry Gilliam

1) Which one of the Monty Python team commented that it was: "A movie so good they named a country after it"?
a) John Cleese b) Michael Palin
c) Graham Chapman d) Eric Idle

2) A computer changed the record of a terrorist named Tuttle to Buttle. Who portrayed him?
a) Bob Hoskins b) Jonathan Pryce
c) Michael Palin d) Robert De Niro

3) The Latin strains of the old song 'Brazil' reverberate throughout the film, but Terry Gilliam claims that his first musical inspiration for the film came from listening to someone singing 'Maria Elena' on the radio. Who was it?
a) Elvis Costello b) Frank Sinatra
c) Luciano Pavarotti d) Ry Cooder

CAT PEOPLE (1942)
Jacques Tourneur

1) Irena Dubrovna dared not consummate her marriage to Oliver (Kent Smith) for fear of awakening the terrible curse of the Cat People. Who portrayed her?
a) Gale Sondergaard
b) Simone Simon
c) Marina Vlady
d) Maria Schell

2) Which country did Irena and her curse originate from?
a) Romania b) Estonia c) Serbia d) Lithuania

3) Name the 17th century poet and priest whose sonnet extract is quoted in the film's final frame:
"But black sin hath betrayed
               to endless night
My world, both parts, and
               both parts must die"
a) John Donne b) Edmund Spenser
c) John Dryden d) William Cowper

DETOUR (1945)
Edgar G. Ulmer

1) What is the occupation of the ill-fated hitchhiker Al Roberts?
a) gas-station attendant b) bartender
c) pianist d) merchant seaman

2) When drug-popping Charles Haskell, Jr. (Edmund MacDonald) picks up hitchhiker Al Roberts en route to Hollywood he reveals a deep scar on his arm. How did he acquire it?
a) in a swordfight b) in a train crash
c) during the Normandy invasion d) his father struck him with a bottle

3) Vera (Ann Savage), the blackmailing femme fatale is strangled to death in a bizarre accident. What happened?
a) she slips on an oil slick and her scarf hooks onto a passing truck b) while decorating a Christmas tree she falls off a stool and her neck becomes entangled in the tree lights c) while drunk she inadvertently wraps a telephone cable around her throat which Al pulls on from the next room d) her string of pearls becomes entangled in a revolving door

DUCK SOUP (1933)
Leo McCarey

1) What is the condition on which Mrs. Teasdale (Margaret Dumont) will donate $20 million to the coffers of the cash-strapped duchy of Freedonia?
a) it will agree to go to war with neighbouring Sylvania b) it will agree to imprison anyone who doesn't comment on her 'beauty' c) it will agree to make Rufus T. Firefly its dictator d) it will agree to a one day working week

2) Who portrayed Ambassador Trentino of Sylvania, the constant butt of jokes and insults from Rufus T. Firefly (Groucho Marx)?
a) George Sanders b) Everett Sloane
c) Louis Calhern d) Monty Woolley

3) Name the dictator who banned the film as he considered it a direct insult to himself.
a) Stalin b) Hitler c) Mussolini d) Enver Hoxha

EASY RIDER (1969)
Dennis Hopper

1) Which role does rock 'n' roll producer Phil Spector play in the film?
a) a hitchhiker b) a dope dealer
c) a rancher d) a sheriff

2) As a symbolic gesture of freedom, Wyatt (Peter Fonda) chucks something into the dust before beginning his journey across America with Billy (Dennis Hopper). What is it?
a) a wristwatch b) his army call-up papers
c) a photograph of his girl d) a diary

3) A consequence of the film's small budget was that there was no money for an original score and classic 60s standards were used instead. Who performed 'Don't Bogart Me'?
a) The Fraternity of Man b) Steppenwolf
c) The Electric Prunes d) The Holy Modal Rounders

ENTER THE DRAGON (1973)
Robert Clouse

1) Who portrayed Roper, the American martial arts expert?
a) John Saxon b) Jim Kelly
c) Bob Wall d) Geoffrey Weeks

2) Lee agrees to enter a martial arts contest on Han's (Shih Kien) fortified island because Oharra (Bob Wall), his second in command, was responsible for the death of one of his family. What relation was the family member to Lee?
a) mother b) father c) brother d) sister

The Movie Quiz Companion

3) A complication arose during filming when Lee performed a kick at great speed. What was it?
a) he almost wrecked the main set b) he broke Obarra's leg c) he knocked himself unconscious for ten hours d) the kick was too fast to be filmed at normal speed

FORBIDDEN PLANET (1956)
Fred M. Wilcox

1) What does Robby the Robot supply in copious quantities to the crew's roguish cook (Earl Holliman)?
a) girls b) bourbon c) U.S. dollars d) beer

2) **Forbidden Planet** is a sci-fi version of Shakespeare's 'The Tempest'. Name the Shakespearian character Dr. Morbius (Walter Pidgeon) doubles for.
a) Prospero b) Ariel c) Caliban d) Alonso

3) Dr. Morbius's nubile daughter, Altaira, has never known a man other than her father and willingly accepts kissing lessons from the crew of the United Planets Cruiser. Who was she?
a) Maria Felix b) Suzy Parker
c) Marion Ross d) Anne Francis

FREAKS (1932)
Tod Browning

1) Circus freaks in Tod Browning's horror classic include the human skeleton, the pinheads, Siamese twins, the bearded lady and the hermaphrodite. What is a hermaphrodite?
a) someone who speaks a lost language
b) someone who never communicates with others
c) someone who has sex with animals d) someone combining the characteristics of both sexes

2) Beautiful circus artist, Cleopatra, seduces and eventually marries Hans the midget to get her hands on his inheritance. What type of act does she perform in the circus?
a) acrobat b) trapeze
c) bare-back rider d) mind-reader

3) After the circus members discover that Cleopatra has been poisoning Hans they savagely mutilate her and turn her into a sideshow freak. Name the attraction they turn her into.
a) Miss Torso b) the legless chicken woman
c) turtle girl d) nature's mistake

GILDA (1946)
Charles Vidor

1) When Rita Hayworth was having problems with the man who became her third husband she blamed producer Virginia Van Upp for creating her in the mould of an unfeasible sex goddess, saying: "It's all your fault. You wrote **Gilda** and every man I've known has fallen in love with **Gilda** and wakened with me." Name the man she was having problems with.
a) Aly Khan b) Orson Welles
c) Robert Ryan d) Richard Conte

2) Who portrayed South American casino owner and Gilda's (Rita Hayworth) villainous German husband, Ballin Mundson?
a) Glenn Ford b) Robert Strickland
c) Brian Donlevy d) George Macready

3) Rita Hayworth had many memorable lines in the film. Can you finish the following: "If I had been a ranch they would have called me............!"
a) the Bar Nothing
b) the Bar Wives
c) the Bar Tender
d) the Bar Sopen

GUN CRAZY (1949)
Joseph Lewis

1) Bart Tare (John Dall), a man with a weird gun fetish, meets sharp-shooting femme fatale, Annie Laurie Starr, at a local carnival side-show. Who was she?
a) Ann Sheridan b) Teresa Wright
c) Ida Lupino d) Peggy Cummins

2) Based on a Saturday Evening Post story by Mackinlay Kantor, the screenplay was credited to Millard Kaufman who fronted for the real screenwriter who was blacklisted at the time by the HUAC. Who was he?
a) Lester Cole b) Carl Foreman
c) Sam Peckinpah d) Dalton Trumbo

3) "The last big one" the duo pull is stealing a payroll from the Armour warehouse where both of them have temporary jobs. What is stored in the warehouse?
a) meat b) beer c) seafood d) furniture

I WALKED WITH A ZOMBIE
(1943) Jacques Tourneur

1) Jacques Tourneur commented: "One day I said to Val Lewton: 'I have an idea. We are going to do a remake of [this film] without telling anyone, simply by radically changing the setting. And that is how **I Walked With a Zombie** came about'". Which film was he talking about?
a) Dark Victory b) Rebecca
c) Jane Eyre d) Spiral Staircase

2) Before dabbling with voodoo, Nurse Betsy (Frances Dee) tries another treatment to bring Jessica Holland (Christine Gordon) out of her catatonic state. What is it?
a) hypnotism
b) electric-shock therapy
c) excorcism d) drugs

3) What does Dr. Maxwell (James Bell) state one has to do before one can turn someone into a zombie?
a) kill them b) make them forsake their religion
c) create a voodoo doll in their likeness d) make an animal sacrifice

INVASION OF THE BODYSNATCHERS (1956)
Don Siegel

1) Sam Peckinpah had a cameo role in the film. Who did he portray?
a) a policeman b) a refuse collector
c) a car salesman d) a meter reader

2) What was the name of the small Californian town which was descended on by aliens?
a) Santa Martha b) Santa Mira
c) Santa Elena d) Santa Perlita

3) What do Miles and Becky (Kevin McCarthy & Dana Wynter) observe the townsfolk off-loading from a truck into their cars?
a) bodies b) plants c) seeds d) pods

JOHNNY GUITAR (1954)
Nicholas Ray

1) The film was based on a novel by a writer who later penned **Cat Ballou**. Who was he?
a) Roy Chanslor b) Barbara Hawks McCampbell
c) Burton Wohl d) John W. Cunningham

2) Who portrayed the virtuous and domineering ranch owner, Emma Small, who is intent on running saloon owner Vienna (Joan Crawford) out of town?
a) Jan Sterling b) Barbara Hale
c) Mercedes McCambridge d) Laraine Day

2) The character portrayed by Scott Brady and his gang hold up a bank in which Vienna is a customer. This leads to false accusations that she participated in the hold-up. What was Brady's character name?
a) The Dancin' Kid b) Johnny Guitar
c) Turkey d) Cole Younger

THE KILLING (1956)
Stanley Kubrick

1) Prior to the racetrack robbery, professional killer Nikki Arcane (Timothy Carey) is given the job of creating a diversion. What does he do?
a) fake a heart-attack b) set fire to a stable
c) shoot a racehorse d) strangle a bookie

2) Another diversion tactic used was a bar-room brawl at the racetrack using wrestler Kola Kwarian. Ex-con Johnny Clay (Sterling Hayden) tracks him down at his local club. What game was he playing there?
a) pool b) chess c) bridge d) ten-pin bowling

3) Who portrayed boastful cashier and gang member, George Peatty, who is married to double-crossing tramp, Sherry (Marie Windsor)?
a) Albert Dekker b) Elisha Cook, Jr.
c) Harry Carey d) Jack Durant

KISS ME DEADLY (1955)
Robert Aldrich

1) At the beginning of the film Mike Hammer gives a lift to a terrified girl who flags him down on a lonely highway. Before she is murdered by her pursuers she informs him she was named after a famous poet, and urges him to "Remember me", a clue which helps Hammer eventually to unlock the mystery from the following lines of verse:
"Remember me when no more day by day
You tell me of our future that you planned:
Only remember me; you'll understand...
For if the darkness and corruption leave
A vestige of the thoughts that once we had..."
Name the poet she was named after.
a) Elizabeth Barrett Browning b) Christina Rossetti c) Mary Shelley d) Emily Dickinson

2) Who portrayed Mickey Spillane's wisecracking, bourbon-slugging private eye, Mike Hammer, whose other screen appearances have included **The Naked Spur**, **Paths of Glory** and **The Dirty Dozen**?
a) Ralph Meeker b) Tom Neal
c) Arthur Kennedy d) George Tobias

3) The "vestige" referred to in the above verse was a key to a locker at the Hollywood Athletic Club. Where did Mike Hammer find the key?
a) inside a Caruso record sleeve b) in the stomach of a corpse c) between the pages of a poetry book d) in a police file

LAST TANGO IN PARIS (1972)
Bernardo Bertolucci

1) After discovering something in their bed, Paul insists on taking it into the kitchen to

The Movie Quiz Companion

put mayonnaise on it. What is it?
a) a spider b) a rat c) a pigeon d) a cockroach

2) At their second meeting in the empty apartment, Paul (Marlon Brando) tells Jeanne, "You and I are going to meet here without knowing anything that goes on outside here. We are going to forget everything we knew - everything." Who portrayed Jeanne?
*a) Veronica Lazare b) Maria Michi
c) Catherine Sola d) Maria Schneider*

3) What is the occupation of Jeanne's boyfriend?
a) film-maker b) waiter c) sailor d) tourist guide

LAURA (1944)
Otto Preminger

1) What does Laura (Gene Tierney) ask cynical newspaper columnist, Waldo Lydecker (Clifton Webb), to endorse for her ad agency on their first meeting at the Algonquin Hotel?
*a) a typewriter b) a pen
c) a desk set d) a swivel chair*

2) Where is the murder weapon hidden in Laura's apartment?
*a) in a cocktail cabinet b) behind her portrait
c) inside a clock d) in the maid's room*

3) Who portrayed police detective, Mark McPherson, who "fell in love with a corpse"?

*a) Glenn Ford b) Van Heflin
c) Dick Powell d) Dana Andrews*

THE LITTLE SHOP OF HORRORS (1961)
Roger Corman

1) Would-be botanist, Seymour Krelboin (Jonathan Haze), creates a talking plant that needs human blood to survive which he names after his girlfriend. What is its name?
*a) Tisha, Jr. b) Samantha, Jr.
c) Alyson, Jr. d) Audrey, Jr.*

2) What type of pain does masochist Wilbur Force (Jack Nicholson) thrive on?
*a) electric shocks b) dental pain
c) kicks to his testicles d) fingernail extraction*

3) How long did it take to shoot the film?
a) 2 days b) 2 weeks c) 2 months d) 2 years

NIGHT OF THE LIVING DEAD (1968) George Romero

1) What is the reason given to explain why the dead were returning to life to eat the living?
*a) radiation from space b) a mystery virus
c) the aftermath of chemical warfare
d) contaminated drinking water*

2) Name the implement used by the little girl to stab her mother to death in the cellar.
*a) a meat hook b) a trowel
c) a scythe d) a garden fork*

3) There is only one infallible method of killing a flesh-eating ghoul. What is it?
*a) setting it on fire b) burying it alive
c) shooting it in the head d) suffocating it*

THE NIGHT OF THE HUNTER (1955) Charles Laughton

1) Where does bank robber, Ben Harper, conceal the stolen money shortly before he is arrested?
a) inside the family Bible b) inside his daughter's doll c) beneath a church pulpit d) inside the belly of a catfish

2) Psychopathic and self-appointed preacher, Harry Powell (Robert Mitchum), sweet-talks his way into the Harper family and marries the widow Willa in his quest to find the $10,000 her dead husband stole. Who portrayed the naive and doomed Willa?
*a) Tuesday Weld b) Claire Trevor
c) Irene Dunne d) Shelley Winters*

3) Fleeing from the clutches of Harry Powell, Willa's children are taken in by Rachel (Lillian Gish), a spinster who cares for homeless children. What does young John Powell give her for Christmas?
*a) his pet mouse b) his father's gun
c) an apple in a doily d) $10,000*

ONCE UPON A TIME IN THE WEST (1969)
Sergio Leone

1) Ennio Morricone wrote the score and gave each of the main characters their own themes, e.g. a harmonica for 'The Man' (Charles Bronson) and a romantic score for Jill (Claudia Cardinale). What instrument was used for Frank's (Henry Fonda) theme?
a) drum b) organ c) electric guitar d) bassoon

2) Italian screenwriter, Dario Argento, collaborated with Sergio Leone and another famous Italian director on the script. Who was he?
*a) Bernardo Bertolucci b) Federico Fellini
c) Vittorio De Sica d) Franco Zeffirelli*

3) One of Frank's (Henry Fonda) three hired killers was the sinister 'Knuckles', who, with his craggy face and sightless left eye assured him a place as a veteran western villain. Who was he?
a) Jack Elam b) Larry Duran
c) John Frederick d) Lionel Stander

OUT OF THE PAST (1947)
Jacques Tourneur

1) Femme fatale, Kathie Moffett, shoots her hoodlum boyfriend Whit Sterling (Kirk Douglas) and disappears with $40,000 with gumshoe Jeff Bailey (Robert Mitchum) in hot pursuit. Who portrayed her?
a) Jane Greer b) Rhonda Fleming
c) Mary Astor d) Rita Hayworth

2) Geoffrey Homes (a pseudonym of screenwriter Daniel Mainwaring) wrote the novel on which the film was based and co-wrote the screenplay. Name the title of his novel.
a) Kiss of the Gallows b) The Gallows of Escondido c) Gallows Fever d) Build My Gallows High

3) In which Mexican town does Jeff Bailey track her down and inevitably fall in love with her?
a) Tampico b) Veracruz c) Acapulco d) Tijuana

PEEPING TOM (1960)
Michael Powell

1) The deranged protagonist in **Peeping Tom** has an abnormal urge to gaze voyeuristically. What term is used to describe this condition?
a) Scopophilia b) Notaphily
c) Spasmophilia d) Argyrophilia

2) A focus puller at a film studio and a clandestine porn photographer, Mark Lewis lures his female victims to their death, while recording the event on film for posterity. Who was the German actor who portrayed Mark?
a) Horst Buchholz b) Hardy Kruger
c) Karl Boehm d) Maximilian Schell

3) Much maligned on its release, **Peeping Tom** was viewed by the critics at the time as little more than goulish pornography. Name the famous film critic who changed his/her mind, stating: "I hated the piece and, together with a great many other critics, said so. Today, I find I am convinced that this is a masterpiece. If in some afterlife conversation is permitted, I shall think it my duty to seek out Michael Powell and apologise."
a) Dilys Powell b) Graham Greene
c) Pauline Kael d) Alexander Walker

PLAN 9 FROM OUTER SPACE
(1959) Edward D. Wood

1) Frequently described as "The Worst Film of All Time", yet nobody could argue against its inventiveness. For instance - what were the flying saucers which attack LA created from?
a) 78 rpm records b) Cadillac hubcaps
c) umbrellas d) upturned pie cases

2) Finnish-born actress, Maila Nurmi, became a cult figure and made a career out of appearing in extremely odd roles - none better than as one of the dead raised to help take over the Earth in Ed Wood's cult classic, **Plan 9 From Outer Space**. By what name was she better known?
a) Carlotta b) Lulu Fishpaw
c) Vampira d) Amber Tussle

3) The aliens in the film plan to take over Earth using 'Plan 9'. What does the plan involve?

The Movie Quiz Companion

a) hypnotising Earthlings b) resurrecting dead Earthlings c) breeding with Earthlings d) kidnapping all Earthlings and burying them alive

QUADROPHENIA (1979)
Franc Roddam

1) The film recounts the empty and aimless existence of Jimmy, a young Mod in 1964 London. Who portrayed him?
a) Mark Wingett b) Gary Duthie
c) Gary Shall d) Phil Daniels

2) Jimmy's idol is an ultra-cool Mod portrayed by Sting who turns out to be a humble hotel bell-boy. What was his character's name in the film?
a) Big Spider b) The Ace Face
c) The Main Man d) Neat Pete

3) Much of the film was shot on location in Brighton, but when the Mod scooter gang first see their bank holiday Nirvana from a crest of a hill, they are not actually looking at Brighton. Where was it?
a) Eastbourne b) Littlehampton
c) Worthing d) Hastings

RESERVOIR DOGS (1992)
Quentin Tarantino

1) Name the veteran Hollywood tough guy who portrayed gang leader Joe Cabot.
a) Lawrence Tierney b) Robert Forster
c) James Haydn d) Joe Pantoliano

2) Tim Roth is an undercover cop who has infiltrated the gang, none of whom know each other and are given false names in case anybody squeals. What is Tim Roth's name?
a) Mr. Orange b) Mr. Brown
c) Mr. Pink d) Mr. White

3) Mr. Blonde (Michael Madsen) captures a cop as a hostage and proceeds to mutilate him and dowse him with petrol to the strains of a 1970's hit. Name its title and performer.
a) 'Hooked on a Feeling' by Blue Swede b) 'Stuck in the Middle With You' by Stealers Wheel
c) 'I Gotcha' by Joe Tex d) 'Fool For Love' by Sandy Rogers

THE ROCKY HORROR PICTURE SHOW (1975)
Jim Sharman

1) When Brad and Janet's car breaks down they seek help at a residence full of alien transsexuals from the planet Transsexual. In which galaxy is the planet Transsexual?
a) Transsexia b) Transshokia
c) Transweirdia d) Transylvania

2) Richard O'Brien wrote the music and lyrics for the film and also played one of the characters. Who did he portray?
a) Rocky Horror b) Riff Raff the butler
c) Dr. Everett Scott d) Ralph Hapschaff

3) What is the ultimate fate of Eddie (Meat Loaf)?
a) he is eaten b) he is turned into a statue
c) he is drowned d) he is electrocuted

SHANE (1953)
George Stevens

1) On whose novel was the film based?
a) Jack Schaefer b) Stuart N. Lake
c) Ernest Haycox d) Barbara Hawks McCampbell

2) When gunfighter **Shane** (Alan Ladd) decides to hang up his guns and help out on the Starrett's Wyoming farm he finds himself attracted to Marion Starrett. Who was she?
a) Loretta Young b) Janet Leigh c) Jean Arthur
d) Linda Darnell

3) Tragically, the actor who portrayed Little Joey Starrett died in a car crash aged only thirty. Who was he?
a) Roddy McDowall b) Scotty Beckett
c) Brandon de Wilde d) Bobby Driscoll

STRAW DOGS (1971)
Sam Peckinpah

1) Peckinpah's most controversial film was strongly criticised for the graphic rape of Amy Sumner. Who portrayed her?
a) Britt Ekland b) Susan George
c) Jane Birkin d) Sarah Miles

2) In which southern English county is the film set?
a) Kent b) Somerset
c) Cornwall d) Devon

3) What is the occupation of Amy's American husband, David (Dustin Hoffman)?
a) mathematician b) architect
c) dentist d) biologist

THE WICKER MAN (1973)
Robin Hardy

1) Devout Christian policeman, and sexually repressed virgin, Sergeant Howie (Edward Woodward), arrives on the remote Summerisle to investigate the disappearance of a schoolgirl. What is her name?
a) Willow b) Alder c) Rowan d) Eurydice

2) During Sergeant Howie's stay at the inn on Summerisle, only a bedroom wall and a stiff prayer saves him from being seduced by the landlord's daughter. What is the name of the inn?
a) The Unicorn b) The Green Man
c) The Maypole d) The Running Hare

3) The Wicker Man in the film stood 60ft high, and incredible as it may seem, such structures did exist and were used to burn sacrificial victims. Name the invader who recorded their use by the pagan Britons in his diaries.
a) Svien 'Fork-Beard' b) Julius Caesar
c) William the Conqueror d) King Canute

WITHNAIL & I (1987)
Bruce Robinson

1) Cracking under the strain of their revolting city life, Withnail and Marwood decide to have a holiday away from it all at Withnail's gay uncle Monty's isolated cottage in the Lake District. Name the cottage.
a) Black Cragg b) Shap Cragg
c) Crow Cragg d) Devil's Cragg

2) When Danny (Ralph Brown) is lamenting that "the greatest decade in the history of mankind is over", he is outraged to discover they are selling hippy wigs where?
a) Tesco b) Woolworth c) C&A d) Harrods

3) The "I" in the title is Withnail's (Richard E. Grant) out-of-work actor flatmate, Marwood. Who portrayed him?
a) Michael Wardle b) James Older
c) Matthew Marsh d) Paul McGann

PERFORMERS

BUD ABBOTT
(William A. Abbott 1895 -1974)
& LOU COSTELLO
(Louis Francis Cristillo 1906 -1959)

1) In which 1948 comedy does Dracula (Bela Lugosi) plan to transplant Wilbur's (Lou Costello) brain into Frankenstein's Monster?
a) Abbott and Costello Meet Frankenstein
b) Abbott and Costello Meet The Killer Boris Karloff c) Abbott and Costello in Hollywood
d) Who Done It?

2) They made their film debut in a 1940 musical comedy. Name the title.
a) Babes on Broadway b) The Boys From Syracuse c) In the Navy d) One Night in the Tropics

3) Which 1952 comedy spoofs the opening of **The Wizard of Oz**, beginning in sepia and changing to colour for the world of make-believe?
a) Jack and the Beanstalk b) Into the Night
c) Pardon My Sarong d) Little Giant

JOSS ACKLAND (1928 -)

1) In 1988 he portrayed wealthy rancher, Sir Henry Jock Broughton, accused of murdering his wife's lover in 1940s Kenya. Name the film.
a) Seven Days To Noon b) Rough Cut
c) White Mischief d) Crescendo

2) What 1979 film connection can you make between Joss Ackland and the writer Paul Theroux?
a) Villain b) Saint Jack
c) Royal Flash d) The Black Windmill

3) In which film did he provide the voice for an animated black rabbit?
a) Animal Farm b) Watership Down
c) The Sleeping Beauty d) All Dogs Go To Heaven

JUNE ALLYSON (1917 -)

1) Name the Hollywood actor (often paired with Ruby Keeler in 1930s musicals) to whom June Allyson was married from 1945 until his death in 1963.
a) Dick Powell b) Al Jolson
c) Guy Kibbee d) George Brent

2) Which 1954 biopic features her portraying the wife of a famous bandleader?
a) Alexander's Ragtime Band b) Meet Danny Wilson c) The Eddy Duchin Story d) The Glenn Miller Story

3) With which 1949 film do you associate her character being married to a one-legged baseball player named Monty (James Stewart)?
a) Made For Each Other
b) The Stratton Story
c) Fear Strikes Out
d) The Jackie Robinson Story

URSULA ANDRESS (1936 -)

1) In 1962 she portrayed the bikini-clad "Honey" in an early James Bond Film. Name the title.
a) Dr. No b) From Russia With Love
c) Goldfinger d) Thunderball

2) What film connection can you make between Ursula Andress and the adventure writer H. Rider Haggard?
a) King Solomon's Mines b) Allan Quatermain
c) Jess d) She

3) Name the western in which she co-starred with Frank Sinatra and Dean Martin in 1963.
a) 4 for Texas b) Rio Bravo
c) Sergeants Three d) The Sons of Katie Elder

DANA ANDREWS
(Carver Daniel Andrews 1912 -1992)

1) The character portrayed by Dana Andrews is one of three innocent homesteaders convicted of murder on circumstantial evidence in William Wellman's 1943 western classic. Name the title.
a) Dodge City
b) Johnny Guitar
c) Duel in the Sun
d) The Ox-Bow Incident

2) In which 1956 film, directed by Fritz Lang, does he deliberately implicate himself as a murderer to prove that circumstantial evidence can lead to wrongful conviction?
a) Each Dawn I Die b) Beyond a Reasonable Doubt c) Witness for the Prosecution d) While the City Sleeps

3) What 1957 horror film, directed by Jacques Tourneur, and based on M.R. James' short story *Casting of the Runes*, cast him as a sceptical scientist whose life is threatened by a black magician?
a) Night of the Demon b) Curse of the Cat People
c) I Walked with a Zombie d) Day of the Dead

JULIE ANDREWS
(Julia Wells 1934 -)

1) In which film does she portray a character who forms a romantic attachment with Lt. Comdr. Charles Madison (James Garner)?
a) The Man Who Loved Women b) Star
c) The Americanization of Emily d) That's Life

2) In 1968 she portrayed the famous musical comedy idol, Gertrude Lawrence, in a film directed by Robert Wise. Name the title.
a) Darling Lili b) Star
c) Thoroughly Modern Millie d) Duet for One

3) Name the 1964 film which won her an AA for Best Actress.
a) The Sound of Music b) Mary Poppins
c) Torn Curtain d) Star

ANN-MARGRET
(Ann Margaret Olsson 1941 -)

1) Which 1975 film cast her as the mother of a "deaf, dumb, and blind kid"?
a) Magic b) The Last Remake of Beau Geste
c) The Cheap Detective d) Tommy

2) She made her 1961 screen debut in director Frank Capra's final film. Name the title.
a) Pocketful of Miracles b) Riding High
c) Here Comes the Groom d) A Hole in the Head

3) In George Sidney's 1963 comedy, **Bye Bye Birdie**, Kim McAfee (Ann-Margret) of Sweet Apple got to meet celebrity Conrad Birdie (Jesse Pearson). What was he?
a) a rock'n'roll singer b) a country singer
c) a disc jockey d) a movie star

GEORGE ARLISS
(George Andrews 1868 -1946)

1) George Arliss won a Best Actor Oscar for his portrayal of a British prime minister in a 1929 biopic. Name the title.
a) Clive of India
b) The Young Mr. Pitt
c) Suez
d) Disraeli

2) What 1937 adventure, which was also his last film, involves Arliss portraying the double life of an English vicar by day and a pirate by night?
a) Night Creatures
b) Doctor Syn
c) The Last Gentleman
d) The Tunnel

3) Which 1935 film cast him as France's cunning Cardinal Richelieu?
a) Under the Red Robe
b) The Iron Mask
c) Cardinal Richelieu
d) The Three Musketeers

PATRICIA ARQUETTE (1968 -)

1) In which film are hooker Alabama Whitman and her boyfriend on the run with $5 million of the mob's cocaine?
a) *Far North* b) *Wildflower*
c) *True Romance* d) *Flirting With Disaster*

2) Name the 1991 drama she starred in which was directed and scripted by Sean Penn who was inspired to write the screenplay after hearing the Bruce Springsteen song 'Highway Patrolman'.
a) *The Indian Runner* b) *Prayer of the Rollerboys*
c) *Daddy* d) *Trouble Bound*

3) In 1993 she portrayed Mattie Silver in John Madden's adaptation of a 1911 Edith Wharton novella. Name the title.
a) *The Reef* b) *The Mother's Recompense*
c) *A Backward Glance* d) *Ethan Frome*

JEAN ARTHUR
(Gladys Greene 1905 -1991)

1) In which 1939 film does she meet naive idealist, Jefferson Smith?
a) *A Foreign Affair* b) *The Plainsman*
c) *Mr. Smith Goes to Washington* d) *Whirlpool*

2) For what film does she play a salesgirl in a New York department store owned by millionaire, Charles Coburn?
a) *You Can't Take It With You* b) *The Devil and Miss Jones* c) *Adventure in Manhattan* d) *Easy Living*

3) In which film did she portray "Calamity Jane"?
a) *The Plainsman* b) *Dodge City*
c) *Carson City* d) *The Kentuckian*

PEGGY ASHCROFT (1900 -1991)

1) Name the title of the David Lean film which won her a Best Supporting Actress Oscar in 1984.
a) *Ryan's Daughter* b) *A Passage to India* c) *A Room With a View* d) *The Europeans*

2) Name the 1959 film in which she portrayed the nun, "Mother Mathilde".
a) *Going My Way* b) *The Singing Nun*
c) *The Nun's Story* d) *The Miracle Worker*

3) In which 1936 film do you associate her with a famous explorer?
a) *Rhodes of Africa* b) *Stanley and Livingstone*
c) *Marco Polo* d) *Seven Seas to Calais*

FRED ASTAIRE
(Frederick Austerlitz 1899 -1987)

1) Fred Astaire and Eleanor Powell co-starred in only one film together. Name the title.
a) *Broadway Melody of 1940* b) *The Band Wagon*
c) *You Were Never Lovelier* d) *Swing Time*

2) Name the title of the film which reunited Fred and Ginger for the last time. Songs included: "They Can't Take That Away From Me", and "Bouncin' the Blues".
a) *The Barkleys of Broadway* b) *Let's Dance*
c) *Funny Face* d) *Easter Parade*

3) In which 1946 film did Fred Astaire and Gene Kelly have their only screen appearance together?
a) *Ziegfeld Follies* b) *Finian's Rainbow*
c) *Blue Skies* d) *Silk Stockings*

MARY ASTOR
(Lucille Vasconcellos Langehanke 1906 -1987)

1) With which film do you associate her portrayal of the mysterious murderess Brigid O'Shaughnessy?
a) *The Great Lie*
b) *The Maltese Falcon*
c) *The Dark Mirror*
d) *The Mask of Dimitrios*

2) For what 1944 film did she portray Mrs. Anne Smith, mother of Esther Smith (Judy Garland)?
a) *Babes on Broadway*
b) *The Clock*
c) *For Me and My Gal*
d) *Meet Me in St. Louis*

3) Mary Astor won a Best Supporting Actress Oscar for portrayal of the spirited concert pianist Sandra Kovac who was pregnant with her supposedly dead ex-husband's child in **The Great Lie** (1941). Name the actress who played the part of the woman who wanted to adopt her baby.
a) *Greer Garson*
b) *Rita Hayworth*
c) *Myrna Loy*
d) *Bette Davis*

RICHARD ATTENBOROUGH (1923 -)

1) Richard Attenborough made his film debut in a WWII naval adventure directed by Noel Coward and David Lean. Name the title.
a) The Cruel Sea b) The Day Will Dawn c) Pursuit of The Graf Spee d) In Which We Serve

2) In which 1960 drama, directed by Guy Green, did he portray Tom Curtis, a factory worker who is terrorised and spurned by his workmates for refusing to participate in an unofficial strike?
a) Code of Silence b) Sworn to Silence c) The Angry Silence d) Trapped in Silence

3) Name the English murderer portrayed by Attenborough in Richard Fleischer's 1971 crime drama, **10 Rillington Place**?
a) Crippen b) Christie c) Jack the Ripper d) Hanratty

GENE AUTRY
(Orvon Gene Autry 1900 -1998)

1) What was the name of the singing cowboy's faithful golden Palomino horse?
a) Champion b) Fury c) Sam d) Streak

2) Name the 1935 film which established his on-screen image and remained the same for ninety-three westerns that followed, ending with **Last of the Pony Riders** in 1952.
a) The Last Roundup b) Tumbleweeds c) Red River Valley d) Boots and Saddles

3) In **Comin' Round the Mountain** (1936) he did something completely out of character for someone who once inscribed a poster of himself thus: "I pledge never to make a picture that you won't be proud to take your son, daughter, mother or father to see. I'll keep them clean". What was it?
a) got drunk b) slapped a girl across her bottom c) kissed a girl d) bared his chest

DAN AYKROYD (1952 -)

1) He was nominated for a Best Supporting Actor Oscar for his role as Boolie Werthan who was adamant his mother should hire a chauffeur in this 1989 comedy drama. Name the film.
a) Nashville b) My Chauffeur c) Prick Up Your Ears d) Driving Miss Daisy

2) In which film do you associate him with being "on a mission from God"?
a) Coneheads b) Dragnet c) The Blues Brothers d) Spies Like Us

3) In 1991 he played distant widower and father, Harry Sultenfass, in the comedy drama **My Girl**. What was his occupation in the film?
a) gravedigger b) executioner c) pathologist d) mortician

LAUREN BACALL
(Betty Joan Perske 1924 -)

1) Lauren Bacall made her film debut alongside Humphrey Bogart in a 1944 drama based on a Hemingway novel. Name the title.
a) Key Largo b) The Big Sleep c) The Snows of Kilimanjaro d) To Have and Have Not

2) In 1956 she portrayed a secretary who marries oil tycoon Kyle Hadley in **Written on the Wind**. She becomes pregnant but isn't sure if the father is Hadley or Hadley's best friend. Who played Hadley?
a) Rock Hudson b) Jeff Chandler c) Lloyd Bridges d) Robert Stack

3) Her first husband, Humphrey Bogart, died in 1957. Who was her second from 1961 to 1969?
a) Jason Robards b) John Cassavetes c) Lloyd Nolan d) Lex Barker

STANLEY BAKER (1927 - 1976)

1) Name the 1953 drama which won him a long-term studio contract and secured his screen career as a working-class hard man and anti-hero.
*a) Hell Below Zero
b) The Cruel Sea
c) Captain Horatio Hornblower
d) Knights of the Round Table*

2) In which film does he portray engineer Lt. John Chard?
*a) Sands of the Kalahari
b) Zulu
c) The Guns of Navarone
d) The Last Grenade*

3) What was ex-con Tom Yately's (Stanley Baker) hazardous occupation in Cy Endfield's 1957 drama, **Hell Drivers**?
*a) racing driver
b) ambulance driver
c) truck driver
d) stunt driver*

The Movie Quiz Companion

ANNE BANCROFT
(Anna Maria Louisa Italiano 1931 -)

1) With which film do you associate her playing the extraordinary teacher, Anne Sullivan, who teaches the blind and deaf Helen Keller (Patty Duke) to communicate through sign language?
a) The Miracle Woman b) Some Kind of Miracle
c) More Than a Miracle d) The Miracle Worker

2) What was the fate of Anne Bancroft's daughter (Sissy Spacek) in the 1986 drama, **Night, Mother**?
a) she shot herself b) she poisoned herself
c) she gassed herself d) she cut her throat

3) In which 1995 romantic drama does she play Finn's (Winona Ryder) great aunt Glady Joe?
a) Home for the Holidays b) How to Make an American Quilt c) Point of No Return d) Malice

BRIGITTE BARDOT
(Camille Javal 1934 -)

1) A former model, Bardot appeared in various nondescript films before attaining stardom and international sex symbol status in a 1956 French drama. Name its title.
a) Act of Love b) La Parisienne
c) Female d) ...And God Created Woman

2) In which 1963 film, directed by Jean-Luc Godard, did Bardot play a character called Camille Javal - her real name?
a) Alphaville b) Contempt / Le Mepris
c) Lola d) A Woman is a Woman / Une Femme est une Femme

3) For what 1955 comedy did Dirk Bogarde co-star with Brigitte Bardot?
a) Doctor at Sea b) Doctor in the House
c) Doctor at Large d) Doctor's Dilemma

ELLEN BARKIN (1954 -)

1) She made her screen debut in a 1982 coming-of-age drama, directed by Barry Levinson, and set in 1950s Baltimore. Name the title.
a) Diner b) The Year My Voice Broke
c) The Flamingo Kid d) Grandview, U.S.A.

2) With which film do you associate her sharing a hot bath with Jeff Bridges in the town of Deadwood?
a) Desert Bloom b) Texasville
c) Blown Away d) Wild Bill

3) Name Harold Becker's 1989 thriller in which she is suspected of being a serial killer by the policeman who falls in love with her?
a) Down By Law b) Bad Company
c) Sea of Love d) Switch

LIONEL BARRYMORE
(Lionel Blythe 1878 -1954)

1) Name the 1931 film which won him a Best Actor Oscar for his role as alcoholic lawyer, Stephen Ashe, who gets racketeer Ace Wilfong (Clark Gable) acquitted on a murder charge.
a) Guilty Hands b) The Unholy Night
c) Public Hero No. 1 d) A Free Soul

2) In 1935 he played a character in George Cukor's version of **David Copperfield**. Who was he?
a) Barkis b) Dan Peggotty
c) Uriah Heep d) Micawber

3) Arthritis confined him to a wheelchair from the late thirties and in 1948 he played crippled hotelier, James Temple, in a crime drama directed by John Huston. Name the title.
a) The Killers b) The Stranger
c) Key Largo d) High Sierra

FREDDIE BARTHOLOMEW
(Frederick Llewellyn 1924 -1992)

1) What 1937 film connection can you make between Freddie Bartholomew and Rudyard Kipling?
a) Little Lord Fauntleroy
b) The Light That Failed
c) Gunga Din
d) Captains Courageous

2) Which 1935 film, directed by Clarence Brown, features Greta Garbo portraying Sergei's (Freddie Bartholomew) mother?
a) Queen Christina
b) Anna Karenina
c) Camille
d) The Painted Veil

3) In 1940 he is stranded on a desert island. Name the film.
a) Robinson Crusoe
b) Treasure Island
c) Swiss Family Robinson
d) Lord Jeff

skirmish at food time

Performers

KIM BASINGER (1953 -)

1) Name the James Bond film which was instrumental in launching this former supermodel's film career.
a) Never Say Never Again b) Octopussy
c) For Your Eyes Only d) A View to a Kill

2) Which film features her as celebrated photographer Vicki Vale?
a) Cool World b) No Mercy
c) My Stepmother is an Alien d) Batman

3) With whom does she portray a character who has a sexual relationship in Adrian Lyne's 1986 erotic drama, **Nine 1/2 Weeks**?
a) Mickey Rourke b) Ray Liotta
c) James Spader d) Jeremy Irons

ALAN BATES (1934 -)

1) In his first major screen role he portrayed Frank Rice, the son of vaudevillian, Archie Rice, in a memorable 1960 drama directed by Tony Richardson. Name the film.
a) The Dance Goes On b) The Music Man c) The Entertainer d) The Singer Not the Song

2) With which film do you associate Basil (Alan Bates) inheriting a lignite mine from his father?
a) Duet For One b) Quartet
c) In Celebration d) Zorba the Greek

3) In **Far From the Madding Crowd** (1967) Alan Bates portrays one of the loves of Bathsheba (Julie Christie). Name the 1971 drama which also cast them as lovers.
a) Doctor Zhivago b) Three Sisters
c) A Day in the Death of Joe Egg d) The Go-Between

KATHY BATES (1948 -)

1) What film connection can you make with Kathy Bates and the Whistle Stop Cafe?
a) Summer Heat b) Come Back to the Five and Dime, Jimmy Dean, Jimmy Dean c) Fried Green Tomatoes d) Misery

2) Kathy Bates and Charles Vanel both portrayed the same police inspector in different versions of the same film in 1996 and 1955 respectively. Name the film.
a) Dick Tracy b) Prelude to a Kiss
c) Shadows and Fog d) Diabolique

3) What 1995 thriller, based on a Stephen King novel, involves Kathy Bates portraying a housekeeper accused of murder which brings her together with her estranged daughter Jennifer Jason Leigh?
a) At Play in the Fields of the Lord b) No Place Like Home c) White Palace d) Dolores Claiborne

ANNE BAXTER (1923 -1985)

1) Which 1950 drama features her as an adoring fan turned secretary to ageing star Margo Channing?
a) Yellow Sky b) One Desire
c) You're My Everything
d) All About Eve

2) Name the 1953 Fritz Lang mystery in which telephone operator Norah Larkin (Anne Baxter) is accused of murdering artist Harry Prebble (Raymond Burr).
a) Beyond a Reasonable Doubt b) The Blue Gardenia c) Secret Beyond the Door d) Human Desire

3) In 1956 the Princess Nefretiri (Anne Baxter) falls in love with a man who is ignorant of his Jewish birth. Name the film.
a) Valley of the Kings b) The Egyptian
c) The Ten Commandments d) The Pharaoh's Woman

WARNER BAXTER (1891 -1951)

1) Warner Baxter was an accomplished silent film actor, but his screen career took off when he won an Oscar for his first ever talkie, **In Old Arizona** (1929). Name the famous western hero he portrayed.
a) Cisco Kid
b) Wyatt Earp
c) Billy the Kid
d) Butch Cassidy

2) In 1936 he played Dr. Samuel Mudd, an innocent man accused of being part of a conspiracy to murder in **The Prisoner of Shark Island**. Name the historical character who is murdered in this film who is based on a real-life character.
a) John Paul Jones
b) Abraham Lincoln
c) Stonewall Jackson
d) Brigham Young

3) What 1934 comedy, directed by Frank Capra, involved his gambling his marriage and future on a racehorse?
a) Rain or Shine
b) Long Pants
c) Broadway Bill
d) Riding High

SEAN BEAN (1958 -)

1) An early screen role for Bean was in a 1986 biopic directed by Derek Jarman in which he was cast as the gambler who has a sexual relationship with a painter. Name the film.
a) Caravaggio b) Wittgenstein
c) Aria d) Sebastian

2) In 1992 he portrayed fanatical Irish terrorist, Sean Miller, intent on killing a CIA agent and his family. Name the film.
a) Innocent Blood b) The Crying Game
c) Patriot Games d) A Stranger Among Us

3) Which 1995 Bond movie features Sean Bean portraying agent 006?
a) GoldenEye b) The World is Not Enough
c) Tomorrow Never Dies d) Licence To Kill

WARREN BEATTY
(Henry Warren Beatty 1937 -)

1) Who was Warren Beatty's leading lady in his 1961 screen debut, **Splendor in the Grass**?
a) Natalie Wood b) Kim Novak
c) Anne Baxter d) Pier Angeli

2) With which 1971 film, directed by Robert Altman, do you associate Warren Beatty running a whorehouse?
a) McCabe and Mrs. Miller b) The Only Game in Town c) Shampoo d) The Fortune

3) He ended up marrying his leading lady in **Bugsy** (1991). Who was she?
a) Dyan Cannon b) Glenne Headly
c) Diane Keaton d) Annette Bening

WILLIAM BENDIX (1906 - 1964)

1) In which 1944 war drama did he portray Gus, a seaman who has his leg amputated without anaesthetic?
a) Lifeboat
b) Battle Stations
c) Two Years Before the Mast
d) Submarine Command

2) Which 1962 Raymond Chandler mystery features him as a de-mobbed sailor returning from the war with a metal plate in his skull and an unreliable memory, trying to help his buddy Alan Ladd extricate himself from a murder wrap?
a) And Now Tomorrow
b) The Blue Dahlia
c) Time To Kill
d) Lady in the Lake

3) For what film did he portray NYC police detective Lou Brody, supportive and soft-hearted partner of troubled detective Jim McLeod (Kirk Douglas)?
a) The Cheap Detective
b) The Hollywood Detective
c) Detective Story
d) Detective

INGRID BERGMAN (1915 - 1982)

1) In the late forties Bergman's Hollywood career and reputation was severely damaged by an illicit affair with an Italian film director whom she eventually married and with whom she had three children. Who was he?
a) Pier Pasolini
b) Francesco Rosi
c) Luchino Visconti
d) Roberto Rossellini

2) She made three films for director Alfred Hitchcock. Name the title of the last one filmed in 1949.
a) Spellbound
b) Under Capricorn
c) Notorious d) Topaz

3) In which 1944 thriller does Scotland Yard detective, Brian Cameron (Joseph Cotten), prevent Paula Alquist (Ingrid Bergman) being driven mad by her husband?
a) Arch of Triumph
b) Saratoga Trunk
c) Gaslight
d) Stromboli

twit dyes roses

Performers

JULIETTE BINOCHE (1964 -)

1) Name the 1988 drama, set in Prague prior to the Russian invasion of 1968, which was instrumental in kick-starting her screen career.
a) Burning Secret b) Dinner For Adele
c) Hail Mary d) The Unbearable Lightness of Being

2) In 1993 she portrayed a woman whose composer husband is killed in a car crash and who has to reconstruct her life. Name the title.
a) Red b) White c) Blue d) Rendez-vous

3) Dr. Stephen Fleming embarks on a steamy affair with his son's enigmatic girlfriend Anna (Juliette Binoche) in Louis Malle's 1992 drama, **Damage**. Who was he?
a) Jeremy Irons b) Alain Delon
c) Elliott Gould d) Michel Piccoli

CLAIRE BLOOM (1931 -)

1) Communist party member, Nan Perry (Claire Bloom), has a doomed affair with British agent Alec Leamas (Richard Burton) in **The Spy Who Came In From the Cold** (!965). What was her occupation in the film?
a) a security officer b) a stripper
c) a librarian d) a prostitute

2) What 1968 drama involves her almost being raped by a mentally retarded man?
a) The Outrage b) The Illustrated Man
c) A Severed Head d) Charly

3) In 1952 she was cast as a young ballet dancer named Terry in a film directed by Charlie Chaplin. Name the title.
a) Limelight b) Gaslight Follies
c) A King in New York d) Monsieur Verdoux

DIRK BOGARDE
(Derek Jules Gaspard Ulric Niven van den Bogaerde 1921 - 1999)

1) The eldest of three children to a Scottish mother and a Dutch father, Dirk Bogarde's place of birth was unusual to say the least. Where was he born?
a) in a potting shed
b) in a London taxi
c) on the pavement outside Harrods
d) in the dining car of the Flying Scotsman

2) With which film do you associate Dirk Bogarde as the father of Judy Garland's illegitimate son?
a) I Could Go on Singing
b) The Singer Not the Song
c) The Stars Are Singing
d) Can't Help Singing

3) In 1965 he portrayed TV news reporter, Robert Gold, in a film directed by John Schlesinger. Name the title.
a) Cast a Dark Shadow b) Accident
c) The Mind Benders d) Darling

HUMPHREY BOGART
(1899 - 1957)

1) Name the 1936 crime thriller which was responsible for putting Bogie's screen career on the map when he was cast as the brutal gangster, Duke Mantee.
a) Crime School b) San Quentin
c) The Petrified Forest d) Midnight

2) In which film is he befriended by a pretty club-footed young girl named Velma?
a) In This Our Life b) High Sierra
c) In a Lonely Place d) It All Came True

3) In **The Barefoot Contessa** (1954), alcoholic has-been director, Harry Dawes (Humphrey Bogart) discovers a beautiful dancer - Maria Vargas - in the slums of Madrid and turns her into a star. Who was she?
a) Audrey Hepburn
b) Cyd Charisse
c) Leslie Caron
d) Ava Gardner

The Movie Quiz Companion

WARD BOND (1903 - 1960)

1) Name the 1941 John Huston mystery which cast him as detective Tom Polhaus who investigates the murder of private eye, Miles Archer.
a) Dead End b) The Maltese Falcon
c) Black Fury d) Chained

2) Which 1946 film features Ward Bond as Bert the cop who attempts to handcuff an angel?
a) For Heaven's Sake b) The Bishop's Wife
c) Angel in a Taxi d) It's a Wonderful Life

3) With which film do you associate his portrayal of the priest Father Peter Lonergan who is more interested in fishing than praying?
a) The Time of Your Life b) The Quiet Man
c) The Mortal Storm d) You Can't Take it With You

HELENA BONHAM-CARTER (1966 -)

1) A frequent star of period 'frock' movies from the Merchant/Ivory stable. Can you name the first film she made for them in 1985?
a) A Room With a View b) The Bostonians
c) Maurice d) Howards End

2) Which 1990 Franco Zeffirelli film involves her portraying a descent into madness?
a) Jane Eyre b) Endless Love
c) Hamlet d) La Traviata

3) In a 1995 comedy she portrayed Amanda, a gallery owner who is unhappily married to a New York sportswriter named Lenny (Woody Allen). Name the film.
a) Scenes From a Mall b) Husbands and Wives
c) Bullets Over Broadway d) Mighty Aphrodite

ERNEST BORGNINE (Ermes Effron Borgnine 1917 -)

1) Name the Robert Aldrich western in which he appeared with Gary Cooper and Burt Lancaster in 1954.
a) Apache b) Vera Cruz
c) Four for Texas d) The Last Sunset

2) In 1953 he portrayed the sadistic Sgt. 'Fatso' Judson who dies in a knifefight with a young soldier named Robert E. Lee Prewitt (Montgomery Clift). Name the film.
a) From Here to Eternity b) The Last Command
c) The Square Jungle d) Torpedo Run

3) With which film do you associate him playing jealous rancher, Shep Horgan, in a 1954 western directed by Delmer Daves, based on Shakespeare's *Othello*?
a) The Bounty Hunter b) The Badlanders
c) Jubal d) Hannie Caulder

CHARLES BOYER (1897 - 1978)

1) For what 1936 historical romance did he play the Archduke Rudolph of Austria who falls in love with a commoner?
a) Anna Karenina b) Mayerling
c) Maxime d) The Magnificent Lie

2) In the 1932 romantic drama, **The Man From Yesterday**, Rene Goudin (Charles Boyer) marries a woman who thinks her former husband is dead. Who was she?
a) Jean Arthur b) Greta Garbo
c) Jean Harlow d) Claudette Colbert

3) In 1938 Boyer made a remake of **Pepe Le Moko**, in which a gangster hiding out in the Casbah is enticed out by a beautiful woman. Name the title.
a) Algiers b) The Desert Hawk
c) Caravan d) The Garden of Allah

KENNETH BRANAGH (1960 -)

1) Name the first film in which he both directed and starred.
a) Mary Shelley's Frankenstein
b) Coming Through
c) Othello d) Henry V

2) In which 1991 mystery did he portray both a detective and a composer?
a) A Midwinter's Tale
b) Dead Again
c) Swing Kids
d) A Month in the Country

3) What 1993 comedy involves the wooing of Benedick (Kenneth Branagh) and Beatrice (Emma Thompson)?
a) Peter's Friends
b) Much Ado About Nothing
c) High Season
d) Love's Labour's Lost

MARLON BRANDO (1924 -)

1) Name the title of Brando's 1950 film debut in which he portrays a wheelchair-bound ex-GI readjusting to life.
a) The Men b) Bedtime Story
c) The Ugly American d) The Fugitive Kind

2) With which 1963 drama do you associate his portrayal of American ambassador, Harrison Carter MacWhite?
a) Bedtime Story b) The Appaloosa
c) Sayonara d) The Ugly American

3) Name the 1959 drama, directed by Sidney Lumet and based on Tennessee Williams' *Orpheus Descending*, which cast Brando as a singing guitarist trying to forget his wild past in a small Mississippi town.
a) The Nightcomers b) The Appaloosa
c) Candy d) The Fugitive Kind

WALTER BRENNAN (1894 - 1974)

1) Walter Brennan won his third Best Supporting Actor Oscar for his role as the infamous Judge Roy Bean in a 1940 western directed by William Wyler. Name the title.
a) The Westerner b) Dakota
c) Law and Order d) Kentucky

2) What film involves Sheriff John T. Chance, Dude, Colorado and Stumpy (Brennan) guarding a prisoner in the town jail?
a) Red River b) Rio Lobo
c) The Big Sky d) Rio Bravo

3) In which film does Doc Velie (Walter Brennan) reveal the whereabouts of a Japanese immigrant's farm to WWII veteran John J. MacReedy?
a) It's a Mad Mad Mad Mad World b) The Far Country c) Bad Day at Black Rock d) How the West Was Won

GEORGE BRENT
(George Brendan Nolan 1904 - 1979)

1) Studio boss, Jack Warner, once commented on a film in which George Brent co-starred with Bette Davis, saying, "Who wants to see a dame go blind?" Name the film.
a) Dark Passage b) Dark Journey
c) Dark Mirror d) Dark Victory

2) New England serial killer, Professor Warren (George Brent), is a strangler who cannot tolerate physically imperfect women, and plans to eliminate his bedridden mother's mute companion, Helen Capell, in the 1946 thriller **The Spiral Staircase**. Who was she?
a) Rosalind Russell b) Rhonda Fleming
c) Dorothy McGuire d) Gene Tierney

3) George Brent was forced to flee his native Ireland because of his political activities during the 'troubles' when he worked with Michael Collins. What job did he perform for Collins?
a) secretary b) driver
c) dispatch rider d) bodyguard

JEFF BRIDGES (1949 -)

1) In 1971 Jacy seduces Duane (Jeff Bridges) for the sole reason of losing her virginity in Peter Bogdanovich's **The Last Picture Show**. Who was she?
a) Karen Black b) Sarah Miles
c) Ellen Burstyn d) Cybill Shepherd

2) For what film did he portray radio DJ Jack Lucas who retires from showbiz and turns to the bottle after one of his deranged listeners commits murder?
a) Fearless b) The Fisher King
c) Cold Feet d) The Morning After

3) With which film do you associate 'The Dude' (Jeff Bridges) getting his carpet peed on?
a) Wild Bill b) Texasville
c) Blown Away d) The Big Lebowski

CHARLES BRONSON
(Charles Bunchinsky 1921 -)

1) Which Bernardo Bertolucci film cast Bronson as a character named 'Harmonica'?
a) Once Upon a Time in the West b) The Conformist c) Little Buddha d) Before the Revolution

2) What is the occupation of Paul Kersey (Charles Bronson), the self-appointed vigilante in **Death Wish** (1974)?
a) policeman b) attorney c) architect d) teacher

3) Bronson's wife died in 1990. A professional dancer, she was often paired with her husband in films which included **Death Wish II**, **Chato's Island** and **The Valachi Papers**. Who was she?
a) Jill Ireland b) Lee Remick
c) Sylvia Sydney d) Jacqueline Bisset

PIERCE BROSNAN (1952 -)

1) In which gritty 1981 crime thriller, starring Bob Hoskins and Helen Mirren, did Pierce Brosnan make his film debut as an Irishman?
a) Lassiter b) The Long Good Friday
c) Beyond the Limit d) Mona Lisa

2) With which comedy do you associate Brosnan as the new boyfriend of a married woman whose ex-husband dresses up as a woman?
a) Mrs. Doubtfire b) The Adventures of Priscilla, Queen of the Desert c) Hairspray d) The Birdcage

3) Pierce Brosnan metamorphosed into James Bond in **GoldenEye** (1995). Who preceded him as agent 007?
a) Timothy Dalton b) Roger Moore
c) George Lazenby d) Sean Connery

NIGEL BRUCE (1895 - 1953)

1) Best remembered for his role as Dr. Watson in 20th Century-Fox's long-running Sherlock Holmes series. Name the 1939 film which was Nigel Bruce's first outing as Holmes' bumbling, but faithful sidekick.
a) The Hound of the Baskervilles b) The Adventures of Sherlock Holmes c) Sherlock Holmes and the Voice of Terror d) Sherlock Holmes Faces Death

2) In which film does the venerable Duke of Rudling (Nigel Bruce) purchase Lassie from her poor masters, Joe and Sam Carraclough (Roddy McDowall and Donald Crisp)?
a) The Magic of Lassie b) Son of Lassie
c) Lassie Come Home d) Courage of Lassie

3) For what 1940 Hitchcock thriller did he portray Major Giles Lacy?
a) Suspicion b) Rebecca
c) Foreign Correspondent d) Jamaica Inn

YUL BRYNNER
(Taidje Khan 1915 - 1985)

1) A circus acrobat who turned to acting, he will be best remembered for his role as the King of Siam in **The King and I** on Broadway and on screen. Name the year the film was released.
a) 1956 b) 1958 c) 1960 d) 1962

2) With which film do you associate his battle with a bandit named Calvera?
a) The Long Duel b) Catlow
c) Invitation to a Gunfighter d) The Magnificent Seven

3) In 1959 he played the title role of Solomon in King Vidor's **Solomon and Sheba**. Who portrayed the Queen of Sheba?
a) Jean Seberg b) Claudia Cardinale
c) Gina Lollobrigida d) Sophia Loren

JACK BUCHANAN (1890 - 1957)

1) Actor, director, producer and dapper song-and-dance man, Jack Buchanan had his first notable screen success when he played a well known detective in a 1925 silent. Name the title.
a) Bulldog Drummond's Third Round
b) Sherlock, Jr. c) Paul Temple in Trouble
d) Sexton Blake Hunts Big Game

2) Which 1953 musical cast him opposite Fred Astaire and Cyd Charisse?
a) Let's Dance b) Funny Face
c) The Band Wagon d) Silk Stockings

3) The title song of which film gave him a hit song in 1932?
a) Break the News b) Goodnight Vienna
c) Yes Mr. Brown d) Sweet Devil

SANDRA BULLOCK (1965 -)

1) What film involved her portraying a hostage on a subway train?

Performers

a) Speed b) Demolition Man
c) When the Party's Over d) The Taking of Pelham One Two Three

2) After saving the life of a mugging victim, who does the man's family mistakenly believe she is in the 1995 romantic comedy, **While You Were Sleeping**?
a) his wife b) his fiancee
c) his secretary d) his boss

3) With which film do you associate her playing a member of the pacifist society of "San Angeles" in 2032?
a) The Net b) Bionic Showdown
c) Two If By Sea d) Demolition Man

ELLEN BURSTYN
(Edna Rae Gillooly 1932 -)

1) In 1974 she won an Oscar for her portrayal of a woman who starts a new life for herself and her young son after her husband is killed in a traffic accident. Name the title.
a) Thursday's Game b) Surviving
c) Alice Doesn't Live Here Anymore d) In Our Hands

2) With which film do you associate her having an adulterous affair from 1951 to 1977?
a) Pack of Lies
b) Same Time, Next Year
c) Something in Common
d) When You Remember Me

3) What special powers does Edna McCauley (Ellen Burstyn) have in the 1980 drama, **Resurrection**?
a) hands-on healing power
b) second sight
c) she could communicate with the dead
d) she could make objects burst into flames

STEVE BUSCEMI (1958 -)

1) In **Reservoir Dogs** (1992) a team of crooks about to pull off a big diamond robbery don't know one another's names but are colour coded for easy identification. Steve Buscemi's character objected to his temporary title. What was it?
a) Mr. Yellow b) Mr. Blonde
c) Mr. White d) Mr. Pink

2) What 1996 crime thriller involves his being hired by car salesman Jerry Lundergaard to kidnap his wife and share in the $80,000 ransom?
a) CrissCross b) Call Me c) In the Soup d) Fargo

3) Name the 1986 film, directed by Bill Sherwood, about New York's gay community.
a) Slaves of New York b) Parting Glances
c) Bloodhounds of Broadway d) Rising Sun

NICHOLAS CAGE
(Nicolas Coppola 1964 -)

1) What 1984 film featured him as Al Columbato, a Vietnam vet whose face is mutilated in the war?
a) Birdy b) The Boy in Blue
c) Zandalee d) Racing With the Moon

2) In John Dahl's 1993 crime thriller he is mistaken for a contract killer hired to kill Lara Flynn Boyle. Name the title.

a) Deadfall b) Kiss of Death
c) Firebirds d) Red Rock West

3) In 1994 he portrayed Secret Service agent, Doug Chesnic, assigned to protect Tess Carlisle (Shirley MacLaine) in **Guarding Tess**. What had Tess's role been in her previous life to warrant the need for a bodyguard?
a) an actress b) a senator
c) a spy d) the US President's wife

JAMES CAGNEY (1899 - 1986)

1) Who was James Cagney's leading lady in the 1934 crime comedy, **Jimmy the Gent**?
a) Bette Davis b) Mary Astor
c) Jean Harlow d) Marlene Dietrich

2) The great song and dance man that Cagney's musical **Yankee Doodle Dandy** (1942) was based on was given a private screening of the film at his home. Afterwards he commented: "My God, what an act to follow!" Who was he?
a) Al Jolson b) Stephen Foster
c) George M. Cohan d) Fred Astaire

3) With which 1955 musical biopic do you associate his portrayal of the gangster known as the Gimp who dominates the life and career of singer Ruth Etting (Doris Day)?
a) Love Me or Leave Me
b) It's Showtime
c) Short Cut to Hell d) These Wilder Years

183

The Movie Quiz Companion

MICHAEL CAINE
(Maurice Micklewhite 1933 -)

1) After a succession of jobs, including those of laundry worker, dishwasher, plumber's mate, and working in a Parisian cafe, he was offered a small part in his first film. Name the title.
a) Steel Bayonet b) Foxhole in Cairo
c) Carve Her Name With Pride d) A Hill in Korea

2) An early bit-part for Caine was as a London policeman directing traffic in a 1962 science-fiction drama. Name the title.
a) The Day the Earth Caught Fire b) Enemy From Space c) Village of the Damned d) The Day of the Triffids

3) Name the 1985 film which won him a Best Supporting Actor Oscar.
a) Educating Rita b) California Suite
c) Hannah and Her Sisters d) Mona Lisa

LOUIS CALHERN
(Carl Henry Vogt 1895 - 1956)

1) Which Marx Brothers film featured him as Ambassador Trentino of Sylvania and constant butt of Rufus T. Firefly's (Groucho) jokes?
a) Monkey Business b) Horse Feathers
c) Animal Crackers d) Duck Soup

2) What was Oliver Wendell Holmes' (Louis Calhern) occupation in John Sturges' 1950 biopic, **The Magnificent Yankee**?
a) judge
b) senator
c) police commissioner
d) admiral

3) Name the film in which Louis Calhern died of a heart attack during filming with Marlon Brando in Tokyo.
a) Reflections in a Golden Eye
b) A Countess From Hong Kong
c) Sayonara
d) The Teahouse of the August Moon

JOHN CANDY (1950 - 1994)

1) In which film does John Candy's screen character confront a schoolteacher, toss her a coin and instruct her to "go downtown and have a rat gnaw that growth off of your face"?
a) Uncle Buck
b) The Great Outdoors
c) Spaceballs
d) Hot to Trot

2) Which film featured him as Chicago cop, Danny Muldoon, who lives with his overbearing Irish mother Rose (Maureen O'Hara)?
a) Splash
b) Ony the Lonely
c) National Lampoon's Vacation
d) Summer Rental

3) John Candy died tragically from a heart attack aged 43 while location filming in Mexico. Name the title of the film he was working on.
a) Wagons East
b) Cool Runnings
c) Only the Lonely
d) Rookie of the Year

CLAUDIA CARDINALE (1939 -)

1) In which 1968 western was former New Orleans prostitute turned landowner, Jill McBain (Claudia Cardinale), hoping to make her fortune from the route of the transcontinental railroad?
a) Shalako b) The Cheyenne Social Club
c) Dirty Dingus Magee d) Once Upon a Time in the West

2) With which film do you associate jewel thief, Sir Charles Lytton (David Niven) attempting to steal a gem belonging to the Indian princess, Dala (Claudia Cardinale), at the alpine resort of Cortina D'Ampezzo in 1964?
a) Bonjour Tristesse b) The Pink Panther
c) To Catch a Thief d) Separate Tables

3) What 1966 western involves four soldiers of fortune, portrayed by Burt Lancaster, Lee Marvin, Robert Ryan and Woody Strode, rescuing her from the clutches of Mexican brigand Jesus Raza (Jack Palance)?
a) The Professionals b) Duel at Diablo
c) Charro! d) Villa Rides

JIM CARREY (1962 -)

1) A former stand-up comedian, Carrey made his film debut in Richard Lester's **Finders Keepers** (1984), but it was a film made ten years later which put him on the road to screen stardom. Name the title.

a venerable coach theft

Performers

a) *Earth Girls Are Easy* b) *The Dead Pool*
c) *Ace Ventura, Pet Detective* d) *Pink Cadillac*

2) In which 1986 Francis Coppola film did he make a brief appearance as a character named Walter Getz?
a) *Peggy Sue Got Married* b) *Tough Guys Don't Dance* c) *Rumble Fish* d) *The Cotton Club*

3) The Riddler (Jim Carrey) is all set to reveal Batman's true identity using the item he shows to Two-Face (Tommy Lee Jones) in **Batman Forever** (1995). What was it?
a) *Batman's birth certificate on microfilm*
b) *a vial containing Batman's thought patterns*
c) *photographs of Batman as an infant* d) *a truth drug*

JACKIE CHAN (1954 -)

1) **Rumble in the Bronx** (1996) was the film which finally convinced world audiences that Jackie Chan wasn't just another chop-socky merchant, but it was shot nowhere near New York. Which city doubled for the Bronx?
a) *Toronto* b) *San Francisco*
c) *Vancouver* d) *Hong Kong*

2) In which 1980 action comedy does Jerry (Jackie Chan) give his girlfriend Nancy (Kristine De Bell) a display of his gymnastic skills when he climbs and swings through the metalwork underneath a bridge?

a) *The Big Brawl* b) *My Lucky Stars*
c) *Police Story* d) *The Protector*

3) With which film do you associate Jackie Chan inserting a videotape of the soft porn movie, **Behind the Green Door**?
a) *The Cannonball Run* b) *Project A*
c) *Heart of the Dragon* d) *Wheels on Meals*

LON CHANEY
(Alonso Chaney 1883 - 1930)

1) Known as 'The Man of a Thousand Faces', to whom or what did Chaney attribute his natural genius for expression?
a) *his pantomime training* b) *his deaf-mute parents* c) *observing street mime artists as a child* d) *studying Japanese theatre*

2) For what film did he portray a sinister ventriloquist? This film was a remake of his 1925 version and his only talkie.
a) *The Unholy Three* b) *The Trap*
c) *The Blackbird* d) *The Monster*

3) With which film do you associate his strapping his arms to his body to play an armless knife thrower?
a) *The Unknown* b) *West of Zanzibar*
c) *The Miracle Man* d) *Daredevil Jack*

LON CHANEY, JR.
(Creighton Chaney 1906 - 1973)

1) His first film of any note, made in 1940, was based on a John Steinbeck novel. Name the title.
a) *The Moon is Down* b) *The Red Pony*
c) *Tortilla Flat* d) *Of Mice and Men*

2) In **The Wolf Man** a pentagram appears on the chest of Larry Talbot (Chaney) after he has been bitten by a werewolf. What is a pentagram?
a) *a three pointed star* b) *a four pointed star*
c) *a five pointed star* d) *a six pointed star*

3) What 1952 film connection can you make between Lon Chaney, Jr., and Gary Cooper?
a) *Vera Cruz* b) *Springfield Rifle*
c) *Dallas* d) *High Noon*

CHARLES CHAPLIN
(1889 - 1977)

1) Chaplin's roots were in London's grimy Victorian streets. In which London borough was he born?
a) *Southwark* b) *Lambeth*
c) *Hillingdon* d) *Hackney*

2) How does the tramp (Chaplin) unwittingly convince blind flower girl (Virginia Cherrill) that he is a millionaire in the 1931 comedy, **City Lights**?
a) *he wears silk gloves* b) *he alights from a limousine* c) *he buys all her flowers* d) *he is thrown out of a five-star hotel*

185

The Movie Quiz Companion

3) In 1952 Chaplin left the U.S.A. for Switzerland. Why?
a) he was accused of tax evasion b) he was accused of Communist sympathies c) for a higher standard of living d) to be nearer his mother's sanatorium

CYD CHARISSE
(Tula Ellice Finklea 1921 -)

1) With which film do you associate her dancing the 'Girl Hunt Ballet' with Fred Astaire in 1953?
a) Funny Face b) Singin' in the Rain c) The Band Wagon d) A Damsel in Distress

2) In 1957 she portrayed a Russian official on a mission to Paris in a film which was a remake of the Greta Garbo classic, **Ninotchka**. Name the title.
a) Silk Stockings b) Deep in My Heart c) It's Always Fair Weather d) Party Girl

3) Name the 1954 musical in which the characters portrayed by Cyd Charisse and Gene Kelly embark on a passionate love affair which bridges two centuries.
*a) The Unfinished Dance
b) Deep in My Heart
c) Twilight for the Gods
d) Brigadoon*

CHER
(Cherilyn Sarkisian 1946 -)

1) Cher made her film debut in a 1965 musical comedy with her now estranged husband Sonny Bono. Name the title.
a) Good Times b) Chastity c) I Got You Babe d) Wild on the Beach

2) In which film did she portray a lesbian named Dolly Pelliker?
a) Silkwood b) The Player c) Mermaids d) Suspect

3) With which film do you associate her having a son who suffers from the rare disease craniodiaphyseal dyaplasia?
a) Faithful b) Come Back to the Five and Dime, Jimmy Dean, Jimmy Dean c) Mask d) Pret-a-Porter

MAURICE CHEVALIER
(1888 - 1972)

1) A former acrobat turned singer, Maurice Chevalier eventually graduated to the screen, where his charm, scene-stealing and romantic accent wooed audiences worldwide. Although he emphasised his thick French accent in English-speaking films his command of English was actually very good, but it was learned in an unusual environment. What was it?
a) in a German prisoner-of-war camp b) in a circus tent in Hartlepool c) at London's Old Vic Theatre d) at the British Embassy in Peking during the Boxer Rebellion

2) Which 1958 musical featured him singing 'Thank Heaven for Little Girls'?
a) Gigi b) Count Your Blessings c) Can-Can d) Pepe

3) With which 1957 romantic comedy do you associate him in the role of private detective, Claude Chavasse, father of Ariane Chavasse (Audrey Hepburn)?
a) A Breath of Scandal b) The Merry Widow c) My Seven Little Sins d) Love in the Afternoon

JULIE CHRISTIE (1941 -)

1) What 1967 film connection can you make between Julie Christie and director François Truffaut?
*a) Stolen Kisses
b) Two English Girls
c) Fahrenheit 451
d) Mississippi Mermaids*

2) In 1967 she portrayed the beautiful Bathsheba Everdene who inherits a farmhouse and is helped to move in by shepherd Gabriel Oak (Alan Bates). Name the film.
*a) The Fast Lady
b) Far From the Madding Crowd
c) The Go-Between
d) Doctor Zhivago*

3) In 1965 she won a Best Actress Oscar for her portrayal of the upwardly mobile Diana Scott in a film directed by John Schlesinger. Name the title.
*a) Billy Liar
b) A Kind of Loving
c) Midnight Cowboy
d) Darling*

Performers

JOHN CLEESE (1939 -)

1) Which film features him as Professor Waldman, a shady 19th century medical lecturer?
a) Rudyard Kipling's The Jungle Book
b) Yellowbeard c) Splitting Heirs
d) Mary Shelley's Frankenstein

2) In which film did he play the voice of a slippery evil cat named Cat R. Waul?
a) An American Tail: Fievel Goes West b) James and the Giant Peach c) All Dogs Go To Heaven
d) Tim Burton's Nightmare Before Christmas

3) What film connection can you make between John Cleese and Cary Grant?
a) they both went to the same Bristol school b) his ex-wife Connie Booth was Cary Grant's stepdaughter c) the character he played in **A Fish Called Wanda** was called Archie Leach d) both made their stage debuts at the Bristol Hippodrome

MONTGOMERY CLIFT (1920 - 1966)

1) After a car crash that paralyzed the left side of his face, his life descended into a haze of pills and alcohol, culminating in a heart attack when he was 45. Name the film he was working on at the time of the crash.
a) Raintree County
b) The Misfits
c) The Young Lions
d) Judgment at Nuremberg

2) Name the actress who said, "He's the only person I know who is in worse shape than I am."
a) Jayne Mansfield b) Marilyn Monroe
c) Judy Garland d) Susan Hayward

3) Montgomery Clift made only one film for Alfred Hitchcock. Name the title.
a) Stage Fright b) Under Capricorn
c) Rope d) I Confess

GEORGE CLOONEY (1961 -)

1) What film connection can you make between George Clooney and the 'Titty Twister' strip joint?
a) Out of Sight b) Red Surf
c) From Dusk Till Dawn d) And They're Off

2) Who was George Clooney's leading lady in the 1997 action drama, **The Peacemaker**?
a) Nicole Kidman b) Bridget Fonda
c) Kim Basinger d) Juliette Lewis

3) For what film did he portray Ulysses Everett McGill, who is told by a blind prophet, "You will find a fortune but not the fortune you seek"?
a) The Perfect Storm b) Return of the Killer Tomatoes c) Unbecoming Age d) Oh Brother, Where Art Thou?

GLENN CLOSE (1947 -)

1) Name the 1982 film, based on John Irving's novel, which was her film debut.
a) The Big Chill b) The World According to Garp
c) The Natural d) Something About Amelia

2) In which film did she portray temperamental opera diva, Karen Anderson, rehearsing a production of Wagner's Tannhauser at the Paris Opera?
a) Meeting Venus b) The Paper
c) Light Years d) The House of the Spirits

3) What 1990 film, directed by Barbet Schroeder, involves Sunny (Glenn Close) narrating the drama from her sickbed?
a) Jagged Edge b) Dangerous Liaisons
c) Immediate Family d) Reversal of Fortune

LEE J. COBB
(Leo Jacob 1911 - 1976)

1) Which film cast him as the Siamese prime minister, Kralahome?
a) The King and I b) The Ugly American
c) Chang d) Anna and the King of Siam

2) In 1957 he portrayed a psychiatrist named Dr. Luther who tries to cure a woman with multiple personalities in **The Three Faces of Eve**. Who was she?
a) Joanne Woodward b) Ida Lupino
c) Gloria Grahame d) Joan Crawford

3) Name the 1957 drama in which No 3 (Lee J. Cobb) re-enacts a murder for No 8 (Henry Fonda).
a) 12 Angry Men b) The Left Hand of God
c) The 49th Man d) 13 Fighting Men

JAMES COBURN (1928 -)

1) In which film is his character known as 'The Manufacturer'?
a) The Magnificent Seven b) The Great Escape c) The President's Analyst d) The Internecine Project

2) With which film do you associate him portraying an employee of ZOWIE (Zonal Organisation on World Intelligence Espionage)?
a) Hudson Hawk b) What Did You Do in the War, Daddy? c) Our Man Flint d) Charade

3) What does Dr. Peter Carey (James Coburn) succeed in doing for a colleague in Blake Edwards' 1972 mystery, **The Carey Treatment**?
a) clear him of a murder charge b) give him a reason to commit suicide c) cover up his negligence d) give him a false alibi

CLAUDETTE COLBERT
(Claudette Lily Chauchoin 1905 - 1996)

1) In **Bluebeard's Eighth Wife** (1938) she becomes the eighth wife of a man (Gary Cooper) who finds it impossible to hold a marriage together. How does Claudette Colbert's character try to make the marriage last?
a) by refusing to consummate it b) by living in a different house c) by having ten children d) by sending her husband off on constant safari

2) Betty and Bob MacDonald (Claudette Colbert and Fred MacMurray) try to eke out a living on their farm in the Pacific Northwest in the 1947 comedy, **The Egg and I**. What line of farming were they in?
a) ostrich farming b) chicken farming c) turkey farming d) duck farming

3) Name the 1934 romantic comedy she starred in which was the first film to win all five major Oscars, including a Best Actress Oscar for herself.
a) Nothing Sacred b) The Gay Divorcee c) It Happened One Night d) Mr. Deeds Goes to Town

JOAN COLLINS (1933 -)

1) Joan Collins made her film debut in a 1951 Frank Launder comedy as a contestant in a beauty contest. Name the title.
a) Lady Godiva Rides Again b) Be Beautiful but Shut Up c) The Moment of Truth d) Object of Beauty

2) With which Hope and Crosby 'Road' movie do you associate her?
a) Road to Hong Kong b) Road to Bali c) Road to Rio d) Road to Utopia

3) In the late seventies she starred in two films based on books written by her sister Jackie, **The Stud** and its sequel. Name the title of the sequel.
a) Paper Dolls b) The Bitch c) Sunburn d) Game For Vultures

RONALD COLMAN (1891 - 1958)

1) Dashing, charming and sophisticated, Ronald Colman was the epitome of the English gentleman. In 1930 he portrayed a gentleman thief based on a character created by novelist E.W. Hornung in *The Amateur Cracksman*. Name the film.
a) Bulldog Drummond b) Raffles c) A Double Life d) The Masquerader

2) With which film do you associate him as law professor, Michael Lightcap, who, while awaiting an appointment to the Supreme Court meets escaped convict Leopold Dilg (Cary Grant) at the lodging house of Nora Shelley (Jean Arthur)?
a) Lucky Partners b) The Light That Failed c) The Talk of the Town d) Champagne For Caesar

3) In which 1935 film does his character utter these lines before his imminent death: "It is a far, far better thing that I do than I have ever done; it is a far, far better rest that I go to than I have ever known."
a) If I Were King b) Condemned c) The Prisoner of Zenda d) A Tale of Two Cities

Performers

ROBBIE COLTRANE (1950 -)

1) In which 1995 film does he portray Valentin Zukovsky, head of the Russian Mafia in St. Petersburg?
a) Shining Through b) The Russia House
c) GoldenEye d) Red Scorpion

2) Which 1989 Shakespearian drama cast him as Sir John Falstaff?
a) Henry V b) Richard III c) King Lear d) Hamlet

3) With which 1993 drama do you associate Robbie Coltrane as the Duke and Jason Robards as King, who attempt to fleece two sisters of their inheritance?
a) Eat the Rich b) The Adventures of Huck Finn
c) The Pope Must Die d) Bert Rigby, You're a Fool

SEAN CONNERY
(Thomas Connery 1930 -)

1) Sean Connery entered the world of acting by pure chance when he auditioned for the chorus of a stage musical while visiting London to enter a 'Mr Universe' contest. Name the musical.
a) Oklahoma! b) Showboat
c) South Pacific d) Kismet

2) In which 1981 film did he portray King Agamemnon?
a) Time Bandits
b) Sword of the Valiant
c) Outland
d) The Wind and the Lion

3) In 1990 he portrayed British subject, Barley Blair, sucked into an espionage caper by the "seriously beautiful" Katya (Michelle Pfeiffer) in **The Russia House**. What was Blair's occupation?
a) diplomat b) publisher
c) college professor d) sports writer

JACKIE COOGAN (1914 - 1984)

1) As a child star Jackie Coogan's most memorable portrayal was in the title role of Chaplin's **The Kid** (1921) who is discovered by Charlie after being abandoned by his mother as a newborn baby. Where did his mother (Edna Purviance) originally leave the infant in the hope of finding a better future for her child?
a) on a police station's doorstep
b) in the back seat of a limousine
c) beside the gates of a mansion
d) under a table at a society wedding

2) From 1937 to 1940 he was married to one of Hollywood's most popular stars, starring in the comedy **Million Dollar Legs** in 1939. Who was she?
a) Betty Grable
b) Alice Faye
c) Myrna Loy
d) Peggy Ann Garner

3) By the late thirties his movie career had petered out, but after the war he revived his success on television becoming a hit in a sixties sit-com. Name the title.
a) I Love Lucy
b) The Dick Van Dyke Show
c) The Addams Family
d) The Beverley Hillbillies

GARY COOPER
(Frank James Cooper 1901 - 1961)

1) Burlesque stripper, Sugarpuss O'Shea, helps stuffy Professor Bertram Potts (Gary Cooper) research his article on slang for an encyclopedia in Howard Hawks' 1941 comedy, **Ball of Fire**. Who played Sugarpuss?
a) Barbara Stanwyck
b) Jean Arthur
c) Mae West
d) Ginger Rogers

2) With which film do you associate him having an off the set love-affair with Amy Jolly (Marlene Dietrich)?
a) Shanghai Express
b) The Scarlet Empress
c) The Blue Angel
d) Morocco

3) On a train destined for Shanghai, mercenary O'Hara (Gary Cooper) laments to beautiful spy Judy Perrie (Madeleine Carroll), "We could have made wonderful music together". Name the film.
a) Saratoga Trunk
b) The General Died at Dawn
c) A Farewell to Arms
d) Now and Forever

JACKIE COOPER (1921 -)

1) In 1931 he portrayed 'Dink', the son of a played out prizefighter called **The Champ**, with an actor he teamed up with in several films, including **The Bowery** (1933) and **Treasure Island** (1934). Who was he?
a) Wallace Beery b) Peter Lorre
c) Walter Connolly d) Buster Keaton

2) Name the film in which he played the title role which was based on Percy Crosby's newspaper comic strip.
a) Li'l Abner b) Palooka c) Mickey Finn d) Skippy

3) What 1934 film connection can you make between Jackie Cooper and Robert Louis Stevenson?
a) Kidnapped b) Treasure Island
c) Dr. Jekyll and Mr. Hyde d) The Master of Ballantrae

KEVIN COSTNER (1955 -)

1) In which film does he tell Madonna her concert was "neat", to which she responds by sticking her finger down her throat?
a) Girl 6 b) Who's That Girl
c) With Honors d) Truth or Dare

2) What 1985 film involves him taking part in the Hell of the West race?
a) No Way Out
b) American Flyers
c) Fandango
d) Revenge

3) Name Kevin Costner's 1993 prison break film which involved a scene in a restaurant called 'Dottie's Squat and Gobble'?
a) A Perfect World b) Table For Five
c) The War d) Shadows Run Black

JOSEPH COTTEN (1905 - 1994)

1) In 1943 he portrayed Uncle Charley, the Merry Widow murderer. Name the film.
a) A Blueprint for Murder
b) Shadow of a Doubt
c) Gaslight
d) Half Angel

2) In which 1953 thriller does Rose Loomis (Marilyn Monroe) plan to kill him?
a) Clash By Night
b) The Asphalt Jungle
c) River of No Return
d) Niagara

3) With which 1942 spy thriller do you associate Turkish intelligence chief Haki informing US Navy engineer Howard Graham (Joseph Cotten) that Nazi agents are out to kill him?
a) Journey into Fear
b) The Last Sunset
c) The Steel Trap
d) Walk Softly, Stranger

TOM COURTENAY (1937 -)

1) Name the Shakespearian play Norman (Tom Courtenay) is desperately trying to get Sir (Albert Finney) ready for in Peter Yates' 1983 drama, **The Dresser**.
a) Othello b) Macbeth c) King Lear d) Hamlet

2) Which 1991 film features him as the father of a mentally incompetent son who is hanged for murder?
a) King and Country b) Billy Budd
c) Let Him Have It d) The Day the Fish Came Out

3) With which 1965 drama do you associate him portraying a poet turned general who states: "history has no room for personal feelings"?
a) Night of the Generals b) Doctor Zhivago
c) A Dandy in Aspic d) Operation Crossbow

JOAN CRAWFORD
(Lucille Fay Le Sueur 1904 - 1977)

1) She was married four times. Her second marriage was to an actor who starred in **Five Graves to Cairo** and **Three Comrades**. Who was he?
a) Charles Boyer b) Farley Granger
c) Franchot Tone d) Tyrone Power

2) In which 1962 thriller does she play a character who suffers a car accident which confines her to a wheelchair for the rest of her life?

190

a) Torch Song b) Possessed
c) I Saw What You Did d) What Ever Happened to Baby Jane?

3) Name the 1945 drama, directed by Michael Curtiz, which won her a Best Actress Oscar for her portrayal of a housewife who evolves into a successful business woman.
a) The Shining Hour b) Untamed
c) Today We Live d) Mildred Pierce

BING CROSBY
(Harry Lillis Crosby 1904 - 1977)

1) Name the film in which he made his screen debut as a band singer with the Rhythm Boys in 1930.
a) The King of Jazz b) Too Much Harmony
c) The Big Broadcast d) Anything Goes

2) What 1962 film connection can you make between Bing Crosby and Peter Sellers?
a) The Road to Hong Kong b) The Magic Christian
c) Let's Make Love d) Heavens Above!

3) In 1944 he won a Best Actor Oscar for his portrayal of the benign priest in Leo McCarey's **Going My Way**. What was the name of the song he sang which also won an Oscar?
a) Aren't You Glad You're You? b) Swinging on a Star c) True Love d) Magic Moments

RUSSELL CROWE (1964 -)

1) For what 1992 drama did he portray neo-Nazi white supremacist gang leader, Hando?
a) Blood Oath b) The Crossing
c) The Efficiency Expert d) Romper Stomper

2) In which 1992 film, directed by Jocelyn Moorhouse, did he portray a dishwasher who befriends a blind photographer?
a) The Sum of Us b) Love in Limbo
c) Proof d) The Quick and the Dead

3) In 1995 he portrayed a mandroid named Sid 6.7 who has been programmed with the personalities of 200 criminals, pursued by cop, Parker Barnes (Denzel Washington). Name the film.
a) Virtuosity b) Hardware
c) Crash and Burn d) Eve of Destruction

TOM CRUISE
(Thomas Cruise Mapother IV 1962 -)

1) For what film did he battle against an evil prince named Darkness?
a) Legend b) Willow
c) The Dark Crystal d) Dragonslayer

2) In 1996 he portrayed professional spy, Ethan Hunt, in **Mission: Impossible**, whose assignment was to prevent the theft of a computer file. What did the file contain?
a) the identities of America's double-agents
b) CIA safe-houses in Europe
c) nuclear missile launch codes d) details of a satellite defence system

3) With which film do you associate his being caught up in the 1893 Oklahoma land rush?
a) Far and Away b) Risky Business
c) The Outsiders d) Losin' It

FINLAY CURRIE (1868 - 1968)

1) What 1949 drama, based on an H.G. Wells novel, involves his character having a bloody altercation with that of John Mills at the Potwell Inn?
a) The Man Who Could Work Miracles b) Kipps
c) The Invisible Man d) The History of Mr. Polly

2) For what 1950 film, directed by Jean Negulesco, did he portray John Brown, Queen Victoria's ghillie?
a) Sixty Glorious Years b) Victoria the Great
c) The Mudlark d) Disraeli

3) In which Michael Powell film, about an island community desperately trying to eke a living from a harsh and desolate landscape which was inspired by the depopulation of St. Kilda in 1930, did Finlay Currie star?
a) I Know Where I'm going b) The Edge of the World c) Gone to Earth d) 49th Parallel

JAMIE LEE CURTIS (1958 -)

1) Jamie Lee Curtis is the daughter of a well known actress. Who is she?

a) Linda Darnell b) Carol Channing
c) Cyd Charisse d) Janet Leigh

2) She made her film debut in a 1978 horror film centred around a murderous stalker. Name the title.
a) Halloween b) Candyman
c) Child's Play d) The Beast Must Die

3) With which 1994 thriller do you associate her being married for fifteen years to a man whom she thinks is a computer salesman but is really a spy?
a) True Lies b) Lies Before Kisses
c) Sweet Lies d) Pack of Lies

TONY CURTIS
(Bernard Schwartz 1925 -)

1) For what film did he portray the obsequious press agent of syndicated columnist J.J. Hunsecker?
a) Meet Danny Wilson
b) Flesh and Fury
c) Sweet Smell of Success
d) Johnny Stool Pigeon

2) Escaped convict, John Jackson (Tony Curtis) was shackled to fellow prisoner, Noah Cullen, in **The Defiant Ones**. Who was he?
a) Kirk Douglas
b) Frank Sinatra
c) Sidney Poitier
d) David Farrar

3) With which Tony Curtis film do you associate Spats Colombo's gang wiping out Toothpick Charlie's gang?
a) Prime Target
b) Some Like it Hot
c) Goodbye Charlie
d) Sweet Dreams

JOHN CUSACK (1966 -)

1) Ten years after standing Debi (Minnie Driver) up on prom night, Martin (John Cusack) returns home for a high school reunion. Name the film.
a) The Grifters b) Grosse Pointe Blank
c) Better Off Dead d) Hot Pursuit

2) For what 1994 comedy did he portray serious young playwright, David Shayne, who will stop at nothing to ensure his success?
a) Broadway Danny Rose b) Neil Simon's 'Broadway Bound' c) Headin' for Broadway
d) Bullets Over Broadway

3) In which 1994 comedy does he become involved in a questionable scheme to manufacture corn flakes?
a) The Road to Wellville b) Breakfast Club
c) Floundering d) Money For Nothing

PETER CUSHING (1913 - 1994)

1) What film connection can you make between Peter Cushing and Laurel and Hardy?
a) A Chump at Oxford b) The Flying Deuces
c) Saps at Sea d) Air Raid Wardens

2) Peter Cushing achieved world-wide fame when he was cast in the title role of Hammer Films' gothic horror movie, **The Curse of Frankenstein**, beginning a long association with the character Baron Victor Frankenstein. How many times did he portray him?
a) 4 b) 6 c) 8 d) 10

3) What was his character name in **Star Wars** (1977)?
a) Chief Jawa b) General Willard
c) Uncle Owen Lars d) Grand Moff Tarkin

WILLEM DAFOE (1955 -)

1) In which 1988 drama did he portray FBI agent, Alan Ward, head of a government investigation into the murders of three men named Chaney, Goodman and Schwerner?
a) Off Limits b) Streets of Fire
c) Absence of Malice d) Mississippi Burning

2) With which film do you associate his making love to Mary Magdalene (Barbara Hershey)?
a) Jesus of Montreal b) Jesus Christ Superstar
c) The Last Temptation of Christ d) The Jesus Trip

3) What 1994 biopic, directed by Brian Gilbert, involved him portraying the poet T.S. Eliot?
a) White Sands b) Poetic Justice
c) Tom & Viv d) The Ghost Writer

BETTE DAVIS
(Ruth Elizabeth Davis 1908 - 1989)

1) With which film do you associate Judith Traherne (Bette Davis) dying from a brain tumour and falling in love with specialist Dr. Frederick Steele (George Brent)?

a) In This Our Life b) All This, and Heaven Too
c) Dark Victory d) The Great Lie

2) Name the Broadway star Davis's Margo Channing character was based on in Joseph L. Mankiewicz's **All About Eve**?
a) Barbara Stanwyck b) Tallulah Bankhead
c) Mae West d) Celeste Holm

3) In which 1944 drama does 'Fanny' Trellis (Bette Davis) agree to a marriage of convenience with a stockbroker?
a) The Bride Came C.O.D. b) Old Acquaintance
c) Shining Victory d) Mr Skeffington

DORIS DAY
(Doris von Kappelhoff 1924 -)

1) In 1954 she starred in a musical remake of Fannie Hurst's 'Four Daughters' with Frank Sinatra. Name the title.
a) Till Clouds Roll By b) Young at Heart
c) Step Lively d) It Happened in Brooklyn

2) Which film featured her singing 'Que Sera, Sera', which won songsmiths Jay Livingston and Ray Evans an Oscar for Best Song in 1956?
a) Calamity Jane b) The Man Who Knew Too Much c) The Thrill of it All d) Caprice

3) In which comedy does she retort: "Mr Allen, this may come as a shock to you, but there are some men who don't end every sentence with a proposition" ?
a) That Touch of Mink b) Move Over, Darling
c) The Pajama Game d) Pillow Talk

DANIEL DAY LEWIS (1958 -)

1) He established himself on screen portraying a homosexual punk in 1985 in a film directed by Stephen Frears. Name the title.
a) Sammy and Rosie Get Laid b) Prick up Your Ears c) My Beautiful Laundrette d) The Hit

2) Which film featured him as a fastidious ninny named Cecil?
a) A Room With a View b) Gandhi c) Stars and Bars d) The Age of Innocence

3) During the filming of **My Left Foot** (1989) he confined himself to a wheelchair and experienced at first hand the humiliation of being dressed, washed and fed by another person. He learned to write and paint with his left foot and his characterisation in the end was so convincing it won him a Best Actor Oscar. On whose autobiography was the film based?
a) Christy Moore b) Christy Cole
c) Christy McCabe d) Christy Brown

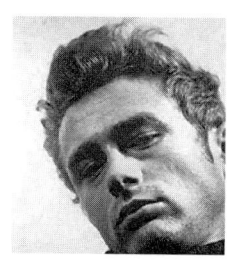

JAMES DEAN (1931 - 1955)

1) Before his career kickstarted he appeared in TV commercials and bit parts. Name the 1953 John Wayne film he appeared in.
a) Trouble Along the Way b) Big Jim McLain
c) Operation Pacific d) Island In the Sky

2) In **East of Eden** (1955) he portrays Cal Trask, the distraught son of the pious farmer, Adam Trask (Raymond Massey). What crop did the family farm?
a) beans b) lettuce c) oranges d) corn

3) The cult of James Dean was such that even the date of his death became the title of a film and was also, incidentally, Dennis Quaid's film debut in 1978. Name the title.
a) July 30, 1955 b) August 30, 1955
c) September 30, 1955 d) October 30, 1955

OLIVIA DE HAVILLAND (1916 -)

1) For what 1948 drama (one of the first films to seriously tackle mental illness) did she portray a young girl's descent into madness?
a) The Snake Pit
b) Shock Corridor
c) Lady in a Cage
d) Fear Strikes Out

2) In 1949 she won a Best Actress Oscar for her portrayal of spinster Catherine Sloper in a film based on Henry James' novel, 'Washington Square'. Name the title.
a) The Heiress
b) In This Our Life
c) That Lady
d) Devotion

3) Name the Daphne du Maurier mystery she starred in with Richard Burton (in his US screen debut) in 1952.
a) Frenchman's Creek
b) My Cousin Rachel
c) Jamaica Inn
d) Rebecca

The Movie Quiz Companion

JUDI DENCH (1934 -)

1) In which film is she a resident of Lansquenet?
a) Henry V b) Chocolat
c) Wetherby d) Jack & Sarah

2) She began her life-long relationship with the Royal Shakespeare Company in 1961 and in 1968 was cast in Peter Hall's screen version of **A Midsummer Night's Dream**. Whom did she portray?
a) Helena b) Hermia c) Hippolyta d) Titania

3) Which Judi Dench film featured an Italianate hideaway overlooking the Solent called Osborne House where she bathed in the sea for the first time?
a) A Handful of Dust b) Mrs. Brown
c) A Room With a View d) Luther

CATHERINE DENEUVE
(Catherine Dorléac 1943 -)

1) In which 1964 film does she portray a character who becomes pregnant to a boyfriend from whom she is separated when he is drafted into the French-Algerian conflict?
a) A Matter of Resistance b) Savage
c) It Only Happens to Others d) The Umbrellas of Cherbourg

2) In François Truffaut's **The Last Metro** (1980), Marion Steiner (Catherine Deneuve) struggles to keep her husband's business from going in Nazi-occupied Paris. What type of business is it?
a) a theatre b) a strip club
c) an antique shop d) a brothel

3) Crown Prince Rudolf falls hopelessly in love with Maria Vetsera (Catherine Deneuve) in the 1968 historical romance, **Mayerling**. Who was he?
a) Oliver Reed b) James Mason
c) Omar Sharif d) Richard Harris

ROBERT DE NIRO (1943 -)

1) In which film did he portray 'Johnny Boy', a street thug in New York's Little Italy who is partial to blowing up mail boxes?
a) New York, New York b) Bloody Mama
c) The Gang That Couldn't Shoot Straight d) Mean Streets

2) What film won him a Best Actor Oscar in 1980?
a) Raging Bull b) The Untouchables
c) The King of Comedy d) The Godfather Part II

3) Name the real-life 1930s producer who inspired De Niro's characterisation of Monroe Stahr in **The Last Tycoon** (1976).
a) Howard Hughes b) Irving Thalberg
c) David O. Selznick d) Carl Laemmle Jr.

GERARD DEPARDIEU (1948 -)

1) In 1990 he was nominated for an Academy Award for his performance in a film based on a play by Edmond Rostand. Name the title.
a) Jean de Florette b) Cyrano de Bergerac
c) Danton d) The Return of Martin Guerre

2) What film connection can you make between Gérard Depardieu and the novelist Emile Zola?
a) La Bête Humaine b) Germinal
c) L'Argent d) Colonel Chabert

3) Which Bernardo Bertolucci film featured him as a Marxist union organiser named Olmo who shared the same birthday with landowner and boyhood friend, Alfredo (Robert De Niro)?
a) Tragedy of a Ridiculous Man b) The Conformist c) The Spider's Strategem d) 1900

JOHNNY DEPP (1963 -)

1) Gene Watson's (Johnny Depp) daughter is held hostage until he assassinates someone in **Nick of Time** (1995). Who is his target?
a) the governor of California
b) the mayor of Los Angeles
c) the U.S. president
d) a CIA agent

2) In **Cry-Baby** he portrays a rock'n'roll delinquent who perpetually grieves over a past tragedy. What was it?
a) the death of his brother
b) a lost romance
c) his parents' divorce
d) his castration in an auto accident

3) In which 1995 drama does he deliver the lines: "What do you know of love? Have you ever loved a woman until milk leaked from her - as if she had just given birth to love itself, and now must feed it or burst?"
a) Ed Wood
b) Benny & Joon
c) Don Juan DeMarco
d) Arizona Dream

Performers

ANDY DEVINE
(Jeremiah Schwartz 1905 - 1977)

1) Throughout his career he was cast as comic sidekick to tall, dark and handsome heroes, notably to a famous screen cowboy whose real name was Leonard Slye. What was he better known as?
a) Gene Autry b) Tom Mix
c) Roy Rogers d) William S. Hart

2) With which film do you associate him as a stagecoach driver named Buck who gives a ride along the trail to the horseless Ringo Kid?
a) Stage to Thunder Rock b) Stage to Fury
c) Last Stagecoach West d) Stagecoach

3) In which western did he portray Link Appleyard, sheriff of Shinbone, who is always in search of a free meal?
a) Dodge City b) The Man Who Shot Liberty Valance c) Pony Express d) Cat Ballou

DANNY DE VITO (1944 -)

1) For what film did he play an asylum inmate named Martini?
a) Psycho II b) The Night Visitor c) Young Einstein d) One Flew Over the Cuckoo's Nest

2) Which film featured him showing off his "important" coin collection, which included the penny he got in change the day he visited the zoo with his father?
a) Throw Momma From the Train b) Wise Guys
c) Tin Men d) Other People's Money

3) In a 1989 comedy he portrayed divorce attorney, Gavin D'Amato, who passes on the following advice to a client: "I get paid $425 an hour to talk to people and so when I offer to tell you something for free, I advise you to listen carefully." He also directed this film. Name the title.
a) The War of the Roses b) Ruthless People
c) Terms of Endearment d) The World's Greatest Lover

CAMERON DIAZ (1972 -)

1) Her 1994 screen debut involved her flirting with a bank clerk while secretly filming the vault for her boss who owns the Coco Bongo Club.
Name the title.
a) Almost an Angel
b) Nuns on the Run
c) Out on a Limb
d) The Mask

2) In which film do her dinner party guests include (amongst others) a male chauvinist pig, a homophobe, an anti-ecologist and a Desert Storm vet?
a) The Last Supper
b) The Meal
c) Thirteen at Dinner
d) My Dinner With André

3) What role did she play in Terry Gilliam's 1998 comedy drama, **Fear and Loathing in Las Vegas**?
a) a bitch-biker
b) a magazine reporter
c) a TV reporter
d) a Highway Patrolwoman

LEONARDO DICAPRIO (1974 -)

1) In the town of Endora, Iowa, "where nothing much happens and nothing ever did", he portrayed a retarded boy, a role for which he was nominated for an Academy Award in 1993. Name the film.
a) What's Eating Gilbert Grape
b) Total Eclipse
c) The Quick and the Dead
d) Critters 3

2) Which 1995 western featured him as a young gunslinger named 'The Kid'?
a) The Quick and the Dead
b) Lightning Jack
c) Posse
d) Tombstone

3) In which film is he forced to pose for a Boy Scout photograph with his tyrannical stepfather while living in a town called Concrete?
a) Honor Thy Father
b) Poison Ivy
c) This Boy's Life
d) Sins of the Father

195

The Movie Quiz Companion

MARLENE DIETRICH
(Maria Magdalene Dietrich
1901 - 1992)

1) In which film does she introduce the song 'Falling in Love Again'?
a) The Blue Angel b) Desire
c) Morocco d) Shanghai Express

2) Name the director with whom she had her most productive creative collaboration, between 1930 and 1935, which included the films **Morocco**, **Shanghai Express** and **Blonde Venus**.
a) Renè Clair b) Fritz Lang
c) Ernst Lubitsch d) Josef von Sternberg

3) Her last appearance on screen was in **Just a Gigolo** (1979) opposite a well known rock star. Who was he?
a) David Bowie b) Mick Jagger
c) Michael Jackson d) George Michael

MATT DILLON (1964 -)

1) Which 1964 drama featured him as a DJ at the Harlem 'Y' Dance?
a) Rumble Fish b) Malcolm X
c) The Outsiders d) Drugstore Cowboy

2) In 1982 he starred in the first of novelist S.E. Hinton's stories to be filmed about the relationship between two brothers. Name the title.
a) Tex b) Over the Edge
c) Little Darlings d) That Was Then, This is Now

3) Which film featured him as Iowa farm boy, J.C. Cullen, who turns into an ace crap shooter?
a) The Flamingo Kid b) Native Son
c) The Big Town d) Target

ROBERT DONAT (1905 - 1958)

1) Name the Alexander Korda film which launched his screen career in 1933.
a) Catherine the Great b) The Private Life of Don Juan c) The Scarlet Pimpernel d) The Private Life of Henry VIII

2) Secret agent Ainsley Fothergill (Robert Donat) helps Countess Alexandra Vladinoff escape the clutches of Russian revolutionaries in the 1937 romantic adventure, **Knight Without Armour**. Who portrayed the countess?
a) Mary Astor b) Marlene Dietrich
c) Anna Neagle d) Margaret Lockwood

3) Plagued by asthma and ill-health in later life, he never fully achieved his expectations on the screen and was seriously ill while making his final film. Name the title.
a) The Winslow Boy b) Captain Boycott
c) The Inn of the Sixth Happiness d) Lease of Life

KIRK DOUGLAS
(Issur Danielovitch 1916 -)

1) Usually portrayed as the cynical hard man he was cast against type in his screen debut as a bespectacled weakling opposite Barbara Stanwyck in a 1946 crime thriller. Name the title.
a) The File on Thelma Jordan b) Cry Wolf
c) Stella Dallas d) The Strange Love of Martha Ivers

2) In which 1962 western does he deliberately start a fight in a saloon in order to get into jail beside his friend to help him escape?
a) The War Wagon b) The Last Sunset
c) Lonely Are the Brave d) The Big Sky

3) Which 1962 drama, directed by Vincente Minnelli, featured him as the washed-up movie star, Jack Andrus, who, when asked why anyone would want to be an actor replies, "That's a good question. To hide from the world. What's the audience doing there but hiding … trading their problems for mine on the screen."?
a) Two Weeks in Another Town b) The Bad and the Beautiful c) On a Clear Day You Can See Forever d) Town without Pity

MICHAEL DOUGLAS (1944 -)

Performers

1) In a 1993 drama, directed by Joel Schumacher, he was given no name, but was known to the police by his licence plate, D-FENS. Name the film.
a) Falling Down b) Radio Flyer
c) Made in America d) Black Rain

2) With which thriller do you associate him suing his boss for sexual harassment?
a) Eyes of an Angel b) Shining Through
c) It's My Turn d) Disclosure

3) In 1979 he starred in **The China Syndrome**, about an attempted cover-up of an accident at a nuclear power plant. What was his occupation in the film?
a) research worker b) TV cameraman
c) private investigator d) night watchman

RICHARD DREYFUSS (1947 -)

1) What film (which incidentally made him a star) involved his character hanging out at Mel's Drive-In?
a) The Goodbye Girl b) American Graffiti
c) Jaws d) Nuts

2) In 1978 he played the wisecracking private investigator, Moses Wine, who, unlike the average screen gumshoe is Jewish, impoverished and has two sons to support. Name the film.
a) The Big Fix
b) Lost in Yonkers
c) Stakeout
d) Let it Ride

3) In which film did he portray 'The Writer', who wrote down his reminiscences from his childhood in Castle Rock, Oregon?
a) The Buddy System
b) The Goodbye Girl
c) Once Around
d) Stand By Me

BOBBY DRISCOLL (1937 - 1968)

1) For which well known animated Walt Disney character did he supply the voice for in 1953?
a) Pinocchio b) Peter Pan
c) The Mad Hatter d) Cruella De Vil

2) One of Driscoll's finest portrayals was as the young cabin boy Jim Hawkins in Walt Disney's 1950 adventure, **Treasure Island**. What was the name of his ship?
a) Hesperus b) Unicorn
c) Hispaniola d) Golden Hind

3) In 1949 he won a special Academy Award for "outstanding juvenile actor of 1949" following a performance as a boy who witnesses a murder in a thriller directed by Ted Tezlaff. Name the title.
a) The Scarlet Cloak b) The Window
c) Identity Unknown d) From this Day Forward

FAYE DUNAWAY (1941 -)

1) The title of the film in which she made her screen debut became a No. 1 hit for The Supremes. Name the film.
a) You Can't Hurry Love b) Where Did Our Love Go c) Baby Love d) The Happening

2) Which film features her as merciless television programmer, Diana Christenson?
a) Broadcast News
b) Dead Pool
c) Silhouette d) Network

3) In 1978 she portrayed a fashion photographer who could foresee murders. Name the film.
a) Eyes of Laura Mars b) The First Deadly Sin
c) Hurry Sundown d) Voyage of the Damned

DEANNA DURBIN
(Edna Mae Durbin 1921 -)

1) In her 1937 musical comedy, **One Hundred Men and a Girl**, what is the occupation of the one hundred men?
a) soldier b) musician c) pirate d) politician

2) What do the sisters portrayed by Deanna Durbin, Barbara Read and Nan Grey accomplish in the 1936 musical comedy, **Three Smart Girls**?
a) they are all top of their college class b) they marry three eligible brothers c) they save their father's antique shop from going under d) they bring their parents back together again

3) Name the actor who gave Deanna Durbin her first screen kiss in the 1939 romance, **First Love**.
a) Louis Calhern b) Van Heflin
c) Fred MacMurray d) Robert Stack

ROBERT DUVALL (1931 -)

1) Name the western legend he portrayed in Philip Kaufman's 1972 biopic, **The Great Northfield, Minnesota Raid**?

197

The Movie Quiz Companion

*a) Billy the Kid b) Butch Cassidy
c) Jesse James d) Wyatt Earp*

2) In which film does he portray the outlaw Ned Pepper?
*a) The Killer Elite b) McQ
c) Ride the High Country d) True Grit*

3) He made his directorial debut in 1983 with a film entitled **Angelo, My Love**. Which American community does it portray?
*a) New York Gypsy
b) Italian American
c) Puerto Rican d) Cajun*

CLINT EASTWOOD (1930 -)

1) In 1955 he played a lab technician in a sequel to **The Creature From the Black Lagoon**. Name the title.
*a) Revenge of the Creature
b) Creature From the Haunted Sea
c) Creatures the World Forgot
d) The Creature Walks Among Us*

2) Name the 1984 thriller in which he plays a cop called Wes Block who likes to make love to women while they are handcuffed.
*a) Tightrope
b) The Enforcer
c) Coogan's Bluff
d) Magnum Force*

3) With which film do you associate Martha (Geraldine Page) amputating John McBurney's (Clint Eastwood) leg?
*a) The Dead Pool
b) Away All Boats
c) Hang 'Em High
d) The Beguiled*

DENHOLM ELLIOTT (1922 - 1992)

1) Which film featured him as a naval officer on HMS Compass Rose, a plucky WWII Corvette Class convoy escort?
a) Sink the Bismarck b) The Battle of the River Plate c) In Which We Serve d) The Cruel Sea

2) In 1985 he played Mr. Emerson who, when moving from his cottage, demands that they "Leave me my portrait of Thoreau". Name the film.
*a) A Room with a View b) The Missionary
c) Saint Jack d) Maurice*

3) With which 1965 drama do you associate him as a prisoner in a Japanese POW camp?
*a) Three Came Home b) A Town Like Alice
c) Prisoners of the Sun d) King Rat*

DAME EDITH EVANS (1888 - 1976)

1) In 1967 she was nominted for a Best Actress Oscar for her portrayal of a senile old lady who believes she is being spied upon in a film directed by Bryan Forbes. Name the title.
*a) The Whisperers b) Whispers in the Dark
c) Whispering Ghosts d) Cries and Whispers*

2) In which version of the Scrooge legend did she play the Ghost of Christmas Past?
*a) Scrooge b) The Muppet Christmas Carol
c) Scrooged d) A Christmas Carol (1951)*

3) With which film do you associate the following dialogue between her character, Lady Bracknell, and Jack Worthing (Michael Redgrave): "Do you smoke?" "Yes, I do," he replies. "Good," she answers. "A man should have an occupation of some sort"?
*a) Tom Jones b) The Importance of Being Earnest
c) The Chalk Garden d) The Last Days of Dolwyn*

DOUGLAS FAIRBANKS
(Douglas Elton Ulman 1883 - 1939)

1) After a successful theatrical career he signed up with Triangle Films for a salary of $2,000 per week in 1915. Name the director with whom he made his first film.
*a) D.W. Griffith
b) Eric von Strobeim
c) Cecil B. De Mille
d) Allan Dwan*

2) Name the studio he founded with Mary Pickford, D.W. Griffith and Charlie Chaplin in 1919.
a) Republic b) Universal c) RKO d) United Artists

3) Which 1920 film cast him as Don Diego de la Vega?
*a) The Americano
b) The Gaucho
c) The Mark of Zorro
d) The Private Life of Don Juan*

symbolic tart roll

Performers

DOUGLAS FAIRBANKS JNR.
(1909 -)

1) Name the actress to whom he was married between 1929 and 1933.
a) Joan Crawford b) Loretta Young
c) Myrna Loy d) Jean Arthur

2) In 1939 he portrayed a cockney sergeant, who, along with two other sergeants (Cary Grant and Victor McLaglen) battles with the followers of Kali. Name the film.
a) Soldiers Three
b) The Lives of a Bengal Lancer
c) Gunga Din
d) The Charge of the Light Brigade

3) With which film do you associate him as a getaway driver for gangster Edward G. Robinson?
a) Little Caesar
b) Brother Orchid
c) Smart Money
d) The Last Gangster

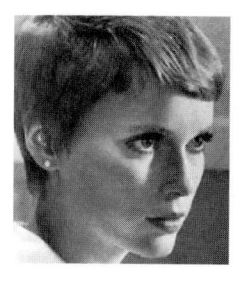

MIA FARROW (1945 -)

1) Over the years she has appeared in numerous Woody Allen films. Name the first one in which she appeared in 1982.
a) A Midsummer Night's Sex Comedy
b) Broadway Danny Rose
c) Zelig d) Stardust Memories

2) Mia Farrow is the daughter of director John Farrow and a well known Hollywood actress. Who was she?
a) Ann Blyth b) Maureen O'Sullivan
c) Olivia De Havilland d) Rita Hayworth

3) Name the film, directed by her father, in which she made her film debut in 1959.
a) Hondo b) The Unholy Wife
c) Alias Jesse James d) John Paul Jones

ALICE FAYE (1912 - 1998)

1) Before her acting career got off the ground she was a nightclub dancer and singer in a well known band, and starred with its leader in the 1934 musical, **George White's Scandals**. Whose band did she sing with?
a) Rudy Vallee b) Artie Shaw
c) Glenn Miller d) Eddy Duchin

2) In which 1938 musical did she give us a rendition of "When That Midnight Choo-Choo Leaves for Alabam"?
a) That Night in Rio b) Music is Magic
c) Hollywood Cavalcade d) Alexander's Ragtime Band

3) With which film do you associate little Barbara Barry (Shirley Temple) running away from home and joining vaudeville performers, Jerry and Jimmy Dolan (Alice Faye & Jack Haley)?
a) On the Avenue b) Sing, Baby, Sing
c) Poor Little Rich Girl d) Stowaway

W.C. FIELDS
(William Claude Dukenfield
1879 - 1946)

1) His misshapen bulbous nose gave him an instant comic appearance, but it was not the proboscis he was born with. How did he acquire it?
a) by jumping from a stationary freight train
b) while being chased by his invalid aunt
c) by diving into a horse trough
d) in a street brawl

2) In 1940 he co-wrote a screenplay with Mae West. Name the title of the film.
a) Klondike Annia b) She Done Him Wrong
c) I'm No Angel d) My Little Chickadee

199

The Movie Quiz Companion

horny games

3) In which film did the following list of accusations appear on a "wanted" poster for W.C. Fields: "Bigamy; passing as the Prince of Wales; eating spaghetti in public; using hard words in a speakeasy; trumping partner's ace; spitting in the Gulf Stream; jumping board bill in 17 lunatic asylums; failing to pay instalments on a strait-jacket; possessing a skunk; revealing the facts of life to an Indian."?
a) The Golf Specialist b) The Bank Dick
c) The Big Broadcast of 1938 d) Poppy

RALPH FIENNES (1962 -)

1) In which 1995 sci-fi thriller does he play con man, Lenny Nero, who, when selling his virtual reality fantasies to an apprehensive businessman explains:
"This is not like TV, only better. This is like a piece of someone's life - straight from the cerebral cortex"?
a) Future Shock
b) Brainscan
c) Strange Days
d) The Blood of Heroes

2) Name the weekly TV quiz show he appears on as the sophisticated intellectual, Charles Van Doren, in the 1994 drama, **Quiz Show**?
a) $64,000 Question
b) Money Talks
c) Reach for the Sky
d) Twenty-One

3) In what film does he undertake a perilous journey to the remote town of Bellingen?
a) The End of the Affair
b) Sunshine
c) Oscar and Lucinda
d) Schindler's List

PETER FINCH
(William Mitchell 1916 - 1977)

1) Which 1950 film, based on Eric Williams' novel *The Tunnel Escape*, featured him as an Australian P.O.W.?
a) A Town Like Alice b) The Wooden Horse
c) The Captive Heart d) King Rat

2) In what 1971 drama, directed by John Schlesinger, was his character involved in a ménage à trois with a heterosexual woman and a bisexual man portrayed by Glenda Jackson and Murray Head?
a) Sunday, Bloody Sunday b) The Divided Heart
c) The Day of the Locust d) The Believers

3) Name the remake of a Frank Capra classic in which he starred in 1973.
a) You Can't Take it With You b) Platinum Blonde c) Broadway Bill d) Lost Horizon

ALBERT FINNEY (1936 -)

1) "All I want is a good time. The rest is propaganda" said Arthur Seaton (Albert Finney) in this 1960 film which is often described as one of the best 'kitchen sink' dramas ever made. Name the title.
a) This Sporting Life b) Saturday Night and Sunday Morning c) Look Back in Anger d) Room at the Top

2) Which 1968 drama featured him as a successful writer with working class roots and Lottie (Billie Whitelaw) for an ex-wife?

a) Under the Volcano b) Two For the Road
c) Charlie Bubbles d) Shoot the Moon

3) What 1951 and 1994 film connection can you make between Michael Redgrave and Albert Finney?
a) The Importance of Being Earnest b) The Lady Vanishes c) The Browning Version d) A Man of No Importance

BARRY FITZGERALD
(William Joseph Shields 1888 - 1961)

1) A part-time actor, he kept on his day job as a civil servant well into his forties until director John Ford invited him to the US in 1936 to recreate one of his stage roles on film. Name the title.
a) The Long Voyage Home b) The Plough and the Stars c) How Green Was My Valley d) Juno and the Paycock

2) In 1944 he won an Academy Award for his portrayal of a priest named Father Fitzgibbon. Name the film.
a) The Bells of St. Mary's b) The Keys of the Kingdom c) Going My Way d) Full Confession

3) In 1952 he portrayed a coachman whose passenger spies a red-haired beauty herding sheep, commenting, "Is that real?" To which Fitzgerald replies that she is "Only a mirage brought on by your terrible thirst!" Name the film.

200

churned beetroot froth

Performers

a) Brigadoon b) The Quiet Man
c) Duffy's Tavern d) Darby O'Gill and the Little People

ERROL FLYNN (1909 -1959)

1) Name the film which launched 25 year old Errol Flynn on the road to stardom in 1935.
a) Captain Blood b) The Adventures of Robin Hood c) The Prince and the Pauper d) The Charge of the Light Brigade

2) The romantic biopic, **The Private Lives of Elizabeth and Essex** (1939), details the love affair of Lord Essex (Errol Flynn) and Queen Elizabeth. Who portrayed the Virgin Queen?
a) Greta Garbo b) Katherine Hepburn
c) Bette Davis d) Olivia De Havilland

3) Name the 1945 war film he starred in which caused outrage amongst WWII veterans on its release and created a diplomatic incident with its suggestion that the USA won the Burma campaign single-handed.
a) Burma Convoy b) Escape to Burma
c) Bombs Over Burma d) Objective Burma!

HENRY FONDA (1905 - 1982)

1) In which 1957 western, directed by Anthony Mann, does bounty hunter and former lawman, Morg Hickman (Henry Fonda), teach rookie sheriff Ben Owens (Anthony Perkins) how to deal with outlaws threatening his town?
a) The Tin Star b) Winchester 73
c) Cimarron d) The Man From Laramie

2) What 1957 film connection can you make between Henry Fonda and Alfred Hitchcock?
a) The Trouble With Harry b) The Man Who Knew Too Much c) I Confess d) The Wrong Man

3) With which film do you associate him encountering a man called 'Harmonica'?
a) My Name is Nobody b) The Cheyenne Social Club c) Once Upon a Time in the West
d) Madigan

JANE FONDA (1937 -)

1) What 1979 comedy western involves Hallie Martin (Jane Fonda) tracking down Sonny Steele (Robert Redford), a man who stole a $12 million thoroughbred from a Las Vegas hotel?
a) The Electric Horseman
b) The Horseplayer
c) Romance of a Horsethief
d) The Horsemasters

2) Name the 1971 crime thriller which won her an Academy Award for her portrayal of a New York call girl.
a) Spirits of the Dead
b) Risky Business
c) Klute
d) California Suite

3) In which film is she given lessons in handling a six-gun by the notorious outlaw, Kid Sheleen?
a) Walk on the Wild Side
b) Cat Ballou
c) Old Gringo
d) Comes a Horseman

JOAN FONTAINE
(Joan De Beauvoir De Havilland 1917 -)

1) In which 1944 romantic drama did Peggy Ann Garner portray her character as a child?
a) The Emperor Waltz b) Rebecca
c) Ivanhoe d) Jane Eyre

2) When Joan Fontaine's character and her married lover are listed as dead in a plane crash they realise they can continue their **September Affair** (1950). Who played the lover?
a) Joseph Cotten b) Stewart Granger
c) Rex Harrison d) Walter Pigeon

3) Name the actor to whom she wrote a **Letter From an Unknown Woman** in 1948.
a) Louis Jourdan b) Charles Boyer
c) Paul Henreid d) Leslie Howard

GLENN FORD
(Gwyllyn Samuel Newton 1916 -)

The Movie Quiz Companion

hope fab rhinoceros invited

1) What film connection can you make between Glenn Ford and Bill Hayley's 'Rock Around the Clock'?
a) Blackboard Jungle b) School for Love
c) Up the Down Staircase d) Rock 'n' Roll High School

2) Farmer Dan Evans agrees to hold outlaw Ben Wade (Glenn Ford) until the arrival of the **3:10 to Yuma**. Who was he?
a) Alan Ladd b) Van Heflin
c) Joel McCrea d) Tyrone Power

3) With which 1956 comedy do you associate his (along with Marlon Brando) being involved with the post-WWII Americanization of Okinawa?
a) Sayonara b) the Nightcomers
c) The Ugly American d) The Teahouse of the August Moon

HARRISON FORD (1942 -)

1) In 1966 he made his inauspicious screen debut in **Dead Heat on a Merry-Go-Round**. What role did he play?
a) a bellhop b) a plumber c) a busker d) a junkie

2) His character's wife disappears on a trip to Paris in Roman Polanski's 1988 thriller, **Frantic**. What was the couple's reason for visiting the city?
a) they were on their honeymoon
b) he was attending a medical convention
c) she was performing at the Paris Opera
d) they were meeting their estranged daughter

3) Humphrey Bogart and Harrison Ford both played the role of billionaire Linus Larrabee in 1954 and 1995 respectively. Name the film.
a) Beat the Devil
b) The Big Shot
c) In a Lonely Place
d) Sabrina

JODIE FOSTER
(Alicia Christian Foster 1962 -)

1) Name the film which won her an Academy Award in 1988 for her portrayal of a rape victim who seeks retribution through the courts.
a) The Accused b) Shadows and Fog
c) Backtrack d) Stealing Home

2) As well as having been a talented child actor and adult actor, she also directs. What was the title of the film in which she made her directing debut?
a) Svengali b) Little Man Tate
c) Home For the Holidays d) Siesta

3) In which film do Paula and Gerome (Natasha Richardson & Liam Neeson) live in a houseboat near her house in order to observe her behaviour at close quarters?
a) One Little Indian b) Freaky Friday
c) It Was a Wonderful Life d) Nell

MICHAEL J. FOX (1961 -)

1) In 1987 he portrayed Joe Rasnick who plays in a rock band with his sister Patti (Joan Jett) in a film written and directed by Paul Schrader. Name the title.
a) Light of Day b) The Hard Way
c) Midnight Madness d) Poison Ivy

2) Farm boy Brantley Foster (Michael J. Fox) started at the bottom of the career ladder in his rich uncle's corporation in **The Secret of My Success** (1987). What department did he work in?
a) the canteen b) the mailroom
c) the typing pool d) the car pool

3) Which film featured him as Lewis Rothschild, White House staff member and quixotic conscience of the President of the United States?
a) The American President b) Wag the Dog
c) The Kidnapping of the President d) Dead Presidents

MORGAN FREEMAN (1937 -)

1) In 1995 he played Somerset, a veteran cop on the trail of a killer named 'John Doe'. Name the film.
a) Seven
b) Clean and Sober
c) Brubaker
d) Eyewitness

2) When Miss Daisy Werthan (Jessica Tandy) is driven across Georgia by her chauffeur, Hoke Colburn (Morgan Freeman) to listen to someone's speech in **Driving Miss Daisy** (1989) she doesn't think to invite him in to the gathering. Who gave the speech?
a) John F. Kennedy
b) Billy Graham
c) Martin Luther King
d) Jimmy Swaggart

3) Critic Pauline Kael asked the question "Is Morgan Freeman the greatest American actor?" after seeing him portray a pimp named Fast Black in 1987. Name the film.
a) Street Smart
b) Streetwise
c) Side Street
d) Streetwalkin'

Performers

CLARK GABLE (1901 - 1960)

1) Clark Gable made his talkie debut in a 1931 western with Hopalong Cassidy star, William Boyd. Name the title.
a) *Texas Trail* b) *Lost City*
c) *Call of the Prairie* d) *The Painted Desert*

2) Who sings 'Dear Mr. Gable - You Made Me Love You' in **Broadway Melody 1938**?
a) *Margaret O'Brien* b) *Shirley Temple*
c) *Judy Garland* d) *Peggy Ann Garner*

3) MGM remade Gable's 1932 drama, **Red Dust**, in which he plays an Indochina rubber worker opposite crude girlfriend Vantine (Jean Harlow). Gable also starred in the 1953 remake with Ava Gardner substituting for Harlow. Name the title.
a) *Strange Cargo* b) *The Hucksters*
c) *Betrayed* d) *Mogambo*

GRETA GARBO
(Greta Gustafsson 1905 - 1990)

a) In which 1932 drama did she retort "I want to be alone" to her secret admirer, Baron Felix von Gaigern (John Barrymore), a line which became associated with her character forever more?
a) *Grand Hotel* b) *Camille*
c) *Queen Christina* d) *Mata Hari*

2) Who portrayed Garbo's lover, Vronsky, in **Anna Karenina** (1935)?

a) *John Gilbert* b) *Charles Bickford*
c) *Fredric March* d) *Basil Rathbone*

3) With which 1939 comedy do you associate her telling Count Dolga (Melvyn Douglas) that love is only "a chemical reaction"?
a) *Wild Orchids* b) *Ninotchka*
c) *Two-Faced Woman* d) *As You Desire Me*

ANDY GARCIA
(Andres Arturo Garci-Menendez 1956 -)

1) Rookie cop, George Stone (Andy Garcia), was singled out for his sharpshooting skills in a 1987 crime drama. Name the title.
a) *The Mean Season* b) *The Untouchables*
c) *Internal Affairs* d) *Hero*

2) Who portrayed his alcoholic wife in **When a Man Loves a Woman** (1994)?
a) *Meg Ryan* b) *Julia Roberts*
c) *Michelle Pfeiffer* d) *Jodie Foster*

3) In which 1989 crime thriller were detectives Nick Conklin (Michael Douglas) and Charlie Vincent (Andy Garcia) assigned to escort a Japanese gangster back to Osaka?
a) *Black Rain* b) *Running*
c) *The Yakuza* d) *8 Million Ways to Die*

AVA GARDNER (1922 - 1990)

1) Stardom came to Ava Gardner after she starred as femme fatale Kitty Collins who manipulated 'The Swede' (Burt Lancaster) in a 1946 crime drama directed by Robert Siodmak. Name the title.
a) *Dark Mirror* b) *Rope of Sand*
c) *Brute Force* d) *The Killers*

2) With which 1951 musical do you associate her portrayal of a mulatto girl named Julie LaVerne?
a) *Carousel* b) *Show Boat*
c) *The Beggar's Opera* d) *An American in Paris*

3) In 1964 she played hotelkeeper, Maxine Faulk, in a film based on a Tennessee Williams play. Name the title.
a) *Sweet Bird of Youth* b) *The Glass Menagerie*
c) *Suddenly, Last Summer* d) *The Night of the Iguana*

JOHN GARFIELD
(Jacob Garfinkel 1913 - 1952)

1) Which film features him as world boxing champion, Charlie Davis, who after his last fight when confronted by gangsters retorts: "So - what are you going to do? Kill me? Everybody dies!" ?
a) *The Square Jungle* b) *Kid Galahad*
c) *Body and Soul* d) *Night and the City*

2) Cora Smith suggests that hired hand, Frank Chambers (John Garfield) murder her husband so they can both live happily ever after on his money in the 1946 crime thriller, **The Postman Always Rings Twice**. Who was she?

The Movie Quiz Companion

an atmosphere affects people

a) Carole Lombard b) Lana Turner
c) Joan Crawford d) Ida Lupino

3) What was greedy Joe Morse's (John Garfield) occupation in **Force of Evil** (1948)?
a) lawyer b) cop c) nightclub owner d) reporter

JUDY GARLAND
(Frances Gumm 1922 - 1969)

1) Judy Garland and Mickey Rooney appeared in nine films together. The first was in 1937. Name the title.
a) Thoroughbreds Don't Cry b) Andy Hardy Meets Debutante c) Girl Crazy d) Strike Up the Band

2) In a 1945 portrayal she meets Cpl. Joe Allen under **The Clock** in New York's Pennsylvania Station and marries him within 48 hours. Who was he?
a) Robert Walker b) Montgomery Clift
c) Dana Andrews d) William Powell

3) In her last film, **I Could Go on Singing** (1963), she arrives in England to claim something or someone from Dirk Bogarde. Who or what was it?
a) her illegitimate son b) incriminating love-letters c) an apology d) her father, whom she had previously believed to have been murdered by the Nazis

JAMES GARNER
(James Baumgarner 1928 -)

1) In which western did he portray veteran lawman Zane Cooper?
a) Support Your Local Sheriff! b) Darby's Rangers
c) Maverick d) Duel at Diablo

2) With which 1963 comedy do you associate his wife returning from the dead after he has remarried?
a) Move Over, Darling b) The Art of Love
c) The Thrill of it All d) Return of a Stranger

3) In the 1964 war drama, **36 Hours**, captured WWII spy Jefferson Pike (James Garner) is brainwashed into believing something. What is it?
a) that he is a German officer b) that the war is over c) that he has assassinated Hitler d) that he executed his platoon

GREER GARSON (1903 - 1996)

1) In 1942 she won a Best Actress Oscar for her role in a film which Winston Churchill described as having "done more for the British war effort than a flotilla of destroyers". Name the title.
a) This Above All
b) The Foreman Went to France
c) Mrs. Miniver
d) In Which We Serve

2) In which 1960 biopic did she portray Eleanor, the wife of Franklin D. Roosevelt?
a) Remember?
b) Blossoms in the Dust
c) Sunrise at Campobello d) Desire Me

3) Which film featured her doing a caricature of Harry Lauder?
a) Strange Lady in Town
b) Random Harvest
c) The Singing Nun
d) Julia Misbehaves

RICHARD GERE (1949 -)

1) In which film does he portray a man who has a love affair with senator's wife, Michelle (Lauren Hutton)?
a) American Gigolo b) Internal Affairs
c) The Cotton Club d) Breathless

2) With which film do you associate him portraying Chicago attorney, Martin Vail, who decides to defend an altar boy accused of murdering a bishop?
a) Intersection b) Beyond the Limit
c) Final Analysis d) Primal Fear

3) Name the 1978 Terence Malick drama which gave him his first starring role.
a) Days of Heaven b) Deadhead Miles
c) Badlands d) Pocket Money

MEL GIBSON (1956 -)

1) Which 1979 film featured him as a policeman who quits the force and seeks revenge for the murder of his wife and child?

204

a) *Chain Reaction* b) *The River*
c) *Mad Max* d) *The Man Without a Face*

2) In Robert Towne's **Tequila Sunrise** (1988) Mel Gibson plays retired drug dealer Dale McKussiac. Who or what does he fear losing most?
a) *his 1955 Pontiac* b) *custody of his son*
c) *the respect of his teenage daughter* d) *his dilapidated beach hut*

3) Name the tyrannical English King, known as Edward Longshanks and played by Patrick McGoohan, who executes William Wallace (Mel Gibson) in **Braveheart** (1995).
a) *Edward I* b) *Edward II*
c) *Edward III* d) *Edward IV*

JOHN GIELGUD (1904 -2000)

1) With which 1936 Hitchcock thriller do you associate him as a spy who is assigned to kill an enemy agent in Switzerland?
a) *The Man Who Knew too Much*
b) *Sabotage*
c) *Secret Agent*
d) *Foreign Correspondent*

2) Which 1964 historical drama, based on a play by Jean Anouilh, featured him as King Louis VII of France?
a) *Becket* b) *Joan of Arc*
c) *The Man in the Iron Mask*
d) *The Lion in Winter*

3) Which 1974 film featured him as Beddoes, manservant to a millionaire named Ratchett?
a) *Murder on the Orient Express*
b) *Arthur*
c) *The Loved One*
d) *Plenty*

LILLIAN GISH (1896 - 1993)

1) What 1955 thriller involves her protecting two orphaned children from the murdering preacher, Harry Powell?
a) *The Cobweb* b) *Night of the Hunter*
c) *Thin Ice* d) *The Unforgiven*

2) Which 1946 western featured her as Laura Belle McCanles, mother of brothers Jesse (Joseph Cotten) and Lewt (Gregory Peck)?
a) *How the West Was Won* b) *Arrowhead*
c) *The Big Country* d) *Duel in the Sun*

3) In which 1919 drama is her screen character beaten to death by her father when he discovers she is having a relationship with a Chinese man?
a) *One Romantic Night* b) *Orphans of the Storm*
c) *Hearts of the World* d) *Broken Blossoms*

WHOOPI GOLDBERG
(Caryn Johnson 1949 -)

1) Her 1985 screen debut was in a film based on a novel by Alice Walker. Name the title.
a) *Clara's Heart* b) *The Color Purple*
c) *Fatal Beauty* d) *Jumpin' Jack Flash*

2) In 1994 she was the voice of Shenzi in Disney's animated tale, **The Lion King**. What kind of animal was she?
a) *a baboon* b) *a hyena*
c) *a zebra* d) *a wildebeeste*

3) Name the film, directed by Jerry Zucker, which won her a Best Supporting Actress Oscar in 1990.
a) *The Long Walk Home* b) *Made in America*
c) *Sister Act* d) *Ghost*

JEFF GOLDBLUM (1952 -)

1) He made his screen debut in a 1974 crime thriller, directed by Michael Winner, as a mugger and a rapist. Name the title.
a) *The Mechanic* b) *Death Wish*
c) *Firepower* d) *The Stone Killer*

2) With which Woody Allen film do you associate him as a party guest of Tony Lacey (Paul Simon) who has forgotten his mantra?
a) *Annie Hall* b) *Manhattan*
c) *Husbands and Wives* d) *Love and Death*

3) In which film does mathematician Ian Malcolm (Jeff Goldblum) visit a mysterious

island with two palaeontologists?
a) Bear Island b) Jurassic Park
c) The Island of Dr. Moreau d) Invasion of the Body Snatchers

JOHN GOODMAN (1952 -)

1) With which film do you associate him playing New York detective, Sherman Touhey, who discovers that people are being murdered after placing ads in a singles magazine?
a) Born Yesterday b) True Stories
c) Sea of Love d) Sweet Dreams

2) For what film did he portray movie showman, Lawrence Woolsey (inspired by real-life producer William Castle), who terrified cinema audiences with gimmicks like electrified seats, dry ice machines and giant ants during performances?
a) Matinee b) Silent Movie
c) Revenge of the Nerds d) Everybody's All-American

3) What 1986 comedy, starring John Goodman and directed by David Byrne of Talking Heads, featured fifty sets of twins, a woman who never left her bed and a happily married couple who had never spoken to each other in fifteen years?
a) True Identity b) True to Life
c) It's All True d) True Stories

ELLIOTT GOULD
(Elliott Goldstein 1938 -)

1) In which 1973 crime drama does a gangster hit his girlfriend with a bottle, warning Elliott Gould's character - "Now that's someone I love. Think what could happen to you"?
a) The Long Goodbye b) The Night They Raided Minsky's c) Getting Straight d) Dead Men Don't Die

2) Name the Robert Altman film in which he appears as himself and is described as "a fairly well-known actor [who] used to be married to Barbra Streisand"?
a) Nashville b) The Player
c) California Split d) Short Cuts

3) With which 1978 comedy do you associate him with a boxing kangaroo?
a) Matilda b) Inside Out
c) The Muppet Movie d) Busting

FARLEY GRANGER (1925 -)

1) Inspired by the real-life Leopold-Loeb murder case, this was Hitchcock's first colour film which involved Philip (Farley Granger) and college friend, Shaw Brandon (John Dall), murdering someone purely for the thrill. Name the title.
a) Young and Innocent
b) The Paradine Case
c) Rope
d) Under Capricorn

2) Farley Granger and Cathy O'Donnell starred as doomed lovers in a film which opens with them kissing and a title which reads, "This boy and this girl were never properly introduced to the world we live in." Name the film.
a) They Live by Night
b) They Drive by Night
c) Night Fall
d) The Night Has Eyes

3) Bruno Antony suggested to tennis pro, Guy Haines (Farley Granger), that they should exchange murders in Hitchcock's 1951 thriller, **Strangers on a Train**. Who portrayed Bruno Antony?
a) Lloyd Corrigan b) Craig Stevens
c) Robert Walker d) Guy Madison

STEWART GRANGER
(James Lablanche Stewart 1913 - 1993)

1) In 1943 he rocketed to stardom in a Gainsborough film studio's costume romp starring James Mason and Margaret Lockwood. Name the title.
a) Waterloo Road b) The Wicked Lady
c) The Man in Grey d) Doctor Syn

2) With which film do you associate him being trapped in a sealed cavern with a woman who discovers the skeletal remains of her missing husband among a vast wealth of diamonds?
a) Moonfleet b) King Solomon's Mines
c) Ashes and Diamonds d) The Clan of the Cave Bear

3) Name the 1947 biopic in which he portrayed violinist Niccolo Paganini.
a) Second Fiddle b) Humoresque
c) Music in My Heart d) The Magic Bow

rare prophecies of lout

Performers

CARY GRANT
(Archibald Leach 1904 - 1986)

1) One of his earliest roles was opposite Mae West in 1933, who reputedly commented when she spotted him on the Paramount lot: "If this one can talk, I'll take him." Name the film.
a) *My Little Chickadee* b) *I'm No Angel*
c) *She Done Him Wrong* d) *Klondike Annie*

2) Name the 1937 screwball comedy, directed by Leo McCarey, where Cary Grant and Irene Dunne portray characters who retreat to a mountain cabin to revive their lost love for each other.
a) *The Awful Truth*
b) *Topper*
c) *My Favourite Wife*
d) *The Last Outpost*

3) In Stanley Donen's 1963 comedy thriller, **Charade**, recently widowed Regina Lambert asks Peter Joshua (Cary Grant) the question, which she also answers, "Do you know what's wrong with you? Nothing." Who was she?
a) *Audrey Hepburn*
b) *Deborah Kerr*
c) *Jean Simmons*
d) *Ingrid Bergman*

HUGH GRANT (1960 -)

1) Which 1987 film featured him as bisexual aristocrat, Clive Durham?
a) *The Dawning* b) *White Mischief*
c) *Maurice* d) *The Remains of the Day*

2) Marianne Dashwood observes "there is something wanting" about Edward Ferrars (Hugh Grant), in Ang Lee's 1995 drama, **Sense and Sensibility**. Who portrayed Marianne Dashwood?
a) *Emma Thompson* b) *Emile François*
c) *Harriet Walter* d) *Kate Winslet*

3) In which 1988 film is Lord James D'Ampton's (Hugh Grant) ancestor said to have slain a 'dragon'?
a) *Restoration* b) *The Lair of the White Worm*
c) *The Dawning* d) *The Beast*

RICHARD E. GRANT (1957 -)

1) With which film do you associate Uncle Monty unexpectedly arriving with food, wine, and designs on Marwood's body?
a) *Suddenly, Last Summer* b) *The Player*
c) *Withnail & I* d) *Hidden City*

2) What film involved his having a talking boil on his shoulder?
a) *How to Get Ahead in Advertising* b) *LA Story*
c) *Hudson Hawk* d) *Warlock*

3) In which 1995 comedy drama does his wife (Imogen Stubbs) die in childbirth, leaving him with a daughter to bring up on his own?
a) *Jack & Sarah* b) *Honest, Decent and True*
c) *Henry & June* d) *Mountains of the Moon*

SYDNEY GREENSTREET
(1879 - 1954)

1) In his 1941 screen debut he frantically shouts, "It's a fake - it's a phoney - it's lead - it's lead - it's a fake." Name the title.
a) *Between Two Worlds*
b) *The Mask of Dimitrios*
c) *The Conspirators*
d) *The Maltese Falcon*

2) Which film featured him as the shifty black marketeer, Señor Ferrari?
a) *Three Strangers*
b) *Casablanca*
c) *Across the Pacific*
d) *Conflict*

3) In the 1949 drama, **Flamingo Road**, he played a corrupt sheriff who imprisons carnival dancer, Lane Bellamy. Who was she?
a) *Joan Crawford*
b) *Rita Hayworth*
c) *Mary Astor*
d) *Gloria Grahame*

The Movie Quiz Companion

rakishly we go

MELANIE GRIFFITH (1957 -)

1) Her 1975 screen debut involved her playing a teenage runaway who is traced to the Florida Keys by LA detective, Harry Moseby (Gene Hackman). Name the title.
a) *Something Wild* b) *Joyride*
c) *Smile* d) *Night Moves*

2) Which film featured her as NYC cop, Emily Eden, who, in order to solve a crime committed in Brooklyn's Hassidic Jewish community lives among them and ends up falling in love with a rabbinical student?
a) *A Stranger Among Us*
b) *Intimate Strangers*
c) *The Stranger Within*
d) *Stranger in Our House*

3) In 1990 she starred in John Schlesinger's thriller **Pacific Heights** with her actress mother. Who was she?
a) Ann Blyth
b) Tippi Hedren
c) Barbara Bel Geddes
d) Joan Bennett

ALEC GUINNESS (1914 - 2000)

1) For which film did he receive a Best Actor Oscar in 1957?
a) *The Lavender Hill Mob* b) *The Bridge on the River Kwai* c) *The Ladykillers* d) *Tunes of Glory*

2) With which film do you associate him portraying Dr. Godbole, a man who accepts fate with a resigned tranquility?
a) *A Passage to India* b) *Murder By Death*
c) *Last Holiday* d) *The Comedians*

3) In which film does mad painter, Gully Jimson (Alec Guinness), decide to adorn the walls of Sir William Beeder's empty flat with his masterpieces, eventually taking over the whole building and leaving it in ruins?
a) *The Horse's Mouth* b) *The Scapegoat*
c) *A Run For Your Money* d) *Hotel Paradiso*

GENE HACKMAN (1930 -)

1) Early in his film career he received his first Oscar nomination for his portrayal of the older brother of a bank robber. Name the film.
a) *Al Capone* b) *Robbery Under Arms*
c) *Machine-Gun Kelly* d) *Bonnie and Clyde*

2) Which film featured him as 'Little Bill' Daggett, the sadistic sheriff of Big Whiskey, Wyoming?
a) *Bite the Bullet* b) *Unforgiven*
c) *Wyatt Earp* d) *Geronimo: An American Legend*

3) In 1995 he played the overbearing captain of the nuclear submarine who reprimands a junior officer for disagreeing with him in front of the crew, saying: "We're here to preserve democracy, not to practice it." Name the film.
a) *Split Decisions* b) *Marooned*
c) *Crimson Tide* d) *Narrow Margin*

TOM HANKS (1956 -)

1) With which film do you associate him appearing on America's Dick Cavett TV show with John Lennon?
a) *Apollo 13* b) *Philadelphia*
c) *Forrest Gump* d) *Punchline*

2) In which comedy adventure does a man named Graynamore (Lloyd Bridges) suggest he become a human sacrifice on an island of restless natives?
a) *The 'burbs* b) *Mazes and Monsters*
c) *Volunteers* d) *Joe Versus the Volcano*

3) In a moving scene from **Philadelphia** (1993), AIDS victim, Andrew Beckett (Tom Hanks) lets his guard down briefly and plays his favourite operatic aria to homophobic lawyer, Joe Miller (Denzel Washington). Who sang the aria?
a) Beniamino Gigli
b) Renata Tebaldi
c) Giuseppe Di Stefano
d) Maria Callas

masochist flee belt hen **Performers**

CEDRIC HARDWICKE
(1893 - 1964)

1) Known for his scholarly and authoritarian roles, which 1940 drama featured him as the humane Dr. Arnold?
a) The Moon is Down b) Forever and a Day
c) Tom Brown's Schooldays d) Things to Come

2) In which film does a reporter from the New York Herald find him after a prolonged absence in Ujiji?
a) King Solomon's Mines b) Valley of the Sun
c) The Keys of the Kingdom d) Stanley and Livingstone

3) Name the 1947 Charles Dickens adaptation in which he portrays Derek Bond's villainous Uncle Ralph?
a) Nicholas Nickleby b) David Copperfield
c) Oliver Twist d) Pickwick Papers

JEAN HARLOW
(Harlean Carpenter 1911 - 1937)

1) Name the Howard Hughes WWI drama which launched her screen career in 1930.
a) Hell's Angels b) Sky Devils
c) Wings d) Flying High

2) During the filming of **Saratoga** in 1937 she became ill and died on June 7, aged 26. What did she die of?
a) cancer b) cerebral oedema
c) tuberculosis d) intestinal haemorrhage

3) In a 1933 George Cuckor comedy, Kitty (Jean Harlow), a former hat-check girl turned social climber, desperately tries to conceal her origins and sound cultured as she converses with refined but faded stage actress, Carlotta Vance (Marie Dressler): "I was reading a book the other day," remarks Kitty "It's all about civilization or something . . . Do you know the guy said machinery is going to take the place of every profession." Eyeing her revealing curves, Carlotta replies, "That's something you'll never have to worry about!" Name the film.
a) Our Betters b) The Virtuous Sin
c) Dinner at Eight d) Girls About Town

WOODY HARRELSON (1961 -)

1) With which comedy do you associate hustler Billy Hoyle's (Woody Harrelson) girlfriend's desire to appear on the TV show 'Jeopardy'?
a) I'll Do Anything
b) No Questions Asked
c) Ted & Venus
d) White Men Can't Jump

2) In which 1995 thriller did he retort, "Buddha consciousness came to me as I was hanging from the 51st floor"?
a) The Cowboy Way
b) Killer Instinct
c) Money Train d) Wildcats

3) In Oliver Stone's **Natural Born Killers** (1994), a film about the media hysteria surrounding two murderers, a teenager being interviewed on television quips enviously: "Mass murder is wrong. But if I WERE a mass murderer, I'd be Mickey and Mallory!" Woody Harrelson was Mickey. Who played Mallory?
a) Juliette Lewis b) Laura Dern
c) Brooke Adams d) Sissy Spacek

RICHARD HARRIS (1930 -)

1) In which film does he portray a character who has an affair with his morose landlady, Mrs. Hammond?
a) The Main Chance b) Caprice
c) This Sporting Life d) Shake Hands with the Devil

2) What drama involves 'Bull' McCabe (Richard Harris) hauling seaweed up a cliff in wicker baskets with his retarded son, Tadgh?
a) Ravagers b) The Field
c) Man in the Wilderness d) The Molly Maguires

3) In Ridley Scott's **Gladiator** (2000) Richard Harris plays an ailing and ageing Roman emperor who is murdered by his jealous son Commodus (Joaquin Phoenix). What was the emperor's name?
a) Marullus Flavius b) Octavius Lepidus
c) Claudius Titinius d) Marcus Aurelius

The Movie Quiz Companion

REX HARRISON
(Reginald Harrison 1908 - 1990)

1) Who or what was British intelligence agent, Gus Bennett (Rex Harrison), trying to get out of Nazi Germany in Carol Reed's 1940 spy drama, **Night Train to Munich**?
a) a Czech scientist b) a code machine
c) a rocket fuel formula d) the plan of a munitions factory

2) For which 1954 film did he portray Saladin?
a) Ashanti b) The Fifth Musketeer
c) King Richard and the Crusaders d) Crossed Swords

3) What 1941 film connection can you make between Rex Harrison and George Bernard Shaw?
a) Major Barbara b) The Devil's Disciple
c) Pygmalion d) Saint Joan

LAURENCE HARVEY
(Laruska Skikne 1928 - 1973)

1) What was the code word which triggered brain-washed Korean war-hero Raymond Shaw's (Laurence Harvey) irrational behaviour in the 1962 political thriller, **The Manchurian Candidate**?
a) thunderbolt b) colossus c) inferno d) solitaire

2) In 1956 he starred in a remake of the classic adventure yarn, **The Four Feathers** (1939), made by the original director, Zoltan Korda. Name the title.
a) Sahara b) Storm Over the Nile
c) East of Sudan d) Serpent of the Nile

3) With which 1960 drama, filmed on location in Brackettville, Texas, do you associate him as Colonel William Travis?
a) The Comancheros
b) Texas Across the River
c) The Alamo d) The Border

JACK HAWKINS (1910 - 1973)

1) For what film did he portray the dauntless Major Warden, head of a WWII sabotage unit?
a) The Bridge on the River Kwai b) The Malta Story c) Rampage d) Guns at Batasi

2) Which film featured his ship being attacked by Macedonian pirates?
a) Land of the Pharaohs b) Ben Hur
c) Duel of the Titans d) Julius Caesar

3) Name the well known actress to whom he was married from 1932 to 1942.
a) Valerie Hobson b) Virginia McKenna
c) Jessica Tandy d) Celia Johnson

STERLING HAYDEN
(Sterling Relyea Walter 1916 - 1986)

1) In the 1950 crime drama, **The Asphalt Jungle**, jewel robber Dix Handley (Sterling Hayden) dreams of buying something back with his share of the loot, something very close to his heart. What is it?
a) his 1948 Buick b) his father's horse ranch
c) his old fishing boat d) his wife's wedding dress

2) Which comedy featured him as the communist-hating General Jack D. Ripper?
a) Dr. Strangelove b) The Optimists
c) Heavens Above! d) What's New, Pussycat?

3) In which 1972 drama did he portray a corrupt police captain who is murdered in an Italian restaurant?
a) Terror in a Texas Town b) The Long Goodbye
c) 1900 d) The Godfather

SUSAN HAYWARD
(Edythe Marrener 1918 - 1975)

1) In which 1952 musical biopic did she portray singer Jane Froman?
a) With a Song in My Heart b) The Lost Moment
c) Race For Life d) My Foolish Heart

2) From who did singer Lillian Roth (Susan Hayward) seek help in the 1955 biopic, **I'll Cry Tomorrow**?
a) Alcoholics Anonymous b) crooked loan sharks
c) the Samaritans d) a devil-worshipping cult

3) In **My Foolish Heart** (1949) Eloise Winters (Susan Hayward) has a WWII romance with soldier Walt Dreiser. Who was he?
a) Alan Ladd b) Dana Andrews
c) Glenn Ford d) Dick Powell

RITA HAYWORTH
(Margarita Carmen Cansino 1918 - 1987)

1) Which 1946 drama, directed by Charles Vidor, featured her singing 'Put the Blame on Mame'?
a) My Gal Sal b) Only Angels Have Wings
c) Blood and Sand d) Gilda

2) Dentist, Biff Grimes, is obsessed with Rita Hayworth in Raoul Walsh's 1941 comedy, **The Strawberry Blonde**. Who was he?
a) Fredric March b) Cary Grant
c) James Cagney d) Walter Pidgeon

3) With which film do you associate her playing the step-daughter of King Herod?
a) The Robe b) Salome
c) Herod the Great d) David and Bathsheba

VAN HEFLIN (1910 - 1971)

1) In the 1936 drama, **A Woman Rebels**, magazine editor Pamela Thistlewaite has an affair with him which results in an illegitimate child. Who was she?
a) Mary Astor b) Katherine Hepburn
c) Jean Harlow d) Joan Fontaine

2) Name the crime drama which won him a Best Supporting Actor Oscar for his role as Robert Taylor's alcoholic buddy in 1942.
a) Black Widow b) Act of Violence
c) Johnny Eager d) The Strange Love of Martha Ivers

3) Which film features him as farmer Joe Starrett battling against the bullying Ryker gang who want his land for grazing their cattle?
a) 3:10 to Yuma b) Santa Fe Trail
c) Tomahawk d) Shane

PAUL HENREID (1908 - 1992)

1) In which film did he portray a character who allows his daughter Tina to live with his former lover, Charlotte Vale?
a) Deception b) Between Two Worlds
c) Now Voyager d) In Our Time

2) Which 1939 film featured him as Herr Staefel, German Master at Brookfield School?
a) Tom Brown's Schooldays b) Jane Eyre
c) David Copperfield d) Goodbye Mr. Chips

3) Whom does he encounter in Curtis Bernhardt's 1946 literary biopic, **Devotion**?
a) the Brontë sisters b) Edith Wharton
c) Jane Austen d) Mary Shelley

AUDREY HEPBURN
(Edda van Heemstra Hepburn-Ruston 1929 - 1993)

1) With which film do you associate her getting "the mean reds"?
a) Funny Face b) Breakfast at Tiffany's
c) My Fair Lady d) Love in the Afternoon

2) Name the romantic comedy, directed by William Wyler, which made her a star and won her a Best Actress Oscar in 1953.
a) Roman Holiday b) Sabrina
c) Charade d) Secret People

3) With whom does she have **Love in the Afternoon,** in Paris in 1957?
a) Gregory Peck b) Cary Grant
c) Gary Cooper d) Kirk Douglas

KATHARINE HEPBURN (1907 -)

1) In which film does Spencer Tracy comment to his buddy: "Not much meat on 'er, but what there is is cherce"?
a) Adam's Rib b) Guess Who's Coming to Dinner
c) Woman of the Year d) Pat and Mike

2) With which David Lean film do you associate her as an ageing spinster who has a holiday romance with Renato Di Rossi (Rossano Brazzi) in 1950's Venice?
a) Summertime b) The Iron Petticoat
c) The Passionate Friends d) Madeleine

3) Name the 1975 western in which she co-starred with John Wayne.
a) McLintock! b) Rio Lobo
c) The Sons of Katie Elder
d) Rooster Cogburn

The Movie Quiz Companion

CHARLTON HESTON
(Charles Carter 1924 -)

1) In 1965 Chrysagon (Charlton Heston) claims his lawful right to sleep with another man's newly wed wife on their wedding night. Name the film.
a) The Savage b) Dark City
c) The War Lord d) Secret of the Incas

2) Lawyer Ramon Miguel 'Mike' Vargas (Charlton Heston) and his new bride Susan narrowly escape a car bomb in the opening scenes of the 1958 crime thriller **Touch of Evil**. Who portrayed Mrs. Vargas?
a) Marlene Dietrich b) Claire Bloom
c) Olivia De Havilland d) Janet Leigh

3) With which film do you associate him portraying a character who causes various plagues to fall upon people?
a) The Omega Man b) The Ten Commandments
c) Beneath the Planet of the Apes d) The Greatest Story Ever Told

VALERIE HOBSON (1917 - 1998)

1) Valerie Hobson developed a reputation as a leading lady with a flair for comedy who personified dignity and class, most notably in David Lean's **Great Expectations** (1946). What was her character's name in the film?
a) Sarah Pocket b) Miss Havisham
c) Mrs. Gargery d) Estella

2) What connection can you make between Valerie Hobson and **Brief Encounter**?
a) she was Noel Coward's first choice to play Laura Jesson b) she was married to producer Anthony Havelock-Allan c) she was an un-credited extra in the station buffet scene d) the film Alec and Laura go to see at the cinema starred Valerie Hobson

3) In which film did she portray the wife of the mad Henry Frankenstein?
a) Frankenstein b) Evil of Frankenstein
c) Frankenstein Conquers the World d) Bride of Frankenstein

DUSTIN HOFFMAN (1937 -)

1) "In the same year that man first flew to the moon and the last American soldier left Vietnam there were still corners of England where lived men and women who had never travelled more than fifteen miles from their own homes." So begins Gordon Williams' book on which Dustin Hoffman's most controversial film, **Straw Dogs** (1971), was based. Name the title of the book.
a) Mortal Fear b) The Gatecrashers
c) The Siege of Trencher's Farm d) City of the Dead

2) Which newspaper do reporters Carl Bernstein (Dustin Hoffman) and Bob Woodward (Robert Redford) work for in Alan J. Pakula's real-life political drama, **All the President's Men**?
a) New York Times b) Chicago Tribune
c) Boston Globe d) Washington Post

3) What Dustin Hoffman film was critic Richard Ebert reviewing when he commented: "...a truly dreadful film, a lifeless, massive, lumbering exercise in failed comedy... the director, has mounted a multimillion-dollar expedition in search of a plot so thin that it could hardly support a five-minute TV sketch"?
a) Lenny b) Who is Harry Kellerman and Why is He Saying Those Terrible Things About Me?
c) Ishtar d) The Tiger Makes Out

WILLIAM HOLDEN
(William Beedle, Jr. 1918 - 1981)

1) In 1955, war correspondent, Mark Elliot (William Holden) falls in love with Han Suyin, a Eurasian doctor in **Love Is a Many Splendoured Thing**. Who was she?
a) Merle Oberon b) Jennifer Jones
c) Ava Gardner d) Loretta Young

2) Name the 1953 P.O.W. camp film which won him a Best Actor Oscar for his portrayal of Sergeant Sefton, a suspected enemy spy.
a) The Bridge on the River Kwai b) King Rat
c) Stalag 17 d) Intimate Strangers

3) "If you had any compassion or love whatsoever for this man you could never call him a cunning drunkard" retorts Broadway director, Bernie Dodd (William Holden) to Georgie Elgin (Grace Kelly), wife of an alcoholic singer (Bing Crosby) hoping for a much-needed comeback. Name the film.
a) The Country Girl b) The Singer Not the Song
c) Born Yesterday d) Golden Boy

elitist oaf ate cow

STANLEY HOLLOWAY
(1890 - 1982)

1) In which 1945 romantic drama does he have his eye on Myrtle (Joyce Carey) the tea lady?
a) This Happy Breed b) Major Barbara
c) Champagne Charlie d) Brief Encounter

2) With which 1947 Dickens adaptation do you associate him as the travelling actor, Vincent Crummles?
a) Oliver Twist b) David Copperfield
c) Great Expectations d) Nicholas Nickleby

3) In which 1951 comedy are bank clerk, Henry Holland (Alec Guinness) and a sculptor named Pendlebury (Stanley Holloway) involved in a chase with a stolen police car?
a) The Titfield Thunderbolt b) The Lavender Hill Mob c) Passport to Pimlico d) The Magic Box

BOB HOPE
(Leslie Townes Hope 1903 -)

1) Bob Hope was born in London at 44 Craighton Road. Which London borough is it in?
a) Greenwich b) Haringey
c) Southwark d) Lambeth

2) He will be best remembered for the 'Road' films with Dorothy Lamour and Bing Crosby, the last of which was **Road to Hong Kong** (1962). Name the first one.
a) Road to Morocco b) Road to Rio
c) Road to Zanzibar d) Road to Singapore

3) Which comedy-western, co-starring Jane Russell as Calamity Jane, featured the Oscar-winning song 'Buttons and Bows'?
a) The Paleface b) Fancy Pants
c) The Lemon Drop Kid d) Alias Jesse James

ANTHONY HOPKINS (1937 -)

1) He made his film debut in 1968 when he was cast as a future English king in **The Lion in Winter**. Name the king.
a) Richard the Lionheart b) Henry V
c) Richard III d) James I

2) For what film did he portray Dr. Frederick Treves?
a) The Road to Wellville b) The Elephant Man
c) Howards End d) Bram Stoker's Dracula

3) With which film do you associate the following dialogue:
"What do you do when you go to bed?"
"I put on my pyjamas and say my prayers and get under the covers."
"Well, then, that's what I want you to do right now, except that when you get under the covers, I'll be there."
a) The Remains of the Day b) 84 Charing Cross Road c) Shadowlands d) Nixon

DENNIS HOPPER (1936 -)

Performers

1) He made his film debut in 1955 as a young thug named Goon in a film directed by Nicholas Ray. Name the title.
a) Rebel Without a Cause b) Hot Blood
c) Run For Cover d) Party Girl

2) In which film does he visit the 'House of Blue Lights' brothel with Wyatt in homage to his dead buddy?
a) Cool Hand Luke b) Johnny Guitar
c) Gunfight at the O.K. Corral d) Easy Rider

3) With which 1986 mystery do you associate him having secret meetings with the 'yellow man'?
a) Colors b) Hoosiers
c) Blue Velvet d) Rumble Fish

BOB HOSKINS (1942 -)

1) Which film featured him as Sgt. Maj. Williams who fought in the British Army against the Zulu nation in the late 1800s?
a) Zulu Dawn
b) Beyond the Limit
c) Royal Flash
d) Young Winston

2) For what film did he portray J. Edgar Hoover?
a) Dillinger
b) Bob Roberts
c) Nixon
d) Chaplin

3) Which film won him the best actor award at the 1986 Cannes Film Festival?
a) Mona Lisa
b) Brazil
c) The Long Good Friday
d) Who Framed Roger Rabbit

213

The Movie Quiz Companion

a thin ghetto hen thief

LESLIE HOWARD
(Leslie Stainer 1893 - 1943)

1) He was killed on 1 June 1943 when his airliner crashed into the sea while returning from a trip to Spain and Portugal. What caused the plane to crash?
a) a thunderstorm
b) the pilot had a heart attack c) engine failure
d) It was shot down by the Luftwaffe who suspected Winston Churchill was aboard

2) In 1942 he portrayed the inventor of the **Spitfire**. Who was he?
a) Barnes Wallis
b) Reginald Mitchell
c) Christopher Cockerell
d) Malcolm Sinclair

3) Phonetics professor, Henry Higgins (Leslie Howard), tries to transform cockney flower girl Eliza Doolittle into a lady of culture in three months in the 1938 comedy, **Pygmalion**. Who was she?
a) Kay Walsh b) Joan Greenwood
c) Jessie Mathews d) Wendy Hiller

TREVOR HOWARD (1916 - 1988)

1) In which David Lean drama did he make his film debut in 1944?
a) One of Our Aircraft is Missing b) The Way Ahead c) In Which We Serve d) The Way to the Stars

2) With which film do you associate him as the drunken coalminer father, Walter Morel, whose son Paul (Dean Stockwell) desperately wants to break away from the tradition of following his father down the pit?
a) Sons and Lovers b) The Stars Look Down
c) How Green Was My Valley d) Coal Miner's Daughter

3) In 1970 he was almost drowned in rough seas while shooting a rowing boat scene in which he portrayed a priest accompanied by village idiot Michael. Name the film.
a) Kidnapped b) The Cockleshell Heroes
c) Outcast of the Islands d) Ryan's Daughter

ROCK HUDSON
(Roy Scherer, Jr. 1925 - 1985)

1) His screen surname was borrowed from the Hudson River. From who or what did he borrow his screen Christian name?
a) the Rock of Gibraltar
b) the Rocky Mountains
c) millionaire J.D. Rockefeller
d) Ayer's Rock

2) Rock Hudson was cast in the remake of a film in 1957, originally made in 1932 with Gary Cooper as the lead. Both were in love with Nurse Barkley. Name the title.
a) The General Died at Dawn b) Wings
c) A Farewell to Arms d) If I Had a Million

3) For what film, adapted from an Alistair MacLean novel, did he portray Cmdr. James Ferraday of the US Navy?
a) When Eight Bells Toll b) Force Ten from Navarone c) Ice Station Zebra d) Bear Island

HOLLY HUNTER (1958 -)

1) In 1987 she portrayed a policewoman who falls in love with a robber when taking his mug shot. Name the film.
a) End of the Line
b) Swing Shift
c) Raising Arizona
d) Copycat

2) Which film featured her as air traffic controller, Donnda Durston, whose pilot boyfriend dies in a crash?
a) Once Around
b) Air America
c) Always
d) Crash!

3) With which film do you associate her travelling to New Zealand for an arranged marriage to a farmer?
a) I Could Never Have Sex With Any Man Who Has So Little Respect For My Husband
b) A Gathering of Old Men
c) The Perfect Marriage
d) The Piano

JEREMY IRONS (1948 -)

1) Name the film, directed by Barbet Schroeder, which won him a Best Actor Oscar in 1990.
a) Reversal of Fortune b) Dead Ringers
c) Kafka d) Betrayal

2) In the 1982 drama, **Moonlighting**, he heads a group of European workmen who are operating illegally in Britain without work permits. When martial law is imposed in their home country he must keep it a secret from them. What nationality are they?
a) Russian b) Polish
c) Czechoslovakian d) Albanian

3) In which film does he bomb a New York department store?
a) Damage b) The Terrorists
c) Die Hard With a Vengeance d) Kansas City Bomber

GORDON JACKSON (1923 - 1990)

1) With which wartime drama do you associate him as a P.O.W. at Stalag Luft 3?
a) The Wooden Horse b) The Great Escape
c) The Captive Heart d) Merry Christmas, Mr. Lawrence

2) What 1949 comedy involved him living on the island of Todday?
a) Wee Geordie b) Against the Wind
c) Whisky Galore d) Millions Like Us

3) In 1984 he played game poacher, Tom Harker, who is hired as a guide by local aristocrat, Sir Randolph Nettleby, in **The Shooting Party**. Who was Sir Randolph?
a) Edward Fox b) James Mason
c) Robert Hardy d) John Gielgud

SAMUEL L. JACKSON (1948 -)

1) Which film featured him as Mister Senor Love Daddy, DJ on the WE-LOVE radio station?
a) Do the Right Thing b) GoodFellas
c) Sea of Love d) The Fastest Guitar Alive

2) What film involved an urgent visit from a clean-up specialist called The Wolf?
a) Kiss of Death b) True Romance
c) Pulp Fiction d) The New Age

3) In which 1996 comedy did he portray boxing promoter the Rev. Fred Sultan?
a) Against the Wall b) Johnny Suede
c) Strictly Business d) The Great White Hype

CELIA JOHNSON (1908 - 1982)

1) She made her film debut in 1942 portraying the naval wife of Captain Kinross (Noel Coward) whose character was based on Lord Louis Mountbatten. Name the title.
a) Stand By For Action b) Sink the Bismarck
c) In Which We Serve d) The Battle of the River Plate

2) With which film do you associate her as Miss Mackay, the dour headmistress of the Marcia Blane School for Girls?
a) The Astonished Heart b) I Believe in You
c) The Good Companions d) The Prime of Miss Jean Brodie

3) In which film does her friend and neighbour, Dolly Messiter (Everley Gregg), interrupt an intimate and heartbreaking farewell?
a) A Kid For Two Farthings b) This Happy Breed
c) Brief Encounter d) The Holly and the Ivy

TOMMY LEE JONES (1946 -)

1) Security specialist, Johnny Gallagher, was assigned to escort military prisoner, Thomas Boyette (Tommy Lee Jones) back to the States in the 1989 political thriller, **The Package**. Who was he?
a) Bruce Willis b) James Woods
c) Burt Reynolds d) Gene Hackman

2) Name the 1994 drama in which he portrayed army Captain, Hank Marshall, a nuclear scientist with a troublesome wife, who explains to his daughters: "What we call love is really the exchange of energy over

time. It's simple quantum mechanics."
a) House of Cards b) Back Roads
c) Black Moon Rising d) Blue Sky

3) In 1994 he portrayed Bible-quoting federal prosecutor, Roy Foltrigg, in Joel Schumacher's crime thriller, **The Client**. What is his nickname in the film?
a) Reverend b) Moses
c) Angel Gabriel d) The Bishop

LOUIS JOURDAN
(Louis Gendre 1919 -)

1) Which 1954 romantic drama featured him as Italian Prince Dino Di Cessi who meets three American women (Jean Peters, Dorothy McGuire & Maggie McNamara) in Rome?
a) Can-Can
b) Three Coins in a Fountain
c) Decameron Nights
d) Dangerous Exile

2) In which 1958 musical did Hermoine Gingold and Isabel Jeans transform a waif into a courtesan to become the mistress of the wealthy Gaston Lachaille (Louis Jourdan)?
a) Funny Face b) The Umbrellas of Cherbourg
c) Gigi d) Les Girls

3) Name the 1982 horror film Roger Ebert is describing: "... the evil villain (Louis Jourdan) drinks the secret formula and confidently waits for it to transform him into a powerful genius, he discovers that the formula doesn't so much change you, as develop what is already latent within you. Therefore, once a horse's ass, always a horse's ass."
a) Swamp Thing
b) It Lives Again
c) The Beast Within
d) The Alchemist

BORIS KARLOFF
(William Henry Pratt 1887 - 1969)

1) William Pratt was twenty-four when he adopted the name Karloff. From where did it originate?
a) it was an old family name b) he saw it printed on the side of a freight train c) it was the name of a circus acrobatic troupe he worked with called 'The Klimbing Karloffs' d) he was once a member of the Karloff Players in Guildford

2) What 1932 horror film involved Roger Penderell and Sir William Porterhouse (Melvyn Douglas & Charles Laughton) attempting to restrain the lecherous mute butler Morgan (Boris Karloff) from going berserk?
a) The Walking Dead b) The Ghoul
c) The Unholy Night d) The Old Dark House

3) A bus crash on a remote Austrian road forces American honeymooners Joan (Jacqueline Wells) and Peter Allison (David Manners) to seek shelter at the house of Hjalmar Poelzig (Boris Karloff), a house built over the ruins of a fort where 10,000 soldiers died. Name the film.
a) The Black Room b) The Raven
c) The Lost Patrol d) The Black Cat

DANNY KAYE
(David Kominski 1913 - 1987)

1) For what musical biopic did he portray jazz trumpeter Loring 'Red' Nichols?
a) The Five Pennies b) Wonder Man
c) A Song is Born d) Knock on Wood

2) With which film do you associate him singing the song 'Ugly Duckling'?
a) The Court Jester b) White Christmas
c) The Secret Life of Walter Mitty d) Hans Christian Andersen

3) In **The Kid From Brooklyn** gentle Burleigh Sullivan (Danny Kaye) accidentally ends up as a prizefighter. What was his former occupation?
a) policeman b) milkman c) taxi driver d) priest

BUSTER KEATON
(Joseph Keaton 1895 - 1966)

1) Which 1924 comedy featured him as an ill-fated projectionist able to walk into and take part in the action revealed on the screen?
a) Sherlock, Jr. b) The Three Ages
c) The Saphead d) The Electric House

2) Name the 1927 film inspired by *The Great Locomotive Chase*, William Pittenger's retelling of a Civil War incident in 1862 when Union soldiers stole a Confederate train.
a) A Southern Yankee b) Three on a Limb
c) The General d) Too Hot to Handle

3) Name the 1952 comedy drama he appeared in with Charlie Chaplin.
a) Around the World in 80 Days b) Limelight
c) A King in New York d) Monsieur Verdoux

DIANE KEATON
(Diane Hall 1946 -)

1) A stock player in numerous Woody Allen comedies, name the film which won her a Best Actress Oscar in 1977.
a) Sleeper b) Manhattan
c) Play it Again, Sam d) Annie Hall

2) Based on Beth Henley's Pulitzer Prize-winning play, which 1986 film featured the reunion of the McGrath sisters (Sissy Spacek, Jessica Lange and Diane Keaton)?
a) Running Mates b) Baby Boom
c) The Good Mother d) Crimes of the Heart

3) In which film does she support her son's ambition to become an opera singer while his father wants him to join the family business?
a) Father of the Bride b) Unstrung Heroes
c) The Godfather Part III d) Shoot the Moon

HOWARD KEEL
(Harry Clifford Leek 1917 -)

1) Name the 1950 musical, directed by George Sidney, which launched his screen career and included songs with unforgettable lyrics like, "Folks are dumb where I come from, They ain't had any learnin'. Still they're happy as can be, Doin' what comes natur'lly."
a) Annie Get Your Gun b) The Kissing Bandit
c) Oklahoma! d) Calamity Jane

2) In which musical comedy does he give Lilli Vanessi (Kathryn Grayson) a spanking?
a) Deep in My Heart b) Rose Marie
c) Kiss Me Kate d) Kismet

3) Which 1963 sci-fi drama featured him using the chimes of an ice-cream vendor's truck to save the world from an alien invasion?
a) The Human Duplicators b) Invasion of the Body Snatchers c) Enemy From Space d) The Day of the Triffids

HARVEY KEITEL (1939 -)

1) After being cast in the leading role of a 1979 war drama, he fell out with the director and was fired on location. The part was eventually given to Martin Sheen. Name the film.
a) The Dogs of War b) Southern Comfort
c) Go Tell the Spartans d) Apocalypse Now

2) Name the 1992 drama, directed by Abel Ferrara, in which his screen character sinks deeper into debt with the Mafia after the Mets beat the Dodgers in the sixth game of the 1988 National League playoffs.
a) Clockers b) The January Man
c) Bad Lieutenant d) Wise Guys

3) A main player in Martin Scorsese's films, what was the first film they collaborated on?
a) Mean Streets b) Who's That Knocking at My Door? c) Boxcar Bertha d) Alice Doesn't Live Here Anymore

GENE KELLY (1912 - 1996)

1) His film debut was opposite Judy Garland in 1942. Name the title.
a) For Me and My Gal b) Ziegfeld Follies
c) Cover Girl d) Thousands Cheer

2) Marjorie Morgenstern falls in love with Noel Airman (Gene Kelly) and cuts herself off from her Jewish background when she changes her name to **Marjorie Morningstar** (1958). Who was she?
a) Mitzi Gaynor b) Natalie Wood
c) Kay Kendall d) Cyd Charisse

3) In 1960 he portrayed cynical newspaper journalist, E. K. Hornbeck, based on the real-life H.L. Mencken who covered the bizarre trial of John T. Scopes in Tennessee in 1925. Name the film.
a) Witness to Murder
b) Xanadu
c) Trial by Jury
d) Inherit the Wind

The Movie Quiz Companion

handmade shoe talent

GRACE KELLY (1928 - 1982)

1) Her film debut was in a 1951 thriller, directed by Henry Hathaway, about a young man threatening to jump off the ledge of a skyscraper. Name the title.
a) Fourteen Hours b) The Long Wait
c) Permission to Kill d) The Suicide's Wife

2) Which Hitchcock thriller features her as high-fashion model Lisa Carol Fremont?
a) Dial M For Murder b) To Catch a Thief
c) Rear Window d) The Trouble With Harry

3) In 1956 she retired from acting when she married Prince Rainier of Monaco. Name the film in which she had her last acting role.
a) High Society b) Dial M For Murder
c) Rear Window d) To Catch a Thief

KAY KENDALL
(Justine McCarthy 1926 - 1959)

1) A well-known screen comedienne of the 1950s, she died of leukaemia two years after marrying a prominent British star. Who was he?
a) Laurence Olivier b) Rex Harrison
c) Alan Bates d) Leslie Howard

2) She will be best remembered for her role as the trumpet-playing Rosalind in a 1953 comedy directed by Henry Cornelius. Name the title.

a) Doctor in the House b) The Constant Husband
c) Genevieve d) Once More With Feeling

3) In 1955 she portrayed Isabelle, Countess of Marcroy, in a historical drama based on a novel by Sir Walter Scott. Name the film.
a) Quentin Durward b) Ivanhoe
c) The Talisman d) Rob Roy

DEBORAH KERR (1921 -)

1) Adept at playing refined ladies, nuns and governesses, she was cast against type and her sweet virgin image laid to rest when she played nymphomaniac, Karen Holmes, in 1953. Name the film.
a) Separate Tables b) The Sundowners
c) Black Narcissus d) From Here to Eternity

2) With which 1956 drama do you associate her as a teacher's wife who has an affair with one of her husband's pupils?
a) Tea and Sympathy b) The Naked Edge
c) Please Believe Me d) The Proud and the Profane

3) In which James Bond film did she portray Agent Mimi?
a) Thunderball b) Live and Let Die c) Casino Royale d) The Man With the Golden Gun

NICOLE KIDMAN (1967 -)

1) On which film shoot did she meet Tom Cruise?
a) Days of Thunder b) A Few Good Men
c) Top Gun d) Far and Away

2) For what 1995 black comedy did she portray a local cable TV weather forecaster in the town of Little Hope?
a) The Bit Part b) To Die For
c) My Life d) Windrider

3) Which 1991 drama, based on an E.L. Doctorow novel, featured her as society girl, Drew Preston?
a) The Wrecking Crew
b) Malice
c) The Drowning Pool d) Billy Bathgate

VAL KILMER (1959 -)

1) With which 1993 film do you associate him playing the ghost of Elvis Presley?
a) Top Secret! b) Real Genius
c) True Romance d) Kill Me Again

2) What film connection can you make between Val Kilmer and the song 'L.A. Woman'?
a) Top Gun b) The Real McCoy
c) Thunderheart d) The Doors

3) In a 1988 fantasy he portrayed a warrior named Madmartigan who is imprisoned in a

218

cage. Name the film.
a) Willow b) Mortal Kombat
c) The Beastmaster d) The Dark Crystal

BEN KINGSLEY
(Krishna Bhanji 1943 -)

1) He won an Oscar for his portrayal of **Gandhi** in 1982, which was his first film appearance since his film debut in an Alistair MacLean thriller in 1972. Name its title.
a) Fear is the Key b) Puppet on a Chain
c) Caravan to Vaccares d) Breakheart Pass

2) Which film featured him as Sherlock Holmes' sidekick and biographer, Dr. John Watson?
a) Without a Clue b) The Return of the World's Greatest Detective c) The Sign of Four d) The Adventures of Sherlock Holmes' Smarter Brother

3) William Snow (Ben Kingsley) and Neara Duncan (Glenda Jackson) devise a daring plan to free captive turtles at London Zoo in a 1985 comedy drama scripted by Harold Pinter. Name the title.
a) Turtle Beach b) The Voice of the Turtle
c) Turtle Diary d) Like a Turtle on its Back

KEVIN KLINE (1947)

1) In which 1990 comedy are hitmen Marlon and Harlan (Keanu Reeves and William Hurt) hired to murder womanizing pizzeria owner Joey Boca (Kevin Kline)?
a) I Love You to Death b) Soapdish
c) Consenting Adults d) The January Man

2) What biopic involved him portraying Douglas Fairbanks?
a) Valentino b) Star! c) Marlene d) Chaplin

3) Who was Dave Kovic (Kevin Kline) employed to impersonate in the 1993 comedy, **Dave**?
a) the U.S. President b) a rock star
c) a nuclear scientist d) a T.V. weatherman

ALAN LADD (1913 - 1964)

1) After years in minor roles he rocketed to fame in 1942 in an adaptation of a Graham Greene novel. Name the film.
a) The Fugitive b) Confidential Agent
c) This Gun For Hire d) Short Cut to Hell

2) Beautiful blonde, Joyce Harwood, comes to the aid of Navy pilot, Johnny Morrison, after he is suspected of murdering his adulterous wife in the 1946 mystery, **The Blue Dahlia**. Who portrayed Joyce?
a) Gloria Grahame b) Dorothy Lamour
c) Bonita Granville d) Veronica Lake

3) With which 1954 adventure do you associate him meeting King Arthur?
a) The Black Knight b) Siege of the Saxons
c) Against All Flags d) Prince Valiant

HEDY LAMARR
(Hedwig Kiesler 1913 - 2000)

1) Name the 1933 Czechoslovakian drama, directed by Gustav Machaty, which was notorious in its day for its explicit nude scenes featuring a young Hedy Kiesler?
a) Seduction b) Nocturno c) Ecstasy d) Jealousy

2) In 1949 she played the title role of Delilah in Cecil B. De Mille's **Samson and Delilah**. Who portrayed Samson?
a) Jock Mahoney b) Victor Mature
c) Russ Tamblyn d) Cornel Wilde

3) In which 1951 spy comedy does she meet Peanuts White (Bob Hope) masquerading as a spy in Tangiers with one million dollars in his money belt?
a) My Favorite Spy b) Never Say Die
c) Spy in Your Eye d) Road to Morocco

CHRISTOPHER LAMBERT
(1957 -)

1) Name the first English word he is taught to pronounce by the Belgian explorer, Captain D'Arnot (Ian Holm), in **Greystoke: The Legend of Tarzan, Lord of the Apes** (1984).
a) father b) mirror c) razor d) river

The Movie Quiz Companion

2) Which 1985 crime drama, directed by Luc Besson, won him a French Cesar for Best Actor?
a) Atlantis b) Nikita c) The Big Blue d) Subway

3) In 1995 he played Rayden, a god from the Outworld. Name the film.
a) Highlander b) Mortal Kombat
c) Fortress d) The Hunted

DOROTHY LAMOUR
(Mary Slaton 1914 - 1996)

1) Which 'Road' film featured Dorothy Lamour, Bing Crosby and Bob Hope singing 'Moonlight Becomes You' with each other's voices?
a) Road to Morocco
b) Road to Singapore
c) Road to Utopia
d) Road to Zanzibar

2) In a 'Road' film, the Hope and Crosby characters ask her to hide them from gangsters, and after listening to them re-capping the plot so far she replies, "OK, boys, I'll hide you." "From the gangsters?" they ask, "No. From the critics." What was the film?
a) Road to Rio
b) Road to Hong Kong
c) Road to Bali
d) Road to Morocco

3) Name the 1952 circus drama in which she played an aerialist who actually swings above the audience on a rope and hung from a metal ring by her teeth.
a) The Greatest Show on Earth
b) The Big Show
c) Man on a Tightrope
d) The Big Circus

BURT LANCASTER (1913 - 1994)

1) A former circus acrobat, Burt Lancaster made his film debut as an ex-prizefighter named 'the Swede' in a 1946 film noir directed by Robert Siodmak. Name the title.
a) Criss Cross b) Conflict
c) Cry of the City d) The Killers

2) In 1963 he portrayed Prince Don Fabrizio Salina, an Italian aristocrat facing up to the realities of Italy's unification in 1860 Sicily. Name the film, which was based on Giuseppe di Lampedusa's novel.
a) Twilight's Last Gleaming b) 1900
c) Seperate But Equal d) The Leopard

3) Which 1963 mystery, directed by John Huston, featured Burt Lancaster portraying a woman?
a) Reflections in a Golden Eye b) The List of Adrian Messenger c) Myra Breckinridge
d) Moulin Rouge

JESSICA LANGE (1949 -)

1) In which film does she share a bed with her friend, Dorothy, whom she suspects as being a lesbian?
a) Frances b) Blue Sky
c) Crimes of the Heart d) Tootsie

2) She made her film debut in a 1976 remake of a 1930s Hollywood classic. Name the title.

a) Mr. Smith Goes to Washington b) The Hunchback of Notre Dame c) King Kong
d) Great Expectations

3) In 1989 she portrayed a criminal attorney who had to defend her own father in court in **Music Box**. What crime was her father accused of?
a) murder b) rape
c) Nazi war crimes d) espionage

MARIO LANZA
(Alfred Arnold Coccozza 1921 - 1959)

1) The star of the 1954 musical, **The Student Prince**, had his voice dubbed by Mario Lanza. Who was he?
a) Edmund Purdom b) Danny Kaye
c) Jeff Chandler d) Fred MacMurray

2) Which film featured him as a fisherman who becomes an opera star with songs such as 'Be My Love', 'The Bayou Lullaby' and 'Boom Biddy Boom Boom'?
a) The Toast of New Orleans b) Serenade
c) The Great Caruso d) That Midnight Kiss

3) In which 1959 film does he fall in love with deaf girl Gloria De Vadnuz (Zsa Zsa Gabr) on the Isle of Capri?
a) Seven Hills of Rome b) Because You're Mine
c) Napoli Bride d) For the First Time

CHARLES LAUGHTON
(1899 - 1962)

1) His first Hollywood movie was a 1932 horror film directed by James Whale. Name the title.
a) Blue Bottles b) The Old Dark House
c) The Invisible Man d) The Kiss Before the Mirror

2) In which film does he utter the memorable line, "The things I've done for England"?
a) The Private Life of Henry VIII b) If I Had a Million c) Payment Deferred d) Mutiny on the Bounty

3) Which film features Norma Shearer as his bedridden daughter?
a) The Tuttles of Tahiti b) Jamaica Inn
c) Rembrandt d) The Barretts of Wimpole Street

LAUREL & HARDY
(Arthur Stanley Jefferson 1890 - 1965
Norvell Hardy 1892 - 1957)

1) What 1937 film involved Stan imitating Claudette Colbert's showing a shapely leg hitchhiking technique in **It Happened One Night**?
a) Way Out West b) Bonnie Scotland
c) Our Relations d) The Bohemian Girl

2) Which film contains the following dialogue:

Stan (answering the 'phone): "Hello? (pause) It sure is."
Ollie : "Well, who was it?"
Stan : "Oh, some fella having a joke... I said 'Hello' and the guy said 'It's a long-distance from Atlanta, Georgia, and I said 'It sure is'..."
Ollie :"I wish there was a way to put a stop to those practical jokers!"
a) Dirty Work b) The Flying Deuces
c) The Fixer-Uppers d) Laughing Gravy

3) Name the 1932 film which won an Oscar for 'Best Live-Action Short Subject, in which Stan kicks a nursemaid (in the rear), who informs a nearby policeman she has just been kicked "right in the middle of my daily duties"?
a) The Music Box b) Saps at Sea
c) Our Wife d) Sons of the Desert

BRUCE LEE
(Lee Yeun Kam 1941 - 1973)

1) Name the 1969 Raymond Chandler mystery in which he co-starred with James Garner.
a) Farewell, My Lovely b) The Long Goodbye
c) The Big Sleep d) Marlowe

2) Lee died during the making of a 1978 action thriller, directed by Robert Clouse. Name the title.
a) Marlowe b) Enter the Dragon
c) The Wrecking Crew d) Game of Death

3) The untimely death of Bruce Lee elevated him into a cult figure. What was the cause of his death?
a) cerebral oedema
b) a heart attack
c) an asthma attack
d) lung cancer

CHRISTOPHER LEE (1922 -)

1) It was his portrayal of **Dracula** (1958) and its many sequels, which eventually brought him screen success. This was a role he initially enjoyed, but he became increasingly dissatisfied with the deteriorating quality of its sequels. How many sequels were there?
a) six b) seven c) eight d) nine

2) In 1998 he maintained this film was the best he'd ever made, describing it as: "... one of the most remarkable films I think probably ever made." Name the title.
a) The Magic Christian b) The Man With the Golden Gun c) The Wicker Man d) 1941

3) With which 1959 Hammer mystery do you associate the disappearance of one of his boots from his hotel room?
a) The Devil Rides Out b) The Hound of the Baskervilles c) The Mummy d) The Man Who Could Cheat Death

JANET LEIGH
(Jeanette Helen Morrison 1927 -)

1) In 1954 she starred opposite her then husband in **The Black Shield of Falworth**. Who was he?
a) Van Johnson
b) David Farrar
c) Gary Cooper
d) Tony Curtis

The Movie Quiz Companion

2) Janet Leigh was "discovered" by a Hollywood star who had spotted a photograph of her and she was duly signed up by MGM in 1946. Name the star.
a) Rita Hayworth b) Norma Shearer
c) Lana Turner d) Jane Russell

3) In which 1962 political thriller, directed by John Frankenheimer, did she portray a woman who meets brainwashed Bennett Marco (Frank Sinatra) on a train and later falls in love with him?
a) The Manchurian Candidate b) Kings Go Forth
c) Never So Far d) Seven Days in May

VIVIEN LEIGH
(Vivien Mary Hartley 1913 - 1967)

1) In 1936 she met and fell in love with Laurence Olivier while making a historical drama directed by William K. Howard. Name the title.
a) Fire Over England
b) Wuthering Heights
c) Lady Hamilton
d) Pride and Prejudice

2) With which film do you associate dancer Myra Lester (Vivien Leigh) giving Captain Roy Cronin her lucky charm which he keeps on his person long after her death?
a) A Yank at Oxford
b) 21 Days
c) Dark Journey
d) Waterloo Bridge

3) In 1946 she played the title role in Gabriel Pascal's historical drama, **Caesar and Cleopatra**. Who portrayed Caesar?
a) Stewart Granger
b) Laurence Olivier
c) Claude Rains
d) Raymond Massey

JACK LEMMON (1925 - 2001)

1) In 1955 he portrayed Ensign Pulver (a role for which he won a Best Supporting Oscar) aboard a WWII cargo ship captained by James Cagney. Name the film.
a) It Should Happen to You
b) Mister Roberts
c) Fire Down Below
d) Operation Mad Ball

2) With which film do you associate Felix Ungar leaving little notes on Oscar Madison's pillow informing him, amongst other things, that they are out of corn flakes?
a) The Odd Couple
b) Buddy Buddy
c) The Out of Towners
d) Grumpy Old Men

3) Insurance clerk, C.C. Baxter (Jack Lemmon) cooks spaghetti for elevator operator Fran Kubelik in Billy Wilder's 1960 comedy drama, **The Apartment**. Who was she?
a) Shirley MacLaine
b) Debbie Reynolds
c) Lee Remick d) Doris Day

JERRY LEWIS
(Joseph Levitch 1926 -)

1) Best known on the screen for his pairing with Dean Martin with whom he made 16 films. Name the title of their 1949 debut.
a) My Friend Irma b) The Caddy
c) The Stooge d) Sailor Beware

2) Name the title character he portrayed in a 1959 musical version of Al Capp's comic strip.
a) Mister Gilfeather b) Count Screwloose
c) Li'l Abner d) Joe Palooka

3) In 1995 Jerry Lewis played famous comedian, George Fawkes, whose son Tommy tries to emulate his success, but fails and returns to his Blackpool roots for inspiration. Name the title.
a) Funny Bones b) Scared Stiff
c) Mr. Saturday Night d) Slapstick (Of Another Kind)

CHRISTOPHER LLOYD (1938 -)

1) In which film does he devise a lethal concoction of turpentine, acetone and benzine known as 'The Dip'?
a) Suburban Commando b) The Addams Family
c) Back to the Future d) Who Framed Roger Rabbit

2) Which 1975 film featured him as an insane asylum inmate named Taber?

hope witchcraft demons homely

Performers

a) *One Flew Over the Cuckoo's Nest* b) *The Fifth Floor* c) *The Dream Team* d) *Crazy People*

3) In 1995 he played 'Pieces', a porno projectionist suffering from leprosy whose body parts frequently fall off. Name the film.
a) *Things to do in Denver When You're Dead*
b) *Walk Like a Man* c) *Eight Men Out* d) *Track 29*

HAROLD LLOYD (1893 - 1971)

1) What was he trying to save from extinction in the 1928 comedy, **Speedy**?
a) NYC's last horse-drawn trolley b) NYC's last gas lamp post c) NYC's last Brooklyn ferry d) NYC's last silent movie theatre

2) Name the 1936 Harold Lloyd film which was remade as **The Kid From Brooklyn** with Danny Kaye.
a) *The Milky Way* b) *The Kid Brother*
c) *Feet First* d) *The Cat's Paw*

3) With which film do you associate his climbing the side of a building as a publicity stunt after the original "human fly" employed to do the stunt is arrested?
a) *Hot Water* b) *Girl Shy*
c) *Safety Last* d) *Why Worry*?

MARGARET LOCKWOOD (1916 - 1990)

1) With which film do you associate Iris Henderson (Margaret Lockwood) telling friends: "I've been everywhere and done everything - what's left for me except marriage?"?
a) *The Man in Grey* b) *The Lady Vanishes*
c) *A Girl Must Live* d) *Trent's Last Case*

2) Who portrayed her highway-robbing partner-in-crime in the 1945 historical romp, **The Wicked Lady**?
a) Dennis Price b) Michael Rennie
c) Stewart Granger d) James Mason

3) What 1940 thriller involved her being allowed to escape from a concentration camp in the hope that she would lead the Nazis to her scientist father?
a) *Night Train to Munich* b) *Cast a Dark Shadow*
c) *Highly Dangerous* d) *Hungry Hill*

CAROLE LOMBARD (Jane Peters 1908 - 1942)

1) Carole Lombard's career was at its peak when she died in a plane crash aged only thirty-three. Name her actor husband at the time of her death.
a) George Raft b) Fredric March
c) Clark Gable d) Joel McCrea

2) In which classic 1937 William Wellman comedy was she supposedly dying from radium poisoning?
a) *Nothing Sacred* b) *In Name Only*
c) *True Confession* d) *To Be or Not to Be*

3) In the 1936 screwball comedy, **My Man Godfrey**, she wins the 'Find the Forgotten Man' contest. Who portrayed the "forgotten" hobo Godfrey?
a) Ray Milland b) Jack Oakie
c) Randolph Scott d) William Powell

SOPHIA LOREN (Sofia Scicolone 1934 -)

1) Producer (and future husband) Carlo Ponti was responsible for discovering and kick-starting her screen career in 1951. Where did he first encounter her?
a) *standing in a bus queue* b) *at a party with her head down the toilet* c) *participating in a beauty contest* d) *sitting in a pavement cafe*

2) Name the title of the film, directed by Vittorio De Sica, which won her a Best Actress Oscar for her portrayal of an Italian mother who is raped by Moroccan soldiers during WWII.
a) *The Key* b) *The Black Orchid*
c) *Five Miles to Midnight* d) *Two Women*

223

The Movie Quiz Companion

3) Who portrayed the destitute Indian doctor she falls for in Anthony Asquith's 1960 comedy, **The Millionairess**?
a) Maurice Chevalier b) David Niven
c) Peter Sellers d) Anthony Quinn

PETER LORRE
(Ladislav Loewenstein 1904 - 1964)

1) Obsessed with Yvonne Orlac (Frances Drake), noteworthy surgeon Dr. Gogol (Peter Lorre) agrees to graft new hands onto her injured concert pianist husband. Who was the previous owner of her husband's new hands?
a) a knife-wielding murderer b) a rapist
c) a strangler d) an axe murderer

2) Name the Hitchcock mystery in which Hungarian-born Lorre made his English-language debut.
a) The Man Who Knew Too Much b) Sabotage
c) Secret Agent d) The Skin Game

3) In which 1941 film did he first appear with Sydney Greenstreet?
a) Passage to Marseille b) The Maltese Falcon
c) Casablanca d) The Mask of Dimitrios

MYRNA LOY
(Myrna Williams 1905 - 1993)

1) Name the series which cast her with William Powell, as sleuths Nora and Nick Charles (and dog Asta), in which she achieves stardom in a series of polished dramas and sharp scripts with lines such as:
Nick - "Oh, I'm a hero? I was shot twice in The Tribune."
Nora - "I reckon you were shot five times in the tabloids."
Nick - "It's not true. He didn't come anywhere near my tabloids."
a) The Saint b) Ellery Queen
c) The Falcon d) The Thin Man

2) With which 1946 film, directed by William Wyler, do you associate her adjusting to the reality of having her husband Al back home safely after WWII?
a) Three Came Home b) The Best Years of Our Lives c) So Ends Our Night d) The Bamboo Prison

3) Name the actor who played pilot Jim Lane who is forced to do an emergency landing on Ann Barton's (Myrna Loy) Kansas farm in Victor Fleming's 1938 drama, **Test Pilot**.
a) Spencer Tracy b) Dick Powell
c) James Stewart d) Clark Gable

BELA LUGOSI
(Béla Blasko 1882 - 1956)

1) Such was the success of his vampire persona that he began parodying his own image to the extent of giving media interviews from an open coffin. When he died in 1956 what was buried beside him in his real coffin?
a) a wooden stake b) a gun loaded with silver bullets c) his Dracula cape d) a crucifix

2) For what 1939 comedy did he portray Soviet Commissar Razinin?
a) Ninotchka
b) Hollywood Hotel
c) Comrade X
d) You Can't Take it With You

3) Bela Lugosi co-starred with Boris Karloff in many classic horror films. Name the film in which they first appeared together in 1934.
a) The Black Cat b) The Raven
c) Son of Frankenstein d) The Invisible Ray

IDA LUPINO (1918 - 1995)

1) In 1939 she portrayed Cockney model, Bessie Broke, who destroys painter Dick Heldar's (Ronald Colman) masterpiece by throwing turpentine at it in a film adapted from a Rudyard Kipling novel. Name the title.
a) The Light That Failed b) Paris Model
c) Portrait of Jennie d) Soldiers Three

2) In which film did she portray gangster Roy Earle's moll, Marie Garson?
a) The Sea of Grass b) High Sierra
c) The Hard Way d) Outrage

3) Lana Carlsen (Ida Lupino) framed truck driver Joe Fabrini for the murder of her husband in Raoul Walsh's 1940 cult classic, **They Drive By Night**. Who was he?
a) Humphrey Bogart b) Spencer Tracy
c) George Raft d) Clark Gable

ANDIE MACDOWELL (1958 -)

1) With which 1989 drama do you associate her screen husband's old college buddy, Graham (James Spader), confessing his impotence to her?

a) Deception b) Green Card
c) St. Elmo's Fire d) Sex, Lies & Videotape

2) For what film did she portray a TV producer who supervises an outside broadcast in a town called Punxsutawney?
a) Unstrung Heroes b) Groundhog Day
c) The Player d) Short Cuts

3) What connection can you make between Andie MacDowell and Maureen O'Sullivan?
a) MacDowell is O'Sullivan's daughter b) they have both played Tarzan's Jane c) they were both 'discovered' by director Frank Borzage d) they were born in the same house

SHIRLEY MACLAINE (1934 -)

1) Name the 1955 film, directed by Alfred Hitchcock, in which she made her screen debut.
a) The Trouble With Harry
b) I Confess
c) To Catch a Thief
d) The Man Who Knew Too Much

2) With which 1958 drama, directed by Vincente Minnelli, do you associate her as the sexually available floozy, Ginny Moorhead, who is in love with unsuccessful novelist, Dave Hirsh (Frank Sinatra)?
a) Kings Go Forth
b) Pal Joey
c) A Hole in the Head
d) Some Came Running

3) Name the James L. Brooks comedy drama which won her a Best Actress Oscar.
a) Terms of Endearment
b) The Apartment
c) Irma La Douce
d) Sweet Charity

FRED MACMURRAY (1908 - 1991)

1) In which film does he ask femme fatale, Phyllis, what is engraved on her anklet?
a) Alice Adams b) The Gilded Lily
c) Double Indemnity d) The Lady is Willing

2) In 1935 he falls in love with a character played by Katherine Hepburn in an adaptation of a Pulitzer Prize-winning Booth Tarkington novel. Name the film.
a) Tiger Rose b) Maid of Salem
c) The Gilded Lily d) Alice Adams

3) Name the 1961 comedy in which his character invents flubber.
a) The Nutty Professor b) The Absent Minded Professor c) Professor Beware d) Bon Voyage Professor

MADONNA (Madonna Ciccone 1958 -)

1) What 1990 film featured her singing the Oscar-winning Stephen Sondheim song 'Sooner or Later (I Always Get My Man)'?
a) Shadows and Fog b) Desperately Seeking Susan
c) Vision Quest d) Dick Tracy

2) Name the film which documented her 1990 Blond Ambition tour of Japan, Europe and the U.S.A.
a) Truth or Dare b) At Close Range
c) Body of Evidence d) With Honors

3) In which film does she play baseball with Tom Hanks?
a) A League of Their Own b) Richie Rich
c) The Babe d) Little Big League

JOHN MALKOVICH (1953 -)

1) Which silent film director does he portray in **Shadow of the Vampire** (2001)?
a) Paul Leni b) Abel Gance
c) F.W. Murnau d) Erich von Stroheim

2) In 1984 he portrayed world weary war photographer, Al Rockoff, who tries unsuccessfully to forge a passport for translator Dith Pran before his inevitable capture at the hands of the Khmer Rouge. Name the film.
a) Heaven and Earth b) Go Tell the Spartans
c) The Killing Fields d) Uncommon Valour

3) With which Woody Allen film do you associate him having a sword swallowing girlfriend named Irmy (Mia Farrow)?
a) Shadows and Fog b) Husbands and Wives
c) Bullets Over Broadway d) Mighty Aphrodite

FREDRIC MARCH (Fredric Bickel 1897 - 1975)

The Movie Quiz Companion

1) With which 1937 drama do you associate him marrying Esther Blodgett (Janet Gaynor)?
a) Smilin' Through b) A Star is Born
c) All of Me d) Strangers in Love

2) Name the romantic biopic which featured him as the poet Robert Browning?
a) When Tomorrow Comes b) The Blood of a Poet
c) Love Affair d) The Barretts of Wimpole Street

3) In 1935 he portrayed Jean Valjean who steals a loaf of bread and is sentenced to ten years hard labour. Name the film.
a) We Live Again b) The Road to Glory
c) The Dark Angel d) Les Miserables

DEAN MARTIN
(Dino Crocetti 1917 - 1995)

1) In 1959 he portrayed a town drunk named 'Dude' who reclaims his self respect through sobriety. Name the film.
a) The Sons of Katie Elder
b) The Stooge
c) Rio Bravo
d) Pardners

2) Name the John Sturges western he starred in which was a wild west version of the old classic adventure yarn, **Gunga Din** (1939).
a) The Ambushers
b) Sergeants Three
c) Who's Got the Action
d) Four For Texas

3) Which 1966 spy comedy featured him as secret agent Matt Helm?
a) The Silencers
b) Murderer's Row
c) Scared Stiff
d) All in a Night's Work

STEVE MARTIN (1945 -)

1) With which film do you associate his being raised by a family of poor black deep south sharecroppers?
a) The Jerk b) The Muppet Movie
c) All of Me d) The Lonely Guy

2) In which film does his wife Joan (Jessica Harper) nurture his peculiar fetish and put lipstick on her nipples?
a) Grand Canyon b) My Blue Heaven
c) Leap of Faith d) Pennies From Heaven

3) Name the 1994 drama, based on George Eliot's *Silas Marner*, about a reclusive miser who communicates with nobody, and lives only for his hoard of gold coins until an orphaned child walks into his life.
a) A Simple Twist of Fate b) The Kids Are Alright
c) Parenthood d) Mixed Nuts

LEE MARVIN (1924 - 1987)

1) What film won him a Best Actor Oscar in 1965?
a) The Dirty Dozen b) The Killers
c) Point Blank d) Cat Ballou

2) Which film features Tom Doniphon shooting him dead in the town of Shinbone?
a) Gun Fury b) Paint Your Wagon
c) The Man Who Shot Liberty Valance
d) The Duel at Silver Creek

3) In which film does he meet the disabled, but tough, no-nonsense war veteran John J. MacReedy?
a) Donovan's Reef b) The Big Heat
c) The Caine Mutiny d) Bad Day at Black Rock

THE MARX BROTHERS
(Chico 1886-1961, Harpo 1888-1964, Groucho 1890-1977, & Zeppo 1901-1979)

1) Name the title of the film with which they made their screen debut in 1929.
a) The Cocoanuts b) Horse Feathers
c) Animal Crackers d) Monkey Business

2) She appeared as Groucho's comic foil in seven Marx Brother's films. Who was she?
a) Margaret Whitton b) Margaret Lacey
c) Margaret Avery d) Margaret Dumont

3) Arguing over a contract Groucho says: "That is what we call a sanity clause", to which Chico replies, "You can't fool me! There ain't no Sanity Claus!". Name the film.
a) A Night at the Opera b) A Day at the Races
c) Duck Soup c) A Night in Casablanca

Performers

JAMES MASON (1909 - 1984)

1) At the height of his career his fan mail was averaging 5,000 letters a week. Name the costume drama which shot him to stardom in 1943.
a) *The Man in Grey* b) *The Painted Desert*
c) *Fire Over England* d) *The Wicked Lady*

2) In which Laurel and Hardy film does he feature as an "Anxious Patron" in 1937?
a) *Swiss Miss* b) *Block-Heads*
c) *Our Relations* d) *Way Out West*

3) In **Pandora and the Flying Dutchman** (1951) he plays a 17th century sea captain who has been condemned to sail the oceans of the world until he finds a woman willing to die for love. After three hundred years he finds salvation in Pandora Reynolds. Who was she?
a) *Jennifer Jones* b) *Claire Trevor*
c) *Ava Gardner* d) *Vivien Leigh*

RAYMOND MASSEY (1896 - 1983)

1) Which film features him as John Cabal, leader of the New World?
a) *Reap the Wild Wind* b) *The Great Imposter*
c) *Under the Red Robe* d) *Things to Come*

2) Raymond Massey earned an Oscar nomination for his portrayal of Lincoln in the 1940 biopic, **Abe Lincoln in Illinois**. He portrayed Lincoln again in a 1962 western directed by Henry Hathaway, John Ford, George Marshall and Richard Thorpe. Name the title.
a) *How the West Was Won* b) *The Plainsman*
c) *The Big Country* d) *Mackenna's Gold*

3) As Black Michael he attempted to thwart his brother, Prince Rudolf's coronation with the help of the villainous Rupert of Hentzau. Name the film.
a) *The Prince and the Pauper* b) *The Queen's Guards* c) *A Royal Scandal* d) *The Prisoner of Zenda*.

WALTER MATTHAU (Walter Matuschanskayasky 1920 - 2000)

1) Name the comedy the following dialogue comes from:
Al Lewis - "You know what your trouble was Willy? You always took the jobs too seriously. It was just jokes. We did comedy on the stage for 43 years. I don't think you enjoyed it once."
Willy Clarke (Matthau) - "If I was there to enjoy it I would buy a ticket."
a) *Grumpy Old Men* b) *The Sunshine Boys*
c) *Hello, Dolly* d) *Goodbye Charlie*

2) In which 1958 Elvis musical did he star as local crime honcho, Maxie Fields?
a) *King Creole* b) *Frankie and Johnny*
c) *Viva Las Vegas* d) *Kid Galahad*

3) In which film did Lt. Garber (Matthau) suggest the following solution to a hijacking: "They're gonna get away by asking every man, woman and child in New York City to close their eyes and count to a hundred."?
a) *Charley Varrick* b) *The Delta Force*
c) *The Taking of Pelham One Two Three*
d) *Passenger 57*

VICTOR MATURE (1915 -1999)

1) In 1954 he starred in a sequel to **The Robe**, as a slave hounded by the mad Emperor Caligula in his search for the holy robe. Name the title.
a) *Demetrius and the Gladiators*
b) *Samson and Delilah*
c) *The Greatest Story Ever Told*
d) *Quo Vadis?*

2) With which 1966 Vittorio De Sica comedy do you associate Victor Mature parodying himself as has-been star Tony Powell?
a) *Marriage Italian-Style*
b) *After the Fox*
c) *Times Gone By*
d) *Miracle in Milan*

3) In which 1947 crime thriller does thief Nick Bianco (Victor Mature) agree to act as a police informer to help bring homicidal maniac, portrayed by Richard Widmark, to justice?
a) *Kiss of Death*
b) *Violent Saturday*
c) *Betrayed*
d) *Affair With a Stranger*

The Movie Quiz Companion

JOEL McCREA (1905 - 1990)

1) Which 1941 film features him as a successful movie director with a string of popular hits, including 'Ants in Your Pants' and 'So Long, Sarong'?
a) They Shall Have Music b) Bed of Roses
c) Sullivan's Travels d) Splendor

2) Tom (an inventor) and Gerry Jeffers (Joel McCrea and Claudette Colbert) are broke. Gerry decides to divorce Tom, marry a rich husband and use his money to finance Tom's inventions. Name this 1942 comedy directed by Preston Sturges.
a) Christmas in July b) The Palm Beach Story
c) The Great Moment d) The Great McGinty

3) Struggling architect Dave (Joel McCrea) is desperate to leave the slum and falls for rich girl Kay, who offers him a paid European vacation in William Wyler's 1937 crime thriller, **Dead End**. Who portrayed Kay?
a) Sylvia Sidney b) Claire Trevor
c) Constance Bennett d) Wendy Barrie

MALCOLM McDOWELL (1943 -)

1) Name the Ken Loach drama in which he made his screen debut in 1967.
a) Poor Cow
b) Wednesday's Child
c) Kes d) The Gamekeeper

2) With which film do you associate him threatening: "One man can change the world with a bullet in the right place"?
a) If... b) The Player
c) Royal Flash d) O Lucky Man!

3) Which Malcolm McDowell film was critic Roger Ebert commenting on when he wrote, "... sickening, utterly worthless, shameful trash... This film is not only garbage on an artistic level, but it is also garbage on the crude and base level where it no doubt hopes to find its audience..."?
a) A Clockwork Orange b) Caligula
c) The Caller d) Tank Girl

RODDY McDOWALL (1928 - 1998)

1) In which film does his father sell his pet dog to the Duke of Rudling?
a) Challenge to Lassie b) Son of Lassie
c) Courage of Lassie d) Lassie Come Home

2) What 1944 film cast him as Francis Chisholm, a young boy who grows up to become a priest (played by Gregory Peck) who devotes most of his life to missionary work in China?
a) Yellow Sands b) The Keys of the Kingdom
c) Oil For the Lamps of China d) The Good Earth

3) In the final scene of John Ford's **How Green Was My Valley** (1941) where Huw Morgan (Roddy McDowall) is walking with his father, Irving Pichel's voice informs us that: "Men like my father cannot die. They remain a living truth in my mind. They are with me still - real in memory as they were real in flesh. Loving and beloved forever. How green was my valley, then." Who portrayed Huw's father?
a) Emlyn Williams b) Barry Fitzgerald
c) Donald Crisp d) Edmund Gwenn

IAN McKELLEN (1939 -)

1) For what 1995 drama does he propose to a widow at her husband's funeral, offering her a ring for her finger lubricated with his own spit?
a) Six Degrees of Separation
b) Restoration
c) Richard III
d) Zina

2) They may be at opposite ends of the acting spectrum, but Ian McKellen once appeared in an Arnold Schwarzenegger action movie.
Name the title.
a) Last Action Hero
b) Total Recall
c) The Running Man
d) True Lies

3) Which 1995 comedy features him as the zealous preacher, Amos Starkadder?
a) The Ballad of Little Jo
b) Windmills of the Gods
c) Plenty
d) Cold Comfort Farm

228

famed oriental hated fat   **Performers**

VICTOR McLAGLEN
(1886 - 1959)

1) He spent most of his career playing brutish but soft-hearted Irishmen, rarely betraying his real roots. What nationality was he?
a) South African b) English
c) Australian d) Dutch

2) One of director John Ford's stock company of actors, he made frequent appearances in his westerns. In which western was Capt. Nathan Brittles (John Wayne) constantly sniffing the breath of Sgt. Quincannon (Victor McLaglen) for signs of alcohol consumption?
a) Fort Apache b) Rio Grande
c) She Wore a Yellow Ribbon d) The Horse Soldiers

3) In 1935 he was awarded a Best Actor Oscar for his portrayal of an Irish drunkard. Name the film.
a) The Informer
b) Duffy's Tavern
c) The Plough and the Stars
d) Juno and the Paycock

STEVE McQUEEN
(Terence Steven McQueen
1930 - 1980)

1) He made his screen debut in a 1956 biopic based on the autobiography of boxer Rocky Graziano. Name the film.
a) The World in His Arms b) Night and the City
c) The Harder They Fall d) Somebody Up There Likes Me

2) With which film do you associate him tracking down the men who killed his parents when he was only a child?
a) The Cincinnati Kid b) Junior Bonner
c) Nevada Smith d) The Hunter

3) In which film did he portray a U.S. sailor aboard a gunboat on the Yangtze in 1926?
a) The War Lover b) The Sand Pebbles
c) 55 Days at Peking d) Hell is For Heroes

BETTE MIDLER (1945 -)

1) Name the 1991 comedy in which she co-starred with Woody Allen.
a) Shadows and Fog b) Bullets Over Broadway
c) Mighty Aphrodite d) Scenes From a Mall

2) Barbara Stone (Bette Midler) is kidnapped in the 1986 comedy, **Ruthless People**, after which her husband Sam tries to buy her back at a discount rate. Who was he?
a) Danny De Vito b) Nick Nolte
c) George Segal d) James Caan

3) What 1979 musical did she star in which was said (unofficially) to mirror the tragic life of Janis Joplin?
a) Divine Madness! b) The Rose
c) Gypsy d) Outrageous Fortune

RAY MILLAND
(Reginald Alfred Truscott-Jones
1905 - 1986)

1) With which 1939 film, directed by William Wellman, do you associate him giving his brother a Viking's funeral?
a) Three Brave Men b) Beau Geste
c) Till We Meet Again d) Bugles in the Afternoon

2) In 1937 he played a no-nonsense English detective who fought clean and tackled villains with a square blow to the jaw accompanied by the phrases, "you vile hound", "blackguard" and "conceited ass". Who was he?
a) Paul Temple b) Bulldog Drummond
c) Nick Carter d) The Saint

3) His greatest acting achievement, for which he won an Oscar, was in the role of the compulsive alcoholic and writer, Don Birnam in 1945. Name the title.
a) Reap the Wild Wind b) Untamed
c) The Lost Weekend d) Easy Living

229

The Movie Quiz Companion

a tensed foe

HAYLEY MILLS (1946 -)

1) The success of her 1959 screen debut secured her a five-year contract with Walt Disney. Name the title.
a) Tiger Bay b) The Moon-Spinners
c) The Daydreamer d) The Chalk Garden

2) What connection can you make between Hayley Mills and Mary Pickford?
a) both portrayed Pollyanna b) both were married to director Roy Boulting c) John Mills was Pickford's Godfather d) Mary Pickford recommended her to Walt Disney

3) Name the 1961 film she starred in which was adapted from her mother Mary Hayley Bell's novel.
a) Summer Magic b) The Family Way
c) The Parent Trap d) Whistle Down the Wind

JOHN MILLS
(Lewis Ernest Watts Mills 1908 -)

1) Peter Colley (John Mills), former pupil of Brookfield School, returned to his alma mater to say farewell to his old master before setting off for the trenches in a 1939 drama directed by Sam Wood. Name the title.
a) Goodbye, Mr. Chips
b) Tom Brown's Schooldays
c) The Browning Version
d) So Well Remembered

2) In which 1944 film does sailor Billy Mitchell (John Mills) ask Frank Gibbons (Robert Newton) for his daughter Queenie's (Kay Walsh) hand in marriage?
a) Dunkirk b) This Happy Breed
c) We Dive at Dawn d) Above Us the Waves

3) Name the 1960 drama, based on the novel by James Kennaway, which won him the Best Actor Award at the Venice Film Festival.
a) Colditz b) I Was Monty's Double
c) King Rat d) Tunes of Glory

ROBERT MITCHUM
(1917 - 1997)

1) Before he launched his screen career he was sentenced to 180 days on the Chatham County chain-gang from which he escaped by simply "walking away". What crime was he charged with?
a) trespassing on railroad property
b) drunk and disorderly
c) police assault
d) passing counterfeit bills

2) Why does gangster Whit Sterling (Kirk Douglas) hire him in Jacques Tourneur's 1947 mystery, **Out of the Past**?
a) to find his missing girlfriend
b) to kidnap a troublesome union leader
c) to fake his death
d) to murder his wife

3) Matt Calder (Robert Mitchum) rescues Kay Weston from a sinking raft in the 1954 western, **River of No Return**. Who was she?
a) Greer Garson
b) Marilyn Monroe
c) Loretta Young
d) Rita Hayworth

MARILYN MONROE
(Norma Jean Mortenson 1926 - 1962)

1) Which film features the following dialogue?:
 - "I come from this musical family. My mother was a piano teacher. My father was a conductor."
 - "Where did he conduct?"
 - "On the Baltimore-Ohio."
a) Niagara b) We're Not Married
c) Some Like it Hot d) The Seven Year Itch

2) In which musical comedy does off-Broadway actress, Amanda (Marilyn Monroe), attend night school to study geography?
a) Let's Make Love b) Love Happy
c) Gentlemen Prefer Blondes d) The Prince and the Showgirl

3) With which film do you associate her as saloon singer Cherie singing 'That Old Black Magic'?
a) River of No Return b) Let's Make Love
c) Bus Stop d) The Misfits

YVES MONTAND
(Ivo Livi 1921 - 1991)

1) In his first dramatic role in a 1952 film directed by Henri-Georges Clouzot, he portrayed a layabout who gets the chance to earn $2,000. Name the title.

eye thrill department Performers

a) Where the Hot Wind Blows b) The Red Inn
c) The Wages of Fear d) The Anatomy of Love

2) In 1960 he made a film with Marilyn Monroe which led to an off-screen affair. Name the film.
a) Bus Stop b) There's No Business Like Show Business c) The Seven Year Itch d) Let's Make Love

3) Name the 1969 political thriller he starred in as 'the deputy', which was based on the real-life killing of Gregorios Lambrakis, a Greek professor of medicine responsible for exposing government corruption.
a) The Confession b) Z
c) State of Siege d) The Fourth Protocol

DEMI MOORE
(Demi Guynes 1962 -)

1) Which 1984 comedy features her as Michael Caine's susceptible daughter, whose father has an affair with her teenage friend?
a) Blame it on Rio
b) About Last Night
c) No Small Affair
d) St. Elmo's Fire

2) Billionaire John Gage (Robert Redford) offers Mrs. Diana Murphy (Demi Moore) a million dollars to spend one night with him in **Indecent Proposal** (1993). Who portrayed her approving husband?
a) Donald Sutherland
b) Oliver Platt
c) John Cusak
d) Woody Harrelson

3) With which 1994 thriller do you associate her being sued for sexual harassment?
a) Disclosure
b) About Last Night
c) The Juror
d) The Seventh Sign

AGNES MOOREHEAD
(1906 - 1974)

1) In which 1951 musical, directed by George Sidney, did she portray Parthy Hawks?
a) Pal Joey b) Kiss Me Kate
c) Annie Get Your Gun d) Show Boat

2) For what film is her spoilt nephew, George (Tim Holt), forced to shut up the family house when the family fortune runs out and seek employment to support himself and his spinster Aunt Fanny (Agnes Moorehead)?
a) The Great Sinner b) The Magnificent Ambersons c) Mrs. Parkington d) Dragon Seed

3) What role did she play in Irwin Allen's 1957 historical fantasy, **The Story of Mankind**?
a) Florence Nightingale b) Nell Gwynn
c) Queen Elizabeth d) Joan of Arc

KENNETH MORE (1914 - 1982)

1) In 1956 he portrayed the legless airman, Douglas Bader, in Lewis Gilbert's biopic, **Reach for the Sky**. What caused the crash at Woodley Aerodrome which resulted in Bader losing both his legs?
a) engine failure
b) birds flying into the propeller
c) bravado aerobatics
d) enemy gunfire

2) Which film featured him as the Ghost of Christmas Present?
a) The Luckiest Man in the World b) Scrooged
c) A Christmas Carol d) Scrooge

3) In which film does he portray Kaiser Wilhelm II?
a) Oh! What a Lovely War b) The Yellow Balloon
c) Sink the Bismarck! d) Scott of the Antarctic

JEANNE MOREAU (1928 -)

1) With which 1965 drama do you associate her hiding Labiche (Burt Lancaster) from the Nazis?
a) The Victors b) Judgement at Nuremberg
c) Scorpio d) The Train

2) What role did she play in George Kaczender's adaptation of a Romain Gary novel - **Your Ticket is No Longer Valid**?
a) a gypsy dancer b) a Parisian brothel madam
c) an assassin d) a trapeze artist

3) For what 1961 drama does she portray a character who forms a ménage-à-trois with Oskar Werner and Henri Serre?
a) La Notte b) Eva
c) Demoniaque d) Jules et Jim

The Movie Quiz Companion

PAUL MUNI
(Muni Weisenfreund 1895 - 1967)

1) Name the 1932 film, directed by Mervin LeRoy, in which prison escapee James Allen (Paul Muni) risks visiting his girlfriend one last time in the film's final scene. "How do you live?" she pleads. From the shadows comes the frenzied reply: "I Steal!". Name the film.
a) The Fugitive Kind
b) They Made Me a Fugitive
c) I Am a Fugitive from a Chain Gang
d) Face of a Fugitive

2) In which 1939 biopic, directed by William Dieterle, did he portray the President of Mexico?
a) Juarez
b) The Last Angry Man
c) Mexican Hayride
d) The Scapegoat

3) His portrayal of a man who made one of the great discoveries of the 19th century won him a Best Actor Oscar in 1936. Name the film.
a) Edison the Man
b) The Story of Alexander Graham Bell
c) Dr. Ehrlich's Magic Bullet
d) The Story of Louis Pasteur

EDDIE MURPHY (1961 -)

1) Name the title of his 1982 feature debut as know-it-all ex-convict, Reggie Hammond.
a) 48hrs b) Hollywood Shuffle
c) Best Defense d) The Golden Child

2) With which film do you associate him being refused a room in a hotel, whereby he claims to be a correspondent from Rolling Stone and accuses the receptionist of racism?
a) Beverley Hills Cop b) The Distinguished Gentleman c) Vampire in Brooklyn d) Harlem Nights

3) Which film featured Eddie Murphy as Clarence the Barber, Saul the old Jew and a singer named Randy Watson?
a) Coming to America b) Trading Places
c) Beverley Hills Cop III d) Another 48hrs

BILL MURRAY (1950 -)

1) In which comedy does he tell his room-mate and out of work actor, Michael Dorsey (Dustin Hoffman): "Don't play hard to get"?
a) Ishtar
b) Madigan's Millions
c) Tootsie
d) John and Mary

2) Name the 1984 drama he starred in, based on a novel by Somerset Maugham, about a young man searching for the meaning of life in the aftermath of WWI.
a) Nothing Lasts Forever
b) Mad Dog and Glory
c) Stripes d) The Razor's Edge

3) Who or what was Bill Murray disguised as when he portrayed a New York bank robber in the 1990 comedy **Quick Change**?
a) a gorilla
b) a clown
c) a hot dog
d) a parking meter

LIAM NEESON (1952 -)

1) Liam Neeson made his screen debut in a 1981 film directed by John Boorman. Name the title.
a) Hope and Glory b) Exorcist II: the Heretic
c) Excalibur d) Angel

2) In 1995 he played the title role in a film on which critic Roger Ebert commented: "I can think of no higher compliment to the movie than that it awakened in me a desire to read [the] novel, although when I failed to find it on my shelves, I was able to live with the disappointment." Name the film.
a) Ethan Frome b) Darkman
c) Rob Roy d) Michael Collins

3) On whose novel was **Ethan Frome** (1993) based?
a) Paul Bowles b) Edith Wharton
c) Taylor Caldwell d) Truman Capote

PAUL NEWMAN (1925 -)

1) In which film does he eat fifty hard-boiled eggs?
a) Cool Hand Luke b) Blaze
c) Winning d) Silent Movie

2) Which film features him trying to persuade a transvestite not to jump off a building, delivering a baby, witnessing his colleagues committing murder and falling in love with a Puerto Rican nurse?

ninth mutating choir

Performers

a) Fort Apache, The Bronx b) The Secret War of Harry Frigg c) The Macintosh Man d) Absence of Malice

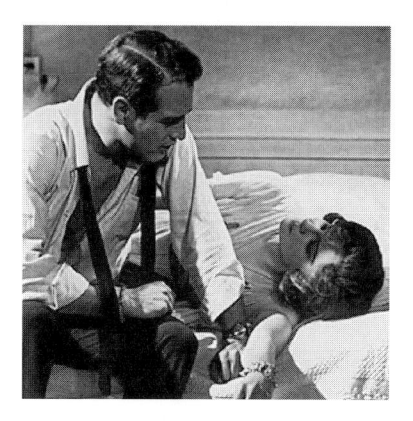

3) Chance Wayne (Paul Newman) had hoped his path to the silver screen lay with fading movie star Alexandra Del Lago (Geraldine Page), but disgusted by her slovenly behaviour, he hits her with some home truths, saying: "You know the big difference between people is not between the rich and the poor or good or evil. The biggest of all differences between people is between those that have had pleasure in love and those that haven't." Name the film.
a) The Prize b) Cat on a Hot Tin Roof
c) The Long Hot Summer d) Sweet Bird of Youth

JACK NICHOLSON (1937 -)

1) For what 1963 low-budget Roger Corman production, based on an Edgar Allan Poe poem, did he portray Rexford Bedlo?
a) The Pit and the Pendulum b) The Raven
c) A Bucket of Blood d) Tales of Terror

2) In which 1987 romantic comedy, directed by James L. Brooks, did he portray TV network anchorman, Bill Rorich?

a) Broadcast News b) Network
c) Goin' South d) Sneakers

3) Military policemen, Buddusky (Jack Nicholson) and Mulhall (Otis Young) are assigned to escort kleptomaniac and unworldly sailor, Meadows, to a naval prison but have lots of fun and frolics en route in **The Last Detail**. Who portrayed the unfortunate Meadows?
a) James Woods b) Will Patton
c) Timothy Bottoms d) Randy Quaid

LESLIE NIELSEN (1926 -)

1) What 1956 film involves him visiting Altair-4?
a) Dark Intruder
b) The Thing (From Another World)
c) See How They Run
d) Forbidden Planet

2) Lt. Frank Drebin (Leslie Neilsen) tries to prevent an assassination attempt on a well known public figure at a Dodgers home game in **The Naked Gun: From the Files of Police Squad** (1988). Who is the public figure?
a) Yasser Arafat
b) the Pope
c) Queen Elizabeth II
d) Elvis Presley

3) Which 1996 comedy features him as Agent WD-40?
a) Spy Hard
b) Rent-A-Kid
c) The Amsterdam Kill
d) Surf Ninjas

DAVID NIVEN (1910 - 1983)

1) David Niven was a great storyteller, but in his best-selling autobiographies, *The Moon's a Balloon* (1971) and *Bring on the Empty Horses* (1975), he never reveals his birthplace. Most movie reference books wrongly list it as Kirriemuir in Scotland. Where was he actually born?
a) Eastbourne b) Glasgow
c) Bognor Regis d) London

2) Name the film for which he won a Best Actor Oscar in 1958.
a) The Guns of Navarone b) Paper Tiger
c) Separate Tables d) The Way Ahead

3) What 1936 film connection can you make between David Niven and the poet Alfred, Lord Tennyson?
a) Dodsworth b) The Real Glory
c) The Prisoner of Zenda
d) The Charge of the Light Brigade

NICK NOLTE (1940 -)

1) In which 1996 crime drama does 1950s LA homicide cop, Hoover (Nick Nolte), inject a hoodlum with a drug overdose?
a) Mulholland Falls b) Extreme Prejudice
c) Another 48hrs d) I'll Do Anything

2) Which film features him as football coach, Tom Wingo, who pours out his painful past

to psychiatrist, Dr. Susan Lowenstein (Barbra Streisand)?
a) For Pete's Sake b) Nuts
c) The Main Event d) The Prince of Tides

3) Name the 1983 drama, set in Nicaragua, during the fall of the Somoza regime, which cast him as a photo journalist who fakes a photograph to aid the guerrillas.
a) Last Plane Out b) Walker
c) Under Fire d) I Love Trouble

MERLE OBERON
(Estelle Merle Oberon Thompson 1911 - 1979)

1) Throughout her life Merle Oberon denied her Eurasian origins. When she became a prolific actress, she passed her mother off as her servant. Listed in most film indexes as born in Hobart, Tasmania (the furthest away place she could think of), where was she actually born?
a) Shanghai
b) Rangoon
c) Bombay
d) Singapore

2) Name the director and producer who launched Merle Oberon's film career and married her in 1939.
a) Herbert Wilcox
b) Alexander Korda
c) Basil Wright
d) Anthony Asquith

3) With which 1933 film do you associate her being beheaded?
a) The Scarlet Pimpernel
b) A Tale of Two Cities
c) The Private Life of Henry the VIII
d) The Dark Angel

GARY OLDMAN (1958 -)

1) In 1987 he portrayed British playwright, Joe Orton, who was murdered by his male lover, in a film directed by Stephen Frears. Name the title.
a) Prick Up Your Ears b) Romeo is Bleeding
c) Meantime d) We Think the World of You

2) Who does Martin (Gary Oldman) try to convince Linda he is in **Track 29** (1988)?
a) her dead husband's twin b) her father
c) her brother d) her son

3) In 1990 he portrayed ex-Korea veteran, Emmett Foley, who was sent to **Chattahoochee**. What type of establishment was Chattahoochee?
a) an army boot camp b) a prison for the mentally ill c) a nuclear test site d) a Sioux Indian reservation

LAURENCE OLIVIER
(1907 - 1989)

1) He was married three times. His second wife was Vivien Leigh, from 1940 to 1960 and in 1961 he married actress Joan Plowright. He married his first actress wife in 1930. Who was she?
a) Kay Walsh
b) Jill Esmond
c) Constance Collier
d) Joan Greenwood

2) In which 1960 drama, directed by Tony Richardson, does Joan Plowright portray his understanding daughter, Jean, telling him that he is "dead behind the eyes"?
a) This Happy Breed b) Bunny Lake is Missing
c) Carrie d) The Entertainer

3) Olivier was badly injured making a film in the 1940s when a horseman smashed into a camera and gashed his lip, leaving him with a scar he would subsequently cover with a moustache. Name the film.
a) Henry V b) Wuthering Heights
c) That Hamilton Woman d) Hamlet

PETER O'TOOLE (1932 -)

1) In Peter Medak's 1972 comedy, the 13th Earl of Gurney (Harry Andrews) returns from the city and accidentally hangs himself leaving his peerage and estate to his insane son Jack (Peter O'Toole). Name the title.
a) Man Friday
b) What's New Pussycat?
c) The Ruling Class
d) The Savage Innocents

2) The king (Peter O'Toole) pleads to his barons in **Becket** (1964): "Will no one rid me of this meddlesome priest? A priest who mocks me. Are all around me cowards like myself? Are there no men left in England?" Name the king he is portraying.
a) Henry II b) Henry III
c) Henry IV d) Henry V

3) Which film featured him as Reginald Johnston, Scottish tutor to Aisin-Gioro 'Henry' Pu Yi?
a) The King and I
b) 55 Days at Peking
c) The Last Emperor
d) China Moon

valuable toe Performers

AL PACINO
(Alfredo James Pacino 1940 -)

1) With which film, directed by himself, do you associate him participating in the battle on Bosworth Field?
a) Revolution b) Scarecrow
c) ... And Justice For All d) Looking For Richard

2) Which film features him as 'Big Boy Caprice'?
a) Scarface b) Carlito's Way
c) Two Bits d) Dick Tracy

3) In which 1973 drama do drifters Lion (Al Pacino) and Max (Gene Hackman) meet on a desolate highway?
a) Bobby Deerfield b) Scarecrow
c) The Panic in Needle Park d) Cruising

JACK PALANCE
(Walter Jack Palahnuik 1919 -)

1) He was awarded a Best Supporting Actor Oscar for his portrayal of Curly the trail boss in 1991. Name the film.
a) Young Guns b) City Slickers
c) Outlaw of Gor d) Tango & Cash

2) Name the 1956 Robert Aldrich war drama in which Jack Palance's unit during the Battle of the Bulge is commanded by the cowardly Eddie Albert.
a) Attack! b) I died a Thousand Times
c) Ten Seconds to Hell d) The Man Inside

3) In the 1952 thriller, **Sudden Fear**, successful playwright Myra Hudson suspects her husband, Lester Blain (Jack Palance), has resolved to murder her. Who portrayed Myra?
a) Barbara Stanwyck b) Loretta Young
c) Shelley Winters d) Joan Crawford

GWYNETH PALTROW (1973 -)

1) In which 1995 biopic does her character's father make a young slave girl pregnant?
a) Jefferson in Paris
b) Cruel Doubt
c) Flesh and Bone
d) Malice

2) Which film features the doomed love affair of Viola De Lessep (Gwyneth Paltrow)?
a) Sliding Doors
b) The Walking Dead
c) Shakespeare in Love
d) Moonlight and Valentino

3) For what film did she portray the pregnant wife of Mills (Brad Pitt)?
a) Seven
b) Cool World
c) Legends of the Fall
d) Kalifornia

GREGORY PECK
(Eldred Gregory Peck 1916 -)

1) Name the 1944 film, directed by John M. Stahl and based on an A.J. Cronin novel, which made him a star.
a) The Keys of the Kingdom b) Hatter's Castle
c) The Citadel d) Beyond this Place

2) What 1945 film connection can you make between Gregory Peck and Salvador Dali?
a) The Macomber Affair b) Spellbound
c) The Valley of Decision d) the Paradine Case

3) Based on John D. MacDonald's novel *The Executioners*, this 1962 thriller involves lawyer Sam Bowden (Gregory Peck) and his family being threatened by a homicidal ex-con called Max Cady. Name the film.
a) Beloved Infidel b) Mirage
c) Cape Fear d) The Stalking Moon

SEAN PENN (1960 -)

1) Name the 1986 adventure he starred in with his then wife, Madonna, set in opium infested 1930s China.
a) Shanghai Cobra b) Shanghai Gesture
c) Shanghai Triad d) Shanghai Surprise

2) What do Daulton and Christopher (Sean Penn and Timothy Hutton) decide to sell in **The Falcon and the Snowman**?
a) government secrets b) counterfeit money
c) pornography d) the Empire State Building

235

The Movie Quiz Companion

3) In which film does prison visitor, Helen Prejean, rebuff his advances, saying: "Death is breathing down your neck and you're playing your little man-on-the-make games."?
a) Bad Boys b) Racing With the Moon
c) State of Grace d) Dead Man Walking

ANTHONY PERKINS
(1932 - 1992)

1) Name the 1957 film in which professional baseball player, Jim Piersal (Anthony Perkins), cracks under pressure from his pushy father (Karl Malden) and the stresses of work and is confined to a state mental hospital.
a) Fear Strikes Out b) Five Miles to Midnight
c) The Lonely Man d) Friendly Persuasion

2) In which film does he grapple with the dilemma of whether to give suicide pills to his wife and child?
a) Logan's Run b) Futureworld
c) On the Beach d) The Day the Earth Caught Fire

3) Which character does he portray in Mike Nichols' **Catch-22**?
a) Maj. Major b) Chaplain Tappman
c) Nurse Duckett d) Doc Daneeka

JOE PESCI (1943 -)

1) Name the film for which he won a Best Supporting Actor Oscar in the role of mobster Tommy DeVito.
a) Goodfellas b) Raging Bull
c) Casino d) A Bronx Tale

2) Which film features him as a lawyer with no courtroom experience and who failed his bar examinations five times, having to defend two innocent college students charged with murder?
a) Backtrack b) My Cousin Vinny
c) The Public Eye d) With Honors

3) In 1995 he played thief and cold blooded killer, Nicky Santoro, who, amongst other fits of wrath, traps a man's head in a vice. Name the film.
a) Casino b) Once Upon a Time in America
c) Lethal Weapon 3 d) Clockers

MICHELLE PFEIFFER (1957 -)

1) With whom was beautician Lurene Hallett (Michelle Pfeiffer) obsessed in Jonathan Kaplan's 1992 drama, **Love Field**?
a) Elvis Presley
b) Jacqueline Kennedy
c) Marilyn Monroe
d) James Dean

2) Which film featured her as nightclub singer, Susie Diamond, whose rendition of 'Makin' Whoopee' on top of a piano was one of the most memorable scenes in the movie?
a) Grease 2
b) Tequila Sunrise
c) The Witches of Eastwick
d) The Fabulous Baker Boys

3) What film connection can you make between Michelle Pfeiffer and lycanthropy?
a) Near Dark
b) Wolf
c) The Howling
d) Innocent Blood

RIVER PHOENIX (1970 - 1993)

1) In which film does he suffer from narcolepsy, a condition characterised by a recurrent tendency to fall asleep in relaxing surroundings?
a) Silent Tongue b) Painted Angels
c) Surviving d) My Own Private Idaho

2) In **Running on Empty** (1988) his parents had been on the run from the FBI for seventeen years for an illegal act they committed when they were student radicals. What was their crime?
a) they blew up a building with the janitor inside
b) they petrol-bombed a bus-load of National Guardsmen c) they sent President Nixon a letter-bomb d) they torched a Highway Patrolman's squad-car

3) River Phoenix's last finished film before his death from an overdose cast him as a young country and western singer named James Wright who hoped to launch his career at Nashville's Bluebell Cafe. Name the title.
a) The Thing Called Love b) A Night in the Life of Jimmy Reardon c) Sneakers d) Dogfight

MARY PICKFORD
(Gladys Smith 1893 - 1979)

1) Who once commented: "It took longer to make one of Mary's contracts than it did to

make one of Mary's pictures"?
a) Adolph Zukor b) Sam Goldwyn
c) D.W. Griffith d) Charlie Chaplin

2) She was awarded an Oscar for her role as flapper Norma Bessant in her first talkie. Name the title.
a) Kiki b) Daddy Long Legs c) Suds d) Coquette

3) Name the 1929 comedy (the only film in which she co-starred with her husband Douglas Fairbanks) of which she said: "The making of that film was my finish. My confidence was completely shattered, and I was never again at ease before the camera or microphone."
a) The Taming of the Shrew b) Little Annie Rooney
c) Sparrows d) The Gay Desperado

WALTER PIDGEON
(1897 - 1984)

1) In which film does he portray the flamboyant impresario, Florenz Ziegfeld, who gets most upset when a performer walks on stage dressed as a pregnant bride?
a) Saratoga b) The Shop Worn Angel
c) Rose of Washington Square d) Funny Girl

2) With which film do you associate him helping to evacuate retreating British soldiers from the beaches of Dunkirk?
a) Hit the Deck b) White Cargo
c) Mrs. Miniver d) Dark Command

3) In 1944 the wealthy Major Augustus Parkington (Walter Pidgeon) marries Susie, who becomes **Mrs. Parkington**. Who was she?
a) Greer Garson
b) Agnes Moorhead
c) Judy Garland
d) Barbara Stanwyck

BRAD PITT
(William Bradley Pitt 1963 -)

1) Hitchhiker, JD (Brad Pitt), has sex with a girl then steals her money in 1991. This scene was dubbed "the $6,000 orgasm" by Pitt. Name the film.
a) Happy Together b) Kalifornia
c) True Romance d) Thelma and Louise

2) Preparing for the character of fanatical animal rights activist, Jeffrey Goines, Pitt attended group therapy sessions and checked into a Philadelphia psychiatric ward for a day. Name the film.
a) Across the Tracks b) Twelve Monkeys
c) The Favor d) Too Young to Die

3) In which film does he look like Death?
a) Meet Joe Black b) Tales From the Crypt
c) Sleepers d) Devil's Own

DONALD PLEASENCE
(1919 - 1995)

1) What 1966 film involved him portraying a member of a medical team attempting to remove a blood clot from the brain of a Czech scientist.
a) The Defection of Simas Kudiraka b) The Two-Handed Spy c) Fantastic Voyage d) The Risk

2) In which film did he work with 'Big X' and 'The Manufacturer'?
a) Halloween II b) You Only Live Twice
c) The Great Escape d) Cul-De-Sac

3) With which John Carpenter sci-fi thriller do you associate him playing the US President who has been hijacked by the underworld?
a) Escape From New York b) Dark Star
c) Starman d) The Fog

CHRISTOPHER PLUMMER
(1927 -)

1) In 1975 he portrayed a newspaper editor who witnesses an "official" document for two British army officers named Peachy Carnehan and Daniel Dravot. Name the film.
a) Aces High b) Conduct Unbecoming
c) Waterloo d) The Man Who Would Be King

2) For what 1969 film, directed by Irving Lerner, did he portray the Inca god-king Atahualpa?
a) The Royal Hunt of the Sun b) Secret of the Incas c) Captain From Castile d) The Mission

3) Which 1979 mystery cast him as Sherlock Holmes and James Mason as Watson on the trail of Jack the Ripper?
a) Murder by Decree b) Hands of the Ripper
c) A Study in Scarlet d) Man in the Attic

SYDNEY POITIER (1924 -)

The Movie Quiz Companion

1) Poitier introduced his big-city detective versus red-neck cop character, Virgil Tibbs, in the 1967 crime thriller, **In the Heat of the Night**. The character appeared for the second time in **They Call Me Mister Tibbs!** (1970). Name the film in which Virgil Tibbs made his third and final appearance.
a) A Piece of the Action b) The Lost Man
c) The Wilby Conspiracy d) The Organization

2) In 1951 he played a young South African preacher named Maimaungu in a film based on a best-selling novel by Alan Paton. Name the film.
a) A Raisin in the Sun b) Cry, the Beloved Country
c) Band of Angels d) No Way Out

3) With which film do you associate him living on Catfish Row in a Charleston waterfront slum?
a) The Defiant Ones b) Edge of the City
c) Porgy and Bess d) A Patch of Blue

DICK POWELL (1904 - 1963)

1) In which film did he wrongly assume he had won $25,000 in a slogan contest?
a) Christmas in July b) Twenty Million Sweethearts c) Happiness Ahead d) Blessed Event

2) Name the 1933 backstage musical he sang and danced in that contained Warner Baxter's much parodied speech: "Miss Sawyer, you listen to me … and you listen hard. Two hundred people, two hundred jobs, two hundred thousand dollars, five weeks of grind and blood and sweat depend upon you! It's the lives of all these people who've worked with you. You've got to go on and you've got to give, and give and give! They've got to like you, got to. You understand? You can't fall down, you can't. Because your future's in it, my future and everything all of us have is staked on you. All right now, I'm through. But you keep your feet on the ground and your head on those shoulders of yours, and, Sawyer, you're going out a youngster, but you've got to come back a star!"
a) 42nd Street b) Stage Struck
c) Footlight Parade d) Gold Diggers of 1933

3) He began his career singing and dancing in musicals, but in 1944 he created a new tough-guy image in a string of successful films noirs. Name the title of the 1944 film which gave audiences their first taste of the new hardboiled Dick Powell.
a) Cornered b) Johnny O'Clock
c) The Ends of the Earth d) Farewell, My Lovely

TYRONE POWER (1913 - 1958)

1) What 1938 musical cast Tyrone Power as bandleader, Don Ameche as pianist and Alice Faye as singer of the Irving Berlin classics, 'Blue Skies,' 'Easter Parade' and 'Oh, How I Hate to Get Up in the Morning'?
a) On the Avenue b) Alexander's Ragtime Band
c) This is the Army d) Carefree

2) For which 1938 biopic did he portray Ferdinand de Lesseps?
a) Suez b) Brigham Young
c) The Eddy Duchin Story d) Marie Antoinette

3) In 1958 he died of a heart attack while making a biblical drama in Madrid. Name the title.
a) Solomon and Sheba b) The Bible
c) David and Goliath d) The Greatest Story Ever Told

ELVIS PRESLEY (1935 - 1977)

1) Presley's autocratic manager, 'Colonel' Tom Parker was said to have felt uneasy about his co-star in **Viva Las Vegas** who matched him in talent and sex appeal. Who was she?
a) Debbie Reynolds b) Ursula Andress
c) Debra Paget d) Ann-Margret

2) Name the title of his 1956 film debut which included the songs 'Let Me,' 'We're Gonna Move to a Better Home,' 'Poor Boy'.
a) Love Me Tender b) Jailhouse Rock
c) Loving You d) King Creole

3) Elvis sang only one song in a 1969 western in an unsuccessful effort to promote himself as a straight actor. Name the film.
a) Flaming Star b) Charro!
c) Gun Fury d) Broken Lance

VINCENT PRICE (1911 - 1993)

1) In which 1959 horror film does Dr. William Chapin (Vincent Price) perfect a process which could successfully extract

'fear' from a person's body in the form of a worm-like creature that could only be killed by screaming?
a) Green Hell b) The Abominable Dr. Phibes
c) The Tingler d) Diary of a Madman

2) Denied a Best Actor of the Year award by the London Critic's Circle, Shakespearean actor Edward Lionheart (Vincent Price) decides to murder his critics using methods inspired by Shakespeare's most gruesome death scenes. Name the title.
a) Theatre of Blood b) The Jackals
c) Curtain Call at Cactus Creek d) House of Wax

3) Before he became typecast in horror roles he was cast in historical costume dramas. Name the 1939 film which cast him as courtier, navigator and poet, Sir Walter Raleigh.
a) Mary of Scotland b) Captain Blood
c) The Private Lives of Elizabeth and Essex
d) The Buccaneer

ANTHONY QUINN (1915 - 2001)

1) Which 1954 drama features him as Zampano, a travelling circus strongman who buys a simple-minded young girl from her mother to assist with his act?
a) The Black Orchid b) Nights of Cabiria
c) The Imperfect Lady d) La Strada

2) In 1952 he won a Best Supporting Actor Oscar for his portrayal of the brother of a character played by Marlon Brando. Name the film.
a) Viva Zapata! b) Guys and Dolls
c) The Teahouse of the August Moon d) On the Waterfront

3) In 1943 he portrayed one of three innocent homesteaders who are hanged by a lynch mob for murder and cattle rustling in a classic western directed by William Wellman. Name the title.
a) Union Pacific b) The Big Sky
c) Cattle Town d) The Ox-Bow Incident

GEORGE RAFT (1895 - 1980)

1) He never denied his underworld connections and in the 1920s he was associated with the Dutch Shultz mob where one of the gang, Bo Weinberg, had a habit of flipping a coin before shooting his victims which Raft used in his portrayal of the gangster Guino Rinaldo in 1932. Name the film.
a) The Bowery b) Jimmy the Gent
c) Johnny Angel d) Scarface

2) An accomplished ballroom dancer, who was his dance partner in **Bolero** (1934)?
a) Ginger Rogers b) Cyd Charisse
c) Carole Lombard d) Loretta Young

3) Who helped him make a daring escape from a courtroom in **Each Dawn I Die** (1939)?
a) Paul Muni b) James Cagney
c) Humphrey Bogart d) Edward G. Robinson

CLAUDE RAINS (1889 - 1967)

1) Why does Dr. Tower (Claude Rains) keep his daughter Cassandra (Betty Field) a virtual prisoner, never allowing her out of the house or to form any lasting relationships in Sam Wood's 1942 drama, **King's Row**?
a) she would eventually go insane b) she was a kleptomaniac c) she committed murder whenever she heard loud noises d) she was a nymphomaniac

2) In 1946, Alexander Sebastian (Claude Rains), with his mother's assistance, attempts to slowly poison his new bride, Alicia. Name the film.
a) Mr. Skeffington b) Moontide
c) Notorious d) This Love of Ours

3) Sir John Talbot (Claude Rains) kills his own son Larry by beating him about the head with a cane in a 1941 horror film. Name the title.
a) The Curse of the Werewolf b) The Wolf Man
c) Cry of the Werewolf d) Werewolf in London

BASIL RATHBONE (1892 - 1967)

1) In 1935 he played the miserable Mr. Murdstone in the screen adaptation of a Charles Dickens novel. Name the film.
a) A Tale of Two Cities b) David Copperfield
c) Scrooge d) The Mystery of Edwin Drood

2) For what 1935 historical drama did he portray Pontius Pilate?
a) Julius Caesar
b) Sins of Rome
c) Roman Scandals
d) The Last Days of Pompeii

3) In which 1939 mystery does cocaine-user Sherlock Holmes (Basil Rathbone) yell to his partner in the closing scene, "Quick Watson, the needle!"?
a) The Hound of the Baskervilles
b) Sherlock Holmes and the Secret Weapon
c) Sherlock Holmes Faces Death
d) Sherlock Holmes and the Voice of Terror

STEPHEN REA (1943 -)

a) In Neil Jordan's directorial debut drama, **Angel** (1982), what does Rea's character exchange for a machine gun after witnessing a murder?
a) a Morris Minor b) two tickets to see Frank Sinatra c) a saxophone d) his record collection

2) Which 1994 Robert Altman comedy features him as star photographer, Milo O'Brannagan?
a) Fool For Love b) Short Cuts c) Vincent & Theo d) Prêt-à-Porter

3) In which film does he befriend a pregnant and unmarried Miss Scacciapensieri (Geena Davis)?
a) Bad Behaviour b) Angie c) The Company of Wolves d) Princess Caraboo

RONALD REAGAN (1911 -)

1) Which film featured "the Yank" (Ronald Reagan) trying to befriend "the Scot" (Richard Todd), a stubborn soldier in an army hospital in WWII Burma with only a few weeks left to live?
a) The Burmese Harp b) Distant Drums c) The Hasty Heart d) The Purple Plain

2) His last film in 1964 was based on a story by Ernest Hemingway, and cast him in the only violent role of his career. Name the title.
a) For Whom the Bell Tolls b) The Sun Also Rises c) The Killers d) The Snows of Kilimanjaro

3) In 1952 he married B-movie actress, Nancy Davis, who became First Lady of the United States from 1981 to 1989. Name the actress (star of **The Lost Weekend** and **The Yearling**) to whom he was married from 1940 to 1948.
a) Joan Leslie b) Kathryn Grayson c) Jane Wyman d) Joan Blondell

ROBERT REDFORD (1937 -)

1) He made his film debut in a 1962 anti-war film set in Korea co-starring with Sydney Pollack and Tom Skerritt. Name the title.
a) War Hunt b) Men in War c) Combat Squad d) Hell in Korea

2) Which film cast him as bisexual film star who marries teenage star Natalie Wood?
a) Barefoot in the Park b) Love With the Proper Stranger c) The Chase d) Inside Daisy Clover

3) With which film do you associate him asking hash slinger Loretta Salino out for a date, unaware she is a highly trained assassin out to kill him?
a) Three Days of the Condor b) The Sting c) The Candidate d) Brubaker

MICHAEL REDGRAVE (1908 - 1985)

1) Name the 1938 mystery in which he has to remember a tune with a secret message vital to the British secret service?
a) The Lady Vanishes b) The Big Blockade c) Secret Agent d) Lady in Distress

2) In which 1942 drama, directed by Roy Boulting, is he haunted by the drowned immigrants of a ship which sank over a hundred years ago?
a) Thunder Rock b) The Sea Shall Not Have Them c) The Green Scarf d) Mourning Becomes Electra

3) For what 1961 horror film, based on Henry James' Turn of the Screw, does 'The Uncle' (Michael Redgrave) hire governess Miss Giddens (Deborah Kerr) to care for his niece and nephew in Victorian England?
a) Shake Hands With the Devil b) Secret Beyond the Door c) Time Without Pity d) The Innocents

VANESSA REDGRAVE (1937 -)

1) Name the British film director to whom she was married from 1962 to 1967?

Performers

a) Guy Hamilton b) Tony Richardson
c) John Boorman d) Terence Davies

2) Which 1984 drama featured her as Olive Chancellor, a repressed lesbian feminist attracted to suffragette Verena Tarrant (Madeleine Potter) who is "unmarried by every implication of her being"?
a) The Bostonians b) Consuming Passions
c) Second Serve d) The Trojan Women

3) In a 1985 drama, directed by David Hare, Jean Travers (Vanessa Redgrave) gives a dinner party. One of the guests is a complete stranger who returns to Jean's house the following day and kills himself. Name the film.
a) Three Sovereigns for Sarah b) Bear Island
c) The Seven Percent Solution d) Wetherby

OLIVER REED (1938 -1999)

1) Arguably more famous for his off-screen hell-raising and heavy drinking than for his acting career, his first starring role was in a 1961 Hammer horror film. Name the title.
a) The Mummy b) The Stranglers of Bombay
c) The Curse of the Werewolf d) The Two Faces of Dr. Jekyll

2) His notoriety made him a familiar face on the chat show circuit, where he would frequently discuss the tattoo on his "mighty mallet". What did the tattoo depict?
a) Blackpool Tower b) a pair of bird's talons
c) an 'I love Mum' dedication d) a dipstick

3) He died of a heart attack in Valletta, Malta, after collapsing during a drinking session in a local bar, during a break from filming. Name the film he never completed.
a) White Squall b) Gladiator
c) Prisoner of Honor d) Severed Ties

KEANU REEVES (1964 -)

1) Although born in Beirut, his unusual Christian name is actually Hawaiian. What does it mean?
a) calm seas brush the sand b) cool breeze over the mountains c) paradise on Earth d) summer rain washes the leaves

2) In which 1990 romantic comedy does he fall in love with his Aunt Julia (Barbara Hershey)?
a) Youngblood b) Freaked
c) Parenthood d) Tune in Tomorrow

3) Which film features him as Neo, a man who might, or might not be, the One who'll lead the world to salvation?
a) Little Buddha b) A Walk in the Clouds
c) Johnny Mnemonic d) The Matrix

LEE REMICK (1935 - 1991)

1) Name the 1957 drama, directed by Elia Kazan, about fascist elements in American culture, in which Lee Remick made her screen debut.
a) The Sea of Grass b) A Face in the Crowd
c) Baby Doll d) Pinky

2) Which 1976 horror film tells the story of Robert and Katherine Thorn (Gregory Peck and Lee Remick) and their son - the Antichrist?
a) Web of the Spider b) Equinox
c) The Devil's Bride d) The Omen

3) In which 1962 drama does her inability to stay sober, eventually resulting in alcoholism, destroy her marriage?
a) Sanctuary b) Days of Wine and Roses
c) A Severed Head d) No Way to Treat a Lady

BURT REYNOLDS (1936 -)

1) Which film was he describing when he commented: "It's the best film I've ever done. It's a picture that just picks you up and crashes you against the rocks. You feel everything and just crawl out of the theater."?
a) Deliverance
b) The Player
c) Nickelodeon
d) Smokey and the Bandit

The Movie Quiz Companion

2) What 1977 film connection can you make between Burt Reynolds and Coors Beer?
a) Rent-a-Cop b) The Cannonball Run
c) Smokey and the Bandit d) Hooper

3) Name the 1988 comedy in which Reynolds co-starred opposite Kathleen Turner in a remake of Lewis Milestone's 1931 classic, **The Front Page**.
a) Switching Channels b) Rough Cut
c) City Heat d) Uphill All the Way

DEBBIE REYNOLDS
(Mary Francis Reynolds 1932 -)

1) Carrie Fisher (her daughter by first husband Eddie Fisher 1955-59) wrote the semi-autobiographical novel, Postcards From the Edge, which was adapted for the screen in 1990. Who played the Reynolds character, Doris Mann?
a) Meryl Streep
b) Dolly Parton
c) Annette Bening
d) Shirley MacLaine

2) In 1964 she portrayed the richest woman in late 1800s Denver in a musical which includes the songs, 'I Ain't Down Yet,' and 'Belly Up to the Bar, Boys.' Name the title.
a) The Affairs of Dobie Gillis
b) Goodbye Charlie
c) The Unsinkable Molly Brown
d) The Second Time Around

3) Tammy Tyree (Debbie Reynolds) falls in love with pilot, Peter Brent, after nursing him back to life following a plane crash in the 1957 comedy, **Tammy and the Bachelor**. Who was he?
a) Tab Hunter
b) Leslie Nielsen
c) Rock Hudson
d) Laurence Harvey

MIRANDA RICHARDSON
(1958 -)

1) She made her film debut in a 1985 biopic, directed by Mike Newell, portraying Ruth Ellis, the last woman to be hanged in Britain in 1955. Name the title.
a) Yield to the Night b) Underworld
c) Dance With a Stranger d) The Innocent

2) Name the 1994 film in which her husband commits her to an institution where she remains for the rest of her life. Her husband, who never visited her, is described by one of the film's characters as an "egotistical little s— who would like to be a saint."
a) Behind Locked Doors b) Tom & Viv
c) Eat the Rich d) Forgotten Woman

3) In a 1992 drama, directed by Louis Malle, her screen husband, Dr. Stephen Fleming (Jeremy Irons), is obsesesd with his son's fiancée, Anna (Juliette Binoche). Name the film.
a) Damage b) Crackers
c) God's Country d) Vanya on 42nd Street

RALPH RICHARDSON
(1902 - 1983)

1) He made his film debut as a parson in a 1933 horror film starring Boris Karloff, an Egyptologist who wants to be buried with a jewel which will give him eternal life. Name the film.
a) The Walking Dead b) The Mummy c) The Black Cat d) The Ghoul

2) In which 1936 film did he portray 'The Boss'?
a) The Stars Look Down b) How Green Was My Valley c) Things to Come d) The Lion Has Wings

3) With which film do you associate a speechless Sangali tribesman with an 'S' branded on his forehead, saving his life in the North African desert?
a) Beau Geste b) The Desert Rats
c) The Four Feathers d) The Lost Patrol

ALAN RICKMAN (1946 -)

1) In 1995 he played Col. Brandon who is smitten by Marianne Dashwood, who, along with her mother and two sisters has been forced into reduced circumstances and must find a husband to remedy the situation forthwith. Name the film.
a) Persuasion
b) Age of Innocence
c) Sense and Sensibility
d) Pride and Prejudice

2) With whom was his girlfriend having a relationship in Stephen Poliakoff's 1991 drama, **Close My Eyes**?
a) her brother b) his wife
c) his father d) her son

3) What did despotic Australian landowner, Elliott Marston (Alan Rickman), hire marksman Matthew Quigley (Tom Selleck) to shoot in the 1990 drama, **Quigley Down Under**?
a) escaped convicts
b) Aborigines
c) gold prospectors
d) kangaroos

TIM ROBBINS (1958 -)

1) For what 1988 comedy did he portray rookie baseball pitcher 'Nuke' LaLoosh?
a) A League of Their Own b) Bull Durham
c) The Bad News Bears d) The Dream Team

2) In which 1992 comedy did he date a dead man's fiancée named June Gudmundsdottir while receiving anonymous postcards threatening his life?
a) The Player
b) Bob Roberts
c) Jacob's Ladder
d) Cadillac Man

3) Name the Robert Altman drama, based on the stories of Raymond Carver, which cast him as a motorcycle cop having an extra-marital affair.
a) Nashville
b) Short Cuts
c) Fool For Love
d) Beyond Therapy

JULIA ROBERTS (1967 -)

1) With which 1993 thriller do you associate her researching the murders of two Supreme Court justices?
a) I Love Trouble b) Blood Red
c) Something to Talk About d) The Pelican Brief

2) From what disorder deos Shelby Eatenton Latcherie (Julia Roberts) suffer in the 1989 comedy drama, **Steel Magnolias**?
a) bulimia b) anorexia c) diabetes d) epilepsy

3) She made her screen debut in 1988 co-starring with her brother Eric in a film set in 1890s California. Name the title.
a) Blood Red b) The Freshman
c) Baja Oklahoma d) Satisfaction

EDWARD G. ROBINSON
(Emmanuel Goldenberg 1893 - 1973)

1) In 1931, after the success of **Little Caesar**, Warner Brothers cast him as a gambling barber in **Smart Money**. Who was the other Warner "tough guy" who starred opposite him in their only film appearance together?
a) Humphrey Bogart b) George Raft
c) James Cagney d) Dick Powell

2) For what 1945 crime drama, directed by Fritz Lang, does Cross (Robinson) steal from his employer and set up his girlfriend Kitty in a Greenwich Village apartment?
a) Scarlet Street b) Flesh and Fantasy
c) The Woman in the Window d) Two Seconds

3) Which film features him as a Hebrew spy for Rameses I?
a) Salome b) Valley of the Kings
c) The Ten Commandments d) The Egyptian

FLORA ROBSON (1902 - 1984)

1) In 1945 she received an Oscar nomination for her role as the mulatto maid of her Creole mistress, Ingrid Bergman. Name the film.
a) The Years Between b) Saratoga Trunk
c) Bahama Passage d) Good Time Girl

2) For which 1937 swashbuckler did she portray Queen Elizabeth I?
a) Fire Over England b) The Sea Hawk
c) Desiree d) Adventures of Don Juan

3) In a 1954 version of **Romeo and Juliet** she played the nurse. Who portrayed Romeo?
a) Robert Donat b) Laurence Olivier
c) Paul Scofield d) Emlyn Williams

GINGER ROGERS
(Virginia Katherine McMath 1911 - 1995)

1) In her 1930 screen debut she spouted the line, "Cigarette me, big boy!" Name the title.

The Movie Quiz Companion

teetotal chef chops puree

a) *Young Man of Manhattan* b) *The Sap From Syracuse* c) *Queen High* d) *Follow the Leader*

2) Which film featured John 'Lucky' Garnett (Fred Astaire) being 'taught' by dance instructor, Penny Carrol (Ginger Rogers) at the Gordon Dancing Academy featuring the Jerome Kern-Dorothy Fields songs "A Fine Romance," "Pick Yourself Up" and the Oscar-winning "The Way You Look Tonight"?
a) *Shall We Dance* b) *Swing Time*
c) *Flying Down to Rio* d) *The Gay Divorcee*

3) Name the title of the film which won her an Academy Award for Best Actress in 1940.
a) *Black Widow* b) *Stage Door*
c) *The Major and the Minor* d) *Kitty Foyle*

ROY ROGERS
(Leonard Slye 1912 - 1998)

1) He first teamed with her in **The Cowboy and the Señorita** (1944) and another nineteen films followed. He married Frances Smith in 1947 after the death of his second wife. By what name was she better known?
a) Googie Withers b) Rhonda Fleming
c) Arlene Wilkins d) Dale Evans

2) In which film does his four-legged friend Trigger share a bed with Bob Hope?
a) *Alias Jesse James* b) *Son of Paleface*
c) *The Lemon Drop Kid* d) *They Got Me Covered*

3) Name his regular grizzled sidekick, whose catchphrase was "You're darn tootin".
a) Gabby Hayes b) Andy Devine
c) Chill Wills d) Walter Brennan

MICKEY ROONEY
(Joe Yule, Jr. 1920 -)

1) In 1937 he portrayed Dan, son of Captain Disko of the Gloucester fleet, who loaned his clothes to rookie fisherman and spoiled brat, Harvey. Name the film.
a) *All Ashore* b) *Little Lord Fauntleroy*
c) *Slave Ship* d) *Captains Courageous*

2) With which 1938 drama do you associate the cocky unrepentant kid, Whitey Marsh (Mickey Rooney), clashing with the benign Father Flanagan (Spencer Tracy)?
a) *The Twinkle in God's Eye* b) *The Big Wheel*
c) *Boys Town* d) *Off Limits*

3) Children of vaudevillians, Mickey Moran (Mickey Rooney) and Patsy Barton (Judy Garland), worked their way through the numbers, 'Where or When,' 'The Lady Is a Tramp,' 'I Cried for You,' 'Good Morning,' and 'You Are My Lucky Star', in a 1939 screen version of a Rogers and Hart musical. Name the film.
a) *Strike Up the Band* b) *Babes in Arms*
c) *Thousands Cheer* d) *Babes on Broadway*

TIM ROTH (1961 -)

1) In 1990 he starred in playwright Tom Stoppard's feature film directing debut, an adaptation of his own play. Name the title.
a) *Rosencrantz and Guildenstern Are Dead*
b) *The Human Factor* c) *A World Apart*
d) *Vincent & Theo*

2) Who portrayed his girlfriend and hold-up accomplice, "Honey Bunny" in **Pulp Fiction** (1994)?
a) Juliette Lewis b) Julia Sweeney
c) Rosanna Arquette d) Amanda Plummer

3) What was Russian-Jewish Joshua Shapira's (Tim Roth) profession in the 1994 drama, **Little Odessa**?
a) taxi-driver b) porno star
c) hit-man d) beachguard

JANE RUSSELL (1921 -)

1) Renowned for her 38-inch bustline, she was once introduced by a well known comedian as "the two and only Miss Russell". Who was he?
a) Bob Hope b) Jerry Lewis
c) Groucho Marx d) Danny Kaye

2) Although she made her film debut in 1943, censorship problems ensured that the film wasn't screened publicly until 1947. Name the title.
a) Double Dynamite b) Young Widow
c) His Kind of Woman d) The Outlaw

3) In which 1953 film did she co-star with Marilyn Monroe?
a) Gentlemen Prefer Blondes b) Don't Bother to Knock c) How to Marry a Millionaire d) There's No Business Like Show Business

MARGARET RUTHERFORD (1892 - 1972)

1) She did not take up professional acting until she was thirty-three when she joined the Old Vic as a student in 1925. What was her previous occupation?
a) nurse b) post mistress
c) librarian d) music teacher

2) Name the film for which she was awarded a Best Supporting Actress Oscar in 1963 in the role of the Duchess of Brighton.
a) The V.I.P.s b) A Countess From Hong Kong
c) I'm All Right Jack d) The Mouse on the Moon

3) To whom does the ancient royal charter belong, which was discovered in old catacombs and given official approval by Professor Hatton-Jones (Margaret Rutherford), renouncing British sovereignty of a London borough and ceding it to France in the 1949 comedy, **Passport to Pimlico**?
a) the Dukes of Normandy b) the Dukes of Burgundy c) the Dukes of Aquitaine d) the Dukes of Lorraine

MEG RYAN (Margaret Hyra 1961 -)

1) She met her future husband while co-starring with him in Joe Dante's sci-fi fantasy in 1987. Who was he?
a) Dennis Quaid b) Tim Robbins
c) Val Kilmer d) Billy Crystal

2) With which 1992 romantic comedy do you associate newly-wed Rita Boyle's (Meg Ryan) body being inhabited by an elderly man?
a) Promised Land b) D.O.A.
c) Flesh and Bone d) Prelude to a Kiss

3) Which film features her as Alice Green, an alcoholic mother of two?
a) Rich and Famous b) French Kiss
c) Armed and Dangerous d) When a Man Loves a Woman

ROBERT RYAN (1909 - 1973)

1) Based on the novel by Herman Melville and set in the Royal Navy of the late 1700s, sadistic master-of-arms Claggart (Ryan) is killed by a young seaman and court martialed for murder. Name the 1962 drama.
a) Moby Dick b) Two Years Before the Mast
c) Billy Budd d) The Trial of Billy Jack

2) For what 1953 western did he portray outlaw killer, Ben Vandergroat, who is relentlessly pursued by bounty hunter Howard Kemp (James Stewart) for the $5,000 reward on his head?
a) The Man From Laramie b) The Naked Spur
c) Winchester 73 d) Bend of the River

3) Name the character he portrayed in Nicholas Ray's 1961 drama, **King of Kings**.
a) John the Baptist b) Pontius Pilate
c) Barabbas d) Judas

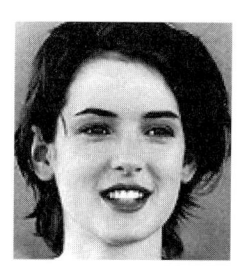

WINONA RYDER (Winona Laura Horowitz 1971 -)

The Movie Quiz Companion

1) With which film do you associate young Myra Gale Brown (Winona Ryder) becoming the bride of 'The Killer'?
a) Heathers b) Beetlejuice
c) Great Balls of Fire! d) Reality Bites

2) In which film does her screen mother tell her: "If you feel your value lies only in being merely decorative, I fear that someday you might find yourself believing that's all you really are. Time erodes all such beauty, but what it cannot diminish is the wonderful workings of your mind."?
a) Mermaids b) The Age of Innocence
c) How to Make an American Quilt d) Little Women

3) Which film featured her as Corky the tattooed cab driver whose movie executive passenger wants to cast her in a film?
a) Night on Earth b) Welcome Home, Roxy Carmichael c) Lucas d) Square Dance

SABU
(Sabu Dastagir 1924 - 1963)

1) Film-maker Robert Flaherty discovered him at the court of an Indian maharajah and cast him in the title role of the 1937 adventure, **Elephant Boy**. What was his position in the maharajah's household?
a) stable boy b) dresser
c) kitchen boy d) gardener

2) In which film does the grand vizier, Jaffar, turn him into a dog?
a) Jungle Book b) Arabian Nights
c) The Thief of Bagdad d) Cobra Woman

3) Who portrayed the native girl he attempted to seduce with the perfume of the **Black Narcissus**?
a) Kathleen Byron b) Merle Oberon
c) Jean Simmons d) Renée Asherson

GEORGE SANDERS
(1902 - 1976)

1) Name the 1950 film in which he portrayed theatre critic, Addison De Witt, a role which won him a Best Supporting Actor Oscar.
a) All About Eve
b) Call Me Madam
c) Bitter Sweet
d) Sundown

2) Which English monarch did he portray in Otto Preminger's 1947 historical drama, **Forever Amber**?
a) James I
b) Richard III
c) Henry IV
d) Charles II

3) For what film did the suave epigram-spouting Lord Henry Wooton (Sanders) inform his friends: "Most people die of a sort of creeping common sense and discover too late that the only things one never regrets are one's mistakes"?
a) The Moon and Sixpence
b) Things to Come
c) Confessions of a Nazi Spy
d) The Picture of Dorian Gray

SUSAN SARANDON
(Susan Tomaling 1946 -)

1) What 1985 mystery involves Long Island housewife and ex-reporter, Judith Singer (Susan Sarandon), investigating the murder of a degenerate dentist?
a) Compromising Positions b) Pretty Baby
c) In Our Hands d) The Other Side of Midnight

2) With which film do you associate her portraying a mother whose child suffers from the incurable degenerative disease adrenoleukodystrophy?
a) Lovin' Molly b) Lorenzo's Oil
c) Pretty Baby d) Something Short of Paradise

3) Who does Sally (Susan Sarandon) befriend in Louis Malle's 1980 crime drama, **Atlantic City**?
a) Burt Lancaster b) Paul Newman
c) Yves Montand d) Al Pacino

ARNOLD SCHWARZENEGGER
(1947 -)

1) What bodybuilding title is Arnie out to win in **Pumping Iron** (1977)?
a) Mr. Universe b) Mr. Olympia
c) The Strongest Man in the World d) The Toughest Man Alive

2) With which film do you associate him seeking vengeance on the evil Thulsa Doom?

heroic texts

Performers

a) *The Running Man* b) *Conan the Barbarian* c) *Total Recall* d) *Red Sonja*

3) For what 1985 action drama did he play a special agent forced to go back into the field when his daughter is kidnapped?
a) *Commando* b) *Kindergarten Cop* c) *Raw Deal* d) *Red Heat*

PAUL SCOFIELD (1922 -)

1) In which film did his character's son appear on a TV show sponsored by Geritol, which cures "tired blood" and makes you "feel stronger fast"?
a) *Hidden Agenda* b) *Network* c) *Quiz Show* d) *Broadcast News*

2) Name the film for which he was awarded a Best Actor Oscar in 1966.
a) *Henry V* b) *A Man for All Seasons* c) *Anna Karenina* d) *The Train*

3) In 1958 he played the part of a man who falls in love with British secret agent, Violette Szabo (Virginia McKenna), who was executed by the Gestapo. Name the film.
a) *Carve Her Name With Pride* b) *Knight Without Armour* c) *Odette* d) *Walk a Crooked Mile*

RANDOLPH SCOTT
(Randolph Crane 1898 - 1987)

1) In which 1935 adventure does he encounter the Flame of Eternal Youth in the land of Kor?
a) *Thunder Over the Plains* b) *She* c) *Island of Lost Souls* d) *The Spoilers*

2) Which film featured him as the "Oregon Kid", a weak caricature of a legendary gunfighter, complete with outrageous stetson, long-haired wig and false beard?
a) *Carson City* b) *The Tall T* c) *Ride the High Country* d) *The Bounty Hunter*

3) Who was his shipmate in Mark Sandrich's 1936 musical comedy, **Follow the Fleet**?
a) Gene Kelly b) Dean Stockwell c) Frank Sinatra d) Fred Astaire

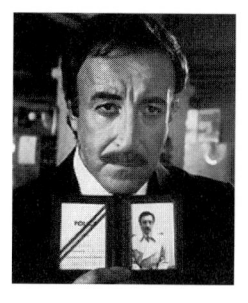

PETER SELLERS
(Richard Henry Sellers 1925 - 1980)

1) Ronald Neame's 1956 spy drama, **The Man Who Never Was**, portrayed the true story of a WWII plot to leak false invasion plans to the Nazis. Whose voice did Peter Sellers impersonate in the final scenes?
a) Field Marshal Montgomery b) Winston Churchill c) General Eisenhower d) King Geo. VI

2) Name the actress with whom he was infatuated in Roy Boulting's 1970 comedy, **There's a Girl in My Soup**.
a) Goldie Hawn b) Sophia Loren c) Britt Ekland d) Lesley-Anne Down

3) He had a chronic heart condition and after a series of heart attacks he collapsed into a coma at London's Dorchester Hotel and died a few days later on 24 July 1980. He was cremated at Golders Green, where, at his own request, a piece of music was played to the mourners. Name the tune.
a) 'Goodbye Cruel World' by James Darren b) 'In the Mood' by Glenn Miller c) 'Goodness Gracious Me' by Peter Sellers and Sophia Loren d) 'Hell Hath No Fury' by Frankie Laine

OMAR SHARIF
(Michel Shahoub 1932 -)

1) Orphan Yuri Zhivago (Omar Sharif) is taken in by the Gromeko family and later marries their daughter, Tonya, in David Lean's **Doctor Zhivago** (1965). Who was she?
a) Susan Hampshire b) Rita Tushingham c) Julie Christie d) Geraldine Chaplin

2) Which one of his films was he talking about when he said: "If you are the man with the money and somebody comes to you and says he wants to make a film that's four hours long, with no stars, and no women, and no love story, and not much action either, and he wants to spend a huge amount of money... what would you say?"?
a) *Mayerling* b) *The Fall of the Roman Empire* c) *Lawrence of Arabia* d) *Genghis Khan*

3) Name the 1976 Pink Panther film in which he portrayed an Egyptian assassin.
a) *The Pink Panther Strikes Again* b) *The Return of the Pink Panther* c) *Revenge of the Pink Panther* d) *Trail of the Pink Panther*

ROBERT SHAW (1927 - 1978)

1) He made his film debut as Flight Sgt. Pulford in a war drama based on the true story of an RAF raid by 617 Squadron in which 53 men were lost, 3 taken prisoner and 8 aircraft went missing. Name the film.

The Movie Quiz Companion

a) *The Way to the Stars* b) *633 Squadron*
c) *Battle of Britain* d) *The Dam Busters*

2) In which film does blond assassin, Red Grant (Robert Shaw), do battle with James Bond?
a) *You Only Live Twice* b) *From Russia With Love*
c) *Goldfinger* d) *Thunderball*

3) With which film do you associate gangster, Doyle Lonnegan (Robert Shaw), losing $500,000 to Henry Gondorff and Johnny Hooker?
a) *Black Sunday* b) *End of the Game*
c) *The Taking of Pelham One Two Three* d) *The Sting*

MOIRA SHEARER
(Moira King 1926 -)

1) In Powell and Pressburger's **The Red Shoes** (1948) a young woman's (Moira Shearer) magical shoes force her to keep on dancing until she almost dies. How do her feet eventually come to rest?
a) they sink into mud
b) they are chopped off with an axe
c) they are held down with chains
d) they are nailed to the floor

2) With which film do you associate her as a young dancer being murdered in a film studio?
a) *Black Tights* b) *The Wrong Box*
c) *Peeping Tom* d) *Murder At the Gallop*

3) Who or what prevented her character from becoming a ballerina in the 1953 drama, **The Story of Three Loves**?
a) a heart condition
b) her domineering father
c) her height
d) her devotion to her only child

NORMA SHEARER (1900 - 1983)

1) Name the film which won her a Best Actress Oscar for her performance as a jilted wife in 1930.
a) *The Divorcee* b) *Private Lives*
c) *A Free Soul* d) *Smilin' Through*

2) With whom did she have a **Strange Interlude** in 1932?
a) Clark Gable b) Cary Grant
c) Paul Henreid d) Gary Cooper

3) In which 1939 comedy, directed by George Cukor, does Chrystal Allen (Joan Crawford) decry Mary Haines (Norma Shearer) and her associates saying: "There's a name for you ladies, but it isn't used in high society - outside of a kennel"?
a) *Their Own Desire* b) *Riptide*
c) *The Women* d) *Idiot's Delight*

MARTIN SHEEN
(Ramon Estevez 1940 -)

1) In 1982 he portrayed Walker in Richard Attenborough's biopic **Gandhi**. What was Walker's occupation?
a) judge
b) police officer
c) consular official d) reporter

2) With which film do you associate him playing Confederate General Robert E. Lee who orders his troops into a suicidal assault against Union trenches?
a) *Gettysburg* b) *Ironclads*
c) *Dances With Wolves* d) *Glory*

3) What is the trapper portrayed by Martin Sheen desperate to retrieve from the renegade Indian (Sam Waterson) he was tracking in the 1979 western, **Eagle's Wing**?
a) his brother's scalp
b) his white stallion
c) his wife
d) the deeds to a silver mine

ALISTAIR SIM (1900 - 1976)

1) He made his film debut at Wembley Studios in a detective thriller called **Riverside Murder**. What character did he portray in the film?
a) a police sergeant
b) a draper's assistant
c) an artist's model
d) a fairground barker

2) In order to legally acquire their inheritance, the characters in the 1951 comedy, **Laughter in Paradise**, have to meet with certain bizarre conditions. What does the character portrayed by Alistair Sim have to do before he can collect his loot?
a) marry the first single girl he meets
b) get himself jailed
c) hold up a bank
d) get a job as a butler

3) Which film features Inspector Cockrill (Alistair Sim) investigating the mysterious death of a postman named Joe Higgins?
a) *An Inspector Calls*
b) *Green For Danger*
c) *Folly to Be Wise*
d) *Escapade*

fictional blend felled homeopath   **Performers**

JEAN SIMMONS (1929 -)

1) Name the British leading man to whom she was married from 1950 to 1960.
a) Stewart Granger b) James Mason
c) Tom Courtenay d) Alan Bates

2) Name the Shakespeare adaptation in which she co-starred with Laurence Olivier in 1948.
a) Hamlet b) Henry V c) Othello d) Richard III

3) Napoleon Bonaparte (Marlon Brando) is in love with Desiree Clary (Jean Simmons), who marries another man in **Desiree** (1954). What is Desiree's occupation?
a) prostitute b) seamstress c) maid d) teacher

FRANK SINATRA (1915 - 1998)

1) In which 1961 drama does Harry (Sinatra) the convict help Father Doonan evacuate a mountain-top children's leper hospital on a volcanic South Sea island?
a) *The Devil at 4 O'Clock*
b) *Higher and Higher*
c) *Kings Go Forth*
d) *The Lost Volcano*

2) Which 1959 comedy featured the Oscar-winning song, 'High Hopes'?
a) *The Tender Trap*
b) *High Society*
c) *Pal Joey*
d) *A Hole in the Head*

3) Drug addict, Frankie Machine (Sinatra), is attracted to his downstairs neighbour, Molly, in Otto Preminger's 1955 drama, **The Man With the Golden Drum**. Who was she?
a) Eleanor Parker b) Jean Kent
c) Kim Novak d) Joanne Woodward

C. AUBREY SMITH (1863 - 1948)

1) With which film do you associate quintessential old soldier, General Burroughs (Smith), spouting repetitively: "All you boys had to do was deal with 'Fuzzy Wuzzy', but The Crimea was different. War was war in those days - no room for weaklings - take Balaclava for instance..."?
a) *The Charge of the Light Brigade* b) *Clive of India* c) *The Four Feathers* d) *The Lives of a Bengal Lancer*

2) What 1938 film, directed by Herbert Wilcox, cast him as the Duke of Wellington?
a) *Sixty Glorious Years* b) *The Yellow Canary*
c) *Victoria the Great* d) *The Lady With a Lamp*

3) In which film does Col. Zapt (Smith) vow that Black Michael (Raymond Massey) will never sit on the throne?
a) *The Prince and the Showgirl*
b) *Queen Christina*
c) *The Prisoner of Zenda*
d) *The Sea Hawk*

SISSY SPACEK (1949 -)

1) In 1980 she was awarded an Oscar for her portrayal of a country music queen, Loretta Lynn. Name the film.
a) *The Coal Miner's Daughter* b) *Hard Promises*
c) *Prime Cut* d) *3 Women*

2) With which 1976 film do you associate her having telekinetic powers?
a) *The Migrants* b) *Carrie*
c) *Raggedy Man* d) *Marie*

3) Why did her screen children cast a spell to make her disappear in the 1994 fantasy, **Trading Mom**?
a) they wanted a replacement mom
b) she was about to be arrested c) their father threatened to kill her d) her dress sense was an embarrassment to them

KEVIN SPACEY (1959 -)

1) Which film features him as aspiring stand-up comic, Dwayne Hanson?
a) *When You Remember Me* b) *Fall From Grace*
c) *Rocket Gibraltar* d) *Working Girl*

2) In which film does he remark: "The greatest trick the Devil ever pulled was convincing the world he didn't exist"?
a) *Seven* b) *The Usual Suspects*
c) *Fall From Grace* d) *Consenting Adults*

3) Name the erotic Parisian diarist with whom he comes into contact in the 1990

249

drama, **Henry & June**?
a) Colette b) Simone de Beauvoir
c) Anaïs Nin d) Monique Wittig

SYLVESTER STALLONE (1946 -)

1) With which **Rocky** film do you associate him coming home and telling his pet turtles, Cuff and Link: "If you guys could sing and dance, I wouldn't have to go through this crap."?
a) Rocky b) Rocky II c) Rocky III d) Rocky IV

2) Name the film in which law enforcer Stallone arrests Fergie (Rob Schneider) for being present at a crime scene:
"But I had only been there five minutes!" Fergie cries.
"You could have jumped out of the window."
"Forty floors up? That would be suicide!"
"But it's legal," says Stallone.
a) Death Race 2000 b) Nighthawks
c) Cobra d) Judge Dredd

3) Rogue cop, Sergeant John Spartan, is defrosted after 36 years of deep-freeze imprisonment into a future where "mellow greetings" have become a substitute for "hello" and everything that could prove harmful, from salt to cigarettes, has been banned. Name the film.
a) Demolition Man b) Assassins
c) Staying Alive d) F.I.S.T.

BARBARA STANWYCK
(Ruby Stevens 1907 - 1990)

1) What 1937 drama involved her glimpsing her daughter's wedding through a window from a rain-drenched street before being moved along by a policeman?
a) Remember the Night b) Stella Dallas
c) Ten Cents a Dance d) The Secret Bride

2) Name the Hollywood heart-throb to whom she was married from 1939 to 1951.
a) Robert Taylor b) William Holden
c) Tyrone Power d) Gregory Peck

3) In 1941 journalist Ann Mitchell (Barbara Stanwyck) concocts a story about an idealistic young man who is going to leap off City Hall on Christmas Eve. The public like the story so much her editor orders her to find a real-life idealist. Name the film.
a) Walk On the Wild Side b) Cry Wolf
c) Ball of Fire d) Meet John Doe

ROD STEIGER (1925 -)

1) In which film does he portray redneck sheriff, Bill Gillespie?
a) Jubal b) The Ballad of the Sad Cafe
c) The Loved One d) In the Heat of the Night

2) Name the 1959 gangster biopic in which he played the title role.
a) Al Capone b) Baby Face Nelson
c) Machine-Gun Kelly d) Dillinger

3) Name the British actress to whom he was married from 1959 to 1969.
a) Virginia McKenna b) Susannah York
c) Claire Bloom d) Jean Simmons

JAMES STEWART (1908 - 1997)

1) Name the film, directed by George Cukor, for which he won a Best Actor Oscar in 1940.
a) The Philadelphia Story b) Mr. Smith Goes to Washington c) Harvey d) Anatomy of a Murder

2) In Ernst Lubitsch's 1940 romantic comedy, **The Shop Around the Corner**, shop clerk and lonely heart, Alfred Kralik (James Stewart), exchanges romantic letters with the mysterious lady of box 237 whom he has never met, but turns out to be his nemesis and fellow staff member, Klara Novak. Who portrayed her?
a) Jean Arthur b) Margaret Sullavan
c) Carole Lombard d) Hedy Lamarr

3) With which 1939 western do you associate him taming the town of Bottleneck without violence and without guns?
a) Destry Rides Again
b) Bend of the River
c) The Man Who Shot Liberty Valance
d) Broken Arrow

Performers

MERYL STREEP
(Mary Streep 1949 -)

1) In which film does Jill (Meryl Streep), the lesbian ex-wife of Isaac (Woody Allen), write a best-selling book about their relationship entitled 'Marriage, Divorce and Selfhood'?
a) A Midsummer Night's Sex Comedy b) Annie Hall c) Manhattan d) Play It Again, Sam

2) Which 1982 drama, based on the novel by William Styron, features her in an Oscar-winning performance about a woman who survives a concentration camp and tries to make a new life in America?
a) Still of the Night b) Julia c) Sophie's Choice d) Plenty

3) When speaking of his love for Francesca (Meryl Streep), photographer Robert Kincaid says to her: "This kind of certainty comes but once in a lifetime." Name the film.
a) Death Becomes Her b) Postcards From the Edge c) She-Devil d) The Bridges of Madison County

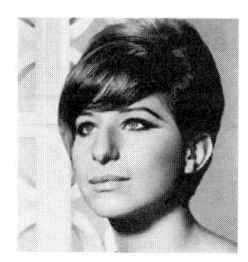

BARBRA STREISAND (1951 -)

1) Her film debut in 1968 won her an Oscar. Name the title.
a) On a Clear Day You Can See Forever b) Hello, Dolly! c) What's Up, Doc? d) Funny Girl

2) "Serious books for Men…picture books for women", shouted the bookseller. In which film is she denied access to scholarship because of her sex?
a) The Main Event b) Yentyl c) The Owl and the Pussycat d) Nuts

3) Which film features her visiting a loan shark to borrow $3,000 to invest in pork belly futures on the stock exchange?
a) For Pete's Sake b) The Prince of Tides c) The Way We Were d) All Night Long

SHARON STONE (1958 -)

1) In which film does Catherine Tramell (Sharon Stone) write a novel about the murder of a rock star, an event which is mirrored in real life?
a) Above the Law b) Deadly Blessings c) Basic Instinct d) Cold Steel

2) With which film do you associate mobster, Ace Rothstein falling in love with her after seeing her image on a TV security monitor?
a) Diary of a Hitman b) Casino c) Year of the Gun d) The Quick and the Dead

3) Where had Cindy Liggitt (Sharon Stone) spent the last twelve years in Bruce Beresford's 1996 drama, **Last Dance**?
a) in a coma b) on Death Row c) on a deserted space station d) in a cave in the Appalachian mountains

DONALD SUTHERLAND (1934 -)

1) Stranded on a Scottish island during WWII, German agent Faber (Donald Sutherland) tells Lucy: "The war has come down to the two of us" in **Eye of the Needle**. Who portrayed Lucy?
a) Kate Nelligan b) Jenny Agutter c) Lesley-Anne Down d) Susan Hampshire

2) What are Jesse Veldini (Donald Sutherland) and his motley collection of drop-outs eager to restore in the 1973 comedy, **Steelyard Blues**?
a) a locomotive b) a Sherman tank c) a seaplane d) a paddle-steamer

3) In which film are wealthy New York socialites, Flan and Ouisa Kittredge (Donald Sutherland and Stockard Channing) taken in by a con man who claims to be the son of Sidney Poitier?
a) Citizen X b) Shadow of the Wolf c) Six Degrees of Separation d) Benefit of the Doubt

PATRICK SWAYZE (1952 -)

1) In 1992 he played Dr. Max Lowe in a film based on Dominique Lapierre's bestselling novel. Name the title.
a) City of Joy
b) Next of Kin
c) Father Hood
d) Three Wishes

2) Which film featured him as a bouncer at the Double Deuce nightclub?
a) Dirty Dancing
b) Steel Dawn
c) Tall Tale
d) Road House

3) What is his occupation in the 1995 comedy, **To Wong Foo, Thanks for Everything, Julie Newmar**?
a) ballet dancer
b) stand-up comedian
c) assassin
d) drag queen

The Movie Quiz Companion

JESSICA TANDY (1909 - 1994)

1) Her Hollywood debut was in Fred Zinnemann's 1944 war drama, **The Seventh Cross**, in the first of many films in which she co-starred opposite her husband. Who was he?
a) Dan Duryea b) Jack Hawkins c) Donald Crisp d) Hume Cronyn

2) What 1991 film connection can you make between Jessica Tandy and the novelist Fannie Flagg?
a) Driving Miss Daisy b) Camilla c) Fried Green Tomatoes d) Foxfire

3) Which 1963 horror film features her living near Bodega Bay with her bachelor son Mitch Brenner?
a) The Mummy b) Children of the Damned c) The Hands of a Stranger d) The Birds

ELIZABETH TAYLOR (1932 -)

1) Her career has mirrored the predictable consequences of stardom: untold riches, drug and alcohol abuse, love affairs and numerous marriages. How many times (to date) has she been married?
a) seven b) eight c) nine d) ten

2) Twice during her career she was awarded an Academy Award for Best Actress. The second time it was for **Who's Afraid of Virginia Woolf?** in 1966. Name the film for which she was awarded her first.
a) Giant b) Suddenly, Last Summer c) Raintree County d) Butterfield 8

3) In which 1952 film does Saxon hero, Wilfrid (Robert Taylor), demand a fair trial for Rebecca (Elizabeth Taylor), who has been accused of witchcraft by the Normans?
a) Ivanhoe b) Knights of the Round Table c) Siege of the Saxons d) The Sword and the Rose

ROBERT TAYLOR
(Spangler Arlington Brugh
1911 - 1969)

1) Saloon gal, Lil Duryea, falls in love with Lt. Richard Perry (Robert Taylor) in the 1937 historical drama, **This Is My Affair**. Who portrayed Lil Duryea?
a) Lana Turner
b) Barbara Stanwyck
c) Norma Shearer d) Hedy Lamarr

2) Adapted to the silent screen in 1915, 1917, and 1921, this Alexandre Dumas tale was brought to the screen again in 1937 co-starring Garbo and Taylor and became one of the great romantic weepies of the golden age. Name the title.
a) Anna Christie b) As You Desire Me c) Camille d) Queen Christina

3) Roman commander, Marcus Vinicius's (Robert Taylor) advances are rejected by his Christian slave, Lygia (Deborah Kerr), because of his Pagan beliefs in a 1951 historical drama directed by Mervyn LeRoy. Name the title.
a) Duel of the Titans b) Julius Caesar c) Androcles and the Lion d) Quo Vadis?

ROD TAYLOR (1929 -)

1) In which film does he meet antagonist and future lover, Melanie Daniels, in Davidson's pet store?
a) Separate Tables b) Hotel
c) The Birds d) Raintree County

2) With which 1961 Disney feature do you associate him as the voice of 'Pongo'?
a) The Incredible Journey b) One Hundred and One Dalmatians c) Old Yeller d) The Shaggy Dog

3) In order to see as much of her as possible, research scientist Bruce Templeton (Rod Taylor) commissions public relations girl Jennifer Nelson to write his biography in Frank Tashlin's 1966 comedy, **The Glass Bottom Boat**. Who was she?
a) Natalie Wood b) Audrey Hepburn c) Doris Day d) Shirley Eaton

SHIRLEY TEMPLE (1928 -)

1) Name the classic 19th century children's story in which she co-starred with Jean Hersholt and Arthur Treacher in 1937.
a) Anne of Green Gables b) Heidi
c) Pollyanna d) Alice in Wonderland

2) With which 1937 comedy drama do you associate her living in a British Army garrison with her widowed mother?
a) Captain January b) The Littlest Rebel c) Wee Willie Winkie d) The Little Colonel

3) In 1949 she starred in a film entitled **The Story of Seabiscuit**. Who or what was Seabiscuit?
a) a fishing boat b) a racehorse c) a parrot d) a seaside resort

TERRY THOMAS
(Thomas Stevens 1911 - 1990)

1) With which film do you associate him on the tiny fly-blown island of Gallardia. which, after the discovery of rich mineral deposits, attracts the interest of major powers.
a) The Mouse on the Moon b) Carlton-Browne of the F.O. c) Too Many Crooks d) Operation Snatch

2) What 1959 comedy, directed by George Pal, involves villains Ivan and Tony (Terry Thomas and Peter Sellers) trying to kidnap the only child of a woodcutter named Jonathan (Bernard Miles)?
a) Private's Progress b) The Brothers in Law c) Lucky Jim d) Tom Thumb

3) In which 1959 comedy does factory personnel manager Major Hitchcock (Terry Thomas) unite with shop steward Fred Kite to protect workers' rights?
a) I'm All Right Jack b) Strange Bedfellows c) Millions Like Us d) The Foreman Went to France

EMMA THOMPSON (1959 -)

1) In which 1993 drama did she portray obstinate lawyer, Gareth Peirce?
a) Peter's Friends b) Henry V
c) Howards End d) In the Name of the Father

2) Name the film for which she was awarded an Academy Award for her portrayal of Margaret Schlegel, born of an English mother and a German father, but not a German "of the dreadful sort"?
a) Maurice b) A Room With a View c) The Remains of the Day d) Howards End

3) In which film is she referred to as a "ravishing boy"?
a) Dead Again b) My Father, The Hero c) Carrington d) Junior

RICHARD TODD (1919 -)

1) Richard Todd and Liam Neeson played the same role in 1954 and 1995 respectively. Name the character they portrayed.
a) Oskar Schindler b) Michael Collins c) Lancelot d) Rob Roy

2) With which 1954 war film do you associate him owning a pet dog named Nigger?
a) The Longest Day b) The Dam Busters c) The Hasty Heart d) D-Day the Sixth of June

3) Name the 1953 live-action Disney drama he starred in.
a) Old Yeller b) The Story of Robin Hood and His Merrie Men c) Treasure Island d) 20,000 Leagues Under the Sea

SPENCER TRACY (1900 - 1967)

1) Name the 1933 drama, directed by William K. Howard, which begins with the funeral of railroad tycoon Tom Garner (Spencer Tracy), and through flashbacks re-evaluates his rags to riches life.
a) The Power and the Glory b) Boom Town c) Man's Castle d) Riffraff

2) Well known for his partnership on and off screen with Katherine Hepburn, name the 1942 comedy, directed by George Stevens, in which they first co-starred together.
a) Woman of the Year b) Pat and Mike c) Keeper of the Flame d) The Sea of Grass

3) Name the 1949 comedy which contains the following dialogue:
- "Shows that what I said was true. There's no difference between the sexes. Man, woman, the same."

The Movie Quiz Companion

- "They are, huh?"
- "Well maybe there is a difference, but it's a little difference."
- "Well you know as the French say - vive la difference!"
- "Which means?"
- "Hurrah for that little difference!"
a) Guess Who's Coming to Dinner b) Adam's Rib c) Father of the Bride d) A Guy Named Joe

JOHN TRAVOLTA (1954 -)

1) In which 1977 film does he dance the night away in Brooklyn's 2001 Odyssey Disco?
a) Grease b) Urban Cowboy c) Blow Out d) Saturday Night Fever

2) With which film do you associate him giving acting lessons on how to look menacing to Hollywood actor Martin Weir?
a) White Man's Burden b) Get Shorty c) Pulp Fiction d) Eyes of an Angel

3) For what 1996 action thriller did he portray a Stealth bomber pilot who plots to steal nuclear weapons?
a) The Devil's Rain b) Broken Arrow c) Staying Alive d) The Experts

LANA TURNER
(Julia Turner 1920 - 1995)

1) In which 1946 crime drama does her doomed death row lover ask a priest: "Father, could you send up a prayer for me and Cora and, if you can find it in your heart, make it so we're together - wherever it is."?
a) Imitation of Life b) Johnny Eager c) Madame X d) The Postman always Rings Twice

2) What film involves producer, Jonathan Shields, seducing actress Georgia Lorrison (Lana Turner) with promises of stardom in a role inspired by the tragic life of John Barrymore's daughter Diana?
a) Cass Timberlane b) Honky Tonk c) A Star is Born d) The Bad and the Beautiful

3) In 1957 she was nominated for an Academy Award for her portrayal of Constance Mackenzie in a drama based on a scandalous novel by Grace Metalious. Name the film.
a) The Merry Widow b) Rich Man, Poor Man c) Peyton Place d) Another Time, Another Place

JOHN TURTURO (1957 -)

1) Name the Depression era social protest playwright and screenwriter on whom the Coen brothers modelled the character of **Barton Fink** (John Turturo) in 1991.
a) Clifford Odets b) William Saroyan c) Eugene O'Neill d) Ben Hecht

2) Which 1994 drama features Jewish New Yorker Herb Stempel (John Turturo) blowing the whistle on 'Twenty-One' to a congressional investigator?
a) Unstrung Heroes b) Do the Right Thing c) Fearless d) Quiz Show

3) For what film did he portray unctuous bookie, Bernie Bernbaum, who begs for his life and then betrays the man who spared him?
*a) Miller's Crossing
b) State of Grace
c) Clockers
d) Raging Bull*

RUDOLPH VALENTINO
(Rodolfo Guglielmi 1895 - 1926)

1) Name the English writer whose desert romance, *The Sheik* (1919) was instrumental in creating the legend of Rudolph Valentino when it was adapted for the screen in 1921.
a) Beatrix Lehmann b) Edith Maude Hull c) Elizabeth Goudge d) R.M. Lamming

2) Which 1921 film, directed by Rex Ingram about two brothers fighting on opposite sides in the Great War, established him as a star?
*a) The Four Horsemen of the Apocalypse
b) Uncharted Seas c) The Conquering Power
d) Beyond the Rocks*

3) What is Valentino's profession in Fred Niblo's 1922 drama, **Blood and Sand**?
a) French Legionnaire b) bullfighter c) slave dealer d) Grand Vizier

JEAN-CLAUDE VAN DAMME
(Jean-Claude Van Varenberg 1961 -)

1) In 1987 he starred in a film about real-life American Ninja Frank Dux, who became the first western martial arts expert to win the prestigious Kumite competition. Name the film.
a) Bloodsport b) Kickboxer c) Street Fighter d) Hard Target

2) In which film does a terrorist not reckon on having to deal with security guard Darren

254

McCord (Van Damme) when he holds the vice president of the U.S.A. hostage during a hockey match between the Chicago Blackhawks and Pittsburgh Penguins?
a) Cyborg b) Double Impact
c) Sudden Death d) Nowhere to Run

3) With which 1991 adventure do you associate him deserting the foreign legion?
a) Lionheart b) No Retreat, No Surrender
c) Death Warrant d) Black Eagle

CONRAD VEIDT (1893 - 1943)

1) Once described as "the man who is built by nature to petrify kings and emperors with a look", Conrad Veidt starred as Baron Karl von Marwitz, opposite Vivien Leigh in a 1937 war drama. Name its title.
a) 49th Parallel b) Contraband
c) The Spy in Black d) Dark Journey

2) Which film featured him as Nazi Major Heinrich Strasser?
a) Dark Journey b) Casablanca
c) Night Train to Munich d) Above Suspicion

3) For what 1919 German expressionist classic did he portray a murderous somnambulist named Cesare?
a) The Cabinet of Dr. Caligari
b) The Gambler
c) Nosferatu
d) Waxworks

ERICH VON STROHEIM (1885 - 1957)

1) After shooting down two French pilots, WW1 German air ace, Von Rauffenstein (Erich von Stroheim), casually invites them to have lunch with him before they are taken to a POW camp. Name the film.
a) Hearts of the World
b) Wings
c) The Lost Squadron
d) Grand Illusion

2) In which WWII drama, directed by Billy Wilder, did he portray Field Marshal Erwin Rommel?
a) The Desert Rats
b) Stalag 17
c) Five Graves to Cairo
d) The Desert Fox

3) In 1932 he co-starred with Greta Garbo in a film about an amnesiac Italian Countess. Name the film.

a) As You Desire Me b) Anna Christie
c) Queen Christina d) Anna Karenina

CHRISTOPHER WALKEN (Roanald Walken 1943 -)

1) He made his film debut playing an electronics expert in a 1972 Sidney Lumet drama about the robbing of an entire Manhattan apartment building. Name the title.
a) The Deadly Affair
b) The Offence
c) Child's Play
d) The Anderson Tapes

2) With which film do you associate him being able to predict the future after recovering from a near-fatal accident which plunged him into a coma for years?
a) Last Embrace
b) At Close Range
c) The Dead Zone
d) Brainstorm

3) Who or what was 'Peina' (Christopher Walken) in Abel Ferrara's 1995 drama, **The Addiction**?
a) a vampire
b) a Colombian drug baron
c) a transvestite nun
d) a lion-tamer

JULIE WALTERS (1950 -)

255

The Movie Quiz Companion

1) With which film's finale do you associate her running a flower stall with her husband outside London's Waterloo Station?
a) *Unfair Exchanges*
b) *Stepping Out*
c) *Car Trouble*
d) *Buster*

2) Name the character she portrayed in **Dreamchild** (1985), about the life of the woman who was the inspiration for Lewis Carroll's Alice.
a) *the Mad Hatter*
b) *a dormouse*
c) *a caterpillar*
d) *a mock turtle*

3) Which film features her as brothel madam, Christine Painter, based on the life of Cynthia Payne?
a) *Prick Up Your Ears*
b) *Scandal*
c) *The Men's Club*
d) *Personal Services*

DENZEL WASHINGTON
(1954 -)

1) For what 1995 mystery is redundant factory employee, Easy Rawlins (Denzel Washington), offered $100 to look for a girl named Daphne Monet?
a) *Devil in a Blue Dress*
b) *Reunion*
c) *Ricochet*
d) *Flesh & Blood*

2) In which 1995 thriller does Parker Barnes (Denzel Washington) track down something or someone who has the personalities of 200 criminals, including the killer who murdered his family?
a) *The Mighty Quinn* b) *Carbon Copy*
c) *Virtuosity* d) *Crimson Tide*

3) Which 1993 Shakespearian comedy cast him as Don Pedro, Prince of Aragon?
a) *Much Ado About Nothing*
b) *A Midsummer Night's Dream*
c) *The Taming of the Shrew*
d) *Twelfth Night*

JOHN WAYNE
(Marion Michael Morrison 1907 - 1979)

1) With which western do you associate Tom Dunson (John Wayne), who, after losing command of his cattle-drive, threatens his stepson Matthew with a warning, saying: "Ye shoulda let 'um kill me, cause I'm gonna kill you. I'll catch up with you. I dunno when, but I'll catch up. Every time you turn around expect to see me, cause one time you'll turn around and I'll be there..."
a) *The Comancheros*
b) *Tall in the Saddle*
c) *Angel and the Badman*
d) *Red River*

2) Name the film which won him a Best Actor Oscar in 1969.
a) *True Grit*
b) *Rio Lobo*
c) *Cast a Giant Shadow*
d) *The Shootist*

3) Lt. Col. Kirby Yorke (John Wayne), the lonely commander of a cavalry outpost harassed by apaches, has the additional problem of dealing with his estranged wife and rookie soldier son in **Rio Grande** (1950). Who portrayed Kirby Yorke's wife?
a) *Loretta Young*
b) *Ida Lupino*
c) *Lauren Bacall*
d) *Maureen O'Hara*

SIGOURNEY WEAVER
(Susan Weaver 1949 -)

1) She adopted the name Sigourney from a character who appears in a well known F. Scott Fitzgerald novel. Name the title.
a) *The Great Gatsby*
b) *The Last Tycoon*
c) *Tender is the Night*
d) *This Side of Paradise*

2) In what 1995 thriller does psychiatrist Helen Hudson (Sigourney Weaver), an expert on serial killers, proclaim: "I'm their damn pinup girl. They all know me"?
a) *Half Moon Street*
b) *Alien 3*
c) *Copycat*
d) *Death and the Maiden*

3) Which 1983 film, directed by Peter Weir, cast her as Jill Bryant, assistant military attaché at the British Embassy in Djakarta?
a) *The Year of Living Dangerously*
b) *Jeffrey*
c) *Eyewitness*
d) *Madman*

ORSON WELLES (1915 - 1985)

1) With which 1956 film do you associate local parson Father Mapple (Orson Welles) preaching a sermon on Jonah from a pulpit shaped like a ship's prow?
a) *Two Years Before the Mast* b) *Moby Dick*
c) *Trouble in the Glen* d) *Crack in the Mirror*

defiling the skill — Performers

2) For what 1942 thriller does he portray Turkish police chief Colonel Haki?
a) *Journey Into Fear* b) *Touch of Evil*
c) *Man in the Shadow* d) *The Black Rose*

3) Name the Shakespearean production he starred in which was shot in only twenty-three days in 1948.
a) *Othello* b) *Macbeth*
c) *Chimes at Midnight* d) *The Tempest*

MAE WEST (1892 - 1980)

1) At the peak of her Broadway career, in 1932, she made her screen debut in a film opposite George Raft, who commented, "She stole everything but the cameras." Name the title.
a) *Night After Night*
b) *Bolero*
c) *The Bowery*
d) *Pick-Up*

2) In 1933 she portrayed Diamond Lil, who, when showing off her jewels to Captain Cummings retorts: "You know it was a toss-up whether I go in for diamonds or sing in the choir. The choir lost." Name the film.
a) *I'm No Angel*
b) *She Done Him Wrong*
c) *Belle of the Nineties*
d) *Go West, Young Man*

3) With which musical comedy do you associate her playing a Salvation Army officer who sings 'I'm An Occidental Woman in An Oriental Mood For Love'?
a) *Klondike Annie*
b) *Goin' to Town*
c) *Every Day's a Holiday*
d) *The Heat's On*

RICHARD WIDMARK (1914 -)

1) What character did he portray in **The Alamo** (1960)?
a) Gen. Sam Houston
b) Jim Bowie
c) Col. William Travis
d) Davy Crockett

2) Name the 1948 western, directed by William Wellman, which involves him entering a ghost town with Gregory Peck.
a) *Yellow Sky*
b) *The Gunfighter*
c) *Two Rode Together*
d) *Duel in the Sun*

3) In 1961 he portrayed prosecuting attorney, Col. Tad Lawson, who was instrumental in sentencing ninety-nine men to prison. Name the film.
a) *Town on Trial*
b) *The Court-Martial of Billy Mitchell*
c) *Massacre*
d) *Judgment at Nuremberg*

ROBIN WILLIAMS (1952 -)

1) In which film does he live in the fishing village of Sweethaven with Shelley Duvall?
a) *The Best of Times*
b) *Popeye*
c) *Mrs. Doubtfire*
d) *Moscow on the Hudson*

2) With which film do you associate him searching for the Holy Grail?
a) *Seize the Day*
b) *Being Human*
c) *The Fisher King*
d) *Club Paradise*

3) Which film features a movement of mute feminists called The Ellen Jamesians, whose name came from a rape victim who had her tongue removed?
a) *The World According to Garp*
b) *The Adventures of Baron Munchausen*
c) *The Survivors*
d) *Shakes the Clown*

BRUCE WILLIS (1955 -)

1) In 1987 he takes Nadia Gates - who has an extremely low alcohol tolerance - on a **Blind Date**. Who was she?
a) Michelle Pfeiffer
b) Andie MacDowell
c) Tara Fitzgerald
d) Kim Basinger

257

The Movie Quiz Companion

2) Which 1991 film, directed by Michael Lehmann, was Variety commenting on when it said: "Ever wondered what a Three Stooges short would look like with a $40 million budget?"?
a) Hudson Hawk
b) Nobody's Fool
c) Look Who's Talking
d) Sunset

3) What was his occupation in Robert Zemeckis's 1992 comedy, **Death Becomes Her**?
a) mortician
b) plastic surgeon
c) rocket scientist
d) pathologist

DEBRA WINGER (1955 -)

1) In which 1990 drama does her husband Port die of typhoid?
a) Everybody Wins
b) Black Widow
c) The Sheltering Sky
d) Forget Paris

2) With which 1993 film do you associate her being taken to the Golden Valley?
a) Urban Cowboy
b) Shadowlands
c) Made in Heaven
d) Leap of Faith

3) What film involved her being the voice of an alien?
a) E.T. The Extra-Terrestrial
b) Dark Star
c) Aliens
d) Deep Space

NATALIE WOOD
(Natasha Gurdin 1938 - 1981)

1) In 1963 she portrayed a character who falls in love with trumpet player, Rocky Papasano, in **Love With the Proper Stranger**. Who was he?
a) Steve McQueen
b) Frank Sinatra
c) Hardy Kruger
d) Tony Curtis

2) Name the actor she married twice, from 1957 to 1963 and again in 1972.
a) Robert Wagner
b) Tony Curtis
c) William Holden
d) Jack Palance

3) In which western did Natalie Wood and her younger sister, Lana, both portray the same daughter of a frontier family who is kidnapped by Indians?
a) The White Squaw
b) Dakota Incident
c) The Searchers
d) The Man From Laramie

JAMES WOODS (1947 -)

1) Name the 1979 crime drama he starred in which was based on the 1963 kidnappings of two Los Angeles policemen and the eventual murder of one of them, which became, after seven years, the longest single criminal court case in California.
a) Against All Odds
b) Eyewitness
c) The Choirboys
d) The Onion Field

2) Which film featured him as Lester Diamond, pimp of high class hooker, Ginger McKenna (Sharon Stone)?
a) Casino
b) Last Dance
c) The Specialist
d) Basic Instinct

3) In David Cronenberg's **Videodrome** (1983), the girlfriend of pirate cable TV programmer, Max Renn (James Woods) deliberately burns herself with a cigarette. Who was she?
a) Debbie Harry b) Piper Laurie c) Drew Barrymore d) Tuesday Weld

TERESA WRIGHT (1918 -)

1) She made her film debut playing the daughter of Bette Davis in a 1941 drama based on a Lillian Hellman play directed by William Wyler. Name the title.

258

a) *Jezebel*
b) *The Little Foxes*
c) *Shining Victory*
d) *Mr. Skeffington*

2) In 1942 she won an Academy Award for her portrayal of Carol Beldon who dies tragically shortly after her marriage in the final scenes of **Mrs. Miniver**. How is she killed?
a) *by a bomb blast*
b) *machine-gunned by a Nazi plane*
c) *in a car crash*
d) *crushed by a collapsing wall*

3) With which film do you associate her Uncle Charlie trying to kill her?
a) *Enchantment*
b) *Pursued*
c) *Shadow of a Doubt*
d) *The Steel Trap*

LORETTA YOUNG
(Gretchen Young
1913 - 2000)

1) She won an Oscar for her portrayal of Swedish country girl, Katrin Holstrom, opposite Joseph Cotten and Ethel Barrymore in the 1947 comedy **The Farmer's Daughter**. What was her occupation in the film?
a) *housemaid* b) *schoolteacher*
c) *prostitute* d) *barmaid*

2) In 1947 Professor Wutheridge (Monty Wooley) gives her a "worthless" Roman coin towards her husband's fund-raising efforts. The coin, however, turns out to be the sole survivor of a hundred which were minted by Julius Caesar when Cleopatra visited Rome. Name the film.
a) *Bedtime Story*
b) *And Now Tomorrow*
c) *Eternally Yours*
d) *The Bishop's Wife*

3) Who portrayed her inventor husband in the 1939 biopic **The Story of Alexander Graham Bell**?
a) *Don Ameche*
b) *Fredric March*
c) *Paul Muni*
d) *Walter Pidgeon*

DIRECTORS

ROBERT ALDRICH (1918 - 1983)

1) Name his 1955 crime drama in which private detective Mike Hammer tracks down the "great whatsit".
a) Too Late the Hero b) The Angry Hills
c) Ten Seconds to Hell d) Kiss Me Deadly

2) For which 1952 film was he assistant director to Charlie Chaplin?
a) A King in New York b) Limelight
c) Monsieur Verdoux d) A Countess From Hong Kong

3) Nunnally Johnson and Lukas Heller scripted the biggest hit of Robert Aldrich's career based on a novel by E.M. Nathanson. Name the title.
a) What Ever Happened to Baby Jane? b) Hush, Hush, Sweet Charlotte c) The Dirty Dozen
d) Flight of the Phoenix

WOODY ALLEN
(Allen Stewart Konigsberg 1935 -)

1) In 1977 he won an Oscar for directing and another for co-writing the script of a film in which his lover always smokes a joint before having sex, to which he responds: "Why don't you take sodium pentothal? Then you could sleep through the whole thing!" Name the title.
a) Everything You Always Wanted to Know About Sex (But Were Afraid to Ask) b) Sleeper c) Annie Hall d) Manhattan

2) Name the 1980 comedy he directed which was a homage to Frederico Fellini's **8½**.
a) Stardust Memories b) Take the Money and Run
c) Love and Death d) Interiors

3) **Citizen Kane** (1941) successfully used the technique of integrating a fictional character into archive newsreels in the film's opening. Which 1983 film directed by Woody Allen does the same?
a) September b) The Purple Rose of Cairo
c) Radio Days d) Zelig

PEDRO ALMODOVAR
(Calzada de Calatrava 1951 -)

1) His first international hit was a 1985 comedy about a Madrid family which includes a glue-sniffing mother whose husband is faking Hitler's memoirs. Name the film.
a) What Have I Done to Deserve This? b) Law of Desire c) Dark Habits d) Pepi, Luci, Bom

2) What act does the retired matador perform as he watches scenes of extreme violence on his VCR in the 1986 comedy drama, **Matador**?
a) ritual suicide b) masturbation
c) copulation with a goat d) sodomy

3) What does Ricky (Antonia Banderas), a former psychiatric patient, want from actress Marina (Victoria Abril) when he kidnaps her in Almodovar's 1990 comedy, **Tie Me Up! Tie Me Down!**?
a) her love b) a part in a movie
c) everyone released from his former psychiatric institution d) for her to listen to his poetry

ROBERT ALTMAN (1925 -)

1) After war service as a pilot he started making industrial films in his home town of Kansas City and directed his first feature film in 1957 which led him into a career in television. Name the title of his first feature.
a) The Delinquents b) The James Dean Story
c) Nightmare in Chicago d) Countdown

2) Ring Lardner Jr.'s script was turned down by a string of directors before Robert Altman made it into a memorable film using unknown actors. Name the title.

a) California Split b) Nashville
c) M*A*S*H d) Short Cuts

3) Which 1974 crime drama was based on a 1937 novel by Edward Anderson, which also formed the basis of Nicholas Ray's **They Live By Night** (1948)?
a) Thieves Like Us b) Fool For Love
c) Remember My Name d) Secret Honor

LINDSAY ANDERSON (1923 - 1994)

1) Its original title was 'The Crusaders' - a film which shifted from institutionalised hell to bizarre realism with many parallels to Jean Vigo's **Zero de Conduite**. It ran out of money before colour filming was completed and shooting had to be finished in black and white. Name the title.
a) Thursday's Children b) if...
c) Nighthawks d) In Celebration

2) Which 1963 Lindsay Anderson film, based on a novel by David Storey, features rugby games which were said at the time to reflect a "microcosm of a corrupt society"?
a) Glory! Glory! b) Wakefield Express
c) Green and Pleasant Land d) This Sporting Life

3) In which 1981 film did he have a cameo role as an anti-Semitic master of a Cambridge college?
a) Prick Up Your Ears b) The Browning Version
c) Chariots of Fire d) The Ruling Class

ANTHONY ASQUITH (1902 - 1968)

1) Son of Britain's Liberal Prime Minister, Lord Asquith, his work was routine and predictable until he co-directed a 1938 comedy with Leslie Howard, based on a George Bernard Shaw play, which established him as a leading British director. Name the film.
a) Dulcimer Street
b) Major Barbara
c) The Devil's Disciple
d) Pygmalion

2) In 1938 he began a collaboration with a playwright. This partnership produced memorable films like **The Way To the Stars** (1945), **The Winslow Boy** (1950), **The Browning Version** (1951), and his last film, **The Yellow Rolls-Royce** (1961). Name the playwright.
a) T.E.B. Clarke
b) Eric Ambler
c) Terence Rattigan
d) R.C. Sherriff

3) In which Anthony Asquith comedy does Gwendolen's mother and Algernon's aunt, Lady Bracknell (Edith Evans), cry out, "Prism! Where is that baby?"?
a) The Importance of Being Earnest
b) The Millionairess
c) Doctor's Dilemma
d) French Without Tears

The Movie Quiz Companion

INGMAR BERGMAN (1918 -)

1) Name the Mozart opera he adapted for the screen in 1974, commenting at the time: "[It] was the best time of my life: you can't imagine what it is like to have Amadeus Mozart's music in the studio every day."
a) The Magic Flute b) Cosi fan tutte
c) The Marriage of Figaro d) Don Giovanni

2) After forty years in the movie business Ingrid Bergman was cast by Ingmar Bergman in a 1978 drama speaking her native language in her final theatrical film. Name the title.
a) The Touch
b) Autumn Sonata
c) The Serpent's Egg
d) The Passion of Anna

3) What was professor Isak Borg (Victor Seastrom) on his way to collect in Lund as he journeyed through the countryside with his daughter-in-law in **Wild Strawberries** (1957)?
a) his wife's ashes
b) an honorary degree
c) a tourist visa for Poland
d) a thesis belonging to a student who had committed suicide

BERNARDO BERTOLUCCI (1940 -)

1) Pauline Kael once said that Bertolucci was the only director to extend an influential French auteur's way of looking at things, instead of just copying him. Which French director was she talking about?
a) Jean Vigo b) Louis Malle
c) Jean-Luc Godard d) Claude Chabrol

2) Which Bertolucci mystery features a young man returning to the small town where his anti-fascist father had been assassinated thirty years previously?
a) The Spider's Stratagem b) Tragedy of a Ridiculous Man c) Accatone d) Before the Revolution

3) In which 1973 film does a husband stand over his wife's dead body observing the mortician's cosmetic make-over, commenting: "Look at you! You're a monument to your mother! You never wore makeup, never wore false eyelashes…"?
a) Partner b) The Conformist c) Luna d) Last Tango in Paris

KATHRYN BIGELOW (1951 -)

1) What was the real identity of the nomadic cowboys in her 1987 horror film, **Near Dark**?
a) werewolves b) vampires c) ghosts d) Martians

2) With which Bigelow film do you associate people wanting to "jack in" by attaching "squids" to their heads?
a) Strange Days b) Point Break
c) Union City d) The Loveless

3) What connection can you make between Kathryn Bigelow and director James Cameron?
a) they are sister and brother b) they were once married to each other c) he appeared in her first short film, **Set-Up**, in 1978 d) Bigelow was originally chosen to direct **Titanic**

PETER BOGDANOVICH (1939 -)

1) In his first feature film, **Targets** (1968), he cast a veteran horror-film star portraying a veteran horror-film star named Byron Orlok. Who was he?
a) Boris Karloff
b) Bela Lugosi
c) Max Schreck
d) Ernest Thesiger

2) Which 1971 drama was set in the West Texas town of Anarene?
a) Nickelodeon
b) What's Up, Doc?
c) Daisy Miller
d) The Last Picture Show

3) With which film do you associate a drifter named Moses Pray?
a) Illegally Yours
b) Paper Moon
c) Saint Jack
d) At Long Last Love

Directors

JOHN BOORMAN (1933 -)

1) His first feature, **Having a Wild Weekend** (1965), was a film which endeavoured to repeat the success of the Beatles' **A Hard Day's Night** (1964) using a chart-topping sixties pop group. Who were they?
a) The Dave Clark Five b) The Rolling Stones
c) The Moody Blues d) Herman's Hermits

2) Which 1974 film was set in a futuristic Ireland of 2293?
a) Where the Heart Is b) Leo the Last
c) Angel d) Zardoz

3) His son, Charley Boorman, had a small part as a Luftwaffe pilot in **Hope and Glory**. In which film did his son live with "The Invisible People"?
a) Beyond Rangoon b) The Emerald Forest
c) Excalibur d) Hell in the Pacific

FRANK BORZAGE (1893 - 1967)

1) Name the WWI romance filmed by Borzage in 1932 in which Lt Frederic Henry (Gary Cooper) falls in love with his nurse, Catherine Barkley (Helen Hayes).
a) A Farewell to Arms b) Wings
c) Today We Live d) Sergeant York

2) In which 1936 Borzage romance did automobile designer Tom Bradley (Gary Cooper) gush to jewel thief Madeleine de Beaupre (Marlene Dietrich): "All I know about you is you stole my car and I'm insane about you."?
a) Desire b) The Shining Hour
c) Stranded d) Hearts Divided

3) Martin Brietner refused to join the Nazi party in Borzage's 1940 drama, **The Mortal Storm**, about the plight of a family in the early years of Hitler's Germany. Who was he?
a) Robert Young b) Robert Stack
c) James Stewart d) Victor Mature

MEL BROOKS
(Melvin Kaminsky 1926 -)

1) In 1968 he was awarded an Oscar for his screenplay for a film which was also his directorial debut. Name the title.
a) Blazing Saddles
b) New Faces
c) Young Frankenstein
d) The Producers

2) Name the Mel Brooks comedy which was a spoof of the work of Alfred Hitchcock and which included classic scenes such as the shower scene in **Psycho**, the climbing scene in **Vertigo** and the shooting scene in **North By Northwest**.
a) High Anxiety
b) History of the World - Part 1
c) The Twelve Chairs
d) Silent Movie

3) Which 1987 comedy parodied **Star Wars** peopled with an assortment of wacky characters including Pizza the Hut, Lord Dark Helmet and President SkroobYogurt?
a) Space Camp
b) Spaced Out
c) Spaceballs
d) Space Raiders

CLARENCE BROWN
(1890 - 1987)

1) One of the great legends of the silver screen claimed Clarence Brown was her favourite director of all time. Who was she?
a) Greta Garbo b) Marlene Dietrich
c) Mary Pickford d) Jean Harlow

2) On whose novel did he base his 1943 comedy, **The Human Comedy**, about a wartime family in small town America, starring Mickey Rooney and Frank Morgan?
a) William Saroyan b) Truman Capote
c) Lilliam Hellman d) Taylor Caldwell

3) In which 1940 biopic does he tell MGM's version of the story of a prolific inventor known as "the Wizard of Menlo Park"?
a) Ford: The Man and the Machine b) The Story of Alexander Graham Bell c) Edison the Man
d) Carbine Williams

TIM BURTON (1958 -)

1) What connection can you make between Tim Burton and Disney's 1987 animated feature, **The Fox and the Hound**?
a) he wrote the original book b) he worked on the film as an animator c) he was the voice of the fox
d) he was one of the screenwriters

2) He made his directorial debut with a 1985 comedy about a simple-minded man whose

The Movie Quiz Companion

a gassed park

search for his stolen bicycle in **Pee Wee's Big Adventure** leads him to a national monument. Name the monument.
a) Mt. Rushmore b) the Alamo
c) the Statue of Liberty d) Alcatraz

3) In which film do Mr. and Mrs. Maitland drown in a car accident?
a) Beetlejuice b) Batman Returns
c) Edward Scissorhands d) Batman

JANE CAMPION (1954 -)

1) Name the New Zealand writer who spent eight years in a psychiatric hospital after being wrongly diagnosed as schizophrenic in Jane Campion's 1990 biopic, **An Angel at My Table**.
a) Jessica Anderson
b) Nancy Cato
c) Elizabeth Jolley
d) Janet Frame

2) About which actor, who starred in a 1993 drama directed by her, was she speaking, when she remarked: "The nice thing about [him] is that he's not a young actor and he's not an old actor, he's ageless in a way... For me, he brought the whole alertness and awareness of the acting tradition, he's one of those people that really live it"?
a) Jack Nicholson
b) Harvey Keitel
c) Bruce Willis
d) Sam Neil

3) Name the title of her 1989 feature debut.
a) The Piano
b) Peel
c) Sweetie
d) A Girl's Own Story

FRANK CAPRA (1897 - 1991)

1) Capra made his feature directorial debut with a film called **The Strong Man** in 1926 starring a well known silent comedian about whom he once commented, "His only ally was God. [He]might be saved by a brick falling on a cop, but it was verboten that he in any way motivate the brick's fall." Name the comedian.
a) Harry Langdon
b) Oliver Hardy
c) Harold Lloyd
d) Buster Keaton

2) Who or what was **Broadway Bill** (1934)?
a) a New York theatrical agent
b) a racehorse
c) government legislation banning flappers dancing on stage
d) a racing schooner

3) Which 1946 drama was based on the story "The Greatest Gift" by Philip Van Doren Stern?
a) You Can't Take it With You
b) Meet John Doe
c) Mr. Deeds Goes to Town
d) It's a Wonderful Life

JOHN CARPENTER (1948 -)

1) What was the **Dark Star** in Carpenter's 1974 sci-fi comedy about the elimination of planets which endangered the human race?
a) a space cruiser b) a terrorist organisation
c) a security code d) a brewery

2) **Assault on Precinct 13** (1976) drew its inspiration from a classic 1959 western. Name the title.
a) The Magnificent Seven b) Silverado
c) Rio Bravo d) Gunfight at the O.K. Corral

3) Name the 1951 Howard Hawks - Christian Nyby sci-fi classic he remade in 1982.
a) It Came From Beneath the Sea of Madness
b) When Worlds Collide c) The Fog d) The Thing

CLAUDE CHABROL (1930 -)

1) Cahiers du Cinéma film critic Claude Chabrol left the magazine after inheriting some money and made his first film which many regard as the first of the French New Wave. Name the title.
a) Les Cousins b) Le Beau Serge
c) A Bout de Souffle d) Le Scandale

2) In which 1959 mystery, starring Jean-Paul Belmondo, does a murderer conduct Berlioz?
a) Le Boucher b) Bluebeard
c) Ophelia d) Web of Passion

3) **The Story of Women / Une Affaire de Femmes** (1988) tells the story of Marie Latour, one of the last three women to die on the guillotine for their acts committed in Vichy France. What did she do?
a) she was a Nazi collaborator b) she was a black marketeer c) she was an abortionist d) she was a spy

MICHAEL CIMINO (1943 -)

1) Name the title of the song which is sung in the final scene of **The Deerhunter** (1978).
a) You're a Grand Old Flag b) God Bless America
c) Over There d) Give My Regards to Broadway

2) Cimino's 1980 feature, **Heaven's Gate**, was budgeted for $7.5 million and ended up costing $36 million. A film synonymous with the word flop, not only was it a catastrophic failure, it also sank the studio. Name the studio.
a) Universal b) United Artists
c) Warner Bros. d) Columbia

3) Clint Eastwood recognized his talents as a writer in the early seventies, and together with John Milius, hired him to write a sequel to **Dirty Harry** (1971). Name the title.
a) The Dead Pool b) The Enforcer
c) Magnum Force d) Every Which Way but Loose

HENRI-GEORGE CLOUZOT (1907 - 1977)

1) What put fear into the hearts of the citizens of a small French town in Clouzot's 1943 mystery, **Le Corbeau/The Raven**?
a) the plague b) a gypsy palmist
c) poison-pen letters d) the local asylum

2) During the Nazi Occupation of France Clouzot wrote a script, based on a Simenon mystery, about French corruption and the film was censured for appeasment. Name the title.
a) Jenny Lamour b) The Truth
c) Female Prisoner d) Strangers in the House

3) After receiving his payment for completing his dangerous mission in **The Wages of Fear** (1952), a joyful Mario (Yves Montand) reaches across the dashboard of his truck for something close to his heart, loses control, and topples into a ravine. What was he reaching out for?
a) a faded postcard of the L'Avenue des Champs-Elysées b) a medal from General De Gaulle
c) a phial of nitroglycerine d) a lucky Metro ticket

JEAN COCTEAU (1889 - 1963)

1) Cocteau's first experimental fantasy feature, **The Blood of a Poet** (1930), takes place in the time it takes for a tall object to topple to the ground and break into pieces. What was the object?
a) a chimney b) a statue
c) a bell tower d) a pylon

2) In which 1949 fantasy is poet Jean Marais escorted to the Underworld by a motorcycling "messenger of death"?
a) The Storm Within b) Beauty and the Beast
c) Orpheus d) The Eternal Return

3) Jean Delannoy directed Cocteau's adaptation of the Tristan and Isolde legend in 1943. Name the title.
a) The Eternal Return
b) Intimate Relations
c) Beauty and the Beast
d) Eagle With Two Heads

FRANCIS FORD COPPOLA (1939 -)

1) Name the low budget horror he directed for Roger Corman about gruesome axe murders in 1963.
a) Night of the Blood Beast b) Tower of London
c) The Terror d) Dementia 13

2) In 1983 he directed **Rumble Fish** which he called an "art film for teenagers". It was shot in black and white except for two things which were red and blue. What were they?
a) Ford Mustangs b) basketball shoes
c) piranha fish d) Diane Lane's breasts

3) Which 1974 drama featured Harry Caul (Gene Hackman) as "the best bugger on the West Coast"?
a) Tucker: The Man and His Dream b) The Outsiders c) The Conversation d) One From the Heart

ROGER CORMAN (1926 -)

1) Francis Ford Coppola, Peter Bogdanovich, Martin Scorsese, John Sayles, Robert Towne, Jack Nicholson, Dennis Hopper and Charles Bronson are just a few of the big names who worked on low budget Roger Corman productions early in their careers. Who starred in **Bloody Mama** (1970), about the exploits of Ma Barker, before he was a known quantity?

The Movie Quiz Companion

a) Bruce Willis b) Harvey Keitel
c) George Clooney d) Robert De Niro

2) In which Francis Coppola film did he portray a U.S. senator?
a) The Godfather Part II b) New York Stories
c) Gardens of Stone d) The Cotton Club

3) What did the gas kill in his 1970 production **Gas-s-s-s** or as it is sometimes known, **Gas-s-s... or, It May Become Necessary to Destroy the World in Order to Save It**?
a) violent men b) all the armed forces of the world c) everyone over the age of thirty
d) everyone who watches television

WES CRAVEN (1939 -)

1) Name the Wes Craven film which was based on Ingmar Bergman's **The Virgin Spring**.
a) Last House On the Left
b) Deadly Blessing
c) The Hills Have Eyes
d) Stranger in Our House

2) Who or what attacks the family during their camping holiday in the 1977 horror film, **The Hills Have Eyes**?
a) giant frogs
b) werewolves
c) flesh-eating insects
d) cannibalistic mutants

3) Which DC Comic hero did he adapt for the screen in 1982?
a) Swamp Thing
b) Captain America
c) Green Lantern
d) Marvel Man

DAVID CRONENBERG (1943 -)

1) Name the 1979 horror film starring Oliver Reed and Samantha Eggar in which Eggar eats her own afterbirth.
a) The Brood b) Crimes of the Future
c) Rabid d) They Came From Within

2) Which William S. Burroughs novel did he adapt for the screen in 1991 which features a scene which actually happened in real life when Burroughs accidentally shot his wife dead while performing a party trick?
a) Junkie b) The Wild Boys
c) Exterminator d) Naked Lunch

3) With which 1996 Cronenberg drama do you associate the dramatic re-enactment of the "Death of James Dean"?
a) Nightbreed b) Into the Night
c) Crash d) Scanners II: The New Order

GEORGE CUKOR (1899 - 1983)

1) He made eight feature films with this well known actress, including her screen debut in **Bill of Divorcement** (1932) and the comedy drama **Sylvia Scarlett** (1935) with Cary Grant. Who was she?
a) Jean Harlow
b) Katherine Hepburn
c) Marie Dressler
d) Greer Garson

2) Clark Gable demanded Cukor be replaced as director of a 1939 film he was starring in because he was homosexual. Name the title.
a) Strange Cargo b) Boom Town
c) Test Pilot d) Gone with the Wind

3) During the making of 'Something's Got to Give' in 1962 the female lead died tragically. Who was she?
a) Jayne Mansfield b) Marilyn Monroe
c) Carole Lombard d) Judy Garland

MICHAEL CURTIZ
(Mihaly Kertesz 1888 - 1962)

1) In 1942 he won an Oscar for his film about a nightclub owner who accidentally bumps into a lover from his past who has since married. Name the title.
a) Garden of the Moon b) Gilda
c) Casablanca d) Night and the City

2) David Niven recalls an incident about Curtiz in his 1975 autobiography: "...his Hungarian-orientated English was a source of joy to us all. High on a rostrum he decided that the right moment had come to order the arrival on the scene of a hundred head of riderless chargers. 'Okay.' he yelled into a megaphone - 'Bring on the empty horses!'" Which film was Niven referring to?
a) The Prisoner of Zenda
b) The Charge of the Light Brigade
c) Gunga Din
d) The Lives of a Bengal Lancer

3) Name the western he directed in 1939 which has one of the biggest and best saloon brawls of the genre and was the inspiration for **Blazing Saddles**.
a) Dodge City
b) The Westerner
c) Destry Rides Again
d) Union Pacific

Directors

CECIL B. De MILLE (1881 - 1959)

1) Whom did he cast in the title role of his 1934 historical drama, **Cleopatra**?
a) Madeleine Carroll b) Paulette Goddard
c) Claudette Colbert d) Greta Garbo

2) Where do the **Four Frightened People** try to survive after their shipwreck in De Mille's 1934 adventure, starring Claudette Colbert and Herbert Marshall?
a) Mont Blanc b) South Pole c) desert d) jungle

3) He made the same film twice. Once in 1923 and again in 1956. Name the title.
a) Samson and Delilah b) Union Pacific
c) The Ten Commandments d) The Buccaneer

JONATHAN DEMME (1944 -)

1) Demme's 1987 film, **Swimming to Cambodia**, is a long monologue by actor Spalding Gray relating his experiences (amongst those of others) of the time he worked on a film in Cambodia. Name the title.
a) The Killing Fields b) Apocalypse Now
c) Welcome Home d) Rambo: First Blood Part II

2) In 1971 he co-wrote and produced the road movie, **Angels Hard as They Come**, which he claimed was a biker version of an Akira Kurosawa classic. Which one was it?
a) Yojimbo b) The Seven Samurai
c) Ran d) Rashomon

3) Name the 1991 drama which won five Oscars, including Best Director for Demme, which was adapted from a novel by Thomas Harris.
a) Traffic b) Philadelphia
c) The Silence of the Lambs d) American Beauty

BRIAN DE PALMA (1940 -)

1) His early feature films, **The Wedding Party** (1966), **Greetings** (1968) and **Hi, Mom!** (1970) were notable for the appearance of an actor who would eventually graduate to superstar status. Who was he?
a) Clint Eastwood b) Jack Nicholson
c) Al Pacino d) Robert De Niro

2) His first commercial success was based on a novel by Stephen King which went on to become a stage musical. Name the film.
a) Carrie b) Get to Know Your Rabbit
c) Wise Guys d) Blow Out

3) Which 1981 mystery featured John Travolta as a sound man for a B-movie company, who, while one night standing on a bridge recording night-time sound effects (owls, bats etc.), witnesses a car plunging into the river, an incident which sucks him into a web of intrigue?
a) Blow Out b) The Fury
c) Dressed to Kill d) Body Double

VITTORIO DE SICA (1902 - 1974)

1) In **Umberto D.** (1952), the eponymous protagonist falls many years behind with the rent for his room, so while he is out at work, his landlady, in order to recoup her losses, rents out his room to second parties. Who are they?
a) lovers b) gamblers c) artists d) musicians

2) In which Italian city is **The Bicycle Thief** (1949) set?
a) Naples b) Rome c) Milan d) Siena

3) What does the old lady find in a cabbage patch in the 1951 fantasy, **Miracle in Milan**?
a) a confused angel b) a newborn baby
c) the Pope's ring d) a statue of the Madonna

WILLIAM DIETERLE (Wilhelm Dieterle 1893 - 1972)

1) Before it was made into a Broadway musical in 1955, Dieterle shot a version of this Arabian Nights-type story with Ronald Colman and Marlene Dietrich in 1944. Name the title.
a) Kismet b) The Student Prince
c) The Desert Song d) The Kissing Bandit

2) Which 1948 film about a painter in love with a girl begins with the prologue: "Since the beginning, Man has looked into the awesome reaches of infinity.... Out of the shadows of knowledge, and out of a painting that hung on a museum wall comes our story, the truth of which lies not on our screen but in your heart."?
a) Scarlet Street b) The Light That Failed
c) Portrait of Jennie d) An American in Paris

3) Maureen O'Hara made her screen debut as a beautiful gypsy named Esmerelda in a 1939 Dieterle drama. Name the title.
a) The Great O'Malley b) Juarez
c) The Life of Emile Zola d) The Hunchback of Notre Dame

The Movie Quiz Companion

EDWARD DMYTRYK (1908 - 1999)

1) Which Raymond Chandler novel, featuring wisecracking gumshoe Philip Marlowe, did he adapt for the screen in 1944?
a) The Big Sleep b) Farewell My Lovely
c) The High Window d) Lady in the Lake

2) With which 1954 drama do you associate the paranoid and cleanliness fanatic, Captain Queeg?
a) The Caine Mutiny b) The Left Hand of God
c) Walk On the Wild Side d) Crossfire

3) In which Dmytryk war drama, based on a novel by Irwin Shaw, does Marlon Brando portray an idealistic German youth who gradually turns into a confused and disillusioned Nazi officer?
a) Soldier of Fortune b) The Men
c) The Young Lions d) The Fugitive Kind

STANLEY DONEN (1924 -)

1) Name the Stanley Donen musical which was based on Stephen Vincent Benét's story, 'The Sobbin' Women'?
a) Funny Face b) Give a Girl a Break
c) The Grass is Greener d) Seven Brides for Seven Brothers

2) Which musical co-directed by Donen features the songs, 'I Feel Like I'm Not Out of Bed Yet', 'Come Up to My Place', 'Main Street', 'Miss Turnstiles Ballet' and 'Pearl of the Persian Sea'?
a) Bedazzled b) Take Me Out to the Ball Game
c) On the Town d) The Pajama Game

3) With which 1955 musical do you associate three demobbed WWII buddies (Gene Kelly, Dan Dailey & Michael Kidd) deciding to have a reunion with each other in ten years' time?
a) It's Always Fair Weather b) This Time For Keeps
c) Damn Yankees d) Deep in My Heart

CLINT EASTWOOD (1930 -)

1) Name the title of his 1971 directorial debut.
a) Play Misty For Me b) The Eiger Sanction
c) Breezy d) High Plains Drifter

2) In 1990 he directed himself in **White Hunter, Black Heart**, about a fictional filmmaker named John Wilson and his desperate attempts to kill an elephant while location shooting in Africa. Which legendary director was Wilson based on?
a) Howard Hawks b) John Huston
c) Cecil B. De Mille d) Raoul Walsh

3) With which film do you associate him as William Munny, a man who has killed women and children in his career as an outlaw?
a) High Plains Drifter b) Joe Kidd
c) Pale Riger d) Unforgiven

BLAKE EDWARDS (1922 -)

1) Best known for his Pink Panther series, what was the last Pink Panther film made by Blake Edwards before Peter Sellers' death in 1980?
a) Revenge of the Pink Panther b) Return of the Pink Panther c) Trail of the Pink Panther d) The Pink Panther Strikes Again

2) David is obsessed with women in the 1983 comedy, **The Man Who Loved Women**, and consults an analyst to help him with his problem but ends up falling in love with her. Who was he?
a) Malcolm McDowell b) Dudley Moore
c) James Garner d) Burt Reynolds

3) Name his actress-singer second wife who starred in many of his films and also writes children's books.
a) Ann Margret b) Petula Clark
c) Julie Andrews d) Mamie Van Doren

SERGEI EISENSTEIN (1898 - 1948)

1) Why do the ship's officers order a group of sailors on the **Potemkin** (1925) to be executed; an act which leads to the crew's mutiny and ignites the 1905 uprising?
a) they refused to shoot civilians
b) they refused to salute an officer
c) they refused to accept a pay cut
d) they refused to eat rancid meat

2) The Odessa steps sequence in **Potemkin** in which a mother is shot and her baby carriage lurches down the steps has been imitated time and again in the cinema. Name the 1987 crime drama which pays homage to the scene.
a) City Heat
b) The Untouchables
c) Scarface d) Al Capone

whinged hormones **Directors**

3) Which film, complete with the Russian Army as extras, re-enacts a historic battle in 1242 against Teutonic invaders on the frozen surface of Lake Peipus?
a) Alexander Nevsky b) Seeds of Freedom
c) Strike d) Ivan the Terrible, Part I

RAINER WERNER FASSBINDER
(Bad Wörishofen 1945 - 1982)

1) Name the title of the third part of Fassbinder's trilogy of life in postwar Germany, which followed **The Marriage of Maria Braun** (1978) and **Lola** (1982).
a) Veronika Voss b) Martha
c) Lili Marleen d) Querelle

2) In which 1974 romantic drama does a sixty year old widow marry a man thirty years her junior?
a) The Merchant of Four Seasons
b) The American Soldier
c) Gods of the Plague
d) Ali - Fear Eats the Soul

3) Fassbinder died in 1982, aged only 36. What killed him?
a) cancer b) heart failure
c) suicide d) plane crash

FREDERICO FELLINI
(1920 - 1993)

1) In Fellini's 1951 solo directorial debut a woman falls in love with a comic-strip hero. Name the title.
a) The White Sheik b) The Greatest Love
c) Without Pity d) Bullet For Stefano

2) With which 1960 film do you associate a statue of Christ being airlifted across Rome by a helicopter?
a) Juliet of the Spirits b) Nights of Cabria
c) Boccaccio 70 d) La Dolce Vita

3) A 1957 drama directed by Fellini won the Oscar for Best Foreign Film and was the basis for the Broadway musical, **Sweet Charity** (1969). Name the title.
a) Nights of Cabiria b) I Vittelloni
c) Amarcord d) La Strada

VICTOR FLEMING (1883 - 1949)

1) Steven Spielberg's **Always** (1989) was a remake of a Victor Fleming's 1943 romantic fantasy about a dead WWII pilot returning to earth to help his girlfriend through her grief and steer her into another relationship. Name the title.
a) Always Remember I Love you b) A Guy Named Joe c) Flying high d) Love Has Many Faces

2) Who portrayed Long John Silver in Fleming's 1934 version of **Treasure Island**?
a) Lewis Stone b) Otto Kruger
c) Wallace Beery d) Charles McNaughton

3) MGM remade this jungle drama in 1953 as **Mogambo**, but the original was shot by Fleming in 1932 with Jean Harlow and Mary Astor fighting over Clark Gable. Name the title.
a) The Devil's Cargo b) Renegades
c) Red Dust d) Mantrap

JOHN FORD
(Sean Aloysius O'Fearna 1895 - 1973)

1) John Wayne became synonymous with the later films of John Ford, but who was the actor who worked closely with him on his early productions (26 in all), and to whom Ford dedicated **3 Godfathers** (1948) ?
a) George O'Brien
b) Ralph Bellamy
c) Wallace Beery
d) Harry Carey, Sr.

2) The sweeping vistas of Utah's Monument Valley were used time and again by Ford as a location for his westerns. Name the last one he shot there.
a) The Searchers
b) My Darling Clementine
c) Cheyenne Autumn
d) She Wore a Yellow Ribbon

3) In 1941 he adapted a popular novel by Richard Llewellyn for the screen. Name the title.
a) The Long Voyage Home
b) How Green Was My Valley
c) The Fugitive
d) They Were Expendable

The Movie Quiz Companion

MILOS FORMAN (1932 -)

1) Name the James Rado - Gerome Ragni - Galt MacDermot hit musical play, set during the age of Aquarius, Forman adapted for the screen in 1979.
a) The Wiz b) Jesus Christ Superstar
c) Hair d) Celebration at Big Sur

2) Which 1984 Milos Forman film was shot in Prague and ends with the protagonist being buried in an unmarked grave?
a) Visions of Eight b) The Fireman's Ball
c) Amadeus d) Taking Off

3) Two film versions of the Choderlos de Laclos novel *Les Liaisons Dangereuses* were filmed within twelve months of each other. The first was Stephen Frears' **Dangerous Liaisons** (1988 / also filmed by Roger Vadim in 1959). What was the title of Milos Forman's 1989 version?
a) The Seduction b) The King's Whore
c) Danton d) Valmont

BILL FORSYTH (1946 -)

1) Which film was inspired by Jack Kerouac's novel, 'Maggie Cassidy'?
a) Gregory's Girl b) Housekeeping
c) Being Human d) Comfort and Joy

2) What was radio announcer, Alan Bird's (Bill Paterson) nickname on his early morning radio show in the 1984 comedy, **Comfort and Joy**?
a) The Bird Man of Bearsden b) Birdy Boy
c) Dickie Bird d) Chirpy Cheep Cheep

3) About which Bill Forsyth film was Vincent Canby talking when he commented, "this is a movie in which just about everybody has a skin problem"?
a) That Sinking Feeling b) Gregory's Girl
c) Comfort and Joy d) Breaking In

JOHN FRANKENHEIMER (1930 -)

1) Burt Lancaster starred in Frankenheimer's 1961 drama **The Young Savages**. Who were the savages?
a) Apache dog-soldiers b) a Harlem juvenile gang
c) student pilots d) kindergarten infants

2) Name the Eugene O'Neill play he adapted for the screen in 1973, depicting the assorted characters of Harry Hope's (Fredric March) saloon.
a) The Emperor Jones
b) The Iceman Cometh
c) Ah, Wilderness
d) Long Day's Journey into Night

3) Col. Martin 'Jiggs' Casey uncovers a military plot to overthrow the government in the 1964 political thriller, **Seven Days in May**. Who was he?
a) Burt Lancaster b) Martin Balsam
c) Fredric March d) Kirk Douglas

WILLIAM FRIEDKIN (1939 -)

1) He began his career in television and made his feature film debut directing a sixties pop group during the summer of love in 1967 with **Good Times**. Name the group.
a) The Birds b) The Mamas and the Papas
c) Sonny and Cher d) Canned Heat

2) For which film was he awarded a Best Director Oscar in 1971?
a) The French Connection b) The Exorcist
c) To Live and Die in LA d) The Night They Raided Minsky's

3) His 1977 adventure, **Sorcerer**, was a remake of a classic French drama. Name the title.
a) The Red Balloon b) Grand Illusion
c) Rules of the Game d) The Wages of Fear

SAMUEL FULLER (1911 - 1997)

1) Sam Fuller, who had been a newspaperman and crime reporter in the 1930s, made a film in 1952 about the world of newspapers in 1880s New York. Name the title.

a) Scandal Sheet b) Park Row
c) Confirm or Deny d) Shockproof

2) Jessica Drummond was a despotic ranch owner who ruled Cochise County with her **Forty Guns** (1957). Who was she?
a) Barbara Stanwyck b) Joan Crawford
c) Thelma Ritter d) Barbara Bel Geddes

3) Who or what was the **White Dog** trained to attack in Sam Fuller's 1982 controversial drama?
a) black people b) policemen
c) crucifixes d) beggars

ABEL GANCE
(Abel Perethon 1889 - 1981)

1) Who or what does railway engineer, Sisif (Severin-Mars), rescue from the train crash in **La Roue** (1922)?
a) a piano b) a dog
c) a baby d) a horse

2) Which 1918 film opens with a mass of soldiers coming together to form the letters of the title?
a) J'accuse
b) Au Secours!
c) Barbe Rousse
d) La Fleur Des Ruines

3) In 1927 Abel Gance shot his 6-hour epic **Napoleon**, which today still stands as one of the great filmmaking feats of the twentieth century. Thirty-three years later, in 1960, he made a film which re-enacted Napoleon's greatest battle. Name the title.
a) The Battle of Austerlitz
b) The Battle of Waterloo
c) The Battle of the Nile
d) The Battle of Neretva

TERRY GILLIAM (1940 -)

1) Name the film which was his solo directing debut in 1977.
a) Brazil b) Jabberwocky
c) Time Bandits d) Monty Python's The Meaning of Life

2) With which Terry Gilliam film do you associate the fastest man on earth who ran to Spain and back for a bottle of wine?
a) Monty Python and the Holy Grail b) The Fisher King c) The Adventures of Baron Munchausen
d) Life of Brian

3) **Time Bandits** (1981) features the maiden voyage of a famous ship. Name the ship.
a) The Mayflower b) The Marie Celeste
c) Titanic d) HMS Victory

JEAN-LUC GODARD (1930 -)

1) With which 1967 drama do you associate an hysterical woman attempting to enter a burning car to retrieve her precious Gucci bag, and a wife eating a stew containing her husband's remains?
a) Weekend b) A Married Woman
c) Lola d) A Woman is a Woman

2) Which Shakespeare classic did he adapt and modernise in 1987?
a) Hamlet b) Macbeth
c) A Midsummer Night's Dream d) King Lear

3) In **Breathless** (1959), small-time crook, Michel (Jean-Paul Belmondo), is pursued by the police for a killing and seeks out refuge with his girlfriend, Patricia. Who was she?
a) Anouk Aimée b) Anna Karina
c) Monique Messine d) Jean Seberg

PETER GREENAWAY (1942 -)

1) In his stylish 1989 drama, **The Cook, The Thief, His Wife & Her Lover**, who played the wife?
a) Tilda Swinton b) Juliet Stevenson
c) Helen Mirren d) Vanessa Redgrave

2) Mr. Neville (Anthony Higgins), a wandering draughtsman, offers to do twelve

drawings of Mrs. Herbert's (Janet Suzman) estate in the 1984 historical drama, **The Draughtsman's Contract**. How is he paid?
a) with as much venison as he can eat served by Mrs. Herbert's naked cook b) after each drawing he is allowed to have sex with one of Mrs. Herbert's parlour maids c) after each drawing there is a special nude ball held in his honour d) with sexual favours from Mrs. Herbert

3) Which film features three women all named Cissie Colpitt?
a) Drowning By Numbers b) The Belly of an Architect c) Prospero's Books d) A Zed & Two Noughts

D.W. GRIFFITH (1875 - 1948)

1) Griffiths made around twenty films a week from 1907 to 1913, usually for Biograph, the film studio from which he disassociated in 1913 following its refusal to let him make his first feature-length film. He eventually made it in 1915. Name the title.
a) Dream Street b) The Birth of a Nation c) San Francisco d) Hearts of the World

2) During which period of history did he set his 1922 drama, **Orphans of the Storm**?
a) American Civil War b) French Revolution c) American War of Independence d) Russian Revolution

3) With which film do you associate the St. Bartholomew's Day Massacre of the French Huguenots in 1572?
a) Intolerance b) Drums of Love c) The Greatest Question d) Way Down East

HENRY HATHAWAY
(1898 - 1985)

1) He began his directing career making low-budget westerns, including **The Last Round-Up**, **The Thundering Hero** and **Sunset Pass**, with an actor who became synonymous with the genre.
Who was he?
a) Randolph Scott
b) Gene Autry
c) Wallace Beery
d) Gabby Hayes

2) In 1953 he directed Marilyn Monroe in a thriller about a wife who plans to kill her husband. Name the title.
a) Hometown Story
b) Clash By Night
c) River of No Return
d) Niagara

3) Which of Hathaway's films was critic Pauline Kael describing when she commented:
"The adolescent boy's fantasy atmosphere is very powerful... part of the picture's romantic charge is its underlying homoeroticism, which comes out in Cooper and Tone's comic camaraderie... But if the movie is morally repugnant, it's also a terrific piece of Hollywood Victoriana."?
a) The Lives of a Bengal Lancer
b) Beau Geste
c) Saratoga Trunk
d) Ten Gentlemen From West Point

HOWARD HAWKS (1896 - 1977)

1) Name the gangster film he directed in 1932 about which writer Ben Hecht and he claimed they had approached the family in the story "as if they were the Borgias set down in Chicago"?
a) Today We Live b) Scarface
c) The Criminal Code d) Barbary Coast

2) Which 1946 film involved him phoning the author because he was baffled by the plot, to which the author replied: "How should I know? You figure it out" and hung up?
a) Monkey Business b) The Big Sleep
c) The Outlaw d) To Have and Have Not

3) With which film do you associate a reporter filing this story over the radio: "One of the world's greatest battles was fought and won today by the human race. Here on top of the world, a handful of American soldiers met the first invasion from another planet. Now, before I bring you the details of the battle, I bring you a warning . . . to everyone listening to the sound of my voice. Tell the world. Tell this to everyone wherever they are: 'Watch the skies! Watch everywhere. Keep on looking. Watch the skies!'" ?
a) War of the Worlds b) It Came From Outer Space c) Day the World Ended d) The Thing (From Another World)

jade has orangutan snot **Directors**

WERNER HERZOG
(Werner Stipetic 1942 -)

1) Name his 1975 biopic based on the life of Kaspar Hauser who is kept chained in a cellar from infancy and suddenly appears in 1820s Nuremberg.
a) Every Man for Himself and God Against All b) Nosferatu the Vampyre c) Signs of Life d) Land of Silence and Darkness

2) Brian Sweeney Fitzgerald, known as **Fitzcarraldo** to the Indians and Spanish, devises a scheme to build an opera house twelve hundred miles upstream from the South American coast. Name the opera singer he planned to bring there to sing.
a) Enrico Caruso b) Emma Calvé c) Clara Butt d) Nellie Melba

3) Name the country **Where the Green Ants Dream** (1984)?
a) India b) Yemen c) Mexico d) Australia

GEORGE ROY HILL (1922 -)

1) Which James A. Michener novel (all 1,130 pages) did he adapt for the screen in 1966?
a) The Bridges at Toko-Ri b) Chesapeake c) Hawaii d) Centennial

2) With which film do you associate Robert Leroy Parker and Harry Longabaugh?
a) Butch Cassidy and the Sundance Kid b) The Sting c) The World of Henry Orient d) Slaughterhouse Five

3) Reggie Dunlop is player and coach to the Charlestown Chiefs, a third-rate hockey team who stop losing and start winning when they learn to play "aggressive hockey" in **Slap Shot** (1977). Who portrays Reggie?
a) Paul Newman b) Chevy Chase c) Robin Williams d) Robert Redford

ALFRED HITCHCOCK
(1899 - 1980)

1) He began his life in the cinema designing title-cards at Islington Studios for its American owners, Famous Players-Lasky. Over the next five years he acquired expertise in most aspects of film production and in 1925 Michael Balcon asked him to direct his first film. Name the title.
a) The Pleasure Garden b) The Lodger c) Blackmail d) The Blackguard

2) Who portrayed caustic fashion journalist, Connie Porter, who cares more for her furs and jewellery than she does for her fellow survivors in **Lifeboat** (1944)?
a) Agnes Moorehead b) Tallulah Bankhead c) Linda Darnell d) Irene Dunn

3) The legendary Hitchcock cameo was born when he needed people "to fill the screen" in **The Lodger**, and cast himself as an extra. Where did he make his appearance in **The Lady Vanishes** (1938)?
a) playing poker on a train b) boarding a train carrying a bass violin c) in a London railway station d) In silhouette, seen behind a door in the Foreign Office

JOHN HUSTON (1906 - 1987)

1) What 1951 film connection can you make between John Huston and author Stephen Crane?
a) The Treasure of the Sierra Madre b) The Battle of San Pietro c) Let There Be Light d) The Red Badge of Courage

2) Which film features an encounter with the warship Louisa?
a) The Wind and the Lion b) Moby Dick c) Beat the Devil d) The African Queen

3) Name his 1987 film which was adapted from a short story in James Joyce's *Dubliners* in which Gabriel Conroy (Donal McCann) muses: "Better pass boldly into that other world, in the full glory of some passion, than fade and wither dismally with age."
a) Young Giants b) The Dead c) Independence d) Victory

JAMES IVORY (1928 -)

273

The Movie Quiz Companion

1) The prolific artistic relationship between James Ivory, producer Ismail Merchant and writer Ruth Prawer Jhabvala, began in 1963 with a comedy about a schoolteacher contending with his arranged marriage. Name the title.
a) The Householder b) The Guru
c) The Delhi Way d) Shakespeare Wallah

2) Name the Henry James novel he adapted for the screen in 1979.
a) The Bostonians b) The Europeans
c) The Aspern Papers d) The Golden Bowl

3) With which Merchant-Ivory production do you associate Darlington Hall?
a) The Remains of the Day b) Maurice
c) Howards End d) A Room With a View

DEREK JARMAN (1942 - 1994)

1) Painter, writer, designer and avant-garde film-maker, he made his first short films while working as a set designer on a Ken Russell production in 1971. Name the production.
a) Savage Messiah b) The Devils
c) Mahler d) The Boy Friend

2) His first full-length feature film, **Sebastiane**, was released in 1976 with English subtitles. Which language is spoken throughout the film?
a) Gaelic b) Breton c) Latin d) Basque

3) In 1991 he adapted for the screen a 16th century play by Christopher Marlowe about a gay king, and included Annie Lennox of the Eurythmics singing Cole Porter's "Ev'ry Time We Say Goodbye." Name the title.
a) Edward II
b) The Last of England
c) Wittgenstein d) Jubilee

LAWRENCE KASDAN (1949 -)

1) Name the Billy Wilder classic to which Kasdan's 1981 crime drama, **Body Heat**, has been compared.
a) Witness For the Prosecution b) The Lost Weekend c) Double Indemnity d) Sunset Blvd.

2) In which 1995 romantic comedy does a jewel thief hide a diamond bracelet in Meg Ryan's luggage?
a) French Kiss b) The Big Chill
c) I Love You to Death d) Grand Canyon

3) In 1981 he wrote the script for a film centred around the broken stone tablets of the Ten Commandments. Name the title.
a) The Holcroft Covenant b) Thou Shalt Not Kill
c) Raiders of the Lost Ark d) Dead and Buried

ELIA KAZAN (Elia Kazanjoglou 1909 -)

1) Criticized for "naming names" to the House Un-American Activities Committee in 1952 during the communist witch hunts, he answered his critics with a 1954 film, of which he later wrote: "When Brando, at the end, yells… 'I'm glad what I done—you hear me?—glad what I done!' that was me saying with identical heat, that I was glad I'd testified as I had." Name the film.
a) The Fugitive Kind b) The Wild One
c) Viva Zapata! d) On the Waterfront

2) In 1947 he was awarded a Best Director Oscar for his adaptation of a Laura Z. Hobson novel about a writer (Gregory Peck) who poses as a jew when writing about anti-Semitism. Name the title.
a) Gentlemen's Agreement b) Pinky
c) The Sea of Grass d) Boomerang!

3) With a screenplay by Harold Pinter and a cluster of stars it was considered by many to be the best screen adaptation of an F. Scott Fitzgerald novel ever made. Name the title.
a) The Great Gatsby b) The Last Tycoon
c) Beloved Infidel d) Tender is the Night

HENRY KING (1886 - 1982)

1) In 1955, Korean war correspondent, Mark Elliot (William Holden), falls in love with Eurasian doctor Han Suyin in Henry King's romantic tale, **Love is a Many Splendored Thing**. Who was she?
a) Jennifer Jones b) Nancy Kwan
c) Merle Oberon d) Gloria Grahame

2) Which 1949 war film depicts the physical and emotional stress of the 918th Bomber Group under the command of the seemingly cold-blooded General Savage (Gregory Peck) in WWII England?
a) Dawn Patrol
b) Twelve O'Clock High
c) Captains of the Clouds d) The Wings of Eagles

Directors

chaotic prancing king

3) Which 1956 Rodgers & Hammerstein musical, directed by King, features the songs "If I Loved You," "June is Bustin' Out All Over," "Soliloquy," and "You'll Never Walk Alone"?
a) Carousel b) Pal Joey
c) State Fair d) Oklahoma!

ALEXANDER KORDA
(Sandor Lazlo Kellner 1893 - 1956)

1) Some say he was inspired to make his 1933 classic after seeing a statue resembling its star and some say it was inspired by a song, which years later became a hit for Herman's Hermits. Name the film.
a) Knight Without Armour b) Sanders of the River
c) The Scarlet Pimpernel d) The Private Life of Henry VIII

2) Who played the title role in his 1948 adventure, **Bonnie Prince Charlie**?
a) Leslie Howard b) David Niven
c) Cedric Hardwicke d) Laurence Olivier

3) Hendrickje Stoffels was the young kitchenmaid who became the mistress of Dutch painter **Rembrandt** (Charles Laughton) in Korda's 1936 biopic. Who was she?
a) Gertrude Lawrence b) Everley Gregg
c) Jean Parker d) Elsa Lanchester

STANLEY KRAMER (1913 -)

1) What do the Italian peasants hide from the Nazis in Kramer's 1969 comedy, **The Secret of Santa Vittoria**?
a) their women b) their gold
c) their wine d) their fireworks factory

2) In the 1947 adventure, **The Pride and the Passion**, British naval officer, Capt. Anthony Trumbull (Cary Grant), retrieves something from the retreating Spanish army to use against Napoleon's forces. What is it?
a) a cannon b) a hot-air balloon
c) a submarine d) a battering ram

3) Name the Nevil Shute novel he adapted for the screen in 1959 which stars Fred Astaire in his first dramatic role.
a) The Far Country b) Lonely Road
c) On the Beach d) No Highway

STANLEY KUBRICK
(1928 - 1999)

1) Kubrick's raw, brutal and technically brilliant depiction of a combat zone during Vietnam's Tet Offensive in **Full Metal Jacket** (1987) was recreated in a London suburb using plastic plants from Hong Kong, ruined buildings, piles of burning tyres, two tanks and two helicopters. Name the location.
a) Old Clapham Hospital b) Woolwich Arsenal
c) Beckton Gas Works d) Battersea Docks

2) Which Kubrick film took its title from Thomas Gray's 'Elegy Written in a Country Churchyard'?
a) Eyes Wide Shut b) Paths of Glory
c) The Shining d) Killer's Kiss

3) **A Clockwork Orange** (1971) is set in a violent Britain of the near future where language is debased and dapper gangs roam bleak landscapes, robbing, murdering and raping. The book's author, Anthony Burgess, called the language 'Nadsat', taken from the Russian suffix for 'teen'. What is the Nadsat word for testicles?
a) yarblockos b) rookers
c) appy polly loggies d) eggyweggs

AKIRA KUROSAWA (1910 -)

1) Name his 1962 crime drama which was based on the Ed McBain novel, *King's Ransom* ?
a) High and Low
b) Throne of Blood
c) Stray Dog
d) The Lower Depths

2) **The Magnificent Seven** (1960) was a western remake of **The Seven Samurai** (1954). Which western did its sequel, **Yojimbo**, inspire?
a) Once Upon a Time in the West
b) A Fistful of Dollars
c) Rio Bravo
d) Shane

3) Which 1985 film was an adaptation of Shakespeare's King Lear?
a) Sanjuro
b) Kagemusha
c) Ran
d) Red Beard

The Movie Quiz Companion

deathbed got unhealthy dog

JOHN LANDIS (1950 -)

1) Landis was charged with involuntary manslaughter in 1983 after a stunt helicopter crashed killing three performers, but he was acquitted in 1987 after a lengthy trial. Which film was he working on at the time of the crash?
a) Twilight Zone - The Movie
b) Coming to America
c) Spies Like Us
d) Trading Places

2) Who portrayed the music store owner who helped **The Blues Brothers** (1980) get their old band back together again?
a) Marvin Gaye
b) Stevie Wonder
c) Smokey Robinson
d) Ray Charles

3) With which film do you associate American tourists, David and Jack, visiting a country inn called The Slaughtered Lamb?
a) Innocent Blood
b) Death Race 2000
c) An American Werewolf in London
d) Into the Night

FRITZ LANG (1890 - 1976)

1) Financed by Howard Hughes, Lang's 1952 western starring Marlene Dietrich was to be called 'Chuck-a-Luck', but Hughes decided the title was all wrong and replaced it with a new one. Name the film.
a) Destry Rides Again b) Rancho Notorious
c) Gun Moll d) The Return of Frank James

2) In which 1952 drama, based on a Clifford Odets story, did he direct Marilyn Monroe?
a) Clash by Night b) Niagara
c) The Asphalt Jungle d) River of No Return

3) Fritz Lang's first American film, a crime drama made in 1936, was described by Graham Greene as "the only film I know to which I have wanted to attach the epithet of 'great'." Name the title.
a) Man Hunt b) You Only Live Once
c) Fury d) The Big Heat

DAVID LEAN (1908 - 1991)

1) In the early thirties he moved to the British-Dominion Studios at Elstree where he became a successful feature film editor, but he turned down offers to direct several quota-quickies, fearing their cheap production techniques could damage his career. In 1942, however, Noel Coward gave him the opportunity to co-direct a film which began his directing career. Name the title.
a) Private Lives b) This Happy Breed
c) Cavalcade d) In Which We Serve

2) Which David Lean drama was inspired by Gustave Flaubert's 'Madame Bovary'?
a) The Passionate Friends b) Madeleine
c) Ryan's Daughter d) Summertime

3) In **The Bridge on the River Kwai** (1957) Colonel Saito welcomes the new prisoners with the address: "In the name of his Imperial Majesty I welcome you. I am the commanding officer of this camp, which is Camp 16, along the great railroad which will soon connect Bangkok with Rangoon. You British prisoners have been chosen to build a bridge across the River Kwai." Who portrayed Colonel Saito?
a) Toshiro Mifune b) Takashi Shimura
c) Masayuki Mori d) Sessue Hayakawa

SPIKE LEE
(Shelton Jackson Lee 1956)

1) His commercial debut was a comedy about a woman (Tracy Camila Johns) and her three lovers, in which Spike Lee portrayed Mars Blackmon, a street hustler with the catchphrase, "please, baby, please, baby, please, baby, please, baby". Name the title.
a) Mo' Better Blues b) School Daze
c) She's Gotta Have It d) The Last Party

2) Which film features Sal, who boasted, "these people have grown up on my pizza"?
a) Do the Right Thing b) Lonely in America
c) Jungle Fever d) Girl 6

3) How do the people known as **Clockers** (1995) earn their livelihood on the streets of New York City?
a) driving high-speed cars b) timing a prostitute's client c) selling drugs "around the clock" d) as 24-hour look-outs for drug dealers

Directors

SERGIO LEONE (1921 - 1989)

1) Leone's directorial debut was a 1960 sword-and-sandal adventure, starring Rory Calhoun, set in ancient Greece. Name the title.
a) The Colossus of Rhodes
b) The 300 Spartans
c) Duel of the Titans
d) Atlantis, The Lost Continent

2) His 1984 drama, **Once Upon a Time in America**, was based on a novel by Harry Grey. Name the title.
a) The Hoods
b) Streetwise
c) A Jewish Childhood
d) Max & Noodles

3) Who portrayed the hunchback on whose neck a match was struck by bounty hunter Colonel Mortimer in the 1966 western, **For a Few Dollars More**?
a) Woody Strode
b) Aldo Sambrell
c) Klaus Kinski
d) Jack Elam

MERVYN LeROY (1900 - 1987)

1) In the 1930s he made a classic gangster film in which the tough and menacing lead, Edward G. Robinson, has to have his eyelids fixed with transparent tape to stop him blinking with fright every time he fires a gun. Name the film.
a) Little Caesar b) Dead End
c) The Public Enemy d) Scarface

2) Who played the title role in his 1936 historical drama, **Anthony Adverse**?
a) Ronald Colman b) Paul Muni
c) Robert Taylor d) Fredric March

3) Who played the title role in LeRoy's 1955 comedy drama, **Mister Roberts**?
a) Tyrone Power b) Henry Fonda
c) James Cagney d) William Powell

ERNST LUBITSCH (1892 - 1947)

1) Lubitsch once said, "Never did I make a picture in which the atmosphere and the characters were truer than in this picture." Based on the play *Parfumerie* by Nikolaus Laszlo, name the title.
a) To Be or Not to Be b) Heaven Can Wait c) The Shop Around the Corner d) If I Had a Million

2) Which 1934 musical comedy was based on the operetta *Die lustige Witwe* by Franz Lehar, Victor Leon and Leo Stein?
a) The Merry Widow b) Maytime
c) Rose Marie d) Naughty Marietta

3) Jewel thief, Gaston Monescula Valle (Herbert Marshall), falls in love with fellow thief, Lily Vautier, in Lubitsch's 1932 comedy, **Trouble in Paradise**. Who was she?
a) Miriam Hopkins b) Gene Tierney
c) Zasu Pitts d) Jeanette MacDonald

GEORGE LUCAS (1944 -)

1) Who played the title role in George Lucas' first feature, **THX-1138**, a sci-fi drama set in the 25th century where drugs are pumped into citizens to curb their sexual appetites?
a) Harrison Ford
b) James Caan
c) Donald Pleasence
d) Robert Duvall

2) The comic book hero created by celebrated cartoonist Alex Raymond was a major inspiration for **Star Wars** (1977). Name the hero.
a) Rip Kirby
b) Commando Yank
c) Spacehawk
d) Flash Gordon

The Movie Quiz Companion

an unscathed oaf foams

3) Who portrayed Terry, the hapless nerd who desperately desires to be "cool" in **American Graffiti**?
a) Charles Martin Smith b) Tim Crowley
c) Ron Howard d) Paul Le Mat

SYDNEY LUMET (1924 -)

1) Name the Eugene O'Neill play he adapted for the screen in 1962, starring Katharine Hepburn and Ralph Richardson.
a) Long Day's Journey Into Night b) The Iceman Cometh c) Days Without End d) Ah! Wilderness

2) Name the prisoner of war drama he directed in 1965.
a) The Fugitive Kind b) The Group
c) The Deadly Affair d) The Hill

3) With which Sydney Lumet film do you associate Howard Beale, seasoned anchorman of the United Broadcasting System whose job is about to be axed?
a) Broadcast News
b) Network
c) Hidden Agenda
d) Bob Roberts

DAVID LYNCH (1946 -)

1) Which David Lynch film featured the "yellow man"?
a) The Grandmother b) Dune
c) Blue Velvet d) Eraserhead

2) The drug spice is traded on a galactic scale in Lynch's 1984 sci-fi adaptation of Frank Herbert's novel **Dune**. What effect does spice have?
a) allows one to live indefinitely b) gives one a fifteen minutes-long orgasm c) allows one to share a partner's dreams d) makes one irresistible to the opposite sex

3) In the final scenes of **Wild at Heart** (1990), Sailor (Nicolas Cage) jumps on the bonnet of a car and bursts into an Elvis song. Name the title.
a) It's Now or Never b) One Night
c) Love Me Tender d) Can't Help Falling in Love

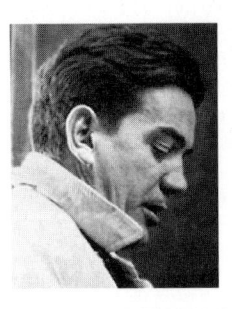

ALEXANDER MACKENDRICK (1912 - 1993)

1) Although his directorial debut film is now considered a classic, it did not make much impact on its release after its West End premier at the Haymarket Gaumont on 16 June 1949. It is now, however, regarded as one of the great Ealing comedies. Name the title.
a) The Ladykillers b) The Lavender Hill Mob
c) Whisky Galore d) Kind Hearts and Coronets

2) Name the 1954 Mackendrick comedy which contains the following dialogue:
Marshall (in plane): "Where do you figure they're headed for?"
Pilot: "It looks like they're putting in to Inverkerran for the night."
Marshall: "Well, tell me: if they thought I thought they were going to Inverkerran, where do you think they'd head for then?"
Pilot: "Strathcathaig, maybe."
Marshall: "I know this sounds silly - but if they thought I'd think they were going to Strathcathaig because it looks as if they're going to Inverkerran - where would they head for then?"
Pilot: "My guess would be Pennymaddy."
Marshall: "Well, if there's such a thing as a triple-bluff, I'll bet MacTaggart invented it. Okay - Pennymaddy."
a) The Ghost Goes West b) The Maggie
c) I Know Where I'm Going d) Wee Geordie

3) Which of his films was he commenting on when he said: "It's too good a book to have been attempted as a film, so it was bound to be second-rate"?
a) A High Wind in Jamaica b) Sweet Smell of Success c) Mandy d) The Devil's Disciple

LOUIS MALLE (1932 - 1995)

1) In the 1987 drama, **Au Revoir, Les Enfants**, the headmaster of a Catholic boys' boarding school in occupied France in 1944 is dismissed and sent to a work camp. What was his crime?
a) embezzling school funds b) molesting pupils
c) sheltering Jews d) promoting communism

2) In which 1980 film did he direct Burt Lancaster?
a) Atlantic City b) Murmur of the Heart
c) Black Moon d) Little Treasure

278

fat sheep polenta

Directors

3) Who portrayed the twelve year old girl who was raised in a New Orleans brothel where her mother is a prostitute in Louis Malle's 1978 drama, **Pretty Baby**?
a) Barbara Hershey b) Drew Barrymore
c) Gail Strickland d) Brooke Shields

DAVID MAMET (1947 -)

1) His 1987 directorial debut involved author and psychiatrist, Dr. Margaret Ford (Lindsay Crouse), becoming involved with a confidence trickster. Name the title.
a) House of Games b) About Last Night...
c) Black Widow d) We're No Angels

2) The mob promises to realize a Chicago shoeshine man's (Don Ameche) dream if he confesses and takes the wrap for a murder he never committed in Mamet's 1984 film, **Things Change**. What was his dream?
a) to own a Chicago pizzeria
b) to own a fishing boat in Sicily
c) to bring his family to America
d) to live on L'Avenue des Champs-Elysées

3) In 1982 he was Oscar nominated for Writing - Screenplay (Based on Material from Another Medium) for a legal drama about medical negligence. Name the title.
a) The Verdict b) Body of Evidence
c) The Client d) Q&A

ROUBEN MAMOULIAN (1897 - 1987)

1) In 1932 he made what was probably the best adaptation of a Robert Louis Stevenson novel ever put on film, but when MGM remade the film in 1941 they bought the rights to the Mamoulian version and buried it for thirty years. Name the title.
a) Treasure Island b) The Master of Ballantrae
c) Weir of Hermiston d) Dr. Jekyll and Mr. Hyde

2) Which Mamoulian historical drama features Garbo uttering the lines: "I'm tired of being a symbol... I long to be a human being. This longing I cannot suppress"?
a) Queen Christina b) Anna Christie
c) Camille d) Anna Karenina

3) In 1957 he directed Fred Astaire and Cyd Charisse in a remake of Garbo's **Ninotchka** (1939). Name the title.
a) Daddy Long Legs
b) Funny Face
c) Finian's Rainbow
d) Silk Stockings

JOSEPH L. MANKIEWICZ (1909 - 1993)

1) Name the 1963 film in which he directed Elizabeth Taylor and Richard Burton.
a) Butterfield 8 b) Who's Afraid of Virginia Woolf?
c) Cleopatra d) The V.I.P.s

2) With which 1950 Mankiewicz drama do you associate Bette Davis' classic line: "Fasten your seatbelts, it's going to be a bumpy night"?
a) The Little Foxes b) Now, Voyager
c) All About Eve d) Mr. Skeffington

3) In 1953 he adapted a Shakespeare play for the screen with a distinguished classical cast which included James Mason and John Gielgud, but in the leading role he cast against type, Marlon Brando, an actor who was in those days nicknamed "The Mumbler" and "The Slob". Name the film.
a) Macbeth b) Henry V c) Julius Caesar d) Hamlet

ANTHONY MANN (Emil Anton Bundmann 1906 - 1967)

1) The western was the genre in which Mann's directorial talents excelled, especially when working with his favourite star, James Stewart. Name the title of their first western collaboration in 1950.
a) Border Incident b) Bend of the River
c) Winchester '73 d) The Tin Star

279

The Movie Quiz Companion

2) Who played the title role in his 1958 western, **Man of the West**?
a) Sterling Hayden b) Gary Cooper
c) Lee Marvin d) Henry Fonda

3) In 1960 he was fired as director from a picture which was subsequently taken over by Stanley Kubrick. Name the film.
a) Spartacus b) Paths of Glory
c) Lolita d) The Killing

VINCENTE MINNELLI
(1910 - 1986)

1) Name the Minnelli musical which features the songs 'Dancing in the Dark,' 'Shine on Your Shoes,' and 'That's Entertainment'.
a) The Pirate
b) The Band Wagon
c) Cabin in the Sky
d) Ziegfeld Follies

2) In 1956 he directed a screen adaptation of an Irving Stone biography about a man who leaves his native country to give religious instruction to Belgian coal miners in 1878, and eventually ends up committing himself to a mental institution. Name the film.
a) Undercurrent
b) The Cobweb
c) The Seventh Sin
d) Lust For Life

3) Which musical won six Oscars: Best Picture, Best Screenplay, Best Cinematography (colour), Best Art Direction (colour), Best Musical Scoring and Best Costume Design (colour), in 1951?
a) An American in Paris
b) Gigi
c) Brigadoon
d) Meet Me in St. Louis

F.W. MURNAU
(Friedrich Wilhelm Plumpe 1888 - 1931)

1) In a 1927 film in which a man is persuaded to drown his wife by his lover, the opening title reads: "This story of a man and his wife is of nowhere and everywhere, you might hear it anywhere and at any time." Name the film.
a) City Girl b) Burning Soil
c) Sunrise d) Journey Into the Night

2) Who portrayed the screen's first Dracula, in Murnau's 1922 classic **Nosferatu**?
a) Gustav von Wangenheim
b) Wolfgang Heinz
c) Alexander Granach
d) Max Schreck

3) Name the title of E. Elias Merhige's 2000 dramatisation of the strange incidents that paralleled the making of **Nosferatu**, starring Willem Dafoe and John Malkovich.
a) Shadow of the Vampire
b) The Velvet Vampire
c) Tale of a Vampire
d) The Vampire Lover

MIKE NICHOLS
(Michael Igor Peschkowsky 1931 -)

1) In which Mike Nichols film does Mr. Maguire (Walter Brooke) offer the advice: "I just want to say one word to you. Just one word. Are you listening? Plastics!"?
a) Carnal Knowledge b) Heartburn
c) The Graduate d) Biloxi Blues

2) He made his directorial debut in 1966 with a film based on a play by Edward Albee about a couple who have invented a son and speak about him as if he were real. Name the title.
a) The Fortune b) Who's Afraid of Virginia Woolf
c) The Day of the Dolphin d) A Day in the Death of Joe Egg

3) What does Eugene Jerome (Matthew Broderick) have to suffer for ten weeks in Biloxi, Mississippi, in the 1988 comedy drama **Biloxi Blues**?
a) cotton picking b) army basic training
c) chronic diarrhoea d) piano lessons

MAX OPHULS
(Max Oppenheimer 1902 - 1957)

1) Name the Max Ophüls' 1951 omnibus film based on three Guy de Maupassant stories: *The Mask*, *The Model* and *The House of Madame Tellier*.

a) *Le Plaisir* b) *La Ronde*
c) *The Reckless Moment* d) *The Earrings of Madame de...*

2) What was the occupation of the beautiful Lola Montes, the eponymous heroine in a film Ophüls made in 1955 recounting a woman's love affairs with numerous men, including Franz Liszt and the King of Bavaria?
a) prostitute b) circus performer
c) gypsy fortune teller d) opera singer

3) Who portrayed Leocadie, the young prostitute in Max Ophüls' **La Ronde** (1950), a film deemed "immoral" by the New York State censorship board?
a) Isa Miranda b) Simone Simon
c) Danielle Darrieux d) Simone Signoret

ALAN PARKER (1944 -)

1) He made his directorial feature film debut in 1976 with a film featuring a femme fatale called Tallulah. Name the title.
a) *Come See the Paradise* b) *Fame*
c) *Bugsy Malone* d) *Melody*

2) Who was the cartoonist employed to do the animated sequences in Alan Parker's 1982 rock musical, **Pink Floyd - the Wall**?
a) Ralph Steadman b) Gerald Scarfe
c) Steve Bell d) Dave Brown

3) George (Albert Finney) and Faith Dunlap's marriage is drifting towards the rocks in **Shoot the Moon** (1982). When Faith's daughter asks: "Why did Daddy leave us?" Faith answers: "I don't think he left you; I think he left me". Who portrayed Faith?
a) Diane Keaton b) Diahnne Abbott
c) Rosanna Arquette d) Ellen Burstyn

PIER PAOLO PASOLINI
(1922 - 1975)

1) Poet, atheist, Marxist and homosexual, Pasolini was one of Italy's greatest post-war film-makers who made his first film in 1961 about the pimps and low-life crooks of Rome. Name the title.
a) *Accatone* b) *Mamma Roma*
c) *La Rabbia* d) *Nights of Cabiria*

2) On whose bawdy tales was Pasolini's octet of stories in **The Decameron** (1970) based?
a) Giovanni Boccaccio b) Geoffrey Chaucer
c) Baldassare Count Castiglione d) Luigi Pirandello

3) His last film before his death (he was beaten to death by a 17-year old boy who claimed he made sexual advances towards him) in 1975 was an adaptation of a Marquis de Sade novel set in Fascist Italy during WWII. Name the title.
a) *Salo, or The 120 Days of Sodom* b) *Pigsty*
c) *Medea* d) *The Witches*

SAM PECKINPAH (1925 - 1984)

1) Who played the title role in his 1972 rodeo comedy drama, **Junior Bonner**?
a) Kris Kristofferson b) James Coburn
c) Steve McQueen d) Paul Newman

2) With which film do you associate ageing lawman, Steve Judd, being hired to escort a shipment of gold from the mining community of Coarse Gold?
a) *Ride the High Country* b) *Major Dundee*
c) *The Wild Bunch* d) *The Ballad of Cable Hogue*

3) Name the Robert Ludlum thriller he adapted for the screen in 1983.
a) *The Holcroft Covenant* b) *The Osterman Weekend* c) *The Icarus Agenda* d) *The Road to Gandolfo*

ROMAN POLANSKI
(Raimund Polanski 1933 -)

2) What does the work colleague of the psychotic Carol Ledoux observe rotting from the heat in her handbag in Polanski's 1965 horror film, **Repulsion**?
a) the head of a rabbit b) a sheep's heart
c) a dead kitten d) a fish head

3) With which film do you associate the paranoid Trelkovsky (Roman Polanski) dressing up as a woman and attempting suicide by throwing himself out of a window?
a) *The Tenant* b) *Two Men and a Wardrobe*
c) *Pirates* d) *Tess*

1) He co-starred with his future wife, Sharon Tate, in a 1967 horror comedy. Name the title.
a) *Andy Warhol's Dracula* b) *The Magic Christian*
c) *Two Men and a Wardrobe* d) *The Fearless Vampire Killers or: Pardon Me, But Your Teeth Are in My Neck*

SYDNEY POLLACK (1934 -)

1) Who played the title role in Pollack's 1977 drama, **Bobby Deerfield**, about a Grand Prix racing driver who falls in love with a dying girl?
a) Robert Redford b) Paul Newman
c) Max von Sydow d) Al Pacino

2) For what 1981 drama does investigative reporter, Megan Carter (Sally Field), print an unattributed story that discredits innocent liquor distributor Michael Gallagher (Paul Newman)?
a) Absence of Malice b) The Drowning Pool
c) The Scalphunters d) The Slender Thread

3) Name his exotic 1975 gangster film, scripted by Paul Schrader, which features world-weary private eye, Harry Kilmer, battling against oriental mobsters.
a) The Shanghai Gesture b) The Yakuza
c) Death Becomes Her d) Year of the Dragon

MICHAEL POWELL (1905 - 1990)

1) **Ill Met by Moonlight** (1957) was based on an actual WWII incident in which partisans kidnapped a German officer. The film's title is a quote from one of Shakespeare's comedies. Name the play.
a) Much Ado About Nothing b) As You Like It
c) Merry Wives of Windsor d) A Midsummer Night's Dream

2) **The Edge of the World** (1937) was Michael Powell's first opportunity to direct something original and imaginative after cutting his teeth on a succession of low-budget quota-quickies. Inspired by the 1930 depopulation of a Scottish island, which could not at that time be used because of its status as a nature reserve, Foula was used instead. Name the original island.
a) Fair Isle b) Benbecula c) Canna d) St. Kilda

3) Who portrayed Theo Kretschmar-Schuldorff, the young German officer who duels with Clive Candy (Roger Livesey) in **The Life and Death of Colonel Blimp** (1943)?
a) Roland Culver b) John Chandos
c) Anton Walbrook d) Niall MacGinnis

OTTO PREMINGER (1906 - 1986)

1) With which 1960 film do you associate the Haganah and the Irgun?
a) Bunny Lake is Missing b) Exodus
c) In Harm's Way d) Saint Joan

2) Name his classic Gershwin musical which features the songs, 'It Ain't Necessarily So' and 'I Got Plenty Of Nothin'.
a) Porgy and Bess b) The Shocking Miss Pilgrim
c) Carmen Jones d) Rosalie

3) For what 1953 POW drama does he portray the sadistic and ostentatious camp commandant, Oberst Von Scherbach?
a) The Password is Courage b) The Cross of Lorraine c) King Rat d) Stalag 17

NICHOLAS RAY (1911 - 1979)

1) Nicholas Ray's first feature was a 1949 Depression-era tale based on Edward Anderson's novel *Thieves Like Us*, with a unique (for its day) opening scene shot from a helicopter. Name the title.
a) The Lusty Men
b) The Savage Innocents
c) On Dangerous Ground
d) They Live By Night

2) In 1955 he directed a film about misunderstood teenagers in which the three leading players were all destined to die tragically in real-life. One drowned, one died in a car crash and one was stabbed to death. Name the film.
a) Run For Cover
b) Born To Be Bad
c) Knock on Any Door
d) Rebel Without a Cause

Directors

3) Cynical Hollywood screenwriter, Dixon Steele (Humphrey Bogart), has an affair with starlet Laurel Grey in the 1950 drama, **In a Lonely Place**. Who was she?
a) Gloria Grahame b) Susan Hayward
c) Joan Fontaine d) Cathy O'Donnell

CAROL REED (1906 - 1976)

1) A well-known British thriller writer, who co-wrote **King Kong**, was instrumental in introducing him to the film world when he asked Reed to supervise his book's screen adaptations. Who was he?
a) John Dickson Carr b) James Hadley Chase
c) Edgar Wallace d) Peter Cheyney

2) He directed his first film, **Midshipman Easy**, in 1934, and seven films later, in 1939, he was to make the film which would secure his reputation as an imaginative talent to watch out for. Name the title.
a) The Third Man b) Night Train to Munich
c) The Stars Look Down d) Kipps

3) What does the little boy believe he has found which can help him work miracles in the 1955 comedy fantasy, **A Kid for Two Farthings**?
a) a leprechaun b) a unicorn
c) a genie d) a wishing-well

ROB REINER (1945 -)

1) Name the title of Spinal Tap's soundtrack album which gets "lots of air play with cuts like 'Sex Farm'" in Reiner's 1984 parody of a rock documentary, **This Is Spinal Tap**.
a) S is for Tap b) Discovering Famous Graves
c) Nightmares of Ecstasy d) Smell the Glove

2) Which 1987 Middle Ages adventure is set in the mythical kingdom of Florin with assorted heroes and villains, including R.O.U.S. - Rodents of Unusual Size?
a) The Swan Princess b) The NeverEnding Story
c) The Princess Bride d) Dragonslayer

3) With which film do you associate novelist Paul Sheldon meeting his "number one fan"?
a) The American President b) The Sure Thing
c) Misery d) Postcards From the Edge

JEAN RENOIR (1894 - 1979)

1) Renoir's 1932 comedy, **Boudu Saved From Drowning**, about the exploits of a tramp who is rescued from the Seine, was remade by Hollywood director Paul Mazursky in 1986, starring Nick Nolte and Richard Dreyfuss. Name the title.
a) Born Again b) Moon Over Parador
c) Down and Out in Beverly Hills d) Life and Nothing But

2) Which 1937 film was banned in Germany by Nazi Propaganda Minister Josef Goebbels who labelled it "Cinematographic Enemy Number 1"?
a) Grand Illusion b) The Lower Depths
c) Rules of the Game d) La Bête Humaine

3) Renoir's first colour film was a 1951 drama, based on a Rumer Godden novel, about a British family in Bengal. Name the title.
a) The River b) A Day in the Country
c) Picnic on the Grass d) The Golden Coach

TONY RICHARDSON (1928 - 1991)

1) "Angry Young Man", Arthur Seaton (Albert Finney), makes his workmate's wife pregnant in the 1960 "kitchen sink" drama, **Saturday Night and Sunday Morning**. His real love, however, is the old-fashioned Doreen Gretton, who refuses to sleep with him until marriage is on the horizon. Who was she?
a) Shirley Ann Field b) Claire Bloom
c) Rachel Roberts d) Julia Foster

2) A 1963 film directed by Tony Richardson won four Oscars, including Best Picture and Director. He declined to attend the award ceremony and later commented, "I didn't go to the awards - not to strike an attitude but because I had never understood their importance in the eyes of the industry and they were never important to me." Name the film.

a) *A Taste of Honey* b) *The Loved One*
c) *The Loneliness of the Long Distance Runner*
d) *Tom Jones*

3) In 1968 he portrayed Lord Raglan, who headed the ill-prepared expeditionary force against the Russians in the Crimea in **The Charge of the Light Brigade**. Who was he?
a) *Harry Andrews* b) *Trevor Howard*
c) *John Gielgud* d) *Ralph Richardson*

ROBERT RODRIGUEZ (1969 -)

1) With which horror film do you associate the crooked brothers, Seth and Richard Gecko, who take a family hostage in Mexico?
a) *From Dusk Till Dawn* b) *Santa Sangre*
c) *After Midnight* d) *Body Parts*

2) In the 1995 anthology film **Four Rooms**, who portrayed the Latino tough guy who checks into a hotel with his wife and their two mischievous children?
a) *Alfonso Arau* b) *Pedro Armendariz*
c) *Antonio Moreno* d) *Antonio Banderas*

3) El Mariachi teams with the sultry and enterprising Carolina (Salma Hayek) in Rodriguez' 1995 **El Mariachi** sequel, **Desperado**. What is her occupation in the film?
a) *district midwife* b) *bookstore proprietress*
c) *tourist guide* d) *car mechanic*

NICOLAS ROEG (1928 -)

1) In 1968 he co-directed a film with Donald Cammell which the studio initially refused to release and which critic Richard Schickel described as "the most disgusting, the most completely worthless film I have seen since I began reviewing." Name the title.
a) *Demon Seed* b) *Performance*
c) *White of the Eye* d) *The Girl-Getters*

2) What was the purpose of marooned alien, Thomas Jerome Newton's (David Bowie) visit to earth in Roeg's 1976 sci-fi drama, **The Man Who Fell to Earth**?
a) *to mate with humans* b) *to find a new planet for his race* c) *to find water for his planet* d) *to find an antidote for a galactic plague*

3) In 1987 she portrayed a woman who answers an advertisement which reads "Writer seeks 'wife' for a year on tropical island" in a film based on Lucy Irvine's autobiographical narrative **Castaway**. Who was she?
a) *Amanda Donohoe* b) *Mimi Rogers*
c) *Theresa Russell* d) *Anita Morris*

GEORGE ROMERO (1940 -)

1) Which 1978 Romero film was critic Roger Ebert describing when he commented: "It is gruesome, sickening, disgusting, violent, brutal, and appalling. It is also (excuse me for a second while I find my other list) brilliantly crafted, funny, droll, and savagely merciless in its satiric view of the American consumer society. Nobody ever said art had to be in good taste"?
a) *Night of the Living Dead* b) *Dawn of the Dead*
c) *Day of the Dead* d) *Creepshow*

2) Who or what was **Martin** (1978)?
a) *a werewolf* b) *a vampire*
c) *a Nazi war-criminal* d) *a feral child*

3) What bursts out of ruthless multimillionaire Upson Pratt's (E.G. Marshall) stomach in the finale of Romero's 1982 horror film, **Creepshow**?
a) *cockroaches* b) *rats* c) *bats* d) *snakes*

KEN RUSSELL (1927 -)

1) Often accused of being tasteless and vulgar, critic Pauline Kael once described him as "a shrill, screaming gossip." His second

film, however, was quite restrained compared to his later works and featured Cockney spy, Harry Palmer (Michael Caine). Name the title.
a) Gambit b) Funeral in Berlin
c) Billion Dollar Brain d) The Ipcress File

2) On whose novel was his 1988 horror film, **The Lair of the White Worm** based?
a) Edgar Allan Poe b) Bram Stoker
c) J. Sheridan Le Fanu d) M.R. James

3) Name his 1991 film which was based on a play called 'Bondage', written by London cabbie, David Hines, who based it on tales related to him by his prostitute passengers.
a) Salome's Last Dance b) Crimes of Passion
c) Women & Men: Stories of Seduction d) Whore

JOHN SCHLESINGER (1926 -)

1) Schlesinger's 1962 feature film debut was based on a 1960s Stan Barstow novel. Name the title.
a) Watchers on the Shore
b) A Kind of Loving
c) Brother's Tale
d) Ask Me Tomorrow

2) With which 1971 drama do you associate the *ménage à trois* of Peter Finch, Glenda Jackson and Murray Head?
a) Sunday, Bloody Sunday
b) The Falcon and the Snowman
c) The Day of the Locust
d) Visions of Eight

3) In the 1987 horror film, **The Believers**, who or what does the cultish religion sacrifice?
a) virgins b) children c) horses
d) those who have never achieved physical perfection

MARTIN SCORSESE (1942 -)

1) Before he discovered film-making Martin Scorsese had seriously considered pursuing another career which contrasted greatly with that of the life of a film director. What was it?
a) airline pilot b) priest
c) ballroom dancer d) geologist

2) The actress who portrayed Mary Magdalene in **The Last Temptation of Christ** (1988) actually introduced Scorsese to the original Nikos Kazantzakis novel. Who was she?
a) Barbara Hershey
b) Laura Dern
c) Ellen Burstyn
d) Rosanna Arquette

3) With which 1978 film do you associate Ringo Starr?
a) After Hours
b) New York, New York
c) American Boy
d) The Last Waltz

RIDLEY SCOTT (1937 -)

1) His first feature, made in 1977, was based on a story by Joseph Conrad. Name the film.
a) Lord Jim b) Legend c) Victory d) The Duellists

2) Critic Roger Ebert summarized a 1987 Ridley Scott thriller in one sentence: "Detective from working-class background falls in love with society beauty." Name the title.
a) The Late Show b) Someone to Watch Over Me
c) The Naked Prey d) Strange Days

3) In 1992 he portrayed explorer Christopher Columbus in Ridley Scott's historical adventure, **1492: Conquest of Paradise**. Who was he?
a) Gerard Depardieu b) Armand Assante
c) Fernando Rey d) Frank Langella

DON SIEGEL (1912 - 1991)

1) Who or what does Major John Tarrant (Michael Caine) try desperately to locate in Siegel's 1974 spy drama, **The Black Windmill**?
a) a radioactive isotope b) his son's kidnappers
c) a rogue plague virus d) the Sultan of Oman's harem

2) Who played the title role in the 1968 NYC crime drama, **Madigan**?
a) Henry Fonda b) Charles Bronson
c) John Wayne d) Richard Widmark

The Movie Quiz Companion

3) Name the 1973 crime thriller in which bank robber Walter Matthau swipes $750,000 of laundered Mafia money and is pursued by hit-man Joe Don Baker.
a) *Jinxed!* b) *Telefon*
c) *Rough Cut* d) *Charley Varrick*

ROBERT SIODMAK (1900 - 1973)

1) Tony Curtis made his screen debut as a gigolo in a 1949 thriller starring Burt Lancaster and Yvonne De Carlo. Name the title.
a) *The Great Sinner*
b) *The Killers*
c) *Criss Cross*
d) *The Suspect*

2) Who played the title role in the 1952 swashbuckling adventure, **The Crimson Pirate**?
a) Errol Flynn
b) Tyrone Power
c) Burt Lancaster
d) Anthony Quinn

3) In **Cry of the City** (1948) two childhood buddies grow up and oppose each other as a policeman and criminal. Name the city featured in the film.
a) New York
b) San Francisco
c) Chicago
d) Denver

STEVEN SPIELBERG (1947 -)

1) Why do Lou Jean (Goldie Hawn) and her husband (William Atherton) speed towards Sugarland, Texas, in a hijacked highway patrol car in the 1974 adventure, **The Sugarland Express**?
a) to retrieve their child b) to appear on local television c) to save the life of a politician d) to have a last hot-dog in the drive-in where they met before it is demolished

2) Name the 1980 John Landis comedy which features him in the cameo role of 'Cook County Clerk'?
a) *The Blues Brothers* b) *Kelly's Heroes*
c) *The Kentucky Fried Movie* d) *Trading Places*

3) On whose Pulitzer Prize-winning book about two sisters who become separated was his 1985 drama **The Color Purple** based?
a) Alice Walker b) Paula Marshall
c) Maya Angelou d) Toni Morrison

GEORGE STEVENS (1904 - 1975)

1) In a 1935 comedy drama, based on a Booth Tarkington story, he cast Katharine Hepburn as a small-town social climber who falls for the wealthy Arthur Russell (Fred MacMurray). Name the title.
a) *Quality Street* b) *Morning Glory*
c) *Sylvia Scarlett* d) *Alice Adams*

2) After the death of their unborn baby, Julie and Roger Adams (Irene Dunne and Cary Grant) decide to adopt a child in a 1941 comedy drama. Name the title.
a) *Love Without Question* b) *Penny Serenade*
c) *Vigil in the Night* d) *A Miracle Can Happen*

3) Who shared a Washington apartment during the WWII housing shortage with Jean Arthur and Joel McCrea in the 1943 comedy, **The More the Merrier**?
a) Edward Everett Horton b) Monty Woolley
c) Eric Blore d) Charles Coburn

OLIVER STONE (1946 -)

1) In his 1981 horror film, **The Hand** (inspired by **The Beast With Five Fingers** (1946)), a cartoonist's hand is severed in an accident and gains a murderous life of its own. Who portrayed the cartoonist?
a) James Woods b) Michael Caine
c) James Belushi d) Warren Beatty

2) Name the film which was based on the real-life experiences of foreign correspondent Richard Boyle.
a) *Salvador*
b) *Year of the Dragon*
c) *Platoon* d) *Seizure*

286

3) **Talk Radio** (1988) was based on the book *Talked to Death: The Life and Murder of Alan Berg* by Stephen Singular and the play created by the actor who portrayed controversial talk-radio host, Barry Champlain, in the movie. Who was he?
a) Michael Wincott b) Alec Baldwin
c) Eric Bogosian d) Robert Trebor

PRESTON STURGES
(Edmund Preston Biden
1898 - 1959)

1) In which 1944 comedy does Woodrow Lafayette Pershing Truesmith (Eddie Bracken) become discharged from the Marines because of hay fever, but rather than face the shame, concocts a story to his mum about being sent overseas?
a) Strictly Dishonorable b) Never Say Die
c) Unfaithfully Yours d) Hail the Conquering Hero

2) In the 1942 screwball comedy, **The Palm Beach Story**, Gerry Jeffers (Claudette Colbert) is running away from her husband (Joel McCrea) when she meets millionaire, J.D. Hackensacker III - who becomes besotted with her - on the train to Florida. Who was he?
a) Eugene Pallette b) Chester Conklin
c) Henry Fonda d) Rudy Vallee

3) Preston Sturges' favourite character actor starred in many of his films, portraying Muggsy-Ambrose Murgatroyd in **The Lady Eve**, the 'sergeant' in **Hail the Conquering Hero**, Officer Kockenlocker in **The Miracle of Morgan's Creek** and in 1946 was Oscar-nominated for his role in **The Jolson Story**. Who was he?
a) William Demarest b) Robert Warwick
c) Arthur Hoyt d) Brian Donlevy

JOHN STURGES (1910 - 1992)

1) Name his 1968 drama based on an Alistair Maclean novel which was reputed to have been Howard Hughes' favourite film.
a) Ice Station Zebra b) Breakheart Pass
c) The Satan Bug d) Fear is the Key

2) Who portrayed Wyatt Earp in John Sturges' 1967 western, **Hour of the Gun**?
a) Robert Ryan b) Burt Lancaster
c) James Garner d) Dennis Hopper

3) What are Chris, Vin, O'Reilly, Lee, Harry, Britt and Chico better known as?
a) The Magnificent Seven b) The Comancheros
c) Quantrill's Raiders d) The Grissom Gang

QUENTIN TARANTINO (1963 -)

1) In which 1994 film, based on a story by Tarantino, does a teenager comment in a TV interview: "Mass murder is wrong. But if I WERE a mass murderer, I'd be Mickey and Mallory!"?
a) Killing Zoe
b) Desperado
c) Natural Born Killers
d) Girl 6

2) In **Four Rooms** (1995), an anthology of four stories set in a lack-lustre hotel linked by Ted (Tim Roth) the bellhop, Tarantino directed **The Man From Hollywood** segment. In the scene where Chester (Tarantino) and his friends are watching an old Hitchcock TV drama where a man bets he can light a Zippo lighter ten times in a row, what was to be his fate if he lost the bet?
a) his finger would get chopped off
b) his wife would be raped
c) his dog would be buried alive
d) he would have to swallow poison

3) Who portrayed bail bondsman Max Cherry, who is hired to get an L.A. stewardess (Pam Grier) out of jail after being busted by the ATF (Bureau of Alcohol, Tobacco and Firearms) in **Jackie Brown**?
a) Lawrence Tierney
b) Robert Forster
c) Tiny Lister
d) Frank Whaley

The Movie Quiz Companion

J. LEE THOMPSON (1914 -)

1) Name his 1959 crime drama, based on the novel 'Rodolphe et le Revolver' by Noel Calef, in which a young Welsh girl witnesses a murder.
a) The Passage b) Tiger Bay
c) The Yellow Balloon d) For Better, For Worse

2) Who portrayed Maria the Resistance leader who is supposedly tortured by the Nazis in Thompson's 1961 war drama, **The Guns of Navarone**? She also portrayed the beautiful and desirable widow in **Zorba the Greek** (1964).
a) Monica Vitti b) Melina Mercouri
c) Katina Paxinou d) Irene Papas

3) Which 1962 thriller was based on John D. MacDonald's novel *The Executioners*?
a) The Weak and the Wicked b) Eye of the Devil
c) Cape Fear d) Woman in a Dressing Gown

JACQUES TOURNEUR
(1904 - 1977)

1) Which film was Tourneur discussing when he commented: "I was the one who suggested that one of the gangsters ought to be killed with a fishing rod. It was more original that way than with a gun, and more importantly, it was more weird..."?
a) Experiment Perilous
b) Berlin Express
c) Out of the Past
d) Circle of Danger

2) After a whirlwind romance with no kissing or sex, and a marriage based on same, a somewhat-stressed out Oliver settles down to life with Cat Woman, Irene Dubrovna, in Jacques Tourneur's 1942 horror classic, **Cat People**. Who portrayed Oliver?
a) Kent Smith b) Ralph Meeker
c) Joseph Turkel d) Jack Holt

3) Name his 1958 horror film which was adapted from Montague R. James's story *Casting the Runes*?
a) Night of the Demon b) The Fearmakers
c) I Walked With a Zombie d) Nightfall

FRANCOIS TRUFFAUT
(1932 - 1984)

1) In **The Woman Next Door** (1981) newly wed Mathilde Bauchard (Fanny Ardant) moves next door to her former lover Bernard, who is now also happily married. Who portrayed him?
a) Gerard Depardieu b) Jean-Louis Trintignant
c) Charles Aznavour d) Alain Delon

2) Name the 1959 film which was the first in Truffaut's autobiographical Antoine Doinel (Jean-Pierre Léaud) series which stretched over twenty years.
a) Love at Twenty b) Stolen Kisses
c) Bed and Board d) The Four Hundred Blows

3) With which 1973 film do you associate him playing a director who is shooting an American-financed film called 'Meet Pamela', with Jean-Pierre Léaud, Jean-Pierre Aumont, Jacqueline Bisset, and Valentina Cortese?
a) The Man Who Loved Women b) Mississippi Mermaid c) Two English Girls d) Day for Night

ROGER VADIM
(Roger Vadim Plemiannikov 1928 -)

1) Which 1968 film, based on the book by Jean-Claude Forest, features a blind angel named Pygar?
a) Love on a Pillow b) The Night Heaven Fell
c) Barbarella d) Blood and Roses

2) Name the film which was responsible for rocketing Brigitte Bardot to stardom and international sex symbol status in 1956.
a) ...And God Created Woman b) School for Love
c) The Bride is Much Too Beautiful d) Female

3) In 1987 he published a book about his relationships, subtitled *My Life with the Three Most Beautiful Women in the World*. Brigitte Bardot and Jane Fonda were two of them. Who was the third?
a) Catherine Deneuve b) Jeanne Moreau
c) Jane Birkin d) Anouk Aimee

Directors

KING VIDOR (1894 - 1982)

1) Who portrayed the alcoholic ex-prizefighter in Vidor's 1931 melodrama, **The Champ**?
a) Wallace Beery b) Buster Keaton
c) Lionel Barrymore d) Lon Chaney

2) Name the A.J. Cronin novel he adapted for the screen which stars Robert Donat as a poverty stricken doctor in the Welsh valleys?
a) Shining Victory b) The Stars Look Down
c) The Green Years d) The Citadel

3) Based on a story by WWI veteran, Lawrence Stallings, this 1925 silent film was considered to be the first serious account of the war and made John Gilbert a star. Name the title.
a) The Big Parade b) What Price Glory?
c) Hearts of the World d) All Quiet on the Western Front

JOSEF VON STERNBERG (Jonas Sternberg 1894 - 1969)

1) Best remembered for his association with Marlene Dietrich with whom he made seven films. Which film features her in an ape costume singing 'Hot Voodoo!'?
a) Blonde Venus b) Shanghai Express
c) The Devil is a Woman d) Dishonored

2) Name the Dostoyevsky novel he adapted for the screen in 1935.
a) The Idiot b) The Devils
c) Crime and Punishment d) The Brothers Karamazov

3) In 1930 Dietrich starred in her first Hollywood film with Gary Cooper commenting: "[He] is pleasant and good-looking. The newspapers have said that Lupe Velez (his girlfriend) has threatened to scratch my eyes out if I come near him. How can I? She sits on his lap between scenes. I don't go close enough, God knows, to see what they're doing, but it looks like they are doing something that is usually done in private." Name the film.
a) Beau Geste b) Morocco
c) Under Two Flags d) The Blue Angel

ERICH VON STROHEIM (1885 - 1957)

1) Which 1925 drama did he adapt from the novel 'McTeague', by Frank Norris, in which a murderer discovers he is handcuffed to his victim in the final scenes?
a) Friends and Lovers b) Crimson Romance
c) Queen Kelly d) Greed

2) Name the actor who flirts with Mae Murray in his 1925 comedy, **The Merry Widow**?
a) John Gilbert b) Conrad Veidt
c) John Boles d) Lewis Stone

3) Harry Carr was Stroheim's script collaborator on a 1928 romantic drama and told Photoplay magazine the same year: "In the story there was to be a motherless girl. Von Stroheim said he couldn't write about a motherless girl - unless he knew what her mother was like. So we had to sit down and spend days manufacturing the life story of a woman who was never intended to appear in the story". Name the film.
a) So Ends Our Night b) Hearts of the World
c) As You Desire Me d) The Wedding March

RAOUL WALSH (1887 - 1981)

1) He started his film career as an actor in 1909 and appeared in D.W. Griffith's **The Birth of a Nation** (1915). Whom did he portray?
a) Abraham Lincoln b) John Wilkes Booth
c) Gen Ulysses S. Grant d) Gen. Robert E. Lee

2) With which 1941 crime drama do you associate the killer, 'Mad Dog Earle'?
a) White Heat b) Roaring Twenties
c) They Drive By Night d) High Sierra

3) Which 1928 film, based on Somerset Maugham's *Rain*, features a carefree prostitute in Pago Pago who comes under the lustful eye of a marine sergeant played by Raoul Walsh?
?

The Movie Quiz Companion

a) *The Lucky Lady* b) *Sailor's Luck*
c) *Sadie Thompson* d) *The Innocent Sinner*

JOHN WATERS (1946 -)

1) Name the title of John Waters' 1981 comedy drama released in 'Odorama' in which the audience was issued with scratch and sniff cards.
a) *Mondo Trasho* b) *Polyester*
c) *Multiple Maniacs* d) *Desperate Living*

2) Which 1988 comedy features the racially segregated 'Corny Collins Show'?
a) *Hairspray* b) *Serial Mom*
c) *Female Trouble* d) *Cry-Baby*

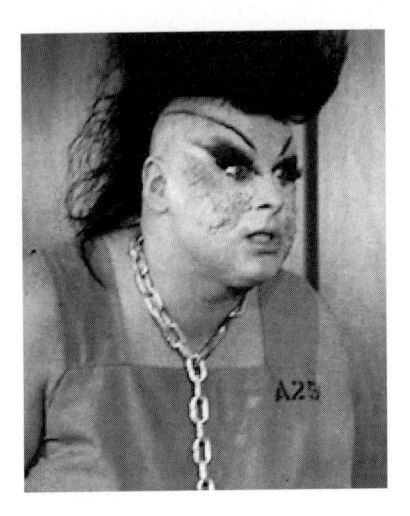

3) Babs Johnson was "the filthiest person alive" who eats dog excrement in the finale of **Pink Flamingos** (1972). Name the 300 pound transvestite who portrayed her.
a) *Divine*
b) *Cookie Mueller*
c) *Danny Mills*
d) *Mink Stole*

PETER WEIR (1944 -)

1) **Picnic at Hanging Rock** (1975), the story of three girls who disappear while on a school picnic, was based on the experience of the author of the book of the same title at Clyde Girls' Grammar School, near Melbourne. Who was she?
a) *Colleen McCullough* b) *Olga Masters*
c) *Rosa Praed* d) *Joan Lindsay*

2) A marriage of convenience ensues when George Faure (Gérard Depardieu) needs a **Green Card** (1990) to enable him to reside in America and Bronte Parrish needs a husband to rent a Manhattan apartment. Who portrayed Bronte?
a) *Meg Ryan* b) *Andie MacDowell*
c) *Helen Hunt* d) *Holly Hunter*

3) Which Peter Weir film was critic Pauline Kael reviewing when she commented: "The young actors are presentable - even admirable - but they're all so camera-angled and director-controlled that they don't have a zit they can call their own"?
a) *Fearless* b) *The Cars That Ate Paris*
c) *The Last Wave* d) *Dead Poets Society*

ORSON WELLES (1915 - 1985)

1) His 1952 adaptation of a Shakespeare play was fraught with budget problems, so much so that on the day he was about to shoot a crucial scene, the costumes hadn't arrived because they hadn't been paid for, but he decided to shoot the scene anyway and relocated it at an old Turkish bath where the actors dressed only in towels. Name the film.
a) *Macbeth* b) *Othello* c) *King Lear* d) *Hamlet*

2) Orson Welles directed himself in the 1946 thriller, **The Stranger**, in which FBI agent, Edward G. Robinson, investigates the past of a seemingly innocent small town professor portrayed by Welles. What does the FBI suspect him of?
a) *bigamy* b) *Nazi war crimes*
c) *espionage* d) *terrorism*

3) Name his 1942 drama, based on a Booth Tarkington novel, which had previously been filmed as a silent in 1925 by Vitagraph, entitled **Pampered Youth** and starring Cullen Landis and Alice Calhoun.
a) *The Lady From Shanghai* b) *Journey Into Fear*
c) *The Magnificent Ambersons* d) *The Black Rose*

WILLIAM WELLMAN (1896 - 1975)

1) In 1927 he directed the first film to win an Academy Award. Name the title.
a) *Wings*
b) *The Jazz Singer*
c) *The Last Command*
d) *The Broadway Melody*

dawn incline ordeal

Directors

2) Fading movie star Norman Maine (Fredric March) meets Esther Blodgett at a Hollywood party and promises to put her in the movies in Wellman's 1937 drama, **A Star is Born**. Who was she?
a) Myrna Loy b) Janet Gaynor
c) Fay Wray d) Gloria Holden

3) Who played the title role in Wellman's 1937 crime drama, **The Last Gangster**?
a) Edward G. Robinson b) George Raft
c) Paul Muni d) James Cagney

WIM WENDERS (1945 -)

1) Name his 1977 mystery, based on Patricia Highsmith's *Ripley's Game*, which cast directors Nicholas Ray, Gérard Blain, and Samuel Fuller as crooks.
a) Hammett b) The American Friend
c) The State of Things d) Until the End of the World

2) Name the title of Wender's last film in his 'road movie' trilogy, following **Alice in the Cities** (1974) and **Wrong Move** (1975).
a) Kings of the Road b) Back Roads
c) Road Games d) Roadside Prophets

3) Travis Clay Henderson had been missing for four years and presumed dead when he is found wandering in the desert in the opening scenes of **Paris, Texas** (1984). Who portrayed him?
a) Harry Dean Stanton b) Dean Stockwell
c) Max von Sydow d) Sam Neill

JAMES WHALE (1889 - 1957)

1) Name the award-winning 1998 film, based on the novel 'Father of Frankenstein' by Christopher Bram, which chronicles the last days of James Whale ending with his tragic suicide by drowning?
a) Gods and Monsters b) To Hollywood With Love
c) Shadow of the Monster d) The Bridegroom of Frankenstein

2) Which 1936 Jerome Kern - Oscar Hammerstein musical, featuring Paul Robeson singing 'Old Man River', did he direct in 1936?
a) Ship Ahoy
b) Rhythm on the River
c) Show Boat
d) Swanee River

3) Who portrayed the effeminate mad scientist Dr. Praetorius in **The Bride of Frankenstein** (1935)?
a) Edward Van Sloan b) E.E. Clive
c) John Boles d) Ernest Thesiger

BILLY WILDER
(Samuel Wilder 1906 -)

1) Billy Wilder was awarded two Best Director Oscars during his career. The first was in 1945 for **The Lost Weekend**. For which 1960 film was he awarded the second?
a) Witness For the Prosecution
b) Some Like It Hot
c) Irma La Douce
d) The Apartment

2) Which 1950 drama was based on the story 'A Can of Beans' by Charles Brackett and Billy Wilder?
a) Sunset Blvd.
b) The Seven Year Itch
c) Ace in the Hole
d) Stalag 17

291

The Movie Quiz Companion

bendy loin dance

3) In which 1948 Wilder film does seductive cabaret singer, Erika von Schlutow (Marlene Dietrich) sing 'Black Market' in a cellar called the Lorelei in Occupied Berlin?
a) *A Foreign Affair* b) *The Lady is Willing*
c) *Follow the Boys* d) *Midnight*

ROBERT WISE (1914 -)

1) Name the title of his 1949 boxing drama, based on the narrative poem by Joseph Moncure March, which features ageing prizefighter, Bill 'Stoker' Thompson (Robert Ryan), who refuses to take a dive.
a) *Body and Soul* b) *Somebody Up There Likes Me*
c) *The Set-Up* d) *The Square Jungle*

2) President of RKO, George J. Schaefer, instructed Wise to reduce an Orson Welles drama, which he considered would be a financial disaster, from 148 minutes to 131 minutes. Wise eventually cut it down to 88 minutes. Name the film.
a) *Citizen Kane* b) *The Lady From Shanghai*
c) *Journey Into Fear* d) *The Magnificent Ambersons*

3) Which film was based on a best-selling 1969 novel by Michael Crichton?
a) *Coma* b) *The Andromeda Strain*
c) *Westworld* d) *The Carey Treatment*

EDWARD D. WOOD, JR. (1924 - 1978)

1) Which Ed Wood feature took 23 years to be released because he couldn't afford the lab processing bill?
a) *Revenge of the Dead* b) *Bride of the Monster*
c) *Final Curtain* d) *The Night the Banshee Cried*

2) In which 1953 drama does Bela Lugosi warn Daniel Davis (Ed Wood) with the words, "Bevare! Bevare! Bevare of the big green dragon that sits on your doorstep... he eats little boys!"?
a) *Glen or Glenda?* b) *Plan 9 From Outer Space*
c) *Necormania* d) *Crossroad Avenger*

3) Ed Wood befriended and employed Bela Lugosi towards the end of his life when his career was in the doldrums and he was a registered drug addict. Who portrayed Lugosi in Tim Burton's nostalgic 1994 tribute to "the world's worst director", **Ed Wood**?
a) Dakin Matthews b) Max Adrian
c) Vincent D'Onofrio d) Martin Landau

SAM WOOD (1883 - 1949)

1) Name the Marx Brothers comedy he directed in 1935.
a) *A Night at the Opera*
b) *Duck Soup*
c) *Animal Crackers*
d) *Horse Feathers*

2) What 1939 film connection can you make between Sam Wood, and author and screenwriter, James Hilton?
a) *Mrs Miniver*
b) *Goodbye Mr Chips*
c) *Random Harvest*
d) *Lost Horizon*

3) "Where's the rest of me?" screams Drake McHugh (Ronald Reagan) to his girl Randy Monoghan (Ann Sheridan) when he discovers both his legs have been amputated after a railroad accident. Name the film.
a) *Our Town*
b) *Kings Row*
c) *The Stratton Story*
d) *Saratoga Trunk*

292

Directors

WILLIAM WYLER (1902 - 1981)

1) On whose novel was **Dodsworth** based, about a retired American couple who visit Europe and discover new moral standards?
a) Nathaniel Hawthorne b) Sinclair Lewis
c) Mark Twain d) Edith Wharton

2) On whose novel was his 1959 epic **Ben-Hur** based?
a) Lew Wallace b) Leon Uris
c) Howard Fast d) Irwin Shaw

3) Name the 1941 drama, adapted from a Lillian Hellman play, about a turn-of-the-century southern family headed by the ruthless and scheming Regina Giddens (Bette Davis) and their attempts to build a cotton mill.
a) The Great Lie b) Little Foxes
c) Of Human Bondage d) Beyond the Forest

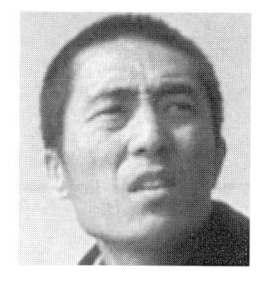

ZHANG YIMOU (1950 -)

1) Name his 1991 film which was based on Su Tong's novel, *Wives and Concubines*?
a) Raise the Red Lantern b) Ju Dou
c) To Live d) Shanghai Triad

2) For what does Wan Qui Ju seek an apology from the head of her village in **The Story of Qui Ju** (1992)?
a) the beating of her husband b) the sexual molestation of her daughter c) the insults aimed at her mother d) being accused of theft

3) Best known internationally for her roles in the films of Zhang Yimou, she is one of China's leading performers who made her film debut in **Red Sorghum** (1987). Who is she?
a) Cao Cuifeng b) Kong Lin
c) He Caifei d) Gong Li

FRANCO ZEFFIRELLI (1923 -)

1) His mother took his name from a Mozart aria - 'Zeffiretti' or 'little breezes' - but when registering his birth it was misspelled 'Zeffirelli'. Name the opera the aria came from.
a) Cosi fan tutte b) The Magic Flute
c) The Marriage of Figaro d) Don Giovanni

2) In 1968 she portrayed seventeen-year-old Juliet in Zeffirelli's **Romeo and Juliet**, described by Pauline Kael as "...banal in [her] youth and innocence as the high-school students [are] in the TV series Peyton Place." Who was she?
a) Esmerelda Ruspoli b) Natasha Parry
c) Gabrielle Anwar d) Olivia Hussey

3) Whose life did he chronicle in the 1973 historical biopic, **Brother Sun, Sister Moon**?
a) Francis of Assisi b) Michelangelo
c) Lazarus d) Charlemagne

ROBERT ZEMECKIS (1952 -)

1) Name the film for which he was awarded a Best Director Oscar in 1994.
a) Forrest Gump b) Death Becomes Her
c) Who Framed Roger Rabbit d) Back to the Future Part III

2) Which 1984 film features best-selling romantic novelist Joan Wilder in Colombia?
a) The Public Eye b) Used Cars
c) I Wanna Hold Your Hand d) Romancing the Stone

3) In 1979 he co-wrote a screenplay with Bob Gale for a film which was directed by Steven Spielberg. Name the title.
a) The Sugarland Express b) 1941
c) Raiders of the Lost Ark d) The Color Purple

FRED ZINNEMANN (1907 - 1997)

1) In 1950 Fred Zinneman introduced a young stage actor to the screen for the first time when he cast him as a paraplegic Second World War hero in **The Men**. This actor later commented: "I had no idea what it was like to be confined to a wheelchair, so I asked to be admitted to the Birmingham Veterans Hospital in Southern California as a paralyzed veteran." Name the actor.
a) Montgomery Clift b) Marlon Brando
c) James Dean d) Rod Steiger

2) Which 1952 film is an allegory on the McCarthy-era witch-hunts?
a) Act of Violence b) The Search
c) High Noon d) The Member of the Wedding

3) In 1960, itinerant couple Paddy and Ida Carmody (Robert Mitchum and Deborah Kerr) featured in a Fred Zinneman drama based on a novel by Jon Cleary. Name the film.
a) The Sundowners b) My Brother Talks to Horses
c) Behold a Pale Horse d) A Hatful of Rain

ANSWERS

THEMES

Aborigines 1B 2D 3B
Abortion 1B 2A 3C
Addresses 1A 2A 3D
Adolescence 1C 2B 3C
Adoption 1D 2A 3B
Aeroplanes 1B 2B 3A
Afterlife 1A 2D 3D
Ageing 1B 2D 3B
Age Reversal & Exchange 1D 2B 3C
Airships & Hot Air Balloons 1D 2A 3A
AIDS & HIV 1A 2A 3D
Ambushes 1A 2C 3C
American Civil War 1D 2A 3A
American War of Independence 1D 2A 3C
Amnesia 1B 2B 3A
Animal Experiments & Vivisection 1A 2D 3A
Anti-Semitism 1A 2B 3B
Apartheid 1C 2B 3A
Arabian Nights 1C 2C 3A
Arabs 1B 2D 3C
Army Life 1D 2A 3A
Arranged Marriages 1A 2C 3B
Art Treasures 1B 2B 3D
Assassinations 1A 2A 3D
Atomic Bombs 1C 2B 3A
Autism 1A 2C 1B
Autobiographical Films 1D 1C 3C
Automobiles 1C 2B 3A

Auto Racing 1D 2C 3A

Babies 1B 2C 3C
Based on a True Story 1B 2C 3A
Basketball 1B 2D 3C
Battle of Britain 1C 2C 3A
Bereavement 1A 2C 3C
Bible, The 1C 2B 3A
Bicycles 1B 2A 3D
Bigamy 1D 2A 3C
Biker Movies 1A 2D 3C
Bisexuality 1A 2D 3B
Blackmail 1C 2B 3A
Black Marketeering 1D 2C 3B
Blaxploitation Films 1C 2A 3A
Blindness 1C 2A 3D
Blitz, The 1B 2C 3C
Blues, The 1D 2D 3A
Boer War 1A 2B 3C
Bombing Raids 1C 2D 3A
Bootlegging & Prohibition 1B 2A 3B
Boxing 1B 2B 3A
Brains 1D 2B 3A
Brainwashing 1B 2B 3A
British Empire 1C 2A 3C
Brothers 1D 2A 3D
Buddhism 1B 2A 3C
Buddy Movies 1D 2C 3C
Buried Alive 1C 2A 3A
Buried Treasure 1A 2B 3B

Buses 1C 2B 3C

Camping 1D 2B 3D
Cannibalism 1A 2D 3C
Car Bombs 1D 2C 3A
Cavalry Charges 1C 2D 3A
Cave Dwellers 1B 2A 3D
Celebrations 1D 2D 3C
Chain Gangs 1D 2C 3A
Chase Movies 1C 2D 3B
Chess 1B 2C 3A
Children & Childhood 1C 2B 3A
Child Custody Disputes 1A 2A 3D
Chivalry, Tales of 1A 2D 3C
Christmas 1A 2B 3A
CIA 1C 2B 3C
Cigars 1B 2A 3C
Cinema Audiences 1D 2A 3B
Class 1B 2B 3C
Climbing Heroes 1B 2B 3B
Climbing Villains 1C 1A 3D
Clocks 1A 2B 3D
Closing Lines 1B 2A 3D
Cold War 1C 2A 3A
Colonialism 1C 2B 3A
Comas 1C 2C 3D
Communism 1A 2B 3D
Computers 1D 2D 3A
Concert Movies 1D 2D 3B
Corrupt Cops 1C 2A 3D

294

Answers

Corpses 1D 2C 3B
Country & Western Music 1A 2D 3A
Courts-Martial 1C 2B 3C
Courtroom Dramas 1D 2A 3D
Cowardice 1C 2D 3A
Crashes, Car 1C 2A 3C
Crashes, Plane 1D 2D 3A
Crashes, Train 1B 2A 3C
Cults 1D 2C 3A
Curses 1A 2D 3C

Dance 1A 2D 3C
Daughters 1C 2C 3A
D-Day Invasion, The 1C 2B 3C
Deafness 1B 2A 3C
Dead - But Not Really Dead 1B 2D 3C
Death Incarnate 1A 2D 3C
Decapitation 1D 2A 3A
Delinquents 1C 2A 3A
Demonic Possession 1B 2C 3D
Department Stores 1B 2B 3B
Depression Era 1B 2D 3A
Deserters 1C 2C 3A
Devil Worship 1B 2C 3B
Disability 1A 2A 3D
Disaster Movies 1A 2D 3B
Disfigurement & Deformity 1C 2C 3C
Disguises 1C 2D 3D
Divorce 1B 2A 3C
Doubles 1B 2D 3B
Dreams 1A 2C 3D
Drowning 1D 2B 3B
Drugs & Drug Addiction 1D 2C 3D
Drunk Scenes 1A 2C 3C
Duels 1C 2B 3A

Earthquakes 1B 2C 3C
Electric Chair & Gas Chamber 1A 2D 3B
End of the World/Post Apocalypse 1D 2A 3D
Epidemics 1C 2C 3B
Eternal Youth & Rejuvenation 1C 2C 3B
Expeditions 1C 2D 3A
Explosions 1C 2D 3C

Family Life 1D 2A 3C
Fascism 1A 2B 3B
Fashion World 1A 2A 3C
Fathers 1D 2A 3B
FBI 1B 2B 3D

Feminism 1A 2B 3A
Feuds 1A 2C 3A
Fights 1C 2B 3A
Fires 1A 2A 3C
Firing Squads 1A 2B 3D
Fishing 1D 2B 3B
Flying 1A 2D 3A
Fog 1D 2A 3D
Foreign Legion 1B 2D 3C
French Resistance 1A 2B 3D
Future, The 1C 2B 3D

Game Shows 1D 2C 3A
Germ Warfare 1A 2B 3C
Getaway Cars 1D 2C 3A
Giants 1B 2A 3A
Gold 1A 2A 3C
Golf 1A 2D 3B
Grandfathers 1D 2C 3D
Grandmothers 1C 2A 3D
Guillotine 1C 2A 3B
Gunfights 1C 2D 3A
Guns 1B 2A 3D
Gypsies 1A 2D 3A

Hallucinations 1B 2D 3C
Heist/Caper Movies 1B 2A 3D
Helicopters 1D 2C 3B
Hijacking 1B 2B 3B
Hinduism 1A 2D 3B
Hitch-hiking 1C 2A 3D
Holidays 1A 2D 3A
Hollywood & The Movie Business 1D 2A 3D
Holocaust 1D 2A 3A
Homecomings 1B 2A 3C
Homelessness 1D 2B 3D
Homosexuality 1D 2C 3D
Horse Racing 1A 2C 3B
Hostages 1D 2B 3A
Hymns 1C 2C 3A

Ice Dramas 1C 2D 3C
Illegitimacy 1D 2A 3A
Illiteracy 1C 2D 3B
Immortality 1B 2B 3A
Impersonation 1D 2A 3A
Impalement 1D 2A 3D
Impotence & Infertility 1D 2B 3A
Impregnable Buildings 1C 2B 3A

Incest 1B 2B 3A
Indians 1B 2C 3A
Infidelity 1B 2A 3C
Inheritance 1B 2A 3D
Insanity 1B 2A 3C
Invasions/Coups d'etat 1C 2B 3D
Invisibility 1A 2A 3C
Islam 1C 2A 3A
Italian Americans 1B 2A 3D

Jail Breaks 1C 2A 3C
Jazz 1B 2B 3C
Journeys & Marches 1A 2D 3C

Kidnapping 1D 2B 3A
Knives 1D 2C 3C
Korean War 1C 2D 3B
Ku Klux Klan 1D 2B 3A

Labour Relations & Strikes 1D 2D 3C
Landslides & Avalanches 1C 2D 3C
Last Rites 1C 2A 3B
Lesbianism 1A 2D 3B
Letters 1D 2A 3D
Long Supposed Dead 1D 2A 3D
Lotteries 1D 2D 3A
Lynching 1C 2D 3B

McCarthyism 1B 2A 3B
Mafia 1D 2D 3B
Marriage Brokers 1B 2A 3D
Martial Arts 1C 2A 3B
Massacres 1B 2A 3D
Meetings 1C 2D 3C
Mexicans 1D 2C 3C
Microfilm 1A 2D 3A
Middle Ages 1C 2A 3B
Millionaires 1C 2A 3B
Miniaturisation 1B 2A 3D
Miracles 1D 2C 3A
Mirrors 1D 2B 3A
Mistaken Identity 1C 2B 3D
Mormons 1A 2B 3A
Mothers 1B 2B 3D
Motorcycles 1A 2C 3D
Movies About Movies 1A 2B 3D
Multiple Personalities 1A 2C 3D
Multiple Roles 1D 2B 3A
Murderers, Real Life 1B 2A 3B

295

The Movie Quiz Companion

Mutation & Metamorphosis 1D 2B 3D
Mutiny 1B 2B 3A
Myths & Legends 1D 2D 3A

Newspapers 1D 2B 3D
Nuclear Energy 1A 2B 3A
Nuclear Weapons 1B 3C 3B
Nudity 1B 2D 3A
Nymphomaniacs 1B 2A 3A

Old Age 1C 2D 3D
Opera 1A 2D 3B
Orphans 1B 2A 3C

Pacifism 1B 2C 3B
Paintings 1D 2B 3B
Personal Ads 1A 2D 3C
Pinball/Video Games 1B 2A 3C
Plagues & Diseases 1C 2B 3C
Plants & Trees 1B 2D 3C
Plastic Surgery 1A 2D 3B
Pornography 1A 2D 3A
Poverty 1A 2B 3D
Pregnancy & Childbirth 1D 2B 3A
Prostitution 1A 2D 3A
Protection Rackets 1A 2A 3C
Psychiatry & Psychology 1A 2C 3B
Punks & Punk Films 1D 2A 3B
Puppets 1B 2D 3D

Quakers 1B 2D 3B

Race 1A 2A 3D
Racism 1A 2C 3B
Radio 1B 2C 3D
Rain 1C 2C 3B
Raj, The 1B 2B 3D
Rape 1A 2A 3B
Reincarnation 1B 2A 3D
Religion 1B 2D 3A
Retirement 1D 2B 3B
Revenge 1C 2C 3A
Revolutions 1C 2D 3B
Rewards 1B 2D 3A
Road Movies 1B 2C 3A
Robberies 1C 2A 3D
Rock 'n' Pop 1D 2A 3D
Rock 'n' Roll 1C 2B 3C
Roller Skating & Skateboards 1A 2A 3D

Sabotage 1A 2A 3D
Sadism & Sadomasochism 1D 2C 3B
Salvation Army, The 1C 2B 3C
Scissors 1D 2C 3D
Secret Identities 1B 2C 3C
Secret Societies 1B 2A 3D
Sermons 1C 2D 3D
Sex 1C 2C 3A
Sex Change 1B 2C 3A
Siamese Twins 1B 2A 3C
Sisters 1C 2B 3D
Skiing 1B 2A 3C
Slasher Movies 1B 2D 3A
Slavery 1A 2A 3B
Small Town Life 1C 2B 3D
Soccer 1C 2A 3C
Soldiers Returning 1A 2D 3B
Solitary Confinement 1A 2C 3B
Sons 1D 2A 3B
Space Exploration 1B 2B 3A
Spanish Civil War 1B 2A 3D
Speeches 1C 2B 3C
Stabbings 1C 2B 3C
Storms 1B 2D 3D
Strangulation 1B 2A 3B
Strikes 1D 2C 3A
Students 1D 2A 3D
Surfing 1A 2B 3C
Suicide 1D 2A 3D
Survival in Wilderness 1B 2A 3D
Swimming 1B 2B 3C

Tattoos 1B 2A 3D
Telekinesis 1B 2B 3C
Telepathy 1D 2A 3C
Telephones 1C 2B 3B
Television 1C 2B 3C
Tennis 1A 2B 3D
Terminally Ill 1A 2B 3D
Thanksgiving 1B 2C 3A
Time Travel 1D 2B 3C
Transplantation 1C 2A 3A
Transvestites 1C 2A 3A
Trapped 1A 2C 3A
Triad Gangs 1B 2D 3D
Truck-driving Movies 1A 2D 3C
Twins 1A 2B 3A

Vietnam War 1D 2B 3A

Vigilantes 1D 2A 3A
Vikings 1B 2A 3D
Voodoo 1B 2A 3D

War Criminals 1D 2C 3A
War Heroes 1C 2C 3D
Wheelchairs 1A 2D 3A
Witchcraft 1A 2C 3D
Witness-to-crime Stories 1D 2B 3A
World War 1 1A 2D 3B
World War II 1A 2A 3C
Wrestling 1C 2B 3A

Year in Title 1A 2B 3D

ROLES

Accountants 1C 2D 3B
Admirals 1C 2A 3A
Advertising Executives 1B 2C 3D
Alcoholics 1A 2B 3B
Aristocrats 1D 2C 3A
Artists 1C 2A 3B
Archaeologists 1B 2D 3B
Assassins 1C 2C 3A
Astronauts 1C 2A 3A
Athletes 1B 2C 3A

Babysitters 1D 2A 3A
Ballerinas 1D 2A 3B
Bankers 1C 2C 3D
Barbers & Hairdressers 1C 2D 3A
Bartenders & Publicans 1D 2B 3C
Baseball Players 1B 2C 3A
Beatniks & Hippies 1C 2D 3C
Bodyguards 1A 2D 3B
Bomb Disposal Experts 1B 2A 3D
Bomber Pilots 1D 2C 3A
Bounty Hunters 1D 2C 3D
Boxers 1A 2B 3C
Bullies 1D 2C 3A
Burglars 1C 2B 3A
Butchers 1A 2C 3D
Butlers 1B 2B 3B

Caretakers & Nightwatchmen 1A 2C 3A
Chauffeurs 1B 2C 3B
Cheerleaders 1A 2B 3A

Answers

Chefs & Cooks 1D 2A 3C
Chorus Girls 1B 2B 3A
Clairvoyants & Fortune Tellers 1B 2D 3A
Clowns 1A 2B 3C
Colonels 1A 2B 3D
Commercial Pilots 1D 2C 3B
Composers, Classical 1C 2B 3A
Composers, Popular 1A 2D 3B
Computer Nerds & Hackers 1A 2A 3C
Confidence Tricksters 1D 2B 3B
Courageous Soldiers 1D 2B 3D
Cowardly Soldiers 1C 2C 3A
Criminals, Master 1D 2C 3A
Criminals, Real Life 1A 2D 3B

Dancers 1D 2D 3A
Dentists 1C 2D 3C
Detectives 1A 2B 3C
Divers 1D 2C 3A
Disc Jockeys 1C 2A 3D
District Attorneys 1A 2D 3B
Doctors 1C 2D 3C
Drill Sergeants 1D 2B 3A
Drug Dealers 1B 2A 3C
Drunks 1C 2B 3D

Editors 1D 2B 3D
Emperors 1A 2C 3C
Engine Drivers 1B 2D 3D
Evangelists 1D 2D 3B
Explorers 1B 2D 3A

Farmers 1C 2D 3D
Fashion Models 1B 2C 3A
Fighter Pilots 1B 2C 3D
Fire-Fighters 1D 2B 3A
Forgers & Counterfeiters 1D 2B 3A

Gamblers 1C 2A 3B
Gardeners 1D 2A 3C
Gangsters 1D 2B 3B
Generals 1C 2B 3C
Gigolos 1A 2C 3D
Gladiators 1C 2C 3A
Gold Prospectors 1C 2A 3D
Governesses 1D 2C 3A
Grave Robbers 1C 2C 3A
Gunfighters 1D 2A 3B
Gun-runners 1D 2A 3C

Headmasters 1C 2D 3B
Highwaymen & Women 1D 2B 3C
Hit Men & Women 1D 2B 3A
Housekeepers 1C 2D 3C
Hunters 1C 2D 3C
Hypnotists 1A 2A 3D

Ice Skaters 1A 2C 3C
Informers 1C 2C 3A
Impresarios 1C 2D 3A
Innkeepers 1C 2C 3B
Insurance Investigators & Sales 1D 2A 3C
Inventors 1C 2A 3D

Jailers 1C 2A 3B
Jesuit Priests 1C 2A 3B
Jewel Thieves 1D 2A 3B
Journalists & Reporters 1D 2D 3B
Judges 1B 2C 3A

Kings 1A 2B 3A

Lawyers 1D 2B 3D
Librarians 1B 2A 3A

Mad Scientists 1D 2C 3C
Magicians 1A 2C 3A
Maids 1B 2A 3C
Matadors 1B 2C 3A
Mayors 1C 2D 3A
Mechanics 1B 2C 3C
Mediums 1A 2C 3D
Mercenaries 1A 2B 3A
Miners 1C 2C 3A
Missionaries 1C 2A 3D
Monks 1B 2D 3C
Mountaineers 1A 2C 3A
Mounties 1D 2A 3C
Movie Directors 1B 2C 3B
MPs 1C 2C 3D
Musicians 1C 2A 3A

Nannies 1B 2C 3C
Nuns 1D 2B 3D
Nurses 1C 2D 3C

Outlaws, Fictional 1A 2D 3A
Outlaws, Real-life 1B 2D 3D

Photographers 1D 2A 3B
Pianists 1B 2A 3A
Pickpockets 1D 2A 3A
Pimps 1C 2D 3A
Pirates, Fictional 1D 2B 3C
Pirates, Real-life 1C 2A 3C
Plastic Surgeons 1A 2B 3A
Poachers 1B 2B 3A
Poets 1C 2A 3D
Police Chiefs & Commissioners 1C 2A 3A
Policemen 1C 2B 3B
Politicians 1D 2C 3A
Popes & Cardinals 1B 2C 3C
Pool Hustlers 1D 2D 3A
Postmen 1C 2A 3B
Preachers 1C 2C 3A
Presidents 1D 2B 3A
Priests 1C 2B 3B
Prime Ministers 1B 2A 3C
Princes 1D 2B 3C
Princesses 1A 2B 3A
Prisoners 1C 2A 3A
Prisoners of War 1C 2B 3A
Private Investigators 1B 2D 3D
Professors 1B 2A 3B
Projectionists 1C 2B 3A
Prostitutes 1C 2D 3D
Psychiatrists 1C 2C 3A

Queens 1C 2A 3B

Racing Drivers 1B 2A 3A
Rustlers 1C 2D 3C

Sailors 1D 2B 3C
Salesmen 1B 2D 3C
Saloon Gals 1C 2D 3C
Samurai Warriors 1C 2A 3A
Santa Claus 1B 2C 3A
School Teachers 1C 2C 3B
Scientists 1C 2B 3B
Sculptors 1C 2D 3C
Sea Captains 1C 2D 3D
Secretaries 1A 2C 3A
Senators 1D 2A 3A
Sheriffs 1A 2D 3C
Shopkeepers 1A 2C 3D
Smugglers 1B 2C 3A
Soda Jerks 1C 2C 3A

The Movie Quiz Companion

Spies & Secret Agents 1D 2C 3B
Sportsmen & Women 1C 2B 3A
Stowaways 1A 2B 3A
Strippers 1A 2D 3C
Surgeons 1D 2A 3A

Taxi Drivers 1C 2B 3A
Terrorists 1A 2C 3C
Texas Rangers 1A 2B 3D
Tramps & Hobos 1B 2B 3B
Truck Drivers 1D 2C 3C
Trumpet Players 1A 2B 3A

Undertakers 1D 2B 3C

Ventriloquists 1C 2A 3A
Vets 1B 2A 3C
Vietnam Veterans 1D 2C 3A
Violinists 1B 2D 3A

Waiters 1C 2D 3C
Waitresses 1A 2D 3B
Witches 1D 2C 3D

SETTINGS

Airports 1A 2C 3D
Airliners 1A 2C 3C
Air-raid Shelters 1B 2A 3B
Ancient Egypt 1D 2D 3A
Ancient Greece 1A 2B 3D
Ancient Rome 1A 2B 3A
Apartments 1D 2C 3B
"Asylums" & "Mental" Institutions 1D 2D 3B

Bakeries 1B 2A 3A
Balconies 1D 2C 3C
Ballrooms 1A 2C 3D
Banks 1D 2A 3B
Banquets & Feasts 1A 2B 3C
Barges 1A 2D 3A
Bathrooms 1D 2C 3C
Battlefields 1C 2A 3B
Beaches 1B 2C 3B
Beauty Contests 1C 2B 3A
Bedrooms 1C 2B 3C
Boarding Schools 1A 2A 3D
Bowling Alleys 1B 2D 3B

Bridges 1C 2D 3A
Brothels 1B 2D 3A
Building Sites 1C 2A 3B

Campfires 1A 2D 3A
Caravans 1D 2D 3A
Carousels & Merry-go-rounds 1B 2C 3A
Car Parks & Parking Lots 1D 2C 3B
Castles 1A 2A 3D
Cattle Drives 1D 2A 3A
Caves 1A 2C 3B
Cellars 1D 2C 3B
Churches 1D 2A 3D
Circuses 1B 2A 3C
Cinemas 1D 2B 3A
Classrooms 1C 2A 3B
Cliffs 1D 2C 3B
Cockpits 1D 2D 3C
Colleges & Campuses 1B 2A 3A
Convents 1C 2C 3A
Courtrooms 1D 2A 3C
Crypts & Tombs 1D 2A 3D

Dams 1D 2B 3C
Dance Halls 1A 2C 3C
Death Cells 1B 2B 3C
Deep South 1A 2D 3B
Department Stores 1D 2A 3C
Desert Islands 1B 2D 3C
Deserts 1D 2B 3A
Devil's Island 1D 2C 3B
Diners 1C 2A 3A
Docks & Waterfronts 1A 2B 3C

Earth's Core 1B 2D 3D
Elevators 1D 2C 3A
Embassies 1C 2B 3D

Factories 1B 2A 3A
Fairgrounds & Carnivals 1D 2C 3B
Farms 1A 2C 3B
Fire Stations 1B 2C 3A
Forests & Woodlands 1C 2D 3A
Forts 1D 2B 3A
Fountains 1A 2B 3A
Foxholes & Shell Holes 1C 2D 3C
Funerals 1D 2A 3C

Garages & Service Stations 1C 2C 3A

Gardens 1C 2A 3C
Graves 1C 2D 3C
Graveyards & Cemeteries 1D 2B 3B
Gyms 1D 2A 3A

Haunted Houses 1D 2B 3B
Heaven 1C 2D 3A
Hell 1C 2D 3B
Hideouts 1C 2B 3B
Hospitals 1C 2D 3C
Hotels 1D 2B 3C
Houses 1A 2A 3B

Islands 1D 2A 3C
Isolated Houses 1C 2C 3B

Jails & Prisons 1B 2A 3C
Jungles 1B 2A 3C

Kitchens 1D 2B 3D

Lakes 1B 2D 3A
Laboratories 1C 2B 3D
Lifeboats 1B 2A 3A
Lighthouses 1D 2B 3D
Limousines 1C 2A 3A

Meetings 1D 2A 3C
Military Academies 1D 2A 3D
Mines 1A 2C 3A
Monasteries 1D 2D 3A
Mountains 1C 2C 3B
Museums 1A 2B 3D
Music Hall & Vaudeville Theaters 1A 2D 3B

Nightclubs 1A 2B 3D
North & South Poles 1A 2D 3A

Ocean Liners 1D 2A 3B
Offices 1C 2D 3A
Oilfields 1D 2A 3B
OK Corral 1D 2B 3C
Old People's Homes & Comm. 1A 2C 3B
Olympic Games 1A 2A 3B
Operating Theatres 1D 2C 3A
Orphanages & Children's Homes 1C 2C 3B
Other Worlds 1B 2D 3B

Parades 1A 2D 3A

298

Answers

Parties 1C 2C 3A
Penal Colonies 1D 2C 3D
Phone Booths 1D 2D 3A
Piers 1B 2A 3A
Plantations 1B 2C 3B
Police Stations 1A 2D 3C
POW Camps 1B 2A 3B
Prom Nights 1B 2A 3C
Pubs 1D 2C 3B
Pyramids 1A 2C 3A

Racetracks 1B 2C 3A
Rafts 1C 2D 3C
Railway Stations 1C 2B 3D
Ranches 1A 2B 3D
Rapids 1A 2B 3D
Red Indian Reservations 1B 2C 3B
Reefs & Icebergs 1B 2C 3A
Restaurants 1D 2B 3D
Rivers 1B 2C 3D
Riverboats & Paddle-Steamers 1A 2C 3A
Rodeos 1A 2B 3D
Rooftops 1B 2D 3C

Safaris 1A 2A 3B
Seances 1C 2D 3A
Seaside Resorts 1C 2A 3B
Sewers & Drains 1B 2D 3C
Sherriffs' Offices 1B 2A 3B
Ships' Cabins 1A 2D 3C
Ships, Cargo 1B 2C 3C
Ships, Naval 1A 2B 3D
Ships, Sailing 1C 2A 3B
Shipwrecks 1D 2A 3C
Showers & Baths 1C 2C 3A
South Seas 1B 2A 3A
Speakeasies 1D 2B 3C
Stables & Barns 1B 2D 3A
Stagecoaches 1B 2D 3D
Stage Doors 1D 2B 3A
Staircases 1B 2C 3A
Submarines 1B 2D 3C
Subway Trains 1D 2D 3B
Summer Camp 1C 2A 3D
Supermarkets 1A 2C 3C
Swamps, Marshes & Mires 1B 2D 3C
Swimming Pools 1D 2B 3A

Taxis 1B 2B 3D

Tents 1C 2A 3C
Theatres 1C 2D 3D
Toilets 1D 2B 3C
Torture Chambers 1A 2D 3B
Trains 1A 2D 3C
Trenches 1A 2D 3B
Tunnels 1C 2C 3A

Undersea Worlds 1B 2C 3B
Universities 1A 2C 3D

Villages 1D 2D 3B
Volcanoes 1A 2C 3C

Wagon Trains 1D 2D 3B
Waterfalls 1A 2A 3D
Weddings 1A 2B 3C
Western Saloons 1C 2A 3A
Windmills 1D 2A 3B

Yachts 1C 2B 3D

Zoos 1A 2A 3B

CHARACTERS

Andy Hardy 1A 2A 3B
Batman & Robin 1C 2A 3A
Batman Villains 1B 2C 3B
The Beatles 1A 2B 3C
Billy the Kid 1D 2B 3A
Blondie 1C 2D 3A
Bond Girls 1A 2D 3B
Bond Villains 1B 2A 3C
Boston Blackie 1A 2C 3D
Bugs Bunny 1B 2B 3D
Buffalo Bill 1A 2C 3D
Bulldog Drummond 1D 2B 3D
Charlie Chan 1B 2C 3A
Davy Crockett 1C 2B 3A
Dead End Kids 1C 2D 3A
Dick Tracy 1A 2C 3D
Doctor Kildare 1B 2D 3C
Dracula 1C 2A 3A
The Falcon 1B 2A 3C
Frankenstein 1B 2C 3D
Freddy Krueger 1C 2B 3D
Flash Gordon 1C 2B 3A

Fu Manchu 1D 2C 3D
General Custer 1B 2D 3D
Henry Aldrich 1A 2B 3C
Hercule Poirot 1B 2A 3C
Hercules 1D 2C 3C
Hitler, Adolf 1C 2A 3D
Hopalong Cassidy 1C 2A 3B
Indiana Jones 1C 2C 3B
Inspector Clouseau 1B 2A 3B
Jack the Ripper 1B 2C 3D
James Bond 1D 2A 3B
Jesse James 1B 2B 3A
Jesus Christ 1A 2C 3B
King Arthur 1A 2C 3D
Lassie 1B 2A 3C
Abraham Lincoln 1B 2D 3D
Lone Ranger, The 1A 2B 3B
Mickey Mouse 1B 2A 3C
Mike Hammer 1D 2A 3C
Miss Marple 1D 2B 3A
Monsieur Hulot 1D 2D 3B
Mr. Belvedere 1C 2A 3B
Mr. Moto 1A 2D 3A
Nancy Drew 1C 2B 3D
Old Mother Riley 1D 2B 3A
Our Gang 1D 2B 3A
Philip Marlowe 1D 2B 3D
Popeye 1A 2C 3B
Rambo 1A 2B 3B
Richard Hannay 1B 2D 3C
Rin Tin Tin 1A 2B 3C
Robin Hood 1D 2B 3A
Rocky 1C 2B 3C
The Saint 1A 2C 3D
Sherlock Holmes 1A 2C 3B
Sinbad the Sailor 1C 2B 3B
Superman 1B 2B 3C
Tarzan 1D 2C 3B
Tom Sawyer & Huckleberry Finn 1B 2D 3B
Wild Bill Hickok 1C 2A 3B
Wyatt Earp 1D 2A 3B
Zorro 1C 2C 3B

CREATURES

Aliens 1D 2A 3C
Alligators & Crocodiles 1D 2C 3D
Androids & Cyborgs 1A 2C 3D

The Movie Quiz Companion

Angels 1C 2C 3C
Apes 1A 2C 3B
Bears 1B 2D 3B
Birds 1D 2D 3A
Blob, The 1B 2B 3A
Buffaloes 1D 2C 3D
Bulls 1C 2A 3B
Camels 1D 2B 3C
Cats 1A 2B 3A
Children Raised by Animals 1C 2B 3A
Crabs & Lobsters 1C 2A 3D
Devil, The 1D 2C 3A
Dinosaurs 1C 2A 3C
Dogs 1A 2A 3B
Dolphins 1B 2C 3A
Donkeys & Mules 1A 2D 3D
Dragons 1D 2A 3D
Dwarfs 1B 2C 3B
Elephants 1A 2C 3A
Fairies & Goblins 1C 2A 3D
Frogs & Toads 1C 2D 3D
Genies 1B 2D 3C
Ghosts 1A 2D 3B
Horses 1A 2C 3D
Human Animals 1D 2A 3C
Insects 1D 2A 3B
Lions & Tigers 1B 2D 3C
Martians 1A 2B 3A
Mermaids 1A 2D 3D
Mice 1D 2C 3B
Mummies 1C 2A 3A
Octopuses & Squids 1D 2B 3D
Pigs 1C 2A 3C
Piranhas 1B 2A 3C
Rabbits 1C 2D 3B
Rats 1C 2B 3B
Robots 1C 2D 3D
Sharks 1D 2B 3D
Snakes 1A 2B 3C
Spiders 1A 2C 3B
Vampires 1C 2D 3B
Werewolves 1C 2B 3A
Whales 1D 2A 3B
Witches 1C 2B 3D
Wolves 1A 2D 3B
Zombies 1D 2D 3A

CLASSIC FILMS

Adventures of Robin Hood, The 1D 2D 3C
African Queen, The 1D 2D 3C
Alfie 1C 2A 3D
Alien 1A 2D 3B
All About Eve 1C 2A 3B
American Graffiti 1D 2C 3A
Apocalypse Now 1D 2B 3C
Back to the Future 1B 2A 3A
Bad Day at Black Rock 1B 2D 3C
Bambi 1D 2B 3B
Big Sleep, The 1B 2B 3D
Blade Runner 1A 2B 3D
Bonnie & Clyde 1B 2D 3B
Bridge on the River Kwai, The 1B 2A 3D
Brief Encounter 1C 2D 3B
Bringing Up Baby 1C 2A 3A
Butch Cassidy & the Sundance Kid 1C 2D 3C
Cabaret 1D 2A 3A
Casablanca 1B 2B 3A
Chinatown 1B 2A 3A
Cinema Paradiso 1C 2B 3B
Citizen Kane 1A 2B 3D
Clockwork Orange, A 1B 2A 3C
Close Encounters of the Third Kind 1C 2A 3B
Day the Earth Stood Still, The 1D 2B 3D
Deer Hunter, The 1A 2D 3B
Double Indemnity 1C 2B 3D
Frankenstein 1A 2B 3B
French Connection, The 1D 2A 3B
Godfather, The 1A 2D 3B
Godfather Part II, The 1D 2C 3C
Goldfinger 1C 2D 3A
Gone With The Wind 1B 2D 3A
Good, the Bad and the Ugly, The 1B 2B 3A
Goodbye Mr. Chips 1C 2D 3B
Goodfellas 1D 2A 3D
Graduate, The 1D 2B 3D
Grapes of Wrath, The 1C 2A 3D
Great Escape, The 1C 2D 3A
Great Expectations 1D 2C 3C
High Noon 1B 2B 3D
It Happened One Night 1D 2D 3B
It's A Wonderful Life 1C 2A 3B
Jean De Florette 1C 2D 3C
King Kong 1D 2C 3A
LA Confidential 1B 2D 3B
Lady Vanishes, The 1B 2C 3A

Ladykillers, The 1B 2C 3D
Lawrence of Arabia 1C 2D 3A
Local Hero 1C 2D 3C
Maltese Falcon, The 1A 2D 3C
Matter of Life and Death, A 1A 2D 3C
Meet Me In St. Louis 1A 2B 3B
North By Northwest 1A 2C 3B
On the Waterfront 1B 2A 3A
One Flew Over the Cuckoo's Nest 1B 2A 3A
Planet of the Apes 1B 2A 3B
Prisoner of Zenda, The 1D 2B 3A
Psycho 1D 2B 3B
Pulp Fiction 1A 2A 3C
Rebecca 1D 2B 3A
Rebel Without a Cause 1C 2C 3D
Searchers, The 1A 2B 3C
Singin' in The Rain 1D 2A 3D
Snow White & the Seven Dwarfs 1A 2C 3D
Some Like It Hot 1D 2B 3D
Sound of Music, The 1C 2D 3A
Stagecoach 1A 2D 3A
Star Wars 1D 2C 3B
Sunset Blvd. 1B 2A 3C
Taxi Driver 1D 2D 3A
Terminator 1C 2A 3D
Third Man, The 1B 2D 3D
39 Steps, The 1A 2C 3B
To Kill a Mockingbird 1B 2B 3D
Top Hat 1D 2B 3B
2001: A Space Odyssey 1B 2C 3C
Vertigo 1B 2B 3B
West Side Story 1D 2A 3D
Whisky Galore 1D 2C 3A
Wild Bunch, The 1D 2C 3C
Wizard of Oz, The 1B 2C 3D
Wuthering Heights 1C 2B 3A

CULT FILMS

Aguirre, The Wrath of God 1A 2B 3D
Badlands 1B 2D 3A
Blow Up 1B 2D 3C
Brazil 1B 2D 3D
CatPeople 1B 2C 3A
Detour 1C 2A 3C
Duck Soup 1C 2C 3C
Easy Rider 1B 2A 3A
Enter the Dragon 1A 2D 3D

Answers

Forbidden Planet 1B 2A 3D
Freaks 1D 2B 3B
Gilda 1A 2D 3A
Gun Crazy 1D 2D 3A
I Walked With A Zombie 1C 2B 3A
Invasion of the Bodysnatchers 1D 2B 3D
Johnny Guitar 1A 2C 3A
Killing, The 1C 2B 3B
Kiss Me Deadly 1B 2A 3B
Last Tango in Paris 1B 2D 3A
Laura 1B 2C 3D
Little Shop of Horrors, The 1D 2B 3A
Night of the Living Dead 1A 2B 3C
Night Of The Hunter 1B 2D 3C
Once Upon a Time in the West 1C 2A 3A
Out Of The Past 1A 2D 3C
Peeping Tom 1A 2C 3A
Plan 9 From Outer Space 1B 2C 3B
Quadrophenia 1D 2B 3A
Reservoir Dogs 1A 2A 3b
Rocky Horror Picture Show, The 1D 2B 3A
Shane 1A 2C 3C
Straw Dogs 1B 2C 3A
Wicker Man, The 1C 2B 3B
Withnail & I 1C 2B 3D

PERFORMERS

Abbott & Costello 1A 2D 3A
Ackland, Joss 1C 2B 3B
Allyson, June 1A 2D 3B
Andress, Ursula 1A 2D 3A
Andrews, Dana 1D 2B 3A
Andrews, Julie 1C 2B 3B
Ann-Margret 1D 2A 3A
Arliss, George 1D 2B 3C
Arquette, Patricia 1C 2A 3D
Arthur, Jean 1C 2B 3A
Ashcroft, Dame Peggy 1B 2C 3A
Astaire, Fred 1A 2A 3A
Astor, Mary 1B 2D 3D
Attenborough, Richard 1D 2C 3B
Autry, Gene 1A 2B 3C
Aykroyd, Dan 1D 2C 3D

Bacall, Lauren 1D 2D 3A
Baker, Sir Stanley 1B 2B 3C
Bancroft, Anne 1D 2A 3B

Bardot, Brigitte 1D 2B 3A
Barkin, Ellen 1A 2D 3C
Barrymore, Lionel 1D 2B 3C
Bartholomew, Freddie 1D 2B 3C
Basinger, Kim 1A 2D 3A
Bates, Alan 1C 2D 3D
Bates, Kathy 1C 2D 3D
Baxter, Anne 1D 2B 3C
Baxter, Warner 1A 2B 3C
Bean, Sean 1A 2C 3A
Beatty, Warren 1A 2A 3D
Bendix, William 1A 2B 3C
Bergman, Ingrid 1D 2B 3C
Binoche, Juliette 1D 2C 3A
Bloom, Claire 1C 2D 3A
Bogarde, Dirk 1B 2A 3D
Bogart, Humphrey 1C 2B 3D
Bond, Ward 1B 2D 3B
Bonham-Carter, Helena 1A 2C 3D
Borgnine, Ernest 1B 2A 3C
Boyer, Charles 1B 2D 3A
Branagh, Kenneth 1D 2B 3B
Brando, Marlon 1A 2D 3D
Brennan, Walter 1A 2D 3C
Brent, George 1D 2C 3C
Bridges, Jeff 1D 2B 3D
Bronson, Charles 1A 2C 3A
Brosnan, Pierce 1B 2A 3A
Bruce, Nigel 1A 2C 3B
Brynner, Yul 1A 2D 3C
Buchanan, Jack 1A 2C 3B
Bullock, Sandra 1A 2B 3D
Burstyn, Ellen 1C 2B 3A
Buscemi, Steve 1D 2D 3B

Cage, Nicholas 1A 2D 3D
Cagney, James 1A 2C 3A
Caine, Michael 1D 2A 3C
Calhern, Louis 1D 2A 3D
Candy, John 1A 2B 3A
Cardinale, Claudia 1D 2B 3A
Carrey, Jim 1C 2A 3B
Chan, Jackie 1C 2A 3A
Chaney, Lon 1B 2A 3A
Chaney Jr., Lon 1D 2C 3D
Chaplin, Charles 1B 2B 3B
Charisse, Cyd 1C 2A 3D
Cher 1D 2A 3C
Chevalier, Maurice 1A 2A 3D

Christie, Julie 1C 2B 3D
Cleese, John 1D 2A 3C
Clift, Montgomery 1A 2B 3D
Clooney, George 1C 2A 3D
Close, Glenn 1B 2A 3D
Cobb, Lee J. 1D 2A 3A
Coburn, James 1B 2C 3A
Colbert, Claudette 1A 2B 3C
Collins, Joan 1A 2A 3B
Colman, Ronald 1B 2C 3D
Coltrane, Robbie 1C 2A 3B
Connery, Sean 1C 2A 3B
Coogan, Jackie 1B 2A 3C
Cooper, Gary 1A 2D 3B
Cooper, Jackie 1A 2D 3B
Costner, Kevin 1D 2B 3A
Cotten, Joseph 1B 2D 3A
Courtenay, Tom 1C 2C 3B
Crawford, Joan 1C 2D 3D
Crosby, Bing 1A 2A 3B
Crowe, Russell 1D 2C 3A
Cruise, Tom 1A 2A 3A
Currie, Finlay 1D 2C 3B
Curtis, Jamie Lee 1D 2A 3A
Curtis, Tony 1C 2C 3B
Cusack, John 1B 2D 3A
Cushing, Peter 1A 2B 3D

Dafoe, Willem 1D 2C 3C
Davis, Bette 1C 2B 3D
Day, Doris 1B 2B 3D
Day Lewis, Daniel 1C 2A 3D
Dean, James 1A 2B 3C
De Havilland, Olivia 1A 2A 3B
Dench, Judi 1B 2D 3B
Deneuve, Catherine 1D 2A 3C
De Niro, Robert 1D 2A 3B
Depardieu, Gérard 1B 2B 3D
Depp, Johnny 1A 2B 3C
Devine, Andy 1C 2D 3B
De Vito, Danny 1D 2A 3A
Diaz, Cameron 1D 2A 3C
DiCaprio, Leonardo 1A 2A 3C
Dietrich, Marlene 1A 2D 3A
Dillon, Matt 1B 2A 3C
Donat, Robert 1D 2B 3C
Douglas, Kirk 1D 2C 3A
Douglas, Michael 1A 2D 3B
Dreyfuss, Richard 1B 2A 3D

The Movie Quiz Companion

Driscoll, Bobby 1B 2C 3B
Dunaway, Faye 1D 2D 3A
Durbin, Deanna 1B 2D 3D
Duvall, Robert 1C 2D 3A

Eastwood, Clint 1A 2A 3D
Elliott, Denholm 1D 2A 3D
Evans, Dame Edith 1A 2A 3B

Fairbanks, Douglas 1A 2D 3C
Fairbanks Jnr., Douglas 1A 2C 3A
Farrow, Mia 1A 2B 3D
Faye, Alice 1A 2D 3C
Fields, W.C. 1D 2D 3A
Fiennes, Ralph 1C 2D 3C
Finch, Peter 1B 2A 3D
Finney, Albert 1B 2C 3C
Fitzgerald, Barry 1B 2C 3B
Flynn, Errol 1A 2C 3D
Fonda, Henry 1A 2D 3C
Fonda, Jane 1A 2C 3B
Fontaine, Joan 1D 2A 3A
Ford, Glenn 1A 2B 3D
Ford, Harrison 1A 2B 3D
Foster, Jodie 1A 2B 3D
Fox, Michael J. 1A 2B 3A
Freeman, Morgan 1A 2C 3A

Gable, Clark 1D 2C 3D
Garbo, Greta 1A 2C 3B
Garcia, Andy 1B 2A 3A
Gardner, Ava 1D 2B 3D
Garfield, John 1C 2B 3A
Garland, Judy 1A 2A 3A
Garner, James 1C 2A 3B
Garson, Greer 1D 2C 3B
Gere, Richard 1A 2D 3A
Gibson, Mel 1C 2B 3A
Gielgud, Sir John 1C 2A 3A
Gish, Lillian 1B 2D 3D
Goldberg, Whoopi 1B 2B 3D
Goldblum, Jeff 1B 2A 3B
Goodman, John 1C 2A 3D
Gould, Elliott 1A 2A 3A
Granger, Farley 1C 2A 3C
Granger, Stewart 1C 2B 3D
Grant, Cary 1C 2A 3A
Grant, Hugh 1C 2D 3B
Grant, Richard E. 1C 2A 3A

Greenstreet, Sydney 1D 2B 3A
Griffith, Melanie 1D 2A 3B
Guinness, Alec 1B 2A 3A

Hackman, Gene 1D 2B 3C
Hanks, Tom 1C 2D 3D
Hardwicke, Cedric 1C 2D 3A
Harlow, Jean 1A 2B 3C
Harrelson, Woody 1D 2C 3A
Harris, Richard 1C 2B 3D
Harrison, Rex 1A 2C 3A
Harvey, Laurence 1D 2B 3C
Hawkins, Jack 1A 2B 3C
Hayden, Sterling 1B 2A 3D
Hayward, Susan 1A 2A 3B
Hayworth, Rita 1D 2C 3B
Heflin, Van 1B 2C 3D
Henreid, Paul 1C 2D 3A
Hepburn, Audrey 1B 2A 3C
Hepburn, Katharine 1D 2A 3D
Heston, Charlton 1C 2D 3B
Hobson, Valerie 1D 2B 3D
Hoffman, Dustin 1C 2D 3C
Holden, William 1B 2C 3A
Holloway, Stanley 1D 2D 3B
Hope, Bob 1A 2D 3A
Hopkins, Anthony 1A 2B 3C
Hopper, Dennis 1A 2D 3C
Hoskins, Bob 1A 2C 3A
Howard, Leslie 1D 2B 3D
Howard, Trevor 1B 2A 3D
Hudson, Rock 1A 2C 3C
Hunter, Holly 1C 2C 3D

Irons, Jeremy 1A 2B 3C

Jackson, Gordon 1B 2C 3B
Jackson, Samuel L. 1A 2C 3D
Johnson, Celia 1C 2D 3C
Jones, Tommy Lee 1D 2D 3A
Jourdan, Louis 1B 2C 3A

Karloff, Boris 1A 2D 3D
Kaye, Danny 1A 2D 3B
Keaton, Buster 1A 2C 3B
Keaton, Diane 1D 2D 3C
Keel, Howard 1A 2C 3D
Keitel, Harvey 1D 2C 3B
Kelly, Gene 1A 2B 3D

Kelly, Grace 1A 2C 3A
Kendall, Kay 1B 2C 3A
Kerr, Deborah 1D 2A 3C
Kidman, Nicole 1A 2B 3D
Kilmer, Val 1C 2D 3A
Kingsley, Ben 1A 2A 3C
Kline, Kevin 1A 2D 3A

Ladd, Alan 1C 2D 3A
Lamarr, Hedy 1C 2B 3A
Lambert, Christopher 1C 2D 3B
Lamour, Dorothy 1A 2B 3A
Lancaster, Burt 1D 2D 3B
Lange, Jessica 1D 2C 3C
Lanza, Mario 1A 2A 3D
Laughton, Charles 1B 2A 3D
Laurel & Hardy 1A 2C 3A
Lee, Bruce 1D 2D 3A
Lee, Christopher 1A 2C 3B
Leigh, Janet 1D 2B 3A
Leigh, Vivien 1A 2D 3C
Lemmon, Jack 1B 2A 3A
Lewis, Jerry 1A 2C 3A
Lloyd, Christopher 1D 2A 3A
Lloyd, Harold 1A 2A 3C
Lockwood, Margaret 1B 2D 3A
Lombard, Carole 1C 2A 3D
Loren, Sophia 1C 2D 3C
Lorre, Peter 1A 2A 3B
Loy, Myrna 1D 2B 3D
Lugosi, Bela 1C 2A 3A
Lupino, Ida 1A 2B 3C

MacDowell, Andie 1D 2B 3B
MacLaine, Shirley 1A 2D 3A
MacMurray, Fred 1C 2D 3B
Madonna 1D 2A 3A
Malkovich, John 1C 2C 3A
March, Fredric 1B 2D 3D
Martin, Dean 1C 2B 3A
Martin, Steve 1A 2D 3A
Marvin, Lee 1D 2C 3D
Marx Brothers, The 1A 2D 3A
Mason, James 1A 2D 3C
Massey, Raymond 1D 2A 3D
Matthau, Walter 1B 2A 3C
Mature, Victor 1A 2B 3A
McCrea, Joel 1C 2B 3D
McDowell, Malcolm 1A 2A 3B

302

Answers

McDowell, Roddy 1D 2B 3C
McKellen, Ian 1C 2A 3D
McLaglen, Victor 1B 2C 3A
McQueen, Steve 1D 2C 3B
Midler, Bette 1D 2A 3B
Milland, Ray 1B 2B 3C
Mills, Hayley 1A 2A 3D
Mills, John 1A 2B 3D
Mitchum, Robert 1A 2A 3B
Monroe, Marilyn 1C 2A 3C
Montand, Yves 1C 2D 3B
Moore, Demi 1A 2D 3A
Moorehead, Agnes 1D 2B 3C
More, Kenneth 1C 2D 3A
Moreau, Jeanne 1D 2B 3D
Muni, Paul 1C 2A 3D
Murphy, Eddie 1A 2A 3A
Murray, Bill 1C 2D 3B

Neeson, Liam 1C 2C 3B
Newman, Paul 1A 2A 3D
Nicholson, Jack 1B 2A 3D
Nielsen, Leslie 1D 2C 3A
Niven, David 1D 2C 3D
Nolte, Nick 1A 2D 3C

Oberon, Merle 1C 2B 3C
Oldman, Gary 1A 2D 3B
Olivier, Laurence 1B 2D 3A
O'Toole, Peter 1C 2A 3C

Pacino, Al 1D 2D 3B
Palance, Jack 1B 2A 3D
Paltrow, Gywneth 1A 2C 3A
Peck, Gregory 1A 2B 3C
Penn, Sean 1D 2A 3D
Perkins, Anthony 1A 2C 3B
Pesci, Joe 1A 2B 3A
Pfeiffer, Michelle 1B 2D 3B
Phoenix, River 1D 2A 3A
Pickford, Mary 1B 2D 3A
Pidgeon, Walter 1D 2C 3A
Pitt, Brad 1D 2B 3A
Pleasence, Donald 1C 2C 3A
Plummer, Christopher 1D 2A 3A
Poitier, Sydney 1D 2B 3C
Powell, Dick 1A 2A 3D
Power, Tyrone 1B 2A 3A
Presley, Elvis 1D 2A 3B

Price, Vincent 1C 2A 3C

Quinn, Anthony 1D 2A 3D

Raft, George 1D 2C 3B
Rains, Claude 1A 2C 3B
Rathbone, Basil 1B 2D 3A
Rea, Stephen 1C 2D 3B
Reagan, Ronald 1C 2C 3C
Redford, Robert 1A 2D 3B
Redgrave, Michael 1A 2A 3D
Redgrave, Vanessa 1B 2A 3D
Reed, Oliver 1C 2B 3B
Reeves, Keanu 1B 2D 3D
Remick, Lee 1B 2D 3B
Reynolds, Burt 1A 2C 3A
Reynolds, Debbie 1D 2C 3B
Richardson, Miranda 1C 2B 3A
Richardson, Ralph 1D 2C 3C
Rickman, Alan 1C 2A 3B
Robbins, Tim 1B 2A 3B
Roberts, Julia 1D 2C 3A
Robinson, Edward G. 1C 2A 3C
Robson, Flora 1B 2A 3B
Rogers, Ginger 1A 2B 3D
Rogers, Roy 1D 2B 3A
Rooney, Mickey 1D 2C 3B
Roth, Tim 1A 2D 3C
Russell, Jane 1A 2D 3A
Rutherford, Margaret 1D 2A 3B
Ryan, Meg 1A 2D 3D
Ryan, Robert 1C 2B 3A
Ryder, Winona 1C 2D 3A

Sabu 1A 2C 3C
Sanders, George 1A 2D 3D
Sarandon, Susan 1A 2B 3A
Schwarzenegger, Arnold 1B 2B 3A
Scofield, Paul 1C 2B 3A
Scott, Randolph 1B 2C 3D
Sellers, Peter 1B 2A 3B
Sharif, Omar 1D 2C 3A
Shaw, Robert 1D 2B 3D
Shearer, Moira 1B 2C 3A
Shearer, Norma 1A 2A 3C
Sheen, Martin 1D 2A 3B
Sim, Alistair 1A 2B 3B
Simmons, Jean 1A 2A 3B
Sinatra, Frank 1A 2D 3C

Smith, C. Aubrey 1C 2A 3C
Spacek, Sissy 1A 2B 3A
Spacey, Kevin 1C 2B 3C
Stallone, Sylvester 1A 2D 3A
Stanwyck, Barbara 1B 2A 3D
Steiger, Rod 1D 2A 3C
Stewart, James 1A 2B 3A
Streep, Meryl 1C 2C 3D
Streisand, Barbra 1D 2B 3A
Stone, Sharon 1C 2B 3B
Sutherland, Donald 1A 2C 3C
Swayze, Patrick 1A 2D 3D

Tandy, Jessica 1D 2C 3D
Taylor, Elizabeth 1C 2D 3A
Taylor, Robert 1B 2C 3D
Taylor, Rod 1C 2B 3C
Temple, Shirley 1B 2C 3B
Thomas, Terry 1B 2D 3A
Thompson, Emma 1D 2D 3C
Todd, Richard 1D 2B 3B
Tracy, Spencer 1A 2A 3B
Travolta, John 1D 2B 3B
Turner, Lana 1D 2D 3C
Turturo, John 1A 2D 3A

Valentino, Rudolph 1B 2A 3B
Van Damme, Jean-Claude 1A 2C 3A
Veidt, Conrad 1D 2B 3A
von Stroheim, Erich 1D 2C 3A

Walken, Christopher 1D 2C 3A
Walters, Julie 1D 2B 3D
Washington, Denzel 1A 2C 3A
Wayne, John 1D 2A 3D
Weaver, Sigourney 1A 2C 3A
Welles, Orson 1B 2A 3B
West, Mae 1A 2B 3A
Widmark, Richard 1B 2A 3D
Williams, Robin 1B 2C 3A
Willis, Bruce 1D 2A 3B
Winger, Debra 1C 2B 3A
Wood, Natalie 1A 2A 3C
Woods, James 1D 2A 3A
Wright, Teresa 1B 2B 3C

Young, Loretta 1A 2D 3A

The Movie Quiz Companion

DIRECTORS

Aldrich, Robert 1D 2B 3C
Allen, Woody 1C 2A 3D
Almodovar, Pedro 1A 2B 3A
Altman, Robert 1A 2C 3A
Anderson, Lindsay 1B 2D 3C
Asquith, Anthony 1D 2C 3A

Bergman, Ingmar 1A 2B 3B
Bertolucci, Bernardo 1C 2A 3D
Bigelow, Kathryn 1B 2A 3B
Bogdanovich, Peter 1A 2D 3B
Boorman, John 1A 2D 3B
Borzage, Frank 1A 2A 3C
Brooks, Mel 1D 2A 3C
Brown, Clarence 1A 2A 3C
Burton, Tim 1B 2B 3A

Campion, Jane 1D 2B 3C
Capra, Frank 1A 2B 3D
Carpenter, John 1A 2C 3D
Chabrol, Claude 1B 2D 3C
Cimino, Michael 1B 2B 3C
Clouzot, Henri-George 1C 2D 3D
Cocteau, Jean 1A 2C 3A
Coppola, Francis Ford 1D 2C 3C
Corman, Roger 1D 2A 3C
Craven, Wes 1A 2D 3A
Cronenberg, David 1A 2D 3C
Cukor, George 1B 2D 3B
Curtiz, Michael 1C 2B 3A

De Mille, Cecil B. 1C 2D 3C
Demme, Jonathan 1A 2D 3C
De Palma, Brian 1D 2A 3A
De Sica, Vittorio 1A 2B 3B
Dieterle, William 1A 2C 3D
Dmytryk, Edward 1B 2A 3C
Donen, Stanley 1D 2C 3A

Eastwood, Clint 1A 2B 3D
Edwards, Blake 1A 2D 3C
Eisenstein, Sergei 1D 2B 3A

Fassbinder, Rainer 1A 2D 3B
Fellini, Frederico 1A 2D 3A
Fleming, Victor 1B 2C 3C
Ford, John 1D 2C 3B

Forman, Milos 1C 2C 3D
Forsyth, Bill 1A 2C 3A
Frankenheimer, John 1B 2B 3D
Friedkin, William 1C 2A 3D
Fuller, Samuel 1B 2A 3A

Gance, Abel 1C 2A 3A
Gilliam, Terry 1B 2C 3C
Godard, Jean-Luc 1A 2D 3D
Greenaway, Peter 1C 2D 3A
Griffith, D.W. 1B 2B 3A

Hathaway, Henry 1A 2D 3A
Hawks, Howard 1B 2B 3D
Herzog, Werner 1A 2A 3D
Hill, George Roy 1C 2A 3A
Hitchcock, Alfred 1A 2B 3C
Huston, John 1D 2D 3B

Ivory, James 1A 2B 3A

Jarman, Derek 1B 2C 3A

Kasdan, Lawrence 1C 2A 3C
Kazan, Elia 1D 2A 3B
King, Henry 1A 2B 3A
Korda, Alexander 1D 2B 3D
Kramer, Stanley 1C 2A 3C
Kubrick, Stanley 1C 2B 3A
Kurosawa, Akira 1A 2B 3C

Landis, John 1A 2D 3C
Lang, Fritz 1B 2A 3C
Lean, David 1D 2C 3D
Lee, Spike 1C 2A 3C
Leone, Sergio 1A 2A 3C
LeRoy, Mervyn 1A 2D 3B
Lubitsch, Ernst 1C 2A 3A
Lucas, George 1D 2D 3A
Lumet, Sydney 1A 2D 3B
Lynch, David 1C 2A 3C

Mackendrick, Alexander 1C 2B 3A
Malle, Louis 1C 2A 3D
Mamet, David 1A 2B 3A
Mamoulian, Rouben 1D 2A 3D
Mankiewicz, Joseph L. 1C 2C 3C
Mann, Anthony 1C 2B 3A
Minnelli, Vincente 1B 2D 3A

Murnau, F.W. 1C 2D 3A
Nichols, Mike 1C 2B 3B

Ophüls, Max 1A 2B 3D

Parker, Alan 1C 2B 3A
Pasolini, Pier Paolo 1A 2A 3A
Peckinpah, Sam 1C 2A 3B
Polanski, Roman 1A 2A 3D
Pollack, Sydney 1D 2A 3B
Powell, Michael 1D 2D 3C
Preminger, Otto 1B 2A 3D

Ray, Nicholas 1D 2D 3A
Reed, Carol 1C 2C 3B
Reiner, Rob 1D 2C 3C
Renoir, Jean 1C 2A 3A
Richardson, Tony 1A 2D 3C
Rodriguez, Robert 1A 2D 3B
Roeg, Nicolas 1B 2C 3A
Romero, George 1B 2B 3A
Russell, Ken 1C 2B 3D

Schlesinger, John 1B 2A 3B
Scorsese, Martin 1B 2A 3D
Scott, Ridley 1D 2B 3A
Siegel, Don 1B 2D 3D
Siodmak, Robert 1C 2C 3A
Spielberg, Steven 1A 2A 3A
Stevens, George 1D 2B 3D
Stone, Oliver 1B 2A 3C
Sturges, Preston 1D 2D 3A
Sturges, John 1A 2C 3A

Tarantino, Quentin 1C 2A 3B
Thompson, J Lee 1B 2D 3C
Tourneur, Jacques 1C 2A 3A
Truffaut, François 1A 2C 3D

Vadim, Roger 1C 2A 3A
Vidor, King 1A 2D 3A
von Sternberg, Josef 1A 2C 3B
von Stroheim, Erich 1D 2A 3D

Walsh, Raoul 1B 2D 3C
Waters, John 1B 2A 3A
Weir, Peter 1D 2B 3D
Welles, Orson 1B 2B 3C
Wellman, William 1A 2B 3A

Answers

Wenders, Wim 1B 2A 3A
Whale, James 1A 2C 3D
Wilder, Billy 1D 2A 3A
Wise, Robert 1C 2D 3B
Wood Jr., Edward D. 1A 2A 3D
Wood, Sam 1A 2B 3B
Wyler, William 1B 2A 3B

Yimou, Zhang 1A 2A 3D

Zeffirelli, Franco 1A 2D 3A
Zemeckis, Robert 1A 2D 3B
Zinneman, Fred 1B 2C 3A

ANAGRAMS
(listed alphabetically)

a borrowing tory kneels
A Tree Grows in Brooklyn
a cocky dark bald bat
Bad Day at Black Rock
a darn soybean dowry
Broadway Danny Rose
a gassed park
Dark Passage
a grovel shawl
Shallow Grave
a gutted hare
The Graduate
a hero flattened a fat maid
A Matter of Life and Death
a high toff deathbed
The Thief of Baghdad
a lust unobserved
Sunset Boulevard
a macho waterfront fish
The Thomas Crown Affair
a mod donut
Odd Man Out
a noble sickly chin
Nicholas Nickleby
a nude joy game
A Guy Named Joe
a resentful mod hairdo
The Island of Dr Moreau
a snippy romp
Mary Poppins

a sunny endeavor
Never on a Sunday
a tensed foe
East of Eden
a thick jam grill
I'm All Right Jack
a thin ghetto hen thief
In the Heat of the Night
a tragicomic omen
Coming to America
a venerable coach theft
The Clan of the Cave Bear
a virgins panty rave
Saving Private Ryan
a washing chore
Anchors Aweigh
a wretched rainy hill
The Railway Children
afternoon hit habit
The Birth of a Nation
agitate the orphan
A Night at the Opera
ah splotchy beer mat
The Palm Beach Story
ah tipsy adolphe hitler
The Philadelphia Story
ailing yam pasta
Play it Again Sam
all noble chefs vegetarian
The Lives of a Bengal Lancer
an atmosphere affects people
Escape From Planet of the Apes
an olde brothel
The Red Balloon
an unscathed oaf foams
Man of a Thousand Faces
ancient lore
Intolerance
anointed hems
Edison the Man
another sweetheart ghost
The Greatest Show on Earth
anti vine blemish
The Invisible Man
any posh ceramic
American Psycho
arrogance by creed
Cyrano de Bergerac

astounding handyman industry rag
Saturday Night and Sunday Morning
avenges hate
Heaven's Gate

ban thy pickles
The Spy in Black
banned ruler
Blade Runner
baronial cafe ware
Lawrence of Arabia
bathrobe of grim warder
Who Framed Roger Rabbit
beer mart mania offer
An Affair to Remember
bendy loin dance
Bonnie and Clyde
brassiere of the lousy vet
The Best Years of our Lives
buy cinerama tea
American Beauty
bygone dog hotel
The Long Goodbye

censorial pet pond
Indecent Proposal
centuries of moth cotton
The Count of Monte Cristo
chaotic prancing king
Picnic at Hanging Rock
churned beetroot froth
The Hunt For Red October
city thieves belche
The Bicycle Thieves
cool butch tent
The Cotton Club
cool clergyman riot
Girl on a Motorcycle
creates hay data
A Day at the Races
creditable organic faith
The Cabinet of Dr Caligari
crippled video fad
David Copperfield
cute mice in paranoia omen
Once Upon a Time in America

dad eyed naked loony
Yankee Doodle Dandy

The Movie Quiz Companion

dam lewd yoyo bar
Broadway Melody
dank nightie
The King and I
dawn incline ordeal
Alice in Wonderland
deathbed got unhealthy dog
The Good, The Bad and The Ugly
debonair cons
Donnie Brasco
decimate nosh
The Comedians
defiling the skill
The Killing Fields
dervish hoot barefoooted nun
The Adventures of Robin Hood
destitute hare aroma refresher
The Treasure of the Sierra Madre
deviant chews owls
Dances with Wolves
did needy penance
Independence Day
dire hate of skeletons
The Sons of Katie Elder
do eat the nipping hen
It Happened One Night
do satellites dot thy hearth
The Day The Earth Stood Still
dread a lame misogynist
Sammy and Rosie Get Laid

eager healers wed
Where Eagles Dare
eager oaf butchered dog
The Red Badge of Courage
earthly lawn rhymes
When Harry Met Sally
elderly silk hat
The Ladykillers
elitist emu omens
Meet me in St Louis
elitist oaf ate cow
A Tale of Two Cities
enormous fancy bar be frock
Rebecca of Sunnybrook Farm
entombed glen repels fern
Gentlemen Prefer Blondes
entwined with hog
Gone With The Wind

essential eels pelts
Sleepless in Seattle
eunuch ant enemy
Cheyenne Autumn
extracting ape toes
Great Expectations
eye thrill department
The Talented Mr Ripley

famed oriental hated fat
A Matter of Life and Death
fat molten leaches
The Maltese Falcon
fat sheep polenta
Planet of the Apes
feces swells costumes
Sweet Smell of Success
fed cute hormones
Curse of the Demon
fetal boy teenager thirteen
The Bitter Tea of General Yen
fetish of retired pet
The Petrified Forest
fetishes act woke witch
The Witches of Eastwick
few shag the parrot
The Grapes of Wrath
fictional blend felled homeopath
The Life and Death of Colonel Blimp
field of wet urinals
It's a Wonderful Life
fiesta worshiped monks
Kiss of the Spider Woman
flash lolly vetoed
Valley of the Dolls
for injured teeth
Return of the Jedi
forfeited her bath
Father of the Bride
four reverent foals
Reversal of Fortune
free patronized nosh
The Prisoner of Zenda
free trophies fitted
The Petrified Forest
frothier fiasco
Chariots of Fire
frothing wino entree
The Towering Inferno

fry joe at reunion
Journey into Fear
fuchsia topic
South Pacific

get foolhardy dingo
The Long Good Friday
ghastly proof
Paths of Glory
gods warts
Straw Dogs
good monster tweeds
Mr Deeds Goes to Town
gothic rave attire
Victoria the Great
gritty flea sandwiches
Angels With Dirty Faces
gritty hen hid bevy
They Drive By Night
gross override
Reservoir Dogs
gusset throbs
Ghostbusters

had tangy radish
A Hard Day's Night
handmade shoe talent
The Old Man and the Sea
hard commoners jeer
Here Comes Mr Jordan
hated the frog
The Godfather
he cheers rats
The Searchers
he fabricated her thigh toggle
The Charge of the Light Brigade
he nice deviant
Death in Venice
he now rotten fart
On the Waterfront
head monastery thief
The Remains of the Day
heathenish bus folk revolted
The Hound of the Baskervilles
heathenish twit minuet
The Man in the White Suit
heavens forgot a nun
The Guns of Navarone

306

Answers

heeds others
The Red Shoes
her hot seeds
The Red Shoes
her portentous horn ached
The Shop Around the Corner
her tenth unfit hog
Night of the Hunter
her thin iced yoghurt
Ride the High Country
heroic texts
The Exorcist
hewn bat gonad
The Bandwagon
his famous liverwort
From Russia With Love
his itchy ego
High Society
hoary dog dung
Groundhog Day
hope fab rhinoceros invited
Robin Hood: Prince of Thieves
hope witchcraft demons homely
The Spy Who Came In From The Cold
hormones heat feet
The Name of the Rose
horny games
Hear My Song
horrendous fetid boot haven
The Adventures of Robin Hood
hoses get ghost wet
The Ghost Goes West
hot van secretion
The Conversation
hothead ant risk
A Shot in the Dark
hug wee nightshirt
Wuthering Heights
hunt my boil
Nil By Mouth
hurls teeth
The Hustler
hut heaters offer
The Four Feathers
hypodermic gobs
Goodbye Mr Chips

ignite a dry red ass
Destry Rides Again

ignorant ass ranter
Strangers on a Train
imprisoned jamboree fetish
The Prime of Miss Jean Brodie
infesting the cavemen
The Magnificent Seven
inflated oil can
LA Confidential
inherit a cat site
Raise the Titanic
inhuman chant eradicated
The Manchurian Candidate
innate mild clergymen
My Darling Clementine
irritating handsome hero flattened
The Great Northfield Minnesota Raid

jade has orangutan snot
Jason and the Argonauts

kangaroo cow clerk
A Clockwork Orange

lee farted on jet
Jean De Florette
lee sells pantie sets
Sleepless in Seattle
lethal bee orchestra
The Three Caballeros
loathsome fetish chant
The Last of the Mohicans
lofty surgeon
Tunes of Glory

maniac doughnut booth
Much Ado About Nothing
masochist flee belt hen
Silence of the Lambs
me sporty family
Play Misty For Me
men repelled ants shit
All the President's Men
mens tormented fear
Terms of Endearment
monthly lavatories bathe wench
The Man Who Shot Liberty Valance
murderous regime hunter
Murders in the Rue Morgue

my fated unreliable tutu
My Beautiful Laundrette
my sad foliage
My Life as a Dog
my wig agony
Going My Way

navel thimble holder
The Lavender Hill Mob
nightmares of absent mince
The Magnificent Ambersons
nihilist spat sap
This is Spinal Tap
ninth mutating choir
Night Train To Munich
noble joke thug
The Jungle Book
nosey papal cow
Apocalypse Now
noticeable cheesy lunch
The Cheyenne Social Club
novelty bear healer
Lonely are the Brave
nubile men oddity
Double Indemnity

ogle worried bat
Waterloo Bridge
oval dingo fink
A Kind of Loving
owl hit newsboy
The Winslow Boy

parenthood diet venues
The Poseidon Adventure
patriotic mop slops
Passport to Pimlico
pee by lunchtime
The Public Enemy
pet trombone enrages chieftain
The Importance of Being Earnest
photogenic fruit arrayed
The Picture of Dorian Gray
priceless thief
The Ipcress File
puritanic oven fat
A Private Function

307

The Movie Quiz Companion

quaint theme
The Quiet Man
queer hen fanatic
The African Queen

racketeer nuns often fish
The Curse of Frankenstein
rakishly we go
Whisky Galore
rampant teeth
The Apartment
randy mummys threaten art
Manhattan Murder Mystery
rare prophecies of lout
The Purple Rose of Cairo
rascals nick bus
Black Narcissus
redeem halcyon television era
Alice Doesn't Live Here Anymore
refreshing roommate cackle
The Miracle of Morgan's Creek
relishing old tuna
The Grand Illusion
respondent coin forger
Foreign Correspondent
riddles of fame
Field of Dreams
roast brains
A Star is Born
rotting paints
Trainspotting

sarcastic man waxes sheathe
The Texas Chainsaw Massacre
scoundrel cooks thirteenth fiend
Close Encounters of the Third Kind
semen eradicates trader
A Streetcar Named Desire
separated ear
Easter Parade
shady vets inhale
The Lady Vanishes
shy frigid liar
His Girl Friday
sick cod horror
Shock Corridor
skirmish at food time
The Mask of Dimitrios

snarling at patios
Last Tango in Paris
snoring rat ran teas
Strangers on a Train
soldiers unworthy death day
Around the World in Eighty Days
solvent grader
Dr Strangelove
sordid swans crashed
Edward Scissorhands
stammering hog shoots twin
Mr Smith Goes to Washington
stifling trophies
This Sporting Life
stunning hinge
The Singing Nun
sweet shaven he farts downwind
Snow White and the Seven Dwarfs
symbolic tart roll
Strictly Ballroom

takeover writhing bed hire
The Bridge on the River Kwai
taste bats beef
Babette's Feast
taverns do harm
Random Harvest
teenagers rot within
The Roaring Twenties
teepee gas chart
The Great Escape
teetotal chef chops puree
The Curse of the Cat People
ten month madmen sect
The Ten Commandments
terrified hens bank often
The Bride of Frankenstein
test thy garbage
The Great Gatsby
the inherent typists
The Thirty Nine Steps
the paternal dad myth
The Lady and the Tramp
the terse wren
The Westerner
theory of retirement
From Here to Eternity
thirteen cent spud
The Student Prince

thorny newts broth
North By Northwest
thy portentous serf
The Nutty Professor
tit caress
Sister Act
to hose fresh water
The War of the Roses
to old erotic dolt
Doctor Dolittle
tolerant farm women unknown
Letter From an Unknown Woman
tormenting measle hater
A Nightmare on Elm Street
touch fake butter
Back to the Future
touches of nudism
The Sound of Music
twit dyes roses
West Side Story

unbutton it my honey
Mutiny on the Bounty

valuable toe
All About Eve
venereal soap sheik
Shakespeare in Love
veterinary dug shaft
Saturday Night Fever
vicars favourite egos
Five Graves to Cairo
vitriol stew
Oliver Twist
vivacious springs
Surviving Picasso

wealthiest ever otter
A Letter to Three Wives
wealthy noodle con
Hollywood Canteen
wed the skeleton
The Lost Weekend
wee hotrod shone
The Wooden Horse
whinged hormones
She Done Him Wrong
whiz team wake libido
I Walked with a Zombie

308

Answers

wicker banjo
Jackie Brown
winner throttles float queen
All Quiet on the Western Front
wino reward
Rear Window
wormy leg was heavenly
How Green was my Valley
wrote pathetic slush
The Last Picture Show
wry aesthetic
Sweet Charity